The Hermeneutics of Sacred Architecture

Volume Two | Hermeneutical Calisthenics

Harvard University Center for the Study of World Religions

Religions of the World
General Editor: Lawrence E. Sullivan

Cambridge, Massachusetts

The Hermeneutics of Sacred Architecture
Experience, Interpretation, Comparison

Volume Two | Hermeneutical Calisthenics
A Morphology of Ritual-Architectural Priorities

Lindsay Jones

distributed by Harvard University Press for the
Harvard University Center for the Study of World Religions

Printed in the United States of America

Library of Congress Cataloging-in-Publication Data

Jones, Lindsay, date.
The hermeneutics of sacred architecture : experience, interpretation, comparison / Lindsay Jones
p. cm. — (Religions of the world)
Includes bibliographical references and index.
Contents: v. 1. Monumental occasions : reflections on the eventfulness of religious architecture — v. 2. Hermeneutical callisthenics : a morphology of ritual-architectural priorities.
ISBN 0-945454-21-X (hardcover : v. 1 : alk. paper)
ISBN 0-945454-22-8 (pbk. : v. 1 : alk. paper)
ISBN 0-945454-23-6 (hardcover : v. 2 : alk. paper)
ISBN 0-945454-24-4 (pbk. : v. 2 : alk. paper)
1. Architecture and religion. 2. Symbolism in architecture. 3. Hermeneutics —Religious aspects. I. Title. II. Religions of the world (Cambridge, Mass.)

NA4600 .J66 2000
726'.01—dc21

00-040716

In memory of Marilyn Robinson Waldman, her counsel, humor, and example.

Contents

Preface to Volume Two

READERS ARE DUE A NOTE OF CLARIFICATION with respect to the relationship between the first volume and this, the second, volume of *The Hermeneutics of Sacred Architecture: Experience, Interpretation, Comparison.* The two are complementary and mutually interrelated, but unequal and not parallel. The present volume is, in one sense, a continuation of the former (which explains why it begins with chapter 13) and, in another sense, a new point of departure. Though they stand more firmly as a pair, either volume may stand also as a viable place to begin (or end) reading about the so-termed hermeneutics of sacred architecture.

Volume 1—*Monumental Occasions: Reflections on the Eventfulness of Religious Architecture*—raises very basic questions about how architecture participates in the production and transaction of meanings, particularly in the context of ritual, and how students of architecture might best come to terms with those productive mechanisms. That volume lays a theoretical foundation for the present work by outlining the advantages of constituting interpretations of sacred architecture, not in terms of the meanings of buildings per se, but in terms of what are designated "ritual-architectural events," that is, occasions in which specific communities and individuals apprehend specific buildings in specific and invariably diversified ways. According to that view, which is built on the proposition that buildings do not have once-and-for-all meanings (irrespective of the common, usually implicit, presupposition that they do), the most rewarding, rigorously empirical version of architectural interpretation and historiography comes in the composition of "ritual-architectural reception histories," which chronicle in and over time the concatenate uses and apprehensions that any substantial work of architecture is certain to engender. Shifting the focus from built forms to the grand and modest "monumental occasions" in which built forms participate does, I argue, make a profound difference.

Volume 2—*Hermeneutical Calisthenics: A Morphology of Ritual-Architectural Priorities*—has a more programmatic tenor insofar as it presents an ample catalog of heuristic questions and possibilities that can serve as an aid to composing the sorts of architectural reception histories proposed in volume 1. Departing from the observation that historians of religions and other largely text-based scholars have usually depended on a quite narrow set of options concerning architecture's functions and mechanisms, this volume is designed to widen and deepen appreciations of the spectacular, too often underestimated diversity of ways in which built forms can express and enhance religious sensibilities, again particularly (but not only) in the context of ritual. Expanding awarenesses of the vast range of possibilities concerning all that architecture can do—largely via aggressively cross-cultural instantiation—ought then to enrich scholars' interpretations of past and present architectures and perhaps (though I venture this prospect with somewhat less certainty) the future creations of practicing architects. Thus, where the first volume provides reflections, a meditation of sorts on the status, workings, and study of religious architecture, this volume moves in a more empirical, demonstrative, and explicitly pedagogical direction. Here, the exposition is more by historical example than by abstraction.

Consequently, numerous viable reading sequences obtain. Because the two volumes together present, and begin to demonstrate, a thoroughgoing program for the hermeneutics of sacred architecture, the most obvious tack would be to start at the beginning of the first one and read through to the end of this one. Alternatively, however, the design of the pair also encourages the possibility that volume 2 might serve as a workable starting point, in which case those readers who require more thorough theoretical underpinnings may feel compelled to consult later the initial volume. Or, as a third possibility, it is likewise plausible to conceive of this volume as an odd sort of manual, sourcebook, or map of alternative interpretive avenues for the interpretation (or perhaps design) of architecture, in which case an even less linear protocol of reading might obtain.

Nonetheless, to reiterate from the introduction to the first volume, as a student of hermeneutics and reception theory, I am fully cognizant of the futility of legislating too completely the order and attitude of readers. As I argue throughout the entire work, books, not unlike buildings and other superabundant cultural productions, nearly always subvert, resist, and rebel against even the most deliberative expectations of their creators. As a kind of consolation to authors and architects, however, I hope also to demonstrate in the course of this project just how often so-labeled misunderstandings and misapprehensions of texts and monuments turn out to be as—or more—interesting and fruitful as those rare occasions when creators and users make a direct connection. Acknowledging, sometimes celebrating, that irrepressible flexibility, the complete two-volume set marks an "open site" at which students of architecture and religion are encouraged to work, construct, and experiment in whatever ways suit their own purposes.[1] To reiterate my invitation from the previous volume, build from it what you can.

Veracruz, Mexico

Acknowledgments

THE COMPOSITION OF THIS WORK has been a prominent, evolving feature of my life for more years than I would like to admit. Initial, now-distant inspirations and impressions have been continually reconsidered, reframed, rejected, and, on occasion, resuscitated. Particularly in the wake of two years living, teaching, and traveling in Asia, I am at this point timorously aware of what a different book would emerge were I just beginning rather than taking stock of my previous literary labors. While some pillars of the project stood firm throughout the long, oft-interrupted construction process, others began to shift and sway. Pressing new questions, more compelling theoretical formulations, and fresher examples constantly announce themselves. With a mushrooming of relevant literature, many of my old complaints about academic approaches to religious architecture now seem overwrought, while concerns that presently strike me as much more urgent are barely broached and never resolved. Neither my perspective nor my field is what it was when I began.

That instability, in ways, provides a contenting justification and unanticipated reward for the exceptionally slow, halting emergence of this work; a sense of discovery and surprise stretched over the entire process. Yet, in other ways, the ceaseless flux of allegiances and priorities evokes a nagging, restless sensation of consternation and discontent. Agreement, even with myself, has proven fleeting. Several sections call for more pruning and revision, but after that I would be certain to want another reworking and then another. Venturing continually to "update" and rejuvenate one's efforts by draping old frames with more suitably fashionable idioms and allusions is definitely futile and probably disingenuous, and I have generally succeeded in resisting that untoward urge. But I must consent, therefore, to being a bit out of style and less than completely satisfied with this latest draft, which masquerades as a finished product. Instead of a final word, this piece positions me to continue ahead with my (re)considerations of the excitingly manifold ways in which built forms work as expressions and evocators of religious sensibilities.

Though all the shortcomings are my own, innumerable contributive influences intersect and collide in the space of this work. Several anxious years as a design student prior to my serious involvements with the history of religions have, I suspect, an important residual effect on my thinking about architecture; and many of my largest debts are to authors and builders I've never had the opportunity to meet. Consequently, I cite here only a very short list of those persons who have had a more certain and tangible influence on the configuration of this project.

Among teachers, the formative influences of Joseph Kitagawa and Mircea Eliade persist as strong and eloquent voices in every debate that I have with myself and others about the past, present, and future of religious studies. Frank Reynolds continues to provide a stabilizing influence; and insights concerning the relations between religion and art acquired years ago by working with Bernard McGinn and Langdon Gilkey remain surprisingly resilient. The influence of master teacher Charles Long, whose presence transforms any event into an occasion of learning, far exceeds that which is evident from sporadic bibliographic credits. It is no coincidence that my comments on the foundational issues of method, comparison, and the estimable role of nonliterary resources in the study of religion appeal so often to the work of Lawrence Sullivan; his influence is large and ongoing. And to Davíd Carrasco, the first to affirm my vague, undergraduate suspicions concerning important connections between architectural design and the history of religions, I owe perhaps my greatest intellectual debt; his very specific critical comments on the entire first volume were only the most recent and direct expression of a profound influence on virtually all aspects of my thinking about the infamous category of "sacred space."

My colleagues in the Division of Comparative Studies at the Ohio State University deserve credit for creating an environment of interdisciplinary stimulation and critical challenge. Conversations with Gary Ebersole in the sole year that we both served in that unit had a lasting impact; he may have been the first to bring to my attention the relevance of reception theory, and his enormous cross-cultural bibliographies on time and space definitely opened innumerable avenues that I would otherwise have missed. I thank Sabra Webber, chair of Comparative Studies for most of the years in which this project took shape, whose generous willingness to sacrifice her own research in order that others of us might advance our own went far beyond the call of duty. And Marilyn Robinson Waldman, a historian of religion of a different stripe and an insuperable model of collegial mentoring, challenged me to reconsider thoroughly what was at issue in the comparative study of religion; choosing to dedicate these volumes to her memory was the simplest part of my task.

Also at Ohio State I have accumulated debts to countless students, most relevantly three sets who, in the early 1990s, participated in seminars on comparative sacred architecture in which preliminary oral and written versions of numerous chapters were field-tested, so to speak. Though some may be surprised to find their names here, all can be assured that their questions, confusions, objections, and occasional affirmations, together with their game efforts at interpreting and comparing specific religious architectures, have proven invaluable. Students that had a particularly strong influence on the ways that I presently conceive of the so-termed hermeneutics of sacred architecture include Mary Beth Crispin Browning, Greg Carter, Janice Glowski, Rory Golden, Tracy Hammer, Jay Hanes, Michael Link, Caroline H. C. Ma, Judson Murray, Beth Parsons, and Jamie Short. Also among that group, Thomas Bremer deserves special note for commenting on the entire manuscript and directing my attention to several places where I had imperfectly coordinated my old interests with newer ones.

Additionally, it was my very good fortune to have this manuscript fall into the hands of Harvard University Center for the Study of World Religions publications coordinator Kathryn Dodgson. My transience during the processes of editing and revision forced upon her an unreasonable share of the factual and bibliographical double-checking of quotations. Her patient and meticulous reading challenged me to reconsider not only my peculiar attachment to various turgid and colloquial phrases but also numerous more substantive questions. Awkwardnesses in composition, word choices, and particularly in the unusual layout of the two volumes invariably mark areas in which her sound judgment ceded to my idiosyncratic wishes. I also thank Hilda Guadalupe Gómez for her energizing support during my wonderful months in Veracruz, Mexico, where I reworked the entire second volume. And to Michio Araki, I express gratitude for orchestrating my productive two-year stint at the University of Tsukuba in Japan, where I made a final set of corrections and revisions. The constant changes in place helped immensely.

Tsukuba, Japan, 24 January 2000

Introduction | A Pedagogical Intent: Comparison and the Cultivation of Architectural Appreciation

> Unlike other visual arts, architecture is an art of life itself expressed in life-sized scale.
>
> Amos Ih Tiao Chang, 1956[1]

> The average reader, leafing through books on the esthetics and criticism of architecture, is horrified by the vagueness of their terms: *truth, movement, force, vitality, sense of outline, harmony, grace, breadth, scale, balance, proportion, light and shade, eurhythmics, solids and voids, symmetry, rhythm, mass, volume, emphasis, character, contrast, personality, analogy*. These are the attributes of architecture which various authors use as classifications without specifying what they refer to.
>
> Bruno Zevi, 1974[2]

> Let's have a look at the books. . . . Perhaps on occasion you have tried to give a semblance of order to your shelves, but every attempt at classification was rapidily foiled by heterogeneous acquisitions.
>
> Italo Calvino, 1981[3]

PUNAVARO, THE INFAMOUS TYRANT-KING of thirteenth-century India, was reportedly so zealously proud of his magnificent city of Patan that he cut off the hands of its architect to ensure that the designer could never again create anything like it.[4] If flattering in some tragic respect, success in fulfilling a client's wishes had, in this case, paradoxically dire consequences. No subsequent, similarly spectacular commission was allowed. The Indian sovereign hoped, via this gratuitous amputation, to guarantee the incomparable architectural supremacy—the uniqueness—of his urban capital.

This second volume—dedicated to synchronic comparisons of sacred architecture, to "significant organization," to the elucidation of patterns, types, and morphologic commonalities (and differences)—finds an ironic futility in that brutal plea for singularity. I will contend instead that no architectural creation, however special, is wholly without important, instructive comparability. I concur, at this stage in my wider program for the hermeneutics of sacred architecture, with Jonathan Z. Smith that, for our present purposes at least, "the 'unique' is an attribute that must be disposed of."[5]

Claims to uniqueness, whether in relation to architectural design or some other phenomenon, are, as Smith demonstrates, much more often political than empirical declarations, asserting a claim to privilege and thus an exemption from critical scrutiny. Endeavors to secure a place beyond the reach of comparative analogy or affinity, not unlike claims to universality, nearly always work, either deliberately or inadvertently, to forestall hermeneutical conversation and critical interpretation rather than to drive it ahead into intriguing, productive new territory. By contrast, nothing, I would wager, expedites understanding so efficiently as comparison. In fact, as I argued in volume 1 (under the rubric of "Modes, Contexts, and Sequences of Architectural Comparison"), we haven't any choice: "All understanding passes through the travail of comparison, conscious or not."[6]

The attitude embraced in this work, then, is that both indigenous ritual experiences and academic interpretations of sacred architecture are inevitably—and fortuitously rather than lamentably—not only occasions of hermeneutical reflection, but also occasions of comparison. Instead of an obstacle to understanding, comparison, that is, strategic negotiations of similarity *and* difference—particularly, I will maintain, widely cross-cultural, morphological comparison—is the most effective of all stimuli to creative and nuanced interpretations of, among other phenomena, specific historical works and configurations of religious architecture.

On those premises, I devote this entire volume to morphological comparisons of architecture. The work consists primarily of eleven essays, preliminary versions of which were initially drafted (well in advance of the actual writing of volume 1) for student consumption in seminars on comparative sacred architecture.[7] The basic pedagogical intent was twofold. The first impetus grew from the observation that religious studies as an academic field has been, and remains, overwhelmingly preoccupied with sacred books, "scripture," and thus with textual exegesis. Too often the operative, taken-for-granted assumption is that we come to know people and religions most fully and most accurately, maybe solely, on the basis of close readings of their literatures. Too often texts alone have been and are regarded as reliable, or even viable, sources for the study of religion, while nonliterary, "alternative vehicles of intelligibility"—preeminently art and architecture—are consigned to a lower evidential tier as supplementary, weaker, less reliable evidences.

But, to reiterate the complaint rehearsed in the first volume (in chapter 9, "Studying Buildings by Decision or Default: Architecture's Evidential Promise"), I contend that by far the greatest obstacle to historians of religions' reliance on works of architecture as primary resources for the study of religion(s) lies not in any inherent deficiency in the genre itself but in our impoverished appreciation of the vast and variegated workings of architecture. Hypersensitive textual exegetes too often remain numb to the vital role of building and buildings as principal means both for expressing and for engendering religious sensibilities. Consequently, and regrettably, those same subtle exegetes fail even to begin capitalizing on the enormous potential of this entire block of nonliterary evidential resources.

As a constructive attempt at redress, then, these eleven essays were designed, first, to awaken students of religion to the manifold and excitingly multidimensional permutations of historical sacred architecture. Enhanced appreciations of the various mechanisms at issue in the design and especially the apprehension of religious buildings, particularly (though not solely) in the context of ritual, could, I imagined, open to students an otherwise neglected realm of source material for the study of religion(s).

The second, closely related pedagogical premise was grounded in a confidence, just reiterated, that comparison—particularly wide-searching, cross-culturally morphological comparison—would provide the most fruitful and expedient means of rectifying those deficient appreciations of sacred architecture. More specifically, the essays and seminars were informed by, and designed to test, the proposition that a widely comparative acquaintance with both specific historical architectures and various disciplinary expositions of architecture, even if that exposure was at points unsystematic and superficial, could jar and jolt, energize and sensitize, students to the marvelously diversified relations between built forms, ritual practices, and religious ideas.

I was impressed, in other words, by the proposition that, as a catalyst to critical and creative interpretations of specific instances of sacred architecture (or of anything), empirical observation is vastly superior to imagination.[8] Students of religion, whether dilettantes or experts, simply cannot summon via their own introspections or personal life experience the crammed catalog of possibilities that are evidenced in actual, empirically documented interactions between people and buildings. Widening the base of historical, cross-cultural, and disciplinary familiarity would, I reasoned, deepen and enliven the interpretation of specific cases. Formerly inconceivable and, I hoped, unprecedentedly productive lines and patterns of inquiry would emerge and would in turn considerably enrich students' more tightly focused and sustained interpretations of specific architectures and architectural situations.

As course materials and impetuses to undergraduate and graduate learning, the essays inspired mixed reviews and issued in mixed, though not altogether unpromising, interpretive results. In subsequent conference situations dominated by faculty participants rather than students, however, where matters of sacred space, place, and architecture made their way into the discussion (as they so often do), I was impressed (sometimes depressed) to note that nearly all my fundamental discontents about our prevailing discourses on sacred architecture obtained in these venues as well. It often seemed that Mircea Eliade, suitably eulogized as "the leading sage in the modern study of sacred space,"[9] had decades ago opened a conversation that captured a huge and hugely enthusiastic audience, but then the dialogue flagged. Though decidedly better informed than our student counterparts, and duly discontent with Eliade in many other respects, professors of religion (and other fields) perpetuated enough of the same methodological problems that I decided to rework the essays one more time (or, in cases, many more times), add an extended introduction (which evolved into volume 1), and then share them with colleagues as well as students.[10]

Occasionally redundant, this work nonetheless presumes all that is presented in volume 1 and, I suspect, might be baffling at points without that foundational background. Though once again commiserating with all those architects whose works I've variously (mis)understood, (mis)represented, (under)appreciated, and sometimes (over)embellished, I have learned (as I explained also in the introduction to volume 1) that I ought not condescend to control too fully the protocols of apprehension that various readers and reading communities will bring to my creations. Consistent with my basically hermeneutical perspective and with my entanglements in reader-response criticism, I realize that even the most carefully crafted books, like superabundant buildings in this respect, are destined to torment, or occasionally to flatter undeservedly, their authors by taking on lives of their own, by embarking on reception careers that evoke all sorts of sentiments and insights that their authors neither intended nor approved. You are invited, then, to appropriate, deconstruct, twist, amplify, and ignore in any selective fashion you see fit—as if readers in our current critical clime need any such urging.

Thirteen | A Morphological Agendum: Organization by Ritual-Architectural Priorities

> The endless variety of phenomena which the history, psychology, and sociology of religion provides us must be organized. Typological categories are designed to do that.
>
> Joachim Wach, 1955[1]

> This tension between the subject's sense of the unique and the methodological requirement of the analogous generates both the excitement and the problematics of historical research.
>
> Jonathan Z. Smith, 1978[2]

> A particular problem of organizational theory is that of avoiding "reification" of the organization, the notion that it has, so [to] speak, organic life and a will, while at the same time keeping in mind that an organization is something more than a mere sum of its constituent parts or members.
>
> Staale Sinding-Larsen, 1984[3]

WORKING IN A PEDAGOGICAL SPIRIT and with an optimistic embrace of morphologic comparison—acting, in other words, on all the methodological complaints and advice that I proffered in volume 1 about respecting the superabundance, "occasionality," and eventful productivity of sacred architecture—this volume is about constructive alternatives. In the previous volume, I expressed deep discontent with comparative orderings of architecture that rely variously on commonalities in formal appearance, building techniques or materials, in geographic location or era of construction, or even in the ethnicity or historical affiliations of the builders—all of which are, from the perspective of a hermeneutical history of religions, (relatively) *in*significant principles of organization.[4] In this volume, I am endeavoring to present practical, constructive suggestions for how we can do better. This is an initiative in "making" and building, an architecture built of architectures.

To describe this sweeping morphological project another way: it takes the conviction (outlined in the first volume) that a hermeneutics of sacred architecture must, of necessity, be constituted (or problematized) in terms of what I term ritual-architectural events rather than in terms of static constructional entities and casts that conviction into a cross-culturally comparative realm, drawing examples and insights from all sorts of historical contexts and academic disciplines. I want to provide, at a quite practical level, the tools and the means to facilitate both nuanced interpretations of specific ritual-architectural occasions and, eventually, the composition of the sorts of creative and critical "ritual-architectural reception histories" that I proposed (in volume I) as the final goal of a hermeneutics of sacred architecture.

To that end, then, this volume outlines, and then adopts for its own structure, an interpretive framework, or a morphology of ritual-architectural events, or, perhaps more properly still, a heuristic framework of *morphs* (that is, forms or, in a sense, types or shapes) of ritual-architectural priorities. This morphological framework (summarized in the chart below and expanded in the appendix) consists of eleven broad categories (and dozens of subcategories) describing the range of alternative priorities that give specific ritual-architectural events their distinctive characters. The classificatory entries to the framework presume to address, in other words, eleven alternative sorts of relationships between monuments and ritual, eleven prospective paths for hermeneutical inquiry, eleven general topics of conversation with which to engage any specific ritual-architectural circumstance in dialogue. This is, then, an exercise in the sort of searchingly synchronic, cross-cultural, and multidisciplinary architectural comparison (outlined in chapter II) that lays a foundation for subsequent, more tightly focused, more rigorously historical analyses of specific cases.[5]

At the risk of inciting a kind of typological terror—at the risk, perhaps, of giving the impression that I have somehow conjured Carolus Linnaeus and George Cuvier back to life and set them to work on a comprehensive classification of sacred architectures rather than biological species[6]—the scope of this portion of my project is, in some respects, unblushingly ambitious, global in fact. In principle, nothing and no place, no historical context, no literary or artistic genre, no disciplinary or journalistic perspective, is exempted as a potential resource for the construction of these alternative, more eventful principles of architectural organization. Moreover, for its subsequent utility, the framework aspires to heuristic relevance, without exception, to *any* human experience of sacred architecture. I will venture immodestly, in fact, that the hermeneutical interpretation of *any* ritual-architectural circumstance, in *any* historical or cultural context, at *any* scale, can be enriched by taking as a point of departure the questions that arise from this morphological framework.

A Morphology of Ritual-Architectural Priorities

I. Architecture as Orientation: The Instigation of Ritual-Architectural Events
   - A. Homology: Sacred architecture that presents a miniaturized replica of the universe and/or conforms to a celestial archetype.
   - B. Convention: Sacred architecture that conforms to standardized rules and/or prestigious mythicohistoric precedents.
   - C. Astronomy: Sacred architecture that is aligned or referenced with respect to celestial bodies or phenomena.

II. Architecture as Commemoration: The Content of Ritual-Architectural Events
   - A. Divinity: Sacred architecture that commemorates, houses, and/or represents a deity, divine presence, or conception of ultimate reality.
   - B. Sacred History: Sacred architecture that commemorates an important mythical, mythicohistorical, or miraculous episode or circumstance.
   - C. Politics: Sacred architecture that commemorates, legitimates, or challenges socioeconomic hierarchy and/or temporal authority.
   - D. The Dead: Sacred architecture that commemorates revered ancestors and/or other deceased individuals or groups.

III. Architecture as Ritual Context: The Presentation of Ritual-Architectural Events
   - A. Theater: Sacred architecture that provides a stage setting or backdrop for ritual performance.
   - B. Contemplation: Sacred architecture that serves as a prop or focus for meditation or devotion.
   - C. Propitiation: Sacred architecture and processes of construction designed to please, appease, and/or manipulate "the sacred" (however variously conceived).
   - D. Sanctuary: Sacred architecture that provides a refuge of purity, sacrality, or perfection.

The Specific Ambitions of Morphology: Methodological Clarifications and Qualifications

So audacious a proposition as relevance to all sacred architectural situations is, to be sure, equally ambitious and vulnerable in the extreme (as well as being decidedly unfashionable). Quickly, though, the pretenses of exhaustive systematization, symmetry, and comprehensiveness dissolve. Closer scrutiny reveals a morphological framework that is, by design, only suggestive and unashamedly lopsided, patchy, idiosyncratic, and uneven.

Morphology is a mode of classification that never fully classifies, a mode of organization that never definitively categorizes.

Not surprisingly, therefore, cocksurety cedes almost immediately to countless qualifications and clarifications—five of which are perhaps the most significant (and all of which come in answer to methodological complaints and demands mapped in volume 1). Because I have already explained, for the most part, the rationale for such a morphological approach —I especially emphasized my version of morphology's quite limited role in a wider hermeneutics of sacred architecture[7]—a succinct review of those preferments ought to suffice.

The Status of the Categories: Heuristic, Empirically Informed Abstractions

Given current—not unwarranted—skepticism about the prospects for any version of typology building to establish "the order of things,"[8] the first important clarification addresses the status of the categories in the morphologic framework, which are, on occasion, advisedly termed "types" of ritual-architectural priorities (though "morph" may be a more accurate if less palatable designation). If "*morphology* literally means an order (*logos*) of forms (*morphē*),"[9] then I have to insist from the outset (on grounds established in volume 1) that my architectural morphology endeavors to describe, and to order, the forms or shapes not of buildings per se but of ritual-architectural events, that is, the "forms" or "shapes" of human experiences or apprehensions of sacred architecture. The entire project presupposes the alternative starting point, bolstered primarily by the hermeneutical perspective of Hans-Georg Gadamer, that the study of architecture must be constituted (or problematized) in terms of ritual-architectural occasions rather than architectural objects.[10]

Moreover, as in many (of the myriad sorts of) typological-morphological enterprises,[11] the organizational categories in this morphology belong to a middle-range of abstraction, that is, to a mode of empirically informed abstraction, which endeavors, still after the timeworn recommendation of Joachim Wach, to mediate between particular historical cases and more generalized (sometimes seemingly universal) patterns or themes.[12] Indebted, with considerable caution, to Eliade's morphological project, and thus to the tradition of Goethe's morphology of plants,[13] the categories in my framework, which derive primarily from empirical observation (not deduction), are heuristic constructs designed to mediate between generalizations and specificities, between idealizations and lived experiences, between abstractions and concrete historical cases.

Speaking in more explicitly comparative terms, the categories are intended to mediate between perceptions of sameness and of singularity, or, in Jonathan Smith's terms, between "the subject's sense of the unique and the methodological requirement of the analogous."[14] To lift lines from Lawrence Sullivan—whose vastly comparative treatment of South American myths, rites, beliefs, and practices provides the best contemporary demonstration of morphological method as applied to religious studies (that is, a morphological approach that both builds upon but then nuances and exceeds Eliade's)—it is a matter of "threading our way between historical circumstances and the general religious condition of humanity."[15]

More specifically, then, the morphologic entries in this framework are designed to balance and weigh both the *commonalities* between individual apprehensions of various architectures, say their shared participation in what I've defined as the twofold pattern of architectural events,[16] and the *idiosyncrasies* of those individual apprehensions. Though we can be certain that there is, on the one hand, no single, ubiquitous theme with which all instances and experiences of ostensibly religious architecture are universally concerned, there are, on the other hand, always relevant, instructive analogies. Claims to absolute uniqueness are counterproductive (even if "true" in some important respect). Consequently, the framework's entries are middle-range abstractions (empirically informed heuristic constructs) in that they direct our attention neither to supposedly universal attributes of (the apprehension of) sacred architecture nor to wholly unique cases. Instead, the categories chart a range of alternative "types," or generalized classes, of concerns and mechanisms—*a set of ritual-architectural priorities*—that inform the way in which various religious built forms are designed, constructed, and, most importantly, experienced.

Furthermore, as in nearly all morphology (though only some versions of typology), my framework, like Sullivan's project, "in the short run . . . forgoes the goal of writing chronological history, stressing similarities and contrasts among symbolic forms rather than the chronological relationships between them."[17] The organizational procedure is, in other words, characteristically morphological, depending as it does, not on temporal, diachronic sequences, but on synchronic, "typological series," which, though sensitive to and informed by specific histories and contexts, are largely *non*historical.[18] Thus, with respect to this morphological ordering of architectures, the organizational juxtapositions are, overwhelmingly, between historically *un*related (and usually geographically noncontiguous) cases.

The Utility of the Categories: Morphs, Types, and Priorities as Leading Questions

The second, related clarification concerns the use and instrumentality of the framework. How does such a nonhistorical organizational program advance the ultimate hermeneutical goal (as outlined in volume 1) of rigorously empirical analyses of specific architectural occasions and then, eventually, the composition of critical ritual-architectural reception histories for specific works and configurations? What is the utility of such a program? What is accomplished? How does it work? And what work does it do?

I have to reiterate my insistence that, as synchronic and provisional comparative categories, these eleven morphological entries, only "types" in a highly qualified sense, are *not* intended as Linnaean classificatory pigeonholes into which various specific cases might be slotted. I reject, for instance, any presupposition that the history of sacred architecture constitutes a coherent whole, "a closed immutable system," or that these categories define anything remotely like a natural or fixed "order of permanent structures."[19] Instead, the entries constitute strictly heuristic possibilities, which thus provide points of departure for interpretation rather than a means of summation. They are preparatory and expendable rather than conclusionary; they have little autonomous value. The morphological entries are offered more in the spirit of Max Weber's provisional "ideal-types"[20] than as "types" in the sense that Wach used them to organize his universalistic conclusions regarding the nature of what he termed types of religious leadership, types of devotion, and types of religious institutions.[21]

This portion of the hermeneutics of sacred architecture is, in other words (also as noted in chapter 11), one of evocative suggestion rather than classification per se. It is an interim stage in what I have termed a sequence of architectural comparisons. This morphology works, colloquially speaking, as a kind of "puts me in the mind of" procedure, an aid to making a segue from one thought to another, particularly where the connection between the two ideas may not otherwise be readily apparent.[22] Moreover, it is, on the one hand, a *defamiliarizing* morphological hermeneutic inasmuch as it is designed to jar us out of interpretive routines and put in doubt any confidence that extant models, such as Eliade's theory of sacred space, have already exposed all the pertinent issues. And it is, on the other hand, a *familiarizing* hermeneutic inasmuch as it helps us to appreciate wider patterns and tendencies in the apprehension of sacred architecture that apply across geographic, temporal, and cultural boundaries.

The primary utility of the morphological categories is, therefore, to evoke or inspire suggestive lines of inquiry into the interpretation of various sacred architectures—to present for consideration patterns of interrogation that might not otherwise have occurred to researchers—rather than to provide a vocabulary for articulating historical conclusions (although, secondarily, they may also serve this latter purpose). These "types" are heuristic devices or tools, prods or stimuli, which are themselves amenable neither to proof nor disproof. Alternatively, in hermeneutical practice, each category ought to be transformed into a question (or set of questions, as outlined in the appendix) whereby researchers ask: how and to what extent is that (type of) priority relevant to the specific case under consideration? The correctness, or "truth," of the categories, to the extent that is even of any interest, ought to be assessed in relation to their success in spurring and facilitating creative, critical, rigorously empirical, hermeneutical interpretations of historical architectures.[23]

In short, operating at this juncture as a generalist, prior to shifting back (in some future project) into a more specialized mode (in my case as a Mesoamericanist), I have as my goal here to generate potentially fruitful hypotheses, the merits and applicability of which I and others may later submit to more sustained evaluation. Entertainment of possibility, ludic playfulness, maybe interpretive mischievousness, all connote the mood of tentativeness and experimentation that should obtain in this medial portion of the hermeneutics of sacred architecture. Again drawing on Sullivan—who claims that his morphology of South American religions, "through sweeping comparisons . . . maps a background against which one may subsequently draw the uniqueness of each tradition with another sort of precision"[24]—my framework, which sometimes has the character of a manual or a workbook, "develops a posture for more sustained reflection on cultural particulars."[25] And, in that more particularistic interpretation, we ought, with an attitude of methodological opportunism rather than loyal allegiance, to be prepared, regretlessly, to dissolve partnership with any of these prim, provisional categories as more serviceable alternatives come to light.[26]

Non–Mutually Exclusive Priorities: Competitions, Overlaps, and Interpenetrations

A third, again closely related clarification involves an insistence that the entries to this morphological framework, as distinct from most versions of typology, are radically non–mutually exclusive. Where, as Sullivan explains, "typology succeeds best where sets of mutually exclusive features can characterize different types,"[27] my morphologic organizational enterprise depends upon—thrives upon—a realization of the interpenetrability and simultaneous applicability of various of the types of ritual-architectural priorities. (This, in fact, explains in large part my decision for an organization rubric according to so-termed priorities, which should connote competing, but not mutually exclusive, interests and concerns.) Particularly as we appreciate the multivocality of symbolic architecture, confinement to specific categories almost never does justice to the complex empirical ritual-architectural realities we hope to describe. Because virtually every ritual-architectural occasion arises from (and then perpetuates) an intensely complex play or competition—a dance if you will—between multiple (often widely diverse) priorities, parameters, interests, aspirations, and limitations, any particular ritual-architectural event participates simultaneously in several of the framework's morphological categories.

Among obvious examples, even in its orthodox apprehension, an Egyptian pyramid, simply by its conception as an eternal abode for a pharaoh who is himself conceived as a god, participates simultaneously in what I term the ritual-architectural commemoration of politics (priority II-C), the commemoration of the dead (priority II-D), and the commemoration of divinity (priority II-A).[28] Moreover, to the extent that the triangular form of the Egyptian pyramid is considered as a cosmic mountain or replica of the universe, what I designate as the homology priority (I-A) becomes relevant; to the extent that the pyramidal form expresses some system of mathematical proportioning, the so-termed conventionality priority (I-B) is applicable; and to the extent that the pyramid is aligned to celestial bodies, the astronomy priority (I-C) obtains. In short, participation in, or instantiation of, one sort of ritual-architectural priority definitely does not preclude participation in the others.

Thus, to cite a somewhat more complex example of non–mutual exclusivity, the effusive Catholic monasteries rebuilt in Central Europe following the Thirty Years' War (1618–1648) likewise span nearly the full spectrum of morphological priorities. Those monasteries served coterminously as repositories of relics, thus ritual-architecturally commemorating the dead (priority II-D); as houses of prayer and meditation, thus instantiating what is coined the contemplation priority (III-B); as centers of theological and historical learning, thus participating in the commemoration of divinity and sacred history (priorities II-A and II-B); as liturgical contexts with a preponderantly "theatric" sort of presentation (as I will define that term in relation to priority III-A); as forums for legislative and economic policy making, that is, for the exercise and commemoration of more explicitly political concerns (priority II-C); and as custodians of newly revived pilgrimage systems, which entailed, among other things, the commemoration of sacred history (priority II-B) in a different sense.[29]

Nevertheless, despite the inevitable overlap and nonexclusivity of (types of) priorities that inform specific ritual-architectural circumstances, in most cases two or three of those categories of concern assert themselves as the dominant priorities, while others are largely irrelevant and still others become significant primarily by their deliberate rejection. To continue with the illustration of European monasteries: generally speaking, the medieval ritual-architectural events staged in the spectacular sanctuary of Cluny, the largest monastery ever built in the West, wove the symbols and heroes of Catholic tradition into liturgical extravaganzas of dripping pomp and splendor—demonstrating, among other things, a close alliance between the commemoration of myth and sacred history (priority II-B) and so-termed theatric modes of ritual-architectural presentation (priority III-A).[30] By contrast, Saint Bernard of Clairvaux, embracing (about the same time) the same Christian historical-mythological themes but disdaining the histrionic excesses of Cluny, initiated the construction of dozens of remote and ornamentless Cistercian monasteries wherein the priority shifted from theatrical liturgy to meditative union with God and perfect conformity to the Rule of Saint Benedict.[31] Bernard's ritual-architectural agenda, in other words, evinced a continued concern for the commemoration of Catholic sacred history and divinity (priorities II-B and II-A), linked in this case with a deep commitment to the priorities of seclusionary sanctuary (III-D) and contemplation (as I define it in relation to category III-B); but, at the same time, Bernard rejected emphatically the theatric modes of presentation (priority III-A), which had been so prominent at Cluny.[32]

This sort of morphology-aided hermeneutical reflection on any particular architectural circumstance, which may at first seem to be taking us further rather than closer to empirical religious realities, is, then, never exhausted by simply ramming the case into some exclusivistic, dovecote-like designation. Instead of fashioning checklists of yes's and no's, the hermeneutical interrogational process should, in every case, entail discussing how and to what extent each of the types of ritual-architectural priorities is pertinent. This is not a quantitative procedure. (And, before long, the tedium of these shorthand designations will, I hope, be somewhat alleviated.)

Nonparallel Categories: The Radical Heterogeneity of Architectural Priorities

A fourth important clarification, which ought to be evident by now, owes to the nonparallel, glaringly heterogeneous character of the eleven morphological priorities themselves. These are by no means collateral categories or commensurate alternatives. To the contrary, the eleven categories of the framework are arranged in three groups, each of which addresses a quite different dimension of the design and, more importantly, the subsequent (and always diversified) apprehensions of sacred architecture. The first of the three sets, which addresses the conservative component, or "front half," of the general twofold pattern of ritual-architectural events, that is, variations on the matter of "architectural allurement,"[33] is framed under the rubric of "*Architecture as Orientation: The Instigation of Ritual-Architectural Events.*" This section concentrates on three alternative strategies for inviting (or coercing) participants into ceremonial occasions, three ways of recruiting both willing and unwilling players into the ritual-architectural game.

The second set—organized under the rubric of "*Architecture as Commemoration: The Content of Ritual-Architectural Events*"—considers four alternative sorts of messages or information that are communicated once ritual participants have relinquished their "spoilsport" status and entered into the ceremonial context. These commemorative priorities explore and organize the range of conversation topics that dialogical ritual-architectural events most often address, that is, the radical component, or "back half," in the general twofold pattern of ritual-architectural events.[34] And the third set, the most diversified collection—designated "*Architecture as Ritual Context: The Presentation of Ritual-Architectural Events*"—considers four other priorities that play against one another in various ways to determine the tone and choreographic staging of particular ritual-architectural performances. These options address alternative modes of ritual-architectural presentation, that is, alternative strategies for constructing the ambience in which the entire ritual-architectural event transpires.

Arranged in this tripartite fashion—the mode of instigation, the nature of the content, and the means of presentation—it may appear as though the proposed method of interpreting architectural events were tantamount to ordering a *comida corrida* (literally, a row or file of food) in a Mexican restaurant as the patron selects a soup, entrée, and dessert from each of three respective sets of options. In hermeneutical practice, however, as one works to analyze specific cases and eventually to compose particularistic ritual-architectural reception histories, nothing so slick is either possible or advisable.

Instead, the tripartite division of the morphological framework, with its uneven medley of entries, stems from an attempt to respect rather than reduce the bizarrely disparate sorts of forces that determine the unique design (and then various subsequent receptions) of any specific ceremonial-architectural circumstance.[35] In the design process, practical matters concerning the strength, cost, and availability of various building materials, for instance, must be factored against the force of cultural fashion, which must be factored against the promulgation of a specific political agenda, which must be factored against the idiosyncrasies of a culture's cosmological vision, and so on. The ritual-architectural design process involves, in other words, reconciling competing priorities of the most omnifarious, often discordant sort. Even when the decision-making process is not explicit and self-conscious (which it seldom fully is), the need to give ritual-architectural expression to rarified theological doctrines must somehow, for example, be reconciled with the more prosaic concerns of engineering stresses and loads; fidelity to the canons of tradition and style competes with geographic and climatic conditions; and propagandistic sociopolitical interests must, in some peculiar way, be balanced against the choreographic potentialities of color, light, and sound. Moreover, remembering the always-considerable dissonance between initial design intentions and the diversity of concatenate apprehensions and receptions of those designs—receptions that invariably rearrange the original builders' and ritual choreographers' hierarchy of priorities—interpretive complexities are exacerbated even more.

Accordingly, the framework—as a heuristic strategy that works to understand and to organize ritual-architectural events with reference to the sorts of priorities that win out in these complex frays of rival forces—of necessity, includes constituent elements (here, the eleven types of priorities) that are as widely and peculiarly variegated as those forces themselves. Unlike those typological procedures that depend upon logical coherence between parallel options, this mottled patchwork is assembled more pragmatically (and more empirically) only for its eventual heuristic utility.

The Role of Examples: Real, Wrong, and Imaginary Sources of Interpretive Inspiration

Fifth and last, because so much of this project takes the form of general propositions followed by illustration via specific "cases," a candid note regarding the status and role of examples is in order. The morphology is filled out with exemplary cases that are deliberately, though unevenly, drawn from different geographic and historical contexts, different kinds of sociocultural contexts, different scales, and different disciplinary perspectives. Eclecticism supersedes elitism. Scholars' (and nonscholars') passing references to the small mounds of sand formed by the hands of Brahmin priests may, in certain instances, prove equally—or more—instructive than long, detailed treatises on huge Gothic cathedrals.[36] Eccentric rather than encyclopedic, each selected example comes at the expense of countless others that might have demonstrated the general point with equal (or perhaps greater) clarity. In past versions, I enlisted different illustrations (and posited somewhat different numbers and configurations of priorities). Were the essays rewritten again, other examples, which have since passed into view, would surely come into play.

At this still-preliminary stage in the wider hermeneutics of sacred architecture, the specific cases, which are in no small measure arbitrary, are rehearsed in the service of expositions of generalized principles. Almost no strong, original, or specific historical conclusions are ventured. Only later in the larger hermeneutical process (and not in this book), say in the detailed interrogation of specific Mesoamerican or Egyptian ritual-architectural events, and then in the composition of rigorously specific ritual-architectural reception histories, does that tension reverse so that generalized categories are manipulated in the service of particularistic analysis.

While every attempt is made to deal responsibly and accurately with historical specifics—to "get it right," so to speak[37]—the reliance on secondary sources from a range of different disciplinary venues, together with the wide cross-cultural foraging for exemplary cases, ensures a measure of inaccuracy and the restatement (sometimes knowingly) of highly contestable hypotheses.[38] Nevertheless, irksome as it may sound, arguable (and even wholly mistaken) interpretations of historical particulars can very often serve as catalysts to highly provocative, exceedingly fruitful—though previously unexplored—lines of inquiry. I proceed, in other words, from the premise (which is actually an empirical observation) that borrowing freely, even pillaging and pilfering, ideas from geographic areas and academic disciplines that lie well beyond one's area of expertise is very often heuristically evocative (and not in principle irresponsible) insofar as it raises fresh hermeneutical questions that enrich subsequent—and presumably more critically well-informed—interpretations of specific materials that do lie within one's area of special competence.[39] Overspilling historical, cultural, and disciplinary boundaries, particularly at this middle point in the interpretive process, refreshes and replenishes rather than contaminates the reservoir of hermeneutical questions.

Furthermore, trafficking as I am in hypothetical possibilities and a kind of interpretive consciousness-raising, insights that derive from nonhistorical, quasi-historical, or even thoroughly "imaginary" sacred architectures are similarly fair game. The architecture of myth, dreams, and fantasy—the splendid temples and houses in the paradisaic city of Tollan, which are described in detail in Aztec lore but apparently correspond to no (single) earthly constructions;[40] or the unbuilt, mythic places of early Judaism, like the prophet Ezekiel's extended "visionary imaginations" of the Garden of Eden or of a future temple in a restored Jerusalem, which, like Tollan, never quite materialize on terra firma[41]—is also deserving of our attention. Idealized Chinese city plans;[42] Plato's prototypes for the layout of Atlantis;[43] Bruegel's painting of the Tower of Babel;[44] the elaborate plan for an ideal, never realized, Carolingian monastery preserved in the library of Saint Gall;[45] the ways in which the "geographic imagination" of mystical Sufi poetry venerates the sacred places of Islam;[46] or, for that matter, Buddhist Jataka tales of the Bodhisattva's mythical efforts as a master architect[47]—none of which describe actual architectural concretizations—can all, nevertheless, raise intriguing hermeneutical questions.

In short, my use and deployment of examples is largely pragmatic and appropriative. In the context of this exploratory hermeneutical stage, ruling on the viability of specific expositions of sacred architecture and resolving historical controversies are, for the time being, less important than expanding and articulating the range of hypothetical alternatives. In that heuristic initiative, along with standing structures, the evocative—if fictive, unbuilt and often unbuildable—architectural creations that reside only in paintings, literature, film, or maybe in the nonwinning entries to design competitions, also lie within our morphological purview.[48]

The Heuristic Rewards of Morphology: Framework-Aided Interpretations and Comparisons

The insidiousness that often accompanies the heuristic triumphs of classificatory systems, "the tyranny of taxonomy" as Bruce Lincoln aptly labels it,[49] has by now been widely exposed (if still under-appreciated). Along with estimable rewards—about which I will be more specific momentarily—there are costs and consequences. Without question, as we work with typologies, taxonomies, and even morphologies, they work on us and on our perceptions of, and interactions with, "others" and their cultural productions. Typological attempts to expand and organize the range of interpretative options can, for instance, work also to constrain those options, to obfuscate and to overdetermine our academic conclusions. As morphological filters heighten some awarenesses, they screen out others. The unsettling irony that our interpretive constructs both open the way and stand in the way of understanding is inescapable.[50]

Expositions and instantiations of typological generalizations via historically and disciplinarily unrelated snapshots, via "scattered pickings from heterogeneous materials," elicit immediately (as they should) the red flags of decontextualization and antihistoricism.[51] As Staale Sinding-Larsen warns, "fragmentary material torn out of context is deprived of what little power of resistance against our efforts it may have possessed."[52] Furthermore, besides sometimes corrupting our scholarly conclusions, Lincoln, bolstered at this point by insights from Michel Foucault, Pierre Bourdieu, and even Emile Durkheim and Marcel Mauss, convinces us that classificatory procedures, along with their salutary "epistemological functions," certainly can work additionally in less "strictly academic" ways as weapons of socioeconomic domination and as means for the "ideological mystifications for political realities."[53] In Lincoln's view, "Taxonomy is thus not only a means for organizing information, but also—as it comes to organize the organizers—an instrument for the classification and manipulation of society."[54]

The perils and potential irresponsibility of erecting high and solid classificatory structures, if increasingly more evident, remain dauntingly real.[55] Nonetheless, on balance, retrieving again the notion of a hermeneutical wager, morphology—of the self-conscious and qualified sort that I am proposing—is, I think, an investment worth making.[56] Qualifications and ambiguities notwithstanding, the interpretation of sacred architecture with respect to these types of ritual-architectural priorities does make heuristic strides in several directions—strides that, I believe, outdistance the considerable risks.

Besides furthering the fundamental hermeneutical, phenomenological incentive for raising the endeavor above the study of buildings per se to that of the human experience of buildings, working with this framework can enhance the interpretation and comparison of sacred architecture in at least four important ways, each of which answers a methodological demand tendered in the first volume: 1) in the realm of intellectual history, the morphology facilitates the critical (re)assessment of other scholars' architectural interpretations; 2) in the realm of cross-cultural comparison, it adduces to more significant (re)orderings and juxtapositions of architecture; 3) in relation to more particularistic analyses, it enables comparisons of the multiple and diverse apprehensions that are at issue in nearly all individual ritual-architectural events; and 4) with respect to the morphology's role in architectural historiography, the framework can expedite the retrieval, and then diachronic comparison and exposition, of the shifting priorities that are manifested over time in relation to a single architectural work or configuration. My morphology can serve, in other words, in a very practical fashion as an aid to composing the sorts of ritual-architectural reception histories that were optimistically imagined in chapter 12.[57]

A succinct elaborative comment about the pregnant possibilities in each of these four arenas should suffice.

Academic Comparisons: (Re)Assessments of Other Scholars' Architectural Interpretations

Not unlike recurrent images of the intrepid anthropologist, always thwarted in his hope of finding that thoroughly pristine, previously unstudied tribe, historians of religions are even less likely to be the earliest to arrive on the interpretive scene. In the interpretation of religious architectures, virtually always we have predecessors. First, then, as one embarks on the (re)interpretation of a specific historical architecture, particularly one that is already well-worked in the academic literature, this morphology provides a means of organizing and assessing the extant interpretations. The morphological framework provides, in other words, a structure and a vocabulary for ordering the issues in academic debates over the supposed uses and meanings of various architectural phenomena. Then, having (re)ordered the relevant history of interpretation along morphological lines, historians of religions (or others) can orient themselves, their approaches, and their considered opinions within that ongoing intellectual history.

Consider, for instance, how this morphology might assist scholars in critically (re)assessing the labyrinthine and unending controversy over the pre-Columbian meanings and ritual usages of the inscribed, upright stone monuments, or stelae, usually two or three meters high, which are particularly abundant in the Petén Maya zone of southern Mexico and Guatemala. Early- and mid-twentieth-century Mayanists, prominently Sylvanus Morley and J. Eric S. Thompson—scholars who eulogized Classic Maya religious practitioners as apolitical, pacific, mystic-minded, time-worshiping astronomer-priests—were insistent that stela epigraphy was exclusively dedicated to nonhistorical, otherworldly cosmological and calendrical themes, that is, as though the overwhelming ritual-architectural priorities were, in my morphologic rubric, homology (I-A) and astronomy (I-C).[58] But then, with the convincingly iconoclastic reinterpretations of Tatiana

Proskouriakoff (about 1960), which really provide the seminal turning point in this debate, Mayanists came to the still-prevailing view that stela inscriptions, while partly cosmological, actually contain a wealth of highly specific genealogical and historical information about the lineages and exploits of individual Maya rulers—that is to say, that the dominant ritual-architectural priorities are actually, in my rubric, the commemoration of sacred history (II-B) and of politics (II-C).[59] Amidst the interminable controversy, however, scholars have likewise imaginatively re-created the Maya "stelae events" as occasions primarily for the commemoration of the dead (priority II-D) or for paying homage to specific deities, as though the commemoration of divinity (II-A) were the premier priority. Other (re)constructions of pre-Columbian stelae events feature most prominently propitiations of health and fertility (priority III-C), while, in still other opinions, a kind of indigenous meditative contemplation (priority III-B) is pictured as the driving concern.[60]

Though hardly a formula for settling such debates, the framework does serve nonetheless as a deft means for arranging the interpretive options, which may at first seem innumerable and scattered but, upon closer inspection, actually fall into a few generalized classes of argumentation. Even more usefully, besides tracking and orienting oneself within these kinds of controversies, morphologically arranged academic debates provide a means for locating instructively parallel debates in other historical contexts and academic fields. Particularly, for instance, when dealing with a largely archaeological context like that of the Classic Maya, for which the empirical evidence is fragmentary in the extreme and contemporaneous literary sources (except for hieroglyphic inscriptions) are very few, an acquaintance with analogous academic disputations concerning the ritual use of iconography and statuary in more accessible, better documented historical contexts can only sharpen one's evaluation of the viability of various options in the long-running Maya stelae debate.

Synchronic Comparisons: Cross-Cultural Juxtapositions and (Re)Orderings of Architecture

Second, with respect to rewards in the realm of synchronic, largely nonhistorical (especially cross-cultural) comparison and in response to my repeated complaints about the relative insignificance of most conventional orderings of architecture,[61] the morphology provides a means of—and thus a means for—fashioning comparative (re)orderings of architecture that do better serve the special interests of hermeneutical historians of religions.

Instead of categorizations and juxtapositions of architecture on the basis of formal, constructional, geographic, or ethnic criteria, the heuristic framework is itself constituted of—and thus facilitates—organizations and synchronic comparisons of architecture on the basis of similarities and differences in ritual-architectural priorities.

By shifting the terms of debate in this way from buildings to the *experience of* buildings, the morphology can, on the one hand, work critically (or *deconstructively*) to expose the naïveté of presuming that formally similar (or even historically related) architectures are necessarily parallel at the level of religious intention and experience. For instance, to cite an obvious example, though Egyptian pyramids and Aztec pyramids happen to have generally resemblant appearances, and are thus often imagined to have served commensurate ritual functions, when analyzed in morphological terms, it quickly becomes apparent, particularly in relation to respective concerns for the commemoration of the dead (II-D), that the two sets of structures actually display profoundly different arrangements of (types of) ritual-architectural priorities.[62] The formal parallels are, from a hermeneutical view, deceptively insignificant.

By the same token, however, on the other hand, the framework can also work *constructively* to facilitate alternative, more "eventful," more (relatively) significant orderings and juxtapositions of sacred art and architecture, particularly between architectures (and other cultural productions) that bear no obvious connection either in terms of outward appearance or the cultural orientations of their respective builders. For instance, to cite another prominent example to which I will return later, if endeavoring to understand the workings of a Gothic cathedral, one might expect, because of the obvious historical and formal connections, to find the closest, most instructive analogues, say, in Renaissance cathedrals. Yet, if we rely on the framework to stage the comparison at the level of ritual-architectural experiences, and especially if we take seriously Abbot Suger's contention that Gothic cathedrals have a special capability to work as "anagogical" props that somehow lift worshipers from the material world to the realm of the immaterial or transcendent (that is, as one particularly vivid sort of manifestation of the contemplation priority, III-B),[63] then we may find, surprisingly enough, that Gothic cathedrals actually have less in common—morphologically speaking—with their historically direct Renaissance successors than with the experience of Tibetan mandalas or perhaps even of Algonquin effigy pipes, both of which also apparently serve as props for meditative devotion (and are thus similarly strong examples of the contemplation priority).[64] Morphology-aided synchronic comparison both exposes the limitedness of a seemingly obvious comparative pairing and, even more helpfully, encourages alternative, less obvious analogues that provide important clues to the transformative mechanism at issue in the Gothic cathedral—clues that are liable to remain largely obscured in the standard juxtaposition of the Gothic cathedral with its solely European counterparts.

Similarly in the realm of synchronic comparison, in addition to evoking productive juxtapositions between historically unrelated, far-spaced cases, such as the Algonquin and the Gothic, the morphology can also provide a means of (re)assessing and (re)mapping contrasts between various regional or "ethnic" architectures within a single wider geocultural area, within pre-Columbian Mesoamerica, perhaps, or traditional Africa. As a kind of cross-*sub*cultural procedure, synchronic morphological comparison can be productive as well, in other words, between architectures that *are* contiguous and historically related. The framework might challenge one, for instance, to move beyond the typical art historical remarks about the characteristic facade decorations and vaulting techniques that are found in various Mesoamerican regions by venturing to articulate those geographic contrasts in terms of more eventful (if decidedly more tentative) generalizations such as the following: the preponderance of wide-open plaza spaces in Central Mexico suggests a strong predisposition for inclusive, theatric modes of ritual-architectural presentation (priority III-A); the Puuc area of central Yucatan is notable for mesmerically complex architectural facades, which would seem designed to foster meditation and introspection (that is, contemplation, priority III-B); while the abundance of tight, almost cavelike architectural spaces in the southern Petén area of the Maya zone seems to be dedicated primarily to esoteric, exclusivistic ritual events (the cultivation of sanctuary as defined in relation to priority III-D).[65] Framed in this fashion —rather than simply as formal, constructional, or stylistic descriptions— these morphologic characterizations, though inadequate as replacements for the more familiar, more certain regional designations, do nonetheless stand as much more intriguing, religiously significant hypotheses, which can then be pursued in any number of ways.

Intra-Event Comparisons: Single Architectural Occasions and Multiple Apprehensions

Third, also primarily in the realm of synchronic comparison, though within a much more tightly circumscribed frame, the hermeneutical interrogational pattern suggested by this morphology (and by the theoretical foundations upon which it is built) ought also to facilitate an appreciation of the multiplicity of apprehensions and meanings that are at issue within nearly any substantial individual ritual-architectural event. As I insisted throughout volume 1, an appreciation of the "autonomy and superabundance of sacred architecture" largely nullifies the empirical viability of any (supposedly) generic, authoritative architectural apprehension or "reception." Even simultaneous receptions of a single architectural event are invariably multiple and diverse. To make that point, I invoked the painfully graphic image of a public Aztec human sacrifice at the Templo Mayor that is variously attended by kings, priest-executioners, visitors, vassals, sacrificial victims, and their onlooking family members—all of whom bring very different preparednesses (or "pre-understandings") to the ritual event, all of whom play very different roles once there, and all of whom thus, quite obviously, experience drastically different sensations.

Proposing, then, that human sacrifice at the Templo Mayor "means," for instance, something about the transience of human existence or of the cosmos, without specifying for whom that meaning obtains, is neither empirically rigorous nor particularly rewarding (though this certainly remains a disappointingly common scholarly practice). Assuredly, the ritual-architectural occasion does not carry the same meaning(s) to all those participants and observers. Thus, instead of bringing the morphology's eleven headings to bear simply on the sacrificial architectural event as a whole, I am recommending that we proceed more pointedly—by submitting, to the extent possible, each of those respective pre-Columbian social constituencies to that pattern of hermeneutical interrogation. Deployed in that fashion, the framework furnishes a heuristic tool to respect and distinguish, and then to talk (and write) about, the simultaneous diversity of ritual-architectural apprehensions in that single event—a diversity that is still too often blurred and squashed.

The viability and relative success of such detailed analyses will depend on several factors. Hermeneutical inquiries based primarily on archaeological and archival resources, as in the Aztec case, present considerably greater difficulties in this respect than those fortuitous occasions in which the architectural event under consideration is available to something like ethnographic participant observation. To suggest a project that could be undertaken via a kind of morphologically aided fieldwork, consider the multiplicity of concurrent apprehensions in the more contemporary ritual-architectural circumstance of a wedding at the renowned Thorncrown Chapel in Eureka Springs, Arkansas, designed by E. Fay Jones and awarded a prize as the best work of American architecture produced during the 1980s.[66]

Were we to direct the morphological pattern of questioning at Jones himself—who cites the "proportioning" and the "ascendancy" of the thirteenth-century Sainte Chappelle in Paris as the explicit inspiration and prototype for his Arkansas design,[67] and who acknowledges a very considerable debt to "organic design principles" derived from his mentor, Frank Lloyd Wright[68]—one arrangement of (types of) ritual-architectural priorities would emerge. Were we to direct the same set of questions to the professional critics who have written so much about Thorncrown Chapel, slightly different arrangements of priorities would probably emerge. But, if we began to canvas along the same morphologic lines the bride, groom, officiants, family members, and guests at the wedding, including women, men, and children—many of whom are wholly unacquainted with (and perhaps largely uninterested in) Jones's pensive allusions to Gothic "architectural theology" and to Wright's design philosophy, but who are nonetheless deeply affected, in some cases irrevocably transformed, by the nuptial proceedings—those constituencies would almost certainly adhere to arrangements of ritual-architectural priorities that are even more widely and variously divergent from that of the architect.

Fay Jones may, then, have succeeded masterfully in his initiative to choreograph visitors' experiences of Thorncrown Chapel, to, in his own words, "move people in a special way."[69] But, consistent with our empirical preoccupations, we ought to remain skeptical that the diverse audiences of his buildings are always moved in quite the ways and directions that he had anticipated. The morphology should enable us to discern and assess the idealized priorities of architects and critics; but, even more rewardingly for empirically minded historians of religions, working with the framework should also foster an appreciation of the always divergent and diverse, on-the-ground priorities espoused by various architectural users—even within the confines of a single ritual occasion.[70]

Diachronic Comparisons: Morphology and Ritual-Architectural Reception Histories

Fourth and finally, casting these concerns for the superabundance of sacred architecture along a temporal axis, and consistent with the historiographic ambitions outlined in chapter 12 of volume 1, this morphological framework can also facilitate diachronic comparison—specifically, the composition of critical and creative ritual-architectural reception histories.[71] In other words, moving now to a slightly higher level of generality, we can use the framework not only to expose diverse architectural apprehensions within a single event but also to chart changes in emphasis and priority over the historical life—or "reception career"—of an enduring architectural work or configuration. Having insisted that revalorizations and (mis)apprehensions that deviate from the idealized expectations of architects and ritual choreographers are often the most noteworthy, and always the most empirically "real," experiences of architecture,[72] I conceive the morphology also as a means of retrieving and assessing that unpredicted and unpredictable concatenation of diverse, appropriative events.

Consider, for instance, the tumultuous and convoluted reception career of a resilient construction like the Temple of Jupiter-Baal at Baalbek in the Valley of Lebanon, which, following its tenure as a major Roman temple, was (to summarize brutally) turned into a basilica by Byzantines, then transformed into a mosque by Moslems, and then destroyed by Mongols before finally being reclaimed, more prosaically, by nomadic Lebanese shepherds as a winter stall for their livestock.[73] Chronicling the political and ethnic affiliations of those successive patrons and recording the successive alterations to the structure's physical form are worthwhile and interesting projects. But recovering, documenting, and evaluating the shifting configurations of ritual-architectural priorities that obtain in the eerily different ceremonial (and unceremonious) events undertaken in each of those phases of the Temple of Jupiter's long reception career—composing a thoroughgoing ritual-architectural reception history for the structure—is, from my vantage, considerably more rewarding and significant. And the framework educes to that more eventful project.

Or, to cite a somewhat more subtle, larger-scale case that could also benefit from morphology-aided historiography, consider the shifting alignments in (types of) ritual-architectural priorities implied by James Duncan's three-stage analysis of the architectural history of the capital city of Kandy, Sri Lanka, prior to, during, and after British colonization.[74] In the precolonial era (before 1815), the capital's claim to urban hegemony was based on its conception as "the city of the [Buddhist] god-king, the center of the universe"; it was imagined, Duncan explains, as "Mount Meru, the city of the gods descended to earth, and the stage upon which the king could display power."[75] At that point, then, Kandy's ritual-architectural program for the announcement of legitimacy and temporal authority (its exercise of one version of the politics priority, II-C) depended upon aggressive utilizations of cosmological symbolism (homology, priority I-A), along with direct and ample allusions to Buddhist sacred history (priority II-B) and conceptions of divinity (priority II-A). By contrast, in the medial era of British colonialism, the Europeans refashioned Kandy's architectural profile in ways explicitly designed to undermine the old symbols of cosmological Buddhist authority and then to make over the South Asian capital according to "a romanticized image of a pre-industrial England"[76]—an eventuality that demonstrates, among other things, continued heavy reliance on monumental architecture to assert the capital's rightful hegemony (politics, II-C), but now via means that deliberately rejected homologized, cosmographic, and (Buddhist) mythological architectural design principles.[77] Then, in the third phase, once Sri Lanka (or more properly Ceylon) had retrieved independence in 1948, Duncan describes an indigenous hope of effecting "the symbolic decolonization of the landscape" via a concerted (not altogether successful) attempt at remodeling the city yet again according to the original notion of a homologized Buddhist polity[78]—morphologically speaking, by reuniting the priority for ritual-architectural assertions of political sovereignty and legitimacy (II-C) with concerns for homology (I-A) along with Buddhist conceptions of divinity (II-A) and sacred history (II-B).

More extended and nuanced morphological analysis would, of course, reveal much greater complexities in all these cases. Operating in this fashion, however—that is, bringing the same matrix of leading hermeneutical questions to bear on each social constituency at the Thorncrown Chapel wedding or on each historical era of the Temple of Jupiter or the Asian capital—holds the interpretive conversation up to the level of events (not buildings) and, moreover, accentuates the multiplicities, changes, and shifting configurations of ritual-architectural priorities, which are so important in crafting a critical architectural reception history. In short, though itself a largely nonhistorical (and admittedly sometimes *not* keenly critical), comparative arrangement, the morphological framework nonetheless lays a foundation for analyses and architectural historiographies that are both rigorously, particularistically historical and highly critical.

Hermeneutical Manuals: Interpretive Instigation, Interrogation, and Imagination

In sum, then, the architectural morphology outlined in this work is a comparative search (primarily) after similarities that, in the end, eventuates in an appreciation of difference. It is an interim stage in the wider hermeneutics of sacred architecture. It is a generalizing, largely nonhistorical endeavor designed, ultimately, to enrich the interpretation of more rigorously contextualized specific historical circumstances. To use its language on itself, the morphology functions as an "instigatory strategy," which initiates, or sets in motion, the interpretive process. Yet, once in motion—once scholars have entered and embraced a hermeneutical conversation with a specific architectural situation—the dialogue can be carried along with a buoyancy of its own that leaves far behind the deceptively neat lines of the eleven-part framework. The morphology of priorities is, therefore, at its best simply a method, a manual, or a guidebook of suggested (and suggestive) interpretive routes. It is a hermeneutical and heuristic tool, more like a hammer or a scaffolding than an encyclopedia, an expendable means to developing the sort of particularistic analyses and comparative ritual-architectural reception histories that would prove satisfying to historians of religions.

Procedurally speaking, then, confronted with any ritual-architectural circumstance, either in person or in a text, either very familiar or startlingly alien—a Jewish wedding, a Hindu fire sacrifice, a presidential inauguration, or, more poignantly still, something like a ruined Mesoamerican pyramid for which there are no contemporaneous texts and no eyewitness accounts describing the indigenous ceremonial proceedings—one might begin the hermeneutical enterprise with consideration of the relevance of each respective category. In other words, if all hermeneutics is dialogical, I am advocating in this case a particularly interrogational hermeneutic. One could commence in an almost rote fashion by asking: How and to what extent might the homology priority (I-A) be relevant to this event? How and to what extent might the conventionality priority (I-B) be relevant to this event? How and to what extent might each of the variations on the commemoration of divinity (priority II-A) be relevant to this event? Which of the modes of ritual-architectural presentation is dominant in this case? Theater (priority III-A)? Contemplation (priority III-B)? Propitiation (priority III-C)? Or sanctuary (III-D)?[79]

I am proposing, in other words, practical, pragmatic solutions to the principal obstacle to reliances on architecture as an evidential resource for historians of religions—namely, our impoverished understanding and awareness of all that architecture, as a nonliterary "vehicle of intelligibility," can do. Convinced by now (particularly by the theoretics of hermeneutic philosophy) of the futility of standing mute before buildings, monuments, and performances waiting for "the facts to speak," the alternative is to approach each ritual-architectural circumstance with an abundance of types, patterns, cross-cultural examples, and analogies in mind. We have to make that interpretive approach as provocative and worthy conversation partners, overbrimming with questions and supposals, though not unduly certain of anything. Such a formulaic procedure, pedantic as it may sound —and personal experience with the interpretation of the ruins of Mesoamerica bears this out[80]—empowers us to break old interpretive habits, to challenge conventional assessments, and to give serious consideration to heretofore neglected possibilities.

In the end, then, the agenda of this volume, which may at first appear so annoyingly encompassing, is, after all, very humble. Mixing metaphors, it is, athletically speaking, simply a stretching and conditioning exercise, the hermeneutic calisthenics if you will that precede the interpretive game. It endeavors only to open new interpretive routes, to raise new questions, to spin out a range of alternatives regarding the ways in which sacred architectures have been (or could have been) experienced in an attempt to enliven our subsequent hermeneutic conversations. In this comparative procedure, then, no magic dwells. Expectations of feeding in data and cranking out interpretations will always be thwarted. This morphology, which can enable pedestrian and essentialist as well as nuanced and critical interpretations of sacred architecture, furnishes no substitute for the creativity, imagination, and hard labor that must always drive the hermeneutic process. But it does, I hope, help to open the way.

Part One | Architecture as Orientation: The Instigation of Ritual-Architectural Events

It all depends on the place a man occupies on the earth. The fortune and misfortune of men can be explained if we remember what connection they have to the land.

Canek: Maya Hero[1]

No duty the Executive had to perform was so trying . . . as to put the right man in the right place.

Thomas Jefferson, 1801[2]

To become completely lost is perhaps a rather rare experience for most people in the modern city. . . . But let this mishap of disorientation once occur, and the sense of anxiety and even terror that accompanies it reveals to us how closely it is linked to our sense of balance and well-being. The very word "lost" in our language means much more than simple geographical uncertainty; it carries overtones of utter disaster.

Kevin Lynch, 1960[3]

THE "RELIGIOUS ACT OF ORIENTATION" has been aptly and succinctly defined as "the fundamental process of situating human life in the world . . . the conscious act of defining and assuming proper position in space."[4] While orientation deals as well with one's situation with respect to time, society, self, and, presumably, with sacred reality, discussions of orientation most often, as in this case, privilege, deservedly or otherwise, the human situation in space. At its most basic, orientation involves finding, both literally and metaphorically, one's place in the world—or, in the case of sacred architecture, actually *constructing* one's place in the world.

Interdisciplinary Perspectives on Orientation

The excitingly diverse and very complex interrelations between orientation, architecture, and ritual, which provide the focus of the next three chapters, has spawned a substantial body of interpretive literature. Notable contributions come from several disciplinary perspectives. A number of historians of religions, for instance, have argued that there is, in fact, an important sense in which orientation *equals* religion. Mircea Eliade considered that the prehistoric act of *homo erectus* merely standing upright, and thereby constituting oneself as a "center" with respect to the four cardinal directions, provides a kind of metaphorical "origin" of religion, and, accordingly, the essential point of departure for his three-volume *History of Religious Ideas;*[5] in his view, "to acquire orientation in the chaos of homogeneity, [is] to 'found the world' and to live in a real sense."[6] Charles Long says that, for his purposes, "religion will mean orientation—orientation in the ultimate sense, that is, how one comes to terms with the ultimate significance of one's place in the world."[7] And Jonathan Smith, affording a similar priority to place and orientation in space for the study of religion, writes:

> the question of the character of the place on which one stands is the fundamental symbolic and social question. Once an individual or culture has expressed its vision of its place, a whole language of symbols and social structure will follow.[8]

Similarly conjoining religion with orientation, among anthropologists, James W. Fernandez, after exploring what he terms the "deictic" tendencies that characterize African religious experience (that is, a fundamental set of locational and directional awarenesses), concludes that "whatever else religion is it is surely, literally, a place to feel at home in space and time."[9] Accordingly, Fernandez argues (less typically) that, besides the orientational functions of traditional rites and cosmologies, the jarringly transformative experiences of colonialism and conversion in Africa also need to be understood as very profound, difficult occasions of "reorientation."[10]

Ancient Mesoamerica, like traditional Africa, another of these so-termed archaic contexts in which, presumably, the "religious experience is a total one,"[11] has also been regularly vaunted for its dedication to orientation and comprehensive orderliness. Scholars working in a host of different disciples have come to impressively similar conclusions. Some half century ago, historian Paul Kirchhoff observed a set of orientational preoccupations that, in his assessment, informed every dimension of ancient Mesoamerican culture, art, and religion. In his view:

> Ancient Mexico is a world of order, in which everything and everybody has a place. . . . Everything has its perfect place, there is a formula for everything. . . . One discovers things that appear to be disorder according to our judgment, but afterwards one discovers a much more fantastic order . . . the orderly structure can be seen in everything. . . .[12]

In the same vein, art historian George Kubler accentuates the extraordinary "monumentality" of Mesoamerican architecture, by which he means not bigness but dexterousness in overriding disorientation and "inscribing some meaning upon the inhuman and hostile wastes of nature."[13] Historian of religions Davíd Carrasco bases his entire inquiry into Mesoamerican urbanism on the premise that the quest for orientation was a causative agent of first importance; in his view, "the story of ancient Mexico is the story of places and symbols of places."[14] Equally sensitive to the complex interwovenness of architecture and orientation, archaeoastronomer Anthony Aveni argues that there was a pan-Mesoamerican "orientation motive," which informed the layout of virtually all pre-Columbian sites, most unmistakably, Teotihuacan.[15] And ethnohistorian Johanna Broda provides an even more eventful appreciation of the encompassment of these indigenous orientational schemes—or "cosmovisions"—when she argues that among the principal functions of pre-Hispanic ritual (I'd say ritual-architectural events) was the transformation of the correspondences between calendrics, myth, society, politics, and ancient Mexican building forms from static abstractions into relevant and lived realities.[16] In Broda's view, pre-Hispanic ritual, in a sense, activated, enlivened, and disseminated an indigenous sensation of encompassing order and orientation.

While the urgency for discovering (or creating) comprehensive systems of order has been most highly touted in these "archaic" contexts, the propensity for encompassing orientation is hardly confined to those situations. Among contemporary Muslims, for instance, even those living in the Western world, the nonnegotiable, shared commitment to orient one's prayer solely toward Mecca—captured so beautifully in the Persian poem that reads, "One God, one direction of prayer, one Prophet, one Book . . ."—remains the most visible sign, to themselves and others, of their participation in a unity of faith.[17]

In fact, though not always so unmistakably as in Islam, many scholars surmise, appropriately I think, that no historical context has been or is exempt from the so-termed orientation motive. Philosopher of science Elisabeth Stroker, for instance, endeavoring to contribute to "the phenomenology of lived space," contends that "being" always implies being oriented in, or "attuned" to, space; for her, orientation in space is neither an option nor a considered decision but an ontological condition, "a pre-reflective orientation toward the world," an "attuned lived experience."[18] Geographers like Yi-Fu Tuan—by accentuating the difference between "neutral, undifferentiated *space*" and "meaningful *places,*" and the seemingly ubiquitous tendency of people in all cultural settings to transform the former into the latter[19]—have similarly implied that the propensity for orienting oneself in the world has more the character of an instinct or a nonnegotiable human exigency, not unlike eating and sleeping, than a reasoned option in which one may or may not participate. Along the same lines, scholars working from a host of different disciplinary perspectives, and in all sorts of historical contexts, have invoked Suzanne Langer's insistence on the absolute human necessity of maintaining a sense of place. She holds that

> a human being can adapt himself somehow to anything his imagination can cope with: but he can not deal with Chaos. . . . Therefore our most important assets are always the symbols of our general *orientation* in nature, on the earth, in society and in what we are doing: the symbols of our *Weltanschauung* and *Lebenanschauung*.[20]

In short, the requirement of finding one's place in space and in the world is, in the judgment of many scholars, integral to the human constitution (as is the need, on occasion, for *losing* one's place).[21]

Orientation, Building, and Architecture

Students of architecture, who similarly affirm this apparently panhuman preoccupation with the discovery and cultivation of order, not surprisingly, have been particularly concerned to accentuate the crucial role of building and buildings in this quest after meaningful orientation. Postulating the ubiquitous necessity of orientation, art historian Titus Burckhardt, for instance, is willing to contend that the construction of sacred architecture at all scales—city, village, temple, and house—and in all historical contexts has invariably been preceded by requisite orientational ritual procedures:

> The rite of orientation is universal in its range. We know that it was used in the most diverse civilizations: it is mentioned in ancient Chinese books, and Vitruvius tells us that the Romans established the *cardo* and the *decumanus* of their cities in this way, after consulting the augurs on the place to be chosen; there are also numerous indications that the same procedure was used by the builders of medieval Europe.[22]

Countless architects and architectural theorists likewise emphasize the sense in which orientation is not simply a passive mode of perception (something discovered or given), but more often is the direct consequence of active and creative manipulation of one's world (something produced or won via hard effort and labor). Christian Norberg-Schulz, for instance, emphasizes the necessity of, in his words,

> supplementing the physical milieu with a symbolic milieu—that is, an environment of meaningful forms. . . . Human life cannot take place anywhere; it presupposes a space that is really a cosmos, a system of meaningful places.[23]

Then, in his subsequent work on "the concept of dwelling," Norberg-Schulz, attaches virtually equal significance to "enclosure" and "orientation."[24] Student of vernacular, or "anonymous," architecture Sibyl Moholy-Nagy similarly holds that, historically, architecture has always been humans' best and most effective strategy not only against the weather but also, and more importantly, against confusion and disorientation; often, in her view, "a planned environment . . . was man's only guarantee against chaos, the antithesis of human effort."[25]

Additionally, historians of more "pedigreed," explicitly religious architecture, though noting occasional exceptions like that of Michelangelo and the Mannerists who validate an atmosphere of doubt, conflict, and tragedy,[26] have nonetheless tended to equate "excellence" in architecture with building programs that exude harmony, regularity, balance, and symmetry —that is to say, buildings that demonstrate seemingly rigorous and perfect orientation. The throne of "harmonious architecture" has occasionally been rattled: postmodernist architects, for instance, launched a vigorous rebellion against static regularity, and iconoclastic theorists like Jonathan Smith have demonstrated that ritual-architectural events in many historical contexts are dedicated to "reflections on incongruity" rather than the celebration of an embracing cosmic order.[27] Yet, even now, irrespective of the widespread enthusiasm for asymmetry, "complexity and contradiction in architecture,"[28] for the most part, harmony, order, and correspondence (however ambiguously defined) remain the watchwords, and often the implicit criteria of success, for both popular and academic assessments of religious architecture.

Orientational Propositions and Reservations

Without question, then, orientation has been and remains a vogue, rather than obscure, topic in all sorts of academic and professional arenas. These next three chapters, which contribute to that ongoing conversation by dealing with the role of orientation in the "instigation" of ritual-architectural events, applaud—with a couple of key reservations—this still-mounting multidisciplinary enthusiasm for both general and specific architectural-orientational studies. On the affirmative side, irrespective of the highly divergent views on the interrelatedness of orientation, architecture, and ritual, I am prepared to accept as working propositions three recurrent and, I think, quite viable (in the sense of heuristically useful) claims: first, that orientation, or the human quest for a "place" in the world, is *the* fundamental religious question in traditional (and perhaps all) cultures;[29] second, that the selective validation of the natural environment and the architectural manipulation of the built environment are the two principal agencies for imposing (or discovering) order in one's surroundings; and third, that rituals, specifically ritual-architectural events, are, as Broda implies, perhaps the most fortuitous occasions in which the harmonious and homologized organizations that are embedded in religious constructions are, in a sense, released, unveiled, and introduced into the life-worlds of ritual participants and spectators. This final point deserves especial emphasis because, while there has been some acknowledgment that orientation in architecture is indispensably related to ritual, systems of architectural-cosmic-social correspondences continue, too often, to be described as ingenious abstractions apart from their performative ritual contexts.

In a more contentious vein, however, the following chapters offer two major challenges or refinements to the enthusiastic linkage of orientation and architecture. First—and this is the most important qualification—despite the crucial role that architecture plays in providing people with a sense of orientation (a point well taken in the current literature), I will insist that almost no ritual-architectural events are exhausted in the simple presentation of generalized world order. Rather, the initial presentation of unity, harmony, and order, which is characteristic of so much sacred architecture, most often functions as the strategy that *allures* ritual participants from their "spoilsport" status into the religio-architectural game.

In other words, I will insist that demonstrative fidelity to cosmic order functions, not as the sum of most (or maybe any) architectural events, but, more often, as the requisite, conservative component that invites (or, in cases, demands) serious consideration of the more substantive component of the architectural event. Cultivating a sensation of orientation and cosmic order, which has primarily to do with fostering a sense of confidence and legitimacy, is only preparatory to the ritual articulation of the very specific privileges, liabilities, and responsibilities that are concomitant with one's particular "place" in that world order. Architecture as orientation, accordingly, is linked throughout these three chapters with the notion of ritual-architectural allurement, that is, with the so-labeled front half of the two-fold structure of ritual-architectural events.[30] (Four subsequent chapters, under the rubric "Architecture as Commemoration: The Content of Architectural Events," will address the back half of the architectural situation.)

The second major challenge stems from a complaint that, while the language of "orientation," "correspondence," "parallelism," "harmony," and "microcosm" permeates, as it should, the literature on sacred architecture, the boundaries and valences of those terms are disturbingly imprecise. In the interest of somewhat greater precision, the next three chapters differentiate between three types of orientation, or three sorts of "harmonious architecture," or, perhaps most accurately (because it admits to the inevitable interpenetrability of the three variations on the theme), three sorts of orientational priorities. In other words, chapters 14, 15, and 16 explicate respectively, and then morphologically instantiate, three alternative catalytic instigatory strategies, three sorts of strategies of ritual-architectural allurement labeled with the following three code terms: homology (priority I-A), or orientation via the correlation of disparate realms of existence; convention (priority I-B), or orientation via conformity to codified architectural prescriptions or historically conventionalized patterns; and astronomy (priority I-C), that is, orientation via ritual-architectural synchronization with sky phenomena.

In each case, the subsequent message (or back half) of the ritual-architectural event wins its audience, or earns its hearing, by a display of respect and fidelity to the cosmic or traditional order. The presentation of harmonious orientation works, in other words, to certify the architectural event as a harbinger of "real," viable alternatives, and not simply as an occasion for promoting idiosyncratic, authoritarian, or expendable frivolities. But, in virtually no case is that announcement of orderly orientation the sum, or even the climax, of the ritual occasion.

As throughout this morphological exercise, the lines of this tripartite division constantly blur and occasionally dissolve. Perhaps, though, as a provisional arrangement, pulling things apart in this artificial fashion may help us, eventually, to put together nuanced and critical assessments of the various strategies of ritual-architectural allurement at work in whatever specific instances we hope to understand.

Fourteen | Homology: Microcosmic Images of the Universe (Priority I-A)

Just as certain limbs of the body are purer than others, so are certain places on earth more sacred—some on account of their situation, others because of their sparkling waters, and others because of their association or habitation of saintly people.

The Mahabharata[1]

The creation of the world is the exemplar for all constructions. Every new town, every new house that is built imitates afresh, and in a sense repeats, the creation of the world. . . . Just as the town is always an *imago mundi,* the house is always a microcosm.

Mircea Eliade, 1949[2]

Architecture . . . constantly plays the seducer. Its disguises are numerous: facades, arcades, squares, even architectural concepts become the artifacts of seduction.

Bernard Tschumi, 1996[3]

TO BEGIN ON WELL-WORKED GROUND, I can outline this first mode of ritual-architectural orientation and allurement—given the shorthand designation "homology" (priority I-A)—by reference to the phenomenological model of sacred space advanced by W. Brede Kristensen, Gerardus van der Leeuw, and, preeminently, Mircea Eliade.[4] For decades this model, at least among historians of religions and at least until fairly recently, endured as the dominant paradigm for interpreting religious architectures. Now, however, times are changing.

Phenomenology and Hierophany: The Discovery, Not Creation, of Sacred Places

Perhaps the most basic and most controversial dimension of this (in)famous model—regarding what actually makes a place "sacred"—is the shared assertion of these phenomenologists that a sacred place is a site at which a god, or some numinous power, *really* has manifested itself. To the dismay of more social scientific students of religion, these theorists, each of whom tends to make a very basic distinction between "archaic" or "primitive" apprehensions of space versus "modern" apprehensions (and then to designate the former as somehow more genuinely "religious"),[5] are willing to take very seriously (too seriously in the minds of many scholars) the possibility that sacred places really are special—and by virtue of the agency of some "Sacred Reality." The interpretations of these phenomenologists presuppose not only that the practicing faithful *regard* certain places, and thus certain built forms, as specially powerful, but that those locales *actually are,* in an ontological sense, exceptional.

Kristensen, for instance, explicitly denied that places are *made* sacred by such human activities as "the utterance of a prayer, the swearing of an oath or performance of a ritual of purification."[6] Explaining the supernatural mechanism of sacred site selection, he contended that "It is rather that this is the place where God dwells and he reveals himself."[7] "Ancient man," he said, was fully confident that "the place where the lightning and the rain have driven into the ground is the seat of divine power."[8] In that premodern view, Kristensen explained, "the holiness of the place *is* the holiness of the god who is worshipped there."[9]

In a similar vein, Eliade, by far the most thoroughgoing spokesman for this position, is even more intimately associated with this notion that "the Sacred" periodically breaks through or "irrupts" into the earthly, "profane" realm, leaving in its wake exceptionally charged places or "hierophanies," that is, "manifestations of the Sacred."[10] He repeatedly insisted on the heterogeneous and "hierophanic" character of the landscape, that is, the sense in which, from the perspective of the so-called archaic consciousness anyway (but likewise, it seems, in Eliade's own perspective), certain geographic places and features—typically mountains, waterfalls, trees, groves, caverns, stones—are somehow intrinsically sacred.[11] Eliade held, in other words, that sacred reality shows itself on earth—but not evenly. Thus, some places are qualitatively more religiously potent than others. In his view, "a sacred place is what it is because of the permanent nature of the hierophany that first consecrated it."[12]

According to this phenomenological perspective, then, human beings (particularly those committed to an "archaic ontology") do *not* create, fabricate, or sanctify particular places. The sacrality of particular sites and features of the landscape is *not,* after the fashion of Durkheim (or, more recently, Jonathan Smith), a matter of social consensus or conditioning, however nondeliberative.[13] No merely human activity is adequate to transform ordinary places into sacred ones. Thus, according to Eliade, sacred places are never, properly speaking, "chosen" by people. Instead, it falls to *homo religiosus* to search for—and to "discover"—those already intrinsically, supernaturally potent places where sacred reality has made its presence felt, and then to orient themselves—and their architectural construction projects—with respect to those charged sites.[14]

In Eliade's view, which promotes that virtual equation of religion and orientation, ("archaic") human beings simply cannot lead meaningful lives in undifferentiated, homogeneous space; they must, in order to participate in "being," and thus become "real," orient themselves with respect to these hierophanic places.[15] There is, in his view, a kind of spatial counterpart to the temporal "terror of history." Accordingly, for Eliade, the rites of augury, geomancy, divination, or "orientatio," which so often precede the building of religious structures (like those addressed by Burckhardt, cited in the introduction to this part), are primarily attempts to *discover* rather than to *create* a sacred precinct.[16]

Moreover, by insisting upon the "autonomy of hierophanies,"[17] Eliade (like Kristensen and van der Leeuw in this respect)—and this goes directly to the matter of ritual-architectural allurement—is afforded a compelling explanation for the widespread, empirically indisputable tendency for religious veneration of outstanding natural features: such features truly have an intrinsic, transnatural magnetism. Furthermore, this interpretive stance has little difficulty explaining the well-documented phenomenon that "rocks, springs, caves and woods venerated from the earliest historic times are still, in different forms, held as sacred by Christian communities today."[18] This "revalorization"—or, I'd say, resilient *allure*—occurs, according to Eliade, because "sacred places will always in some way or another reveal themselves."[19] The prestige of those places is permanent because it does *not* depend upon arbitrary or simply social human choices, even of an unconscious sort.[20]

Eliade's (In)Famous Model: Mythical Archetypes, *Imago Mundis*, and *Axis Mundis*

With this controversial notion of the heterogeneity space and the "autonomy of hierophanies" as a foundation, Eliade constructs his notoriously comprehensive model of sacred space on the basis of three particularly prominent pillars, all of which he attributes to the interactivity of the archaic consciousness and "the Sacred," all exceedingly well-known. First is the notion of adherence to celestial or mythical archetypes, which manifests itself in a pervasive tendency among *homo religiosus* to conduct their lives—and thus to build their buildings—in imitation of mythical, "primordial" patterns (a phenomenon that will actually be even more germane to my exposition of the architectural commemoration of sacred history [priority II-B]). Second, and more directly relevant to this first morphological entry (homology, priority I-A), is the related notion of *imago mundi,* which entails a similarly widespread tendency among "the religious" to conceive their cultural productions, most poignantly their architectural constructions, as microcosmic replicas of the wider macrocosm. And third is the notion of *axis mundi,* a preoccupation with the symbolism of the center and the cardinal compass directions, which is manifested in an even more pervasive tendency among "primitives," to conceive of one's self, one's habitations, and one's houses of worship as situated at the Center of the World. (This "centering" phenomenon, while generally relevant to the homology priority, has been so widely discussed and instantiated that I can largely dispense with rehearsing it again in this context.[21])

Architecturally speaking, these three interrelated principles coalesce in Eliade's poignant contention that, for the *homo religiosus,* the construction of any structure—whether at the scale of houses, temples, villages, cities, or even whole regions—is patterned after the cosmogony, the original creation of the world, and is thus tantamount to the founding or (re)creation of a new world. In his redoubted formulation:

> *If the world is to be lived in,* it must be *founded*—and no world can come to birth in the chaos of the homogeneity and relativity of profane space. The discovery or projection of a fixed point—the center—is equivalent to the creation of the world.[22]

Consequently then, according to Eliade—and it is really this portion of his wider model that constitutes the quintessence of what I am designating as the homology priority—there is a widespread, in his generalizing vision virtually panhuman, incentive to design and conceive of architectural forms as literal images of the world, downsized (microcosmic) models of the entire universe or earthly replicas of the cosmos at large—in other words, as *imago mundi*s.[23] Thus, every occasion of building, whether a simple domicile or a sumptuous temple, can be rewarding and deeply meaningful (from the perspective of the "archaic consciousness") insofar as it is an occasion to reiterate the (mythical) creation of the world, to create a new "little cosmos," and thereby to participate again in the freshness and purity of "the primordial time of beginnings."[24]

Though derived originally from his studies of Hinduism and the ancient Near East, specifically Babylon, neither Eliade nor his inheritors have been at all timid in extending this model of homologized or microcosmic architecture into countless other cultural contexts. (Samplings of the impressively long list of exemplars from the work of Eliade and others will be enumerated below.) Instead of limited utility, then, the more serious problem has been the uncritical ease with which scholars have latched onto Eliade's scheme as a would-be interpretive panacea for speedily explaining all sorts of monuments in virtually every historical context. Because Eliade's model seemed to provide a coherent way of talking about sacred space in so many different situations (many of which he himself never addresses), the incautious tendency, literally for decades, was to follow Eliade's universalizing lead by applying this model wholesale to any and all historical contexts—seizing here on a mythical archetype, there on a hierophany, and everywhere on *axis* and *imago mundis*.

Recovering Eliade: Heuristic Options and (Would-be) Interpretive Panaceas

The repute of this marvelous, once-canonical model is now on the decline, as it perhaps should be. At present a spectrum of opinions stretches between two extremes: At one end are fully faithful enthusiasts, now probably consisting more of non–historians of religions who have happened onto Eliade's theory and remain impressed, sometimes seemingly intoxicated, by its suggestive power in the realms both of studying and of making architecture; epigrammatic, usually uncritical invocations of Eliade continue to abound, for instance, in the writings of architects and designers.[25] At the other extreme are detractors so thoroughly disenchanted with Eliade's entire *Religionswissenschaft* project, for one reason or another, that they feel compelled to jettison all allusions to his celebrated terminology of sacred space except to expose, and presumably repair, the distortions promulgated by what they regard as its insidious theoretical hegemony.[26]

For my morphological purposes, however, a middle ground—defined primarily by two qualifications (or actually three, counting one to which I will return at the chapter's end)—provides the most serviceable critical stance. First, with respect to the supposed "autonomy of hierophanies," which is itself enough for many scholars to abandon Eliade's hermeneutic scow, I would wager that this model's heuristic utility for the critical interpretation of specific historical cases is *not,* after all, contingent on the acceptance (or rejection) of some apparently theological claim regarding the existence or active agency of "the Sacred." Even those students of religious architecture who are less inclined than Eliade to afford sacred places any intrinsic supernatural ontological status (and that includes most contemporary academics) are nonetheless willing to grant that, at least from the perspective of the devotees, the site selection of a place of worship is very often—though certainly not always—imagined as the purgative of a supernatural rather than a human agency.[27] As an ontological or universally applicable proposition, Eliade's notion of hierophany may be unpalatable (perhaps even, as some feel, insidious); but it remains, at the very least, useful in describing one sort of internal ritual-architectural logic wherein designers and worshipers imagine as their first priority the *discovery,* then acknowledgment, of some (seemingly) intrinsically powerful site.[28]

Second, and even more basically, I would insist that, in the context of a morphology of ritual-architectural priorities, this rightfully renowned theory of sacred space must be understood as directing our attention to one major set of concerns—but only one among many. Instead of the original, "primordial" or "really real" human mode of organizing sacred space from which all other modes were subsequently to evolve (or *de*volve as Eliade might lead us to believe), the phenomenon of homologized space and architecture deserves a prominent place alongside several other heuristic options. Despite the unfettered universalizing language, and despite the wide cross-cultural relevance of the patterns that Eliade presents, those patterns are, with respect to other historical architectures, as Gregory Alles demonstrates in the case of Greece, almost wholly irrelevant.[29] Some cases, and some dimensions of the experience of sacred architecture, are illumined by Eliade's interpretive frame; but many others, even within supposedly "archaic" contexts, are not. Eliade delivers less than he promises, and much less than a remedy to all our interpretive troubles.

Nonetheless, in my current initiative to assemble and organize provocative, though always limited and open-ended questions, Eliade's utility remains formidable in the extreme. Particularly (but not exclusively) with respect to this first mode of orientation and allurement (homology, priority I-A), Eliade's work—and specifically his famous concept of the *imago mundi*—remain singularly helpful.[30] My recommendation is, then, that we neither impose Eliade's model as the authoritative yardstick against which all variously "desacralized" architectural configurations are measured (as he himself seems to want us to do) nor consign the old model to the interpretive scrapheap (as many of his critics demand). Instead of the sole prepotent paradigm, his theory becomes for us one rich hermeneutical resource among others. My suggestion is, in other words, that the provocative, only sometimes relevant, terminology of *imago mundi,* "cosmogrammatic," and "microcosmic" architecture, together with that of *axis mundi* and even hierophany (all of which are most relevant in my rubric to the homology priority), be transformed into heuristic questions—and then situated alongside ten other sets of similarly limited heuristic queries.

The Exposition and Instantiation of Homology: Innumerable Contexts and Scales

With those caveats, then, the principle of homology and homologized architecture, which enjoys such a high profile in Eliade's writing, most definitely deserves our considered attention. As revealed either by his work or by others', the logic and effectiveness of homologized building schemes depend upon a "cosmological conviction," a confidence (characteristic particularly of "locative" worldviews) in an encompassing world order, and a commitment to attune all dimensions of life to that order.[31] This urge to respect, or sometimes *effect,* an all-embracing unification between the disparate spheres of existence provides the basis for those fabulous architectural-cosmological systems that (endeavor to) unite microcosm and macrocosm through elaborate correlations—or homologies—of celestial phenomena, biological species, colors, parts of the body, seasons of the year, systems of polity, mythicohistorical events, and architectural forms.

Roxana Waterson, for example (who does not appeal directly to Eliade), has documented the exercise of such a cosmological conviction in the house plan of the Sa'Dan Toraja of Indonesia, a domicile that is explicitly conceived and constructed as a reduced version of the entire Toraja cosmological system. Thus, in this case, the east end of the building corresponds to the rising sun, to the color yellow, to the right hand, to a certain set of fecund deities (*deata*) and life-enhancing rituals, and to shared social prosperity. The west side of the Toraja house, by contrast, corresponds to the setting sun, to red and black, to the left hand, to death and the ancestors, to a set of mortuary rituals, and to social division and competition.[32]

Eliade's own innumerable examples of such homologized structures, to mention but a few, range over such far-flung contexts as the Siberian Samoyed, the Ainu of Japan, the Khasi of Northeast India, the Hamilitic peoples of North Africa, the Canadian Algonkian, and the Delaware

Indians, whose "big house" stands for the world in the sense that its floor *is* the earth, the four walls *are* the four quarters, and the roof *is* the sky.[33] The global illustration of cosmogrammatic architecture, both by aficionados of Eliade and by others with very different epistemological starting points, has been truly awe-inspiring. Even a brush with the overstuffed literature on homologized architecture reveals a spectacular range of viable exemplary cases. The gigantic mandala architectures of Borobudur in Java, for instance, and Angkor Thom in Cambodia;[34] in India, the ancient pilgrimage city of Banaras and any number of Hindu temples patterned after the mythical Mount Meru;[35] Tibetan monasteries;[36] and the three-tiered *yaka calai* room where the South Indian fire sacrifice (or *yakam*) is performed have all been interpreted, not unconvincingly, as architectural cosmograms.[37] Likewise, the humble though symbolically munificent houses of the Atoni on the Indonesian island of Timor;[38] Sudanese Dogon longhouses and the vernacular architecture of West Africa;[39] the Salteaux Indian villages of Manitoba, along with Shoshone and Ute sun dance lodges;[40] and even Shaker meetinghouses in the eastern United States, notwithstanding the profound differences among those structures and cultural contexts, have all been illumined similarly (in a morphological sense) as human constructions that mirror the cosmic order.[41]

Furthermore, the incentive for homologization seems to manifest itself on every conceivable scale. In Japan houses, temples, and even the whole of the island-country, conceived as a "divine nation," have been elucidated as literal images of the universe.[42] Recent studies of Mesoamerican "cosmovision" (noted earlier) reveal an exercise of the homology priority at virtually every scale of pre-Columbian architecture:[43] Joyce Marcus has hypothesized a regionally homologized scheme among the Classic Maya (not unlike the Inca *ceque* system, discussed below) wherein Tikal was the grand ceremonial capital, which had dynastic links with four regional capitals that were geometrically positioned to correspond with the four divine brothers (or *bacabs*) of Maya mythology, who bore the sky respectively in the north, south, east, and west.[44] At the scale of individual sites, besides numerous four-quartered pre-Columbian cities of the sort featured in urban geographer Paul Wheatley's seminal work,[45] there is ample evidence that both pre- and post-Hispanic Maya villages were arranged with four principal entrances, often guarded by four *balams,* or jaguars.[46] Likewise, individual buildings at a number of Maya sites have been interpreted as "miniature models of the universe";[47] and the Aztec Templo Mayor is only one of numerous arresting examples of cosmogrammatic construction in the Central Mexican area.[48] Even the constituent elements of pre-Columbian buildings—for example, tripartite columns correlated with heaven, earth, and underworld—are, in many cases, homologized constructions.[49] And finally, at an even smaller scale, the ritual accoutrements in Mesoamerican architecture—for instance, offertory boxes and incesario lids—are often designed as homologized cosmograms.[50]

Homologized Houses, Empires, and Rituals: Two South American Examples

Assuredly, then, the literature is overbrimming with instances of homologized architecture, many, but hardly all, of which have been interpreted with direct reference to Eliade's model. Two final South American examples, treated in slightly greater detail, may, however, help to clarify how this incentive to homologize actually works, particularly in relation to ritual, as a means of ritual-architectural orientation and allurement. In both cases, the morphological themes typically associated with the homology priority (I-A)—hierophanic space, mythical precedents, the symbolism of the center and cardinal directions, and, particularly, parallelism between micro- and macrocosm—are unmistakably pertinent.

First, the Barasana longhouse (also not among Eliade's own examples), owing to its accompanying ritual data, constitutes a particularly rich exemplum for the type of architectural event that has as its priority the embodiment and expression of a homologous correspondence that embraces the various realms of an organic universe.[51] As anthropologists Stephen and Christine Hugh-Jones have so carefully documented, for the Barasana, a group of some three hundred in Northwest Amazonia, the universe is itself a house.[52] According to Barasana myth, in the beginning there were no people inside the universe-house until *Yeba Meni,* their anaconda ancestor, entered from the east and swam upriver to the *Pira-parana,* the center of the world. There, *Yeba Meni* reversed its direction, and then, either by vomiting them out of its mouth or by transforming and dissecting its body, created the respective constituencies of the He People, the protohuman ancestors of the Barasana. Their order of creation both gave rise to the hierarchic ranking of the different sibs and determined where they and their human descendents should reside on earth.

The most important event in Barasana religious life is, then, the He House ritual in which shamanistic powers, hallucinogenic drugs, and contact with sacred objects are enlisted to reenact this sequence of mythical events. In the context of this august occasion, the built form of the maloca, or longhouse, will, in an important sense, *become* the universe and the mere humans inside will *become* the He People, or first ancestors. Stephen Hugh-Jones explains how, in preparation for the periodic event, the Barasana maloca, a structure some eighty feet long by forty feet wide with a tent-like gable roof, is explicitly conceived and constructed as a microcosm of the whole universe: the roof is the sky, the house posts are mountains that support the sky, and the floor space is the earth.[53] Inside there are two overlapping symbolic geographies: one concentrically based on center and periphery, the other on front and back. Both geographies are meticulously homologized with reference to distinctions between sacred/profane, male/female, social life/domestic life, consumption of food/production of food, daytime/nighttime, and so forth.[54] Furthermore, there is a vertical correlation between the elevations of the longhouse, the layers of the Barasana cosmos, and the religious disposition of each layer.[55]

For the performance of the He House proper, Barasana individuals form an anaconda-like line and march into the center of the universe-house, where, in reiteration of the successive creations of their ancestors, they split apart and move to their respective places in the architectural cosmos. The ritual is required, in other words, to activate and reaffirm the otherwise static arrangement of spatial, mythological, and social associations.

The pre-Columbian *ceque* system of Cuzco, Peru, provides an even more breathtaking instance of the homology priority, and one that pushes the homologizing agenda to a regional scale.[56] R. T. Zuidema's meticulous studies of the sociopolitical dimensions of the *ceque* system, and more recently of its archaeoastronomical dimensions, demonstrate a fabulous density of systematization.[57] Specifically, he explains how the whole of the Inca empire was integrated via an intensely elaborate network of some four hundred stone shrines, or *huacas,* which were positioned along arrow-straight sightlines—or *ceque*—some up to fifteen kilometers long and all of which converged, like the spokes of a wheel, upon the Coricancha, or Temple of the Sun, at the center of the capital city.

Though at points almost impenetrably (but justifiably) detailed, Zuidema's researches reveal, in brief, that the regional domain of Cuzco was divided by an east-west axis into upper (*Hanan*/northern) and lower (*Hurin*/southern) moieties, each of which was halved again to produce four quarters, or *suyus.*[58] Each *suyu,* or socioterritorial quarter, possessed an ordered number of *ceque* lines, which in turn corresponded both to particular social (sub)groups and to the "descendants" affiliated with particular (usually long-deceased) Inca emperors. Residents were thus assigned a special connection with the mythicohistorical era in which their respective emperor-forebear had reigned. With the entire imperial region partitioned in this fashion, like an enormous pie that had been sliced out from its center over and over again (along the invisible *ceque* sightlines), territories and neighborhoods were, in other words, carefully correlated with respective sociopolitical privileges and obligations, as well as with colors, occupations, tribute responsibilities, kinship and marriage groups, mythological and historical events, seasons and holidays in the festival calendar, and, not inconsequentially, sky phenomena.

More edifying at the moment than the details, however, is the realization that here as well it was periodic ritual that activated the otherwise latent homologized system. We learn from Zuidema, whom I again savagely summarize, that each *huaca* on a given *ceque* was worshiped on its own day, thus constituting an occasion to draft the inhabitants of that respective territory into special ceremonial roles and, thereby, to provide (or force upon) them a forum for reminding themselves and others of the rights and duties concomitant with their particular place in the empire.[59] Moreover, whole groups and combinations of *ceque* were connected with larger divisions of time, which would, it seems, likewise have served to engender and clarify the network of socioeconomic and religiopolitical relations. In short, the *ceque* system, whether serving primarily as a means of state-sponsored domination or, as Eliade would probably propose, of meaningful social and even cosmic orientation (or as both perhaps), the transformation of that fantastic scheme from cartographic abstraction to lived reality would have depended, almost assuredly, on the exercise of its ritual dimensions.

Closing Thoughts: Homology as a Strategy of Ritual-Architectural Allurement

As even this brief sampling well demonstrates—and one should not be left with the erroneous impression that the homology priority (I-A) is strictly the preserve of traditional or "archaic" contexts[60]—the cross-cultural history of sacred architecture, both at its most spectacular and most modest extremes, abounds with examples of homologized building. The documentation of architectural projects that work to replicate the cosmos, and thus to effect a unification of disparate realms of existence, has been, in short, thoroughgoing and indisputable. Therefore, in the end, it becomes less significant (for me) to announce once again the international pervasiveness of homologized architecture and the wide applicability of Eliade's phenomenological conception of the *imago mundi*—a task already widely embraced with aplomb and success—than to guard against being lulled to believe that Eliade's model of sacred space explains more than it actually does.

To reiterate, simply noting the slick "fit" between this famed model—noting, for instance, in the case of Tenrikyo religion in Japan (again not among Eliade's own examples) that "It is interesting and even surprising that here the phenomenologists' description of the meaning of sacred places remarkably holds true"[61]—and then accepting as a final conclusion something about the generic correctness, or "truth," of the formulations of Kristensen, van der Leeuw, or Eliade, does almost nothing to advance our understanding of the empirical workings of specific sacred architectures. We can, however, benefit greatly in that empirical regard by mining those theorists for provisional heuristic questions—if, that is, we remain vigilantly cognizant that the priority for homologization and cosmic unification is, for all its importance, but one of a number of competing priorities that assert themselves in the design (and experience) of any religio-architectural situation. In fact, the enumeration of ten alternative, less well-documented types of ritual-architectural priorities in the subsequent sections of this volume is, among other things, a concerted effort to counteract any interpretive lethargy or overconfidence that Eliade's model can "explain it all." Homology and the so-termed cosmological conviction are *not,* in every case, preeminent concerns.

Nevertheless, as but one set of design parameters among many, the cultivation of "harmony with the cosmos" does still retain a distinctive prestige. It is, in most instances, actually less a rival alternative alongside other ritual-architectural priorities than a substratum underneath. That is to say, homologized architectures, like the Barasana longhouse and the Peruvian *ceque* system, do articulate a cosmological conviction for generalized unity and cosmic wholeness; but, invariably—and this is that third large qualification to which I referred earlier—we have to appreciate that such cosmic articulations are virtually always the *beginning* of an architectural event's significance rather than a summation of its total significance.

The construction of homologized architecture is, in other words, most often a strategy of ritual-architectural allurement. The display of fidelity to cosmic dictates, in most situations, serves as that essential conservative component of allurement or instigation, the so-labeled front half of the ritual-architectural event that sets the process in motion. By demonstrating its integral involvement in the cosmological fabric, a cosmogrammatic monument (or a city or a territory) ought to be perceived as reliable, legitimate, and worthy of a serious consideration, and, thus, the associated ritual-architectural events ought to be appreciated as occasions of transhuman, cosmic consequence. If, as Bernard Tschumi maintains, "architecture . . . constantly plays the seducer,"[62] then presentations of homology are among architects' most powerful and most oft-used tools of seduction.

Mesoamerican examples again provide a vehicle for making the point. Huge pyramid-temples, such as the Castillo at Chichén Itzá, which has so many obviously calendrical referencings that it could well function as a kind of didactic text for the space-time machinations of the northern Maya, or the Pyramid of the Niches at El Tajin, Veracruz, with its 365 recessed compartments that must have been correlated to the days of the solar year, are unmistakable exercises of the homology priority (I-A).[63] Of that there is little question. Yet, these exercises in spatiotemporal unification through architecture do not, I think, constitute the total meaning of these monuments. More likely, these irrefutable displays of homologized unity were intended to convince the assembled pre-Hispanic audiences that these monuments, and even more the ritual activities that transpired on and around them, were legitimate, important, and deserving of serious attention. Such unifying displays work primarily to capture the interest of onlookers and to invite their participation. The initiative at homologization constituted, in other words, whether at Chichén Itzá and El Tajin or among the Barasana and Inca, an important element in the *instigation* of ritual-architectural events—events that, once the spectators had been lured into involvement, would have proceeded (in the back half of those occasions) to articulate more substantive messages about such issues as pre-Columbian conceptions of divinity and sacred history (priorities II-A and II-B), or perhaps about particularistic socioeconomic and political responsibilities (that is, priority II-C), all themes that will be addressed in subsequent chapters.

In sum then, homologized architecture works in concert with, rather than at the expense of, other ritual-architectural priorities. Where applicable, it sets the stage and calls the assembly to attention. The significance of homologized architecture and exercise of what I'm calling priority I-A is almost never exhausted in the simple pronouncement of some static cosmic order (as too many Eliadean interpretations imply). Much more often, the architectural creation of an aura of cosmological correspondence is the strategy (actually one among several strategies) that lures—or allures—participants and spectators away from their status as spoilsports and into the ritual game. Homologized architecture engenders trust and respect, and thereby opens people to the kind of receptivity, or suspension of disbelief, that is requisite to transactions of meaning and transformative experiences of architecture. And therein lies the greatest relevance of homologized architecture, and thus of Eliade's work, for this morphological framework of ritual-architectural priorities.

Fifteen | Convention: Codified Prescriptions of Order (Priority I-B)

> In the Doric, the symmetrical proportions are distinguished by the following rules. . . . The aperture of the doorway should be determined by dividing the height of the temple, from floor to coffered ceiling, into three and one half parts and letting two and one half thereof constitute the height of the aperture of the folding doors. . . .
>
> Vitruvius[1]

> Art [in India and elsewhere, and especially hieratic art] is by definition essentially conventional (*saṁketita*). . . . Conventionality [in art] has nothing to do with calculated simplification . . . or with degeneration from representation.
>
> Ananda Coomaraswamy, 1934[2]

> The game of architecture is an intricate play with rules that one may accept or reject. . . . To differentiate between rules and ropes is irrelevant here. What matters is that there is no simple bondage technique: the more numerous and sophisticated the restraints, the greater the pleasure.
>
> Bernard Tschumi, 1996[3]

FEW ARCHITECTS WOULD DISPUTE that theirs is a profession encumbered by many rules, both written and unwritten. Even famously independent autodidacts, such as the Mexican Luis Barragan, winner of the 1980 Pritzker award (described as an architectural equivalent of the Nobel Prize)—who, like Frank Lloyd Wright, Mies van der Rohe, and Le Corbusier, can attest with no regret whatever to a complete avoidance of formal architectural training—cannot claim to work outside of systems of conventionalized architectural design.[4] The "mechanism of architecture," which depends upon a twofold juxtaposition of order and variation, of conformity with and departure from expectations, requires that all (successful) architecture, even that produced by the most fiercely individualistic designers, is rule-bound.[5]

To accept, however, as Ananda Coomaraswamy (among many) persuades us, that all art and architecture, particularly in explicitly "hieratic" manifestations, is, in some measure, conventionalized, is not to imagine that the sway of convention is everywhere the same. Canons of tradition face serious competition in both the design and the experience of sacred architecture. This chapter, though, is dedicated to the exposition of a second mode of ritual-architectural orientation and allurement in which adherence to codified prescriptions and prestigious mythicohistoric precedents, usually in some direct and explicit way, does become the preeminent concern (a prospect that I designate "convention," or priority I-B).[6]

In the cross-cultural, cross-disciplinary survey of that theme, three sorts of indigenous claims to the authority of standardized architectural stipulations emerge as most conspicuous: 1) that there are certain universally applicable rhythms and proportions, observable in the workings of nature and mathematics, for example, that ought then to be replicated in architecture; 2) that a god, variously conceived, has decreed certain ritual-architectural prescriptions, which ought then to be observed in architectural design; and 3) that prestigious forebears, "the Ancients" as it were, again variously conceived, have established definitive patterns that ought to be replicated in one's contemporary architecture. Heuristically useful, in historical practice these suboptions, even more than most of my morphological categories, are non–mutually exclusive and, as we will see, constantly intersecting.

Overlapping Options: Conventionalized and/or Homologized Orientation

Otto von Simson argues that the symbolism of the Gothic cathedral has been misunderstood.[7] In his attempt to remedy that error he articulates what amounts to a heuristic distinction between architecture conceived as a literal image of the universe (homology, priority I-A) and architectural adherence to codified prescriptions of order that were "discovered" by earlier generations and canonized by tradition, that is, one seminal variation on the convention priority.[8] Von Simson repeatedly describes the Gothic cathedral, which in his opinion attains its classic expression at Chartres, as a "symbol of heaven," a "'model' of the cosmos," and an "image of the Celestial City"—all metaphors that connote homologized architecture.[9] Yet, he argues persuasively that the nature of the relation between the symbolic cathedral and the larger cosmos is not, as Hans Sedlmayr has contended, "representation," and even less is it "optical illusion."[10]

Alternatively, according to von Simson, the built form of the cathedral and cosmos are linked by what he calls "the tie of analogy." He argues, in other words, that a particular set of abstract laws of measure and proportion, deemed "universal" by the Western Christian tradition, were considered to inform both the universe at large and the physical form of the cathedral. Accordingly, the architectural configuration of the Gothic cathedral is, from this perspective, conceived not so much as a kind of three-dimensional representation of the universe, that is, as a microcosmic reflection of the macrocosm (as in the case of the homology priority, I-A), as it is a reflection of a commitment to replicate traditionally validated standards of "Augustinian aesthetics of number and proportion," that is, a design initiative more aptly connected to the convention priority (I-B).

This distinction between homologized architecture and building programs that take conformity to the standards of convention as their first priority—and, even more, the *experience* of these two modes of ritual-architectural orientation—is hardly absolute.[11] More likely, the pair marks two points on a single (perhaps developmental) continuum.[12] Often, meticulous systemizations of space and proportion that arise originally from the direct, largely empirical observations of geometry, music, human anatomy, or nature (sky phenomena, for instance), or maybe even from some divine revelation, actually (as subsequent examples will show) owe their lasting prestige to processes of historical amplification and canonization. Orientation in these latter cases, then, has less to do with (even supposed) replications of the cosmos (homology, priority I-A) than with claims to be "doing it as it has always been done" (that is, convention, priority I-B). Yet, even in those many contexts in which, eventually, rote conformity to conventionalized codes and stipulations comes to matter most, the operative mode of ritual-architectural instigation continues to depend upon the presentation of an aura of reliability, stability, and incontestably legitimate order. In each of the sorts of orientational procedures along this spectrum, the ideals (or at least appearance) of world harmony, of correspondence between disparate realms of existence and of synchronization with the prevailing rhythms of the universe, are paramount.

Still, the contrast between these first two morphological categories is significant. Where the builders of the Barasana longhouse, a choice exemplum of the homology priority, express their confidence and commitment to world harmony by actually constructing a microcosmic duplicate of the universe, participants in this second type of orientational strategy make their bid for orientational legitimacy by conformity to abstract principles that, often even by their own admission, carry the authority granted by history and tradition. As two different morphologically distinct modes of allurement, homologized architecture is prestigious and reliable because it (seemingly) conforms to a (super)natural, cosmological scheme; conventionalized architecture, by contrast, is prestigious and reliable because it conforms faithfully to rules and principles that enjoy some historically sanctioned pedigree. Again, concrete examples provide the best explication.

Renaissance Rulebooks: Secret Rhythms, Magic Numbers, and Manuals of Proportion

When, in the West, this idea of reproducing in architecture the secret rhythms and proportions of the universe actually originated has been a matter of considerable debate. Vincent Scully suggests postclassic Greece;[13] Whitney Stoddard argues for a Romanesque origin;[14] von Simson's work affords that privilege to the Gothic, while Rudolf Wittkower connects this preoccupation with the emergence of the Renaissance.[15] It is in Renaissance Italy, however, and in the proliferation of manuals of proportional building standards that this priority for conventionalization finds perhaps its most lucid, Western illustration. The quintessence of this Renaissance architectural tradition, and thus a prime exemplar of the convention priority, is Leon Battista Alberti (1404–1472).[16]

Unsurpassed as a master at integrating abstract principles and practical construction processes, Alberti's greatest contribution was not a particular building, but a handbook for the working architect.[17] Reworking the famous architectural treatise of Vitruvius, Alberti's *De re aedificatoria* (1485) is the most prestigious in a distinguished line of Italian rulebooks that includes, among others, the hugely influential sixteenth-century manuals of Sebastiano Serlio,[18] Giacomo Barozzi da Vignola,[19] and Andrea Palladio.[20] Conformity to the practical prescriptions of proportion and style outlined in these manuals, whether duteously or selectively, far exceeded the bounds of ecclesiastical architecture of Italy or, for that matter, of the Renaissance era. Moreover, the abundant (and continuing) legacy of these building manuals represents, among other things, a giant reservoir of buildings—particularly institutional buildings—whose plea for legitimacy is based on precisely this orientational strategy of fidelity to historically canonized standards of architectural design (one version of the convention priority).

The ascendancy of rarified proportionality and architectural rulebooks in the Italian Renaissance was, not inconsequentially, abetted by a congenial and all-encompassing theoretical orientation. The God of the Renaissance (by contrast to that of the Middle Ages) was conceived as the

"Great Artificer of Nature," himself an architect who had fashioned the cosmos according to immutable metric laws.[21] Moreover, scientific Copernican cosmology confirmed the Renaissance confidence in a universe that was systematically and rationally ordered according to abstract, general rules, the "first principles of Nature." Though operative everywhere (and ultimately the consequence of God's perfect creation), these immutable laws were considered to make themselves most available to empirical discovery in the proportions of geometry, in the harmonic tones of music, and in the measurements of the human body[22]—all of which were diligently scrutinized by the doyen of this tradition, Alberti.[23] For Alberti, then, space was neither heterogeneous nor hierophanic (in contrast to Eliade's "archaic ontology"); instead, it was a thoroughly consistent substance that could be endlessly dissected, arranged, and rearranged. Thus, architecture, for Alberti, as for Vitruvius,[24] became a science of partitioning space according to the harmonic patterns of nature, a science in which, as Wittkower explains, the supreme priority was proportion, that is, discerning, and then replicating in built forms, the correct relationship of parts to the whole.[25]

The continued influence of Alberti's manual, and probably even more so that of Palladio, is impressive to be sure. Perhaps even more notable in the modern era, however, was Le Corbusier's attempt, almost half a millennium later, to revive this tradition of architectural proportionality with his famous "modular" system, based on the "golden section" and the "golden triangle."[26] Though (as I will note toward the close of this chapter) Corbusier's expectation for the experiential impact of standardized forms seems rather more modest than that of Alberti, his notion of harmonious architecture, like Alberti's, does rely heavily and explicitly on analogies to mathematics, music, and especially to the proportions of the human body.[27]

Axiomatic Stipulations and Architectural Legalism: Cross-Cultural Instantiations

If Renaissance conceptions of proportionality and architecture lent themselves particularly to codification, innumerable earlier and later traditions, most operating with very different epistemologies, likewise evidence the embrace (or imposition) of similarly formulaic, sometimes "legalistic," principles of design. The Babylonian Code of Hammurabi (1793–1750 B.C.E.), for instance, contained both explicit directives about techniques and styles of construction and severe penalties in the case of noncompliance.[28] Ancient Egyptian manuals on the "correct" construction and decoration of temples also abound, most ascribed to legendary twenty-seventh-century B.C.E. savant Imhotep.[29] Moreover, archaeological evidence suggests that both statuary and pyramids in this context were constructed according to a grid system of rectangles and isosceles triangles so as to provide what J. G. Davies calls "absolute formal clarity,"[30] or what Gottfried Richter terms "a mathematical experience."[31]

Or, in the case of the nonrectilinear layout of ancient Greek cities, which were built prior to the emergence of Hippodamian grid systems—Athens, for example—initial academic impressions of orderlessness have since given way, again primarily on the basis of archaeology, to realizations that Greek urban planners were, at least by the sixth century B.C.E., adhering to very different, though similarly rigorous, rules of architectural spacing. C. A. Doxiadis maintains that each ancient Greek city's layout was developed on-site and in response to the peculiarities of the landscape, but that, in all cases, the determining orientational factor was "the human viewpoint."[32] Doxiadis believes that once a pivotal spot from which some idealized patron would have apprehended the city was established, usually at the main entrance to the site, buildings were arranged according to sightlines and geometrically derived angles of vision from that privileged point. Thus, instead of haphazard, in his view, "the organization of every [Greek city] site was entirely rational and could be immediately comprehended from the entrance."[33]

The Abrahamic faiths also provide strong, diversified—and continuing—exemplification of the convention priority. Islam and especially Sufism, particularly in relation to a vibrant tradition of "symbolic and qualitative mathematics," provide a surfeit of architectural design solutions like those in the dome of Persian Shaykh Lutfullāh Mosque or the colonnade of Maydān-i-Shāh, both of which are conceived as reiterating celestial, universal rhythms and proportions.[34] Famously apparent, for instance, in the Dome of the Rock, the strategic manipulation of basic geometrical shapes—circles, squares, and octagons or, in three dimensions, cubes and conical and spherical domes—is evidenced as well in virtually all Muslim regions and eras.[35] That kind of cosmo-mathematical design logic, profoundly different presuppositions notwithstanding, is, morphologically speaking, quite like its Renaissance counterpart.

Additionally, however, Islamic materials are heuristically helpful in bringing to our attention a somewhat different—though definitely not mutually exclusive—permutation on the convention priority: namely, ritual-architectural conventions revealed by a god or divinely inspired individual. Instead of being adduced primarily via observations of nature or mathematical calculations, in some cases Muslim design standards and proportions are understood to have been delivered directly by Allah, and then recorded in sacred scripture. The general, divinely sanctioned layout of the mosque, for instance, was laid down in the Qur'an, so that conformity to architectural prescriptions constitutes a willful act of submission to Allah (thus merging the priority of adherence to convention [I-B] with that of the commemoration of divinity [II-A]).[36]

In Judaism, though matters of proportioning and geo-mathematical design are considerably less prominent, this divinely inspired variation on the conventionality theme in which a god delivers the design directives, which are subsequently recorded in scripture, finds more direct parallels: Both the Torah itself and the halakic (religious-legal) literature address in detailed fashion innumerable "religious commands with a spatial import," including the boundaries of the land of Israel; Sabbath restrictions on travel; urban, village, and agricultural land usage; ecological and environmental issues; the construction of buildings suitable for the provision of specific religious functions; and even building details, such as the plan, window placement, and location of houses and synagogues so as to avoid "visual damage."[37] Moreover, as Yossi Katz's researches confirm, such Jewish spatial and architectural policies ought to—and do—remain operative, in principle, in the erection and organization of Orthodox neighborhoods and settlements during the modern era and even to the present.[38]

And, among Christianities, besides substantial continuities with these ancient Jewish architectural conventions,[39] and besides Alberti's Western tradition, Eastern Orthodox churches, and especially icons, if they are to be efficacious in transmitting divine grace to human devotees, must be configured according to traditional formulas.[40] Demonstrating the tremendous resilience of these canons of proportion for Orthodox iconography and church design, for which patrons likewise claim divine inspiration, the "Painter's Manual" by Dionysios of Fourna (written during the Turkish occupation of Greece, circa 1670–1745) continues to be meticulously followed even now both in Eastern Europe and in the construction and icon painting of Orthodox churches in the United States.[41] In these cases, though, because of the overwhelming number of storiological biblical themes in the iconography, the most prominent linkage is between the convention priority (I-B) and that of the commemoration of sacred history (II-B).

Asian Parallels: Chinese *Feng Shui* and Hindu Manuals of Proportion

In Asia, endorsements of anything like the Renaissance notion of homogeneous space are rare. Here, the features of the landscape are, traditionally, nearly always perceived as heterogeneous and hierophanically charged (thus blurring even more any clean distinction between the priorities of homology [I-A] and convention [I-B]). Codified architectural prescriptions are, nonetheless, constantly invoked to make certain that buildings—and the experience of buildings—are efficacious, legitimate, and, consequently, alluring.[42] From the realm of "imaginary architecture," a Jataka tale, for instance, recounts that when the Bodhisattva himself was acting as an architect in one of his previous lives, even he could not rely on his personal whims or self-expression; instead, even the Enlightened One—like every other master craftsman—was obliged to consult the canonical rules of tradition.[43]

One of the most salient Asian exemplifications of conventionalized building comes in the axiomatic stipulations outlined in association with the much-discussed Chinese geomantic practice of *feng shui* (literally, "wind and water").[44] As the most explicitly architectural dimension of a stunningly complex tradition of divinization, numerology, and prognosticative "magic squares,"[45] the ancient art of *feng shui* entails, as Jeffery Meyer explains, "diagnosing" the topography of the potential site of a grave, a building, or a city and then prescribing—in consultation with such ritual and divination texts as the *Chou li* (The rites of the Chou dynasty) and the *I ching* (Book of changes)—how best to harmonize the vital energies, or "cosmic breaths" (*ch'i*), set up by these new constructions with the energies inherent in the existing natural and built features.[46] In addition to establishing favorable sites and pleasing architectural configurations, *feng shui* is, moreover, a method for discerning the causes of human illness and suffering. Thus, beyond any simply aesthetic considerations, adherence to traditional orientational prescriptions in this case is a very pragmatic strategy for the avoidance of danger and the enhancement of health and prosperity.[47]

Furthermore, this resilient, partly shamanistic, partly Taoist tradition of *feng shui* geomancy (which continues to be widely practiced) was eventually overlaid with—rather than superseded by—the Confucian cosmological orientation of the cult of the emperor, which defined that sovereign as the "Son of Heaven" and his place as the *axis mundi* (a blending that demonstrates, among other things, an intersection of the ritual-architectural priority for conventionality [I-B] with those of homology [I-A] and the commemoration of politics [II-C] and even divinity [II-A]).[48] It was, in fact, the cross-fertilization of these multiple orientational schemes and priorities that eventuated in the thoroughgoing "cosmomagical," "astro-biological" design principles of centrality, axiality, and rectilinearity that Paul Wheatley regards as characteristic of all traditional Chinese capitals, including Beijing.[49]

If outwardly similar, the idealized plan of the traditional Indian city—articulated in equally detailed building manuals, the *Shilpa Shastra*—is quite different from that of the Chinese walled city. Nelson Wu, for one, considers that the two urban configurations "differ in every respect."[50] Yet, morphologically speaking, the ancient Hindu science of building (*vastu*)—which, like *feng shui* (or even Japanese *hogaku* [literally, "direction-angle"]), obtains with respect to domestic as well as explicitly religious constructions, at all architectural scales and in all phases of the construction process[51]—does, nonetheless, provide more marvelous instantiation of rigorously conventionalized building. Moreover, irrespective of the profoundly divergent epistemologies, the prescriptions for correct temple proportioning in the *Shilpa Shastra* are strikingly similar in tone to those in the treatises of Vitruvius and Alberti. For example, one among countless, relentlessly detailed passages in the *Shilpa Prakasha,* a medieval Orissan text on temple architecture, reads:

> Hear in what manner the various parts of the [Hindu] shrine are disposed.
>
> Adding together the sides (breadth and length) of the shrine, the produce of that operation in numbers multiplied by three,
>
> And that number divided by four: the result in aṅgulas determines (the height) of the wall-base in the form of a vīthī-pīṭha (plain base) on all four sides (of the temple).[52]

Rules and Design: Asian Adherence to and Deviation from Canonical Prescriptions

Within the same Indian tradition, in addition to the narrative design stipulations of the *Shilpa Shastra,* there are also schematic diagrams or mandalas, most notably the *Vastupurusha Mandala* (or "metaphysical plan"), which provide parameters for the design and layout of traditional houses, villages, cities, and, preeminently, Hindu temples.[53] Though there are innumerable versions, virtually all such drawings, which are appropriately regarded as cosmograms, or maps of the cosmos, mirror the square shape of the created universe as conceived in early Indian cosmology (thus exhibiting again the homology priority [I-A] as well as that of conventionality [I-B]). The simplest has a square divided into nine smaller squares, in which the central square corresponds to the "center of the world" while the eight peripheral squares correspond, respectively, to the cardinal directions and the four intermediate directions.[54] More elaborate versions of the *Vastupurusha Mandala* have grids of 8 x 8, 9 x 9, 10 x 10, and so on, with some containing as many as 1024 square subdivisions, or *padas*. Yet, in an important sense, all versions are interchangeable: Stella Kramrisch, for instance, concludes that, irrespective of which of these schematic renditions is put into practice, the Hindu temple, whatever its size, wherever its location, "is built in principle on the same plan, [the ritual diagram known as] the *Vastupurusamandala*."[55]

More instructive with respect to ritual-architectural orientation and allurement than the specific configurations of these traditional formulae and cosmogrammatic diagrams is, however, the vigorous debate concerning just how exactingly—and *why*—Hindu builders actually adhere to such stipulations. Some scholars emphasize that "nothing that is seen on the [Hindu] temple is left unsaid in the verbal tradition nor is any of the detail arbitrary or superfluous."[56] In this view, the *Shilpa Shastra* contains such explicitly programmatic directives that "the workmen believed that it was impossible to fail if the codes were faithfully followed."[57] Similarly stressing the necessity of meticulous compliance, Coomaraswamy, addressing the certain karmic ramifications of (in)fidelity to the canons of Indian image-making, holds that "images made as directed, with all their members complete, are attractive and merit-yielding; those [made] otherwise are destructive of life and ever increase sorrow."[58]

Tempering this notion of rote conformity, George Michell, in contrast to Coomaraswamy, contends that the building texts that comprise the *Vastu Shastra* are more likely "the theoretical writings of theologians, the learned brahmans, than manuals of architectural and artistic practice."[59] In this view, these abstract discourses are rarely concerned with the sorts of technical information on which craftsmen would directly rely. Instead, Michell believes that "their true function [is] as a collection of rules that attempts to facilitate the translation of theological concepts into architectural forms."[60] In the same vein, Kramrisch contends that the *Vastupurusa Mandala* "is a metaphysical plan of the temple," but that "this does not imply an identity of the actual plan of the temple with the mandala."[61] In her opinion, by the time the great Hindu temples were actually built, the drawing of this mandala had become, rather than a utilitarian guide to construction, "an architectural rite."[62]

Michael Meister, however, cross-checking the texts with the actual architectural forms, challenges Kramrisch's (and Michell's) intimation that the *Vastupurusa Mandala* was not directly related to the actual layout of the great Hindu temples. His alternative conclusion is that this mandala grid actually did provide the architect a very practical—yet exceedingly flexible—tool, a "proportioning diagram" or "secret device," which allowed both considerable variability and a strong continuity over some ten centuries of Hindu temple building. Thus Meister concludes (in terms that largely collapse distinctions between homology [I-A] and convention [I-B]) that,

> by preserving the ritual grid, the architect preserved the sanctity of the ritual altar, mimicking in his act that of the priest constructing the altar, itself the re-creation of a continuing cosmic creation.[63]

Even so, this final scholarly view (the most appealing from my perspective) suggests, consistent with the familiar twofold pattern of ritual-architectural events, that these esteemed Indian textual and diagrammatic formulae have enjoyed such endurance largely because they serve as vehicles, on the one hand, for fashioning demonstrable, alluring continuity with convention (and, in this case, with cosmogonic precedent) and, on the other hand, for enabling productive, somewhat more idiosyncratic departures from convention.[64]

Deliberate Archaisms and Mythicohistoric Precedents: Mesoamerican Examples

Before summing up with respect to the convention priority, we benefit by another brief digression through materials pertaining to ancient Mesoamerica. Though there is some emergent evidence of pre-Columbian concerns for abstract architectural formulae and proportionality,[65] in this context a different, more straightforward, probably more cross-culturally pervasive (and perhaps more persuasive) variation on allurement via conventionality comes to the fore: namely, the deliberate imitation of built forms, configurations, or motifs lifted from esteemed predecessors (or contemporaries), often at a considerable remove in either space or time. "Real" historical descent lines are not required. The authority—and thus "allure"—of deliberately derivative ritual-architectural styles and practices of this sort derive less from their apparent correspondence to universal cosmomagical rhythms, or to divinely decreed design requirements, than—to accentuate a third option—from their (apparent) correspondence to patterns employed by prestigious mythicohistoric precursors.[66] As noted, however, those heuristic suboptions definitely are not mutually exclusive.

Mesoamerican architecture is hardly unique in placing a premium on unoriginality. Among many obvious examples of architectural mimicry, virtually all Orthodox churches are patterned after the supreme prototype of Hagia Sophia, and so many Sikh temples have been directly modeled after the Golden Temple in Amritsar in northern India that it has been described as "the sheet anchor of the stylistic index of the entire range of Sikh architecture."[67] Even Alberti's claim to legitimacy, his careful anatomical and arithmetical studies notwithstanding, was based largely on a presumed continuity with Vitruvius and "the Ancients."[68]

Mesoamerica is nonetheless impressively thick with unmistakable instances of anachronistic and cross-regional architectural imitation.[69] Particularly intriguing, morphologically speaking, are those circumstances in which urban alignments that originate as empirical, "functional" astronomical references (thus exemplifying the astronomy priority [I-C]) are subsequently imitated, sometimes centuries later, in contexts where those traditionally revered systems are totally irrelevant to empirical celestial phenomena (thus evincing instead the convention priority [I-B]). An orientational pattern uniquely relevant to the Honduran skies of the pre-Hispanic city of Copán, for example, was duplicated at several other Maya sites where the same celestial views would *not* have been possible.[70] Or, even more famously, the 17 degrees east-of-north orientation of Teotihuacan, which probably originated in response to the movements of the Pleiades with respect to the mountains surrounding that particular site, was mimicked as a nonoperative alignment by a whole family of sites, including several built hundreds of miles away in mountainless Yucatan, nearly a millennium after the collapse of Teotihuacan.[71]

In many other cases, however, Mesoamerican exercises in ritual-architectural appropriation (again as in countless other cultural contexts) were much less subtle. Often, distinguished building styles or sculptural techniques were simply copied with little modification or imperfectly synthesized with additional well-known pictographic elements into some sort of eclectic iconographic program—thereby, at least in the hopeful expectations of designers, partaking in the prestige associated with those revered, if involuntary, donors.[72] In the obvious case of the Aztecs, who were desperate to overcome a specter of illegitimacy, their shrewd imitations of Toltec art and architectural forms, which constituted by far the most highly regarded of available mythicohistoric models, proved to be among their most expedient strategies for fashioning a distinguished pedigree, even where no actual bloodlines existed.[73] Instead of innovation, which might have intensified alienation and resentment, visitors to the grand ceremonial precinct of Tenochtitlan were thus confronted with unequivocal replicas of familiar and highly respected Toltec architecture, deliberate archaisms that were deployed to impress and legitimate. Those visitors were forced to acknowledge, in Gadamer's terms, a "continuity of tradition," perhaps even a "self-recognition" or homecoming of sorts,[74] which, to the extent this plagiaristic ploy worked, required even reluctant spectators to give serious consideration to the religiopolitical program of Aztec civic ceremony, however objectionable it may at first have appeared.[75]

Experiencing Proportionality: The Transformative Consequences of Conventionality

There is, then, ample and irrefutable cross-cultural evidence of sacred architecture that not only participates in conventionalized patterns (as all assuredly does), but takes its form primarily in direct and explicit response either to codified prescriptions or to prestigious mythicohistoric precedents. The nature of the human *experience* of conventionalized architecture, and particularly of architectonic proportioning, is, however, a rather more contestable issue—especially since explicit, detailed knowledge of the conventions at issue is virtually always highly restricted. Meister, for instance, aptly demonstrates in the case of the complex Hindu system of proportioning based on the *Vastupurusha Mandala*—and this would assuredly apply as well to the arcane divinations of *feng shui* geomancy, the geometric calculations of Greek site planning, or the precise proportioning rules of Orthodox icons—that only a very elite set of specialists has even a rudimentary command of the operative abstract principles.[76] As Meister suggests, few people are cognizant of the logic behind the architectural forms in which they live their daily lives; fewer still explicitly understand the subtleties of the structures in which they worship.

And yet, if the precise standards of "correct" proportioning and orientation are, in most cases, either secret or at least highly privileged knowledge, how then do the great majority of untutored ritual participants experience these architectural conventions? Is fidelity to the dictates of tradition of any significance to them? And how, if at all, do these recondite conventions work on their sensibilities to effect anything like a transformative religious experience?

If historically verifiable answers to those questions are elusive (another understatement), intriguing, heuristically provocative proposals (as befit an exercise in "hermeneutic calisthenics"), nearly all vaunting the fortuitous consequences of correct proportioning, are quite common. Alberti, suggestive here by his extravagant assessment of the transformative potential of the experience of skillfully wrought art and architecture, marks one endpoint on the spectrum. In his roseate view, perfectly proportioned architecture (or painting or sculpture) engenders a nearly magical, certainly transrational sense of realization and fulfillment. No preparatory training, no culturally specific cultivation of taste nor experiential conditioning is required. Simply for any person, however unschooled in the theoretics of design, to stand in the face of beautiful—that is, rightly proportioned—works of art, according to Alberti, automatically effects a profound transformation in that spectator and "contributes to the honest pleasure of the mind."[77]

Similarly grand claims for the spontaneous effect (and affect) of right proportioning survive in Umberto Eco's endorsement of the aesthetics of Thomas Aquinas, wherein a felicitous system of proportion, which is "sensible and basically quantitative," like that at work not only in the shapes and colors of nature, but also in well-made music and thus, presumably, architecture, "produces an immediate feeling of pleasure."[78] Though somewhat less spectacularly, Le Corbusier likewise seems to believe that a well-designed building, that is, one reiterative of bodily proportions, can have a nonreflective, almost automatic impact on one's sensibilities insofar as it creates an eminently liveable, "humanized" environment, the means by which the human "compels inhuman nature to his need."[79] Or, in the more speculative case of ancient Egyptian pyramids, where we are told that careful adherence to standardized proportions engendered a "mathematical experience" or a sensation of "absolute formal clarity," the imagined experiential results are again more modest, though apparently similarly effortless.[80]

In accounts of Sufism, by contrast, the contemplative experience of arithmetical forms and shapes requires both greater exertion and more direct mediation through explicitly intellectualized processes, but the experience also reaps more profound rewards. In this case, meditating on geometric architecture, "one [among many] of the gates through which we move to the knowledge of the essence of the soul,"[81] can, we are told, enable Muslims "to traverse the path from the exoteric to the esoteric . . . from the sensible to the intelligible world . . . from the manifest (*ẓāhir*) to the hidden (*bāṭin*),"[82] an experiential prospect that will be addressed more fully with respect to the contemplation priority (III-B). Or different still, *feng shui* planning emerges from most secondary accounts, however (in)accurately, as a kind of thoroughgoing preventive maintenance program undertaken by people explicitly concerned about the impact of the natural and built environments on all aspects of their mind-body health and destiny, thus implying an experiential process more self-conscious than that imagined by Alberti but less esoteric than Sufi meditation. Moreover, the solicitation and remuneration of *feng shui* specialists seem to imply a forthright admission by all concerned that the pragmatic rewards of conformity to ritual-architectural conventions are *not,* in this context, contingent on precise knowledge of those conventions.

Accounts of Hinduism also suggest, at points (as do all of the options just rehearsed), that the fruits of fidelity to traditional formulae are largely pragmatic and anthropocentric insofar as they issue in some sort of *human* catharsis, improvement, or realization: we hear, for instance, that "the welfare of the community and the happiness of its members depend upon the correctly proportioned temple" and that only work completed "according to the rules" will gain the desired merit for its builders.[83] But Hindu materials also present at least two other, even more fascinating alternatives. The first is a kind of reversal of the familiar logic of microcosmic construction wherein the functioning of the cosmos at large is actually conceived as a reflection of the earthly architecture (rather than architecture being a reflection of the cosmos). One Indian architectural text, the *Mayamata,* explains that "if the measurement of the temple is in every way perfect, there will be perfection in the universe as well."[84] People will, in other words, benefit from correct temple proportions but, in this instance, only indirectly via the betterment of the cosmos at large.

The second, similarly suggestive notion holds that it is the gods, no less than humans, who are favorably impressed—or allured—by the correct proportioning of the temple. Thus, we read repeatedly in the Hindu literature that only by conformity to conventional rules will builders succeed in creating an architectural space that is pleasing enough to a divinity that he or she will take up residence there, making his or her presence manifest, and thereby affording the worshiper direct access to otherwise inaccessible divine powers.[85] Moreover, though their respective conceptions of divinity depart radically, Indian ritual-architectural logic is not altogether unlike (in a morphological sense) those explanations of Orthodox Christian art, which stress that God will transmit divine grace only through iconographic and architectural forms that demonstrate meticulous conformity to conventionalized standards.[86] The god of Christianity, too, may be subject to the allurement of proportionality.

Suspicion and Retrieval: The Allurement and Apprehension(s) of Conventionality

Upon reflection, it is striking that otherwise very widely divergent indigenous and academic accounts are in such general accord concerning the beneficent ramifications of conventionalized architecture, and particularly of rigorous proportioning. Imagined results range from the pleasing to the positively stupendous. If, however, one exercises a critical hermeneutic of suspicion, two sociological observations especially ought to engender some doubt about such strictly benign repercussions. First, as I've stressed, access to the particulars of these sorts of architectural schemes are, in nearly all cases, highly restricted to certain elite social constituencies. And second, these sorts of design prescriptions are, by nature, configured explicitly to reinforce and perpetuate (not challenge or subvert) the religio-artistic and, thus it would seem, the sociopolitical status quo. There is, therefore, little doubt that conventionalized sacred architectures, which are nearly always executed (sociologically speaking) from the top down, besides contributing to "the honest pleasure of the mind," are, to a considerable extent, instruments for the maintenance of political and economic privilege. Ulterior motives for such building practices are not difficult to imagine.

To expose and make explicit both the deliberate and inadvertent socioeconomic abuses consequent of faithful adherence to ritual-architectural conventions (themes that will resurface in chapter 19 on politics [priority II-C]) is, therefore, an important task, and, if perhaps neglected during the era in which Mircea Eliade's theory of sacred space held sway, one to which historians of religion are now devoting increasing energy.[87] Forcing into view the pernicious patterns of exploitation and privilege perpetuated by conventionalized ritual-architectural practices can in itself be, for some, a rewarding project; it ought to be, for all, a component of one's interpretive oeuvre. A critical hermeneutics of sacred architecture can, however—and should—also do more; again the requirement of balancing skeptical hermeneutics with one of retrieval and replenishment asserts itself. Consequently, I close these thoughts on architectural conventionality, more in the spirit of the latter with suggestions for two additional, though equally critical, heuristic trajectories. Both reflect the methodological program outlined in volume 1; both thus recommend correctives to more standard (less eventful) practices of architectural interpretation.

The first, which bears directly on the matter of allurement (perhaps obvious at this point), requires that we appreciate the important, but still quite limited, role that conventionalized built forms and practices play in the context of wider ritual-architectural programs. My reiterative contention has been that, like homologized building (I-A), building that reflects the convention priority (I-B) in any of its permutations—whether conceived as conforming to universal principles and rhythms, to divinely delivered sanctions, to the precedents of prestigious mythicohistoric forebears, or perhaps to all of those simultaneously—serves primarily as a mode of ritual-architectural instigation. Thus, again like the homology priority (and, as we'll see, like astronomically informed orientations [priority I-C]), copying and adhering to the architectural standards of tradition seldom, if ever, constitute the total raison d'être of an architectural program.

We err in imagining (as many interpreters implicitly do) that obviously conventionalized design elements—a carefully proportioned Doric entryway or a geometrically tiled mosque dome—constitute the substance or main message of a ritual-architectural program. Far more often, such formulaic elements work primarily in a preliminary fashion to cultivate an impression (often deservedly) of credibility, legitimacy, or pedigree, which convinces people that the proceedings undertaken here and the pronouncements delivered here carry the force of history and tradition. Conventionality (in the sense I've defined it), like homology, belongs overwhelmingly to the front half of the twofold pattern of ritual-architectural events, which invites or sometimes coerces participation in and serious consideration of what subsequently follows.

Thus, to condemn conventionality in architecture, particularly in large-scaled public constructions, too quickly as insidiously conservative (again, as many interpreters are wont to do) deprives us of a fuller understanding of its role in the mechanism of ritual-architectural experience. Such "tried and true" architectural conventions, such deliberately staid strategies of instigation, can actually open the way to ritual-architectural events that (in their back halves) provide among the most pregnant of forums, the most charged of opportunities, in which to air all sorts of more substantive issues—including, quite often, protests and challenges to the prevailing sociopolitical status quo. Ritual-architectural events instigated in this fashion can facilitate continuity, but they may also bring about change. Stodgily conservative architecture may, on occasion, actually play a vital role in social and cultural innovation.

The second heuristic suggestion arises from very basic concerns about respecting the superabundance of sacred architecture and, more directly, from my call for the composition of particularistic, rigorously empirical ritual-architectural reception histories.[88] It is vital that we remember that nearly all those extravagant assessments concerning the transformative magic of perfect proportions and formulaic design were delivered either by the perpetrators of those systems—say, Renaissance architect-thinkers or Christian and Sufi theologians—or by scholars well versed in those elite traditions, such as exegetes of Hindu building manuals. We have at our disposal, for most historical contexts, much less empirical confirmation of the liberating wonders of proportionality from the perspective of the unschooled who are supposedly so fortuitously transformed and improved by it.

Accordingly, as a methodological principle, we must appreciate that such elite discourses on architectural design, though not spurious, cannot be regarded as authoritative—particularly in the sense of empirical descriptions of specific peoples' basic experiences of concrete built forms. Such elite discourses belong almost exclusively to what I have termed highly idealized protocols of ritual-architectural apprehension, which correspond primarily with the initial intentions and expectations of designers and only imperfectly, if at all, to subsequent, always "revalorative" experiences of multivocal religious architectures.[89] The richly evocative descriptions of the transformative experience of conventionalized architectures cited in this chapter belong, almost unanimously—though this is too easily forgotten—to a hypothetical or intentional realm rather than to an empirical one.

That is not to suggest, however, that such orthodox and academic accounts be simply dismissed, nor merely dismantled to expose the implicit claims to privilege. That would be a profound loss. Instead, in this hermeneutics of sacred architecture, expositions like Alberti's theorizing on the effect of a Renaissance cathedral constitute, as it were, the initial salvos in the reception career of that built form, and thus are positioned as early entries in the architectural reception history of that monument. The less abstract, lived experiences of Alberti's contemporaries constitute a different sort of protocol of architectural apprehension, and thus (to the extent that we can access those experiences) become later entries in that reception history. The revalorative apprehensions of the cathedral's proportions by twentieth-century visitors, and by architectural historians like Rudolf Wittkower, constitute additional protocols, and thus additional historiographic entries, and so forth.

As stressed in volume 1, from a largely empirical frame, the idiosyncratic, irregular (mis)apprehensions unforeseen by Alberti, the supposed (mis)understandings of right proportioning—the very existence of which Alberti's universalizing rhetoric would lead us to deny—though decidedly different from the orthodox party line (and usually much harder to retrieve), are no less interesting, valid, or deserving of academic hermeneutical scrutiny.[90] In short, empirical studies will have to conclude that no measure of dedication to the rules of conventionality is adequate to subdue the superabundance and autonomy of sacred architecture.

Sixteen | Astronomy: Predictions and Enhancements of Nature (Priority I-C)

What's on the earth is in the stars; and what's in the stars is on the earth.

Stanley Looking Horse, circa 1985[1]

[T]he universality of sky symbolism in the history of religions would seem to suggest that the sky has expressed more fully than any other symbol at least a part of the religious experience of life.

Peter C. Chemery, 1987[2]

It is as though we all pursue that which we find interesting rather than that which was important to the people whose astronomies we are studying. After all, ancient astronomy was what it was and it may have meant something entirely different to its practioners than either scientist or social scientist can conceive.

Anthony F. Aveni, 1989[3]

INNUMERABLE EARLY STUDENTS OF RELIGION, from Charles François Dupuis to the "Panbabylonianists" to F. Max Müller, Raffaele Pettazzoni, E. O. James, and even Mircea Eliade, placed the human experience of the sky and of sky phenomena—sunrises, sunsets, phases of the moon, thunderstorms, Venus observations—at the very center of their theories of religion.[4] But then preoccupations with connecting celestial observations and religion flagged. Since the 1970s and in the wake of loud debate surrounding Stonehenge's (mis)identification variously as a lunar observatory, a calendar, or a "neolithic computer," there has been, however, by all assessments, "an explosion of new interest in the astronomical knowledge of ancient and contemporary non-Western cultures."[5] Thus, at present, with that curve still rising, the subtle relations between ritual, architecture, cosmology, and celestial phenomena are being appreciated with unprecedented sophistication, particularly by scholars in the interrelated fields of archaeoastronomy, ethnoastronomy, and astroarchaeology.[6]

In response, then, to a not inappropriate query as to why architectural orientation with respect to the sky is singled out for special treatment when orientation with respect to such other natural features as waterways, mountains, or caves, is not, I would provide a pair of responses, both heuristically pragmatic. Remember first that morphology ought not be a slave to symmetry; this framework makes no pretense to evenness or to comprehensiveness. In fact, where only rarely in the hermeneutical interrogation of explicitly religious architectures will one come to entirely negative responses as to the relevance of the heuristic questions inventoried under the homology rubric (priority I-A), and virtually never will all of the variations on the convention priority (I-B) be irrelevant, we should be prepared to find many specific instances in which the astronomy priority (I-C) is of little or no consequence. Astroarchitectural orientation is definitely, in some imprecisely statistical sense, the least widely applicable of these three modes of ritual-architectural allurement (though again I stress the non–mutual exclusivity of all options).

Second, the frequent irrelevance of astronomy notwithstanding, the still-mounting interest in studying celestial orientations, alignments, and putative horizon indications, especially but not only at megalithic sites, opens the way for this entry to the framework. In precisely the evocative spirit of this morphological project, the "explosion" of interest in connections between human constructions and the sky has generated a flurry of fresh questions that scholars should and are bringing to bear on old, well-worked but hardly exhausted specific cases. In innumerable contexts, most dramatically at archaeological sites in Britain and the Americas, architectural features and configurations that were long assessed as oddly skewed, quaintly aesthetic, or simply haphazard are being reassessed (sometimes too zealously) as astronomically significant. Hermeneuts benefit, then, irrespective of the historical contexts in which they are working, by adding to their interrogational oeuvre these only occasionally relevant astronomical questions.

"Science or Symbolism?" Revalorizations and (Mis)Understandings of Ancient Astronomy[7]

The long, sometimes turbulent, sometimes turgid debate concerning British megaliths, particularly Stonehenge, has been, without question, of singular importance in reviving enthusiasm in these issues.[8] Scholars trained both in the "numerate disciplines" of astronomy and surveying and those from the social sciences, particularly archaeology, simultaneously embraced the study of stone rings and rows to create a field that would demonstrate, at every step, the mixed triumphs and tribulations of interdisciplinary work.[9] In some happily idealized collaboration, the former would supply "reliable archaeoastronomical evidence," which the latter could then situate in sociohistorical (and religious) contexts. In practice, however, interpretations of Stonehenge clustered in two largely antagonistic camps.[10] On one side, astronomers and surveyors (re)conceived the great stone circle primarily as an astronomical observatory; the relevant lineage on this side is usually traced from the early twentieth-century work of Norman Lockyer, through that of A. Thom, A. S. Thom, Gerald Hawkins, and others.[11] On the other side were archaeologists, notably R. J. C. Atkinson, Glyn Daniel, and Jacquetta Hawkes, who (re)conceived the famed standing stones primarily as a "ceremonial center," that is, a construction designed to facilitate religious or magical ritual.[12]

Replaying the old Stonehenge saw, however briefly, serves to remind us of several pertinent points. According to a viable formulation reiterated by several of the more self-critical participants in the debate, we ought to notice—and grow suspicious—that each strain and generation of investigators, in a sense, (re)discovers a Stonehenge that (re)affirmed the preeminence of their own personal and disciplinary concerns.[13] Or, in my rubric, the abundance and diversity of Stonehenge explanations testifies again to the "superabundance" and "inexhaustibility" of nearly all substantial built forms. In that frame, those various interpretive options and their countless permutations constitute successive "revalorizations" or creative (mis)apprehensions in the ongoing reception career of a superabundant Stonehenge, all of which belong to roughly the same nonindigenous protocol of architectural apprehension and all of which reflect much more heavily the overt prejudices and covert "pre-understandings" of modern investigators than those of the initial builders and users of the megalith, whoever they may have been.[14]

Most specifically, we should notice that the untoward antithesis between "astronomical observatory" and "ceremonial center" actually provides a forum in which to reflect upon and debate two much broader issues: first, the timeworn controversy concerning the intellectual capabilities of "primitive peoples" and "how natives think," and thus, in this case, their ability (or lack thereof) to have orchestrated sophisticated celestial alignments; and, second, an even wider sort of ambivalence about modern science, which is reflected in scholars' presumptions of incompatibility between Stonehenge's "scientific" purposes (its function as an instrument for the accumulation of practical, systematic, and precise knowledge) and its "symbolic" or "religious" purposes (functions that are assessed, by contrast, as impractical, imprecise, and unproductive forms of knowledge).[15]

If megalithic revalorizations of this sort are mildly useful in sorting through certain contemporary anxieties (which is certainly debatable in itself), this scientific/religious dichotomy has proven, for the purposes of empirical research, counterproductive in the extreme. Mirroring the layering of hermeneutical situations, there is kind of layering of distortions here.[16] In one respect, decidedly positivistic students of megalith astronomy are, not unlike their modern counterparts in other fields, vulnerable to now-familiar postmodern (and hermeneutical) charges of a kind of insidious self-deception by failing to acknowledge their own deviations from strict empiricism. But, in this case, there is additionally a more specific, more ironic problem surrounding the unwillingness (or inability) of those researchers to appreciate the other-than-strictly-empirical propensities of ancient astronomers. That is to say, ironically, the same scholars that express their disappointment over native astronomers' deviations from empiricism fail to realize their own parallel departures from "pure observation." In a Gadamerian idiom, we could accuse protagonists in the (early) archaeoastronomy debates of failing to appreciate the implicitly hermeneutical (nonpositivistic) nature of both native astronomers' interpretive interactions with the sky and with their own scholarly machinations. From that angle, Anthony Aveni's recent title, *Conversing with the Planets,* connotes a particularly fortuitous advance.[17]

Nonetheless, for too long archaeoastronomical researchers would not (or could not) appreciate that, in archaic astronomy, whether in northern Europe, pre-Columbian America, or elsewhere, the quest after "empirical data" was nearly always subsumed by wider orientational agendums of conventionalized and/or homologized unification of space, time, society, and polity. If moderns regard observational objectivity as a goal (albeit unrealizable), it is for ancient astronomers (perhaps more honestly) at most a means. The Maya's unmistakably willful distortion of observed celestial cycles provides a strong case in point.[18] Their propensity for invariably "cheating" or "twisting" the empirical data to their ulterior purposes—particularly via prestidigitations that work to synchronize sky phenomena both with the recording of past events and with the scheduling of future ones—has been for decades a continued source of consternation and disappointment to Western scholars. Early Mayanist Sylvanus Morley, for instance, termed the practice "chronological coercion," and Alfred Tozzer assigned it the even more telling label of a "mass compulsion neurosis."[19]

The Maya (and other traditional people) had, in these assessments, what was often described as an irritating tendency to blur astronomy and astrology.

Increasingly, however, more scholars (even those still hesitant to acknowledge the hermeneutical nature of their own work) are becoming much more sensitive to, and thus affirming of, the alternative, non-positivistic (I would venture hermeneutical) nature of ancient astronomical "observation." On the basis of both building alignments and astronomical references in hieroglyphs at the Maya site of Palenque, Linda Schele, for example, contends that theirs was "a different type of astronomy, in which the goal was to interlock cosmic cycles and visual phenomena with the functions and definitions of Palenque rulership."[20] Coming to similar conclusions regarding pre-Columbian astronomy in central Mexico, Johanna Broda also cautions against the ethnocentrism of trying to wrestle apart the "scientific" from the "religious." Alternatively, in Broda's phrasing, we must "put the emphasis on the particular mental and social processes by which astronomical observations became immersed in myth and ritual, thus leaving behind the terrain of 'objective' scientific knowledge."[21] In indigenous contexts, conventionality (priority I-B) and homology (I-A) are seldom divorced from astronomy (I-C).[22]

Morphological Conjunctions and Astronomical Alliances: Cross-Cultural Samplings

Perhaps the most obviously astronomically informed sacred architectures are actual observatories, of which there are countless notable cross-cultural exemplars.[23] Yet, even in those cases, the incentive is virtually never confined to the strictly empirical observation of natural processes.[24] Instead, astroarchitectural features nearly always work in an ancillary or supplemental role that furthers the pursuit of other ritual-architectural priorities. Often, astronomical references are a component in a more widely encompassing program of ritual-architectural homologization (I-A), as in the case of the celestial alignments that are integrated into the regional cosmogram of the Incas' *ceque* system.[25] Other astroarchitectural programs are homologizing insofar as they provide earthly, microcosmic, or even pictographic replicas of celestial phenomena: in China, the Han dynasty's makeshift capital city of Ch'ang-an became known as Tou-ch'eng, the "City of the Dippers," because its irregular urban layout was presumed to replicate on a reduced scale the shape of the northern and southern "Dippers," or

"Pei-tou" and "Nan-tou."[26] Or, in a similar vein but on a much smaller scale, nearly all Maya houses have fireplaces formed of three stones that correspond to a three-star constellation that the Maya call *ac ek,* "turtle stars" (and that Western astronomers identify as Orion's belt).[27]

Other manifestations of the astronomy priority (I-C) work more like the convention mode (I-B) insofar as they depend *not* on downsized representations of sky phenomena, but on abstract, astronomically derived rhythms and alignments.[28] In Rome, for example, while the suburban areas were oriented cardinally, the urban core was rotated some 36 degrees to bring the major avenues into line with the path of the sun on the summer and winter equinoxes, thereby distinguishing that zone as special and, it seems, especially sacred.[29] In fact, often, as with the continued preference for orienting Christian churches to the east, which is only sometimes rationalized in terms of the apparent solar imagery of the *risen* Christ (an association that in other cases is explicitly rejected), celestial orientations are actually more a matter of historical conventionality than direct interaction with sky phenomenon.[30]

Nevertheless, whether coupled more tightly with homologized replication or conventionalized practices, astroarchitectural features invariably serve in the front half of a ritual-architectural program, thus providing the instigatory preparation for exercises of the more substantively commemorative priorities. The interactions between astronomy and the commemoration of divinity (priority II-A), for instance, are especially rich: Sometimes religious buildings simply provide ritual contexts for the worship of distant celestial bodies, variously conceived as supreme beings, mythological heroes, or "storm gods," such as Zeus, Indra, Rudra, Baal, Jupiter, and Thor.[31] In other cases—the Incas' Coricancha with its *Punchau,* or golden face-like statue of the sun,[32] or the temple at Rhodes in ancient Greece, one of the seven wonders of the world, which also housed an enormous anthropomorphic figure of a sun god[33]—built forms provide an earthly habitation, a home away from home as it were, to which some celestial deity can descend and take up residence, often in an image to which prayers, sacrifices, offerings, and solicitations for advice are addressed. Or, in other pairings of astronomy and divinity commemoration, the entire architectural form itself is conceived as an earthly manifestation of a sky god, as instantiated in some venturesome interpretations of the famously controversial Nazca lines,[34] or of the quarter-mile-long earthworks of the Serpent Mound in Ohio, which may (or may not) reproduce the shape of, and thus in some sense *become,* a celestial serpent.[35]

Astroarchitectural features that are connected especially with the ritual-architectural commemoration of myth and sacred history (priority II-B), though often inseparable from the previous option, provide another morphological possibility. Among Native Americans, Africans, Polynesians, and Australian aborigines, for instance, constructions (and thus rituals) are often directed toward personified celestial phenomena that are conceived as the animal and humanoid protagonists in their sacred stories.[36]

Or sometimes, as evidenced in the widespread practice of catasterism (the transfer of human beings or deified ancestors to heaven, usually in the form of a constellation), it is the interactions between astronomically aligned architecture and the worship of esteemed ancestors (the commemoration of the dead, priority II-D) that are most salient. In regard to this pairing, which is also closely related to the divinity option, even the simple graves of Neanderthals seem to have been oriented east-to-west along the path of the sun.[37] Benjamin Ray's "new interpretation" of Stonehenge, while acknowledging the importance of celestial alignments, actually assesses the larger significance of the monument in terms that resonate more with the older, "memorial-to-the-dead" interpretations.[38] And, in the same vein, according to Aubrey Burl's analysis, Stonehenge and other British megaliths were astronomically referenced neither primarily to honor sky gods nor to collect predictive data, but instead principally in the interest of actually incorporating the sun and moon into rituals concerned with dead ancestors and fertility.[39]

Moreover, the tie between astronomically aligned architecture and political authority (priority II-C) is also, in some cases, especially tight. Perhaps owing to the sun's apparent omniscience and "leadership" in the sky, the cult of the sun, for instance, is very often linked to notions of imperial kingship, and, consequently, is most developed in "high cultures" —the pre-Columbian Americas, ancient Egypt, Greece, Rome, and Mesopotamia, where the sun temple at Babylon was known as "the house of the judge of the world."[40] Or, in ancient China, as in so many contexts (notably among the Classic Maya), the scheduling of imperial rites was carefully synchronized with periodic celestial phenomena, so that it is hardly surprising that the Son of Heaven's ritual hall, or *ming-tang,* served both as an astronomical observatory and as the "palace of Great Instruction" from which the orders of government were dispensed.[41]

In short, though the astronomy priority is often notable primarily either by its complete irrelevance or, more interestingly, by its extreme selectivity,[42] it is very easy to assemble a widely cross-cultural spray of celestially informed, ostensibly religious architectures. To arrange them in any heuristically useful fashion is, however, much more difficult. The heterogeneity of apparently relevant samplings strains the notions of "significant organization" and morphological similarity, and may leave one wondering what, if any, more general heuristic questions might be adduced from such diversity. How, for instance, can we imagine astronomically informed orientation as a mode of ritual-architectural allurement distinct from the other two morphologic options? Wherein lies the singularity of the astronomy priority? And what insights and questions can we adduce from these comparative materials that might enrich our more particularistic architectural studies in other contexts?

The remainder of this chapter attempts to answer that frustration via the exposition and illustration of two plausible answers to those important questions: the first bears on matters of time, timing, and predictions of nature; the second, on ritual-architectural "enhancements" of nature.

Allurement via Prediction: Sensations of Passive Harmony and Active Control

As strategies of allurement, those instances of celestially referenced architecture that play upon abstract rhythms and cycles have much in common with the convention mode (I-B), while those that reproduce microcosmic versions of constellations could actually qualify as subspecies of homologized architecture (I-A). Unlike either of those two orientational modes, however, the astronomy priority (I-C) usually issues in architectural configurations that, though significant, are *not* constantly operative. Owing to the dynamic movement of the heavenly bodies themselves, astroarchitectural features and alignments are, in nearly every instance, only periodically relevant; they are, in short, only occasionally operational. Moreover, it is that highly restricted, intermittent—though also highly regularized—applicablity that gives those features their special effectiveness as components of allurement. Celestially informed architecture facilitates a special binding of space and time and a special sense of orientation to the future unequalled by either of the other possibilities.

The unique potentiality of astroarchitectural configurations as strategies of allurement (or actually as a distinct morphological option) rests, then, most of all on the power of prognostication—the capacity to predict the future—that is inherent in those configurations. Where homologized and conventionalized architectures initiate ritual-architectural events with announcements of harmony and reliability, astronomically referenced architecture, which also allures via presentations of harmony and reliability, has the additional capability of instigating participation by seizing upon predictable celestial phenomena to confirm the right and propitious timing of those ritual events.

By capitalizing on a foreknowledge of sky phenomena, and thus making preparations on the basis of informed anticipation of a specific celestial occurrence, astroarchitectural events enable their ritual participants to move beyond orientation with respect to the conventions of the past (I-B) and beyond orientation with respect to the homologous correspondences of the present (I-A). Astroarchitectural events (I-C) afford those involved a special opportunity to participate, as well, in a sense of place with respect to a predictable and presaged future.

Though the correlation of convention, homology, and astronomy modes with, respectively, orientations to the past, present, and future, is an oversimplification, the (morphological) contrasts are nonetheless (heuristically) instructive. It is, in fact, this often public demonstration of an ability to see into the future—the power of prediction—that sets astronomical orientation apart from the other modes of allurement (and thus provides us with an alternative pattern of hermeneutical questioning to apply in the areas of our special concern). Moreover, while the sundials, gnomons, and "medicine wheels" built by hunting peoples provide modest exemplifications of astronomically predictive architecture,[43] it is no coincidence that, as Peter Lancaster Brown notes, the most elaborate architectures of prediction, such as British megaliths and Maya monuments, are associated with agricultural cultures.[44]

Mircea Eliade explains this connection via his repeated insistence that the "discovery" of agriculture engendered a new consciousness of the periodicity or redundancy of time. In his words, this new, profoundly different approach to life required that

> . . . [the agriculturalist], above all, had to perfect his technique for calculating time. . . . From then on, the cultivator had to make his plans several months before they were to be implemented, had to perform, in exact order, a series of complex activities in view of a distant and, especially in the beginning, always uncertain result: the harvest.[45]

According to this historical hypothesis, the heightened chronologic demands of agriculture were then echoed by similarly intensified astronomical preoccupations. The cycles of the sun, moon, planets, and stars—

which provide "by far the most dependable regularly occurring natural events"[46]—were examined with unprecedented care and used to demarcate standardized intervals between both agricultural and associated ritual activities. In Eliade's view, this new consciousness of the redundancy of time had profound ramifications, moreover, for the conception of space and building: specifically, these developments were decisive in the emergence of both megalithic architecture and the homologized patterns of construction that he then finds so globally pervasive.

Though ruling on the historical merits of this hypothesis is outside my present purview, I would wager, however, in a morphological vein (and contrary to Eliade), that this pervasive idea of "circular" or "rhythmic time," which is inherent in the neolithic agricultural lifestyle, does *not* actually find its most direct architectural analogue in the symbolism of the center and the construction of *imago mundis* (that is, in the agenda of the homology priority [I-A]). Alternatively, the more exciting ritual-architectural ramification of this new "conceptualization of duration,"[47] and thus new capabilities of prediction and prognosticative foreknowledge, would seem to be (more in the spirit of the astronomy priority [I-C]) a similarly new opportunity for choreographing a ritual-architectural experience of orientation with respect to the future. In both cases, the unification of calendrical time and architectural space is paramount, but there is a specialness in the incorporation of the periodicities of sky phenomena into the ritual-architectural situation that deserves greater accentuation.

In other words, where many interpretations of neolithic-megalithic architecture, like Eliade's, blur the contrast between what I term "homologized" and "astronomic" (and, for that matter, "conventionalized") architectural programs, I am urging that, for heuristic reasons especially, we highlight those contrasts. Though the distinction is morphological rather than developmental (that is, a distinction that provides us with heuristic questions rather than historical answers), I would submit that two qualitatively different sorts of experience of architecture are at issue here. Where adherence to the homology priority (and that of convention) connotes faithful conformity to cosmic rhythms, the efficacy in prediction concomitant of the astroarchitectural design provides a more commanding sense of orientation.[48] Instead of dutiful acquiescence with the natural and supernatural patterns, the power of prediction—the experience of a largely predictable universe—moves humans beyond the level of simple continuity with nature to a sensation (however illusory) of discontinuity with and dominance over their environment.[49] To expropriate van der Leeuw's distinction between "passive harmony" and "active control," the power of prediction allows one to transcend the sensation of being "caught up in and ruled by a rhythm," and instead enables one "to subjugate the world by mastering a rhythm."[50]

Allurement via the Ritual-Architectural Enhancement of Nature: Mesoamerican Examples

Consideration of this alternative, more aggressive way of interacting with cosmo-celestial rhythms, which is admittedly very difficult to document empirically, guides our attention to a second, especially provocative feature of many astronomically based strategies of allurement, and one that is somewhat easier to ascertain. Here we should note that, though virtually everyone, particularly in agricultural contexts, is aware of the phases of the moon and the turn of the seasons, even in those contexts, the subtleties of celestial prognostication—predictions of eclipses and comets, helical risings of the Pleiades, the appearance and disappearance of Venus—are (not unlike the nuances of conventionalized building prescriptions) the province of an elite few. Accordingly, the potentialities for using—and abusing—predictive astronomy as a compelling (or compulsory) means of ritual-architectural instigation, either benignly or as a tool for religio-political manipulation, are enormous.

In some traditional Chinese cases, in fact, according to Nancy Shatzman Steinhardt's analysis, ceremonial events were orchestrated so as to perpetrate the notion that it was the imperial authorities who actually controlled the weather and the celestial rhythms, rather than being controlled by those forces. She cites, for instance, a passage in the *Li chi* (Book of rites) that reads:

> when they presented their offerings to God [at that felicitous spot that they had chosen for their capital] . . . the winds and rains duly regulated, and the heat and cold came each in its proper time, so that the sage (king) had only to stand with his face to the south and order prevailed all under the sky.[51]

To advance and sustain such grand cosmopolitical claims requires more than synchronization with the predicted sky phenomena; it requires as well—and this is the point to be stressed—the strategic ritual-architectural *enhancement* of those natural phenomena. Ancient Mesoamerica, by virtue of a uniquely fortuitous combination of archaeoastronomical, epigraphic, ethnohistoric, and ethnographic evidences, provides the best opportunity, even better than the British megalithic evidence, for illustrating how that sort of contrived, ritual-architectural augmentation of natural processes could actually work.[52] In this rare instance, hermeneuts of pre-Columbian ruins can, for once, be the donors rather than recipients of provocative heuristic questions.[53]

In a cultural context challenged both by endemic, highly volatile politico-military competition and by what is often assessed as an almost pathological obsession with divination, prognostication, prophecy, omens, oracles, and sortilege,[54] ancient Mesoamericans, even more than most agriculturalists, labored with a special unease about the uncertainties of the future. Cosmic calamity, by nearly all accounts, seemed an imminent possibility, and thus prediction a matter of especial import. Against that backdrop, pre-Columbian sovereigns, often it seems, seized upon predictable celestial occurrences and startling meteorological "coincidences," which could then be fashioned into (seemingly) divinely sanctioned imperatives to acknowledge the seriousness and legitimacy of their religiopolitical ritual programs.

This indigenous strategy of celestial opportunism variously exploited the unique topographical and astronomical configurations of each site: at Palenque westward-looking phenomena, particularly sunsets, were favored;[55] at La Venta on the Gulf Coast, in consonance with other feline imagery, the Olmec oriented their buildings toward a constellation of stars that seemed to form a cat's mouth;[56] and at Teotihuacan the melodrama of violent seasonal thunderstorms was integrated into the agricultural rites of the rain god Tlaloc and the solar year.[57] In other cases, the ritual-architectural invitation (or demand) was made even more emphatic by synchronization with multiple, simultaneously occurring sky phenomena.[58]

In all these cases, however, the experience of "natural" occurrences in the sky, particularly in ritual, was "artificially" enhanced by ingeniously constructed architectural forms. In other words—and again, this is the point that must be emphasized—while the relevant movements of celestial bodies transpired "naturally," that is, irrespective of human intervention, strategically configured built forms and ritual procedures were indispensable to the very powerful human experience of these natural phenomena. The potency, and thus religious and political expediency, of those apprehensions of "nature" depended in ancient Mesoamerica (as elsewhere) upon a choreographed collusion of natural processes and humanly constructed forms. In short, without the supporting architecture and careful ritual timing, there were no remarkable views.[59]

Among the most dramatic Mesoamerican exemplars of this sort of astroarchitecturally contrived allurement is the biannual phenomenon of the "serpent of light," which "descends" the huge Castillo pyramid at Chichén Itzá each spring (and fall) solar equinox.[60] In this much-discussed case (which some regard as a stroke of luck rather than orientational prowess), the stepped pyramid is (re)constructed in such a fashion that twice a year in the late afternoon, as the sun sets, the nine tiers of the pyramid cast the distinctive zigzag pattern of light and shadow line along the structure's own north stairway, a pattern of elongated triangles that resembles an undulating snake and is thus usually identified as Quetzalcoatl (or Kukulcán), the mythical Plumed Serpent who is so closely associated with this site.

As an astroengineering feat, this architecturally contrived hierophany, the "Castillo equinox event" if you will, even if cynically assessed as a colossal manipulation, remains impressive to the huge contemporary audiences that are drawn to the site each spring. To pre-Columbian audiences, it must have been even more so. What needs accentuation in the context of the present discussion, however, is the indisputable fact that the notorious "serpent of light" is *not,* after all, a natural phenomenon; it is a humanly fabricated effect—a ritual-architectural enhancement of natural celestial movements. In the absence of the built form, nothing of special consequence happens in the Chichén Itzá plaza on the biannual occasions of equinox. Without the architecture, the luminous snake never appears.

One last, less famous but more subtle Mesoamerican circumstance in which a simultaneity of sky phenomena is hewn into an irrefusable offer to enter the closed world of the religioarchitectural proceedings, and thus to consider seriously the directives articulated there—ineloquently labeled the "Copán Temple 22-Sun-Venus-maize-kingship event"—may serve both to clarify this matter of nature enhancements and to focus the wider issue of ritual-architectural allurement.[61] The broader archaeoastronomical layout of Copán, a massively complex Maya site on the Guatemala-Honduras border, has been explained in several ways.[62] The scheduling of this particular (albeit hypothetical) religiopolitical ceremony, however, exploited the annual coincidence of two natural celestial phenomena: the first involves the sun's passage along a baseline that bisects the Main Acropolis and connects two outlying stelae (or "outliers") positioned some four miles apart on either side of the Copán Valley;[63] the second involves the (re)appearance of Venus on the horizon after its disappearance during the rainy season, an occurrence to which a slit-like aperture window on the west side of Temple

22 seems to have been specifically oriented.[64]

The one evening each year when these solar and Venus phenomena coincide, not incidentally about twenty days before the advent of the rainy season, is the scheduled date for what art historian Mary Miller believes, on the basis primarily of ethnohistorical evidence, was an elaborate rite of ascension or reaffirmation of kingship.[65] According to Miller, Temple 22 was both the ritual palace of the royal family and an architectural replica of the cosmic Earth Monster, a built symbol of the earth itself. On this most propitious day, in the context of this ceremonial reaffirmation, the king would enter the "Earth Monster doorway" of the royal temple—a metaphor for the sowing of maize—and then, in an intricate series of ritual movements, the king would, as he emerged from the building, "sprout" and "grow."

There was, in other words, a masterful orchestration (or astrohomologization) of the career of the king, the return of the rainy season, the act of sowing maize, the (re)appearance of Venus in the aperture window, and the setting of the sun along the baseline of the outliers. Moreover, the twofold pattern of ritual-architectural events is especially evident. First, a spectator standing in front of Temple 22—our epigrammatic pilgrim perhaps—would have been "opened" by the witness of the celestial coincidence of Venus and the sun, which thus served as the conservative, catalytic, instigatory component of the ceremonial event. Then, once involved, that spectator would have encountered as the component of variation and new information—the back half of the event—an announcement concerning the specific agenda of agricultural duty and political loyalty to the Copán king. In one fabulous, triply significant stroke, the king, having bound himself into the very cosmological fabric of the universe, was legitimated; the timing and, moreover, cosmic responsibility to sow and reap maize was affirmed; and the peripheral territory of the outliers was integrated with the civic ceremonial center of Copán.

Closing Thoughts: Inconclusive Morphologies of Ritual-Architectural Allurement

I have in these first three chapters, in the interest of enlarging our catalog of hermeneutical options, worked to isolate—and to compare—three morphologically distinct strategies or modes of ritual-architectural allurement. This third option, the exploitation of predictable sky phenomena (astronomy, priority I-C)—epitomized by the Classic Maya's ingenious synchronization of built forms, ceremonial actions, and celestial movements at Palenque and Copán—provides a means of eliciting ritual participation that is different in several respects from the invitations proffered either by the replication of microcosmic images of the universe (homology, priority I-A) or by strategic conformity to the standards of tradition (convention, priority I-B). Instigation of ceremonial occasions via astronomically aligned architecture constitutes perhaps the most spectacular, but definitely least widespread, of the options; often astronomy is completely irrelevant. Where the effectiveness of all three modes of allurement depends upon clear presentations of order and legitimacy, astroarchitectural strategies, if the least common, are, in all likelihood, the most emphatic in calling potential participants to attention and announcing that indifference and noninvolvement are no longer options. Celestial references, by drawing into the ritual-architectural context heavenly bodies that are, paradoxically, universally accessible but always beyond reach, "everywhere present yet imperturbable,"[66] have special virtues in issuing the ultimatum that noncompliance with the subsequent ritual agenda could have dire and even cosmic consequences.

Moreover, relevant examplars suggest that astroarchitectural orientation may exceed the other modes of allurement insofar as it confers an experience that transcends that of passive harmony with the order of the world and facilitates (the sensation of) a more commanding, more audacious orientation of predictive control and domination; natural processes are not only observed, but manipulated and enhanced. There is also compelling evidence that astronomically referenced architectures, which may at first seem to provide the most natural, least affected mode of allurement, often, upon closer inspection, prove to be even more sociopolitically contrived than those associated with the homology or convention priorities. Be that as it may, astroarchitectural configurations appear to be limited, precisely like the other two modes, insofar as celestial orientations also serve primarily in that preliminary, instigative role that sets the ritual activities in motion but virtually never constitutes the total significance of the ceremonial program. All three orientational modes belong overwhelmingly to the initial component of the twofold pattern, which encourages involvement but has only limited substantive value.

In the end, however, all such forgetive comparisons between the different categorical modes of allurement—comparative formulations that are really third-, fourth-, and fifth-order abstractions—are largely incidental. I cannot stress too often that the important test of this morphologic arrangement does *not* lie in generating conclusive or even provisional similarities and contrasts between (or within) its various abstracted categories; those idealized observations are simply the hermeneutical preliminaries, the stretching and tuning before engaging the more tightly contextualized, and thus more fully rewarding, interpretive task. The classificatory impulse is a means rather than an end. The far more significant measure of morphological success lies, therefore, in generating the heuristic questions, the patterns of hermeneutical interrogation, that will enrich and drive forward rigorously empirical analyses of particularistic ritual-architectural situations.

Asking general questions can help in that sort of pointed, critical initiative: How and to what extent are the respective homologized, conventionalized, and astronomical options relevant to the strategies of allurement operating in whatever specific ritual-architectural circumstance you may be interrogating? Which is most prominent? And which is notable by omission? But more detailed, more challenging hermeneutical inquires can help even more. With respect to the astronomy priority, for instance, I am urging interpreters to inquire more specifically: If astronomical features are important in the particular sacred architecture you are studying, with which of the other orientational and commemorative priorities is the astronomical initiative most closely aligned? Are there predictive elements to that ritual-architectural situation that engender orientational sensations that might be better characterized as "active control" of the future than as "passive harmony" with past practices and present cosmic realities? And, in that particular situation, are there ways in which ritual choreographers rely on built configurations in order to enhance the observation of sky phenomena and, thereby, enhance the "naturalness" of their ritual-architectural agenda?

This first part, "Architecture as Orientation," which concentrated on the front half of the experience of religious architecture, is, therefore, a morphologic classification deliberately without conclusions. It strings out an array of leading questions, which often may lead nowhere, but, one hopes, will occasionally serve as stimuli to fresh interpretive insights. With equally modest ambitions, attention now shifts in part 2 to the back half of the ritual-architectural situation, to the component of variation, innovation, and informational content, all embraced under the title "Architecture as Commemoration."

Part Two | Architecture as Commemoration: The Content of Ritual-Architectural Events

A traditional monument, as the origin of the word indicates, is an object which is supposed to remind us of something important. That is to say it exists to put people in mind of some obligation they have incurred: a great public figure, a great public event, a great public declaration which the group had pledged itself to honor.

J. B. Jackson, 1980[1]

But beyond this pedigreed "history in stone" exists an [anonymous] architecture that transmits a different aspect of life. It testifies to the aspirations of the group. Its buildings tell not the official but the private history of a culture—the unending struggle for physical and spiritual survival of anonymous men. Indigenous buildings speak the vernacular of the people.

Sibyl Moholy-Nagy, 1976[2]

Monumentality . . . always embodies and imposes a clearly intelligible message. It says what it wishes to say—yet it hides a good deal more. . . .

Henri Lefebvre, 1991[3]

RITUAL-ARCHITECTURAL EVENTS ARE, by definition, never content to leave things and thoughts as they are. Where hermeneutical experiences of architecture are initiated on the basis of confirming apprehensions of world order and continuity with conventionalized expectations, the productivity of those occasions depends upon the sometimes exhilarating, often discomforting confrontation with "strangenesses" and unfamiliar possibilities. Such occasions enable—and often force to recognition—insights about oneself and one's world that had been, prior to that point, unknown, even inconceivable. Strategically choreographed experiences of architecture have, then, an exceptional capability (different from but not less than that of written texts) for presenting new information, for retrieving forgotten meanings, and for facilitating participation in otherwise inaccessible realms.[4]

Stressing the ontological dimensions of such occasions, Hans-Georg Gadamer would remind us that successful or "happy" solutions in architecture, even more than in the literary arts, are "genuinely productive": they "add something new to the spatial dimensions of a town or a landscape," something new that issues in transformations of human consciousness and even "increases of being."[5] For Gadamer, interactions with architecture, even more adeptly than the reading of texts, enable what was not, to come to be. Or, stressing the always-comparative aspect of such occasions, Marilyn Waldman, not incompatibly, would remind us how architectural events can serve as forums not simply to recycle and dispense old ideas, but to produce *new* knowledge, to construct *new* meanings, and to reconfigure prevailing religiosocial alignments into *new* ones.[6] Yet, in either formulation, experiences of architecture—via the strategic juxtaposition of old and new, order and variation, similarity and difference—have a rare, maybe singular, appetency for facilitating changes of a most diverse and consequential sort.

Where the chapters in part 1, "Architecture as Orientation," explored various strategies of allurement for drawing people into these transformative events (the front half of the architectural situation), attention in these next four chapters, under the rubric "Architecture as Commemoration," turns to the manifold diversity in the substantive content—the *messages*—of ritual-architectural events (the back half, or the component of variation and new information). This section asks: What, once the pilgrim and the pyramid are engaged in dialogue, is the topic of conversation? What sorts of things do the ritual participants learn that they had not known before? And how are they and their worlds different after the event from before? In short, what commemorative, communicative possibilities do experiences of sacred architecture offer?

Hortatory Monuments: Specificity, Diversity, and Obligation in the Experience of Architecture

As Gadamer suggests, experiences of architecture can, not unlike rites of passage, work as mechanisms of progressive growth, improvement, or "world expansion."[7] Moreover, not unlike other ritual occasions, architectural events can be liberating insofar as they play havoc with the neat succession of time and the boundedness of physical space by invoking—or commemorating—circumstances and personages from the past and future as well as the present. In apprehensions of the commemorative dimension of sacred architectures, mythical realms can be visited, dead ancestors revived, deities engaged in conversation, and impending epochs lived and tested. The salutary possibilities for expansion of horizons and emancipation from habitudes are enormous—but, I would accentuate additionally that ritual-architectural encounters of this sort can also be limiting and confining.

These architecturally abetted space-time flights are not simply occasions for generalized adoration and wonderment; and neither is compliance with the alternatives such occasions present an entirely voluntary matter.

Those two qualifications are perhaps especially apparent in the experience of what J. B. Jackson terms "traditional monuments," which, in his view, are "supposed to remind us of something important . . . to put people in mind of some obligation they have incurred."[8] Reaffirming the sensations of challenge and particularity that are characteristic of the back half of the ritual-architectural situation, Jackson maintains that the potency of such explicitly commemorative monuments lies not in their generalized "aesthetic quality," but in the pointed challenges and demands that they issue: in their power "to recall something specific . . . to remind us of obligations, religious and political."[9] Such monuments, he says, do not, in the end, please and console people; instead, they alert people to what they should do and how they should act. In his apt phrase, "traditional monuments" have a "hortatory" function, urging upon those who encounter them the acceptance of "an obligation to be discharged to avoid future trouble."[10]

Consequently, that the "mute texts" of architecture are often derided for their vagueness as "vehicles of intelligibility," for their stuttering and imprecision as modes of communication, is, I think, an unfair and untoward assessment.[11] Alternatively, as innumerable specific illustrations will demonstrate, experiences of what I term loosely the "commemorative dimension" of sacred architecture lay before ritual participants and spectators information that is, often, both very specific and highly prescriptive (or sometimes proscriptive), information that compels people to change not only the way that they think, but also how they act and interact with others. The informational disclosures transacted in apprehensions of commemorative architecture include insights not only about deities, cosmology, and mythology (which also carry obligations), but about ancestral history, ethical standards, systems of religiopolitics, and apportionments of socioeconomic power—all of which entail highly specific responsibilities. In short, work of many sorts is accomplished by capitalizing on the special communicative and transformative capabilities of architecture.

The Means and Messages of Commemorative Architecture: From Pedantic to Profound

If the specific informational and commemorative themes with which ritual-architectural events deal are enormously diverse, cross-cultural study makes immediately apparent that so too are the means of commemorative presentation. Presentational ploys run the gamut from the subtly suggestive to that of face-slapping bluntness. At the bluntly didactic end of the spectrum, the work of Bohemian architect Johann Blasius Santini Aichel (1677–1723) provides a particularly clear instance of unsubtle, allegorical architecture. Synthesizing Gothic and baroque modes, Santini Aichel worked to erase all ambiguity by designing, for example, a number of emblematically shaped constructions that included monastic buildings in the form of the abbot's initials, a court in the shape of a lyre, and a chapel to the Virgin at Obyetov that had a tortoise-shaped plan to betoken constancy.[12] Even more indelicately commemorative was the votive chapel that Santini Aichel designed to house the tongue of John Nepomul, a saint supposedly martyred for his refusal to utter the secrets of the confessional—that dedicatory plan featured five "tongue-shaped" altar niches.[13]

Equally transparent pedagogy via architecture was likewise employed by the Cholas of Tamil Nadu in their chariot-shaped *mandapa,* a Hindu temple designed complete with wheels and yoked horses and elephants to facilitate "the celestial ride";[14] or in the boat-shaped Durga temples, which are similarly intended to "symbolically ferry [the pilgrim] away from this world to 'the other shore.'"[15] Often, in fact, architectural elements have informational agenda that is no less direct than that of written texts: Consider, among countless examples, the memorial or "hero-stones" of India;[16] the monuments of American Civil War battlefields;[17] the didactic stained glass of Christian Europe; or Maya stelae, which are cloaked with detailed epigraphic inscriptions that refer to specific deities, cosmologies, historical events, and places.[18]

Furthermore, architecture can be even more categorically informational, or maybe propagandistic, when constructed deliberately in the direct service of a specific ideology. The House of Successions, for example, was built at the turn of this century in Vienna by a group of then-iconoclastic designers as a kind of revolutionary architectural manifesto, a self-proclaimed "template of art" to express their alternative aesthetic and moral principles, thus providing a caricature of the didactic potentialities of architectural form.[19] Only slightly less unabashed in their presentation of commemorative information are those sculptural architectures—like the forthcoming examples of Egyptian pyramids and classical Greek temples—that eschew almost entirely their function as sheltering spaces in favor of "monumental" exterior volumes that few if any ritual participants are allowed to enter. Morphologically similar, the impassable "simulated" or "fake temples" of the Río Bec Maya area in Yucatan, sculpted into edifice-sized deity masks with impossibly steep stairways leading up the face-like facades to false doorways, are, presumably, designed first and foremost to display the attributes of the god.[20] Or, exemplifying the aggressive exploitation of architecture's teacherly potential in a totally different and much lighter vein is the oft-cited case of the little stand on Long Island that sells ducks and duck eggs and, accordingly, is itself shaped like a duck.[21]

Obviously, then—from divinities to ducks—not only the means of architectural commemoration, but the range of issues that built forms can memorialize or commemorate is tremendously diversified, from the highly rarified to the decidedly mundane. At the rarified end of the spectrum, built forms have been enlisted in the commemoration or exploration of all manner of subtle theological themes, as in Michelangelo's Sistine Chapel, which, in John Dixon's view, provides a pictographic-architectural presentation of "the full range of human life."[22] Even the simplest architectural form potentially carries very profound messages, as in the case of the rude little hut of the Indian ascetic, which has been interpreted as "a metaphor for spiritual potentiality, for the possibility of the aspirant to ascend from this world toward a different level of realization."[23]

Yet, at the less ethereal end of the spectrum, commemorative architecture likewise may give voice to a wide range of very basic concerns, such as fertility or agricultural fecundity: The main axis of the Aegean palaces at Pylos, for example, was aligned with a conical hill and the cleft peak of Mount Mathia (that is, with landscape features that symbolize the goddess), so that, according to J. G. Davies, "the sexual symbolism is undeniable."[24] The Coricancha, or "Golden Enclosure," in the heart of pre-Columbian urban Cuzco—described by sixteenth-century chronicler Pedro de Cieza de León as a kind of artificial garden paradise where the stems of leaves, corn cobs, llamas, and even clods of earth were reproduced in fine gold—seems to have been a kind of ritual-architectural acknowledgment of the agricultural, peasant foundations of the Inca empire.[25] And, in a similar vein, the much discussed representation of modest Maya houses in the superelaborate stone friezes at the urban sites of Uxmal, Labná, and Kabah may similarly have been a nostalgic architectural ode to a simpler, more pastoral life-style.[26]

Cautionary Notes: (Non)Substantive, Inadvertent, and Superabundant Commemoration

In short, scholars working from a range of disciplinary perspectives have already well documented architecture's aptitude and versatility for communicating all sorts of information; and the next four chapters should redouble the realization that architecture works differently, but not less effectively, than texts in the transaction of religious ideas and obligations. As in the consideration of architecture as orientation, however, a couple of cautionary notes are in order, each of which both complicates and enlivens the rigorously empirical hermeneutic of specific historical cases.

The first involves ascertaining, to the extent possible, designers' motivations for the deployment of *apparently* informational architectural elements, and thus ascertaining the always limited role of those elements in the wider ritual-architectural program. In this respect, I have maintained that one of the most important and most difficult (and thus most often misconstrued) aspects in the analysis of specific sacred architectures comes in differentiating between those elements that belong to, respectively, the front and back halves of that architectural situation; identifying which elements are working primarily in the service of allurement and which are working in the service of communicating specific information and obligations is not always easy. Moreover, the instances most liable to cause difficulty in this regard are those in which the architectural situation under consideration explicitly imitates and borrows elements from some earlier ritual-architectural program. As noted in relation to the convention priority (I-B), such cases of architectural mimicry and appropriation are common in the extreme, but the motivations are neither obvious nor at all uniform.[27]

We can look once more to ancient Mexico for two contrastive cases that illustrate the problem.[28] First, Postclassic Maya revitalization movements apparently went to great pains to refurbish and re-erect Classic-era monuments as a means of similarly retrieving those older and presumably purer religious practices.[29] Here, architectural imitation seems to have proceeded as a concerted effort to revive intact the entire form-meaning, ritual-architectural package, as it were. In this case, then, substantive, informational elements were appropriated with the express intention of maintaining, or reviving, their full symbolic and informational value; such architectural elements as pictorial iconography of animals and deities, which had originally worked in the back half of the Classic-era events, were, in this case, resituated so that they would work again in that substantive role in Postclassic ritual-architectural events.

By contrast—and this is by far the more common circumstance—the Maya designers of Chichén Itzá fastidiously copied architectural elements from the distant site of Tula (and elsewhere), in the interest, it seems, of fashioning an eclectic, alluring aura of legitimacy.[30] Thus, pictographic representations of mythological figures and military orders that had been integral to the shockingly novel message of Tula's ritual-architectural program were, at Chichén Itzá, largely emptied of their informational content and redeployed simply as constituent elements in a conventionalized program of allurement. At Chichén Itzá, elements that had originally served to communicate important messages were, in a sense, demoted from the back half of the architectural situation to the front. And, because that happens so often, hermeneuts should be on guard against being seduced into imagining that all ostensibly informational elements really are, in an empirical sense, the architectural bearers of important information. In short, we need to beware of mistaking *apparently* informational elements, which are actually working as largely nonsubstantive components of conventionalized allurement, for the actual content of the occasion.

A second and closely related cautionary note arises even more directly from the superabundance and autonomy of sacred architecture; this by-now familiar point bears particularly on the charting and composition of the architectural reception histories of specific works.[31] Here we should keep in mind that even where interpreters succeed in recovering the explicit motivations of designers, those idealized intentions constitute only one of several very different protocols of architectural apprehension. The disparity between the creators' expectations and the eventual, always diversified apprehensions of their creations is, in fact, the most apparent in the realm of the content of architectural events.

Thus, on the one hand, even buildings that are designed for the most utilitarian, seemingly informationless purposes—barns, warehouses, lean-tos, or lighthouses—invariably transcend their strictly prosaic purposes to become, irrespective of overwhelmingly pragmatic design decisions, bearers of all sorts of substantive messages and meanings. It is not only tortoise-shaped chapels, mausoleums, and war memorials that commemorate by carrying important and diverse information to indigenous users, and thus to curious scholars. The vernacular, "non-pedigreed architecture" on which Sibyl Moholy-Nagy trains her attention, especially domestic constructions and workplaces, do much more than simply shelter the activities of life and labor; the intimate relations that people develop with the vernacular constructions of their everyday lives enable those built forms to serve both as repositories of their old aspirations, dreams, and values and as provocateurs of new ones. In Moholy-Nagy's assessment, "anonymous architecture . . . testifies to the aspirations of the group. . . . Indigenous buildings speak the vernacular of the people."[32] Empirically oriented hermeneuts ought, then, to be cognizant and attentive to the estimable communicative potential of what are, in a sense, only inadvertently meaningful buildings.

We need, on the other hand, to keep in mind that even the most deliberately didactic and memorializing monuments have superabundant commemorative and informational potentials that far exceed, and occasionally undermine, the sign-posting presentation of pedagogically, politically, or moralistically explicit agenda. As I've reiterated, even highly self-conscious building programs, intent on exploiting architecture's communicative and propagandistic virtues, will, apparently without exception, evoke highly diversified and often unintended, even unwanted, meanings and messages.

Thus, as stressed in the final chapter of volume 1, rigorously empirical hermeneuts ought not express their disappointment at the uncooperative sloppiness with which people "misconstrue" the meanings of their own sacred architectures; nor, worse still, should interpreters perpetuate the tacit denial, the art historical fiction, that such idiosyncratic (mis)understandings are rare, when they are in fact the rule rather than the exception; and nor should hermeneuts conclude from the pervasiveness of such unanticipated (mis)apprehensions that architecture, as a less-than-literary genre, is an enfeebled, unreliable medium of communication. Instead, if empirical hermeneutical description remains our goal, we ought to fix our strongest interpretive attentions directly on those creative revalorizations of architecture. It is there, in those multifarious (mis)apprehensions, not in the design studio, that we will gain the most direct insight into the workings of sacred architecture and into the people who are making it work.

With those caveats, then, I again adopt morphology and the strategic arrangement of specific cross-cultural examples as a means to laying a foundation for the sorts of particularistic hermeneutical inquiries that can attend to all protocols of architectural apprehension, eccentric as well as idealized. In order to assemble relevant heuristic questions, the diversity of messages and meanings that ritual-architectural events are especially inclined to explore is surveyed in terms of four thematic issues: the commemoration of divinity (priority II-A), of sacred history (priority II-B), of politics (priority II-C), and of the dead (priority II-D). Of the three broad sets of heuristic inquiries ventured in this framework—orientation, commemoration, and ritual context—it is this intermediate set that invariably elicits the most straightforward responses.

Seventeen | Divinity: Bodies, Abodes, and Abstractions (Priority II-A)

> The [Hindu] temple is at once the notion of God, the dwelling of God, the body of God, and the holy act of man utilizing tangible substance to realize all these abstract ideas.
>
> Nelson I. Wu, 1963[1]

> To medieval man the cathedral was truly the house of God, in a very real and awesome sense for us to understand today.
>
> Wim Swaan, 1984[2]

> Jesus answered them, "Destroy this temple, and in three days I will raise it up." The Jews then said, "It has taken forty-six years to build this temple, and will you raise it up in three days?" But he spoke of the temple of his body.
>
> John 2:19–21[3]

IMMEDIATELY UPON THEIR ARRIVAL in the New World, sixteenth-century Spanish conquistadors and priests were, among other challenges, forced into the hermeneutical initiative of "making sense" of the strangeness of the apparently religious architecture of the Aztecs and other indigenous peoples.[4] Cross-cultural comparison and analogies to the Old World "idolaters" figured large in their interpretive initiative, as classically educated friar-chroniclers, intimately familiar with one perspective on the Greco-Roman pantheon of anthropomorphic deities, worked to correlate the divine presences of the Aztec world with their similarly non-Christian, "pagan" counterparts.[5] Equipped with that sparse reservoir of morphological options, Spanish attempts to force various works of native architecture into some framework of coherence were invariably initiated on the basis of, and often largely confined to, solicitations of answers to one question: To which god is this temple dedicated?

The continuity between those colonialist interpretive efforts and our own attempts at understanding is discomforting. More specifically, there is considerable unease in the observation that the same brusque, over-determining question remains, five hundred years later, foundational, often summational, for most casual and many academic inquiries into the sacred architectures of Mesoamerica and elsewhere. The presumption that "religious architecture" in all contexts is built first and foremost to facilitate interactions with supernatural beings and forces (however imaginal), to honor and petition gods (however conceived), continues to enjoy wide currency. "Houses of god" remains the most common heading under which to organize comparative studies of sacred architecture.[6]

To put a keener edge on the often intimate relations between gods and buildings will require not only the less normative, more critical temper that will enable greater sensitivity to the cultural specificity of conceptions of the divine. It will require also a firmer, wider base of morphological options, a more nuanced map of relevant cross-cultural cases and academic analyses, from which we can generate more and better heuristic questions concerning the ritual-architectural commemoration of divinity (priority II-A). Understandable antipathy in some quarters toward the privilege of Hellenic analogies notwithstanding, Greek materials can provide an advantageous point of departure.

Greek Gods and Temples: Three Variations on a Theme

Architectural historian Vincent Scully maintains that "all Greek sacred architecture explores the character of a god or group of gods."[7] With that bold claim as his basis, his expansive treatment of the historical development of the Hellenic architectural tradition presents, not just one imagining of the relations between buildings and gods, but actually a whole series of variations on the ritual-architectural commemoration of divinity. Moreover, Scully's work serves our purposes especially well by virtue of his uncommon respect for what I call the eventfulness of architecture.[8] He frames (or problematizes) his inquiry, not simply in terms of the built forms of ancient Greece, but also in terms of the religious disposition that spawns a particular architectural form, the ceremonial occasion of its use, and, particularly, the integration of the built form with the surrounding landscape. Together these elements—the architectural construction, the human mindset that created it, the occasion of its use, and the natural landscape in which it is situated—constitute the appropriate unit of study, or what Scully refers to (not unlike a ritual-architectural event) as "one ritual whole."[9]

From Scully's frame, then, the historical development of Greek sacred architecture emerges as a series of expressions and explorations of the relationships between nature (or the landscape), humanity, and divinity—between "the earth, the temple, and the gods." In the earliest phase, the great Cretan palaces, the paradigm of which is at Knossos, embody and celebrate the central tenant of Minoan religion—namely, an unquestioning reverence for a great nurturing goddess of the earth. Therefore, the siting, orientation, and design of the Minoan palace are all coordinated in such a manner that the building is literally, even magically, identified with the actual body of the earth goddess; in Scully's evaluation, the architectural fabric, in fact, actually *was* the goddess.[10] Thus, while humanly constructed, the Cretan palace had, as Nikos Kazantzakis agrees, a life and personality of its own: "this palace [at Knossos] grew and proliferated in the course of time, slowly, like a living organism. . . ."[11]

Later, however, according to Scully, the Mycenaean culture witnessed a transition toward a more "human centered view of experience" and thus a movement away from the conception of a magical unity between the goddess and the architecture that had dominated Minoan planning.[12] By Homeric times, nature was perceived more as hostile than venerable, and the conception of divinity was characterized by a plurality of gods who, aside from immortality and fantastic power, were not too different from human beings (a view more like that which the Spaniards expected to find in Aztec Tenochtitlan).[13] These Homeric, preclassic conceptions were, Scully says, reflected in the archaic Greek temple that, rather than itself "being" a deity, *houses* the image of a deity. The preclassic temple represented, in other words, the presence of a god rather than the literal body of the god. Yet, by its sculptural qualities, the temple made visible the otherwise hidden character of the god.[14]

The historical development from body, to abode, to abstraction culminates in the classic Greek temple, which is, in Scully's assessment, "the ultimate refinement of the Stone and Bronze Age tradition."[15] The classic Greek temple, like much of Mesoamerican sculptural architecture, rejected almost entirely the function of "elaborated shelter" and the facilitation of activities in favor of the commemorative presentations of a conception of divinity.[16] These classical forms, then, provided ritual contexts only in a highly restricted sense.[17] The temples of Hera, Demeter, Artemis, and Aphrodite, for instance, were not designed spatially as interior rooms; nor were they intended as backdrops to ritual performance. Instead, they were, according to Scully, "articulated sculptural bodies," and as such, "personifications" and commemorations of a deity's attributes.[18] Employing a purely abstract, transhuman scale (a strategy again very similar to that apparently employed by the pre-Columbian Maya in the Río Bec–Chenes area of Yucatan), the classic Greek temple at once denied human entry and delivered a theological statement about the nature of divinity and about the nature of humanity's and nature's relatedness to divinity.

In Scully's analysis, then, the evolution of Greek architecture demonstrates a continuum stretching from literal to abstract strategies for the ritual-architectural commemoration divinity. While again willing to abstain on the historical merits of the (re)construction, I can, in a more synchronic vein, extract from Scully's work a triad of morphological variations on the theme of deity commemoration: 1) architecture conceived as the body of the god; 2) architecture conceived as the abode of the god; and 3) architecture conceived as the abstract representation of the god's attributes. This neat, alliterative division of three variations on a theme, three alternative expressions of the priority for commemorating divinity (II-A), is, as usual, only heuristic and thus, as we'll see momentarily, not at all mutually exclusive.

Hindu Temples and the Interpenetrability of Morphological Options

Where, in Scully's analysis of Greek sacred architecture, those options are stretched out on a timeline, the multivocal phenomenon of the Hindu temple—which provides perhaps the most vivid and most variegated of all exemplars of the ritual-architectural commemoration of divinity—makes especially clear the plausible simultaneity and interpretability of all three possibilities. The Hindu temple, as George Michell explains, "is designed to bring about contact between man and the gods; it is here that the gods appear to man."[19] Thus, quite obviously, even to Western observers, the Hindu temple is, in one sense, like the preclassic Greek temple, a "house of god," an earthly residence where the gods, usually manifest in the form of an anthropomorphic image, make themselves visible and accessible to human devotees.[20]

In India, however, this ritual-architectural incentive for constructing a divine residence to which a god might be lured, and then visited and propitiated, or entertained as a royal guest, takes innumerable forms. A very humble variation on that ploy is evident in the dilapidated shelter, decorated only with a cheap eight-by-ten-inch print of the goddess Durga via which a solitary ascetic summons and worships the deity.[21] But the same concern for summoning and sheltering the divinity likewise engenders those magnificently elaborate temples, notably the huge rock-cut temple at

Ellora, which are built as replicas of Shiva's mythological mountain home of Kailasa with the expectation that the god will come to reside there and will dispense his favors on the builders and patrons.[22] Or, in other cases, the expectation of divine recompense is less apparent (or at least less direct) than a motive simply to provide a built environment in which the resident deity can be pampered via some extreme demonstration of hospitality: At Tiruanaikka, near Tiruchirapalli in Tamil Nadu, for instance, Shiva, who is *abhisekha-priya* (fond of ritual bath), is indulged by an *unda-deul* (or sunken shrine) temple in which the sanctum floor is laid below the level of the water table so that it is nightly flooded and then manually baled out before worship each morning.[23]

Besides functioning as the earthly residences for the gods, and thus as sheltering spaces for the interactions between anthropomorphic divinities and their devotees, Hindu temples can, however, also be identified with the divinity in a much more direct sense (and thus at that point to function more like Cretan palaces than preclassic temples). To draw again on Michell: "the [Hindu] temple is not only a *place* of worship but also an *object* of worship. The divinity that is revealed within the sanctuary may also be revealed in the very fabric of the temple itself."[24]

Sometimes, in fact, the direct identification of the "body" of the Indian divinity (and the human body as well) with the architectural form has been conceived as so complete that, according to K. V. Soundara Rajan, the erection of the physical form of the Hindu temples was considered as "the emergence of the corporeal body and vesture of God, replete with flesh, bones, tendons, and nerves, and breathing with life. The temple itself was looked upon as God transcreated."[25] In those cases, divinity is manifest not only in the anthropomorphic images sheltered within the temple, but in the entire architectural construction itself. The whole Hindu temple, in a very graphic sense, *becomes* the divinity or, more anthropomorphically still, as Stella Kramrisch suggests, "the monumental embodiment of the [primordial cosmic 'man'] Puruṣa."[26]

Having accentuated the more-than-metaphorical identification between divinities and buildings, interpreters of Hindu temples are, however, also careful to impose an important qualification: Behind this conspicuously anthropomorphic imagery, Indian logic dictates that there is always an ultimate reality without form, a divine reality (*brahman*), which is formless but which, by virtue of the Hindu conception of cosmic parturition, may take on an infinity of temporal forms—including architectural forms.[27] The Hindu temple, then, is a monumental embodiment not simply of the cosmic body of Purusha, but, moreover and somewhat paradoxically, the architectural form is likewise the manifestation of that formless "supreme reality" that is *brahman*. The Hindu temple provides, in other words, a "place for *brahman*," or a place where the formlessness of *brahman* might be experienced, a place of transit, a ford or crossing place (*tirtha*) where worshipers are allowed to transcend this present illusory world and participate in that which is eternal.

Thus, in addition to the conceptions of the Hindu temple as the *abode* of the god (like preclassic Greek temples) and more graphically as the *body* of the god (like Cretan palaces), the Hindu temple participates in the more abstract sort of ritual-architectural commemoration of divinity with which Scully credits the classic Greek temple. In Nelson Wu's summarizing formulation, the temple is at once the dwelling, the body, and "the notion of God."[28] The Hindu temple provides, in Kramrisch's phrase, an architectonic manifestation of ultimate reality or of "the Essence": "it is the form of Consciousness itself."[29] And, consequently, the ritual-architectural experience of the Hindu temple can provide a kind of realization or awakening insight both into the human condition in this illusory world and into the means toward transubstantiation or release from this world (*moksha*). The architecture of the temple expresses both the existential problem and a possible solution.

In sum, the multivocality of the Hindu temple thus serves a double purpose in the present morphological project. The exemplum of the Hindu temple is incisive in exposing the artificiality and nonexclusivity of the various morphological categories and subcategories (an observation redoubled when one remembers the piquancy with which Hindu temples also exemplify the homology [I-A] and convention [I-B] priorities). Yet, at the same time, the complex case of the Hindu temple also demonstrates the productivity and utility of such provisional distinctions. When these various heuristic options are allowed to collapse (as do most interpretations of the Hindu temple), the specialness of the Hindu temple, particularly as compared to other non-Indian sacred architectures, is obfuscated rather than illumined. Holding apart those artificial distinctions enables us to see the fairly obvious sense in which Hindu temples are "houses of god," which so often serves as a kind of interpretive default mode, but it also forces to recognition those less obvious possibilities, which are too often neglected. Moreover, even in India, all permutations of divinity commemoration are not equally relevant to all social constituencies, to all occasions, or to all regions, and those heuristic distinctions provide us with a means and a vocabulary for addressing those empirical contrasts: in South India, for instance, the notion of temple as shelter for the divinity seems to be accentuated, while North Indians emphasize this notion of the temple as a "door" or crossing place (*tirtha*) from this world toward a divine realm beyond form.[30]

Reminded once more, then, of the limitedness of this medial stage in a wider hermeneutics, I can, borrowing from Scully and these Indologists, work roughly from the literal to the abstract (though without, I hope, implying any evolutionary scheme)[31] to provide some reflections on and examples of each of the three principal variations on the ritual-architectural commemoration of divinity (priority II-A).

Architecture as the Body of God: Personified Landscapes and Earth Monsters

First, with respect to the equation of architecture (broadly speaking) and deities (again broadly speaking), we should take note of a fairly widespread tendency to identify features of the natural landscape, "the architecture of nature" as it were—mountains, stones, trees, lakes, and crags—with specific divine or mythological beings.[32] Australian aborigines, for example, seemingly define any piece of country by the presence and activities of mythic beings so that, according to Ronald M. Berndt, "In a sense, such land not only locates but also identifies a particular deity; the one is a necessary condition of the other."[33] Similarly suggesting an equation of places (either built of unbuilt) and divinity, Father Cobo was fascinated and disturbed by the way that the seventeenth-century Indians of Peru seemed to use the same two terms—*vilca* and *guaca*—"to mean not only any god or idol, but also all places of worship, such as temples, graves, and any other place that was venerated and where sacrifices were made."[34] And the "primitive" Japanese are likewise credited with a "personification" or "divinization" of natural features insofar as trees and rocks were identified with various deities; thus, with respect to certain Japanese shrines (or *iwakura*), like that of the Takimatsuri-no-kami and the Okitama-no-kami, we hear that "the deity resides in a rock or in stones, and there are no sanctuary buildings at all."[35] (In these cases, though, it would appear that the rock is conceived more as the abode of the deity than as its actual body.)[36]

Be that as it may, we find considerably more direct, more explicitly architectural parallels to Scully's interpretation of Cretan palaces and to the Hindu equation of whole buildings with divinities in the rich indigenous

American tradition of "theomorphizing architecture." Outstanding in this respect are the serpent-mouth or dragon-throated temples of the Río Bec–Chenes and Puuc Maya regions of Central Yucatan, wherein entire buildings were fashioned into enormous deity masks, complete with eyes, noses, and tooth-lined doorways, a luridly elegant effect that Paul Gendrop describes as "mythical surrealism."[37] Suggesting a kind of "triple identification," Eric Thompson argued that these anthropomorphic, face-like temples were, in one sense, architectural reiterations of the Maya conception of a house-like universe (thus foregrounding a microcosmic or homologized building agenda [priority I-A]) and, at the same time, architectural representations of the celestial creator deity, Itzam Na or Iguana House, "the greatest god of the Yucatec Maya" (instantiating also a version of divinity commemoration [priority II-A]).[38]

In the wake of more current Maya research, which has put in doubt Thompson's contention that Itzam Na stood at the head of a Maya pantheon of gods,[39] the dragon-throated temples of Central Yucatan now seem less likely to be embodiments of a supereminent creator god than representations of the earth itself, or of an "earth monster"—a prospect that makes them an even closer morphological parallel to the Cretan palace's conception as the body of the Minoan earth goddess. Imagining a symbolic equation between earth(-deity) and architecture, Elizabeth Benson hypothesizes that these distinctive structures facilitated what I might term a "serpent-mouth temple event," wherein entry into the mouth doorway amounted to a kind of symbolic death as one is swallowed up by the earth monster and thus transported into a "cosmologically defined world"; but then, upon exiting through the god mouth, the ritual participant "re-enacts the ancient emergence from the primordial cave, from the earth," and thus (not unlike the metaphorical sense in which the king "sprouted" in the Copán Temple 22 event, discussed in chapter 16) experiences the catharsis of rebirth.[40]

The much-discussed kivas of the American Southwest, which facilitate a still more explicit (re)entry and exit from the earth, are also amenable to the eventful sort of interpretation suggested by Benson.[41] Plausible but uncertain interpretations of the so-called effigy mounds of North America, huge raised earth sculptures of animals and birds like the quarter-mile-long Ohio Serpent Mound, suggest that these were even more enormous embodiments of deities (or mythological figures).[42] Innumerable other Mesoamerican constructions, though widely variant in scale and appearance, have likewise been plausibly interpreted as "theomorphs" or architectonic deities, particularly (but not exclusively) earth monsters. Among especially notable examples, the famous "zoomorphic boulders" of Copán and Quirigua have been interpreted as Maya gods and culture heroes in the form of grotesque reptile, bird, and mammal composites,[43] or, more recently, as representations of "crouching earth monsters or sky deities with humans seated among their snake like coils";[44] Johanna Broda considers that "on the mythological level the Templo Mayor, the sacred mountain, was the earth itself, the earth as a voracious monster devouring human victims and blood";[45] a heavy, elaborately sculpted portal at Copán has been interpreted as a "sky monster," which thus presents the possibility for entry into a different sort of religiocosmic realm;[46] and, on a somewhat larger scale, because the full layout of the Olmec ceremonial center of La Venta seems to depict a gigantic jaguar mask, the suggestion has been made that the entire complex may have been identified with a feline deity.[47]

Architecture as the House of God: Deity Domiciles and Sacred Shelters

With respect to the second, more sheltering set of expressions of ritual-architectural commemoration of divinity, pre-Columbian Mesoamerica again provides innumerable examples of architectures that "house" deities, perhaps the most dramatic being the specially designed sanctuary of the Aztecs where the "gods" of conquered peoples were installed as slaves in cells, niches, and, in some cases, wooden cages.[48] Karen Bassie-Sweet also notes that "When the Maya built a temple or pyramid near or on a cave site or water shrine, they were creating a house that replicated the deity's home at the mythological mountain, thus duplicating a cosmological concept."[49] Looking more cross-culturally, however, J. G. Davies notes that the majority of the terms used for explicitly religious buildings—in Hebrew, *beit Elohim* ("house of God"); in Greek, *naos,* from *naio* ("to dwell in"); in Latin, *domus dei* ("a god's home"); and in Sanskrit, *devalaya* (a residence of god)—emphasize this quality of a divine dwelling.[50] This notion of providing domiciles for deities can, nevertheless, take many forms.

Often, as in the architectural re-creation of Shiva's mythological home of Mount Kailasa at Ellora (or as in the Maya case just cited), the building is constructed as an earthly replica of some celestial divine dwelling. The Temple of Solomon, for instance, is described in the Letter to the Hebrews (8:5, 9:23 RSV) as "a copy and a shadow of the heavenly sanctuary" and as "copies of the heavenly things."[51] From a medieval Christian view, the Gothic cathedral was "truly the house of God," which, according to Wim

Swaan, "was conceived as no less than the earthly embodiment of the heavenly Jerusalem."[52] And the ziggurat form of ancient Babylonia, evincing a similar sheltering function, is routinely described as

> a representation of the celestial hill upon which the Babylonian gods were supposed to dwell, crowned with a temple in which a god was supposed to lodge when he came to earth for the service of humanity. . . .[53]

In Japan, the *yama* (or model mountain) is an architectural replica of the deity's dwelling place, "constructed to receive the deity temporarily."[54] And, blending these first two variations on the architectural commemoration of divinity (that is, bodies of god and abodes of god), Kenzo Tange explains how, from a very early period, Japanese used rice straw ropes (*shimenawa*) to delimit sacred areas, which, presumably, "both signified the space occupied by the deities and symbolized the deities themselves."[55]

The sense in which the deity is actually present in these divine dwellings (or in the image or statue that the dwellings house) is also conceived in a variety of very different ways. Often, elaborate rituals are performed to induce the deity to come into, or to reside in, the humanly constructed forms, whether buildings, statuary, or paintings. In the case of Tibetan Buddhist monasteries, for example, not only does the Lamaist word for temple, "lha-k'an," mean "God's house,"[56] but also, more specifically, individual rooms throughout the monastery are regarded as habitations or shelters for specific deities. Thus, as Romi Khosla explains, after each sacred room is built,

> elaborate ceremonies are conducted to invite the deity to inhabit its dwelling place. The room can only have a religious function if the deity is considered to be present. If the deity chooses to depart from its dwelling place then the senior Lama is compelled to rebuild the temple.[57]

David Freedberg has collected a wide and fascinating sampling of consecration rites wherein inanimate constructed objects are imbued with life: in ancient Egypt (as in Babylonia or Sumer and Assyria), the final stage in making an image of a god consisted of "the rite of the Washing and Opening of the mouth," whereby the image was identified and invested with the life of that divinity; and, in a parallel fashion among Theravada Buddhists of Sri Lanka, the fashioning of a statue of the Buddha culminates with the painting of the eyes, the *netra pinkama,* or "eye-ceremony"—"the very act by which it is brought to life."[58] Similarly, Coomaraswamy explains that, in Hinduism,

> on the completion of an image, its eyes are "opened" by a special and elaborate ceremony. Thus, it is clearly indicated that the image is to be regarded as if animated by the deity.[59]

And, drawing on a more proximate circumstance, Fred Clothey recounts the performance of the *pratistha,* a Hindu ceremonial process by which icons can be embodied with the fullness of the divine, in which the deity Venkateshvara was physically transported from India and resituated in his new home in the Penn Hills Temple near Pittsburgh.[60]

This perception of the deity's actual presence in the temple accounts, then, for those Hindu architectural events in which divine images are washed, fed, or caressed—all practices that the resident gods are said "to enjoy."[61] Such extremely anthropomorphic conceptions are, however, hardly unique to India. Scholars consider that in ancient Egypt, prior to the establishment of the Pharaonic dynasty (about 3200 B.C.E.),

> no doubt every town had its own "house of the god" where the deity was believed to dwell, and prayers, lustrations, offerings and gifts were made to him daily, accompanied by dancing, music and processions.[62]

Or, in Greek oracle temples, the god—Apollo in the case of Delphi—was considered sufficiently present (at least in certain seasons) that he could be consulted about important personal and political questions.[63] The extent to which Greek statuary of the gods was invested with life, and thus potentially dangerous as well as beneficent, is even more apparent in the abundant stories and representations of the chaining of the stone images of Ares, Hera, Dionysius, and other Greek deities to prevent their escape or transfer of residence (a circumstance that is, in a sense, parallel to the Aztec capture and enslavement of deity images).[64] And, in the same vein, whether accessed as passionate conviction or facile sentimentality, there is certainly no shortage of accounts (both antique and brand new) of Christian images (both three- and two-dimensional) speaking, weeping, and waving.

Architecture and the Attributes of God: Iconoclasm and Aniconism

Consideration of a third, more abstract set of variations on the ritual-architectural commemoration of divinity, a set of design solutions more resemblant to those that Scully sees in the classic Greek temple or that Wu sees in Hindu expressions of "the notion of God," leads us into the intricate problems of iconoclasm, aniconism, and doctrinal proscriptions against representing god. Particularly striking are innumerable categorical denials, from widely spaced cultural contexts, that god is in any especial sense present *in* the building, let alone *is* the building. Though, empirically speaking, this may be an empty category—since theoretic claims to such radical anti-anthropomorphism are almost never sustained in lived interactions with religious arts and architectures—the contenders for inclusion in this morphologic option are nonetheless many.

Most prominently, the Abrahamic religions—Judaism, Christianity, and Islam—by virtue of a shared insistence on the unity and transcendence of God, and thus an (ostensibly) deep enmity for idolatry, are each vexed by the awkward task of commemorating God without depicting God.[65] The Bible and the Mishnah both deliver strong prohibitions against any anthropomorphic representation of God, and, consequently, many Christians (like Jews in this regard) argue strenuously that "the church is *not* a house for the deity: rather it is a house for the *people* of the deity," a meetinghouse for the community of the faithful.[66] Some (though hardly all) Christians would, in fact, go so far as to insist that:

> It can hardly be too strongly emphasized that the only good reason for building a church is to provide shelter for a worshipping community, a place where the Church, in the biblical sense, may offer to God the one "full, perfect, and sufficient sacrifice, oblation and satisfaction for the sins of the whole world."[67]

Islam, even more often, is credited with the total avoidance of deity images or images of the Prophet, a prohibition that ostensibly serves to affirm the transcendence of Allah, "since the Divine Essence cannot be compared with anything whatsoever."[68] Strange morphological bedfellows, some tribal contexts—for instance, the Maori, the Nupe of Western Africa, and the Australian Walbiri—have been credited with a similarly complete avoidance of visual imagery.[69] And likewise, even in India, we routinely (though now, it seems, inadvisably) hear about an aniconic period in early Buddhism in which images of the historical Buddha Shakyamuni were entirely prohibited; in that familiar view, subsequent worship of anthropomorphic Buddha figures is almost strictly a result of foreign Greek influences and is nearly always glossed as compromising the original purity of the tradition.[70]

Theological imperatives and anthropological reports of iconographic abstinence notwithstanding, closer consideration of each of these historical contexts reveals that the alleged aniconism is almost never realized in actual practice. Highlighting the discrepancy between orthodox injunctions and empirical practice, Freedberg, in fact, makes a compelling argument for some sort of fundamental human predisposition for representing that which is important, "an ever-present impulse to image," so that "the will to image figuratively—even anthropomorphically—cannot be suppressed."[71] Exploring the tension between "our need for images" and "our fear of images," Freedberg contends that the widely circulated notion that certain cultures (usually monotheistic or "primitively pure" cultures) totally avoid images in their art and architecture is actually a fiction, "a deep and persistent historiographical myth," which seldom if ever corresponds to the historical reality. He argues that, "abstinence from figuring the deity does occasionally occur, but for the rest the notion of aniconism is wholly untenable."[72] Alternatively, he holds that: "objects of worship and veneration are inevitably visualized; such visualizations must then be made real and material; and that in turn reinforces the ever-present impulse to image."[73]

Thus, if we look past doctrinal prohibitions against figurative imagery and past arguable academic accounts of aniconically "pure" contexts and concentrate on more fully empirical interactions with buildings, we discover that these ostensibly iconoclastic traditions, instead of exempting themselves from participation in the ritual-architectural commemoration of divinity, actually demonstrate a set of especially creative and subtle permutations on this priority.[74] (Remember, though, that in the present construction of morphology, both the idealized injunctions of orthodoxy and arguable academic interpretations, as well as the diversity of "real," historically observable architectural apprehensions, are all regarded as viable and instructive resources.)[75]

As regards the widely circulated postulate of a complete avoidance of anthropomorphic images of Shakyamuni in early Buddhist art, there is now controverting evidence that images of the Buddha were made and worshiped from the very beginning.[76] Art historian Susan Huntington's compelling work on the intellectual history of that notion suggests, in fact, that there really were no doctrinal proscriptions against the creation of such works and that the notion of a "pure," strictly aniconic early Buddhism is largely a Western construction (or aspiration) based on a "misunderstanding of the thematic content of the art [of that period]."[77] Nonetheless, the ever-presence of images should not be allowed to dissuade us from taking seriously Buddhist claims that those anthropomorphic elements facilitate neither the worship of the person nor the divinity of the Buddha, but rather his teaching or his example, the Dharma—an eventuality that suggests that (some) Buddhist temples are not houses of god per se, but, in a more subtle variation on the commemoration of divinity priority, ritual-architectural expressions (or commemorations) of ultimate truth.

By the same token, in Islam, despite categorical prohibitions against any depiction of divinity that might detract (or distract) from Allah's transcendence, it is quite clear that the (super)nature of divinity is, nevertheless, regularly, if somewhat indirectly, addressed in Muslim art and architecture. According to Lois Ibsen al-Fārūqī, for instance, while "the Muslim artist is never involved with a depiction, however stylized or abstracted, of God Himself," Muslim art most assuredly does attempt to "disclose an intuition" of the nature and transcendence of God.[78] She says that, in Islam,

> the aesthetic realm, the beautiful, is that which directs attention to Allah . . . this transcendence-obsessed culture sought, through the creation of the beautiful, to stimulate in the viewer or listener an intuition of, or an insight into, the nature of God and of man's relation to Him.[79]

The aniconic attitude typically afforded Jews, not infrequently (mis)-characterized as "a people who lacked artistic inclination," similarly masks a more ambivalent attitude toward the potentiality for artistic and architectural commemorations of divinity.[80] Besides the prohibitions in Exodus against idolatry ("You shall not make a carved image for yourself . . ."), the Torah likewise describes in detail an elaborate "tent of the presence," which the Israelites were to build as a cultic center for God's worship. Thus, according to some Jewish traditions, the Temple of Solomon was built, in conformity to divine directives revealed to David, as a fixed dwelling place for the *Shekhina,* "the Divine Presence on earth," for which Moses had prepared a moveable dwelling.[81] If presumably "only metaphorical," the residential imagery is unmistakable.

Early Christians also strenuously resisted any intimation that God's divine presence could be contained within an earthly architectural form; in their view, which seems to accuse Jews of claiming to "house" God, the built Temple of Solomon was to be replaced by "the body of Christ."[82] Nevertheless, in Christianity as well, endemic controversy over how best to observe strictures against idolatry and, simultaneously, to capitalize on the unique potentialities of art and architecture issues in, among other consequences, a variegated spectrum of creative solutions to the problem of the ritual-architectural commemoration of divinity. Compare, for example, the profound differences in the relationships between built form and Christian divinity in each of the following: the Byzantine church, which affirms the Neoplatonic notion that spiritual power might actually be present in material objects such as icons;[83] the Gothic cathedral, whose discourses into light and height, in a somewhat less direct fashion, accentuate the remote majesty and maybe fearful judgment of God;[84] and the Quaker meeting-house, which, in all its simplicity, "witnesses to a being who is to be known in the midst of life, who is not separate, whose dwelling is within human-kind, offering fellowship."[85]

Perhaps the most morphologically direct Christian parallel to the Hindu conception of the temple as the body of Purusha is the cross-shaped plan of the basilica that, according to medieval liturgists, represents, in a quite literal fashion, the physiognomy of the crucified lord. In their view:

> His head corresponds to the apse with its axis to the East, His outstretched arms are the transepts, His torso and legs are at rest in the nave, His heart lies at the principle altar.[86]

And a similarly direct parallel to the abstract sense in which the classical Greek temple commemorates the attributes of a specific divinity comes in those many church designs that express and celebrate the Christian conception of divinity, that is, the Trinity. The triangular-shaped Austrian Baroque Church of the Trinity at Stadl-Paura (1714–25), to cite but one among countless relevant exemplars, has not only three identical facades, each framed by three towers, but also three main portals and three altars, each of which is explicitly dedicated to a member of the Trinity.[87]

Closing Thoughts: Specificity and Superabundance in Divinity Commemoration

As in ancient Greece, then, the wealth of variety in the history of Christian building well demonstrates that architectural forms can do much more than simply express (or elicit) the generalized presence of divinity. Architecture, on the one hand, again challenging the supposedly singular communicative potentialities of texts, can articulate highly particularistic intricacies and details concerning respective, culturally specific conceptions of God and reality.[88] Even now, proscriptions against idolatry still intact, Christians remain confident that their "theological visions" and conceptions of divinity can be accurately and fruitfully expressed in architectural form.[89] Arguably, the rarefied notion of the Trinity, and the specific privileges and obligations that are the consequence of faith in that Christian notion, have, in the past two thousand years, reached and impressed more multitudes via ritual-architectural than via literary expressions. Architecture assuredly can speak with force and precision about even the most subtle of theological doctrines.

Yet, on the other hand, the history of Christian building, particularly the frequent controversies and proclamations of ecclesiastical authorities regarding the "correct" spiritual attitude toward images and art, also demonstrates especially well the superabundance and autonomy, the rebellious flexibility, of architectural commemorations of divinity. Churchly distress over popular, too-literal enthusiasm for artistic representations of saviors, saints, and virgins is legendary. The redundancy of correctives in that regard belies the reliability of art and architecture's communicative potential and exposes the endemically wide disparities between the official teachings concerning appropriate perceptions of artistic, architectural expressions of divinity and the creatively idiosyncratic apprehensions of "ordinary people."[90] Over the long run, neither the church-goers nor the built theologies prove themselves very faithful to original religioartistic intentions.

Moreover, also with respect to superabundance but in a tighter time frame, Christianity studies like Staale Sinding-Larson's exceptional work on iconography and ritual show that, even where painted, carved, and built configurations do work precisely as designers and ecclesiastical authorities anticipate, hermeneuts ought not presume static, one-to-one correspondences between architectural elements and divine attributes. Ritual-architectural expressions of divinity are not codes that can be deciphered and translated back into words. Where Sinding-Larsen stresses that an icon, particularly in the context of ritual, "is not one solid unchangeable and undifferentiated entity,"[91] the same is true, if somewhat less obvious, for the hard stone, steel, or glass elements of architecture. Where Sinding-Larsen explains the fascinating, speedy malleability whereby the meaning of an iconographic image of Christ changes several times even within the course of a single mass—"the connotations may change from that of the Trinity to that of the present God, to Christ's presence in the eucharistic bread and wine, and so forth"[92]—we need to appreciate that, paradoxically enough, the meanings and valances of sturdier architectural expressions of the attributes of God, such as ceilings, sculpted doorways, and windows, can also be significantly rearranged within the span of a few eventful, liturgical moments.

In sum, then, one working definition with which to differentiate sacred architecture from other sorts of building (a distinction that I am not usually inclined to make) may be that—whether as the body, the abode, or the abstract expression of a god—religious structures always commemorate some conception of the divine, the exceptional. Consequently, there is, at one level, a unity to experiences of sacred architecture insofar as some permutation of the ritual-architectural commemoration of divinity (priority II-A) is always at issue. But, even a brief cross-cultural survey reveals spectacularly diverse means and ends in that regard; there are, in fact, manifold possibilities even within any single architectural configuration. If, therefore, that staid old standard—to which god is this temple dedicated? —is a dangerously prejudicial interpretive starting point, it is much less adequate as a summational hermeneutical interrogation.

Eighteen | Sacred History: Myths and Miracles (Priority II-B)

> For mythical thinking the relation between what a thing "is" and the place in which it is situated is never purely external and accidental; the place is itself a part of the thing's being, and the place confers very specific inner ties upon the thing.
>
> Ernst Cassirer, 1955[1]

> [E]very individual feature of Ayer's Rock is linked [by Australian aborigines] to a significant myth and the mythological beings who created it. Every tree, every stain, hole and fissure has meaning.
>
> Amos Rapoport, 1975[2]

> Above all else, sacred place is "storied place.". . . Without exception, the sacred place is the place rich in story.
>
> Belden C. Lane, 1988[3]

PARTICULARLY IN SO-TERMED ARCHAIC CONTEXTS, the original cosmogony, the fabulous adventures of mythical ancestors and culture heroes, and the miraculous (and some not so miraculous) happenings of the post-primordial era meld into a single, unbroken course of "sacred history."[4] These stories, which usually draw in some uneven measure on the sources of inspiration, imagination, and empirical occurrence, often run, with fits and starts, from the very creation of the world through to the present. Along the way, such seamlessly, roughly interwoven mythicohistoric stories provide not only entertainment, but the rationales, the models, the paradigms, and the patterns both for "how things are" and, more importantly, for "how things should be." Accordingly, the memory of one's sacred history—even in not so archaic cultures—is among the foremost of spiritual responsibilities. Moreover, as John Ruskin urged via his mid-nineteenth-century declaration that "there are but two strong conquerors of the forgetfulness of men—poetry and architecture,"[5] building and buildings have a special dexterity in fulfilling that mnemonic charge. Architecture is and should be, according to Ruskin and a host of others, an embodiment of history, characterized by a "richness of record."[6]

That builders in all cultural contexts, particularly where religious and public works are concerned, have accepted the challenge of memorializing, in one way or another, important episodes and individuals from their respective mythological and historical pasts has never been in doubt. The same Western investigators who took for granted that the pre-Columbian constructions of Middle America must have commemorated native "gods" were similarly confident that figural elements in that architecture and decoration were "undoubtedly mythologic" or "mytho-esthetic motifs."[7] Nineteenth-century explorer of Maya ruins John Lloyd Stephens, for instance, who was always concerned to reign in the extravagant assessments of his less "scientific" antiquarian predecessors, risked no loss of credibility in his speculation that "each figure [in the so-called Governor's Palace at the site of Uxmal] was perhaps the portrait of some cacique, warrior, prophet, or priest, distinguished in the history of this unknown people."[8] No one questions that the collusion between the paired incentives to build and to remember the past, among the Maya or elsewhere, has been prolific.

The present morphological challenge, therefore, as in the case of divinity commemoration (priority II-A), is not to persuade hermeneuts of the deep and wide importance of the ritual-architectural commemoration of sacred history (priority II-B); that much is already taken for granted. Alternatively, the more urgent requirement is for some heuristically significant organization of the unwieldy diversity of built configurations that express and preserve mythical, miraculous, and historical circumstances.

Perhaps the most cross-culturally common constructional manifestations of those concerns are countless stage-like arrangements whereupon sacred architectures co-opt (or retrieve) the roles of museum, school, and especially theater by facilitating the performance, and thus re-experience, of the dramas of myth and history. Bishop Landa, for instance, could, on the one hand, dismiss the low square stages or "dance platforms" that he observed in the remains of nearly every pre-Columbian Yucatecan plaza with the condescendingly eventful, sixteenth-century surmise that these must have served their "pagan" Maya patrons as the tribunes on which "farces were represented, and comedies for the pleasures of the public";[9] but we, on the other hand, could note as well that nearly all Christian churches (Landa's included), however diverse in other respects, are likewise designed, to a considerable extent, as ritual-architectural "stages" for the reiteration and reenactment of the sacred drama of Christ's life and passion. Architecture, then, whether in indigenous or European contexts, very often abets the commemoration of sacred history primarily in an *in*direct fashion—by providing the ritual context and supporting backdrop against which mythicohistorical stories can be (re)told and (re)enacted again and again.[10]

Yet, in addition to this ancillary stage-setting function, there are also many more direct and more ingenious ways in which various peoples have exploited architecture's rare potential for expressing and retrieving the dramas of their respective sacred histories. In addition to amphitheatric settings for mythical dramas, consider in turn these four variations on the sacred history theme: ritual-architectural commemorations of cosmogony, of mythological (or mythicohistorical) episodes, of mythological (or mythicohistorical) individuals, and, finally, of the places where mythological or miraculous events transpired. Again, the organizational strategy denotes categories that are, if hermeneutically provocative, largely artificial and thoroughly intertwined.

Cosmogonic Commemorations: Constructional Embodiments of Creation

Mircea Eliade's (in)famous, incessantly repeated claim—that "*every construction or fabrication has the cosmogony as paradigmatic model.* The creation of the world becomes the archetype of every creative human gesture"[11]—is certainly (and deliberately) an overstatement. Nonetheless, the abundance and diversity of relevant cross-cultural instantiations does lend credence to that hyperbolic announcement. The erection of the Hindu temple, for example, Eliade's own archetype, entails a construction process that is explicitly correlated (or homologized) with the cosmogonic myth of the dismemberment of the primordial body of Purusha, and thus with the symbolism of sacrificial death and rebirth. Repeatedly, then, the bringing into being of a new Hindu temple is described as "the re-creation of a continuing cosmic creation," or as the reiteration of the creation of the universe.[12]

Occasionally, the construction of Christian churches is similarly likened to the (re)creation of a cosmos out of chaos wherein, according to one interpretation:

> The building materials, wood, brick or stone, correspond to the *hyle* or *materia prima,* the plastic substance of the world. . . . The tools used to shape the crude materials accordingly symbolize the divine "instruments" which "fashion" the cosmos out of the undifferentiated and amorphous *materia prima.*[13]

And, J. B. Jackson ventures the not implausible suggestion that the contemporary American fascination with green lawns and gardens, and with preserving wilderness areas, stems from an urge to participate in some fashion in the cosmogonic archetypal garden of Eden, "to restore as much as possible the *original* aspect of the landscape . . . [to retrieve] a golden age, a time of beginnings."[14]

There is, however, no shortage of more certain instances of the ritual-architectural commemoration of cosmogony. The architectural arrangement of the moat-encircled Angkor Wat in Cambodia is an unmistakably direct expression of a Southeast Asian creation story: The balustrades of the causeway over the moat to the city gates are formed by rows of giant stone figures who are holding an enormous nine-headed serpent that, in Buddhist myth, was used to churn the world into existence. By virtue of the architectonic presence of these mythical protagonists, according to Robert Heine-Geldern, "the whole city became a representation of the churning of the primeval milk ocean by gods and demons, when they used the serpent king Vasuke as a rope and Mount Meru as a churning stick."[15]

Likewise, both Egyptian and Mesopotamian temples have been interpreted as direct architectural embodiments of cosmogony: The temple of Atum-Re at Heliopolis was, in consonance with Egyptian cosmogonic traditions, supposedly built to mark and depict the first mound to rise out of the watery abyss on which Atum-Re stood when he began the work of creation; and in Sumer, "the ancient temple of the god Enki at Eridu was reputed to be founded upon the *abzu* or primordial deep of the sweet waters."[16] And the pre-Columbian Incas, employing a very different strategy of architectural commemoration of cosmogony, fashioned a cult temple out of live rock at Pacaritombo (literally, "Origin Lodge") to designate the emergence cave from which culture hero Manco Capac and his followers began their mythical journey to found the eventual imperial capital of Cuzco.[17]

Interpretations of ancient Mesoamerica, where the cycles of creation and destruction were a constant concern, likewise provide numerous variations on the architectural concretization of cosmogony. Michael Coe hypothesizes that the reliefs of deity heads projecting from a sea scene on the Temple of Quetzalcoatl at Teotihuacan "represent the initial creation of the universe from a watery void through a series of dual oppositions."[18] And Karl Taube likewise finds explicitly cosmogonic symbolism in the architecture of Teotihuacan—in the Temple of Quetzalcoatl, the Pyramid of the Sun, and in the Tepantitla murals—symbolism that he considers parallel to that of the Pueblo kivas of the American Southwest.[19] The cave paintings of Olmec creation scenes at Juxtlahuaca and Oxtitlán in Guerrero, some of the oldest known in the New World, likewise evince the Mesoamerican propensity for enlivening and sustaining their cosmogonic traditions through architecture.[20] The famed Aztec Calendar Stone has, for decades, been recognized as "a record of the cosmogonic myth of the Aztecs and the creations and destructions of the world."[21] And art historian Richard Townsend, working in a particularly eventful mode, explores the intricately homologized relations between Aztec kingship, architecture, landscape, seasonal cycles, and ritual movements, before concluding that:

> Indeed, the long [annual] pilgrimage of the kings to the mountaintop [of Mt. Tlaloc on the outskirts of the capital of Tenochtitlan] and its source of life, and their return with a boon to the cities of the Valley suggest the enactment of an ancient cosmogonic myth.[22]

Memorializing Mythical and Miraculous Episodes: Occurrences as Recurrences

Besides commemorations of the original creation of the world, many ritual-architectural events memorialize "later" mythological and miraculous episodes in the careers of deities, culture heroes, and saints. Vivid and multifarious cross-cultural examples abound. The architectural reiteration of a mythical building episode provides for us a particularly relevant phenomenon: the periodic (re)construction and ceremonial dedication of the finely built *tongkonan,* or family "origin houses," of the Sa'dan Toraja in Indonesia is explicitly conceived as the reiteration and commemoration of the occasion of the construction of the very first *tongkonan* by their mythical ancestor Tangdilino'.[23] Navajo sandpainting rituals, similarly constructional though very different sorts of "architectural" events, not only recall but actually rejuvenate, the *Diyin Dine 'e* and other deities by depicting and recounting their most significant episodes.[24] And, to cite a rough parallel in which the prospects for renewal depend more on killing than building, numerous interpreters have recognized not only the sense in which the Aztecs' Templo Mayor was conceived as a built replica of the mythico-cosmic mountain of Coatepec but, moreover, the sense in which public human sacrifices, particularly of large numbers of victims, graphically reiterated the sequence of mythical events on Mount Coatepec wherein war god Huitzilopochtli was born in full military regalia and then immediately slew his traitorous four hundred brothers and sister Coyolxauhqui.[25] Aztec executioners apparently threw the body parts of sacrificial victims down the temple steps, just as Huitzilopochtli had scattered his siblings' limbs on the mythical mountain.

Often, however, the episode being commemorated has more the character of a one-time "historic" miracle, even a fairly recent one, than of an occurrence understood to have transpired deep in some timeless primordial era or dimension. Vierzehnheiligen, a German church built over the spot where, in 1445, a shepherd had a vision of the Christ child surrounded by fourteen other children, later interpreted as the Fourteen Saints in Time of Need, is one of many clear examples of that pattern.[26] And, in Islam, the Dome of the Rock, constructed on the summit of the Mount Moriah site already revered by Jews and Christians as the place where David had his altar and Solomon his temple, preserves the footprint of Muhammad and marks the spot where Muslims believe he ascended, one night in (roughly) 620 C.E., with the archangel Gabriel on his eagle-winged horse to visit the seven heavens.[27] Moreover, the singularity of the Dome of the Rock notwithstanding, there is a sense in which every dome in the Muslim world works to recall and commemorate that episode of Muhammad's ascent to heaven, the *mi'raj,* or Night Journey.[28]

India provides further dramatic instantiation of the ritual-architectural commemoration of both mythical and miraculous episodes. Fred Clothey terms a whole set of South Asian ceremonials (and their attendant architectural contexts) "theofests," that is, festivals designed explicitly to commemorate some aspect of a god's activity, to distinguish those ritual occasions from "ecofests," which commemorate some important agricultural or astronomical event.[29] Surinder Mohan Bhardwaj is even more helpful in finetuning this morphological suboption of "episode commemoration" when he notes an indigenous Indian distinction between, on the one hand, those sacred sites (*asura tirthas*) that are associated with (mythical) circumstances in which various Hindu gods destroyed demons and thus restored moral order and, on the other hand, another "type" of sacred site (*arsa tirthas*), which are consecrated by virtue of the (miraculous) austerities, penances and sacrifices of human saints and sages.[30] Among the most spectacular exemplars of the first category, the elaborate Pallava-style relief carving of the Descent of the Ganges at Mamallapuram (near Madras) fixes forever the mythological moment when Shiva permitted the life-giving waters of the Ganges to flow to earth, an episode that is punctuated and enlivened by a waterfall curtain that flows directly over the relief.[31] In Indian Buddhism, however, which is likewise thick with explicitly commemorative art and architecture, the paradoxically ordinary-exceptional status of Gautama makes it more difficult to maintain any distinction between the ritual-architectural commemoration of human versus superhuman episodes: the rock-cut temples of Ajanta, for instance, sheathed by magnificent narrative frescoes, are among innumerable Indian Buddhist configurations that preserve episodes in both the historical and "mystic" life of the Buddha.[32]

Turning to the West, there are, of course, thousands of European monuments memorializing significant (though not necessarily miraculous) religiopolitical episodes, such as the Arch of Titus in Rome, which was erected about 70 C.E. on the Forum Romanum to commemorate the victory of Titus over the Jews.[33] Here we can note, however (which is not to say that the same does not apply in non-Western contexts), that commemorative sacred art and architecture, particularly in specifically religious contexts, does considerably more than simply record or "fix" mythical and miraculous episodes, thus making them accessible to recall or intellectualized memory. Many interpreters insist, appropriately, that in addition to that documental function, the apprehension of various architectural configurations, particularly in the context of ritual, can also provide means of "reactualizing" the relevant episodes; worshipers not only learn or remember what supposedly happened, they are allowed, in a sense, to be present and to participate in those happenings, episodes that belong somehow to both the past and the present. In the ritual experience of commemorative architecture, mythicohistoric occurrences are, according to several accounts, transformed into recurrences.

M. E. Kenna, for instance, explains how the various entrances that the priest makes from the sanctuary into the body of the church during the course of the Orthodox liturgy allow the congregation to witness, in a "symbolic" fashion,

> [the] actual entrances made by Jesus during his earthly life—such as the entry into Jerusalem—as well as entrances that are spiritual interventions—such as the Incarnation.[34]

In a similar vein, Howard Hibbard considers that the explicit intention of Bernini's theatrical baroque sculpture-architecture was, in most cases, to freeze the climactic moment of some mythic or saintly story—but not simply in hopes of documenting such occurrences; instead, Bernini's greater ambition was to (re)capture in art the emotion of that defining moment so that viewers could, for themselves, re-experience and participate in the sensibilities of the original protagonists.[35] And likewise, John Dixon astutely (and eventfully) emphasizes that paintings like those of Michelangelo in the Sistine Chapel do not just provide a record of mythicohistorical events; more poignantly, such paintings effect the possibility of a participatory reenactment of those sacred events. Dixon explains that

> [The painting in the Sistine Chapel] is not simply a representation of the process of redemption. . . . It is a translation of the redemptive action into a form that makes possible the participation of the worshipper.[36]

Mythicohistorical Personages: Ritual-Architectural Expressions of Excellence

In other cases, the priority is not actually the ritual-architectural commemoration of a particular sacred historical episode, but, instead, the acknowledgment of an individual personage from within the respective corpus of stories. Where humans and human-like individuals are the most obvious foci of such commemorations, deities, animals, "other mythical beasts," and even personified plants and natural features are likewise relevant contenders. Though the distinction between individuals and their activities is nearly always blurry, it does bring to our attention an importantly different, if somewhat less frequent, morphological possibility.

Sikh shrines, for instance, are known as *gurdwaras*, that is, "doors," or seats, of the guru, because they are, in almost every case, associated with some particular individual sage, or guru.[37] Thus, while early Sikh shrines did not conform to any specific architectural style—some were simply humble residences before a guru sanctified them by his visit or temporary residence there, and other much more elaborate (and more strictly commemorative) shrines were erected a long time after the spot was sanctified by the guru's presence—a shrine's connection to a specific sage was critical. Accordingly, rather than tracing any evolution in architectural style or construction technique, Sardar Surinder Singh Johar considers that the most significant principle of organization for his survey and comparison of Sikh shrines ought to be their respective associations with the individual renowned gurus—for instance, the shrines of Guru Nakak, the shrines of Guru Arjan Dev, the shrines of Guru Teg Bahadur, and so on.[38]

A number of Buddhist shrines also seem to demonstrate less of a concern to commemorate specific episodes in the Buddha's career, either in his final lifetime or some other realm, say, in the way that those episodes are detailedly depicted in the storiological reliefs in the lower levels of

Borobudur,[39] than to praise his person or, at any rate, his personal example (the Dharma). As Edward Conze notes, *caityas* (a general term for any Buddhist sanctuary or shrine) are "always connected with the person of the Buddha himself, although the connection may be a very indirect one. . . ."[40] In that spirit, then, countless stupas, or gravemounds, were constructed (at least originally) to house relics of the Buddha: one of the most famous temples of Indochina, the Shwe Dagon Pagoda at Rangoon, was built specifically to enshrine eight hairs given by Gautama himself to two Buddhist merchants.[41] Subsequently, stupas were built to enshrine the remains of other Buddhist sages considered to have transcended the cycles of birth and death, though in these cases as well the most prominent association is apparently between a shrine and, ironically, a selfless individual rather than any specific episode or activity (aside from that of exemplary meditation).[42]

Likewise demonstrating the priority of a kind of cult of personality over that of commemoration of specific events and achievements, the reliquary geography of late medieval Europe, particularly in the wake of the post-Tridentine enthusiasm for miracles and relics, was overlaid with dozens of monuments dedicated to specific heroes and heroines of Catholic sacred history.[43] Recalling or reliving the particular eventualities by which a saint earned canonization (which in some cases seem to have been nearly forgotten) could become less urgent than simply, via relics and remains, establishing a direct connection with that holy individual. Even the wide enthusiasm for visiting the Cappella della S. S. Sindome, for instance, which was built specifically to safeguard and display the Holy Shroud of Turin (in spite of the shroud's authenticity having been officially denied by the Church in the later Middle Ages), seems to be born more of a generalized veneration for the person of Jesus than from any particular event (except, perhaps, the Resurrection).[44]

The morphological possibility of commemorating mythicohistorical individuals rather than their specific accomplishments is perhaps illustrated more clearly by the less explicitly religious, but exceeding common, life-like statues of military and political leaders, standing motionlessly, hands at their sides, in parks or in front of civic buildings; or, in the same morphic category would be person-specific memorializing edifices like the Lincoln and Jefferson Memorials or the Washington Monument. These sorts of individualized architectural commemorations usually have more the character of lifetime achievement awards, as it were, than of prizes won in a single occasion of glory or distinction. Personalistic monuments of this sort usually express, and then engender, a generalized admiration for the moral fortitude, honesty, strength of personality, or wisdom in statecrafting of individual (mythico)historic leaders without, however, placing in the foreground one specific incident that demonstrates those personal attributes.

Often, architecture works, in other words, not unlike mythical narratives, as a forum in which to assemble, concentrate, and personify—in one individual—a host of abstract qualities of excellence, thereby making those otherwise elusive qualities accessible to participation and imitation. Honesty, valor, integrity, incorruptibility, rectitude, and perspicacity are, as idealized conceptions, too intangible to serve as practical guides for right behavior and decision making; but when personified in an individual, however fictively, those abstractions are transformed into tangible prototypes for ethical conduct and, in the cases of gurus, saints, and saviors, for conducting one's worshipful life. Ritual-architectural events can, then, enable worshipers not only to be present at mythicohistoric episodes but also, in an important sense, to identify with, and sometimes actually become, the actors in those sacred stories.

Mythical Places: Contact with and Commemorations of the Sites of Sacred History

Another very important, perhaps more obviously distinct variation on the commemoration of sacred history is that set of ritual-architectural events in which the featured priority is neither the facilitation of an actual reenactment of episodes from sacred history nor even the commemoration of specific saints or mythicohistorical heroes, but is, instead, simply the marking of or connection with the supposed site—the place—of a mythical or miraculous occurrence. Australian aborigines (as noted) have a tremendously detailed set of correlations between the features of the landscape and the mythical beings and episodes that brought those features into being;[45] but this morphological suboption involves other sorts of circumstances in which the very places and locales, almost irrespective of attendant narratives, come to be revered in themselves. Sometimes, in other words, the significance of the "where" of sacred history can transcend even the "what" and the "who."[46]

In an appropriate turn of phrase, Diana Eck, for instance, describes how, at the pilgrimage site of Banaras on the Ganges, "mythology becomes geography";[47] simply to be there (especially to die there), at that efficacious place, is what matters most.[48] Many pilgrimage journeys to the presumed site of a mythical or miraculous event, not only in Hinduism but in many traditions, are, in fact, motivated less by an interest of reiterating or even remembering sacred historical personages or circumstances, which may indeed have been largely forgotten, than by rather more pragmatic concerns: to touch the magically potent earth or relics, to drink the restorative water, to petition for health and fertility, to fulfill vows or, as in the case of pilgrimages to oracles, to solicit advice and information.[49]

This fascination with the real estate of sacred history is apparent at any number of pilgrimage sites: Lourdes, Mecca, and the great shrine of the Virgin of Guadalupe outside Mexico City are only the most spectacular of hundreds of strong examples.[50] As participants in this morphological suboption (among others), it is important to note that, though each of these famous destinations owes its original prestige to some sequence of exceptional events—a sequence of events that remains always important—the stories of those circumstances are very well known even before pilgrims leave home; few new details regarding the apparitions of virgins at Lourdes and Guadalupe, or Abraham's and Sarah's movements at Mecca are liable to be learned by making those respective trips. But there is, as perhaps best encapsulated in the hajji's reiterative prayer upon arriving at the precinct of the Ka'bah—"I am here, O Lord! I am here"[51]—a more affective, trans-intellectual need for direct contact with the site, the geographic locus, at which one's sacred history was made.

Often, then, ritual-architectural design solutions take their characteristic forms with the express purpose of facilitating this sort of grassroots fascination for visitation and taction with the physical evidence and miraculous precincts of one's sacred history. The formative power of pilgrimage to Rome, for instance, has ramifications at every scale of the built environment: At the relatively small end on the spectrum, the annular crypt, an architectural element that became a hallmark of early medieval church building, first arose as a device to make Saint Peter's relics visible and easily accessible to pilgrims, yet safe from handling and abuse.[52] At the level of buildings, the characteristic basilica form was adopted by Christians in sixth-century Rome largely as the direct and ingenious architectural solution to the problems caused by floods of pilgrims.[53] And on a regional scale, Richard Krautheimer has shown that pilgrimage, particularly in the adept hands of Gregory the Great, was perhaps *the* decisive force in Rome's ascension to political and religious hegemony, and in the contouring of medieval Europe generally.[54]

Besides the obvious (and enormous) set of instances in which people feel compelled to journey to the site of some exceptional sacred historical event, the urge to commemorate the geographic places of, to use William McNeill's term, "mythistory" likewise manifests itself in a variety of creative strategies for somehow transferring the miraculous power of that place elsewhere or, in a sense, "bringing the place home."[55] Pilgrims routinely carry away reproductions of miracle-working images, water, or amupullae filled with substances associated with the site in hopes that they might somehow maintain contact with that powerful place.[56] Ronald Grimes provides an even more graphic image of this urgent desire literally to lay hands (or feet) on the geographic context of one's sacred history in his description of those contemporary pilgrims who journey to the small New Mexican village of Chimayo to obtain dirt, which they then bring home to eat (a practice termed geophagy) and to mix with saliva to make the sign of the cross on their children's foreheads. In Grimes's interpretation, "space becomes objectified as land . . . tierra del Santo [sacred soil] . . . and insofar as space becomes objectified as land one can 'carry space' back with him in the form of a jar of dirt."[57]

Albeit a radically different historical context, the same sort of fascination with the turf of sacred history is demonstrated in a more explicitly architectural fashion by the exploits of Saint Helen, the mother of Constantine the Great. According to legend, Helen returned from Jerusalem's Mount Calvary with a shipload of the earth upon which Christ had shed his blood at the Crucifixion; though she originally placed that venerable dirt on the floor of her own room, it eventually came to underlie the chapel dedicated to her in the Basilica of Santa Croce at Rome.[58] Consequently, by virtue of what Irving Lavin calls the "topographical transfusion" of Jerusalem to Rome (or what I might connect with homologizing architecture [priority I-A]), that chapel itself, the whole basilica, and even the whole of Rome could be understood as the second Jerusalem, in fact, "the truer Jerusalem," where the Lord was crucified a second time in Saint Peter.[59] Or, in yet another profoundly different context, Edward Linenthal recounts how designers of the United States Holocaust Memorial Museum, in their attempt to construct a building that would force visitors to "leave" Washington, D.C., in order to journey into the crucial memory of the Holocaust, not only reproduced the "hard industrial forms" of the Nazi death camps, but also brought thousands of pairs of victims' shoes and even soil from those camps, which was then placed at strategic places in the memorial and, in some cases, overlaid with soil taken from American military cemeteries, "because their soil symbolizes the end of darkness and the beginning of hope."[60]

In Hinduism, to borrow both Surinder Mohan Bhardwaj's phrase and assessment, this "transferring of sanctity" from a mythologically significant place to somewhere else is "a quite frequent phenomenon."[61] Thus, where the sacred abode of Shiva may, in some mythicogeographic sense, lie at the origin of the Ganges in the Himalayas (specifically at Mount Kailasa), Bhardwaj explains that

> the quality of sanctity of the Ganga and of the Himalayas seems to have been transferred in part to other rivers and other mountains respectively. Every mountain top can be a local abode of Śiva or his consort Śakti. Every river can be a local Ganga.[62]

In perhaps the most spectacular (and most specifically architectural) manifestations of this urge to "bring home" the places of one's sacred history, whole buildings and even towns have, on occasion, been reproduced elsewhere. In the fifteenth century in the town of Varallo in Piedmont, Italy, Friar Minor Bernardino Caimi orchestrated the construction of a whole series of chapels (some forty-five are extant at this point), which, complete with remarkably lifelike statues and paintings, replicate the most famous sites of the Holy Land and depict in stunning detail scenes of Christian sacred history from Eden to the Crucifixion and burial of Jesus. According to Freedberg:

> [Caimi's] aim was to evoke, in a natural setting, the holy places he himself had visited, Bethlehem, Nazareth, Mount Tabor, and Jerusalem, and especially the various sites of the Passion—Gethsemane, Mount Sion, and Golgotha.[63]

By virtue of this incredible effort in architectural replication, Varallo, in an important sense, becomes the Holy Land, and visitors are allowed not simply to remember or recall Christ's Passion but to relive and participate in it—to be there once again—in a most palpable sense.

Other more modest versions of Caimi's spectacular facsimile were subsequently constructed around northern Italy.[64] The notion of creating a "New Jerusalem," albeit less verisimilitudinously, was embraced even by iconoclastic Protestants from John Calvin to the American Puritans, Shakers, and early Mormons.[65] And, in South America, Padre Cicero Romao Batista, himself a reputed miracle worker, undertook a project that did rival Caimi's ambitious play on this theme when, early in this century, he initiated the construction of an elaborate facsimile of Jerusalem at Juazeiro do Norte, Brazil, complete with a Via Sacra (the Rua do Horto) by which hundreds of thousands of pilgrims continue to make their entry into the city.[66]

Avoidances of and Restrictions on the Artistic Commemoration of Sacred History

As cross-culturally prevalent and variegated as strategies for exploiting architecture's potential for commemorating mythicohistorical episodes, personages, and places are, we ought also be alert, as in the case of divinity commemoration (priority II-A), for those historical circumstances (and those academic interpretations) in which exercises of the sacred history priority (II-B) are most notable by omission or by highly restricted relevance. Scholars working in several contexts have noticed major discrepancies both in the extent to which and the means by which various cultures commemorate "mythistory" in art and architecture. Case in point, the Hindu architecture of Southeast Asia—Java and Cambodia particularly—is, generally speaking, assessed as more concerned with, and more adept at, depicting mythological episodes than is the Hindu architecture of India. George Michell, for instance, noting particularly the spectacular architectural embodiment of creation stories at Angkor Wat, says, "Striking among the qualities of Hindu temples outside India is their ability to create an architectural layout that embodies elements of myth."[67]

Likewise in Mesoamericanist studies, where very often (much too often) problems of historical (re)construction have been solved on the basis of a presumed "polarity" or radical contrast between the pre-Hispanic peoples of the Maya zone and those of Central Mexico, one of the defining diagnostics for differentiating between those two groups has been an imagined antithesis between what I would term their relative interests in the ritual-architectural commemoration of sacred (and not-so-sacred) history.[68] Put bluntly (and in my rubric), prevailing stereotypes for most of the twentieth century held that cerebral, otherworldly Maya artists were obsessed with the cosmomagical matters associated with the homology priority (I-A) and wholly uninterested in depicting any storiological themes, least of all those that would record their leaders' military and political exploits; the Maya, in other words, supposedly cared little for commemorations of sacred history (priority II-B). The Machiavellian Mexicans, by contrast, had precisely the opposite priorities, and thus produced an art that was dominated by highly particularistic (though also presumably highly idealized and mythologized) accounts of worldly events. On those grounds, then, the extensive artistic oeuvre of a pre-Columbian city such as Chichén Itzá, imagined as a site where these two groups met head-to-head, was for decades bipartitioned into non-narrative components, which were assigned to indigenous Yucatecan Maya artists, and the more explicitly representational and informational art (also deemed more "secular")—especially murals depicting battle scenes and statues of well-armed warriors—which were credited to invading Central Mexican Toltecs.[69]

Though in hindsight that oversimple Maya-Mexican bipartitioning has proven distorting in the extreme, Mesoamericanists continue to contend, not inappropriately I think, that there are significant regional and "ethnic" discrepancies with respect to indigenous inclinations for artistic commemorations of narrative sacred history. Art historian John Graham, for instance, recognizes a great enthusiasm for recounting narratives in Izapan art (in the Chiapas-Guatemalan highlands), but a decided disinterest in story-telling among the arts of the Olmec and Lowland Maya.[70] In his assessment of Izapan art, "the chief purpose seems to have been the depiction of narrative scenes often depending to a great extent on movement and dramatic action for their clarity and effect"; Olmec art, which is preoccupied with monumentality and with full, swelling masses, and Maya art, which favors elite portraiture, are, by contrast, Graham concludes, patentedly "non-narrative."[71]

Generalizations like Graham's—of a Maya preference for elite portraiture over depictions of narrative, for example—suggest that, rather than indifference for artistic commemorations of sacred history (as older ideas had held), their priorities were more individual-specific than episode-specific. Moreover, where it may be, as Tatiana Proskouriakoff claimed fifty years ago, that in Maya sculpture and architecture "action is seldom depicted and always restrained in character,"[72] a wider study of Maya art would reveal much greater enthusiasm for depicting thoroughgoing narrative sequences (both mythical and more strictly "historical") in other artistic genres, say, vase painting, codices, and murals.[73] And, perhaps most importantly, because such assessments are usually based almost strictly on analyses of extant pre-Columbian art objects, largely disconnected from any ritual context, we ought to keep in mind that the associated performative movements, recitations, and songs may have reflected quite different priorities. Nevertheless—and this is the most relevant point in the present context—the willingness to entertain seriously the possibility that commemorations of sacred history, and specifically of narrative episodes, might be significant most by omission provides us a good hermeneutical example.

Mythistory Commemoration as the Back Half of the Architectural Situation: A Maya Example

Before closing, more extended treatment of another pre-Columbian Maya situation, based on the political mythology of the Chiapas site of Palenque, can serve several purposes: to offset further any categorical evaluation of Maya art and architecture as static and otherworldly, to segue into the next chapter's consideration of the commemoration of temporal authority (politics, II-C), and, most significantly, to remind us how commemorations of sacred history (II-B) belong primarily to the back half of the twofold pattern of ritual architectural events.

According to art historian and epigrapher Linda Schele's elaborate (and unusually eventful) analysis of Palenque, the first three rulers of the Late Classic era—Pacal the Great, Chan-Bahlum, and Kan-Xul—were not simply all-powerful sovereigns; they were the protagonists of a "mythology of kingship," which established the patterns to which all later rulers were obliged to adhere.[74] The major constructions of these primogenitorial rulers—the Temple of the Inscriptions, the Group of the Cross, and the north buildings of the palace—functioned, according to Schele, as "texts" to articulate the paradigmatic mechanisms for the exercise and transference of royal power. In her phrasing, "the orientation of the buildings housing the monuments of the three rulers is designed to repeat the mythological pictures of the ascension and death events."[75]

Moreover, the way in which Schele imagines the pre-Hispanic kingship rituals that were performed at these three buildings conforms very neatly to the twofold pattern that characterizes ritual-architectural events generally. With respect to the front half of the ceremonial event, Schele describes how the lords of Palenque seized upon astronomical occurrences—in this case, solstice sunset phenomena—to achieve the "right timing" that demonstrated the cosmic import of their mythicopolitical proceedings. The choreographed experience of solstice phenomena, in other words, served as the instigatory strategy (an exercise of the astronomy priority [I-C]), which, to the extent that it worked (as Schele assumes that it did), drew "spoilsport" spectators into the ritual-architectural game, and thus promoted a sympathetic hearing for the very practical program of information that was to follow. Schele summarizes the pragmatic effect of the careful timing of the royal rites this way:

> [both the Temple of the Cross and the Temple of the Inscriptions are situated] so that large numbers of people could and can view the [solstice] hierophanies. The generality of the events, the accessibility to them, their dramatic characterization and their grandiose scale and publicness argue for a direct linkage between the perceptions of the real events in the heavens and the mythology that explained the relationship of man to the cosmos and the function and identity of rulers.[76]

We could take issue with the intimation that the alluring sky phenomena ("the real events in the heavens"), the relevant views of which actually depend on "architectural enhancements of nature," are more ontologically firm than the relevant mythology.[77] But Schele's intimation (which I would emphasize more fully than she has) that there was, in the apprehension of this ritual-architectural event, a transition from sensations of generalized wonderment to specific obligation is particularly apt. If the occasion began with a confirming, legitimating reminder of the kings' and the celestial bodies' shared participation in a comprehensive world order, once drawn into the royal proceedings, the spectators were treated to a docket of very specific—obligatory and challenging—information about the relations between cosmos, kings, and citizenry (that is, the back half of the ritual-architectural event). Thus, the royal rites of Palenque provided information not simply about the distinguished mythicohistorical exploits of the past and present hero-kings of Palenque (the commemoration of sacred history, priority II-B), but, likewise, unambiguous information about the appropriateness of these kings' continued hegemony, about the responsibilities of vassalage, and about the dire consequences of dissent or rebellion (the commemoration of political authority, priority II-C).

Closing Reservations: The Complexities of Myth, History, Narrative, and Ritual

Where there may be major discrepancies in relative enthusiasms for artistic depictions of narrative, it is difficult if not impossible to imagine a "religious" architecture that declines entirely to participate, in one fashion or another, in the ritual-architectural commemoration of sacred history (II-B). As in the cases of the convention priority (I-B) and divinity commemoration (II-A), some variation on this theme is virtually always relevant. In fact, because the prestige of buildings and places so often depends upon their associations with the circumstances and protagonists of sacred history, it is hardly surprising that enterprising Hindu (or Sikh) priests, for instance, will go to almost any length to establish (or to construct) a link between their local places of worship and some portion of the "greater" Sanskritic tradition.[78] Grafting a place and a building into one's sacred history works to enhance immeasurably the potency and appeal of the ritual activities that transpire there.

Moreover, along with exceptionally wide relevance, the ritual-architectural commemoration of sacred history might also appear, at first, to be the most tractable of the morphological options so far considered. Outlining a five-step checklist that separates stage-like configurations for the reenactment of sacred history from ritual-architectural commemorations of cosmogony, and then from commemorations of mythicohistorical episodes, individuals, and places may reinforce that illusion of simple manageability. Sustained hermeneutical inquiry into specific historical cases and the composition of rigorously empirical ritual-architectural reception histories should, however, quickly dispel any pretense of interpretive ease as one is drawn into a snarl of the history of religions' most time-honored and difficult problems. Among countless complications, all of which would have to be resolved on a case-specific basis, let me highlight four.

First, there are the by-now familiar, still very important caveats concerning the provisional and non–mutually exclusive status of this and other morphological headings. As the synchronization of astronomy, mythology, power politics, buildings, landscapes, and rituals at Palenque demonstrates so well—an imbrication that is hardly unique to the Classic Maya—the commemoration of sacred history constantly overlaps and interpenetrates with virtually all of the various categories in this framework. Even less easily isolated are those five subdivisions on the theme. Identifying sacred historical elements in a ritual-architectural program—whether episodes, individuals, or places—will, then, be a preliminary rather than culminating interpretive move.

Second and more specifically, trafficking in concerns about the relations between architecture and the stories of sacred history immediately ensnares one in decades of debate concerning the relations and distinctions between various narrative genres—fables and legends, allegories and parables, canonical versions of the past and subversive folk tales, and that most infamous pairing of all, myth and history. Difficulties may be conveniently sidestepped or delayed by appeals to coinages like "mythicohistorical" or McNeill's "mythistory," but interpreters will eventually need to attend to the fact that, sometimes, the actors and activities being "commemorated" belong to some qualitatively different, transnatural (mythical) space-time dimension, while in other situations the actors and activities have a more fully human and plainly historical status. Though in virtually all instances we encounter some degree of the "mythologization" of history (or less often a "historicization" of myth), heuristic separations between myth and history remain salient.[79]

Third, reflections on ways in which artistic and architectural allusions to either myth or history are, in an empirical sense, experienced and apprehended, particularly in the context of ritual, draws one also into similarly timeworn controversy concerning the most appropriate ways of imagining and describing both the relations between myth and ritual and the relations between ritual participants and their respective sacred narratives. Extant theories provide us a host of generalized possibilities, most that afford the privilege to myth over ritual, in which cases, rituals are imagined variously as retelling, reenacting, or "reactualizing" myth. In those cases, then, ritual-architectural apprehensions of sacred history may be conceived variously as pedagogical occasions of learning and remembering, or as more existentially challenging occasions of "reliving" and participating in mythical dimensions and realities. Fewer interpreters afford the privilege to ritual, in which case myth and sacred stories are imagined as derivative and etiological of ritual practice. Tough decisions regarding which, if any, of those generically theoretical (non–mutually exclusive) possibilities provides the most suitable empirical descriptions will, again, require resolution on a case-specific basis.

And fourth, the superabundance of architecture asserts itself in a couple of particularly noteworthy ways in relation to the commemoration of mythicohistorical episodes and individuals. Many (probably most) ritual-architectural solutions address, by design, multiple layers and dimensions of the pertinent sacred history. Most Mexican Catholic churches, for example the seventeeth-century cathedral at Cuernavaca, commemorate, at one level, via images of Mary and Christ, the universalistic story of Jesus' birth, teaching, death, and resurrection. At another level, there are also allusions to a more specifically Mexican Catholic mythistory, epitomized most obviously by ubiquitous images of the Virgin of Guadelupe. But at yet another level, invariably more idiosyncratic decisions are made to foreground certain individuals and episodes from the larger corpus of Christian stories: at Cuernavaca the walls are covered with paintings depicting, plate by plate, an ill-fated attempt to Christianize Japan, which eventuated in the crucifixion of Saint Matthew and several other Franciscan friars by their Japanese would-have-been converts. Moreover, those narrative presentations are overlaid again by large, portable banners that address seasonally significant holidays and associated elements of the Christian story and, at Cuernavaca, matters pertaining to more specifically political current events.

As a consequence of this deliberate layering of mythicohistorical allusions, the Cuernavaca cathedral, like most substantial ritual-architectural contexts, presents not one but numerous different stories, each of which is subject to innumerable different interpretations. The combination of sacred historical overlays and the multiplicity of experiential options within any one of those multivocal narrative layers provides, then, for enormous flexibility in the apprehension of what transpires there. Detailed empirical surveys, perhaps something like exit interviews of the young and old, male and female, rich and poor worshipers (and tourists) departing on a single Sunday evening mass, would reveal, I'm sure, considerable disagreement as to which of the available stories had proven most compelling and even wider disagreement as to the theological meanings, religiopolitical messages, and ethical lessons that those stories had served to demonstrate. Particularly where narrative modes of expression are involved, the spectrum of (indigenous and academic) interpretive conclusions, or "readings" of the situation, is very wide indeed. Thus, while the ritual-architectural commemoration of sacred history (priority II-B) might appear at first to be among the most refreshingly straightforward of the morphological options, in actual fact, the perplexities of rigorously empirical hermeneutical interpretations are, in these cases, particularly intense.

Nineteen | Politics: The Legitimation of Authority (Priority II-C)

> There seems to be some reluctance to "drag politics" into architectural history.
>
> John Maass, 1969[1]

> Although ritual was (and is) a cultural resource employed in the creation and maintenance of symbolic worlds of meaning, it was (and is) also used as a political tool in the competition for and the control of the seat of power.
>
> Gary Ebersole, 1989[2]

> Because space is the common framework for all activities, it is often used politically in order to give an appearance of coherence through the concealment of its social contradictions.
>
> Bernard Tschumi, 1996[3]

POLITICAL LEADERS, TIME AND AGAIN, have demonstrated enormous confidence in elaborate architecture as a deft "vehicle of intelligibility" for their expressions of power.[4] Thucydides reflected that "If Athens should [be deserted, and nothing should be left of it but its temples and the foundations of other buildings,] its power would, I think, be conjectured double what it is."[5] Louis XIV, apparently inspired by the Assyrian conqueror Sargon's glorific palace at Khorsabab, proclaimed his own immodest hegemony by placing his bed at the center of the palace of Versailles, upon which roads from Paris and a host of other places converge.[6] With equal audacity, Napoleon promulgated the equation of the global destiny of France with its role as the legitimate guardian of all the world's art treasures by constructing the Louvre to display cultural booty expropriated from all over Europe and north Africa.[7] One of the earliest of Hitler's many appeals to architecture (and ritual), his Haus der Deutschen Kunst in Munich, with its long, straight row of columns, which have been likened to "the faceless integers of a totalitarian crowd," served as an architectural announcement of "the clean and orderly Germany that the builder could guarantee if only we obey."[8] And, demonstrating continuing confidence in the propagandistic power of public monuments, the Victory Arch in Baghdad, constructed in the late 1980s by the Baath regime, displays two monumental crossed swords held by gigantic hands constructed from plaster models of Saddam Hussein's own arms, a "monstrous magnification of part of the ruler's own body."[9]

Moreover, explicitly "religious" architecture, usually by linking worldly and otherworldly authorities, has proven an especially felicitous means for the expression and manipulation of political sentiments. Abbot Suger, for instance, ostensible "founder" of Gothic architecture, undertook his massive rebuilding of the Abbey of Saint-Denis largely to promote his grand political design for France and the Capetian monarchy.[10] And the Fifty New Churches, built in London and the suburbs in the early eighteenth century, besides their otherworldly significances, were, according to Kerry Downes, monuments to the Tory government and to Queen Anne, as well as to the High Church party of the Church of England.[11]

Also, in India, traditionally, "architecture served [the rulers] as their most spectacular and accredited publicity agents and promoters,"[12] and thus Indian families who had amassed wealth by various commercial means found their most apt vehicle to status and prestige in the sponsorship of massive Hindu temple constructions.[13] So too, the homologized *ceque* system of Cuzco was not only a cosmologically sensitive layout but, moreover, Pachacuti's grand ritual-architectural design for the political integration of the Inca empire.[14] Similarly, the cosmogrammatic mandala organizations that characterized the "galactic polities" of Southeast Asia represent an even more extreme linkage of architecture and polity;[15] Heine-Geldern explains, for example, how, in the Hinayana Buddhist empires of Burma, Siam, and Cambodia, the power of kingship, in an important sense, resided not in an individual, but in the palace—in the built form—itself.[16] It is, in short, as Henri Lefebvre observes, "small wonder that from time immemorial conquerors and revolutionaries eager to destroy a society should so often have sought to do so by burning or razing that society's monuments."[17]

Each of these cases, together with thousands of others, testifies to the munificent collusion of politics and buildings, a strategic alliance evidenced in even the most categorically "religious" constructions. There is, in other words, an enormous fund of ritual-architectural events that features as a (perhaps *the*) leading priority the manipulation of public sentiments, the validation of socioeconomic inequities, the glorification of suzerains, and/or the legitimation of their suzerainties—in sum, the commemoration of temporal authority (in shorthand, politics, priority II-C).

From Hierophany to Hierarchy: Belated Appreciations of Sociopolitical Context

Scholars in social scientific fields have long assumed that the prime significance of religious architecture, particularly large-scale public monuments, lies in the sociopolitical manipulation of its intended audience. Historians of religions, however, owing in large part to the domination of Mircea Eliade's phenomenological model of sacred space, took the opposite tack insofar as they neglected, even deliberately excised, matters of politics from their interpretations of specific religious places and buildings. There was, in a sense, an overcorrection. Because Eliade, intent on recovering the "irreducibly religious," tended to concentrate so heavily on the supposedly transhistorical symbolism associated with religious places and constructions—*axis mundis*, *imago mundis*, hierophanies, and so on (that is, concerns associated primarily with the homology priority [I-A])—in his work, according to contemporary critics, "Sacred space is stripped of politics and real history."[18]

Yet, from Eliade's own perspective, since the sacrality and prestige of a pilgrimage site, for example, is ultimately the consequence of a sudden "eruption of the Sacred" into the otherwise "profane" world, then it is that ontologically distinct "hierophanic" character that constitutes both the essence of the sacred site and, thus, the appropriate focus of hermeneutical attention.[19] From an Eliadean frame, scholars ought to acknowledge the existence of the political entanglements of such places, as in the ways in which Gregory the Great exploited medieval pilgrims' fascination with journeying to Rome; but those must be assessed as largely derivative phenomena, which probably signal the forces of "secularization" and "desacralization" of foundational manifestations of the sacred. For historians of religions of that ilk, to concentrate on the politics of place was to risk seduction away from the specifically religious aspects of the place, which it was their special charge to bring to the fore.

More recently, however, as well exemplified by Roger Friedland and Richard Hecht's 1991 study of centuries of Jewish-Muslim contestation over the wall and platform in the Old City of Jerusalem, and by numerous interpreters' concentration on the category of "contested space," growing numbers of scholars have very self-consciously shifted attention from the religioaesthetics to the "politics of sacred space."[20] To the extent that the designation of certain places and buildings as sacred is conceived more as a consequence of sociological and historical dynamics than of a *homo religiosus*'s visceral response to some supernatural agency—a position forced to prominence especially by Jonathan Z. Smith—then the political and socioeconomic factors that Eliade regarded as derivative and incidental actually become the matters of the greatest academic concern. From this perspective, interrogating the politics of site selection and the subsequent manipulations of those sites in the service of material and cultural organizations of power is the first rather than last order of scholarly business. Though resistance remains strong in some quarters, scholars of religion who now argue that "sacred space is socially constructed"[21]—that the supposed sacrality of revered places is inevitably an expression of sociopolitical hierarchy rather than of uniquely religious hierophany—are expressing the prevailing rather than iconoclastic position.

Though in similarly belated fashion, the fields of art and architectural history have also come to display greater attentiveness to matters of politics and social context.[22] Likewise reticent (though on somewhat different grounds) to "reduce" works of art and architecture to socioeconomic causes, through the 1980s architectural historians nonetheless became increasingly determined to relate buildings to the cultural and political contexts in which they were constructed and used and were thus increasingly receptive to the notion that "there is a direct and obviously predictable relation between social and economic conditions and architectural forms."[23] Such acknowledgments, which often intimated more resignation than resolve, were, though, usually accompanied by warnings against embracing too quickly the Marxist (and, to an extent, Hegelian) presupposition that art and architecture—as "expressions" or "reflections" of a reality that is essentially historical and evolutionary in character—will conform to the same laws that determine the evolution of socioeconomic and cultural institutions. Architectural historian David Watkin, for instance, on the one hand, advocated greater attention to social context but, on the other, cautioned that:

> . . . it remains far from clear to what extent and in what ways [social, political, and economic history] is reflected in architecture. Sometimes there seems to be a direct connection, at others very little, so that it is difficult to establish any set of laws or range of predictions.[24]

In the past two decades, then, some students of religious architecture have been dragged into consideration of the sociopolitical dimensions of sacred space, while others have vigorously applauded what they regard as the overdue rescission of an apolitical exemption that had been wrongly granted to artistic and religious cultural productions in the first place. In fact, some apostates from Eliade's interpretive frame, freshly fortified (or maybe befooled, depending on your perspective) by more materialist orientations, have, either avowedly or implicitly, adopted the stance that, in virtually all cases, it is political ambitions and interests (broadly speaking) that constitute the "real reasons" that determine the characteristic configurations and usages of specific works of religious architecture. In that lopsided view, what I term the commemoration of politics (II-C) is declared the winner in the competition of ritual-architectural priorities even before specific cases are considered (not unlike the way in which Eliade was prepared to announce the global supereminence of the homology priority).

Alternatively, my position holds that it is an appreciation of the sometimes antagonistic, sometimes synergistic play between multiple and very different sorts of priorities—explicitly and implicitly political concerns among them—that is required to deliver critical, empirically satisfying descriptions of specific sacred architectures and architectural histories. Or, to phrase it differently, the important requirement of "contextualization" (or problematization) of specific rituals and architectures with respect to matters of social and political hierarchy ought not be fulfilled at the expense of decontextualization with respect to the also culturally specific "contexts" of indigenous cosmology, mythology, and conceptions of divinity.

In hopes, then, of allowing politics a suitably prominent place, but not untoward domination, in this hermeneutics of sacred architecture, the wide range of relevant possibilities, which include the machinations of conquerors and kings along with subtler, more modest built expressions of disparities in power, is provisionally arranged, first, according to a distinction between architectural configurations that reflect and perpetuate the currently prevailing social hierarchy versus those that work to challenge, change, or undermine the status quo. Then I address three more explicitly governmental alternatives: ritual-architectural glorifications of specific leaders; ritual-architectural facilitations of the daily operations of government; and, finally, ritual-architectural demonstrations of the strength and stability of religiocivic institutions.

Reflecting, Reinforcing, and Perpetuating the Status Quo: Scales and Heights

Beginning even on so modest a scale as the relative size of the grass mat (*okidatami*) on which a Japanese court official is allowed to sit,[25] there is a host of ways in which architectural arrangements very clearly reflect—and thus to a considerable degree reinforce and perpetuate—systems of social stratification. Occasionally, the religioarchitectural expression of social hierarchy is inconspicuous, indirect, generalized, and completely unnoticed by all but a few sensitive observers. Father M. C. Niebarn, for instance, makes the perhaps overimaginative conjecture that "the stones of the walls" of medieval Christian churches "were symbolic of the simple faithful, while the pillars, piers and buttresses symbolised the great mystics and teachers or 'the kings and the powerful ones of the earth, whose duty it is to support and uphold the Church by their intellectual and moral power.'"[26] Yet, even in such seemingly innocuous, probably inadvertent cases, correlations between built forms and social constituencies ought not to be dismissed as incidental and without significance.

Often, however, particularly in explicitly religious architectures, such as early New England Puritan meetinghouses, the spatialization of social hierarchy is much more overt and detailed. In that fascinating situation, on weekdays, the centrally located meetinghouse provided the architectural forum for the facilitation of the community's day-to-day governmental operations (another subtype of the politics priority, discussed below); in that space-time ambience the democratic principles of one man–one vote were meticulously guarded. But on the sabbath, a committee whose duty it was to "dignify the meeting" by assigning every member of the congregation a proper place—based on age, sex, wealth, birth, learning, and public service—enforced a sociospatial hierarchy of the most rigid and glaring sort. As Edmund Sinnott explains:

> All, to be sure—men, women, children, Indians, servants, and slaves—were admitted to the meetinghouse, and in the early days were compelled to attend services; but once inside, distinctions among them were rigidly enforced. . . . Just as some seats were evidently much better than others, so were some people considered superior to their fellows, and it was the essence of the Puritan's social philosophy to give the best men the "foreseats" and to reserve for the lesser individuals those that were farther back and less desirable in other ways.[27]

Residential, less explicitly religious architectural arrangements—at all scales—can also reflect deliberate and unmistakable socioeconomic hierarchies. At the scale of individual buildings, Paul Oliver's descriptions of the carefully circumscribed spaces for respective male and female activities in the Navajo hogan or the distinct men's and women's entrances into the Amazonian Tukanoan community house are only a couple of the most obvious of innumerable instances in which social distinctions, particularly along gender lines, are fully integrated into complex homologized systems of mythological, cosmological, and spatial correlations.[28] Roxana Waterson's impressively detailed study of the houses of the Sa'dan Toraja provides an even clearer example. She shows that these structures, like the houses of many Indonesian groups, in addition to their more obvious sheltering and explicitly ceremonial functions, play essential social roles as "a focus of kinship groupings," as "embodiments of a traditional system of rank," and even as "advertisements for the power of the ruling nobility."[29] According to Waterson, Toraja social distinctions are expressed not only in the relative sizes of the houses, but also in a hierarchy of adornment in which only the small group of highest ranking nobles (the *tana'bulaan,* or "golden stake") are allowed to cover fully their *tongkonan,* or "origin-houses," with carving; lesser nobles (the *tana'bassi,* or "iron stake") could carve the upper portion of their houses, while the majority of Torajans were required to leave their considerably smaller houses unadorned.[30]

At the scale of settlements, Oliver also provides several examples of traditional layouts that reflect both the unity and internal inequality of communities. Presumably symbolizing everyone's shared participation in the community, all of the huts in the camp of the nomadic African Rendille, for instance, have entrances facing the main access to the compound; but, reflecting the social differentiation within the group, those huts are also arranged "in an order of seniority that reflects the sub-clan and status of the occupants."[31] A notable, somewhat larger-scale parallel comes in the concentric sociospatial arrangement of sixteenth-century Yucatecan Maya villages, like Mayapán, where Bishop Landa observed that

> the houses of the lords and priests [were at the center of the city, near to the temples], and then those of the most important people. . . . [Then] came the houses of the richest and those who were held in highest estimation nearest to them, and at the outskirts of town were the houses of the lower class.[32]

Or, at a still larger urban scale, Robert Carmack describes a virtual equation of the social and architectural organizations in the Quiché Maya capital of Utatlán in Guatemala, where "buildings occupied by the lineages became as important symbolically as the lineages themselves—hence the name *nim ja* ('big house') as the general term for lineage."[33]

At an even larger urban scale, the layout of traditional Beijing conformed to an idealized cosmological plan in which the nonnegotiable realities of Chinese social hierarchy were fully integrated into a complex (and alluring) network of homologized, conventionalized, and astronomical references; among particularly salient features were separate gates and roadways for nobles and commoners so that visitors were sorted according to social class even before entering the Imperial City.[34] In traditional India, the rigid caste stratification of Hindu society was similarly reflected not only in the horizontal layout of the city, but also vertically—in the relative heights of the dwellings of each class. Thus, according to Andreas Volwahsen, the house of a Sudra (slave or servant) could not exceed two and a half stories, a Vaisya (merchant) up to four, Kshatriyas (warriors) up to five and half, Brahmins up to six and a half and, finally, the residence of a king could reach up to seven stories.[35]

Correlations of physical height and "high places" with social status (and perhaps relative sacrality) do, in fact, provide the most cross-culturally common means of expressing and, to that extent, perpetuating social rankings via architecture. To mention just four wide-spaced examples: The pre-Columbian site of Xochicalco in a hilly region of Morelos, Mexico, is arranged with a succession of increasingly higher and more exclusive plazas so that people at the top can look down upon all that is happening below while those at the bottom (both socially and physically) are totally excluded from what happens above them.[36] In Islam, it is noteworthy that while a mosque or *madrasah* (a college) is seldom built on a raised platform (*socle*) —because in those cases "the equality of the horizontal plane is sought"[37]— by contrast, the palace complexes of Islamic states like Shi'ite Iran, which consolidate temporal and spiritual authority, maintain and extend the pre-Islamic notion of a raised throne, and thus "are placed at the symbolic head of the city and normally at its highest location."[38] Jean DeBernardi suggests the additional prospect that height differences can be used to express socio-spatial hierarchies that apply to divine as well as human beings; she describes how, in China, various disparate entities are all organized into categories of "above" and "below" (*shang/hsia*), which are then reflected in ritual-architectural design:

> Most basically, it is seen in worship in any temple in which the Lord of Heaven is worshiped in an elevated shrine; Buddhas, Lao Tzu, deified heroes, and ancestors on an intermediate level altar; and the Earth gods in a shrine on the ground beneath the altar. If ghosts are worshiped, these are worshiped at the back door or at the "foot" of the front door.[39]

Finally, the expression of social differences in terms of differentiations in architectural heights is even more elaborate in ancient Japan. In the context of his intriguing "phenomenology of floors," Arata Isozaki explains that

> in a land like ancient Japan, where religious-ceremonial and governmental functions were actually synonymous, the differences in level between the ground floor and the raised floor stood for social differences that evolved in the presence of vesting and sanctifying the state.[40]

Implying a set of homologized socio-religio-architectural correspondences, Isozaki goes on to explain that, generally speaking, the ground level was considered vulgar and was thus associated with commoners (who are, in fact, referred to as "people below the ground"), while elevated floors were considered sacred and typically were associated with the aristocracy and imperial family (or the "people above the ground"). Accordingly, the act of ascending a stairway (or of being prohibited from ascending) takes on significant social and political as well as religious connotations:

> Just as the Shinto priest had to ascend a staircase to the shrine during ceremonials, so it became necessary to ascend a staircase to reach the floor level of the homes of the aristocracy. . . . People of low social rank who for one reason or another might be invited to [the raised-floor] mansions of the great were usually not allowed to mount the staircase; they must have experienced a sense of inferiority and oppression.[41]

Suspending, Undermining, or Overriding the Status Quo: Subversives and Conquerors

Where architecture is particularly adept at reinforcing prevailing socioeconomic arrangements, there are also instances in which even explicitly religious architectures can provide a means for variously suspending, undermining, or overriding the status quo.[42] In deliberate protest against the exclusionary practices of the Hindu caste system, and thus in direct contrast to the architectural forms that supported that institutionalized inequality, the design of the Indian temples of Sikhs and Baha'is, for example, delivered an equally explicit architectural statement of openness to any and all that wished to enter. The first task of Arjun, the guru who assumed leadership of the Sikhs in the late sixteenth century, was to erect a temple on what would eventually become the site of the Golden Temple, or Harimandir, the most sacred shrine of the Sikhs. Yet, reflecting—or actually announcing—the eclectic and inclusivistic priorities of the Sikhs, instead of building the temple on a high base in the Hindu style, Arjun had it built in a depression so that worshipers had to go down (rather than up) steps in order to enter it; moreover, he provided four entrances, presumably "symbolic of the new faith which made no distinction between the four

Hindu castes."[43] The Golden Temple, as Pardeep Singh Arshi explains, "has four doorways which symbolize the access to the temple available to people of all rank and creed."[44] Half a millennium later, in the same spirit of social as well as spiritual inclusiveness, the sparkling white North American Baha'i Center in Winnetka, Illinois, is built with nine sides, since nine, being the largest unit number, symbolizes the unity and inclusive synthesis that Baha'i wishes to bring to humanity.[45]

In Islam, characteristic mosque designs that, on the one hand, announced Islam's distinctiveness from other faiths, on the other hand, expressed its radically egalitarian ideals. In a sense reversing the Puritan pattern, in which the worship context provided a lens for bringing status differences into the sharpest possible focus, the Muslim worship space erased or suspended, if only temporarily, the social distinctions that obtained in the outside world. As Madeline Zilfi explains in the context of her study of Ottoman "politics of piety":

> Every mosque, however modest, represented the community of Islam, the communal focus of the most fundamental tenets of the faith. The mosque was inherently egalitarian . . . profession of the faith was enough to enable one to secure a place alongside fellow believers, take part in mosque rituals and even address the assembled congregation. Ulema, Sufis, mosque preachers, and laymen from the Sultan and his courtiers to tradesmen and sweepers, mixed in rites common to all Muslims. Ritual and liturgy, condemning social distinctions, in such moments erased them.[46]

Architectural configurations may, in other cases, provide more overt statements of independence, indignation, or perhaps, depending on your perspective, impertinence. Donald Robertson describes, for instance, how an attempt by imprudent Tlatelolcan builders to construct their own local pyramid on a grander scale than the Templo Mayor of their contemporaries and close neighbors, the Aztecs, was considered so gross an affront that the latter were compelled to respond militarily.[47] Or similarly, in Japan, one particular style of *katsuogi* (the tapered wooden cylinders set crosswise along the ridges of Shinto shrines) had been conventionalized into "a symbol of authority," and was thus the exclusive preserve of the highest royalty; accordingly, when a certain local lord had the procacity to build for himself a dwelling with a *katsuogi* roof treatment that imitated that of the imperial residence, the emperor Yuryaku was so enraged that he promptly sent an envoy to burn it down.[48]

Though often with similarly frustrated results, social activists in numerous, more contemporary contexts have also tried to capitalize on architectural design as "a peaceful tool of social transformation, as a means of changing the relation between the individual and society by generating new lifestyles."[49] Architect and theorist Bernard Tschumi cites the largely failed attempt of the Russian revolutionary "social condensers" of the 1920s, who hoped via the creation of "minimal cells" and community kitchens to foster new sorts of relationships between people, as a precedent to his own inquiries into the question: "How could architects avoid seeing architecture and planning as the faithful product of dominant society, viewing their craft, on the contrary, as a catalyst for change?"[50] Tschumi himself, then, experimented, particularly in Western urban settings, with "counterdesign" and a "guerrilla architecture" that would serve as a means of demystification by revealing the dehumanizing effects of "the capitalist organization of space" and then demonstrating, alternatively, that "it is possible to build fast and cheaply with building methods that are in contradiction with the economic logic of the system."[51]

Such experimental, counterhegemonic, "guerrilla" practices open up to historically oriented hermeneuts the important morphological possibility of social subversive architectures. But the limited success of such practices —reflected in Tschumi's own observation that "spatial organization may temporarily modify individual or group behavior, but [that] does not imply that it will change the socioeconomic structure of a reactionary society"[52]— impresses us more strongly with the serious limitations of architecture as an instrument of social protest or revolution, limitations that owe in large part to the inordinate expenditures required for substantial building projects.[53] It is, in fact, I suspect (to raise a point to which I will return at the close of this chapter), the subversive use and apprehension (or, on occasion, destruction) of always-superabundant, preexisting civic and public constructions, rather than the erection of new forms, that provides architecture's greatest utility to social revolutionaries. That is to say, it is particularly in the "ritual" dimension of ritual-architectural events, that there is "space" for social protest.[54]

Be that as it may, considerably more prominent (and more often successful) instantiations of architecture's potential for contesting and rearranging prevailing social conditions are those undertaken by competing, similarly powerful, and well-endowed constituencies. Reminiscent of the competition between various European municipalities for the grandest Gothic cathedral (or, for that matter, between contemporary cities for the highest skyscraper), Raymond Sidrys argues that monumental constructions of the ancient Maya functioned as highly visible symbols of national prestige, labor organization, and political power, and as such were the megalithic pawns in a shrewd tournament of "competitive building" between the rival chiefdoms of the Early Classic northern lowlands.[55]

Even more prominent are those instances of reliance on large-scale architecture to announce or confirm the ascendancy of a new (or not-so-new) pattern of hierarchy over another that is already in place. The transitions of power in Istanbul, for example, "twice the capital of a world power," have deliberate, spectacular (and explicitly religious) architectural counterparts in the Hagia Sophia and the Suleymaniye Mosque, which continues to represent not only the height of Ottoman architecture but also a kind of golden age in Islamic history.[56] Built more than one thousand years later but just one mile from the Hagia Sophia, which had itself represented the triumph of Byzantium in the days of Justinian, the Suleymaniye was conceived explicitly by esteemed architect Sinan as a structure that would surpass the Hagia Sophia both visually and technically, and, thus, among other things, confirm the political conquest of the Byzantine city by the Ottoman Turks.

As a means to social transformation, then, architecture has, not surprisingly, served more successfully in the hands of kings, conquerors, and colonialists, who work from the top down as it were to override competing polities, than in the hands of popular revolutionaries working from the bottom up to undermine prevailing social norms. Building, especially of the monumental sort, is, in the main, a weapon of the enfranchised rather than the disenfranchised. In the century before Christ, the first Roman emperor, Augustus, for instance, used his enormous resources to have eighty-two temples recast in the Greco-Roman style, and a whole "second population" of Greek statuary erected in Rome to announce the success of his invasion and the establishment of his empire.[57] Thus, by late antiquity, as H. P. L'Orange observes, there was a structural (maybe homological) correspondence between Roman polity, art, and architecture in which all were arranged with perfect uniformity and symmetry around the emperor.[58] Not unlike the Inca, who superimposed their conventions of architectural order on all that they conquered, the Romans relied very heavily on manipulations of the built environment in pursuit of their aspiration to regularize the full extent of the world.[59]

Yet, as the convoluted history of Rome, and particularly the battle in the early Christian era for what Richard Krautheimer terms "the conquest of the center," further demonstrates that, even with ample backing, there are severe limitations on the ways in which political-architectural maneuvering can work to foment significant social change.[60] Krautheimer explains that, while Constantine, the first Christian emperor, like Augustus, took great pains to announce the ascendancy of his new orientation by constructing highly prominent Christian churches, the fact that Constantine was forced to build both the Latern papal palace and Saint Peter's on the periphery of the city rather than at the classical center actually symbolized failure rather than success in genuinely Christianizing Rome. According to Krautheimer, it was not until the Middle Ages that the map of Rome does finally bespeak a Christian victory insofar as, by that time, there had been an ironic reversal wherein Saint Peter's and the Borgio quarter had become the real estate of preeminence, and the once coveted Capitoline Hill precinct was almost completely neglected.[61] To invoke an idiom familiar to historians of religions, eventually, the religiopolitical periphery had become central and the old center was abandoned; but Constantine's ineffectual building program was, at most, one of many factors that precipitated that change.[62]

Ritual-Architectural Instruments of Statecraft: Three Morphological Options

Moving toward a set of more explicitly governmental variations on the ritual-architectural commemoration of temporal authority (priority II-C), we find particularly helpful organizational clues in George Cowgill's subtle studies of the dynamic interrelations between building and polity in the early Mesoamerican capital of Teotihuacan, and particularly in his reflections on what he calls the "cross-cultural ethnoarchaeology of public architecture."[63] Though not employing the terminology of hermeneutics, Cowgill's work, which concentrates specifically on the Ciudadela, the extensive building complex generally believed to have been the governmental seat of Teotihuacan, nonetheless has the character of a ritual-architectural reception history: instead of presuming once-and-for-all architectural meanings, he attempts to trace the changing political functions (or, perhaps, the shifting ritual-architectural priorities) of this complex of buildings over time.

Briefly summarized, according to Cowgill's hypothesis, the Ciudadela was originally the center of Teotihuacan's routine administration and political management. But, as Teotihuacan grew in population and complexity, the Ciudadela was soon too small to house the day-to-day affairs of the city. Yet, because of the building's even more significant role as the physical embodiment of the stability and intransigence of the Teotihuacan state, rather than modifying and expanding it enough to keep pace with the increasingly complex bureaucratic routines of a growing city, those mundane functions were moved to other quarters, and the Ciudadela accepted a more "symbolic," less quotidian role. Cowgill concludes, moreover, that, unlike the state palaces of many other pre-Columbian peoples (notably those at Chan Chan, the Chimu capital on the northern coast of Peru, where each new ruler constructed a new residential complex that was forever identified with his individual persona),[64] the Ciudadela was dedicated to the legitimation of the Teotihuacan state in general, not to the glorification of any individual ruler.[65]

As a fresh reading of the Ciudadela, Cowgill's analysis is provocative and original.[66] Even more heuristically useful, however, is the implied distinction between what amounts to three additional generalized (though decidedly nonparallel) morphological variations on the ritual-architectural commemoration of temporal authority: configurations that glorify a particular ruler; those that facilitate the daily operation of a government; and those that function in some manner as symbolic announcements of the strength and stability of religiocivic institutions. Furthermore, as Cowgill himself demonstrates very well in the case of Teotihuacan, there is nearly always a lively interplay between these three oddly heterogeneous, logistical, and ideological concerns, each of which is, on occasion, most noteworthy for having been omitted or superseded. Paying particular attention, then, to the way in which these three variations on the theme of the sacred architecture as an instrument of statecraft play against one another, consider cross-cultural exemplifications of each.

Glorifications of Specific Rulers: Divine or Human, Present or Past

First, with respect to the suboption that Cowgill found notably absent in the Ciudadela, famed architectural historian Sir Banister Fletcher observed, and no one has disagreed, that "Many of the world's greatest rulers have been [Architecture's] patrons and some, like Rameses the Great, have used Architecture as the symbol of their personal power."[67] Moreover, leaders of considerably lesser rank and world celebrity—tribal chiefs, local ministers, county commissioners, precinct captains, and university presidents—may all find in building an apt means of personal aggrandizement. Though academic acknowledgments of this possibility are common in the extreme (most of the previous chapter's comments about cults of personality and commemorations of mythicohistorical individuals are relevant here), perhaps the most striking, explicitly religiopolitical exemplars are connected with various notions of divine kingship.

In ancient Egypt, while all pharaohs were apparently identified either with the god Horus or with the sun god Re (thus blending commemorations of politics [II-C] and divinity [II-A]), the individuality of each ruler was also very important: The Sphinx, for instance, appears to be an "idealized portrait statue" of an individual pharaoh, namely, Chephren; the Ramesseum, the mortuary temple of Rameses II to which Fletcher referred, was decorated with scenes of his personal military triumphs and a colossal statue of his likeness, some fifty-seven feet high; and the Great Pyramid at Giza was essentially a royal tomb built about 2600 B.C.E. specifically by and for Cheops.[68] Moreover, following Cheops's efforts, each successive pharaoh seems to have at least planned a pyramid for himself down through the end of the Middle Kingdom (1600 B.C.E.) when, for whatever reason, different priorities seem to have asserted themselves so that the concept of a one-to-one correspondence between rulers and buildings was abandoned in favor of less conspicuous burial places.[69]

In numerous instances, then, the ritual-architectural glorification of individual rulers—particularly when the sovereign himself or herself initiates it—is primarily in the interest of establishing or confirming the divine authorization of that living leader's temporal authority. The eleventh-century Hindu sovereign Rajendra, for example, erected a temple to Shiva in his capital city of Gangaikondacholapuram that featured relief carvings in which he depicted himself receiving a floral garland of victory directly from the god Shiva and his consort Parvati, thus presumably announcing the divine sanction of Rajendra's conquest of Bengali armies and the northward extension of his empire.[70] In Java and Cambodia, the relationship between Hindu temple building and kingship is even closer than in India. Here, too, the careers of individual kings and gods were thoroughly interwoven in the iconography of temples that were, as Michell explains, "dedicated simultaneously to the god and the king himself";[71] though, in Southeast Asia, suggesting an additional morphological slice, it appears that usually it is the royal *office* rather than the momentary officeholder that is regarded as most deserving of ritual-architectural commemoration.[72]

In many other cases, instead of directly legitimating the status or activities of a currently active ruler or even the office, the first priority is the posthumous ritual-architectural memorialization of the mythicohistoric exploits of a particular sovereign (which thus links the politics priority especially to commemorations of the dead [II-D]). Note among thousands of relevant exemplars the case of the two widowed queens of the Chalukyan king Vikramaditya II who, in the middle of the eighth century, built temples to Shiva at the royal site of Pattadakal in South India to commemorate the victory of their past husband over the neighboring Pallava ruler.[73] Sometimes, then, what matters most in such posthumous memorials is an architectural record of the accomplishments of the sovereign, though in other situations the commemoration is effected by somehow preserving or displaying the leader's physical remains. Among equally numerous examples of that sort, the variously interpreted Late Minoan palace at Hagia Triada near Phaestos (resembling the general arrangement of the palace of Minos at Knossos, though on a much smaller scale) was apparently built to house the mortal remains of a Minoan priest-king who was worshiped as "an apotheosized royal hero who had been transported by griffins and accompanied by goddesses to the realms of the gods and there deified."[74]

While there is little need of rehearsing more examples—because this is a permutation on politicized architecture that has escaped almost no one's attention—it is worth noting how heuristically productive, and sometimes controversial, comparative inquiries along this line have been. It is, for instance, precisely the presence (or absence) of this sort of individuated commemoration of rulers that has, in large part, sustained the notorious debate about the intended significance of pre-Hispanic Maya stelae and hieroglyphs. Old guard Mayanists, intent on imagining Classic Maya priorities as strictly cosmological and apolitical, insisted that these monuments "are in *no* sense records of personal glorification and self-laudation like the inscriptions of Egypt, Assyria, or Babylonia";[75] a middle ground has claimed that Maya art and architecture, more like Southeast Asia, commemorate religiopolitical offices but not individual rulers;[76] but the presently prevailing consensus, which, suspiciously consistent with wider academic trends, lifts political priorities to the very top of list, makes a compelling argument that the Maya glyphs and monuments depict, more than anything else, the accomplishments and descent lines of specific historical rulers.[77]

Facilitations of Routine Governmental Activities: Contexts of Decision Making

The second and third possibilities that can be extracted from Cowgill's work—ritual-architectural facilitations of the routine government affairs and symbolic expressions of a government's strength and stability—correlate roughly with architecture's specially dual participation in the realms of the prosaically utilitarian and the "artfully" transutilitarian.[78] Though the two sorts of functions are never entirely distinct, they are often in tension: religiocivic architecture may, on the one hand, work like sculpture to express bureaucratic ideals and identities; but, on the other hand, we ought to note also architecture's less glamorous, more indirect, tool-like function in sheltering, facilitating, and thus in important ways influencing the routine processes of government.[79]

Faced with the prospect of rebuilding the House of Commons after World War II, Sir Winston Churchill's impassioned plea against changing from the conventional rectangular shape to a circular chamber, for example, demonstrated, among other things, how specific architectural configurations, in addition to providing built expressions of abstract governmental or jurisprudential ideals, can intrude in very tangible ways on how and when lawmakers speak, and how they take responsibility for what they say. Where a round room would have had an advantage in connoting some egalitarian democratic ideal, Churchill recognized that there was an unmistakable correlation between one's political affinities and the seat one occupied on the right or left of the four-sided chamber. Thus, he argued:

> the party system is much favored by the oblong form. It is easy for an individual to move through those insensible gradations from Right to Left [in a circular assembly], but the act of crossing the Floor is one which requires serious consideration.[80]

Against some resistance, Churchill eventually won his case. Moreover, Churchill's victory demonstrated, as does Cowgill's analysis of Teotihuacan, that ritual-architectural decisions are not infrequently made first and foremost in the interest of furnishing a (ritual) context for the practical exigencies and stylized conversation of political debate, legislation, and law enforcement.

The tension between expediting the pragmatic affairs of the state and the other two more explicitly commemorative functions is even more clearly instantiated in Minoru Ooka's account of the evolution of early religiocivic Japanese architecture. Ooka explains that, in very ancient Japan, prior to sustained interactions with China, each new emperor, as the head of a theocracy that united religious and political functions in one person, selected a new site for the imperial palace upon his ascension to the throne, thus effecting a unique identification between the reign of an individual and a specific place; no capital continued for more than one era. At that point, then, of the three morphological suboptions, the leading priority would seem to have been the ritual-architectural glorification of an individual sovereign, and the correlation of the power of the state with the divine personhood of a specific emperor.

Ooka's analysis suggests, however, that, as contact with the Asian mainland became more frequent, and especially after the seventh-century C.E. Taika Reforms worked to establish a more centralized administration and state sponsorship of Buddhism, the importance of both of the other two suboptions increased dramatically: day-to-day administrative demands intensified tremendously and institutional "matters of prestige" became, as Ooka says, "rather more important."[81] Together those forces militated against periodic relocation of authority according to the idiosyncratic predilections of each emperor until, in 710 C.E., the decision was made to establish a permanent capital at Heijokyo (presently Nara). At that point, in my morphological idiom, the priority for glorifying individual leaders was superseded both by the practical requirements of administration and, looking ahead to the third suboption, by more expressly "symbolic," elocutionary sorts of ritual-architectural statecrafting, which would enable a clearer demonstration of the strength, stability, and transpersonal continuity of Japanese governmental institutions. To that end, in 741 C.E., Emperor Shomu erected a gigantic bronze statue of Vairocana Buddha in the main temple at Heijokyo, a statue that, according to Tamaru Noriyoshi, functioned as "at once a symbol of the magnificent universe and of the centralized state"; moreover, relying again on architecture to confirm the longer reach and wider relevance of that new religiocivic orientation, Shomu also initiated the building of a network of state-subsidized Buddhist temples (*kokubunji*) in each outlying province.[82]

Symbols of Strength and Stability: Integration, Identity, and Intimidation

The last religiocivic suboption provides the most vivid, voluminous, and often most violent set of exemplars of the ritual-architectural commemoration of temporal authority. In many circumstances, as in the preceding Japanese example, architecture is employed as a mechanism of political integration, a means of persuading reticent people in peripheral territories of their necessary respect for and allegiance to a hegemonic center. Architecture, in those cases, is intended to shape disparate, perhaps antagonistic interests into some common concerns. In ancient China, for instance, *ming-tang* served not only as ritual halls and celestial observatories (discussed above in regard to astronomy [priority I-C], but also as tools for religiopolitical standardization, which were apparently constructed in outlying areas "only at those times when the emperor needed to invoke the most powerful imperial symbolism, usually to make legitimate his usurpation of imperial authority."[83]

Or, in the pre-Columbian Americas, while this sort of religio-architectural standardization in the interest of integration seems to have been much more of a priority for Inca rulers than for either their Maya or Aztec counterparts,[84] the Quiché, for example, the most powerful Highland Maya state, in a sense effecting a kind of symbolic exportation of the center, marked the extent of their imperial penetration into peripheral territories with garrisons that were scaled-down copies of the civic buildings of their capital, Utatlán.[85] In other cases, extensive systems of raised causeways, like that which radiates from Dzibilchaltún, a Maya site in northern Yucatan, were constructed apparently less as pragmatic transportation or communication routes than as symbolic statements of a superlocal integration of society and politics.[86] Even the Aztecs, notorious for their disinterest in refashioning the spirituality of conquered peoples (tribute collection, it seems, superseded any priority for conversion) did, on occasion, resort to architectural announcements of authority, as at the rock-cut site of Malinalco where they overlaid the symbols of their eagle and jaguar military orders on the earlier structures.[87] In each of these and many other situations, the manipulation of sentiments depended upon twofold juxtapositions of familiar, heterogeneous local ritual-architectural elements with less familiar, but much more homogenized elements associated with a larger centralized authority.

Often then, especially where centralized authority is imperiled or expanding—most poignantly in relation to the processes of conquest and colonialism—mechanisms of ritual-architectural statecraft can become very important in establishing a persuasively clear sense of identity and legitimacy. Salient in this respect are the numerous instances inventoried earlier in relation to allurement via conventionality (priority I-B), particularly those like the insecure Aztecs' imitation and expropriation of the prestigious Toltec building style in which ritual-architectural means figured large in the construction of an impressive (if fictive) pedigree that would convince ruled and rulers alike of the propriety of Aztec supereminence over the Valley of Mexico.[88] Much closer to home, and more similar than some may want to admit, is the pedigree construction evidenced in the widely eclectic design of the public spaces of the United States capital, where, as Michael Blakey has noted:

> the [Washington, D.C.] Mall's architecture symbolizes the heritage, stability, and power of the United States through the use of Greco-Roman motifs, with which we should note the presence of a feudal European "castle" and an Egyptian obelisk.[89]

The same, of course, could be said for thousands of less prominent instances of American (religio)civic architecture.[90]

In other cases, the persuasiveness of other ritual-architectural depictions of religiocivic identity and control depends less on mythicogenealogical allusions than on blunt intimidation. Architectural decorations such as those that depict kings standing on the necks of captives on ancient Far Eastern conquest monuments,[91] or the grim reliefs of two mailed knights standing on the heads of vanquished Maya natives above the doorway to Spanish conquistador Francisco de Montejo's colonial palace in Merida, Yucatan, are, of course, legion.[92] In a more strictly architectural pre-Hispanic case from the same area, the Cocom Maya ruler of Mayapán, showcasing the dire consequences of rebellion against his authority, apparently held his subsidiary lords as public hostages in thirteen colonnaded halls at the civic core that were, in turn, correlated (or homologized) with thirteen dependent provinces.[93] Or, exemplifying even better the possibility of performative evocations of terror, Mesoamerican human sacrifice was, at least in part, as John Pohl and others have concluded, the ritual-architectural climax of politically motivated power struggles that "served as public demonstrations of power."[94]

Irrespective of the wide pervasiveness of this morphologic suboption, one last circumstance, the contrast between the earlier and later British colonial capitals in India, ought to help dispel any presupposal concerning the reliability of such deployments of ritual-architectural intimidation in effecting actual sociopolitical transformations. The original British colonial palace, in Calcutta, is characterized as "aggressively foreign," insofar as there was a deliberate rejection of any indigenous elements whatever; but overt intimidation was *not* apparently a leading design determinant. Michael Edwardes suggests that the principal concern at that point was the definition of a British self-identity that was thoroughly distinct from, and presumably superior to, that of native India:

> [The old British palace in Calcutta was] designed not so much to impress Indians—which at the time did not seem necessary—but to convince the

> British themselves, at the beginning of their empire, that they had really arrived, that they were in fact *rulers* with palaces just like the rulers of Europe, the only criterion that counted.[95]

By the 1900s, however, more secure in their self-identity as colonizers, but also apparently more committed to manipulating the Indian sensibilities, the British opted to move their base from Calcutta to Delhi, the site where, not inconsequentially, "already, the capital cities of seven previous conquerors survived in various stages of collapse."[96] This strategic relocation and the colonial architecture of New Delhi, foremost the second royal palace, or Viceroy's House (the Rashtrapati Bhavan), optimistically termed "the last major example of architectural imperialism,"[97] if perhaps accommodating a few more indigenous elements (though not many), also demonstrated a considerably stronger initiative to impress and intimidate the local population, and thus to reaffirm in the most forceful terms "the assertion of the unfaltering determination to maintain British rule in India."[98] Ironically, however—perhaps testifying again to the autonomy of monumental architecture and to its decided limitations as a vehicle to real social change—less than twenty years after the dedication of New Delhi in 1931, India won its independence and the the Viceroy's House came to serve as home to the democratically elected president of India.

Closing Thoughts: Sacred and Profane Religious Architecture

Closing out this quick reconnaissance of the vast area of ritual-architectural commemorations of sociopolitical authority (priority II-C), three points are most deserving of attention. First, regarding the morphologically interesting prospect of thoroughly apolitical religious architectures in which this priority would be wholly irrelevant, we must conclude, empirically and historically speaking, that there are none. Paradoxically and unavoidably, even ritual-architectural configurations designed to capacitate the complete avoidance of worldly political affairs—say, monastic communities or hermit refuges—make significant political statements. Moreover, academics that counterpoise "religion" and "politics," and thus equate the politicization of sacred architecture with "secularization," or with some notion of degradation from a more "genuinely religious" condition, are participating in another sort of polemical social commentary. Neutrality in the affairs of politics (broadly speaking) is not an option. All sacred architecture is to that extent profane.

Moreover, if historians of religions, not unlike other humanities and social scientific scholars, are already increasingly attentive to the disparities of power that either quietly or loudly assert themselves in every sort of situation, historical or academic, they ought to note that "religious architecture" is actually more, not less, implicated in matrixes of sociopolitical power than most others sorts of cultural productions. The special case of architecture among the arts—its dual fraternity in "the functional" and "the aesthetic," what Gadamer termed its "duality of decorative mediation," and thus architecture's "mercenary" entanglements in facilitations of the mundane and expressions of the profound[99]—intensifies rather than lessens the requirement that even explicitly religious constructions always be interpreted in relation to the sociohistorical contexts in which they are created, used, and maybe misused. In short, matters of hierarchy and socioeconomic interest must be appreciated as one among numerous sets of competing ritual-architectural priorities that impinge on every ritual-architectural situation. To privilege the political dimensions of sacred architecture as always foundational and determinative, that is, to assume that those are the always-winning priorities, will astrict and forestall rigorously empirical descriptions and analyses of specific historical cases; but avoidance of these issues, which is still probably a more widespread problem, is certain to prove much more obfuscating.

The second point bears on the twofold pattern of ritual-architectural events and the necessary juxtaposition of expressly political content with other seemingly apolitical concerns. This is sacred architecture in its most aggressively rhetorical mode, and the persuasiveness of its pointed social, political, and economic messages depends, nearly always, on their apparent interwovenness into much broader, less contentious homologized (I-A), conventionalized (I-B), and occasionally astronomical (I-C) orientational programs. In politically charged architectural events, then, the characteristic twofold transitions from familiar to strange, from conservative to radical, from sensations of similarity to acceptances of difference, from general to specific, and from voluntary to obligatory are especially evident.

Art historian Richard Townsend's analysis of Aztec coronation at the Templo Mayor exemplifies particularly well the characteristic pattern wherein conventional, noncontroversial elements are used to instigate a ritual-architectural event that subsequently details a highly specific program of political authority and obligation.[100] Townsend considers, in other words, that the rulers of Tenochtitlan were deeply concerned with the incorporation of ancient ritual-architectural elements as well as the invention of new ones. Consequently, the Templo Mayor and its royal rites presented, in his view, the masterful integration of "an architectural vocabulary that was traditional" (the front half of the architectural event) with an original, innovative expression that was specific to the time and needs of the Aztec imperial context (the back half of the situation). Embedding the particulars of the political agenda within the more generalized, incontestable canons of convention improved enormously the prospects that the demands of the *huey tlatoni,* the Aztec chief speaker, would not be perceived as aberrant, opportunistic, or exploitative. To the contrary, Townsend explains that this juxtaposition of old and new elements

> . . . allowed the events of a present, unfolding history to be perceived as an inevitable, preordained outcome of a cosmic process that had been established since the time of origins, since the beginning of things.[101]

In short, even glaringly intimidating ritual-architectural commemorations of temporal authority, if they are to succeed in their expressly political purposes, must appear as other than expressly political.

Third and finally, we should note that the superabundance and autonomy of architecture, and the hermeneutically dialogical character of the experience of architecture, assert themselves in distinctive ways with respect to the commemoration of politics—ways that severely limit architecture's utility as an instrument for either the maintenance or the disruption of sociopolitical hierarchy but that provide hermeneuts with some special opportunities. Were, as some behavioralist interpretations suggest (and many art and architectural historical interpretations presume), there greater certainty and homogeneity in people's responses to particular configurations of space and art, then architecture might serve more effectively and more reliably in directing the course of social change; moreover, the interpretation of architecture would be a much more straightforward affair.[102] But, as I have stressed in relation to always-diverse protocols of ritual-architectural apprehension, the reception careers even of fastidiously planned monuments are invariably characterized by unpredicted, and largely unpredictable, twists and, as it were, "turns of events."[103]

Nonetheless, while, as Jacques Maquet suggests, "it may be expected that totalitarian regimes [would be] afraid of the freedom of thought stimulated by the polysemic character of visual symbols," preeminently by multivalent architectural forms,[104] we actually observe the opposite. The history of sacred and civic architecture is, on the one hand, packed with instances in which those in power have seized upon the seemingly enormous potential of monumental architecture to further their own patterns of privilege. Totalitarian leaders and governments—who also seem decidedly neglectful of the superabundance of architecture—have been the most energetic of builders; and doubtless, particularly when coupled with similarly aggressive ritual choreography, architecture has often proven highly serviceable in that role.

Yet, on the other hand, I would accentuate that users of architecture are neither so passive nor so compliant as to allow complete or even regular success in such manipulative agendums. Too many studies (albeit inadvertently) conflate sovereigns' and designers' hopeful expectations for how their creations will influence audience sentiments with the actual empirical apprehensions of those creations (not unlike the pervasive tendency of students of religion to proceed as though rituals always "work").[105] The present hermeneutics of sacred architecture, however, which constantly foregrounds the usually underestimated "share of the beholder" and the always active role of ritual participants in the production of architectural meaning, leads us to anticipate *dis*continuity between original design intentions and subsequent apprehensions rather than continuity. It is very difficult to know how often, and for whom, strategic building programs like those of Augustus, Constantine, British colonialists in India, or the Aztecs, in a sense, backfired and thus engendered disdain and resentment rather than respect, or to know when those events misfired and thus inspired no strong response (which seems a less likely prospect in those cases). One must suspect, however, that it is in the realm of ritual-architectural politicking and propaganda that the always significant gap between the idealized apprehensions imagined by designers and the on-the-ground apprehensions of the faithful and not-so-faithful is at its very widest.

For kings and architects, such discrepancies and infelicitous efforts at engineering public opinion via ritual-architectural means are disappointing failures that present policy problems. For most students of religiocivic architecture, those disparities and miscues are never seriously considered. But for critical, empirically minded hermeneuts, intent on respecting the superabundance of architecture, those resistant and revalorative apprehensions are exceptionally telling and fortuitous occasions, which will mark decisive turning points in their ritual-architectural reception histories. For hermeneuts, it is in the aggressively dialogical apprehensions of politicized architectural events, when audiences assert their own priorities rather than passively ingesting those of sovereigns and suzerains, that we will find the most pregnant opportunities for penetrating to those audiences' lived perceptions of religious architecture and of the world.

Twenty | The Dead: Memorials, Stones, and Bones (Priority II-D)

> A universal custom among all Indian nations was to pay more attention to the dwelling that they were to have after death than the one they had during their lifetime.
>
> Father Bernabé Cobo, 1653[1]

> The funeral practices of other nations are full of oddities in which impiety often borders on the ridiculous.
>
> Arthur Mercier, 1855[2]

> Architects generally do not love that part of life that resembles death: decaying constructions—the dissolving traces that time leaves on buildings—are incompatible with both the ideology of modernity and what might be called conceptual aesthetics.
>
> Bernard Tschumi, 1976[3]

THE FABULOUS ABUNDANCE AND DIVERSITY of extravagant religio-architectural manifestations of the fascination, fear, and awe of death—tombs, vaults, sepulchers and sarcophagi, morgues and mausoleums, gallows and graves—lend considerable support to the venturesome surmise that "Man is instinctively that improvising architect who is as much concerned with his installation in the beyond, his residence in eternity, as with his temporal habitation."[4] In fact, amazed at just how often the dead are more esteemed architectural clients than the living, travelers and anthropologists have, for centuries, marveled at those many contexts in which people deny themselves any semblance of bodily comfort in order to construct sumptuous dwellings for their dead.

In seventeenth-century Peru, for instance, Father Bernabé Cobo was simultaneously dazzled and repulsed by the embalmed bodies of Inca nobles that were provided with lavish accommodations, attended by large numbers of servants, escorted on tours to visit their similarly deceased counterparts, and honored as the most eminent guests at important ceremonies where they were seated in a row according to their seniority and treated to the best food and drink. In Cobo's condemnatory description, "the beastly act of venerating the bodies of the dead" reached such outrageous proportions that even the native chieftain Huascar Inca complained that "the dead had taken over the best of everything in his kingdom."[5] In the same region, chronicler Pedro de Cieza de León had recorded similar impressions of the immense funerary monuments that surround Ayaviri by Lake Titicaca: "the place is worthy of note," he wrote, "especially the great tombs which are so numerous that they occupy more space than the habitations of the living."[6]

Amidst the poverty of twentieth-century Haiti, Sibyl Moholy-Nagy was likewise profoundly impressed by the "highly artistic originality" and massive construction of the royal sarcophagi—in which no form is ever precisely duplicated—which, ironically, stood directly beside thoroughly dilapidated domestic dwellings.[7] Raymond Decary, surveying a similar sort of situation in the high plateaus of Madagascar, was awed that the Kiboris willingly devoted their entire lives to building a house for their dead. In that context, according to Decary:

> The habitation of the living man may be poor, even wretched, but the tomb on the contrary has to be vast and attract attention. . . . The eternal abode has to stand out for its solidity and fine appearance. . . . The tomb is visible wealth, and some ruin themselves in building it.[8]

Or in West Africa, the elaborately decorated two-story dwellings of the Tamberma of northern Togo provide another circumstance in which facilitations of the activities of daily life constitute much less important design parameters than the crucial, prearranged role that those houses will play in elaborate funeral performances upon the death of male and female elders.[9]

If the commitment to building for the dead is not always so overpowering, manifestations of the ritual-architectural commemoration of the dead (priority II-D) are, nonetheless, spectacularly diverse. Moreover, as in the realm of divinity commemoration (priority II-A), where one confronts an enormous cross-cultural diversity in respective conceptions of "gods" and the supernatural, here hermeneuts must deal with enormously varied, culturally specific notions not only of death, afterlives, ghosts, spirits, and relations to one's ancestors, but also of personhood and human bodies. Cross-cultural morphological comparisons of funerary practices and constructions pose especially difficult problems. As Joseph Kitagawa counseled, it is important for historians of religions working in any specific context to ask, and to take seriously responses to, the question: just how dead are the dead?[10]

At any rate, whether assessed in this case as mildly managed chaos or relatively significant organization, I can add to the assemblage of heuristic questions by reviewing some of the more salient variations on the commemoration of the dead in terms of three especially uneven sets of morphological possibilities.[11] First, in order to broaden the category and accentuate some of the less obviously relevant circumstances, is a brief discussion of a few ritual-architectural configurations that somehow honor and memorialize the dead, variously conceived, without, however, relying on the placement or display of actual bodily remains. Second are a couple of sections exploring ritual-architectural configurations, particularly megaliths, that somehow (re)embody or (re)actualize the dead, again, largely irrespective of physical remains. Here the challenge is to entertain the possibility of the actual "transmutation" of ancestors into architectural, usually stone constructions; in these cases, built forms, in some important sense, *are* the dead. And third is consideration of a series of variations on more explicitly funerary architectural practices, most of which do depend heavily on the ritual-architectural accommodation and strategic location of bones and body parts. These are architectural configurations designed in order that the dead—or, often, very active "undead"—are variously housed, pampered, transported, confined, or obeyed. Again, the distinctions in this chapter are especially provisional, and thus by no means absolute.

Bodiless Memorializing: Honoring Mythical Ancestors and the Fully Dead

Where the prospect of ritual-architectural commemorations of the dead may first summon images of burials, crypts, and coffins, we ought to note as well that there are countless viable candidates for participation in this category in which actual bodily remains play a small, incidental, or no role at all. Bodiless architectural memorials to the deceased are diverse and quite common, though the precise ontological status of the dead honorees is one of those areas in which culturally specific (and often individually specific) notions of anthropology and cosmology intrude in especially strong ways. Of the many different ways that the dead might be memorialized and commemorated in architecture—largely irrespective of bodily remains—two radically different possibilities merit special comment: one that largely nullifies the importance of preserving bodies on the basis of "archaic-mythological" presuppositions, and another that minimizes the significance of posthumous bodies on a more modern Western epistemological basis.

The first, maybe inobvious alternative concerns the commemoration of mythical ancestors, or what might be termed "the dead that never lived." As noted in relation to the ritual-architectural commemoration of mythico-historical personages (one variation under the rubric of sacred history [II-B]), not only are the "dead individuals" that are commemorated in architecture virtually always, to some extent, mythologized—quite often, the honored "dead" have a *strictly* imaginal, mythical status.[12] To be an esteemed ancestor does not always require, in other words, that one has first lived as a human being. In those cases, then, bodily remains are largely irrelevant because the honorees never have enjoyed (or endured) an earthly human existence. Death, for them, is not a condition of after-human-life but of an ongoing mythical existence.

The architecture of the Dogon, famously described in Marcel Griaule's *Conversations with Ogotemmêli,* exemplifies this intriguing morphological possibility.[13] Among this West African people, the eight generations of esteemed "ancestors" that play such a crucial role in their mythological traditions, and thus in the spatial layouts of the villages and dwellings, are "the dead" who have never, in any plainly human sense, lived. Among innumerable architectonic concessions to these mythological ancestors, Ogotemmêli explained to Griaule that the eight rows of ten niches on the front wall of a Dogon house represent "the eight ancestors and their descendents, numerous as the fingers on their hands"; these eighty niches are "the homes of the ancestors, who occupy them in order of birth beginning with the highest rows," and thus should never be closed, "for the ancestors need to breathe the outdoor air."[14] Additionally, the characteristic Binu sanctuary of the Dogon, explicitly described by Ogotemmêli as a "tomb," is erected to honor an ancestor, Binu, whose name is "a contraction of two terms, one of which means 'gone' and the other 'come back.'"[15] Thus, according to Griaule's gloss of the Dogon view, while the esteemed figure of Binu "was apparently dead, that is to say, gone to another world, then returned to the world of men, to his people to protect them and to succour them,"[16] it is also the case that Binu and the other "ancestors" who are so fastidiously referenced in the constructions of the Dogon at no time lived and breathed as humans. The design of Dogon houses and sanctuaries depends, then, on rigorous orientation with respect to a body of stories about the (never-lived) dead but not with respect to bodily remains.[17]

Moreover, in that very broad sense, nearly any instance of ritual-architectural pedigree-building via the appropriation or imitation of previous art styles and elements—of which my reiterative example of the Aztec appropriation of the quasi-historical Toltecs' pedigree via the imitation of Toltec building styles is one—constitutes a kind of commemoration of the (largely mythic) dead. In such cases, former styles of art and architecture, and, to that extent, former "peoples"—even those whose identity is primarily or wholly mythical or legendary—are honored, memorialized, and, thus, resuscitated and given new lives. Imitative architectures keep the otherwise dead styles and dead peoples of the past alive. And if, as I will suggest without great originality in the conclusion to this chapter, commemorations of the dead are primarily for the living, then the imaginal, nonhistorical status of the honored dead may not pose a serious problem.

A second, quite different variation on this morphological possibility reflects the removal of bodily remains from the crux on commemorations of the dead by virtue of more modernist, secularized presuppositions about life, death, myth, and history. These cases, evident primarily in the modern West, involve ritual-architectural commemorations of what might be termed "the fully dead," that is, noteworthy political, military, or religious heroes or heroines who have lived and died in the recent or remote historical past. These honorees are individuals (or groups) who lived unambiguously human lives but who, after death, are no longer expected to exercise any direct influence on this-worldly affairs. Integrating bodily remains directly into these sorts of memorializing works of architecture (for instance, by building the monument directly over a grave), may occasionally provide an effective means of summoning the memory of a specific revered person. More often, however, actual physical remains are regarded as largely incidental—not because the bones and body parts are not available (as in the case of strictly mythical ancestors), but because, according to the culturally specific anthropologies working here, the essence of personhood is generally considered to lie somewhere in consciousness, in "the mind" as it were, rather than in the materiality of the body.

As a morphological possibility,[18] ritual-architectural commemorations that arise in relation to heavily rationalized notions of death and the dead usually have a decidedly museum-like or pedagogical, non-"magical" quality insofar as there is no expectation of initiating a dialogue with the dead, no great fear of the dead, little effort to placate the dead, and not even a strong sense of responsibility in meeting the expectations of the dead. The deceased in these cases are respected but remote; the gulf between life and death is especially wide; these are the most completely dormant of the dead. Though the honorees in these cases (like strictly imaginal ancestors) also qualify as mythicohistorical personages, the manipulations of mythologization transform those historical individuals into idealized (mythic) paradigms of some sort. These mythicohistoric dead often become (as noted earlier) foci for consolidating and personifying attributes of excellence in leadership and life, and thus, in the context of architectural memorials to them, may engender admiration and serve importantly as exemplary models.[19] But these fully dead deceased persons, quite unlike numerous of the undead that we will encounter momentarily, are not imagined as animated agents of any sort; and, since these fully dead do not do anything per se, their posthumous (non)existences require no architectural support. Ritual-architectural memorializing in these cases, again, quite obviously, serves the interests of the living rather than the dead.

More specifically, then, monuments to the fully dead, which have a particularly text-like character (very frequently complete with written commentaries), often acknowledge a group of deceased and a particular circumstance of collective death. Conspicuous examples include Holocaust museums, battlefield monuments commemorating the heroic demise of a specific battalion or company, and war memorials like the Washington, D.C., Vietnam Veterans Memorial, which is well distanced from both the actual place of death and the remains of the dead to which it alludes.

Also falling into that category of collective, bodiless commemoration are thousands of constructions like the monument overlooking the Gulf of Mexico from the port city of Veracruz, erected in 1987 to honor all of the sailors of the world who have offered their lives to the sea, or the perpetually burning flame on the bank of the Scioto River in Columbus, Ohio, which commemorates all the city's firemen who have died in the line of duty—neither of which is accompanied by any actual bodily remains. Though individuated apprehensions of such monuments are diverse in the extreme, and in these cases the sensations of nonintellectualized affect are often especially intense, nonetheless, the museumological incentives of remembering and learning about the (fully) dead are more prominent than those of placating or communicating with posthumously active presences. People usually visit these collective memorials in order to think about the deceased, but not to speak with them.

Even more often, such commemorations of the dead are individual-specific, though here the range of relevant possibilities widens further still. Frequently, the commemorative means are anthropomorphic and representational, relying on statues, busts, portraits, or photographs. Similarly common are nonanthropomorphic means, say, the exceedingly common practice of attaching individual names either to explicitly religious buildings, like chapels, or to less explicitly religious constructions, like stadiums, hospitals, bridges, streets, or plazas and parks. Parts of buildings—new additions, balconies, windows, furniture—are also very commonly dedicated to the memory of individuals whose physical remains are variously buried or disposed of elsewhere. Relevant exemplars of this sort of bodiless ritual-architectural memorializing are, in short, too numerous and too obvious to require additional elaboration.

Megalithic Embodiments of the Dead: The Transmutation of Ancestors into Stone

Other sorts of bodiless ritual-architectural memorializing of the dead are not nearly so obvious. Sometimes, in addition to reliances on architecture (and ritual) to facilitate a remembrance of the dead, or maybe to provide a locus for participatory imitation of the excellence of the mythicohistorical dead, there is a more intense and direct identification between the honored dead and the built forms. There is, in some contexts, an important sense in which built forms actually *are* the dead—though here as well the presence of bodily remains is (or may be) largely incidental.

Stonehenge and the other heavily studied megalithic monuments of Western Europe, and particularly Aubrey Burl's refreshingly eventful treatment of those notoriously controversial structures and their supposed ritual usages, provide an excellent point of departure into consideration of this morphological possibility wherein, sometimes, dead ancestors are actually identified with, or "transmutated" into, architectural, specifically stone constructions.[20] Entertaining the plausibility of numerous interpretive alternatives,[21] Burl nonetheless comes to the conclusion that far and away the most important incentive in the construction and use of these megalithic monuments was continued communication with deceased ancestors. In support of his interpretation, Burl proposes a roughly chronological, five-stage evolution. If suspect as an empirical historical reconstruction (a matter on which I will again abstain), Burl's scheme is, without question, morphologically provocative testimony to the complexity and heterogeneity of the relations between megaliths and the dead.

In brief, Burl considers that the original Paleolithic practice of simply burying the dead under the hearths of their cave domiciles (stage 1) was eventually supplanted in the Neolithic Age by family mortuary houses in the form of long earthen barrows (stage 2).[22] Gradually, in a third stage, the great megalithic mounds came to serve not only as tombs but also as temples or worship spaces, shrines where rituals were performed to honor the dead and ask for their assistance.[23] Eventually, however, in response to expanding ritual demands, chambered tombs and long mounds were abandoned entirely in favor of the famous stone circles and henges (stage 4). And then, in a fifth stage, the Bronze Age, a disenchantment with the efficacy of stone circles spawned three new sorts of ritual-architectural conceptions: monuments that more explicitly commemorated the passing of individual chieftains;[24] avenues of standing stones through which funeral processions could pass;[25] and low circular banks of rubble that served to enclose cremation cemeteries.[26]

In Burl's view (and in my idiom), there was, then, over time, both a dynamic play of competing ritual-architectural priorities and considerable fluctuation with respect to attitudes toward death and the dead. The very strong incentive to express and expedite those respective mortuary views via suitable built forms and ritual practices remained, however, quite constant. Burl argues, in other words, that all variations on British megaliths were essentially accoutrements of necromancy, so that every development in ancient European necrotic belief was echoed by, or reflected in, a ritual-architectural response. Thus, in his view, even the indubitable astronomical alignments of European megaliths, particularly lunar orientations, were primarily mechanisms for communicating with the dead.[27]

That portion of Burl's assessment—the primacy of ancestor worship in these contexts—is not particularly unusual. Writing in the 1920s, Gordon Childe came to the dour conclusion that, in megalithic culture, where "superstition absorbed all their energies," "the cult of the dead overshadowed all other activities."[28] And much more recently and more specifically, historian of religions Benjamin Ray, after paying careful attention to the complex developmental history of Stonehenge (and noting Burl's work), concludes that "the several configurations of Stonehenge do, in fact, suggest a single, underlying ritual function: the periodic coordination of solar and (possibly) lunar cycles with the remains of the dead."[29]

More specifically (and morphologically) interesting, however, is Burl's intimation that, where in certain of these funerary design solutions the facilitation of direct interaction with and preservation of bodily remains was paramount, in other "stages," most notably stone henges and circles, the materiality of human bodies was not nearly so important. In those cases—which much better instantiate the morphologic possibility of bodiless memorializations of deceased persons—it is more appropriate to imagine the megalithic architectural constructions as embodying, "transmutating," or "transubstantiating" the dead, rather than simply entombing the dead.

Intimations of that intriguing, though subtler, possibility are made more explicit and amplified in the work of other scholars. Robert Heine-Geldern, for example, considered that the megalithic monuments of Western and Northern Europe served, in a pervasive Neolithic cult of ancestors, as architectural manifestations of the human hope that one's person would be remembered, perhaps immortalized, through the agency of stone, a memory "fixed" in the rock.[30] Similarly, Mircea Eliade invoked his work on lithic symbolism to explain that, whereas the houses of Neolithic peasants in these contexts were modest and ephemeral, the dwellings for the dead were built of stone so as "to last forever."[31] For Eliade (and, he thinks, for Neolithic people), slabs of stone reveal duration without end, modalities existing independently of temporal being, which thereby constitute an inexhaustible reservoir of vitality and power. Thus, he contends that

> [in megalithic religions] the ideas of perenniality and of continuity between life and death are apprehended through the exaltation of the ancestors as identified with, or associated with, stones.[32]

Additionally, Lawrence Sullivan who, like Burl and Ray, wants to accentuate that the astronomical referencing of British megaliths was ultimately in the service of commemorations of the dead rather than some sort of prescientific collection of empirical sky data, contends that, in these cases,

> the meaning of the religious perception of the heavens is involved with the megalithic religious experience of the dead, of stone, of space ordered permanently in stone, of the Earth, and of fertility; for these are the realities brought together in megalithic material sites.[33]

Thus, while there is certain archaeological evidence of actual human remains in, at, and around Stonehenge and the other megalithic monuments, hermeneuts ought also to give serious consideration to the less obvious, but maybe more acute alternative that the dead were even more "present"—more "alive" and available for communication—in the actual stones themselves. In that case, the huge stones did not simply mark the spot of ancestral burials, say, in the manner of giant tombstones; nor would those constructions have been conceived primarily as some sort of posthumous housing for the (un)dead. More poignantly, and more significantly as a morphologically distinct variation on the ritual-architectural commemoration of the dead, in those instances the dead would have been more directly identified with or transubstantiated in the stones.[34] In an important sense, the architectural forms *are* the dead and, thus, at some point, the presence or absence of the actual bodily remains of the dead is not a matter of great moment.

Architectural Conquests of Death: Stone, Wood, Wax, and Other Embodiments of the Dead

Once again, then, architecture demonstrates its special status among the arts and among other vehicles of intelligibility, such as texts, speech, music, and dance. Monumental constructions particularly, by virtue of their size, stability, and apparent permanence, emerge as an especially—perhaps uniquely—suitable means of expressing and combatting human anxiety about death. In Henri Lefebvre's challengingly expansive terms:

> The most beautiful monuments are imposing in their durability. A cyclopean wall achieves monumental beauty because it seems eternal, because it seems to have escaped time. Monumentality transcends death, and hence what is sometimes called the 'death instinct.' As both appearance and reality, this transcendence embeds itself in the monument as its irreducible foundation; the lineaments of atemporality overwhelm anxiety, even—and indeed above all—in funerary monuments.[35]

Moreover, if massive scale and expressions of an "intense aversion to littleness" provide one particularly effective means of engendering sensations of durability and thus deathlessness,[36] it has traditionally been, of course, stone, as in the case of megalithic menhirs and dolmens, that, by its hardness and seeming invulnerability to the ravages of time, has provided the most prized building material. Eliade, who interprets so many religious phenomena as human strategies against a ubiquitary "terror of history" (a stance that implies, in other words, that different religions are in large part alternative solutions to existential anxieties about death), is only one of countless scholars to note the special power of rocks and stones to elude time and death, or at least to cultivate a sensation of atemporality (or transtemporality), and thus of deathless life. Artist and theorist Adrian Stokes, reflecting on the uniquely reciprocal complicity between the builders and stone, which he eloquently terms "stone-blossom," also observes that raw stone has a life of its own, a flower-like potential "to push itself forward," or "to bloom" in the hands of an artist.[37]

Furthermore, British megaliths are only the most spectacular of countless historical exemplifications of the conceptualization of (un)dead ancestors as residing, literally and permanently, in rocks and stones.[38] Mesoamericanist Doris Heyden notes a similar confidence among ancient Mexicans that their ancestors were embodied, and apparently living on, in rocks and stones. She writes that

> stone was worshiped in many parts of Mesoamerica, especially flint and obsidian, and some groups believed themselves to be the descendants of great rocks, the way others saw their primeval forebears as trees.[39]

Quiché Maya documents repeatedly allude to the stone that Nacxit (their name for Quetzalcoatl, the mythical plumed serpent) gave as a gift to those tribes when they departed the mythic city of Tulán Civán. This stone, "which the [Quiché] kings and the people worshipped [and which] they used in their incantations," was enshrined in the Great Edifice of Tohil in their capital city of Utatlán and guarded as the paramount symbol of authority and sovereignty because it was the tangible, pertinacious link to their revered and authenticating "Toltec" ancestry—as the *Popol Vuh* says, the "reminder of their fathers."[40]

India, as well, evinces the quest after the transephemeral via architecture in rock-cut temples that, whether scooped (cut-in) or monolithic (cut-out), are revered for their permanence.[41] According to I. W. Mabbett, Hindu shrines can be conceived, in a quite literal fashion, as the "live bodies" that house the souls of (un)dead ancestors:

> often [a Hindu shrine's] life is an embodiment of the soul of a real human being, a deceased chieftain, ruler, dignitary, or human sacrifice, for whom his new home is regarded as a lodging in exactly the same way as was his body during his life.[42]

Likewise affording stone a special prestige, in Japanese Shinto, rocks, often in conjunction with trees, were worshiped as deities and considered symbols of eternity.[43] And Cistercians similarly embrace strict, unadorned stone construction for their monasteries because of its unadulterated purity and precisely because of this connotation of temporal intransigence.[44] In all these very different historical situations, building and "making" in stone—perhaps epitomized best, but hardly uniquely, by hulking megaliths—become a prime architectural strategy for "conquering death," for keeping alive one's forebears and assuming continued relations with them by creating efficacious contexts for ritual dance, procession, and sacrifice.

Its clear suitability for expressing eternity notwithstanding, stone is not the only medium for the ritual-architectural embodiment of the dead. Among the Baoulés, along the Ivory Coast of Africa, the soul of the dead is apparently incorporated (or transubstantiated) in a wooden stool, "which captures the vital force when it escapes from the body."[45] Or, in other contexts, rather more obviously, death may be transcended and the dead transubstantiated in more anthropomorphically veristic paintings and statues. David Freedberg describes stunningly verisimilitudinous wax and papier-mâché images (*boti*) made from casts of living bodies and from the faces of the dead, which were installed by the hundreds in the Christian churches of Italy in the fifteenth and sixteenth centuries. These "living reconstitutions of the dead" eventually evolved more into tourist attractions than devotional contexts; yet, Freedberg opines that, even now, "we are arrested by these [incredibly lifelike wax] images at least partly out of fear that they might just come alive, just open their mouths, just begin to move."[46]

Moreover, Freedberg suggests that, in the wake of the woodcut, the printing press, and the consequent reproducibility of images, the unique prestige of stone was largely undermined:

> Away with the monuments of stone! We need them no longer. Because of the fact of reproduction, every image has become reality and is a witness of what is, what has been, and therefore what will always remain.[47]

We are, in fact, left with the somewhat disquieting possibility that, in stone's stead, photography (and now maybe some sort of computer-generated imaging) may currently provide the most expeditious medium for the transubstantiation of the dead. Roland Barthes, for instance, observed that "photography has something to do with resurrection," and, consequently, as Freedberg explains, Barthes actually sought for the replenishment of the "being of his mother" in his favorite photograph of her:

> Barthes loved the reality of the photograph because in it he saw the death of his mother transcended. In his gazing at it, she was not just restored; she existed again. . . . The picture is reality; it is not bad, or misleading, or deceiving, or even weak copy. . . .[48]

Bones and Burials: Assiduous Treatments and Accommodations of Bodily Remains

Besides these various transmutations of the dead into stone, wood, wax, photographs, or whatever, an even larger and more prominent set of manifestations of the ritual-architectural commemoration of the dead involves the meticulous treatment of the actual bodily remains of deceased people. Having emphasized that in certain situations the whereabouts of the physical human remains might actually be incidental to the ritual-architectural commemoration of the dead, I direct attention now to an even wider collection of more explicitly funerary alternatives in which the careful storage or containment of bones and body parts is absolutely crucial.

Chinese *feng shui* geomancy provides both a quintessential exemplar and an apt point of departure. The intensely detailed axiomatic stipulations of *feng shui* planning and design, as noted earlier with respect to one permutation of conventionalized architecture (priority I-B), depend upon the combined purgatives of a marvelously rich tradition of prognostication and numerology and the fundamental place of ancestor worship in traditional China.[49] In this view, the deceased—and specifically their osseous remains—continue to exercise enormous influence on the affairs of the living. There are, in fact, very dynamic and intricate relationships between the physical remains of the dead and the health and prosperity of their live descendants, relationships that are mediated via the flow and exercise of forces, or *ch'i,* variously described as vital natural energies, "cosmic breaths," or "local currents of cosmic breath."[50] According to one explanation:

> Every living body is a concentration of energy [or *ch'i*]. The energy condenses and forms bones. When a man dies, only the bones remain. Therefore it is a principle that a buried corpse can influence latently its descendants by returning the energy from the bones. . . .[51]

Moreover, also as noted earlier, built as well as natural features intrude upon this delicate equipoise of energies, so that any additional construction or alteration of the landscape constitutes both considerable danger and a potentially fortuitous opportunity. Accordingly, the first task of the Chinese geomancer, and the first priority in *feng shui* spatial planning, is to decipher or "diagnose" the topography of the potential site of a grave, a building, or a city. Then, having discerned the current status of the convoluted relations between *ch'i,* bones, and the living, the geomantic designer (in consultation with ritual and divination texts) must imagine and "prescribe" ways in which new architectural configurations, including burials, can not only respect and harmonize with currently prevailing energies, but also exploit the interactive, "umbilical" connections between living descendants and dead ancestors.[52] Success in strategic orientation with respect to bones (among other factors), whether at the scale of regions, villages, or, especially, individual domiciles, ought, then, to eventuate not only aesthetically pleasing designs, but also mitigations of illness, suffering, and anxiety.[53]

Obviously, this notion that the physical remains of ancestors—usually but not always bones[54]—play a very vital role in the lives of the not-yet-deceased is hardly unique to the Far East.[55] Furthermore, confidences that deceased persons, who are often conceived as anything but apathetic and inactive, continue to have energetic involvements in earthly affairs are invariably manifested in elaborate ritual-architectural solutions designed, in one way or another, to placate and accommodate those (un)dead. Though again the wide divergences and cultural-specificity of necrotic presuppositions complicate comparative matters enormously, some appreciation of the wealth of morphological possibilities may emerge from staccato consideration of a half dozen of the most promiment ways of conceiving of mortuary constructions: as domiciles; as resting places; as vehicles of transport, gates, or "crossing places"; as prisons; as palaces; and as memorials and museums.

Mortuary Domiciles: Pampering and Housing the (Un)Dead

In numerous tribal situations, upon the death of one member of a household, the entire remaining family will abandon their house to that dead individual; or, as in the case of the Fulani compounds of Bé in Cameroon, even if the deceased is actually buried in a different location, the living family members nonetheless feel compelled to move to a new dwelling, leaving the old structure to "die," decay, and eventually disappear.[56] Among the Navajo, for instance, Paul Oliver notes that the domicile hogan, by virtue of its intense cosmo-socio-spatial layout, is not only "the symbol of life" that is "at the heart of much of the people's spiritual and behavioural values," but also a built expression of their attitudes toward death: "when an occupant dies the body is taken out through an opening made in the north wall, and the hogan is abandoned and allowed to collapse; with death the spirit and material of the hogan rejoin the earth."[57]

In many other situations, though, connoting perhaps the most elemental of ritual-architectural commemorations of the dead, family members who die are simply interred in their own houses, after which the living and the deceased continue to share the same dwelling: both ancient Greeks and Romans, among countless examples, buried their dead beneath stone floors of their homes, until hygienic considerations prevailed.[58] More common still, and apparently indicative of an even stronger sense of continuity between earthly and afterlives, are those situations in which the dead repair to specially built "house-tombs," which are essentially replicas of their former residences. Such funerary domiciles are designed, in other words, so that the (un)dead are able to carry on their posthumous affairs much as they had before. Assyro-Babylonian literatures, for instance, refer to graves variously as "the house of shades," "the house of dust," or "the house from which he who enters does not leave"; and, Michel Ragon observes in the context of his exceedingly rich study of the architectural spaces of death that "Indeed the Assyro-Babylonian burial places are conceived as veritable houses in which the dead man is supposed to go on living."[59]

Even more famously, the Etruscan tomb was also "a veritable underground house, with its own door and a staircase, or a corridor sloping down to an apartment";[60] not surprisingly, then, when Pál Kelemen was struck by the accoutrements of domesticity included in the pre-Columbian Zapotecan tombs of Oaxaca, Mexico, he compared them explicitly to the Etruscan graves of Tuscany and Umbria.[61] Similarly, the pagan Gallo-Romans, according to Ragon, "believed that death was merely a continuation of life and that the only change would be in one's way of life, that it was a kind of removal from one residence to another"; they too imagined that "one lived in the tomb as in another residence."[62] Consequently, in that context, people were buried with all of the domestic supplies and household utensils required to carry on their routine affairs: "[the] dead were served with food and drink, in the same dishes and the same jugs. And children were buried with their small furniture."[63]

In other contexts, whole cities were constructed to facilitate the lifelike activities of the (un)dead, with grid plans that corresponded exactly to the layout of the cities of the living. The immense necropoles of forty to fifty thousand tomb-houses in Bosnia and Herzegovina, for instance, constituted much more dense populations than the present-day villages in that area.[64] And at Thebes, a vast necropolis some two and a half miles long, likewise included dwellings for the enormous staff of live workers whose sole function was to serve and protect the (un)dead citizenry.[65]

Mortuary Refuges: *Tomb Wombs, Final Resting Places, and Places of Waiting*

Where somewhat less continuity between life and death is imagined, rather than indulging the continuing domestic needs of the (un)dead, tombs provide a place for the deceased simply to sleep quietly and unaccosted, without, however, involving themselves in the daily affairs of the living. Claude Lévi-Strauss, for instance, observes that:

> Some societies let their dead rest; provided homage is paid to them periodically, the dead refrain from troubling the living. . . . It is as if a contract had been concluded between the dead and the living; in return for being treated with a reasonable degree of respect, the dead remain in their own abode, and the temporary meetings between the two groups are always governed by concern for the interests of the living.[66]

Often then, to insure that the dead are not wandering homeless, tombs and burials provide a permanent, peaceful refuge. Moreover, particularly where human beings are considered as autochthonous (that is, born out of the earth or created out of dirt or clay), inhumation in the earth or burial in caves (or in built structures that patently resemble caves) provide ritual-architectural strategies for completing the eternal cycle of life and death by returning bodies whence they came. Contradistinct, in other words, to the notion of "fixing" the dead in stone, presumably so that they might maintain an eternal earthly presence, cave burials and flat, modestly marked graves in the earth seem to be design solutions born of a more direct, maybe more humble acceptance of the transience of earthly life and of some variation on the circular cosmological notion of ashes to ashes, dust to dust.

Providing this sort of final resting place, and thus effecting a kind of closure to the life cycle, the womb-like entrance to the burial chamber at Hagar Qim, Malta, among many examples of architectural grottos, was sealed with a portable slab, "which increased the temple's resemblance to a cave, natural or man-made."[67] The cave-burials of the Greeks, the famous catacombs in Rome, and the countless crypts in the Christian churches of Europe have all likewise been interpreted as (maybe latent) reflections of an abiding fascination with the earth as "universal uterus" from which people are, in some sense, born and then ultimately return.[68] Moreover, the enduring notion of funerary gardens, the continuing concern of contemporary planners to integrate cemeteries into the natural environment, and even the practice of laying flowers at burials have all, not implausibly, been linked with the "vegetal setting of death," that is, with a need to close, via specific ritual-architectural practices, the cycle of life and death by returning dead bodies back to nature and to the earth.[69]

In other situations, however, the pervasive notion that death is simply a kind of sleep, from which the dead will eventually awaken into a different and presumably even more real sort of "life" that is eternal, requires that burial places provide a temporary rather than final and permanent place of repose. Tombs and burials may, then, be variously conceived as temporary abodes, places of waiting, or, crudely stated, holding pens. Generally speaking, for Jews, Christians, and Muslims, for instance, the tomb has been considered only a transitional, provisional resting place where the body sleeps until resurrection (or condemnation, as the case may be). Martin Luther, for example, reviving the belief of the primitive church that death was merely a "deep, untroubled sleep" prior to the resurrection of the body, thus considered the grave a "bed of repose."[70]

Funerary Vehicles of Transport, Gates, and Crossing Places for the Dead and the Living

Closely related to the conception of graves as transitional places is the similarly pervasive notion that a burial provides a kind of ford, or "crossing place," or a gate or antechamber, through which the dead make their passage to the otherworld. The Egyptian *Book of the Dead,* among many relevant exemplars, details the funerary constructions and rituals that will guarantee a "happy crossing" to the other side.[71] Reflecting even more vividly this notion of a posthumous passage that requires some ritual-architectural support is the conception of the crypt itself as the vehicle of transport that facilitates the "final passage" or "last journey" of the dead, most typically, across a perilous swamp or river: Polynesians, for instance, used floating tombs; on Madagascar, prior to the eighteenth century, kings were buried in wooden canoes; the ancient Egyptians gave coffins the shape of boats;[72] and the Saxon ship-burials of the Vikings similarly suggest some sort of architectonic transport to the otherworld.[73]

Another, significantly different variation on the notion of the tomb as a place of transition or ritual-architectural "crossing place" comes in those burial constructions that are understood not only to facilitate the passage of the dead to some other world, but to provide the living also with an opening to transcendent realms or, if you will, "a springboard for access into the other world."[74] In this very common conception, burial places work in much the same way that Eliade describes the prestige and allure of "centers" and *axis mundis* as "points of ontological transition";[75] that is to say, burials of this sort are regarded as uniquely privileged points of entry and accessibility, thresholds or openings through which access from the earthly plane to heavenly and netherworlds, impossible in ordinarily peripheral places, becomes possible, perhaps even unavoidable—and perhaps for live persons as well as dead ones.

More specifically, burial mounds are, on occasion (usually in relation to homologized notions of space [priority I-A]), conceived as architectonic reconstructions of a primeval mountain: the primordial source from which all life arises, as in Egypt; or the center of the world, as in China. Or, in countless situations, notably in the pre-Columbian Americas, burials and dedicatory caches that include substantial quantities of human remains along with masks, food, figurines, vessels, musical instruments, weapons, ornaments, and other "gifts to the gods" were regularly emplaced within major cosmogrammatically referenced monuments not only on the occasion of the original construction but with each substantial remodeling. Paying special attention to "the religious significance of the gifts [of the Mexica]," archaeologist Leonardo López Luján has recently made an intensive study of over one hundred distinct offerings, nearly all of which included human skulls and bones, that were recovered in the various stages and structures of the sacred precinct of the Aztecs' Templo Mayor.[76] And Michael Coe, among others, has made the interesting observation that the pre-Columbian Maya also not infrequently used their monumental constructions as "burial grounds" insofar as they often excavated new graves into much older substructures.[77]

Storing and preserving bodily remains in such contexts serves both to confirm and, in some cases, to enhance greatly the cosmological prestige of those sites as gaps and passageways into (or for communication into) other higher and lower orders of reality.[78] The presence of skulls and bones amplifies and intensifies a monument's status as a cosmomagical center. Thus, in their redoubled significance, such places come to serve as ports of entry for the dead to travel to their more permanent cosmic destinations, and, often more importantly, those places also provide propitious sites for the living to interact with other-than-earthly powers and entities. Stressing this possibility of accessibility to the transcendent via mortal remains, Ragon challenges the conventional wisdom that the Egyptian pyramids were "houses of the dead" and that the mummified corpses were intended to forestall the putrefaction of the body (in which case they would instantiate the suboption of funerary domiciles, just discussed) and contends instead that Egyptian graves were primarily "a sort of apparatus for communicating with the beyond." In his view, "The Egyptian tombs . . . were merely a receiver, a medium, intended to receive psychic radiation from the beyond" and "The mummy was merely a pivot intended to trap the 'astral body'" (or the psychic double).[79]

This prevalent confidence that human remains and burial sites, even when they are not conceived as the "center of the world," provide uniquely opportune contexts for communicating with otherworldly realms is also evidenced among the Greeks, who actually slept in tombs "in order to dream of the dead and to question them."[80] Additionally, the exceedingly widespread practice of burying church leaders and especially martyrs near or inside Christian churches was typically understood to benefit the living as well as the honored dead by holding open the channels of communication between earthly and heavenly realms; thus, in that tradition, pilgrims journey to reliquaries and mausoleum-churches with the expectation that their petitions, whether directly relevant to the specific individuals inhumed there or not, should nonetheless be made more effective simply by the proximity of the dead.

Buddhist pilgrims likewise consider that the efficacy of their offerings and meditations is enhanced immeasurably by journeying to a stupa (or, in Tibet, a *chorten*), where relics of the Buddha and his disciples are enshrined (though, somewhat paradoxically, even where these monuments are constructed as cenotaphs, that is, empty graves without bodily remains, they nevertheless provide efficacious points of contact between the sacred and profane).[81] And, in Hinduism, traditionally among the most effective means of accumulating religious merit is pilgrimage to those *tirtha*s (that is, "sacred fords" or "crossing places") that are specifically suited to the performance of rites for the deceased; in the assessment of Surinder Mohan Bhardwaj, the most important of these Hindu sacrifices to the dead is the *sraddha*, and perhaps the most desirable *tirtha* for its performance is Gaya.[82]

Mortuary Prisons and Places of Confinement: Policing and Incarcerating the (Un)Dead

Providing a kind of inverse to this notion of ritual-architectural crossing places of extraordinary access between ontological realms is the conception of tombs as prisons or as places of confinement. In these cases, incentives to venerate the dead are tempered, sometimes superseded, by a fear of the dead. Whether death and the dead are conceived as a source of pollution or some other jeopardous malady, often there is a sense of urgency that the worlds of the dead and the living ought to remain as wholly separate from one another as possible. In many situations, then, the first priority in funerary architecture is to establish and enforce strict boundaries between the terrestrial and subterranean (or superterranean) realms, and thus to insure proper disposal of the dead so that they do not "come back" and harm the living.

Michel Ragon provides several graphically relevant examples of acute antagonism between the living and the dead: Greeks who mutilated their dead enemies to prevent them from taking revenge; Chinese who were vastly outnumbered by a population of dead that "dominated and terrorized" them; and Tibetan lamas who feared that the souls of the dead pursued both people and animals to rob them of their "vital breath."[83] In each of these contexts, Ragon explains how burial strategies were designed to police and to incarcerate the dead. Thus where, in some situations, a heavy stone over a tomb may symbolize eternity and closure as the deceased repair to a womb-cave to complete their journey "from dust to dust," ponderous grave constructions in these cases seem to have been born more of an incentive to entrap the dead and to prevent still-threatening corpses from rising and "getting away."[84]

The Assyro-Babylonian burial place (as noted above) was a house where the dead kept on living, but it was also, invariably, "a house-prison, a house intended to make the dead man disappear and to prevent his return."[85] And, perhaps most famous in this regard, the massiveness of tombs in Haiti, besides insuring their permanence, guarantees an appropriately restricted interaction between the living and the dead; in Moholy-Nagy's phrasing, "not only can the ancestor not take flight, shirking his protective duties, but also no voodoo charm cast by malice can penetrate this 'castle.'"[86]

Mortuary Palaces: Facilitating Posthumous Exercises of Authority

In addition to all these strategies for sheltering, shipping, visiting, and incarcerating deceased persons, we ought also to take note of those many circumstances in which ritual-architectural priorities for commemorating the dead (II-D) merge even more thoroughly with those of the commemoration of politics (II-C). Far more often than not, the privileges and privations of social hierarchy are considered to persist beyond death. Sovereigns of high rank in this world are afforded similar prestige in death, and thus indulged with tombs and burial spaces that are not only sumptuous residences and/or memorials, but, in effect, palaces from which they might continue their postmortem reign over the living and where their vassals might continue to pay them homage.

Most famously, Egyptian pyramids are routinely explained as constructions designed to cater to the pharaoh's posthumous exercise of authority. In fact, implying that these kings were considered more potent in death than in life, scholars have contended that, in ancient Egypt, "kings were ritually murdered in their prime lest, in their declining years, their lessening vigor cause a sympathetic lessening of the kingdom's strength."[87] Whether death actually enhanced the pharaoh's status is debatable, but the pyramid of Djoser (Zoser), for instance, complete with two eye-level holes in the wall—the mummified pharaoh's "windows on the world"—was most probably built to provide a context for the jubilee ceremony (or *heb-sed*) whereby the deceased king retained his vigor and influence over the affairs of the living.[88] Or, similarly, the Egyptian tomb of Seti I, at Abydos, has been described as "a subterranean palace in which the pharaoh could transform his coffin into a throne and preside over the assembly of his vassals and attendants, walled up at the same time as himself."[89]

Evincing the same ironic notion that the prestige and worldly participation of the king were actually enhanced rather than terminated by death, the ancient Peruvians also went to spectacular lengths to keep their dead sovereigns "alive." In addition to the remarkably skilled embalment of Inca lords—"some of the [mummified] bodies lasted this way for two hundred years"[90]—more fascinating still is Father Cobo's account of how "during their lifetimes, all of the kings and lords of the Inca class were in the habit of each making a statue that depicted its owner."[91] These statues were greatly venerated not only as the lord's "brother" (*guauque*) but as a kind of double that family members were instructed to treat as if it were the lord himself. Consequently, during his lifetime each Inca would build houses and assign servants to his respective *guauque,* and then, after the lord's death, the family was to continue dressing and feeding the *guauque,* bringing it out for all solemn festivals—in short, treating the *guauque* in every way as if it were alive and still carrying on its rule.[92]

More provocative testimony to the perpetuating postmortem authority of deceased kings comes in the Temple of the Inscriptions at Palenque, an enormous pyramid and "funerary temple" built over the meticulously preserved bodily remains of the seventh-century Maya Lord Pacal.[93] The raft of alternative interpretations of this much-discussed pyramid-temple-tomb would actually (and not necessarily inappropriately) bring to the fore not only several variations on the ritual-architectural commemoration of sacred history and politics (priorities II-B and II-C), but also virtually every permutation of the commemoration of the dead.[94] In the context of the present discussion of the morphological possibility of posthumous exercises of religiopolitical control, however, it is particularly notable, first, that Pacal's sumptuous sarcophagus, which has been described as "a small cosmic house inside a large cosmic model," was equipped with all the royal accoutrements and retainers due an active king.[95] Moreover, according to John Carlson's hypothesis, both the strategic placement of the "bone element" in the iconography of the sarcophagus lid and the "psychoduct" (a hollow stone tube that runs from Pacal's subterranean crypt up to the temple floor) were artistic-architectural contrivances designed to enable the (un)dead king to send posthumous guidance or, perhaps, in the manner of the *ch'i* forces of *feng shui,* to channel the "life, breath, and soul" of Pacal to the living.[96]

It may be difficult to imagine that even after his death Lord Pacal actually continued to hold court in the Temple of the Inscriptions and to exercise control in Palenque's ongoing political process (as Egyptian and Inca kings supposedly did); it is, however, much easier to appreciate how the presence of his carefully preserved remains, together with the etiological iconography, worked to punctuate the clear and legitimate line of succession from the entombed king to his living progeny. This dual purgative for honoring a dead ancestral sovereign and at the same time exploiting him to legitimate the temporal authority of his living, breathing descendants—a tension that is probably at work in virtually all ritual-architectural commemorations of deceased rulers—likewise seems to animate the stupendous tombs of Monte Albán and Mitla in the Zapotec-Mixtec region of Oaxaca. In the Oaxacan cases, not only are the bodily remains of esteemed rulers preserved in elaborately decorated masonry vaults that form the foundations of the temples (that is, the part of those structures that Kelemen compared to the house-like Etruscan tombs),[97] but stone sculptures apparently representing those same deceased lords were displayed, as it were, upstairs in the temples' worship spaces.[98]

This practice of both burying the dead in the substructure and exhibiting stone effigies of them in the superstructure of the same construction, which is what seems to be happening in the Oaxaca tombs, is morphologically interesting insofar as it represents, among other things, a juxtaposition of two principal manifestations of the commemoration of the dead: the reverential treatment of the actual royal remains and the transmutation of ancestors into stone, in this case into statues, or "idols." Moreover, via this kind of redundant commemorative strategy, even if the deceased sovereigns do not actually continue their active rulership (and one ought to exercise some suspicion about that even in the infamous Egyptian and Inca cases), the vivid display of genealogical continuity with their now-dead forebears provides a silent sanction that adds immeasurably to the legitimacy of those presently in power.

Funerary Memorials and Museums: Rationalizations, Ethical Examples, and Identity Constructions

Of course, many funerary practices, say of the ash-scattering sort, have no strictly architectural components. Moreover, not infrequently, the winning priorities in funerary architecture would seem to be pragmatic concerns for the preservation of space and hygiene: The catacombs of Rome, for instance, despite their possible conception as "earth-wombs," and notwithstanding romantic stories of their use as refuges from persecution, emerge from Fabrizio Mancinelli's rather more prosaic account as the largely utilitarian solution of Christians and Jews to the problem caused by a preference for burial rather than cremation that was made increasingly difficult in a city where space was limited and suburban land costly.[99] In that case, then, popular accounts of early Christians huddled in these subterranean tombs in order to worship surreptitiously and avoid the harassment of Roman authorities constitute primarily creative "revalorative" architectural apprehensions, which may serve to inspire subsequent generations of believers but are much less reliable as historical explanations.

Furthermore, sometimes, as among Cistercians, the veneration and visitation of the bodily remains of saintly and heroic individuals are actively discouraged. Thomas Merton explains, for example, that:

> When [in the Middle Ages] some of the Cistercian saints began to acquire reputations that attracted pilgrims to their tombs, the monks walled up the doors that gave access to their places of burial and suppressed the accounts of their miracles.[100]

In other cases, where especially rationalized attitudes toward the status and disposal of nonliving bodies obtain, exerting oneself to indulge or even memorialize the dead is regarded as a completely wrongheaded proposition. Compte de Volney, for instance, upon traveling from France to visit the pyramids of Egypt in 1783–85, was thoroughly repulsed and even saddened by their distribution of ritual-architectural priorities. In Volney's impassioned assessment:

> It is pitiful to think that in order to construct a vain tomb, an entire nation had to be tormented for twenty years; one shudders at the thought of all the injustices and vexations it must have cost to transport, to cut, and to pile up so much material. One feels indignation against the extravagance of the despots who ordered such barbaric works. . . .[101]

Often then, particularly in the context of modernist, Protestant and/or "secular humanist" orientations, we observe sentiments to the effect that "Death is no longer an event to be celebrated by major ceremonial, the grave no longer a place to be marked by substantial architectural or sculptural monuments."[102] Where rationalized splits of mind and body prevail, notions that a person's essence or life force might persist in his or her bodily remains are largely untenable. Funerals and cemeteries, then, may provide contexts in which the accomplishments and character of the dead are acknowledged and remembered, and perhaps some poignant ethical examples or life lessons are extracted from his or her biography; and such occasions may thus advance important historiographic, pedagogical, and maybe grieving purposes. But the incentive to serve the supposed needs of the deceased at the expense of those of the living is regarded as variously pointless, perverted, and probably pernicious. From this modernist perspective, which brings us full circle in this morphological survey to the sorts of bodiless memorializing with which I began, once again the actual presence of bones and body parts is (ostensibly anyway) largely incidental, reduced now to a quaintly anachronistic vestige of former beliefs in the more literal animation of bodily remains. Burial constructions and practices, in this rationalized frame, ought to be tailored solely to the requirements of the living.

Nonetheless, even in presumably secularized ambiences, complete indifference with respect to the handling and preservation of bodily remains appears to be another of those intriguing morphological possibilities in which, aside from isolated cases, few if any empirical, historical exemplars actually participate fully. Even where seemingly strictly pragmatic and rationalized parameters dominate—that is, where the priorities of the living unapologetically supersede those of the dead and where there is little or no expectation that deceased persons will continue to play a direct and active role in the affairs of this world—nevertheless, more extramundane, less palpable concerns invariably intrude, in which case ritual-architectural commemorations of the dead may take on the character of memorials or, at times, museums.

Among the most vehement and violent rejections of the notion of architecturally accommodating the (un)dead, and particularly of the practice of indulging kingly cadavers and thus posthumously perpetuating their social prestige, occurs during the French Revolution. In that context, earlier commitments to eulogize wealthy and powerful individuals with suitably grand burials were flatly rejected—reversed in fact—in favor of an even more fierce, frenzied insistence upon "the equality of the dead," which manifested itself in "a posthumous massacre of kings, queens, princes, and princesses."[103] The sumptuous burial places in the royal abbey of Saint-Denis, among many others, were thoroughly trashed, and the remains of the once-honored dead dragged from their privileged repose and irreverently pitched into common graves.

Extending this "rationalization of space" and the "secularization of cemeteries" further still, in 1864, Baron Haussmann made a grandiose proposal to expedite burial and free up much-needed space in Paris by eliminating all the graveyards within the city and deporting the dead by rail to a huge outlying cemetery at Méry-sur-Oise. As Haussmann explained:

> The transportation of the coffins would be carried out by special trains using the same equipment as the ordinary trains. . . . Every day, trains, whose number, composition, and service would be fixed according to the recognized requirements of the population, would take visitors to the Great Necropolis.[104]

In this way, space would be saved, the health hazards of decaying corpses mitigated, and the funerary business could be run as expeditiously as any other commercial enterprise. To Haussmann's considerable surprise, however, presumably enlightened Parisians flatly rejected his eminently practical proposal. He was criticized as "an Anglophile Protestant," and Léon Vafflard, funeral contractor for the city of Paris, declared that while, in England, "the body seems to be regarded as a parcel, which one is in a hurry to get rid of and which the entire population sees pass by without paying the slightest attention," that sort of glib necrotic warehousing would never suffice in France.

Thus, as Ragon explains, after seemingly showing no interest in their burials for years and, in fact, leveling all signs of the perpetuity of social hierarchy in death, Parisians nonetheless abhorred any tampering with their cemeteries. This indignation, however, not surprisingly, continued to reflect the priority of the living over the dead. That is to say, the cemeteries were apparently cherished at this point, not because they provided the (un)dead a comfortable posthumous accommodation or because human bones opened a crossing place into alternative orders of reality, but because those cemeteries provided the living with a sense of history or perhaps national identity. As Ragon writes:

> Parisians now regarded their cemeteries as museums. They refused to let anyone lay a finger on them. . . . And the three Paris cemeteries of the nineteenth century, contravening laws still in force, stayed where they were, becoming more and more like museums.[105]

Closing Thoughts: Timeless and Time-Bound Architectures of the Dead

The range of alternative manifestations of the ritual-architectural commemoration of the dead (priority II-D) is, in sum, dizzying. Partial coverage is achieved via the three-step consideration of bodiless memorializations and remembrances of the dead, transmutations or embodiments of the dead, and then strategic accommodations of bodily remains; but here, perhaps more than for any other of the framework's categories, admissions of the inadequacy and provisional status of this arrangement of morphological options are in order. Nevertheless, four pertinent points of clarification and methodological recommendation may provide a measure of closure.

First, hermeneuts ought to remember that where the careful architectural preservation or containment of bodily remains provides virtually certain evidence of the exercise of this priority, the absence of bodily remains is much less certain evidence of its irrelevance. Tombs, burials, charnel houses, sarcophagi, and mausoleums are the most obvious expressions of a reliance on building and built forms in response to anxieties about death and dying, but very often the commemoration of the dead proceeds irrespective of bodily remains.

Sometimes, as in the case of Dogon houses and sanctuaries, the deceased honorees are mythical ancestors, "the dead that never lived," who thus have no bodily remains. Sometimes, as in relation to modern Western anthropological presuppositions, personhood is sufficiently disconnected from one's physical human body that bodily remains may be regarded as largely incidental to the respectful remembrance and commemoration of the dead. And the phenomenon of megaliths, which raises the possibility of re-embodying or transmutating the dead into stone forms and constructions (or other media), arguably presents another sort of pervasive strategy for memorializing the dead largely irrespective of human remains. Moreover, sometimes, as in the case of the Tamberma funeral performances, the most important dimensions of the ritual-architectural commemorations of the dead are neither bodily remains nor built forms, but performative gestures and movements.[106] In short, we ought not be lulled into concentrating too exclusively on the preservational status of bones and body parts.

The second point, which bears on the twofold pattern of ritual-architectural events, is an acknowledgment (too little emphasized in this short discussion) that commemorations of the dead, far more often and more effectively than any of the other three sorts of commemorative priorities, can also serve as largely nonsubstantive strategies of allurement. That is to say, memorializations of the dead can, on the one hand, belong to the back half of the ritual-architectural situation insofar as they entail articulations of specific information and obligations in ways that are parallel to, and often complementary with, commemorations of divinity (II-A), sacred history (II-B), and especially politics (II-C). As noted, allusions to the dead are, for instance, often inextricable from ritual-architectural remembrances of mythicohistorical individuals and glorifications of specific individual rulers. But, in many other situations, the presence of human remains or architectural embodiments of ancestors actually functions much more like the orientational, instigative priorities of homology (I-A) and especially convention (I-B), which typically manifest themselves in the front half of the architectural situation. In those circumstances, allusions to the dead work primarily to sanctify, legitimate, and enhance the respectability and credibility of the ensuing occasion, encouraging beholders to take seriously what transpires in that context. Often, the emplacements of bodily remains—in the vaults of saints beneath Christian churches, in the caches entombed in nearly every Mesoamerican pyramid, or in the graves of soldiers at war memorials—operate more like a strategy of allurement than an expression of content-specific information.

On many occasions, such as a rountine Sunday mass in the Cuernavaca cathedral, there will be no direct mention at all of the martyrs or ecclesiastical leaders who are buried immediately within the ritual context. Those commemorations of the dead contribute little or nothing to the substantive content of that occasion; they supply no challenging new information, as one now should associate with the back half of a ritual-architectural event. But the presence of those relics and remains do nonetheless work in an important, if indirect, fashion to make the service more august and more compelling, more effective and probably more affective. When Zapotecan or Maya sovereigns delivered their religiopolitical policy statements from atop constructions in or beneath which their predecessors were buried, those funerary configurations served in that sort of ancillary, alluring role, not unlike other homologized and conventionalized features, to make the occasion convincing and powerful. Or, when an American president selects Arlington Cemetery or the Vietnam Veterans Memorial as the site from which to speak, most often the dead, though probably acknowledged in those cases, are nonetheless serving primarily as the backdrop, the conservative, alluring dimension of the ritual-architectural situation that legitimates, enhances, and adds force to the viability of some new proposal or expenditure that is being announced. In short, it is not surprising that there has so often been competition and intrigue over the ownership and control of bones and relics; nor can such preoccupations be passed off as the morbid, vestigial superstitions of archaic and medieval mentalities. Particularly in highly politicized events, demonstrations of affiliation with the dead have been, and continue to be, among the most persuasive of ritual-architectural instigatorial devices.

The third and fourth points, the former having to do with "the special case of architecture" and the latter bearing again on "the superabundance of architecture," are essentially inverses of one another. Here, hermeneuts ought to recall, in the first respect, that architecture's special status among the arts—most saliently in this venue its solidity and apparent imperishablity—makes building, particularly in stone, an especially suitable response to the phenomena of death and dying. Monumental architecture, as numerous theorists and historians have noticed, has an apparently singular capacity for the expression of eternity, or at least for fostering an illusion of escape from or supersession of time and, thus, in Eliade's terms, for assuaging the "terror of history."

Henri Lefebvre, for instance (as noted earlier), maintains that "Monumentality transcends death, and hence what is sometimes called the 'death instinct.'"[107] Invoking the example of the renowned Empress's Tomb in the Taj Mahal, which was built by Shah Jahan both as a tribute to his beloved wife and to alleviate his own sorrow at her premature passing, Lefebvre goes on to make the apposite observation that "Every bit as much as a poem or a tragedy, a monument transmutes the fear of the passage of time, and anxiety about death, into splendour."[108] Though in general agreement with Lefebvre, I could object with respect to this third point of clarification that his commendation of architecture's capability for confronting (or maybe deflecting) the challenge of death is actually too conservative, too understated. I would venture that architecture succeeds in mitigating anxiety about death, not simply "every bit as much" as literature or, for that matter, as painting, music, or dance, but much more effectively. As countless, endurant cross-cultural historical exemplars from British megaliths to Egyptian pyramids and Hindu rock-cut temples would attest, architecture connotes endlessness and imperishability—in a sense, deathlessness—like no other art.

But, on the other hand—and this is the final point of clarification—Lefebvre is helpful in providing the following qualification of his claims concerning the estimable ability of architecture, specifically that of a monumental sort, to effect conquests of time and death:

> Monumental 'durability' is unable, however, to achieve a complete illusion. To put it in what pass for modern terms, its credibility is never total. It replaces a brutal reality with a materially realized appearance; reality is changed into appearance.[109]

The deathlessness of architecture is, Lefebvre suggests, an illusion that, albeit compelling, cannot be sustained indefinitely. Or, to phrase it more in the idiom of this Gadamerian hermeneutics, architecture's seeming timelessness avails it of no exception from its full existence in time and history. Though monumental built forms nearly always far outlast their human creators, and thus to that extent transcend artistic intentions and specific historical contexts, the *apprehensions* of those forms (which is, after all, where our hermeneutical gaze ought to be trained) are fully situated in specific historical contexts. Again with respect to commemorations of the dead, the paired superabundant autonomy of sacred architecture and the eventfulness of specific apprehensions of architecture assert themselves in decisive ways.

In other words, as the radically subversive expropriation of burial monuments during the French Revolution ought to remind us, funerary architecture actually intensifies rather than freezes or flattens the potential for revalorization that resides in virtually all substantial works of architecture. The meanings of monuments and buildings that are expressly designed to memorialize the dead are not more stable or "timeless" than those of other constructions. In fact, because such explicitly commemorative forms often have such long reception careers, and because they so often evoke especially intensified, personalistic emotional responses, the succession of actual receptions engendered by architectural configurations that are originally built to and for the dead is particularly heterogeneous and idiosyncratically variable. While the physicality of architectural commemorations of the dead may be uniquely durable, the same claim to stability and constancy cannot be made for the perceptions of those physical forms.

Irrespective of the original intentions and cosmological presuppositions of their builders, the spectacular pyramid-tombs of Egypt, for instance, eventually evoked revulsion rather than respect; the grand commemorative tombs of Saint-Denis eventually became symbols of social repression; and the cemeteries of Paris, beyond simply accommodating the otherworldly existences of dead individuals, became politicized pawns in a struggle of the living for national identity. Likewise telling (though not unusual) are self-conscious observations like that of Jacques Maquet when his contemplative apprehension of the tomb of Napoleon in the Paris church of Saint-Louis issued in an exceptionally powerful sensation of "life as an overwhelming force" that, to his initial surprise, seemed to have nothing to do with the French general and emperor; in Maquet's muse, "Looking at Napoleon's tomb, I had forgotten Napoleon."[110] So too, Stonehenge, Palenque's Temple of the Inscriptions, and the Taj Mahal, all thriving tourist destinations at this point, now engender a spray of sometimes forceful, sometimes frivolous sensations that reflect very strongly the preoccupations of travelers and scholars but only faintly, if at all, the original dedicatory intentions of those ritual-architectural commemorations of the dead.

Funerary monuments, therefore, provide an apt and summational closing to this four-chapter inventory of sacred architecture's relative strengths and limitations as a communicator of substantive messages and meanings. Monuments to the dead reconfirm that, where architecture may seem to enjoy some singular status in facilitating extrications from history and escapes from time and death, any emancipation from sociohistorical context is figmental, a mirage of sorts. No more than the other arts, no more, for instance, than the famously ephemeral expressions of improvisational jazz or sand paintings, can architecture—or, properly speaking, *specific empirical apprehensions* of architecture—claim an exemption from the situatedness and impingements of sociohistorical contexts. The specific prejudices, interests, and contingencies of particularistic historical ambiences, the decisive hermeneutical force of preunderstandings, intrude no less strongly on dialogical experiences of architecture than on any other genre. In fact, the purgative for permanence, which is so characteristic of architectural commemorations of the dead, has actually eventuated, albeit inadvertently, in a spectacular fund of monuments that demonstrate in particularly piquant terms the mechanisms of ritual-architectural superabundance and revalorization with which the present project is so much concerned.

In the end, the situated, interested, and revalorative apprehensions that punctuate the convoluted and on-going ritual-architectural reception careers of these infamous funerary monuments—the strategic ways in which contemporary persons interrogate these monuments so that they will speak to their contemporary concerns—reconfirm the unoriginal insight that architectures of the dead are primarily for the living. In the end, the timeboundedness of sacred architecture supersedes its apparent timelessness.

Part Three | Architecture as Ritual Context: The Presentation of Ritual-Architectural Events

Moulding clay into a vessel, we find the utility in its hollowness;
Cutting doors and windows for a house, we find the utility in its
empty space.
Therefore, the being of things is profitable, the non-being of things
is serviceable.

Lao-tzu, *Tao-te-ching*[1]

It was for the performance of liturgy that any church was ever built.

Staale Sinding-Larsen, 1984[2]

The essence of construction lies neither in piling up layers of building materials nor in ordering them according to a plan, but solely in the fact that when we set up a new space another atmosphere opens up, precisely through what is set up.

Mark Wigley, 1993[3]

THE MENDICANT ORDERS EMERGE from Wolfgang Braunfels's survey of European monastic architecture as something of a special case. Committed to peregrination rather than building, originally neither Saint Francis nor Saint Dominic reflected particularly upon the layouts of their houses, nor did the question possess any great importance in the eyes of their immediate successors. Braunfels explains that, consequently:

> The fruit of this casualness toward what they considered superficial was the adoption [by Franciscans and Dominicans] of the traditional Benedictine scheme for all their establishments.[4]

The significance of cases of this sort notwithstanding—and the subsequent development of highly distinctive Franciscan and Dominican architectures, particularly in the New World, belie that even they constitute anomalies in this regard[5]—nonchalance about the built environment in which one practices the religious life is an exception rather than the rule, even (in fact, especially) among monastic communities. Inevitably—whether it entails simply sweeping the ground clean, cordoning off a sacred precinct, or constructing some sort of elaborate monumental edifice—the first step in a collective ritual celebration involves the requisite sanctification of place, the preparation of some sort of ritual context wherein the subsequent ceremonial activities might proceed with due decorum, efficacy, and efficiency.

Religious architecture, then, epitomizes in a particularly strong fashion, the irony suggested by Lao-tzu and so many architectural critics and designers that the greatest significance and utility in construction, whether of molded clay vessels or of grand cathedrals, often lies not in the solid masses themselves but in the hollowness they create, in the spaces, contexts, ambiences, and significant voids that come to being via the processes of construction.[6] In fact, the space of ritual, the preparative engineering of a ceremonial milieu, is scrutinized with all or more of the rigor that applies to the scheduling of the ceremonial event, the consecration of the ceremonial paraphernalia, and even the careful selection of the ritual participants.

Four Modes of Ritual-Architectural Presentation: The Play and Contest of Priorities

By way of organizing the plethora of strategies whereby architecture participates in concocting an efficacious context for ritual, which is considerably more difficult than ordering either the instigatory strategies or the manifold content of various ritual-architectural events, the final four chapters isolate and instantiate four alternative modes of ritual-architectural presentation, or four types of presentational priorities. These are, in other words, four alternative ways of describing the interactive relationship between human ritual participants and built ritual contexts.

In each case, unassuming terms are assigned somewhat more technical designations: "Theater" (priority III-A) will refer to ritual-architectural configurations that serve as backdrops or stages for the performance and spectatorial viewing of ritual dramas. "Contemplation" (priority III-B), which here takes on an especially specific meaning, directs attention to configurations in which architectural forms and features themselves serve as foci or props for devotion. Under the rubric of "propitiation" (priority III-C), I will accentuate circumstances in which the construction (or sometimes destruction) process itself, even more than the use of the end product, has the character of ritual. And last, "sanctuary" (priority III-D) will designate ritual-architectural configurations that serve as built (or occasionally found) refuges of perfect order or pristine sacrality.

Where the initial three chapters, on architecture as orientation, focused on the range of instigatorial strategies that usually operate in the front half of ritual-architectural events, and the next four chapters, on architecture as commemoration, addressed the range of messages that are most likely to be expressed in the back half of those events, these final chapters, on *architecture as ritual context,* are trained on alternative modes of presentation, or perhaps means, of ritual-architectural choreography, which usually apply more generally to the entire twofold ritual-architectural situation. Though insisting from start to finish in this hermeneutical prolegomenon that the interpretation of sacred architecture be constituted (or problematized) in terms of events and situations, not in the static forms or meanings of buildings, it is at this point in the project that we traffic most closely to matters of formal appearance and composition. Often, in fact, the hermeneut's challenge is to capitalize on largely formal (noneventful) academic observations, translating and extending them into more suitably situational, eventful terms.

Moreover, though fashioning morphological categories that are strictly parallel is nowhere a primary concern in the building of the present framework, this last set of entries is considerably more heterogeneous than either of the previous sets. Two sorts of tensions are, nonetheless, particularly important in framing the distinctions between the various presentational alternatives. First is a tension between what might be conceived as *indirect* versus *direct* experiences of sacred architecture. In indirect apprehensions, architecture facilitates the efficacy of ritual proceedings by providing a background ambience that participants experience in an important though tacit fashion, often with little or no conscious awareness of the specific shapes, colors, and textures of the built forms; direct apprehensions of sacred architecture, by contrast, are those in which ritual participants deliberately and very explicitly engage the architectural forms, often as the principal foci of attention in their devotional practice. The second tension is between what might be termed *inclusive* ritual contexts, designed in large part to beckon and entice even reticent, reluctant spectators into involvement in the ritual proceedings, as opposed to *exclusive* ritual contexts, wherein the architectural forms serve primarily to restrict access, isolating the ritual proceedings both from the prosaic surroundings and from some other-than-elect constituency.

With respect to those tensions, the theater mode (III-A) may be characterized as indirect and inclusive; the contemplation mode (III-B) is direct and either inclusive or exclusive; and sanctuary (priority III-D) is indirect and exclusive. Reflecting the special unevenness of this group, however, the propitiation mode (III-C), because it refers more often to the apprehension of construction processes themselves than to the subsequent experiences of those completed ritual contexts, is not really illumined by the indirect/direct or inclusive/exclusive dynamics. In short, no simple binary oppositions can account for the present quadripartite arrangement.

Note, then, that where the commemorative priorities provide the most straightforward patterns of hermeneutical interrogation, and the orientational priorities somewhat less direct lines of interpretive questioning, these presentational priorities are, by far, the least straightforward. Illusions of comprehensiveness and systemization (which nearly always are illusions in the case of morphology) are less easily sustained at this point. Again constituting heuristic, empirically formed abstractions, these four possibilities denote especially fluid, permeable boundaries. Sometimes they work together in various combinations, sometimes independently, and often they are in direct competition.

Unapologetically mismatched, then, these options belong together in the framework, not because they are parallel terms, but because, in hermeneutical practice, as I hope to demonstrate, they have proven to play off one another in very productive and intriguing ways. Entertaining the heuristic questions that are a consequence of this four-part division can, I think, both stimulate productive comparisons of several sorts and, eventually, reveal innumerable dimensions of individual sacred architectures that might otherwise have escaped our attention.[7]

Twenty-one | Theater: Pomp, Procession, and Pageant (Priority III-A)

In all the long catalogue of superstitious rites that darken the pages of man's history, I cannot imagine a picture more horribly exciting than that of the Indian priest, with his white dress and long hair glotted with gore, performing his murderous sacrifices at this lofty height, in full view of the people throughout the whole extent of the city.

Diego López de Cogolludo, 1688[1]

[The Hajj is] a symbolic demonstration of the philosophy of the Creation of Adam . . . a simultaneous show of many things; it is a "show of creation," a "show of history," a "show of unity," a "show of Islamic ideology," and a "show of the Umma" (Nation). Allah is the stage manager. The theme portrayed is the actions of the people involved. Adam, Abraham, Hagar, and Satan are the main characters. The scenes are the Masjid-ul-Haram [the sacred mosque], the Haram area. . . . Lastly, the player of the roles in this "show" is only one—and that is you [a Muslim].

Ali Shariati, 1977[2]

When emotion enters design, it is not an end in itself but a mode of persuasive communication that serves a broader argument.

Richard Buchanan, 1989[3]

THE FUNDAMENTAL PROBLEM for the study of pre-Columbian Mesoamerican architecture—not unlike the study of sacred architecture elsewhere—has been the disengagement of monuments from ritual, the dissevering of edifices from events. Confronted by the magnificent processional ways and "pageant-spaces" of ancient Mexico, however, even those reporters who were usually content with formal descriptions have been swept into imaginative (re)creations of the supposed histrionics of pre-Columbian ritual-architectural performances.[4] In the imagination of colonial writer López de Cogolludo, the ruins of Yucatan conjured up simultaneously fascinating and repulsive images of the "horribly exciting" spectacle of Maya human sacrifice.[5] And for Bishop Landa, whose own minatory orchestrations of sixteenth-century Inquisitional ritual-architectural events demonstrated a "superb theatrical sense,"[6] those same ruins evoked a scene of the "great show and company of people," which, in his view, must have accompanied the steamy dramaturgy of Maya public ceremony.[7]

Similarly, in the nineteenth century, explorer Frederick Catherwood's imagination filled the still ruins of the Yucatecan Maya with "great exhibitions of pomp and splendor," while his traveling partner, John Lloyd Stephens, likewise envisaged "the theatre of great events and imposing religious ceremonies" that must have characterized pre-Columbian Yucatan.[8] Also in the heart of the southern Maya zone, the obviously amphitheatric arrangement of the main court of Copán, bounded on three sides by artificial ramparts and low platforms and on the fourth by a three-hundred-foot-wide stairway, has inspired equally graphic imaginings of ritual spectacle and panache: Francisco de Fuentes (circa 1700) pictured "the great circus of Copán";[9] Herbert Spinden wrote that "the plaza [of Copán] is surrounded by a stepped wall as if it were a sort of theatre";[10] and Pál Kelemen, invoking a direct parallel to the theatrical Baroque churches of Bernini (discussed below), described the Copán plaza as

> an ideal arena. . . . Baroque it is—in feeling, in its complication of design and ebullience of detail, in the dramatic dynamics of its whole conception, in the untrammeled freedom of its execution . . . a ceremony witnessed here must have been immensely awe-inspiring.[11]

Though these simultaneously enthusiastic and condescending assessments of pre-Columbian ceremonial showmanship are almost certainly filtered through modern Western ambivalences about ritual, particularly about the supposed "ritualism" with which indigenous people conduct their religious lives (a set of problems to which I will return later in this chapter), the choreographic contrivance to seduce and to shock that they describe is the hallmark of, for lack of more precise terminology, the "theater" mode of ritual-architectural presentation (priority III-A). At best high drama, at worst garish pretension, where the theater priority dominates, ritual-architectural events begin by taking one's breath and then proceed, via religioperformative thespianism, to convey their messages.[12] This is ritual-architectural choreography—stage-setting and composition—in its most obvious sense.

Architecture, Emotion, and Liturgy: Ritual-Architectural Cultivations of Affect

Though attending to only a small slice of what belongs to the multidimensional phenomenon of theater, as a distinct morphological option, the technical, somewhat eccentric designation of "theatrical presentation" in this case directs attention to ritual-architectural configurations that are *inclusive* insofar as the incentive is more often to cajole spectators into involvement than to restrict access to the proceedings (as is the case with the sanctuary mode [III-D]). Moreover, such theatric presentational means, by heuristic definition (and in contrast to the direct engagements of the contemplative mode [III-B]), enhance apprehensions of architectural events in an *indirect* fashion insofar as they pertain to the configuration of stages, backdrops, ambiences, and atmospheres for performative activities. The built forms themselves, in such cases, are not, by and large, objects of the direct circumspections of ritual participants.

Furthermore, it is with the theater mode that we are drawn most fully into a swirl of subtly interrelated themes concerning not only performance and persuasion but, more specifically, architecture's and ritual's relationships to emotion, sentiment, and sensory stimulation—themes concerning what Raymond Williams terms "structures of feeling"[13] or James Fernandez calls "feeling tone."[14] Here we are trafficking in the affective dimension of the experience of sacred architecture, the evocation of awe, wonderment, and sensibility. In their affect, theatrically presented architectural events are those that work, in very concerted ways, to make an impression, to influence, touch, impress, sway, and persuade the assembled audiences and participants.

The relationships between architecture, ritual, and emotion are, however, exceedingly complex, to say the least.[15] And, though such sentiments as happiness, surprise, fear, anger, disgust, and sadness have been—only arguably—deemed "universal emotions,"[16] the increasing appreciation that emotions, too, are invariably embedded in socially constructed, culturally specific categories complicates (and, again, enlivens) the prospects for cross-cultural comparison.[17] Nevertheless, that the design of ritual-architectural events in virtually all contexts is informed, to some important extent, by concerns for theatrical choreography and for the cultivation of some sort of affective response is difficult to dispute. In ritual-architectural design processes, the provocation of emotion—the incentive to move people, to incite feelings or passions—is one more component in the always oddly uneven contestation between such factors as allegiances to tradition, fulfillments of theological and cosmological responsibility, exercises of socioeconomic interest, as well as allowances for more obviously practical factors like climate and the physical limitations of particular building materials and techniques. Not infrequently, in fact, the demands of liturgical stagecrafting, which provides one (among many) particularly conspicuous manifestation of the theater priority, overpower all other parameters of design.

Historical case in point, the competition and interaction between circular and longitudinal European church plans, and particularly the controversy and eventual rejection of Bramante's sixteenth-century design for the round rebuilding of Saint Peter's in Rome, illustrates very well a complex play of ritual-architectural priorities and the eventual victory of theatric—in this case, liturgical—considerations. In his account of that controversy, Rudolf Wittkower argues that the shift from the basilican cross form to centralized church plans was the architectural expression of a fundamentally changed conception of the godhead that separated the Middle Ages from the Renaissance: the medieval Christ was the "Man of Sorrows" who had suffered on the cross for humanity and the Latin cross plan was the symbolic expression of his crucifixion; by contrast, the Renaissance Christ was the essence of perfection and harmony, the "Pantocrator," whose truth and omnipotence were best captured in a mathematical architecture of centers, circles, and spheres.[18] Moreover, Wittkower notes that Christian martyria were also traditionally circular in plan.

Thus, whether Bramante conceived of Saint Peter's as an enormous martyrium for the Father of the Church (and thus primarily as an exercise in the commemoration of the dead [priority II-D])[19] or as an architectural symbol of God's perfection (and thus primarily as a commemoration of a specific conception of divinity [priority II-A]),[20] his original idea called for a centrally planned building. In either case, the circular plan was severely criticized as inadequate to the needs of ecclesiastical ceremony: it had no adequate sacristy, few chapels for the worship of individual saints, and, worst of all, no nave, a feature essential to house a large congregation and to provide a suitable setting for processions.[21] After several attempts at compromise, round symmetry was thus jettisoned in favor of the Latin cross plan—the most propitious stage for grand processionary ritual—that exists as Saint Peter's today.

The resistance to centrally planned churches, in other words, stemmed largely from the liturgical, and to that extent affective, potency that the basilican plan had demonstrated in the Romanesque period. The longitudinal shape, originally borrowed from the form of the pagan Roman basilica, had endured hundreds of years of transformation and refinement to bring it into accord with the demands of Christian liturgy, an evolution that perhaps culminated in the third abbey church of Cluny (1088–1130).[22] The similarly shaped Cluny church demonstrates even better than Saint Peter's the ascendency of theatric, liturgical priorities insofar as gigantic scale, munificent lavishness, and sublime symbolism collaborate in a longitudinal basilica that was designed, above all, to provide the backdrop for grandiose procession and ceremony. Of the single-minded agenda at Cluny, Braunfels writes:

> building was to one end only: the life of the monks was almost exclusively devoted to the celebration of liturgy, to such long-drawn-out services that by comparison meditation and study were virtually, and bodily labor wholly, neglected.[23]

To caricature Cluniac monks as "liturgical animals" who proceed through their ritual routines with thoughtless, automatous efficiency is too simple;[24] one could likewise argue that the ostentations of Cluniac liturgy were for the "glory of God" (thus providing, among other relevant possibilities, strong instantiations of the divinity [II-A] and propitiation [III-C] priorities). There is, of course, a good deal more at issue in Cluny ceremony than the pandering and provocation of emotion. But, even so, the lavish liturgical and building program of Cluny does provides us a quintessential exemplar of the theatric mode of ritual-architectural presentation. One needn't travel into the pre-Columbian jungles of Yucatan to discover circumstances in which the cultivation of affect stands very near the top of the list of ritual-architectural priorities.

Theatrical Modes of Allurement: Inclusion, Exhortation, Anthrocentrism, and Appearances

Theatric ritual-architectural presentation is, then, at least as I define the working morphological category of priority III-A, concerned primarily with appearances rather than actualities, with evoking an emotive human response rather than soliciting some divine agency or conforming to some cosmic dictate. As in Bates Lowry's assessment of the intended effect of Brunelleschi's Renaissance architecture as "the presentation of a visual image whose total form was dictated by a concern for how it would appear to the eye of the human observer,"[25] we are dealing here with a decidedly affective and anthrocentric set of concerns.

Also relevant is the much-discussed practice of "entasis" at the Parthenon, wherein nearly all the critical lines of the building have been substantially curved so as to appear straight: columns, for instance, are cigar-shaped so as to appear perfectly tapered, and doorways deviate from genuine rectangularity so as to appear rectangular. While typically applauded as evidence of an "almost unbelievable subtlety and sophisticated knowledge on the part of the Greek architects of the Periclean period,"[26] this willingness to sacrifice arithmetically exact dimensioning in the interest of an *appearance* of perfect regularity demonstrates, moreover (and more relevant to the present discussion), the ascendency of the priority for theatrical presentation. In both the Parthenon and Brunelleschi's work, what matters most is the *affect* of the building on the human observer, how it appears and how it moves those people who interact with it.

Given this preoccupation with manipulating the perceptions of onlookers, the priority for theatrical presentation announces itself particularly in the realm of ritual-architectural allurement, that is, in the front half of the ritual-architectural situation. Theatrical strategies of allurement, moreover, are especially adept in those circumstances wherein there is a concerted effort to induce the participation of reluctant spectators, that is, to coerce onlookers out of their passivity and into active involvement in the ritual proceedings (a coercive initiative that, as we will see in the following sections, is not characteristic of the other three modes of ritual-architectural presentation). Furthermore, if invariably dedicated to openness and inclusion rather than privacy and exclusion (precisely the antithesis of the sanctuary priority [III-D]), there are, of course, any number of very different sorts of choreographic contrivances that might work (or might fail) to elicit the participation of spectators—including those onlookers who may initially be indifferent or even hostile to the associated ritual proceedings.

Artificially, but perhaps to some heuristic benefit, the range of instigative choreographic options can be arranged according to three sorts of theatrical configurations: first, stationary architectural events in which an ensemble of ritual actors performs on some sort of fixed stage or "pageant-space" for an assembly of onlookers; second, processional or ambulatory architectural events in which ritual actors move past an essentially fixed audience; and third, more actively participatory processional architectural events in which both the principal ritual actors and spectators are moving together in a promenade or parade.[27] Brief instantiation of each heuristic suboption should suffice.

Stationary Audiences and Stages: Performance and Pageant Spaces

Not unlike tens of thousands of theater, classroom, and church layouts where a seated audience faces a stage or podium of some sort, the Great

Plaza of the Zapotec-Mixtec site of Monte Albán in Oaxaca provides a clear exemplar of this first, very familiar sort of configuration. This plaza is specially instructive in this regard, however, because, despite being located on a mountaintop, rather than exploit the pregnant vistas and direct visitors' gazes outward to the exquisite landscape, it seems designed to do just the opposite. Thus, in Jorge Hardoy's assessment, Monte Albán's most outstanding feature is "its negation of topography and natural environment"; in his view, the arrangement of buildings and platforms "takes control of the space," apparently in the interest of achieving its choreographic ideal—namely, the creation of an amphitheater that would enclose large gatherings of people and rivet their attention inward on the performative drama of Zapotecan ritual.[28] It was, in fact, Monte Albán's ruined but still sumptuous Great Plaza that inspired a typically impassive William Henry Holmes to muse that "Civilization has rarely conceived anything in the way of amphitheatric display more extensive and imposing than this,"[29] an assessment reechoed a hundred years later when George Kubler was moved to a similarly uncharacteristic flourish on "the stirring fusion of stone and ritual . . . the sumptuous life of religious pageantry" that must have transpired on the platforms and stairways of Monte Albán, "the most grandiose of all American temple centers."[30]

Nonetheless, if allurement—and thus the success and productivity of ritual-architectural events—depends upon transforming initially uninterested spectators into committed "players," then these fixed amphitheatric arrangements pose a special challenge. As Peter Hammond complains in the context of his study of Christian liturgy and architecture (and as nearly every preacher's and teacher's personal experience can confirm), such stationary audience-and-stage configurations are very prone to engender lassitude and passivity instead of active involvement. Spoilsports abound in such arrangements and are often allowed to remain largely indifferent to the proceedings being staged in front of them.

Commenting on what might be required to make such circumstances successfully alluring, Walter Gropius (speaking about the design of theaters proper) maintained that, in order to work, there must be "no separation between stage and auditorium."[31] The architect must, according to Gropius, use "all possible spatial means capable of shaking the spectator out of his lethargy, of surprising and assaulting him and obliging him to take a real, living interest in the play."[32] Nonetheless, Gropius was optimistic that a coordination of the architectural elements of the theater could, in fact, effect "a unity between actor and spectator." He wrote that

> by erasing the distinction between "this side" and "that side" of the footlights, between the stage and the auditorium: by bringing the events of the drama among the audience: by animating the theatre through the creation of a three-dimensional space instead of a flat "stage-picture" . . . [the architect should be able] to extend the scene being enacted on the central stage, so as to encompass the spectators and to bring them in some way within it.[33]

Hammond, then, who argues that Christian worship, even when configured as a sermon-like interaction between one standing speaker and many similarly still listeners, ought to be an essentially "corporate activity," applauds both Gropius's reasoning and its application to more specifically religious architecture. Gropius's tack provided, in fact, according to Hammond, "a very precise description" of the aim that was realized, with varying degrees of success, in the abundance of modern Christian churches, both Catholic and Protestant, beginning in the 1950s, which have been based on circular or elliptical plans in order to facilitate a communal liturgy in which all are actively involved.[34]

Be that as it may—and rearranging a still-stationary audience may significantly enhance the allure of such situations—I would nevertheless counsel that, where configurations of this sort obtain, empirically oriented hermeneuts need to be particularly diligent in noting as well those many impassive (non)participants who take their seats but withhold their committed involvement. Here, especially, failures in allurement outnumber successes.

Ambulatory Actors, Stationary Audiences: Spectatorial Parades and Processions

The second, similarly familiar morphological suboption—that of more ambulatory arrangements that feature parades or processions past a largely stationary audience or reviewing stand—affords somewhat different, but probably greater opportunities for allurement, to the extent that, as Richard Buchanan notes in the context of his discussion of the element of emotion or pathos in a "design argument," "Much feeling is conveyed in the experience of movement. . . ."[35] Examples of ritual-architectural strategics that exploit the special, seemingly intrinsic beguilement of movement and parade are endless.[36] A particularly strong case in point, historian of religions Gary Ebersole, accentuating the religiopolitical effectiveness of the ritual processions of early Japanese royalty, "complete with the requisite fanfare and entourage of courtiers and servants," notes both the prevalence of these royal excursions and the powerful effect (and affect) on the audience: "To be able to carry a large number of people and things in one's trail is a public expression of power and prestige."[37]

Again, relevant exemplars are too many and too obvious to require much comment. Note, however, that in Mesoamerica, countless murals and reliefs depict equally spectacular pre-Columbian royal and military processionary events—in all likelihood, no less propagandistic than their Japanese counterparts—and the sumptuous avenues and causeways that grace nearly every ancient city, usually leading nowhere, are so far oversized for their simple utilitarian functions that they can only have served as ceremonial roads, or *via sacres*.[38] Confronted by the legacy of this stupendous pre-Hispanic tradition of ritual ambulation in the garishly elaborate processions of nineteenth-century Mexican Catholics, English traveler William Bullock was forced to admit that "in order and regularity, in the grandeur of the vestments, and in the silver and gold . . . the processions of Rome, or any other city in Europe suffer much in comparison."[39]

And, besides the sumptuous allure of military parades or all manner of public royal processions, the internationally common practice of processing through the streets with the image of a saint or deity demonstrates yet another very common set of permutations wherein theatrically staged processions are enlisted to draw spectators into the proceedings. Processions in the context of Hindu festivals, for instance, may have a special allure for certain lower segments of the community because deity images that are typically housed within the sanctuary of temples, and thus that are ordinarily inaccessible to commoners, are brought outside into the streets, affording devotees a rare opportunity to present flowers, food, or other offerings directly to the god or goddess as it is carried in procession.[40] Here as well, though, we have to imagine that failures to stir onlookers out of their passivity and into active involvement are at least as common as successes.

Ambulatory Actors and Audiences: Participatory Processions and the Experience of Movement

The third suboption—situations in which audience members themselves are physically appropriated into the actual processionary movement—provides a considerably expanded set of stratagems for success in allurement. As Hammond noted in relation to his consternation at the pervasive modern tendency to replace the open spaces of Christian churches with fixed seating,

> one of the surest ways of breaking down the psychological barriers to lay participation in the liturgy is to get people out of their pews. The procession to the font might well involve the movement of the whole congregation to the baptistery. This would stress the fact that the whole of the church building is a liturgical space. . . .[41]

Also, as exemplified in the quotation from Islamic philosopher Ali Shariati that introduced this chapter, the entire pilgrimage to Mecca may be conceived as a kind of fully participatory, in a sense audienceless, "show" in which all of the pilgrims are the "players of the roles" who follow the stage direction of Allah.[42] Likewise, architectural mazes and labyrinths like those in Minoan palaces, the apprehensions of which demonstrate with particular clarity the twofold pattern of ritual-architectural events, are alluring and can provide exhilarating experiences of choreographed movement by juxtaposing a sensation of order with a kind of "delight in being temporarily lost."[43] J. G. Davies, for instance, considers that the baffling choices of direction in the mazeways of Minoan palaces present a challenge, and thus a rewarding experience. As one proceeds through such a palace, Davies imagines that:

> . . . there is a feeling that a problem is being solved, akin to finding the answer to a riddle, except that in this case it is not so much a matter of the intellect nor just of visual perception but of bodily motion. Indeed the essence of a labyrinth is movement; such a structure only takes on meaning as you walk through it.[44]

Or, instantiating a somewhat calmer (though still obviously twofold) set of ambulatory architectural apprehensions, the carefully choreographed walks along the roofed corridors that connect the various buildings in a Chinese classical garden likewise provide the visitor with alternating sensations of passage and rest.[45] The meticulously mapped ascent of Borobudur, or any number of mandala temples in Tibet or Southeast Asia, also epitomize this sort of very purposeful, architecturally abetted ritual meandering.[46] And, albeit in a very different context, one more example comes in Le Corbusier's attempt to exploit the potentialities of allurement via procession with a system of absolutely fixed routes through the Maison La Roche, whereby he hoped to gain choreographic control over the temporal as well as the spatial experience of the building.[47]

In all these cases, then, theatrical allurement entails making people, in fully physical ways, move. This is theatrical ritual-architectural allurement that tugs people into involvement by the arm (or legs) rather than by the conscience or heartstrings. In these more viscerally participatory configurations, the distance, both figurative and physical, between spectators and actors collapses entirely as onlookers are compelled, as it were, from the curb directly into the parade.[48] Here, onlookers are no longer simply looking on; they, too, are performers, experiencing the ritual circumstance in the most direct of fashions. The option of passivity is removed. Though still hermeneutical (and still comparative), in these more actively first-hand apprehensions, the ritual-architectural experience is a sensory and kinesthetic one in which considerably less imagination and empathy are required. The difference between the previous two suboptions and this one is, in short, the difference between watching and reflecting on a dance and dancing.

Theatrical Presentations of Meanings and Messages: Augmentations of Intensity

While the priority for theatrical presentation (III-A) is especially apparent in orchestrations of ritual-architectural allurement, the potency of such strategics is hardly exhausted in that instigatory function. Though theatric modes often (and not always inappropriately) connote a kind of contentless flash and meretriciousness, such means may also play a very effective—albeit usually indirect—role in communicating the precise sorts of information and obligations associated with the back half of the ritual-architectural situation. That is to say, where contemplative presentational modes (III-B) rely on direct apprehensions of built forms to transact ideas and meanings, theatric modes (as they are defined in this context) are more like sanctuary modes (III-D) insofar as both contribute to the articulation and dissemination of messages and meanings *in*directly, via the construction of supportive ambiences and, in this case, especially via the cultivation of "affect."

In other words, if, as Lawrence Sullivan and others contend, what sets (ritual) performance apart from brute behavior is, in part, a "quality of knowledge" experienced in those situations, theatric arrangements provide among the best means for fashioning the kinds of atmospheres necessary for the acquisition of this special sort of knowing and awareness.[49] Heightening emotion heightens receptivity both to transintellectual sensory apprehensions and awarenesses (of the sort Sullivan is emphasizing) as well as to the more plainly cognitive ideas and responsibilities that I arranged under the rubrics of the four commemorative priorities. Thus, where sanctuary modes work in the realm of atmosphere enhancement by quieting the ritual context and screening out distractions, theatric modes intensify the ritual context by turning up the volume, as it were, sharpening the focus, and exaggerating the contrasts.

Cross-referencing morphological possibilities brings to light ritual-architectural commemorations of the dead (II-D), of divinity (II-A), of sacred history (II-B), and especially of temporal authority (politics, II-C) that are, by that definition, patently "theatrical." Consider brief illustrations of each.

Theatrical Commemorations of the Dead: Tamberma Mortuary Histrionics

Among countless compelling instances of theatrical ritual-architectural commemorations of the dead (which thus demonstrate the fusion of priorities II-D and III-A),[50] Suzanne Preston Blier's analysis of the architecture and staging of the funeral performances, or *Tibenti* (literally, "The Dance of Drums"), of the Tamberma of northern Togo in West Africa provides a particularly strong example.[51] Working from a "dramaturgical perspective," Blier explains that the two-story houses of the Tamberma are designed to function not simply as residential quarters but, in the event of a death in the household, as multiple stages or backdrops for the variously public and private scenes that are acted out over the course of their highly elaborate funeral performances.

Tamberma houses, in other words, serve a kind of double duty: first, as domiciles for the living, and then, subsequently, as theatrical contexts for the enactment of funeral dramas for those same residents.[52] Floor plans, roof supports, window and doorway configurations, as well as the decorative elements of the Tamberma houses are all designed according to their eventual roles in these funeral performances. The landscaping and orientation of the structures also are determined by the potential need for the precise staging and lighting of performance spaces within each house; and front yards are designed to accommodate audiences to the funerary dramas that may, in some cases, number several hundred people.[53]

According to Blier, following the death of a male or female elder, a full cast of funeral actors is drafted, including an "Earth priest" who will represent the village founder, "guardians of death" who will ensure that the drama runs smoothly, a gravedigger, surrogate family members, persons representing the adversaries of the deceased man, and even an orchestra. An intricately choreographed set of performances ensues, often with several scenes occurring simultaneously on different stages within the theater-house for different audiences. In Blier's words:

> The various members of the funeral cast contribute as artists to the play's overall aesthetic image through their carefully choreographed movement patterns and through their use of the house facade for the arrangements of scenery.[54]

As the mortuary play unfolds, the audience, in a sense, witnesses an explication of the Tamberma ontology of death: the funeral actors first publicly mourn the loss of the former inhabitant of the house-stage; then they reinitiate the deceased into various religious associations of the village; and then they brusquely send away his or her soul so that it will leave for the world of the ancestors. Finally, usually three days later, the funeral actors dramatize the Tamberma confidence in a linkage between death and regeneration by encouraging the deceased—now a revered ancestor—to return and to foster children in the families of his or her descendants.[55] According to Blier, the native audience, already veteran observers of this sort of ritual-architectural funerary event, then critiques such dramaturgical dimensions of the performance with respect to its aesthetic merit, the size of the production, the wealth of the scenery, the number of people in attendance, the "script" interpretation, and the intensity of the drama. Shabbily choreographed funerals may be deemed "dull and joyless," while well-staged obsequies are discussed for years.[56]

Theatrical Commemorations of Divinity: Dramaturgy in Deity Domiciles

Though perhaps a somewhat less salient combination, some commemorations of divinity (priority II-A) are also markedly enhanced by elaborately theatrical presentational means. Those many circumstances (noted above) in which deity images are paraded around in lavish public processions would, for example, seem to provide obviously relevant exemplars. More specifically, an instance like that of the sumptuous ritual transport of the ancient Egyptian sun god, Amon-Ra—wherein the image of the god, accompanied by singers, dancers, and a great retinue of other gods, was carried along the two-mile, sphinx-lined avenue from Karnak, Amon-Ra's residence, to Luxor, the "pleasure-palace" where he was subsequently feted and entertained—would seem to constitute a particularly spectacular and public "theatrically presented" commemoration of divinity.[57]

Morphological analyses of the multiple modes of presentation at issue in this sort of parading of deity images, or, for that matter, in apprehensions of deity images that remain in more stationary poses, are, however, rather more complex than they might at first appear. On the one hand, to the extent that the painted or carved representations of god displayed in these situations are apprehended in a very direct fashion—say, as though beholders imagine themselves in a kind of active conversation with divine entities, as is often the case—that dimension of the occasion is, morphologically speaking, actually a stronger demonstration of the sort of unmediated apprehensions of works of art and architecture that are associated in the present scheme with the contemplative presentational mode (III-B). On the other hand, the less direct, and thus more properly theatrical, dimension of the occasion (that is, the exercise of priority III-A) involves the choreographic organization of the wider ritual ambience—the composition of pathways and viewing spaces, lighting, timing, costuming—all factors that may go largely unnoticed in an explicit fashion, but that serve in an important, albeit ancillary fashion to enhance the more direct apprehensions of the specific character and aspects of the deity.

By the same token, if we recall the tripartite division of morphological options outlined in chapter 17 relative to the commemoration of divinity (priority II-A)—that is, architectures conceived, respectively, as the body of a god, as the abode of a god, or as the abstract representation of the attributes of a god—we can note that, in both the first and third of those options, full works of architecture such as Cretan palaces or classical Greek temples provide giant sculptures that are usually admired from the outside rather than ritual contexts into which worshipers enter, and thus, to that extent, actually serve much like very large-scale images of deities.[58] In those sculpture-like variations on the ritual-architectural commemoration of divinity, worshipers, generally speaking, fix their attention directly on the building per se in order to interact with, or perhaps better understand, their respective conceptions of divinity, a mode of apprehension that is again better characterized as contemplative than theatrical.

It is, then, in relation to the medial, more residential morphological option, wherein gods are conceived as visiting or inhabiting a built form—"houses of god," as it were—that we can observe the most common, most piquant, and most specifically relevant linkages of theatrical presentation and divinity commemoration.[59] In these cases, it should be particularly apparent that theatrical modes of presentation (as defined with respect to priority III-A) are not working in the direct expression of information but, rather, indirectly, via construction and/or enhancement of a ritual atmosphere that intensifies the sensations of a deity's actual presence. To retrieve relevant examples from that section of chapter 17 that dealt with abodes of gods, Hindu temples (in some senses), the Temple of Solomon, Tibetan Buddhist monasteries, and Greek oracle temples, among many viable examples, could all be interpreted as circumstances in which the prospects for directly dialogical interactions with divinities are facilitated, enhanced, and intensified by decidedly theatrical strategics and configurations.[60]

Theatrical Commemorations of Sacred History: Bernini's Architectural Thespianism

The dramatic conventions of storytelling and playacting invariably associated with the reiteration of myths and miracles ensure a rather more common, straightforward pairing between the priorities of theatric presentation and of commemorating sacred history (II-B). Here again, examples abound. Consider, for instance, the obvious relevance of the ubiquitously staged renditions of Jesus's birth and death, respectively, at Christmas and Easter—productions that run the full gamut from campy to sublime.

Perhaps no circumstance is, however, more famously poignant in this regard than the emotive stagecrafting of Baroque architecture, and especially the work of its most renowned artisan, Gian Lorenzo Bernini.[61] A sculptor by trade, Bernini's preoccupation in his later years became architecture and the creation of whole environments that could embody his sculptural ideal: namely, the production of art that invites the spectator to be moved, which provides an occasion for enlightenment and inspiration, not, in this case, through liturgy, but via direct participation in the reality of various episodes in Catholic sacred history. "In Bernini's churches," as Wittkower writes, "the architecture is no more and no less than the setting for a stirring mystery revealed to the faithful by sculptural decoration."[62] Bernini's is an affective agenda that, in Gottfried Richter's assessment, is certain to stir the emotions of any who experience it: "If we have experienced Baroque architecture inwardly, we understand its innermost secret, and as we stand facing it we will probably feel like proclaiming this 'Holy open mystery!' aloud."[63]

Bernini, in other words, achieves this emotive ideal by freezing in art the "crucial moment" of various myths and miracles. Captured in art, climactic sacred historical circumstances thereby become accessible to the spectator, and their full significance is forced into recognition. The mystical experience of Teresa of Avila, for instance, is concretized in his fabulous sculpture, the *Ecstasy of St. Teresa* (1645–52); and the passion and resurrection of Christ are ossified, and thus reactualized, in the architectural space of the Crossing of Saint Peter's. In Irving Lavin's words:

> the Christ figure charges the physical space of the Crossing with the meaning of a dramatic action: we are actually at Jerusalem and salvation is being achieved before our eyes.[64]

Thus, while the informational content of Bernini's architecture deals primarily with the commemoration of the circumstances and individuals of Catholic sacred history (priority II-B), his manner of presentation relies upon the histrionic devices, emotional pleas, and arousal of astonishment that are characteristic of the theater priority (III-A).[65] Curves, movement, color, and light—a fusion of painting, sculpture, and architecture—all collaborate in Bernini's architectural thespianism as demonstrated in his small church of Sant'Andrea al Quininale in Rome (begun 1658),[66] and, on an unrivaled scale, in his design for the piazza in front of Saint Peter's, the large space where crowds gather for the papal benediction from the Vatican palace. This huge oval plaza is flanked by two free-standing colonnades, likened by Bernini to the outstretched arms of the Church welcoming the faithful—a ploy that epitomizes perfectly the inclusiveness and exhortation typical of the theatric presentational mode. Though only a portion of Bernini's plan was actually built, its deft enhancement of the drama of papal benediction makes it among the most compelling of all public ritual spaces.[67]

Theatrical Commemorations of Politics: Balinese Theater States and Japanese Funerals

Bernini's staunch ritual-architectural advocacy for the papacy and the Catholic Church (he actually worked for a whole series of popes) also had, of course, a profoundly political dimension. Yet, not surprisingly, where the content of ritual-architectural programs becomes even more explicitly political—particularly in relation to competing claims of authority and delicate transitions in leadership, or where newly acquired power needs legitimation—utilizations of theatrical choreography have proven perhaps their most efficacious of all. In short, theatrical modes of presentation (III-A) and commemorations of politics (II-C) are an exceedingly common and, it seems, highly effective combination.

A quintessential example comes in Clifford Geertz's study of what he terms "the theatre state" in nineteenth-century Bali, wherein, according to his interpretation, pomp and pageantry did not simply represent the state or reflect its power arrangements, they *were* the state, "the thing itself," its very essence.[68] Lavish and dramatic court ceremonialism so dominated the Balinese *negara* that Geertz is able to conclude that "power served pomp, not pomp power."[69] Moreover, instantiating with similar clarity the more ambulatory manifestations of the collusion between drama-like presentation and political content, elsewhere Geertz discusses the sense in which theatrically staged public processions in many stratified societies, not just in Southeast Asia, provide among the most efficient demonstrations of charisma, of order, and, most especially, of extending the boundaries of the state's hegemony and clarifying matters of sociopolitical status. Geertz writes:

> [Royal processions] locate the society's center and affirm its connection with transcendent things by stamping a territory with ritual signs of dominance. When kings journey around the countryside, making appearances, attending fetes, conferring honors, exchanging gifts, or defying rivals, they mark it, like some wolf or tiger spreading his scent through his territory, as almost physically part of himself.[70]

In the same vein, Gary Ebersole, following Geertz (who, Ebersole notes, follows Edward Shils who follows Max Weber), emphasizes the crucial role of publicly performed ritual poetry in the Japanese royal family's sweeping attempt to reform the government and to consolidate its power during the volatile Taika era (645–710 C.E.).[71] Specifically, Ebersole carefully analyzes the religiopolitical dimensions of the ritual-architectural events surrounding the practice of double burial (or *mogari no miya*) rituals wherein, upon the death of a sovereign, the royal corpse was first deposited temporarily in a *moya,* or "mourning house," and only later transported to a permanent burial site.[72] This temporary internment, a "liminal period par excellence," which lasted variously from two months to over six years before the final burial, created a situation of danger and great uncertainty. Ebersole explains that the *mogari no miya* ritual created, in effect, a kind of stage setting—both a place and a time—"a time of opportunity, a time for maneuvering for position at all levels of the hierarchical court society."[73]

According to Ebersole's account, the death of the Japanese sovereign, in other words, threw the sociopolitical hierarchy into immediate disarray—but, at the same time, the subsequent funerary rituals also generated a theater-like forum for acting out the "politics of death" and for initiating "the process of establishing a new order."[74] Thus, while the funerary poetry and elaborate public rituals performed during this specially opportune period did provide some occasion for the expression of personal emotions of grief, he emphasizes even more strongly that, "The rituals of temporary enshrinement were . . . also vehicles for political maneuvering in the immediate aftermath of the sovereign's death and a venue for actors engaged in political theatre."[75] Again, epitomizing the inclusive, suasive, often coercive tendencies associated with such presentational strategies, decidedly dramaturgical means were enlisted to articulate and legitimate (however successfully) contentious claims to authority and to force upon probably highly resistant audiences the specific obligations consequent to those configurations of power.

The Constitution and Choreography of the Audience: Strategic Recruitments of Beholders

Before closing, Ebersole's interpretive treatment of Japanese funerary practices suggests one last issue pertinent to both theatrical modes of allurement and expressions of content that deserves at least brief comment: namely, the careful choreographic composition of the audience as well as of the ritual-architectural place, performers, and performance itself. Who is watching and listening, what motives they have for attendance, and thus what characteristic expectations and preunderstandings they bring to the occasion are always important considerations both for indigenous ritual-architectural choreographers and for hermeneuts bent on composing critical architectural reception histories. But in heavily politicized circumstances like those that Ebersole describes or, say, religiocivic Aztec human sacrifice, the strategic recruitment of audience members takes on a special urgency.

In ancient Japan, for instance, not just locally competing parties but also emissaries and official delegations from the various Korean kingdoms, China, and elsewhere were invited to attend the *mogari no miya* rituals, which, as Ebersole explains, made these ceremonials, among other things, superb occasions for the royal court to cultivate and hone international relations.[76] Operating on their own turf, so to speak, the Japanese tailored their royal rites to exploit as fully as possible the rare assemblage of this highly eclectic audience. Likewise, in the Aztec case, even nineteenth-century historian William Prescott, among the first to bring the "horrid wonders" of the Aztec ritual to North American readers, despite his inclination to characterize the "barbarian" Mexicans as superstitious heathens rather than astute politicians, nevertheless imagined the gory showmanship of human sacrifice at the Templo Mayor was intended more for the human audience than for the actual participants (let alone for the deities of Mesoamerica). In Prescott's Victorian prose:

> From the construction of [the Aztecs'] temples, all religious services were public. The long processions ascending their massive sides, as they rose higher and higher toward the summit, and the dismal rites of the sacrifice which were performed there, were all visible from the remotest corners of the capital, impressing on the spectator's mind a superstitious veneration for the mysteries of his religion, and for the dread ministers by whom they were interpreted.[77]

The romantic excesses of Prescott notwithstanding, state-of-the-art excavation and interpretation of the Templo Mayor have done little to dispel his vision either of the lushness of the ceremonial theatrics or of the inclusivistically public character of the proceedings. Ethnohistorian Johanna Broda recently explained how each successive Aztec ruler enlarged the Templo Mayor, not in its entirety, but in a fashion that produced an increasingly spectacular frontal view;[78] as with the Parthenon, it was anthrocentric appearances that mattered most. Moreover, Broda recounts how, in the wake of each preferment, selected lords of allies and enemies alike were then invited—or forced—to witness extravagant inaugurations that began with displays of the architectural embellishments and tributes of luxury goods from the conquered provinces and then climaxed in massive human sacrifices of captives from resisting populations.[79] Davíd Carrasco, too, has emphasized that the Templo Mayor ceremonials were, among other things, spectacular "dramas of intimidation" wherein motion, color, sound, and gesture were all choreographed with a very specific audience in mind:

> The ritual extravaganza was carried out with maximum theatrical tension, paraphernalia and terror in order to amaze and intimidate the visiting dignitaries who returned to their kingdoms trembling with fear and convinced that co-operation and not rebellion was the best response to Aztec imperialism.[80]

In short, at Tenochtitlan, as in ancient Japan, the intensification of the meanings and messages transacted in public ritual theater, and thus the political expedience of those occasions, was enhanced immeasurably by extending strategic, compulsory invitations not only to local and loyal constituencies but, probably more importantly, to representatives from peripheral and competing polities.

Closing Thoughts: Ritualism and the Ill-Repute of Theatrical Architecture

Consideration of the theatric mode of presentation (priority III-A), and particularly this notoriously close relationship between religiopolitical propagandizing and highly dramatic ceremonialism, raises innumerable larger issues relative to the present hermeneutics of sacred architecture. Four uneven but important clarifying comments, which distinguish this morphological category from the other three presentational options, will, however, have to suffice.

First are very brief observations concerning decidedly theatric ritual-architectural events' conformity to and departure from the idealized, Gadamerian exposition of experiential and transformative apprehensions of sacred architecture that was outlined in volume 1. In that respect, we should note, on the one hand, how instances of theatrical staging seem to demonstrate in an obvious—even quintessential—fashion my reiterative claims concerning the eventfulness or occasionality of architecture and, therefore, the inextricability of architectural meaning and the performative occasions in which that architecture plays an active, dynamic role.[81] That is to say, we find in these historical examples seemingly strong confirmation of Hans-Georg Gadamer's proposition that the presentation or performance of a work of art, not only in the obvious cases of poetry readings, plays, and musical recitals, but for every type of art—architecture included—is something intrinsic, not incidental: "for in this [performance]," he explains, "is merely completed what the works of art already are: the being there of what is represented in them."[82] If architectural meaning is always situational and always contingent on performance, theatrically staged architectural events would seem to demonstrate that with the greatest clarity.

Moreover, as is particularly evident in relation to these last, heavily politicized examples, we should note that ritual-architectural events couched in this theatric mode epitomize more clearly than any others what Gadamer termed the "double mediation" of architecture, or what I glossed as the characteristic twofold pattern, wherein "productivity" and "transformation" require that a work first draw (or allure) the attention and admiration of the viewer and then challenge that viewer with the requisite "enlivening effect."[83] Thus, where transactions of meaning in each of the other presentational modes will, generally speaking, depend upon more voluntary, self-motivated, often more individualistic sorts of instigative means, it is the theater mode that shows best architecture's potential for persuasion, coercion, and manipulation even against considerable resistance. Though matters subtle and sedate may also be presented "theatrically," the viability of that blusterous two-stage scenario—in which the epigrammatic pilgrim is first "yanked" into involvement with the pyramid and then "played hard," and thus issued an irrefusable offer to see the world in a new light (or, in Gadamer's terms, to "be" differently)—depends upon the sorts of hortatory presentational strategies discussed in this chapter.[84]

On the other hand, though, by stressing the ambience-enhancing role of architecture in these theatric cases, and thus the only indirect apprehension of built forms and configurations, the sense in which people interact with works of architecture in a dialogical or "playfully" hermeneutical fashion (as was so heavily stressed in volume 1) is somewhat complicated.[85] The dynamically reciprocal, to-and-fro metaphors of conversation and play between people and built forms, between that pilgrim and the pyramid, are strained. Alternatively, this is architecture in, to use another of Gadamer's terms, its most "decorative" mode: here, built configurations' first role is to "give shape to space" and to provide the felicitous spatial arrangements that embrace the representational arts of poetry, music, acting, and dancing; only secondarily does theatric architecture "assert its own perspective."[86] Here, then, the hermeneutical experience of architecture entails the dialogical engagement of the full ritual context rather than of the built forms per se. Committed ritual participants continue to play active, questioning roles; but the addressees of their hermeneutical interrogations are more properly conceived as the ritual actors and actions themselves, not the shapes, designs, and colors of the architecture per se. (The next chapter should demonstrate that built features *are* much more accurately conceived as hermeneutical "conversation partners" in the case of the contemplation mode [III-B].)

The second and third comments, which actually translate into the strongest methodological recommendations, involve, respectively, the exceptionally common aspersions that highly theatrical ritual-architectural programs draw from contemporaneous critics and then the even more routinely pejorative appraisals delivered retrospectively by academic students of religion and architecture. Reviewing these materials one cannot help but notice that assessments of highly theatrical ritual-architectural programs—which trigger images of flash, glamour, zest, spice, savor, and thus connotations of superficiality and disingenuousness—are far more often condescending than congratulatory. Loud and profound, sensuous and sublime, gaudy and godly strike many as impossible combinations. No other presentational mode, no other ritual-architectural priority in fact, elicits nearly such fierce and frequent disapprobation. Though the reasons for such hostility are complex and varied (and again the close alliance between politics and theater is telling), with this morphological option especially, it is imperative that hermeneuts assay not only enthusiastic exercises of the theatric mode (III-A), but also vehement avoidances. Indifference and lukewarm embraces of dramatic presentational means are considerably less common than either of the extremes.

If theatric architecture in all contexts is, then, vulnerable to charges of vulgarity, superficiality, and degeneracy, it is those (in)famously extreme exemplars like the emotive stagecrafting of Bernini or at Cluny that elicit the most polarizing evaluations. In the eyes of its patrons and priests, the opulent theatrics of Cluny, for instance, honed and refined over several generations, were unprecedentedly successful in evoking the desired flood of emotions, a masterful design solution to abet Christian liturgy and worship. Yet, from other, still-Christian perspectives, the very same agenda was condemned as wholly misguided and inappropriate. Among the most articulate critics, Saint Bernard, for example, espoused a radically different arrangement of ritual-architectural priorities and, thus, was certain that the ostentation of Cluny was an obstacle to spirituality rather than an enhancement. According to Bernard,

> . . . the soaring heights and extravagant lengths and unnecessary widths of the churches, . . . their expensive decorations and their novel images, . . . catch the attention of those who go to pray, and dry up their devotion.[87]

In Saint Bernard's remarks, then—and even more in his own Cistercian monastic building program (a featured example below in relation to the sanctuary priority [III-D])—we are apprised of a wide and very enduring strain of Christian architecture that strives in a most deliberate fashion to absent itself from the theatrical mode (at least as I have defined it). Embracing plainness over grandeur, the design tradition epitomized by Bernard's Cistercians and their Trappist inheritors, not unlike the great majority of Protestant architectures in this respect, does *not* aspire to foster an emotional sense of wonderment. The inclusivism and affectivity characteristic of the theatric priority are, in those orientations, intentionally jettisoned in favor of exclusivistic and very private ritual spaces. Instead of summoning sensations of God's glory and might, Bernard's concern was with engendering a deep, silent awareness of the divine's universe-infusing presence. Thus, rather than stimulate emotions, the Cistercian ritual context was intended to quiet them and to effect a calm and a clearheadedness. In Bernard's building program, for which we could find many cross-cultural morphological parallels, the theater priority was significant most of all for its suppression and subversion.

Along with attending to historical circumstances in which highly dramatic presentational modes are deliberately squelched, which will require an aggressive "hermeneutic of retrieval," even more challenging—and this constitutes the third and probably most signal cautioning note—is undertaking the sort of critical "hermeneutic of suspicion" required to interrogate and expose the endemic, deep ambivalence toward theatric approaches that is evident in so many scholarly accounts of sacred architecture. Like Bernard in this respect, modern students of religion, anthropology, and architecture have, in other words, tended to evaluate theatricality, whether in Catholic or non-Western contexts, not as a sign of "high culture" and sophistication, but, quite to the contrary, as a symptom of superstitiousness, rigorless sentimentality, and, in some cases, even barbarity.

Though the relevant intellectual history is dense in the extreme (and well beyond the scope of the present discussion), there is no question that this is an area in which the modernist, colonialist, and particularly Protestant biases of "academic" religious studies assert themselves in especially insidious ways. Often, in fact, in Western academic parlance, as the incisive work of Catherine Bell and Talal Asad has shown, "ritual" (perhaps calling it "ritualism" would make the point more bluntly) has been designated—and denigrated—as a kind of emotion-driven, bodily and sensuous, "thoughtless action" and then counterpoised to more supposedly responsible, disciplined, intellectualized (that is, more rationalized and Protestant-like) exercises of religiosity.[88] In that still-pervasive contrapositioning of thought and action, belief and ritual, mind and body, rationality and emotion, an organization of knowledge that usually works implicitly rather than explicitly, theatrical and affective practices of the sort addressed under this morphological option are invariably situated on the pejorative (that is, thoughtlessly ritualistic) side of the divide.

To invoke one last Mesoamerican illustration, consider the untoward but enduring proclivity of Western scholars to polarize, on the one side, the pre-Columbian peoples of Central Mexico, particularly the Toltecs, whose ritual-architectural program has routinely been (mis)represented as the region's most superficial, showy, and insincere (that is, the most patently "theatrical"), over against, on the other side, the Classic Maya, who have been, with equal regularity, lauded as the most mystical and cerebrally sublime of New World natives.[89] Though, empirically speaking, current research suggests that those two sets of indigenous peoples actually embraced theatric modes of presentation with roughly the same measure of enthusiasm, the polarizing stereotypes, particularly of the early and mid-twentieth century, painted the Classic Maya as adhering to a thoroughly apolitical and peaceful "spirituality," orchestrated by highly intellectual, time-worshiping astronomer-priests; their supposed ritual-architectural priorities were introverted, otherworldly, and esoteric—that is, impressively nontheatric. Toltecs, by contrast, were pictured as the barbarian bullies of the ancient Mesoamerican world whose unscrupulous Machiavellian tendencies and shameless ritual propagandizing issued in a flashy but shoddily executed architecture that was, in Miguel Covarrubias's oft-cited assessment, "meant to impress but not to last."[90]

In this (historically improbable) view, the infiltration of the unsubtle Toltec style into the Maya zone was signaled by an unprecedented "spaciousness of planning," a non-Maya commitment to "maximum spectator participation, pomp and ceremony," and the replacement of Maya philosopher-priests by "gloriously robed" Toltec officiants who were more adroit at stimulating the senses than the intellect.[91] Ignacio Bernal's condescending conclusion regarding the inferiority of the consequent gimcrack and "hybrid" style, as opposed to that of the "pure" Maya, is typical:

> Toltec-Maya art produces a very spectacular architecture and sculpture, colorful but at the same time more superficial and emptier than those of the Classic [Maya] period; it is a nouveau-riche art suitable to the taste of warriors who have lately achieved power.[92]

More recent interpretations, however, belie nearly all those Maya versus Toltec contradistinctions.[93] In this case, then, which is extreme but hardly unique, purportedly academic diagnoses of the theatrical (or nontheatrical) character of a ritual-architectural program are actually less empirical descriptions of indigenous historical realities than normative codes that reflect (usually inadvertently) scholars' own ambivalences about the relationship of "ritualism" to spirituality, or maybe to governmental authority. Or perhaps, as Catherine Lutz and Geoffrey White suggest, the routine disapprobation of decidedly affective ritual presentations is born of a perceived antipathy between science and emotion, or a post-Enlightenment tendency to equate sentiment with irrationality, and thus to see emotions as, "if not symptoms of the animal in the human, at least disordering and problematic."[94] In any case, emotive, theatric architecture marks an area in which hermeneuts who aspire to rigorously empirical accounts must exercise a special level of critical self-consciousness both in their reliance on secondary accounts of the dramatics of sacred architecture and in their own interpretive descriptions.

Finally, the fourth note of caution, which looks ahead to the next presentational options, is a simple reminder that complexity, ornateness, and ostentation in architectural forms are by no means definitive signs that the prevailing mode of presentation and apprehension is exclusively, or even primarily, of the theatrical sort (at least as I've defined priority III-A). Always, as each historical example forces to recognition, multiple modes are intersecting and working simultaneously. Moreover, in each of the next two morphological options—contemplation (III-B) and propitiation (III-C)—we will encounter two very viable, but also very deliberately nontheatrical, explanations for the commitment to ostentation and "Baroque-like" architecture, whether in Mesoamerica or elsewhere.

Twenty-two | Contemplation: Props for Devotion (Priority III-B)

> The visible world was made to correspond to the world invisible and there is nothing in this world but is a symbol of something in the other world.
>
> Abū Ḥāmid al-Ghazālī, eleventh century[1]

> [T]he distinctive character of the contemplative mental mode is not clearly recognized in the common Western construction of the human psyche. Intellectuality and affectivity, volition and action are easily distinguishable concepts in our ordinary communication. Contemplation is not. Yet contemplation is what confers on aesthetic objects their unique function, and fascination, in our lives.
>
> Jacques Maquet, 1986[2]

> We may no longer have much leisure to contemplate the images before us, but people once did; and they turned contemplation into something useful, therapeutic, elevating, consoling, and terrifying. They did so in order to attain a state of empathy. . . .
>
> David Freedberg, 1989[3]

IN PUEBLA, A STATE IN CENTRAL MEXICO famously abundant with spectacularly tiled, carved, and stuccoed colonial churches, two modestly sized but stupendously decorated exemplars stand out: Santa María Tonantzintla and Santuario San Francisco Acatepec.[4] As though the winners in some tournament to create the most crowdedly ornamental facades and surfaces, the interior of each of these small nineteenth-century churches features literally hundreds of small cherubic faces scattered through a riot of gold-leafed Churrigueresque decoration in which Catholic motifs are integrated with indigenous ones. Upon entering either structure, the first in a chain of sensations is an experience of affectivity as visitors are stunned or surprised by its decorative, histrionic hyperbole. Sitting in the back near the door, one hears a gasp from nearly everyone that enters, particularly if this is their first time.

The initial sensation of these Mexican churches, which can be overwhelming, is of that emotive sort characteristic of the experience of the theater mode (III-A). But then, very likely, this very same fantastic array of angelic visages sustains continued interest as the patron's attention fastens on one, or on a series, of the exuberant elements in the decoration as a kind of mandala-like object of meditation. That is to say, the beholder's mode of architectural apprehension, the nature of her relationship to the built forms, can shift, perhaps in the matter of a few moments, from that of the theatrical sort to that which is characteristic of what we can now consider under the rubric of the "contemplation mode" (priority III-B).[5]

Where, in most cases, sacred architecture contributes to the experience of ritual indirectly, either by crafting constructional elements into a stage for the performance and witness of ritual enactments (as in the theater mode [III-A]) or by providing an environment of distractionless purity (as in the sanctuary mode [III-D]), this chapter addresses a sort of ritual-architectural presentation in which the link between building elements and ritual participants is direct, immediate, and unmitigated. These are ritual-architectural events that depend on the explicit devotion of, or sustained meditative attention on, the actual physical forms of the architecture itself. The so-termed contemplation priority, in other words, concerns architecture that serves variously as an object of concentration, a prop or focus for devotion, an aid to spiritual exercise or ascent, a support, or a guide—in short, a direct catalyst of religioritual experience.

Contemplation as the Direct and Purposeful Experience of Architecture

It is important, then, right at the onset, to define contemplation in a quite specific, if somewhat limited and idiosyncratic fashion.[6] The term contemplation usually connotes a whole complex of ideas related to meditation, rumination, metaphysical introspection, spiritual concentration, and mystical ascent—all of which are certainly relevant to the present discussion. Moreover, not infrequently, "aesthetic contemplation" of works of art and architecture is conceived as a "meditation-like" process. In the terminology of Jacques Maquet, for instance, the "contemplative encounter" between art object and beholder, though less methodical, intense, and "radical" than meditation per se, is nonetheless "a special mode of consciousness," irreducible either to cognition or to affectivity, which participates in the character of meditation insofar as it entails a "disinterested engrossment" or, in Harold Osborne's terms, a "weakening of the ego," "nonattachment," or a "reduction of self-interest."[7]

That view, too, is quite pertinent, particularly because it accentuates (as

I would) the sense in which, to use more explicitly hermeneutical (Gadamerian) phraseology, the "productivity" of contemplations of art and architecture is largely contingent on a measure of self-abandonment and acceptance of vulnerability as one enters "the closed world" of the work, accepts the wager that the situation offers, and thus commits to abiding by rules that may be less than pleasant. I concur, in other words, with Maquet's contention that, to an important degree, "Selflessness makes contemplation possible and thus is reinforced by contemplation," and, therefore, that the transformations effected by contemplative apprehensions of works of sacred architecture, not unlike other "insight-oriented processes," are neither fully predictable nor always felicitous.[8]

Yet, for my heuristic purposes, the embrace of contemplation as a distinct morphological category subsumes only a portion of that wide cluster of issues related to meditation and art-induced insight. The tighter focus here is on those ritual-architectural circumstances in which human beings engage directly and deliberately the actual architectural forms as part of their spiritual exercises. Simply stated, just because people are meditating, even if that deep mentation is somehow supported by built forms (which nearly all meditation is), does *not* necessarily mean that they are participating in the contemplation priority (III-B) as it is being defined here. My concern at this point is not with contemplation, meditation, and ritual ratiocination broadly speaking, but rather with those ritual-architectural circumstances in which devotion is facilitated by the explicit and purposive apprehension of artistic and architectural elements and configurations.

Of the four presentational alternatives, here, then, the image of the pilgrim in face-to-face, to-and-fro interactive dialogue with the pyramid is at its most appropriate. Here, the conceptualization (about which I have often complained) of works of art and architecture as "texts" that are "read" and deciphered is at its least inadequate.[9] Here, the experience of architecture is at its most obviously hermeneutical insofar as it entails an exegetical occasion of crisis-driven reflection wherein people are struggling to "make sense," and to drive ahead to meaning. This is, in short, the most intellectualized, least sensuous of the four modes of presentation and apprehension.

Given this specific, heuristic definition of contemplation, David Freedberg's work on the "image-assisted meditation," if expanded to include the engagement of all sorts of architectonic forms, not just representative art, provides a concise statement of precisely the sort of experiential mechanism that "contemplative" ritual-architectural presentations are usually intended to facilitate:

> The aim of this kind of meditation is to grasp what is absent, whether historical or spiritual. It is predicated on the view that since our minds are labile, meditation profitably begins in concentration. By concentrating on physical images [or perhaps on an architectural form], the natural inclination of the mind to wander is kept in check, and we ascend with increasing intensity to the spiritual and emotional essence of that which is represented in material form before our eyes—our external eyes and not the eyes of the mind.[10]

Thus, where the contemplation priority may find its most glamorous instantiation in highly self-reflective, rarified, and esoteric introspections of monks and mystics, this mode of ritual-architectural presentation manifests itself also, as we should see, in the most unremarkably mundane, pedantic, and popular of devotions—direct and purposeful interactions with paintings, posters, banners, stained glass, statues, stelae, and totem poles, as well as with geometrically decorated floors, domes, and towers. And, because the fabulous tradition of Asian mandala architecture—particularly the stupendous monument of Borobudur in Java—encompasses the full range of these highly rarified and more pedestrian sorts of manifestations, it provides us, I think, an advantageous point at which to begin an inventory of pertinent permutations on the theme.

Mandala Architecture: Contemplative Presentation and Apprehension Par Excellence

Mandalas, in perhaps their simplest form, are two-dimensional diagrams that (as discussed in relation to the homology priority [I-A]) represent, at once, maps of the entire universe and of human consciousness itself. The famous mandala paintings that hang in Tibetan monasteries, beyond a merely decorative or even pedagogical function, serve very pragmatically as aids to devotion, or as objects of contemplation. By concentrating on these two-dimensional, microcosmic paintings, Buddhist monks "enter" the world that is represented there and thus are allowed to "travel" through the larger macrocosm, and, in an important sense, to make the cathartic ascent of the mythical Mount Meru, which corresponds both to the center of the world and to the center of one's being.[11] In Guiseppe Tucci's Jungian language, these mandalas serve as "the concretization of a psychological state," that is, as "psycho-cosmogrammata that lead the neophyte by revealing to him the secret play of the forces that operate in the universe and in us, on the way to reintegration of consciousness."[12] In Romi Khosla's words, "The initiated *arhat* seeking to realize the mandala is compelled to concentrate upon it and enter within it so as to eventually merge completely with the central deity within."[13]

In addition to these flat, cosmogrammatic wall hangings, the mandala concept is likewise expressed in a more explicitly architectural fashion in the layout of the entire Tibetan monastery. Thus, moving through the monastery itself becomes a figurative sort of journey around the universe, or, perhaps, more psychologically speaking, around one's consciousness. As Kholsa explains:

> The Tibetan temple within the compound of the monastery is also a mandala. Just as the disciple mentally enters the spiritual realm of the diagram through concentrated meditation, he too, by physically entering the temple, arrives within a spiritual realm.[14]

This architecturalization of the mandala concept materializes on a still grander scale in the cosmogrammatic monuments of Angkor Wat in Cambodia and Borobudur in Java. Again, in these fabulous constructions, the sweep of relevant morphological options is nearly complete. These multivalent mandala temples are certainly, as Tucci wrote, concretizations of mental states and, as Eliade explained, homologized maps of the universe (exercises of the homology priority, I-A); and the geometrical regularity of their plans conforms to all sorts of abstract and standardized prescriptions and conventions (thus instantiating priority II-B).[15] Likewise, the galleries through which one enters each of these monuments are replete with representations and allusions to Southeast Asian cosmology and mythology (commemorations of sacred history, priority II-B); and, Angkor Wat, especially, displays as well the important episodes from the military career of leaders such as King Suryavarman II (commemorations of politics, priority II-C).[16] Furthermore, the whole of Borobudur is often interpreted as an elaborate stupa and, as such, an architectural "substitute" for the Buddha, thus evincing both commemorations of the dead (priority II-D) and of divinity (priority II-A).[17] Borobudur has, in fact, been praised as "the most complex and sophisticated conception of deity in the whole history of religious iconography."[18] Nevertheless, as monumental vehicles for devotion, or, as Tucci would claim, "means of psychic integration," these architectural mandalas are instructive in the present context most of all as quintessential exemplars of the contemplation mode of ritual-architectural presentation (III-B).

The issues crystalize especially in the experience of ascending Borobudur. This huge and symmetrical construction, which was originally attached to a Mahayana monastery (where we can imagine that particularly esoteric apprehensions of the monument prevailed), eventually came to constitute both the literal and figurative climax to the spiritual peregrinations of all sorts of Buddhist pilgrims. Thus, where reading a Tibetan painted mandala diagram, say, in a stationary seated posture, requires concentrating on its pattern and effecting a kind of "liberation through sight" typically reserved for initiated *arhats*,[19] the analogous, though perhaps more flexibly egalitarian, sort of spiritual transformation that Borobudur facilitates requires that pilgrims literally walk along the circuitous paths of the ninth-century shrine.

Capitalizing again (as noted in the previous chapter, with respect to participatory processions) on the special ritual-architectural potentialities that arise in relation to actual bodily movement,[20] this ambulatory transformative experience proceeds in several stages. At the base of Borobudur, according to Hiram Woodward's helpfully eventful account, the pilgrim is confronted with nearly two miles of didactic reliefs of the elementary laws of cause and effect, intimations of the punishments and rewards held within the monument. From there, the pilgrim enters a "monster gate"—thus formally initiating the ritual-architectural event—and begins to climb through a series of four corridor-like galleries that encircle the monument, creating spaces open to the sky but otherwise closed off to the outside world. These galleries are lined with life-sized images of the Buddha and with a succession of relief panels based upon the life and enlightenment of Gautama and on the *Gandavyuha Sutra,* a Mahayana text telling the story of the edification of a pilgrim named Sudhana.[21] Emerging from this confining space and passing through a second monster doorway, the pilgrim is finally granted an open view of the great crowning stupa, encircled by seventy-two smaller stupas, each containing an image of the Buddha and, perhaps, symbolizing the seventy-two elements, or *dharma*s, of existence.

Woodward, insisting that the meaning of Borobudur be interpreted against "an international Buddhist context," finds an important analogy between the two main levels of the huge Javanese monument and the two complementary mandalas of Japanese Shingon Buddhism.[22] He believes, in other words, that Borobudur actually consists of a pair of superimposed mandalas: the dim lower galleries correspond to the "womb mandala," the real world or the trial, while the upper open terraces and apical stupas correspond to the "diamond mandala," the ideal world as known by the *bodhisattva*s, the reward for lessons learned in the dark galleries.[23] Thus, according to Woodward, ascending the monument entails a preparatory sort of education, a daunting experience of confinement, and then, finally, at the top, a crowning sense of freedom and exhilaration. Upon emerging into the open air at the summit of the monument, Woodward imagines that "even the visitor who has understood little from the reliefs in the galleries should be deeply stirred."[24]

Though the specific analogy to Shingon Buddhism will not persuade everyone, Woodward's eventful interpretation of the pilgrim's experience of Borobudur does illustrate very clearly the profoundly transformative potential of this sort of monument.[25] Furthermore, his discussion helps here by foregrounding the specific mechanism of growth and change that is more generally characteristic of contemplation modes of ritual-architectural presentation and apprehension: beyond simply creating a dramatic ambient background (as in the case of theater [III-A] or sanctuary [III-D] modes), the reliefs and built forms of Borobudur—like the images in the two-dimensional mandala diagrams—are engaged directly and deliberately. The art and architectural elements are, in this case, absolutely indispensable to the pilgrim's spiritual ascent; the transfigurement of the pilgrim, when the work of the monument succeeds, is not one that could have happened otherwise.

Cross-Cultural Instantiation: Persian, Mesoamerican, Egyptian, and Hindu Parallels

If the presentation and idealized apprehension of Borobudur provide a superlative exemplar of the contemplation mode, scholars have likewise noted a very similar sort of logic at work in any number of other historical contexts—from the East, the West and, if too infrequently, in indigenous and tribal settings. Nader Ardalan and Laleh Bakhtiar, for instance, explicitly discuss the incorporation of "the concept of the mandala" into the Sufi tradition of Persian architecture as a means of "structuring," and thus facilitating, Sufi contemplative ascents from "the Manifest" (*ẓāhir*) to "the Hidden" (*bāṭin*).[26] Though usually (maybe unfairly) consigned to the fringe of pre-Columbian art history, a few scholars have employed Jungian perspectives to interpret Mesoamerican decorative motifs, particularly Quetzalcoatl and the quincunx pattern at Teotihuacan, as mandala-like symbols that functioned as props for psychic unity and reinterpretation.[27] Early this century, pathfinding Americanist Eduard Seler interpreted portions of the Codex Borgia, a set of Mixtec pictographs and hieroglyphics, after the fashion of a mandala;[28] and Eric Thompson, on occasion, described the intentionally circuitous route and manipulation of open and closed spaces in Maya planning in a manner that recalls the pilgrim's path at Borobudur.[29] Neither proposal, however, received a very enthusiastic reception.[30]

A more sustained exploration of this sort of possibility comes in Gottfried Richter's expansive interpretation of the experience of Egyptian temples, which (if again contestable as an accurate rendition of ancient Egyptian sentiments) likewise features the direct engagement of architectural forms facilitating a mandala-like ascent to self-realization. Richter, who stresses the uniformity over thousands of years in the way that Egyptian temples were built, describes "*the* architectural experience of Egypt" as a kind of initiatory journey, a series of repeated "enterings" wherein individuals moved along a windowless shaft-like passageway, through a succession of portals, from room to narrower room, until, "finally, in the lowest and narrowest of all the rooms, one may enter the holy of holies and stand face to face with the god himself."[31] In other words, according to Richter (who at this point echoes Tucci's psychological interpretation of the mandala), penetrating the Egyptian temple becomes a process of crossing a series of thresholds that exist both in the physical architecture and in one's consciousness, crossings that Richter construes as "experiences of waking up."[32] He writes:

> [The experience of] these temples must have been a tremendous education toward self-awareness, guiding man into new and almost unbearable inner movements and experiences. The closer a man came to it, the more this wall pushed its way into him. Its gesture forced him deeper and deeper into his own physical body.[33]

Interpretations of the experience of Hindu architecture—where, very often, "temples and shrines are meant to be looked at, and their decoration to facilitate meditation"[34]—provide even stronger continuity with the contemplative mechanism that is at work in the experience of mandala architecture. Discussions of Hindu architecture also reaffirm and underscore the wide range of ways in which the contemplation priority intersects with other ritual-architectural concerns. At one level, for instance, not unlike the educative reliefs in the lower levels of Borobudur (or of medieval Christian stained glass, discussed momentarily), Hinduism's fabulously rich tradition of storiological sculptural and mural ornamentation exemplifies the merger of a contemplative presentation with the commemoration of all sorts of mythical and sacred historical themes (priority II-B). More interestingly still, the homologous equation of the very substance of the walls and architectural form of the Hindu temple with the body of the divinity, or

Purusha, the supreme principle, epitomizes the pairing of contemplative presentational strategies and the commemoration of divinity (priority II-A).[35] Stella Kramrisch, for example, emphasizing the homologous equation of the built form with the very body of the divinity, is emphatic that the Hindu temple, beyond simply providing an ambience for worship, though certainly it does that, should itself be worshiped:

> The temple is the house of the divine presence and its very body. The temple itself, therefore, should be worshiped as *puruṣa,* the essential and unchanging and unaffected Principle of all things. . . .[36]

Thus, when George Michell describes the Hindu temple as "a place of transcendence, a place where man may progress from the world of illusion to knowledge and truth,"[37] he is actually talking about the ritual-architectural facilitation of spiritual illumination in at least two quite different senses: in his own apt phrasing, "the [Hindu] temple is not only a *place* of worship but also an *object* of worship."[38] The Hindu temple, in other words, facilitates a transformative experience indirectly by providing an ambience of purity and a refuge from the distractions of the profane world (an expression of the sanctuary priority [III-D]); but (and more relevant here), the worshiper's spiritual transformation is likewise facilitated more directly in the apprehension of the temple as an "object of worship," that is, by focusing one's attention purposefully and explicitly on the architectural forms themselves (thus exemplifying once again the contemplation mode [III-B]).[39]

Imperfect Generalizations: Voluntary Participation and Esoteric Content

Though each of these historical exemplars of the contemplation priority introduces special, idiosyncratic problems, together they also suggest a provisional—that is, strictly heuristic—set of general criteria by which this mode of ritual-architectural presentation might be distinguished from other possibilities, particularly from more theatrical modes (priority III-A). All of these generalizations will, however, as subsequent examples demonstrate, prove nearly as instructive by their imperfect correspondence with empirical cases as by their neat concurrence. These are general precepts with myriad exceptions.

First, regarding allurement, and thus the front half of these ritual-architectural events, accounts of Southeast Asian mandala architectures and their morphological parallels suggest that the contemplative mode usually relies on quite different means for instigating participation in ceremonial proceedings than that which is characteristic of the theatric mode (III-A). Where theatrical presentation most often involves inclusive strategies of allurement that coax people into involvement—not infrequently, cajoling, inciting, beckoning, begging, and even coercing unwilling spectators to participate—by contrast, contemplation ritual-architectural events (more like the sanctuary [III-D] and propitiation [III-C] modes in this regard) are usually (which is not to say always) instigated more spontaneously and voluntarily. Worshipers in these contemplative sorts of ritual-architectural circumstances, like pilgrims to Borobudur, for instance, routinely involve themselves, not because they were forced or tricked into doing so, but because they are inclined to see the situation as an opportunity for personal improvement or for fulfillment of a social or religious obligation.

The success of contemplative modes of architectural allurement usually depends, in other words, on devotees who enter into the situation of their own volition, either electively or in compliance with some sense of responsibility. Participating in the paradox that informs so many meditative practices, contemplative beholders, on the one hand, as Maquet and Osborne suggest, need to be selflessly disinterested, "non-attached," and, to an important extent, egoless; they must forfeit spoilsport status and make themselves vulnerable to risks and somewhat uncertain ramifications.[40] But, on the other hand, their participation is, as a general rule, undertaken with deliberate resolve, ardor, eagerness, and hopeful expectations of personal spiritual progress or reward.[41] Here participants' preunderstandings are, most often, couched in expectancy and readiness; ironically, selflessness, in many instances, serves self-interest. Thus, where theatric instigation, generally speaking, combats resistance, contemplative instigation usually capitalizes on enthusiasm.

Regarding the back half of such ritual-architectural situations, I can hazard an even more venturesome set of heuristic generalizations—rules with even more prominent exceptions—in relation to the sorts of information, meanings, and messages that are transacted via contemplative modes of presentation, again particularly in contrast to more theatric modes. Where the physical forms featured in contemplative modes of presentation (that is, the actual buildings and architectural decorations) often rival their theatrical counterparts in complexity and elaboration, and often exceed them in attention to ornamental detail, the content of those ritual-architectural events in which priority III-B prevails is, again generally speaking, more cerebral, more explicitly philosophical or metaphysical, more individualistic, and thus more self-reflective and more idiosyncratic. These are the most characteristically pensive apprehensions of sacred architecture.

Furthermore, given the voluntary and individualistic tenor of most contemplative events, albeit another very imperfect generalization (and I will note some exceptions below), such presentational strategies are less inclined to be concerned with commemorations of socioeconomic, temporal authority (that is, politics, priority II-C) than with commemorations of sacred history (priority II-B) and, even more, with explorations of spiritual and transcendent knowledge (broadly speaking, the commemoration of divinity, priority II-A). Instead of endorsing worshipers' positions in the world, contemplative ritual-architectural modes very often present props for devotion that, by their direct apprehension, facilitate devotees' escape from worldliness to otherworldliness. Thus, where the commemoration of divinity and the exploration of abstract conceptions of ultimate reality (one important strain of the divinity priority, II-A) was actually the least likely pairing with theatric modes of presentation (III-A), it is precisely in this more cerebral and explicitly metaphysical realm that the contemplation mode asserts itself most strongly.

Abrahamic Ambivalences and Qualifications: Judaism and Islam

If heuristically useful, these are, to be sure, highly vulnerable generalizations. Working through a more specific set of manifestations of the contemplative mode—namely, those that arise in relation to the interminable controversies over idolatry and iconoclasm in each of the Abrahamic traditions—should, however, provide some important qualifications. As noted in relation to the commemoration of divinity (priority II-A), ritual-architectural choreographers operating in each of the traditions of Judaism, Christianity, and Islam are vexed by a tension between, on the one hand, explicit and official theological injunctions against relying on art and architectural forms as props, or maybe crutches, for devotion, and, on the other hand, the inevitable appeal to the inspirational quality of art.[42] Total abstinence from artistic expression is, by virtually all assessments, an opportunity missed. Again, then, as in the case of divinity commemoration, instead of wholesale avoidance of art-abetted devotional activity, these monotheistic traditions issue in qualified endorsements of contemplative modes of presentation that are nuanced in particularly provocative and telling ways.

In Judaism, for instance, there is a perpetual insistence, on the one hand, that "art is not employed or enjoyed for its own sake, nor certainly as an object of worship."[43] Yet, there is, on the other hand, a receptivity to the notion that the art work that embellishes religious manuscripts and ceremonial objects, along with synagogue architecture and decoration, can, and thus should, facilitate a "beautification of the commandments."[44] Thus, historically, Jews, even while respecting biblical prohibitions against representational art, have been, as David and Linda Altshuler note, quite willing to acknowledge that art and architecture have a major role to play in "bringing meaning and emotion to religious observance," and thus enhancing the "fulfillment of God's revelatory instructions to Israel, the Jewish people."[45]

Islamic architecture—where one observes an even more striking juxtaposition of inexorable proscriptions against representational art with equally ardent enthusiasms for profuse, intensely detailed floral and geometric decoration—provides a still more interesting case with respect to the contemplation priority. While in Islam, as in Judaism, there is an absolute prohibition against any depiction of God, however stylized or abstracted, there is nonetheless an approval of the notion that Islamic works of art and architecture can, and thus should, "disclose an intuition of *tawḥīd,*" that is, a respectful awareness of the unity or oneness of God.[46] Therefore, while Muslim artists fastidiously avoid any veristic depiction of human or naturalistic elements, they employ a plethora of geometric, calligraphic, and stylized floral motifs to create artistic abstractions that work, in Lois Ibsen al-Fārūqī's words, "to stimulate in the viewer . . . an intuition of, or an insight into, the nature of God and of man's relation to Him"[47]—a strategy that qualifies, after all, in my rubric, as an exercise of contemplative presentation (priority III-B) in the interest of divinity commemoration (priority II-A).

Titus Burckhardt also works to explain how this seemingly contradictive stance concerning the (non)reliance on art and architecture in Muslim devotion is resolved in actual practice. In his view, the creation of an art without images is a direct means of dissolving anything corresponding to images in the mental order and any fixation of the mind on an object of desire.[48] Thus, rather than using decorative elements to summon images to mind—images, for instance, of divinity or of sacred historical events—Islam choreographs an experience of art and architecture that does precisely the opposite, that is, an experience that dismantles and dissolves any image that might detract from an appreciation of God's incomparable transcendence. Instead of fixing attention on a single image (as an icon or a mandala does), the abstract decorations in and on Islamic buildings are meant, according to Burckhardt, to engender a dynamic sort of contemplation by keeping the eye constantly moving over the geometric infinitude of patterns without ever being caught. Instead of simplicity, infinitesimal detail and complexity guide a process in which, to cite al-Fārūqī again, "each movement, each change of direction in the pattern, catches the eye of the viewer and draws him persistently along to new areas. . . ."[49] Burckhardt's assessment of the contemplative apprehension of the abstract and interlaced geometry of the arabesque designs that decorate the walls of certain mosques provides a particularly piquant example:

> . . . for a Muslim the arabesque is not merely a possibility of producing art without making images; it is a direct means for dissolving images of what corresponds to them in the mental order, in the same way as the rhythmical repetition of certain Koranic formulae dissolves the fixation of the mind on an object of desire. In the arabesque all suggestion of an individual form is eliminated by the indefinity of a continuous weave. . . . Thus at the sight of glittering waves or of leafage trembling in the breeze, the soul detaches itself from its internal objects, from the "idols" of passion, and plunges, vibrant within itself, into a pure state of being.[50]

Sufi Architecture and Contemplation: The Hidden within the Manifest

Architects in the Sufi tradition—not surprisingly, given their confidence in the notion that "all of creation is an emanation from the One" and, consequently, that there is a commonalty of structure and proportion that permeates all things[51]—embrace contemplative modes of ritual-architectural presentation with even greater exuberance than designers within mainstream Islam. Sufi practitioners, who tend to believe that the physical or visible world is but "a symbol and image of the spiritual world," are usually dedicated to transcending this sentient world in order to participate in that higher and "more real" invisible world.[52] Thus, from their perspective, works of art and architecture—especially, though not actually too differently from other earthly objects, whether constructed or found—are valued not in and of themselves, but for their pragmatic utility as "symbols" or vehicles that facilitate this quest after permanence within change, after the hidden within the manifest, and after unity within multiplicity. In the mystical phrasing of Abū Bakr:

> . . . the foremost and truest fact about any form is that it is a symbol, so that when contemplating something in order to be reminded of its higher realities the traveler is considering that thing in its universal aspect which alone explains its existence.[53]

In principle, then, from this vantage, any form or image—a rock, the head of a nail, or the crudest sketch—might potentially serve as an object of Sufi meditation, a stance that may actually demonstrate the most radical possible endorsement of the contemplation priority. Yet, in practice, those works of art whose creation is perceived as divinely inspired provide particularly dexterous foci for contemplation, capable of leading one back to their source (or "Source"), that is, to some eternal principle of unity.[54] Moreover, owing to the Sufi confidence in all-pervasive parallelism between the visible and invisible, art and architecture that conform to presumably universal systems of geometrical and mathematical proportioning serve as especially effective objects of devotion, or as "guides to the eternal and concrete essences that reside in the Divine Order" (thus demonstrating an especially tight link between the contemplation priority and those of homology [I-A] and convention [I-B]).[55]

Furthermore, Sufism enriches the inventory of variations on this morphological option by providing strong exemplifications of contemplative presentation and apprehension at virtually all scales. Calligraphy, for example, as "the embodiment of the Word of God" and thus the most sacred art in Islam, whether in manuscripts or employed as architectural decoration, can guide one's meditative ascent to a higher plane of awareness and into the realm of the infinite, as can the diminutive but detailed floral and geometric designs on jewelry, small brass trays, or woven carpets.[56] At an only slightly larger scale, Sufi contemplation on the painting in Persian miniatures—by acting as kind of intermediary "imaginal world" through which one must pass on the contemplative journey from this sentient, temporal world to an eventual participation in the infinite and eternal—provides an especially tight morphological parallel to the workings of mandala diagrams (or to Abbot Suger's understanding of the contemplative ascent facilitated by the elements of the Gothic cathedral, discussed in the next section).[57]

More specifically architectural, and at the scale of individual buildings, for al-Ghazālī, even the Ka'bah itself serves as an object of contemplation that might lead the contemplative mind on from the sensible to the intelligible, from the *ẓāhir* ("the Manifest") to the *bāṭin* ("the Hidden") of a form. Thus, he explained that:

> The Ka'bah is an outward symbol in this material world of that Presence not seen by the eye, which dwells within the Divine world, just as the body is an outward symbol of this phenomenal world, of the heart, which cannot be seen by the eye, for it belongs to the world of the Unseen, and this material, visible world is a means of ascent to the invisible, spiritual world for him to whom God has opened the door.[58]

And, widening the frame even further by concentrating on the urban layout and evolution of Isfahan in Iran, Ardalan and Bakhtiar contend that precisely the same logic that animates the creation and apprehension of the Persian miniature, the garden carpet, and the design of arabesques and individual buildings manifests itself at the scale of whole cities.[59] They maintain that, from the Sufi perspective, "the *why* of all creativity, its hidden aspect, remains eternally the same."[60] From a Sufi view, the same mystic principles—and thus the same opportunities for strategic cultivations of direct, purposive, and contemplative engagements of art and architecture—operate in all realms and times, and at all scales.

Christianity: Art-Abetted Ascents, Anagogical Illumination, and Gothic Contemplation

Finally, in the third Abrahamic faith, the never-ending controversy regarding the appropriate role of art and architecture in Christian devotion has issued in a whole series of very explicit statements that either vigorously endorse or, with equal pertinacity, reject entirely what I am describing as the contemplation priority (II-B). Early Christian writers like Eusebius and Augustine strenuously resisted the Neoplatonic position that artistic images of divinity are both appropriate and necessary aids in the step-by-step spiritual ascent to the realm of pure intellect and spirit, and that, in fact, as Neoplatonists held, "without images the divine remained inaccessible to ordinary mortals."[61] By the early Middle Ages, however, most Christians had come to endorse precisely that position—and thus to endorse the utility of so-termed contemplative modes of ritual-architectural presentation.[62]

Appealing most often to the plenipotent fifth-century formulations of Dionysius the Areopagite regarding the means by which one progresses from "the visible" to "the invisible"—that is, the Areopagite's theory of "anagogical illumination"[63]—a whole series of medieval Christian theorists made the case that, rather than providing obstacles to spirituality, works of art can facilitate, and perhaps are indispensable in, the upward climb from the material to the mental, and then on to the spiritual: "from the gross circumscribed object to that which is uncircumscribable."[64] Gregory the Great, for instance, not only tolerated but vigorously encouraged the use of images of Christ in private, solitary meditation. Thus, responding in 599 C.E. to the query of the recluse Secundinus, Gregory wrote:

> Your request [for images] pleases us greatly, since you seek with all your heart and all intentness Him, whose picture you wish to have before your eyes, so that, being so accustomed to the daily corporeal sight, when you see an image of Him you are inflamed in your soul with love for Him whose picture you wish to see. We do no harm in wishing to show the invisible by means of the visible.[65]

The same medieval Christian confidence that images and works of art could facilitate a "transport from the material to the immaterial" found a more public, more spectacular—and more strictly architectural—climax in the Gothic cathedral. Abbot Suger's innovative design for the abbey church at Saint-Denis, near Paris, often described as "the first Gothic cathedral," provides the preeminent heuristic example, particularly because Suger produced a manuscript that thoroughly documents what he hoped to achieve with his massive twelfth-century building program. Among the most fortuitous documents in architectural history, Suger's treatise makes explicit both his intention to adapt fully the Pseudo-Areopagite's metaphysical theory of anagogical illumination to the realm of architecture and his own self-satisfaction in having succeeded.[66] Invoking beautifully expansive language, Suger explained how contemplation of the architectural elements of Saint-Denis, the precious stones and altar ornaments, lifted him out of his quotidian boundedness, up to a "strange region" of ethereal bliss, which lies somewhere between heaven and earth. Few statements capture better what is at issue in this presentational mode than Suger's poetical account of his own personally transformative apprehension of Saint-Denis:

> When—out of my delight in the beauty of the house of God—the loveliness of the many-colored stones has called me away from external cares, and worthy meditation has induced me to reflect, transferring that which is material to that which is immaterial, on the diversity of the sacred virtues: then it seems to me that I see myself dwelling, as it were, in some strange region of the universe which neither exists entirely in the slime of the earth nor entirely in the purity of Heaven; and that by the grace of God, I can be transported from this inferior to that higher world in an anagogical manner.[67]

Suger, then, like the designers of Borobudur's massive gilded surfaces, flamboyant narrative reliefs, and hundreds of Buddha statues,[68] contrived at Saint-Denis, in every way possible, to construct an atmosphere of sumptuousness and ostentation. The dramatic effect is unmistakable, and there is most assuredly an appeal to the senses. Yet, the (anticipated) experience of the Gothic, again like that of Borobudur, is *not* primarily of the affective, theatric sort (priority III-A); nor is it simply a sensation of quietude like that engendered by the hermetic architectural spaces that I will be discussing in relation to the sanctuary priority (III-D).[69] Rather, at both Saint-Denis and Borobudur, the relation between the human and the architectural forms is (intended by designers to be) more direct. The artistic forms are "effective symbols"[70] insofar as they are specifically responsible for evoking a transformative experience—an experience that Suger considered not simply as psychological but as religious.

To the extent Suger prevailed in his grand plan (again, success and failure would have to be assessed on a case-by-case basis), meditating directly on the shiny surfaces of the Gothic cathedral, and preeminently on the light that filters through the stained glass, induces a trance-like state, a memorizing sensation described by Erwin Panofsky as "spiritual illumination."[71] The constructed elements of the cathedral were intended as, in Gadol's terms, "referential symbols";[72] as, in von Simson's phrasing, "object[s] of mystical contemplation . . . gateway[s] leading the mind to ineffable truths";[73] or, in Suger's own words, as "anagogical windows [that] urge us onward from the material to the immaterial."[74] Art is not only a helpful guide to transcendence; it is indispensable. For Suger, the only route to God is through material things.

Weak Rules, Strong Exceptions: Esoteric and Popular, Apolitical and Expedient, Scripted and Spontaneous

Beginning to move toward summational comments, I might note again that reflections on contemplation, and on meditation and mysticism, nearly always—but only sometimes appropriately—summon to mind images of isolated, world-renouncing anchorites, spiraling through their recondite metaphysical gyrations largely oblivious to the more prosaic workings and workers of the world. And, designating Asian mandala architecture as the guiding exemplar of this mode of presentation and apprehension (priority III-B) may exacerbate those limiting imaginings. These Abrahamic instances, however, and especially Suger's massive building agenda, ought to help us by undermining nearly all of those stereotypes. The exceptions to the "imperfect generalizations" tendered earlier are maybe stronger than the rules. A morphological resemblance in strategies of presentation is, to be sure, no guarantee of commonalities in other respects. In fact, so-termed contemplative modes of presentation can be deployed, as readers should by now have noticed, to considerable advantage in ritual-architectural programs that are, in most other important respects, profoundly different, perhaps even antithetical.

For example, while such presentational modes are very often espoused for their special effectiveness in guiding abstract, esoteric, and individuated mediations—as in Gregory the Great's advocacy for images to advance the deep and eremitic ruminations of Secundinus—in other situations precisely the opposite is true. In these latter instances, contemplative presentation (in the technical, if atypical, use of that term) is favored for its special efficacy in facilitating the popular devotions of the unlettered segment of the community, neophytes, and even children. Thus, effective as the use of art forms and images proved in the solitary meditations of mystical contemplatives, the medieval Catholic confidence in the process of ascent from the visible—particularly visible art and architecture—to the invisible was hardly the exclusive preserve of reclusive ascetics in pursuit of arcane truths. Quite to the contrary, Gregory himself likewise affirmed the popular and pragmatic role of art in the spirituality of unschooled commoners, arguing that: "Images are to be employed in churches, so that those who are illiterate might at least read by seeing on the walls what they cannot read in books."[75]

Likewise, the politically astute and pragmatic-minded Suger, friend and counselor to both Louis VI and Louis VII, similarly embraced contemplative modes of ritual-architectural presentation, not primarily for their suitability in fostering sophisticated intellectualizing, but because of what he perceived as their genuinely catholic appeal, and thus religiopolitical expediency. Suger, a dedicated servant of the royal, military, and national state as well as the Church, believed that art and architecture had the potential for working an almost magical transformation on learned and unlearned souls alike, a changed outlook that would not only recast and refine their status as responsible Christians but also as loyal French citizens.[76]

Suger's exhortative agenda, then, calls to our attention a set of ritual-architectural events that (contrary to the generalizations ventured above), while relying on patently contemplative modes of presentation, are neither elitist nor apolitical. Suger's strategies of allurement were enterprisingly and manipulatively inclusive rather than exclusive: "he wished to accommodate as great a crowd as possible."[77] Where theatrically staged events (III-A) are invariably *inclusive* inasmuch as they encourage and sometimes demand that even reticent spectators get involved, and where the sanctuary priority (III-D) invariably issues in ritual-architectural events that are *exclusive* insofar as participation is restricted to some elite few, contemplative modes (III-B) may be adopted either in the interest of inclusion (as in the case of Suger's Gothic program) or exclusion (as in the esoteric meditations of Sufis).

Moreover, as regards the content (or back half) of these Gothic events (again, contrary to the aforementioned generalizations), it is clear that Suger endeavored not only to delineate otherworldly Catholic conceptions of divinity and sacred history (priorities II-A and II-B) but also to bring people into the fold of the Church and the Capetian monarchy, a strategic initiative of the most aggressively political sort (priority II-C). So, too, subsequent Christian theorists, for instance Aquinas and Bonaventure, who are even more explicit than Suger about the pragmatic utility of art-assisted devotion for ministering to the unlettered, advocated such "contemplative" means as depicting the exemplary behavior of saints in paintings or stained glass primarily in the service of promulgating doctrinally prescriptive and educative rather than abstruse meanings and messages.[78]

Aesthetic contemplation may, then, very often and not inappropriately insinuate the rarified attitudes of detachment and indifference to the worldly affairs of society about which Maquet and Osborne write.[79] In actual (empirical) fact, however, the most prevalent utilizations of such contemplative choreographic ploys in Christianity (not unlike other traditions) have probably always come in relation to much more straightforward, pedagogical, religioritual tasks, such as introducing catechists to the beliefs and practices of the Church or guiding the attentions of a congregation through the various topics of the corporate liturgy.

Furthermore, if such presentational means are particularly apt to the wide dissemination of carefully scripted, institutionalized policies and concepts, we can be sure that the superabundance of such didactic elements also issued in widely divergent, unpredicted but not necessarily unproductive apprehensions. Hermeneuts must, therefore, strive to talk about "objects" of contemplation in nonobjectifying, eventful, and situational ways.[80] Where attendees to a medieval Saint-Denis mass not infrequently understood, say, the altar and eucharistic chalice, in precisely the orthodox manner prescribed by the clergy, we have to imagine, as Sinding-Larsen suspects, that at least as often those elements evoked much more spontaneous, private, and highly idiosyncratic understandings. In his view, the iconographic images in medieval (and probably contemporary) Catholic churches, besides working as the purveyors of Church doctrines, served frequently to "hold the attention of or at least 'distract' in a positive manner the bored congregation during the much-deplored long liturgical proceedings in which it often did not have much share."[81] And, from the perspective of this hermeneutics of sacred architecture, unscripted, noncompliant apprehensions of that sort, while often better characterized as daydreamings than acquisitions of churchly knowledge, are, nonetheless, both fully deserving of academic attention and of the morphologic label "contemplative."

Finally, one last spectrum of diversity subsumed within this morphological option also deserves note. Though I have stressed that contemplation modes of presentation very often issue in artistic and architectural forms of splendor, elaboration, and detail that rival those enlisted in the theatric (III-A) or propitiatory modes (III-C)—Suger's Gothic program again provides an obvious exemplar—ritual-architectural foci of contemplation may also be of the plainest and simplest sort. For their tea ceremony, the Japanese, for instance, "prefer a space devoid of anything save one work of art to concentrate attention."[82] Or, more radically still, in a Zen rock garden, objects that, at first glance, appear as little more than randomly strewn sand and boulders work as powerful aids to devotion or "self-annihilating contemplation" precisely because of their (seemingly) arbitrary and rough hewn forms.[83]

Or sometimes—and recall here that the crucial heuristic criterion for contemplative presentation and apprehension is direct, sustained interaction between worshipers and "architectural elements" (broadly speaking) rather than any specific sort of formal or visual quality—fully natural features like sunsets, waterfalls, and sheer cliffs, in addition to evoking an immediate sense of awe, may likewise serve as the foci of extended devotion or meditation. One may, for instance, reflect at great length and to considerable advantage on the designful pattern of cracks and fissures in some pristine canyon wall, or on the forces that must have brought that pattern into being. Ironically significant as well are those accidental or inadvertent architectural props for devotion: Given the amount of time that devotees spend gazing downward, the potentially evocative importance of the textures, patterns, cracks, and scuffs on church floors, for example, is much underrated. And, by the same token, even a water-stained wall or the back of a pew that has been vandalized by a penknife may become the habitual focus of some worshiper's attention, and, as such, peculiarly enough, surpass the very carefully designed altar or stained glass in transformative power. Correlations between fancy and contemplative, not unlike presumptions that such presentational means are always esoteric and apolitical, are, in short, dangerously oversimple.

Closing Thoughts: The Abrahamic Ambivalences and Distortions of Academe

Albeit in skewed and sometimes inobvious ways, academic religious studies also reflects very strongly Abrahamic, particularly liberal Protestant, ambivalences about ritual, about contemplation and meditation, and especially about art-assisted devotion. Closing remarks, then, are confined to quick cautionings concerning the uneven ways in which matters relevant to this mode of ritual-architectural presentation and apprehension are (mis)represented in the scholarly literature. To avoid simply replicating these prejudices, critical hermeneuts of sacred architecture—those working simultaneously in the modes of retrieval and suspicion—ought to be especially self-conscious concerning three, somewhat conflicted but widely operative, kinds of distortions.

First, where (as noted last chapter) rationalist and Protestant biases issue in a tendency to denigrate theatric modes of ritual-architectural presentation (III-A) as "ritualistic," superficial, and meretricious, there is, in the case of contemplation and meditation, at least within large quarters of modern (and postmodern) religious studies, a very marked tendency in precisely the opposite direction. Contemplative and especially "mystical" practices (vaguely and broadly defined), whether observed in Western or Eastern contexts, because they are presumed to constitute the most highly intellectualized, nuanced, explicitly cognitive and cerebral strains of those traditions (particularly in contrast to the seemingly basely emotive and bodily character of theatric ritual practices), routinely garner very generous academic reviews. Contemplation and meditation are judged the most hard thinking, the most responsibly self-controlled of devotional approaches, the most sophisticated and highly evolved. Moreover, the perception (only sometimes correct) of such activities as nonthreateningly apolitical and "specifically religious" also enhances this aura of sincerity and discipline; contemplation is, it seems, if impractical, at least benignly harmless. These are the abstrusely metaphysical cogitations of spiritual experts, "worshipful" or "prayerful" activities that barely qualify as "ritual"—again, the opposite of theatrically choreographed events.

There has been and remains, then, ironically, a kind of Western romanticization, sometimes exoticism, of the mentalist introspection associated with contemplation, particularly in the case of Asian religions. Oddly, from a liberal Protestant frame, mysticism especially, which seems to correspond most closely to the counterinstitutionalized, personalistic, and otherworldly "essence" of "spirituality," continues to enjoy a special privilege in the comparative history of religions. In these meditative-mystical practices, according to the presumptions of many academic assessments, the superficial differences of cultural specificity are erased and the transhistorical crux of religion laid bare. And thus, from one scholarly sight line, contemplation of all sorts, including that involving art and architecture, is granted a noncritical, overgenerous commendation.

The second tendency, however, which pulls in nearly the opposite direction, reflects that strain in Abrahamic religion that is never fully persuaded the merits of art-assisted religiosity outweigh the potentially idolatrous dangers. Medieval Catholic Saint Bernard, for instance—while dedicated to meditation and contemplation in the general sense—because of his contemporaneity with Suger and explicit criticism of the anagogical Gothic approach, provides an especially revealing example of the (almost) wholesale rejection of artistic accoutrements to devotion, and thus of the so-labeled contemplation priority (III-B).[84] Discussed more fully in relation to the sanctuary priority (III-D), suffice it to note here that Saint Bernard's diatribes against the luxuriant dramatics of Cluny's ritual-architectural program (that is, against theatric modes, III-A) apply likewise to Suger's notion that one's Christian aspirations might require the use of artistic or architectural props for devotion.[85] Yet, iconoclast that he is, even Bernard provides a highly qualified, if condescending, endorsement of contemplative presentational modes by acknowledging their usefulness among the spiritually immature. Bernard says: "Bishops have a duty toward both the wise and foolish. They have to make use of material ornamentation to rouse devotion in a carnal people, incapable of spiritual things"; but he then quickly explains that, as monks, "we no longer belong to such people," and, thus, art is necessarily more distracting than inspiring for the contemplative practice of serious Cistercians.[86]

Modern scholars of religion, then, who also like to imagine themselves as "no longer belonging to such people," often lump contemplative approaches (III-B) together with theatric ones (III-A), and then dismiss both with the same broad brush as superstitious, sophomoric, and irreflectively gullible—that is, the virtual opposite of individuated, self-critical, meditative introspection. From that more obviously Protestant-informed perspective, art-assisted contemplation of the sort explored in this chapter *is* ritualistic, a kind of lingering legacy of (or similarly puerile parallel to) medieval, magicomechanistic delusions concerning the supposed inherent efficacy of sacramental actions and objects. Thus, instead of a free pass, the interpretive description of historical instances of decidedly contemplative presentation, such as the Gothic cathedral or the monument of Borobudur, which are delivered by scholars with these leanings, are likely to exercise roughly the same sort of condescending filters and distortions to which the theatric mode is so vulnerable. In these cases, contemplative modes are dismissed too soon rather than elevated too high.

The third and last cautioning note calls attention to the very serious underrepresentation of indigenous peoples as exemplars of this morphological option—a failing that obtains both in the present discussion and in the wider anthropological and religious studies literature. Of the four presentational options, there has been by far the greatest unwillingness to give due consideration to the viability of contemplative modes of presentation and apprehension (III-B) in so-called archaic, traditional, or tribal contexts. Despite the wide acknowledgment of pervasive strategies of this sort in the "great world religions" (from which I, too, have drawn most of my examples), and particularly in the exoticized Asian traditions, interpreters of sacred architectures outside those major faiths very seldom appeal to this sort of explanation. Here, then, Christocentric and modernist biases are laced with colonialist ones insofar as Euro-American researchers have had particular difficulty in imagining that indigenous peoples might have the inclination or wherewithal to undertake the sort of deep, abstract thinking required of contemplative modes of ritual-architectural apprehension.[87] Native peoples' ritualized interactions with art objects and constructions have been routinely diagnosed as "fetishism" (which brings them under the force of the pejorative, condescending distortions of contemplative modes), but *not,* with rare exceptions, as "mysticism" (which would bring them under the sway of the more romanticizing distortions of this mode).[88]

If the root causes and genealogies of such academic prejudices are again complex in the extreme, the absence of this sort of interpretive tack in the pertinent literature is easily observed. As noted, Western students of ancient Mesoamerica, for instance, have constantly acknowledged a powerfully histrionic quality in pre-Columbian architecture (that is, the applicability of the theater priority [III-A]) and, though with somewhat less frequency, have likewise provided explanations that suggest the propitiatory (III-C) and sanctuary (III-D) modes.[89] Yet, aside from condemnatory assessments of pre-Hispanic peoples as "heathen idolators" who trained their devotion on carved stones without ever looking beyond those "graven images" (which actually does imply their involvement in one version of the contemplation mode [III-B]), the possibility that the elaborate ornamentation that accompanies so much pre-Columbian architecture might have served primarily as objects of direct and sustained devotion, or as mandala-like guides to meditation, has seldom been seriously considered—a disturbing omission to be sure.

This hesitancy to explore the possibility that the effusive geometric decoration of pre-Columbian (and other native) architectures might have functioned as aids to rarefied contemplation or mystical meditations—like that at Borobudur, in Persian mosques, or in Gothic cathedrals—raises important questions (too large to address at present) regarding the insidiously colonialist ways in which Western scholars have tended to imagine and represent indigenous peoples, their spiritualities, and their religio-artistic productions. But, more circumspectly and more relevantly here, the situation could also be construed as a hermeneutical challenge, as a test case for the sorts of cross-culturally, evocatively morphologically comparative enterprises advocated in this project. First, via a rigorous hermeneutic of suspicion, we can expose and complain of the inadequacy of extant interpretations; but then, we can also undertake a more recovering, replenishing hermeneutic by transforming this chapter's historical instantiations into heuristic questions as a means by which to explore the very real possibility that, in one way or another, contemplative modes of ritual-architectural presentation and apprehension have, in fact, been operative in such indigenous historical contexts as ancient (or contemporary) Mesoamerica. Searchingly morphological comparisons, in this case particularly, provide a foundation on which to build empirically rigorous and specific interpretive descriptions.

Twenty-three | Propitiation: Building as Offering (Priority III-C)

> Here are the petitions to their gods, when they prayed, and this was the supplication of their hearts: Lord God, remember us as who are thine; grant us health, give us children and prosperity so that the people shall increase and serve thee, give us water and good weather so that we may maintain ourselves and that we may live; hear our petitions, receive our prayers; help us against our enemies; give us ease and rest.
>
> Bartolomé de las Casas, circa 1550[1]

> Nay, I do not want marble churches at all for their own sake, but for the sake of the spirit that would build them. . . . It is not the church we want, but the sacrifice; not the emotion of admiration, but the art of adoration: not the gift, but the giving.
>
> John Ruskin, 1849[2]

> But unlike pure engineering where the objective is efficiency and economy in construction, architecture is something deeper.
>
> Amos Ih Tiao Chang, 1956[3]

"PROPITIATION," A TERM ENCUMBERED by especially thick Jewish and Christian valances, usually implies winning the favor of some higher authority, gaining or regaining an aura of good will, petitioning, placating, or conciliating a superior—particularly a deity but perhaps a demon, ancestor, or spirit—that has been offended. Propitiative ritual, then, is usually in the service of cultivating, maintaining, or restoring some sort of favorable inclination or condition of harmony. Appeasing and assuaging, making peace and begging pardon, soothing and dulcifying, quenching and quelling conflict are often the watchwords of propitiation; it may, however, also involve a more aggressively interested, more strategic negotiation to some advantage, a haggling, bartering, or bribing of superhuman partners or adversaries.

Propitiation, therefore, a dissatisfyingly imprecise designation for priority III-C, touches upon a whole nexus of loosely interrelated forms of ritual practice: from offering and oblation to petitionary sacrifices and fertility rites; healing, cleansing, and exorcism; worship, supplication, thanksgiving, and expressions of gratitude; atonement, pleas for forgiveness, expiation, and vindication; and thus exercises of penance, fasting, flagellation, or other forms of self-mortification. Frustratingly inclusive, this is the most widely framed (and least parallel) category in the entire morphology. Yet, because this complex of concerns intrudes so heavily on so many—perhaps most—ritual-architectural programs, and even more because so many commentators—perhaps too many—have invoked "begging for divine favor" as their primary solution to the problem of what is at stake in the ceremonial usage of specific sacred architectures, this is a necessary and, I hope to show, provocative adjunct to the heuristic framework.

The propitiation priority, as I am framing this set of heuristic options, is *not,* then, a mode of ritual-architectural presentation in quite the same sense as theater (III-A), contemplation (III-B), and sanctuary (III-D). Though still concerned with ritualized apprehensions of architecture, this inventory of relationships between propitiation and building calls attention to a range of motivations, or set of incentives, for making and using architecture that can intersect or overlap with virtually all of the other priorities in the morphology. With respect to allurement, for instance, many decidedly propitiatory architectural events—notably, seasonal planting or harvest ceremonials—are initiated according to regularized astrobiological schedules (and thus closely linked to the homology [I-A] and maybe astronomy [I-C] priorities). Others—say, rites performed in preparation for hunting or even war—are often timed not only in response to situational crises but according to time-worn traditional schedules and historical precedents (thus linking propitiation especially to the convention priority [I-B]). Or, in other contexts, ritual-architectural propitiations are undertaken with more generalized indemnificatory purposes, in Robert Redfield's phrase, "just in case."[4] With respect to the more content-specific back half of the architectural situation, to propitiate, a tellingly transitive verb requiring a direct object, may entail most often ritual petitions directed at deities and/or revered ancestors (thus linking those propitiatory rites with commemorations of divinity [II-A] and/or the dead [II-D]). But ritualized propitiation might also be aimed at mythological culture heroes or even temporal rulers (whereupon commemorations of sacred history [II-B] or of politics [II-C] are the closest links).

Owing to the wide, virtually ubiquitous, relevance of broadly propitiatory concerns, aspirations to comprehensiveness with respect to this priority are particularly futile. Nonetheless, the unwieldy mass of relevant themes and variations can be provisionally organized via a bipartite but very uneven division between: propitiatory uses of standing architecture, which, though already very widely acknowledged, are often seriously distorted; and the somewhat more neglected senses in which architectural construction itself is, in one way or another, conceived as propitiatory ritual. The first set of possibilities, though perhaps relevant in some respect to nearly all ritual-architectural events, is dispatched fairly quickly. The lion's share of the chapter is, then, devoted to the second, more explicitly constructional set of alternatives wherein the "ritual contexts" most at issue are not those delimited by the (supposedly) finished architectural forms, but by the contexts of building and "making."

Propitiatory Uses of Architecture: Visions and Delusions of Negotiated Exchange

Patently propitiatory uses of standing architecture are, not surprisingly, particularly conspicuous in the monotheistic traditions, which feature conceptions of a personal, largely omnipotent, and not altogether unreasonable god with whom devotees might enter into an essentially conversational sort of negotiative exchange. The covenantal relationship between the People of Israel and Yahweh provides perhaps the best example of this sort of earthly-Otherly contractual arrangement. In Judaism, though appeals and solicitations to God might ostensibly be offered from everywhere, the Western Wall in Jerusalem, originally a mere retaining support for the Temple Mount enclosure but now the most sacred of Jewish sites, provides a special point of delivery for such human-divine communiqués. Daily, therefore, this stupendously superabundant built form, initially not even part of the actual temple structure, is host to a wide array of explicitly propitiatory ritual-architectural events.[5]

Regarding the apprehensions of this unelaborate but inexhaustibly meaningful architectural feature, Mordechai Ha'cohen explains that Jews are confident that, if they pray at the Western Wall, "the Holy One, blessed be He, forgives them all their sins."[6] Pilgrimaging to the Wall enables one to petition directly to God, because, according to tradition, "it has been decreed in Heaven that it will never be destroyed. . . . Because the Divine Presence will never depart from the Western Wall."[7] A ceaseless flow of Jewish pilgrims visits the "Wall of Tears," as non-Jews refer to it, to pray, cry, or "wail." Epitomizing a particularly intimate interactive exchange between buildings and beholders, pilgrims come here, Ha'cohen says, to caress and kiss the stones, to inscribe their names or write them in ink and paint, "to drive nails into the cracks between the stones as a talisman," to deposit the clothing of their dead relatives, and to write their own special petitions on pieces of paper and insert them into cracks in the Wall—"in the hope that [these] would thus be continually before Him, whose presence rests on the Wall."[8] In these cases, then, ritual-architectural propitiation is based upon a kind of logic of exchange between a personal god and his "chosen people," a confidence that devotional investments will reap a return, that demonstrations of compliance with one's juridical obligations to God will engender some appropriately reciprocal response on the part of the divine.

Though a suitably empirical description for (at least some) pilgrims to Jerusalem, extrapolating this kind of negotiative logic of propitiation into other cross-cultural contexts is another of those interpretive possibilities—often linked closely to the hackneyed query, to which god is this temple dedicated?[9]—that is made problematic more by its incautious overuse than by its neglect. In Mesoamericanist studies, for example, from the earliest colonialist encounters, the most standard of all explanations of pre-Columbian ritual-architectural events has been built upon the presumption that huge pyramid-temples and modest shrines alike were built primarily as "adoratorios," places for petitioning and dickering for the favor of deities.[10] Consequently, whether appropriate or not, the most prevalent explanation of indigenous ceremonials, from spectacular pre-Hispanic public sacrifices to the still-ubiquitous burning of copal incense—epitomized in Bishop Bartolomé de las Casas's oft-cited rendition of a petitionary prayer the Maya of Guatemala supposedly recited during their human sacrifices[11]—has been, and remains, to imagine such practices as occasions for human devotees to enter into a kind of dialogical bartering with their deities. Indians too, it has generally been presumed, not unlike Jewish pilgrims to the Western Wall, feel a compulsion to build and to ritualize as a means of honoring and exploiting their contractual relationships with the gods.

Eric Thompson, for instance, argued that, "essentially, Maya religion is a matter of a contract between man and his gods."[12] Redfield contended that Yucatec folk religion was based on a detailed "keeping of accounts" with gods, saints, and *yuntzilb* (the protectors of the fields and woods) and on a "preservation of balance expressed in offering and ritual performance."[13] Thomas Lee, Evon Vogt, and George Foster each describe a "bargaining process" between Highland Maya and the supernatural.[14] And Joyce Marcus argues that, among Zapotecs, "all relationships—whether with ancestors, animals, other Zapotecs, or supernaturals—were considered reciprocal, with something offered in return for every concession."[15]

More recently, Johanna Broda, too, has proposed that Aztec human sacrifice, in addition to more obviously politicized motives within the state cult, was also conceived as a kind of "debt payment" to the rain and mountain gods, or as a magical act of reciprocity according to the principle of *do ut des* ("give that you may receive").[16] She explains that, in the context of agricultural or fertility cults:

> [human sacrifice] denoted an act of reciprocity with the deities that represented natural phenomena; that is, the gods of rain and the mountains, the goddesses of sweet and salty water, the maize deities, and the earth goddess. The natural phenomena that were "negotiated" were water, rain and agricultural growth.[17]

According to this logic of reciprocal ritual negotiation, the ritual sacrifice of children, for instance, involved an exchange of one "precious liquid"—the blood of children—for another "precious liquid," rain.[18]

The pervasiveness of these sorts of mercantile metaphors in the literature on Mesoamerica—or in the literature on numerous other indigenous contexts—while not wholly untoward, has nonetheless a tendency to overdetermine and seriously distort empirical native priorities. The language of negotiation and bargaining (and, to a lesser extent, reciprocity), for one, too often presupposes personalistic Abrahamic or "pagan" conceptions of divinity and thus obfuscates other alternatives.[19] That indigenous rituals were operating with the logic of pleading and ransoming favor from a "pantheon" of temperamental "gods," for instance, seemed eminently plausible to Spanish Catholic friar-chroniclers who, consequently, missed almost entirely those nonanthropomorphic conceptions of divinity for which they had less semblant comparative counterparts.[20] As the recent and masterful work of Alfredo López Austin demonstrates, for centuries Western scholars have been dealing with a distressingly thin slice of the subtle Nahautl conceptions of divinity, space, time, and human bodies, and have thus remained largely blind to the nuanced religiocosmological logic of indigenous ritual practices.[21]

Hermeneuts ought, therefore, to remain alert to the many contexts in which propitiatory ritual-architectural events are undertaken, largely irrespective of any expectation of winning the benignity of a personalized supernatural presence. The notion of haggling one's way to some bilateral understanding with god, or of purchasing divine favor, which is usually a pejorative accusation about someone else's religious reasoning rather than a self-description of one's own, is, for instance, largely irrelevant also in most forms of interiorized meditation, most broadly "magical" or alchemical practices, or in the godless but thoroughly reliable reciprocations of karma —all of which could nevertheless be relevant to the propitiation priority (III-C). Even the old interpretive line that prehistoric rituals were based on a logic of "sympathetic causation"—epitomized by E. O. James's now unpopular contention that prehistoric hunters acted out the desired sequence of events ritually in the context of cave-sanctuaries or rock-shelter shrines so as to ensure the subsequent success of the actual expedition[22]—raises the heuristic possibility of propitiatory architectural events and dances performed not so much in hopes of eliciting the assistance of deities as manipulating more directly the course of future events.

Another relevant, more compelling possibility (which probably better approximates what was happening in most pre-Hispanic Aztec rites) are those ritual-architectural events that are conceived as strategic exercises in channeling impersonal, fluid-like spiritual energies and cosmic forces, again largely irrespective of solicitations of godly requital. Both Jonathan Smith's polemical work on Melanesian cargo cults and Irving Goldman's reassessment of Kwakiutl potlatch redistribution suggest a devotional logic wherein, instead of conversation partners with the gods, ritual participants conceive of themselves as integral elements in something like a "cosmological system of circulation," an all-embracing cosmic system of mutual relatedness and equilibrium.[23] Consequently, instead of buying or begging for divine favor, ritual-architectural events in these situations, which might also be properly classed as propitiatory, arise from both an obligation to participate in the larger cosmic system by offering and exchanging and a confidence that one's actions in the human realm will "provoke a corresponding response in all associated realms."[24]

In sum, then, instead of offering a fittingly detailed inventory of variations on the propitiatory use of standing architecture—the first, exceedingly broad set of expressions of priority III-C—(too large a task for the present venue), we must settle here for a word of caution. Though perhaps virtually all substantial ritual-architectural events are at least vaguely propitiatory in the widest sense of the term (a dimension of those events that should not go unnoticed), problems of cultural-specificity are, in this respect, as with commemorations of divinity (priority II-A), particularly intense. Instead, then, of replicating the familiar error of transferring into cross-cultural contexts some vaguely generic "Judeo-Christian" model of petitionary ritual, critical hermeneuts would be better advised to examine the interminably contestatory reinterpretation among Jews, Christians, and even Muslims themselves concerning what is at issue in being the "People of the Covenant"[25]—which should serve, among other purposes, as a warning against settling too easily for some glib conception of the ritualized give-and-take between people and gods.

Building as Propitiatory Ritual: Rationales for Nonexpedient Construction

Where standing architecture works in many ways to accommodate expressly, if widely diverse, propitiatory ritual practices, we need also to consider a second, quite different, more often neglected set of manifestations of priority III-C: namely, the sense in which acts of construction—the making and building of architecture—are themselves conceived as offertory or propitiatory rituals. The ritual context that matters most in these cases is the context of production; and thus the (indigenous) hermeneutical experiences of architecture that matter most are the experiential apprehensions of the meaning and significance of one's participation in construction processes. The finished product, while no doubt engendering a large measure of satisfaction, is of less consequence than the fabricatory processes. As one major component of our hermeneutics of sacred architecture, therefore, we need to embrace, as too few scholars have, what is more properly the hermeneutics of building than of buildings.

If Eurocentric notions of bargaining and negotiation can lead, on occasion, to distortions of the propitiatory usages of indigenous architectures, it is quite likely modernist presumptions concerning the seemingly commonsensical goals of cost effectiveness and expedience in construction processes (including those that obtain in the case of explicitly religious buildings) that are largely responsible for the failure to appreciate fully the significance of deliberately tedious, laborious means of architectural production. Walter Gropius, for instance, gave voice not only to the abstract ideals of the "New Architecture" of the Bauhaus but to pragmatic attitudes of most working contractors when he campaigned incessantly for simplicity and economy in building, a "rationalized construction" that could raise buildings quickly and with the least expenditure of effort.[26] For most critics, then, it seems only fair that interpretation is delayed until a work of art of architecture is completed. What is done is nearly always privileged over the doing. Yet, surveying the cross-cultural history of architecture—and remembering the apparent "uselessness" of many architectural productions[27]—we quickly discover countless fascinating circumstances in which the erection of "religious" buildings seems to have been undertaken with precisely the opposite priority—that is, nonexpedience or, better, "transexpedience."

One rationale (among many) for embracing the inobvious ideal of maximizing rather than minimizing effort in the construction process is provided by John Ruskin's nineteenth-century exposition of the first of his "Seven Lamps of Architecture," the "Lamp of Sacrifice." In the course of his universalistic recommendations for architects, Ruskin defines the Lamp of Sacrifice, first, in a negative fashion, as "the opposite of the prevalent feeling of modern times, which desires to produce the largest results at the least cost," and then, in a positive fashion, as an architectural aspiration that "prompts us to the offering of precious things merely because they are precious, not because they are useful or necessary."[28] According to Ruskin's puritanical reasoning, architectural beauty derives less from a building's conformity to some aesthetic criteria than from the tangible demonstration of commitment and sincerity; and thus, conversely, to have been easily or inexpensively produced abrogates a building's effectiveness and appeal. He argues, in other words, "that we should consider an increase of apparent labor as an increase of beauty in the building."[29] In his view, instead of streamlining any part of the building process, success in building is directly proportional to the toil, the costliness of materials, and the sacrifice that produced it.

Though few circumstances actually match Ruskin's extreme recommendation for nonexpedience, many building projects—though underwritten by a range of quite different rationales—do reflect parallel sorts of abnegations of efficiency. In the next sections, the countless variations on this theme of transutilitarian, propitiatory ritual construction (the second broad set of expressions of this priority) can, for the sake of heuristic exposition, be organized according to three broad impulses: building for periodic renewal; building as a demonstration of devotion; and building as a strategic investment or petition of divine favor.

(Re)Building for Periodic Renewal: Constructional Reiterations of Cosmogony

This first set of suboptions, which involves the cultivation of an experience of periodic regeneration via building or renovation, can take a number of forms. Very often, however, such practices are based upon an explicit analogy between the construction of a building and the creation of the world. This notion of constructional reiterations of the cosmogony (which thus merges the propitiatory priority [III-C] with that of homology [I-A] and the commemoration of sacred history [II-B]), a relentless emphasis in the work of Mircea Eliade, has been amply documented in countless contexts.[30] In India, to cite Eliade's own most prized example, the elaborate ritual prescriptions applied to building materials, craftsmen, and techniques of temple construction are all couched in explicit metaphors of founding a new world; and, once erected, even if structurally sound, the very brick, mortar, and timber members of those Hindu temples are subject to periodic ritual renewal.[31] Or, among dozens of well-documented tribal examples, the repetitive (re)construction of Barasana longhouses[32] and of the sun dance lodges and *hocokas*, or camp circles, of the Oglala Sioux have likewise been interpreted by both natives and nonnatives as exercises in the construction of microcosmic universes, and thus ritual reiterations of their respective creation myths.[33]

The notion of construction as a reiteration of cosmogony may even apply, albeit in less obvious ways, in Judeo-Christian traditions. Intriguingly, Mieke Bal explains that the verb that describes the creation of gender in Genesis 2:22 is the same verb that refers specifically to architecture and the construction of buildings, thus raising the possibility that, in some sense, each Judeo-Christian act of construction is a reiteration of cosmogony.[34] And, accentuating both the homologous correspondence between "the Christian temple" and the cosmos and the ritual nature of its construction, Titus Burckhardt is much more explicit in his contention that there is an important sense in which the construction of a Christian sanctuary reproduces once again the original creation:

> Like the cosmos the temple is produced out of chaos. The building materials, wood, brick or stone, correspond to the *hyle* or *materia prima,* the plastic substance of the world. . . . The tools used to shape the crude materials accordingly symbolize the divine "instruments" which "fashion" the cosmos out of the undifferentiated and amorphous *materia prima.*[35]

Closely related to construction that is conceived as a deliberate reiteration of the cosmogony are those manifestations of the propitiatory priority in which perfectly serviceable structures are periodically (or perpetually) rebuilt according to a calendrically regular schedule. In Mesoamerica, for instance, the practice of routinely moving, remodeling, or rebuilding, not because buildings are worn out in any physical sense but (apparently) to facilitate a sense of regeneration, has been well documented at all levels of society. At the domestic level, Bishop Landa was struck by the Yucatecans seemingly inordinate changes in residence and, moreover, by their annual compulsion for sweeping up and destroying nearly all their household utensils only to replace them with near duplicates at the first of the new year.[36] At a more public scale, Alfred Tozzer, among many, wondered at the pan-Maya evidence of "an almost feverish restlessness to demolish and rebuild or to cover up a smaller by a larger construction."[37] And, in Central Mexico, the pyramid of Tenayuca, where each of six major campaigns of enlargement and remodeling may (or may not) have corresponded to the conclusions of fifty-two-year calendar cycles, has been the classic example of regularly scheduled pre-Columbian rebuilding.[38]

Perpetual, Regularized Rebuilding: Permanence and Impermanence at Ise

Instances of routinized rebuilding are, then, prevalent around the world. Yet, because perhaps no circumstance demonstrates more pointedly this permutation of the propitiation priority than Japan's Grand Shrine of Ise, a context in which the notion of periodic rebuilding is elaborated into that of virtually constant building, it deserves somewhat fuller consideration. In addition to a number of auxiliary shrines, this pre-Zen religious center is built around two major shrines, roughly identical in form. The most important, the Naiku (Inner Shrine) is dedicated to Amaterasu, the sovereign solar deity who is ancestress of the imperial line. The other major shrine, the Geku (Outer Shrine), located some five miles away on the opposite side of the Isuzu River, is dedicated to Toyouke, the archaic food goddess.[39] These unpainted, unadorned wooden shrines have a formal clarity that has been described variously as "heroic simplicity,"[40] as "an architecture of rare and clean power,"[41] and even as "plain to the point of artlessness."[42] There are no great sculptures, no polychrome, no intricate spaces to fathom.

Nevertheless, Ise has persevered literally for centuries as perhaps the most prestigious of Japanese shrines. Moreover, not inconsequentially, owing to faithful adherence to the custom of rebuilding the shrines every twenty years, the visage of the major constructions has been maintained virtually unchanged for that entire time.

Obviously then, Ise is another of those circumstances that demonstrate an exceedingly complex play of ritual-architectural priorities: Because of its special associations with the imperial family and with the mythology of

Amaterasu, admixings and variations on the priorities of politics (II-C), divinity (II-A), and sacred history (II-B) are especially relevant. Moreover, Robert Ellwood's detailed explication and interpretation of the Kanname-sai, or Harvest Festival, an annual first fruits ceremony in which a whole series of offerings is made to each of Ise's two major shrines and then over the next several days to all the lesser shrines within the system, provides marvelous instantiation of the propitiatory use of standing architecture, discussed at the outset of this chapter.[43] Still more striking, though—and the phenomenon that makes Ise a quintessential example of this more explicitly constructional permutation of the propitiation priority—is the enduring practice of ceremonially dismantling and rebuilding the shrine buildings of Ise every twenty years.

In Kenzo Tange's account of this ongoing, rightfully renowned renovation, we learn that adjacent to each of the two main shrines is a fenced enclosure that serves as the "alternate site," where, after dismantling the buildings every twenty years, brand new copies of the old wooden shrines are (re)built.[44] In other words, alongside the structures currently in use, a new group is perpetually being constructed in the image of the existing ones. Each stage of the veritably ceaseless construction process is meticulously regulated. Fully ten years prior to the actual rebuilding, the Mountain Entrance rites formally initiate the garnering of precisely the right wood in precisely the right way:

> Carpenters in spotless white repair to the sacred forests on the Kiso Mountains to cut new timber. They bathe frequently; if blood should fall on any stick, it would be rejected.[45]

Then, as Tange explains, each stage of preparation—hauling the materials, staking out the site, breaking the ground, setting the primary pillars—proceeds according to similarly fastidious (and often secret) ritual regulation. Upon completion of the new shrines (that is, every twenty years), the process culminates with the ceremony of *sengushiki,* an intricate set of rituals and a spectacular procession of musicians and priests with offerings and torches, wherein the actual divine presence (the *yata kagami,* or mirror, supposedly given by Amaterasu) is transferred from the twenty-year-old shrine to its fresh replacement. The two-decade-old structure is then completely dismantled and its site readied for the next rebuilding.[46]

Remarkably, since the end of the seventh century, when the imperial family first instituted the rites associated with the rebuilding of these shrines, the constructional routine has been carried out some sixty times—

that is, for more than a thousand years.[47] Accordingly, the buildings currently standing at Ise are virtually identical to the ones that stood there at least as early as 685 C.E. While the ceaseless rebuilding does mitigate any sagging, warping, or weathering that might compromise the aesthetic effect of the whole, the regularized rebuilding of Ise is obviously not dedicated simply to the preservation of old buildings as such. Beyond merely keeping the shrine in good repair, Ellwood emphasizes the transutilitarian and regenerative effect of the repetitive rebuildings. Taking an Eliadean tack, he interprets the periodic reconstruction as a "rite of the defiance of temporal decay and historical change":

> For the historian of religion, the Grand Shrine of Ise and above all the Ritual Year rebuilding displays how a religious institution which is, in [S. G. F.] Brandon's phrase, a "ritual perpetuation of the past" can at the same time be an effective statement of perpetual newness, of the overcoming of time and hence of the immediacy of the timeless transcendent Holy.[48]

Moreover, to accentuate a point that Ellwood does not address, the ritual dismantlement of the architecture (another permutation on the propitiatory priority addressed more fully in a moment) may be as important at Ise as the process of reconstruction. Noboru Kawazoe's astute interpretation of Ise, more helpful than Ellwood's in this respect, suggests that the regularized rebuilding is not, after all, an attempt to conquer time, as in the case of Western monuments that are intended to last forever. Instead, quite to the contrary, the endless process is, in Kawazoe's view, an acknowledgment of impermanence. According to this interpretation, the juxtaposition of ephemeral wooden materials with the permanent, invariant style of Ise provides a kind of ritual-architectural expression of the Shinto philosophy of the transience of all worldly things (thus suggesting, among other things, a merger of the propitiation priority [III-C] with a particularly nuanced commemoration of ultimate reality or divinity [priority II-A]). In Kawazoe's phrasing:

> It was the style, not the actual structures embodying it, that they sought to preserve for posterity. Everything that had physical, concrete form, they believed, was doomed to decay; only style was indestructible. . . . [Or] to go one step further, what the Japanese wanted to preserve was not even the style as such in all its details but something else, some intangible essence within the style.[49]

Strategic, Irregular Rebuilding: Politics, Available Resources, Life Crises

Regenerative rebuildings do not, however, always proceed with the sort of calendrical precision demonstrated at Ise. Often, instead of following regularized cycles of time, ritual rebuildings are correlated, for instance, with transitions in political leadership, thus directing our attention to yet another important subset of variations on the propitiatory priority that are linked especially to the commemoration of temporal authority (politics, priority II-C). For example, looking once more to ancient Mesoamerica, almost immediately upon ascending to the throne, each of seven successive Aztecs rulers felt compelled to refurbish substantially the already spectacular Templo Mayor.[50] The same sort of reliance on architectural construction and refurbishment to sanction a change in leadership, that is, to announce emphatically both the end of one era and the fresh and legitimate beginning of another, is also evident in seventeenth-century chronicler M. A. Tovilla's description of events in the wake of the passing of the Maya lord of Utatlán: "when the king died," Tovilla writes, "they rewhitened all the streets and palaces inside and out, and painted new histories."[51]

Similarly, countless tribal peoples rely on construction, not simply as a means of periodically engendering a generalized sense of starting afresh, but also to formalize and legitimate a transfer of authority. Among the Tongo of South Africa, when a headman dies, not unlike when a village is struck by lightning or when the adjacent land has been exhausted, a ritual specialist invokes astragalomancy (the use of divining bones) to select a fresh site, consummates that choice by sexual intercourse, and then embarks upon a lengthy process wherein the old village is "broken to pieces" and the new village erected and sacralized. The new beginning effected by relocation and rebuilding allows the Tongo to experience what has appropriately been described as "a phoenix-like opportunity for rebirth of the community with the rebirth of the village" and, more specifically, redirects their allegiance to a new headman.[52]

Sometimes, in less overtly politicized situations, the processes of periodic renewal via ritual-architectural construction proceed on an irregular schedule imposed by the availability of resources. The humble Otomi, sedentary peasants of the high plains of Mexico, for example, though apparently enamored of the idea of renewal via building, took down and replaced their temple on a highly sporadic schedule that was determined more by economic than ecological or cosmic factors.[53] And Roxana

Waterson explains how the status of origin-houses of the Indonesian Sa'dan Toraja (the extravagantly dramatic funerals that are staged in these houses was discussed in chapter 21) is greatly enhanced by repeated rebuildings that take place, not on any regularized schedule, "but whenever the descendants of the house feel they can afford it."[54]

In many situations, the regenerative potential of building is invoked on a similarly irregular schedule, but in response to personal transitions or life crises or perhaps as a very palpable demonstration of one's cultural affinities or ethnic identity. Waterson goes on to explain that Toraja natives who have left their home villages for the city are even more concerned than the indigenous residents who stayed behind to return periodically and rebuild their traditional origin-houses as a means of publicly reaffirming their "Torajaness." She considers that

> the reconstruction of an origin-house provides a dramatic means of asserting a "Toraja" identity, which now has to be defined within the context of the cultural diversity of modern Indonesia.[55]

Similarly alluding to the way in which construction can foster a very personalized sense of identity, satisfaction, and renewal—as evidenced perhaps in the seemingly universal enthusiasm that children have for inhabiting the makeshift forts and tree houses of their own creation—Paul Oliver emphasizes that in many tribal societies, "all members of the community are expected to have the knowledge and the dexterity to be able to construct their own dwelling."[56] In those contexts, then, construction provides one of the principal avenues both to personal self-fulfillment and rejuvenation and, owing to those sorts of roof-raising activities that require communal cooperation, to a collective sense of accomplishment and renewal. Oliver's quite viable implication is, in other words, that something very important—an opportunity for self- and group-expression and for periodic renewal—is lost when, in modern societies, the construction process becomes the unique preserve of a few specialists.[57]

Building as a Demonstration of Devotion: Expressions of Gratitude, Commitment, and Adoration

A second, closely related subset of constructional permutations on the propitiation priority is comprised of building processes that are undertaken, largely without expectation of reward, as demonstrations of devotion, that is, building that arises in response to religioritual incentives, such as a desire to give thanks for some good fortune, to fulfill a sacred contract, or, more generally, simply to display worthiness and humility. Thus, besides fostering a human experience of renewal, transexpedient building projects might also be initiated variously as sacrificial offerings, as tangible expressions of a community's commitment to supernatural authority, as admissions of dependence and createdness, or, in Evelyn Underhill's term, as signs of "pure adoration."[58]

Among the most obvious expressions of this sort of devotional building is that set of shrines and monuments that are erected explicitly as expressions of gratitude in the wake of some miracle or good fortune. In ancient Babylon, for example, "it became the first duty of kings to build, endow or embellish a temple in recognition of the services rendered to them by the divine powers."[59] Equally unmistakable are those constructions built expressly as recompense for some serious transgression. The white marble Jain temple at Mount Abu in western India, for instance, was built, so the story goes, as an act of penance by Vimala, a minister to the Solanki ruler Bhima I, who, in his capacity as commander of the army, had caused considerable bloodshed in pacifying a rebellious principality.[60]

There are, however, countless, more subtle variations on this basic theme of an architecture of adoration in which expedience in construction is an almost totally foreign priority. Often, particularly where anthropomorphic conceptions of the sacred prevail, seemingly extravagant building projects are initiated (or justified) primarily in the interest of offering a "gift to god," and only secondarily in order to furnish an enduring ritual context in which devotees might subsequently pursue their religious lives. By deliberately and dramatically placing (supposedly) divine interests before human ones, toilsome construction processes provide builders with forums, times, and places—ritual contexts of another sort—in which to prove their worth and their willingness to sacrifice both for one another and for god. The threadbare congregations of Poland in the 1980s, for instance, by transforming their scant resources and a state-induced shortage of materials into "the largest increase in Christian churches anywhere in the world [during that decade]," provided not only inspiration to other Christians but evidence to the enduring potential of construction as a means for the expression and reaffirmation of religious commitment.[61]

Moreover, given the logic of this sort of offertory architecture, expeditiousness in completion is not nearly so important as proceeding through the (ritualized) construction process in a fashion that demonstrates a commitment to, in some sense, "give one's best to God." In these cases, means supersede ends. Herod's rebuilding of the Temple in Jerusalem, for instance, was complicated immensely by twin commitments to use massive stones, which would evoke a sense of "God's presence Everlasting," and to forestall completion rather than expedite the process with iron tools, iron supposedly having been created to "shorten the days of man."[62] Or, a world away, in the Shaker community of Pleasant Hill, Kentucky, while vehemently rejecting the notion that their finished meetinghouses could themselves serve as objects of devotion—Shakers were, in other words, adamant in their rejection of the contemplation priority (III-B)—these Christians nonetheless explicitly described the communal and meticulous construction of those plain white structures as collective demonstrations of devotion to God.[63]

Or, though in terms of formal appearance it is difficult to imagine a more drastic contrast to the starkness of Shaker design, even the ongoing construction of Barcelona's fantastically elaborate Sagrada Familia, the Expiatory Temple of the Holy Family, begun in 1882 and still just 40 percent complete, may, morphologically (and generously) speaking, participate in the same sort of propitiatory logic. When architect Antoni Gaudi supposedly dismissed queries regarding the exorbitant costs and decades of construction that would be required to complete his phantasmagoric, art nouveau creation by noting calmly, "My client isn't in any hurry," the designer would seem similarly to be espousing the notion that sacred architecture is intended primarily for God, and only secondarily for human use.[64]

Art for the Wholly Other: The Viability of Apolitical Architecture

There is, of course, particularly in the case of spectacular public monuments like that of the Sagrada Familia, the strong likelihood, even inevitability, that professed motivations of godly devotion (that is, exercises of this particular permutation of the propitiation priority [III-C]) are laced with or "contaminated" by ulterior, more pragmatic sociopolitical incentives (that is, by expressions of the politics priority [II-C]).[65] Highly visible exercises of apparent reverence and selflessness can certainly serve as effective means of social and economic manipulation. For already-suspicious postmodern hermeneuts, however, warnings of that exploitative prospect are probably less urgent than entreatments to take very seriously the real (that is, empirical) viability of architectural projects that *are* undertaken expressly and foremost for transhuman, supernatural, or cosmic consumption, as it were. Sincere compliance with what are perceived as divinely mandated design directives at the expense of more obviously tangible sociopolitical interests—both as a heuristic possibility and as a historical reality—ought not to be dismissed too quickly.

Pursuing this interpretive tack, which is consistent with a hermeneutic of retrieval, requires one to entertain, for instance, the ironic but definitely plausible possibility that the ostentatious, the intricate, and the high in sacred architecture—beyond their significance as bold signs of human accomplishment or of political hegemony—may serve, alternatively or additionally, as built demonstrations of humility and of the acknowledgment of designers' and builders' subservience before the divine.[66] Accordingly, many of those displays of ornamentation and supra-utility alluded to earlier in relation to the theatric (III-A) and contemplative (III-B) modes of ritual-architectural presentation—Gothic cathedrals that were hundreds of years in the making, baroque spaces of unbelievable complexity, or the temple of Karnak, perhaps the largest of all human constructions—may likewise be, in the apprehensions of at least some specific audiences, stupendous offerings to their respective gods. Spectacular constructions like St.-Denis and Borobudur, in addition to being aids to contemplation and expressions of political interests, might be viably interpreted as monuments to the vicissitudinous inconvenience the faithful will endure to express modesty and abasement before the sacred—and thus as strong participants in this devotional permutation of the propitiation priority. Paradoxically, in architecture, the sumptuous, as well as the simple, can be an expression of humility and acquiescence.

Perhaps the most compelling empirical evidence of the sincerity of such offertory, largely apolitical ritual-architectural incentives—art for the Wholly Other—is provided by the near or complete inaccessibility of so many elaborate artistic and architectural works and elements.[67] British historian of religion S. G. F. Brandon, for example, puzzled over the unmistakable discrepancy between the obviously didactic motives behind something like medieval Christian stained glass and "the more mysterious nature of the motives operative in Palaeolithic art" because, in the latter case, "most of its products are situated in the innermost recesses of caves, most difficult of access and enshrouded in complete darkness."[68] Brandon concluded, and I agree, that, "Quite obviously paintings so positioned were not intended for instruction or decoration."[69] Neither would those largely obscured works have served as cultic accoutrements, except to highly restricted audiences on quite rare occasions; and neither, therefore, would they have been very effective vehicles for the manipulation of social policy or opinion. Nor does "aesthetic pleasure" impress Brandon as sufficent explanation, leaving propitiative—offertory and sacrificial—purposes, or "religio-magical motives," as, if arguing by subtraction, the most feasible possibilities.[70]

Similarly vexed by the logic that eventuated in caches of pristine, carefully preserved masks, vessels, musical instruments, figurines, and ornaments in virtually every pre-Hispanic structure, Mesoamericanists are, on the one hand, thrilled and grateful that so many fine "works of art" (a particularly inept term at this point) were stowed and thus saved. Yet, on the other hand, viewed from a Western perspective, such recondite troves can also engender perplexity and a melancholic sense of waste and misspent effort as one realizes that even in the era of their creation almost no persons were allowed to see and appreciate these splendid objects. Immediately and permanently stashing such treasures seems, from a modernist perspective, ludicrous, a thriftless squandering of talent and energy, and thus, for some, evidence of the true strangeness and impracticality of indigenous priorities.

Cast in a more affirmative light, however, the quality and quantity of "gifts," as López Luján terms them, which have been retrieved from Mesoamerica's ubiquitous dedicatory caches,[71] have forced scholars to acknowledge a strain of pre-Columbian building, artistry, and religion that seems to stand in nearly diametrical opposition to the ritual-architectural pomp, panache, and shameless propagandizing for which this historical context is so often credited (or condemned).[72] This less obviously political, seemingly more propitiatory religioartistic strain, which secreted away its most elaborate productions for the exclusive peruse of divine patrons (whether conceived as gods or deified ancestors), reversed the priority of inclusivistic theatric display (III-A) and largely abstained from the presentation of the sorts of built objects and decoration that might have served as props to ongoing devotion (as in the case of the contemplative mode, III-B). Alternatively, this strain embraces a logic of propitiatory devotion (a permutation of priority III-C), which shows itself in those elaborately carved downsides of sculptures that, once positioned, are forever hidden from human view; or in those magnificent Olmec masks, never meant for public display, which were buried almost immediately upon being made;[73] or in those Maya murals that were stowed deep in caves, in Ian Graham's words, "like Ghirlandajo's frescoes . . . painted for the eyes of gods, not men."[74]

Additionally, more strictly architectural evidence of the currency of this version of propitiative construction comes in the similarly widespread pre-

Columbian practice of covering over whole pyramidal structures with later and larger ones, in which case sculptural and decorative elements were more often carefully preserved and sealed in, like huge-scaled offertory caches, than salvaged to expedite subsequent constructions. Likewise, the sheer size of buildings and monuments speaks to the relevance of this sort of propitiatory incentive: Many indigenous constructions, particularly in Central Mexico—the gargantuan Pyramid of the Sun at Teotihuacan and the even larger pyramid at Cholula, for example—have engendered the respect of scholars and travelers, not for their beauty or craftsmanship, but primarily for the tremendous outlay of labor, the apparent sacrifice and commitment, that was required to erect them.[75]

Finally, this sort of transexpedient logic of offertory construction is evident also in the redundancy of decoration that invariably embellishes those over-big monuments. Reflecting on what seemed odd native priorities at the Oaxaca site of Mitla, turn-of-the-century explorer W. H. Holmes, for instance, pondered the fabulous intricacy of the geometric facades before concluding that "the amount of work involved was great, but these strange people were evidently not adverse to work."[76] Especially perplexing to Holmes was the fact that so much of that artful exertion was hidden in sealed tombs. For that reason, though, if for few others, pre-Columbian builders might have won the condescending approval of Ruskin, who insists that even though some portion of a building may be entirely concealed from human view—as in the sculpted designs on the backs of the statues or on the wall surfaces of a corridor that is too narrow for a person to pass—it cannot "lawfully" or "honestly" be left unfinished. Failing to attend with equal care to those surfaces that lie outside of people's view, from Ruskin's perspective, amounts to "trickery and dishonesty," a kind of deceit against God.[77] Ironically, then, for architectural "decoration" that issues from this version of the propitiation priority, unlike the decorative elaborations associated with theatric, anthrocentric modes of presentation and apprehension (III-A), appearances are *not* what matter most.

Ritual Destruction and Defacement: Ceremonial Ruinations of Art and Architecture

Even more pointed testimony to the viability and broad distribution of this sort of offertory "art for the Other" is provided by the startlingly widespread phenomenon of the deliberate ritual destruction of art and architecture. Very often (as noted in chapter 19), the ritualized demolition of monuments and buildings is initiated as a sign of intimidation or in order to formalize either a forcible or peaceful transition of authority. Reflecting on the difficulties, but considerable interest, in writing "a history of toppled monuments," Robert Harbison reminds us that absenting the landscape of, say, carved and cast images of Stalin, most of which were wrecked in dramatically public fashion, makes an obvious sort of political statement.[78] As folklorist Sabra Webber notes, well-timed destructions and burnings—of books, flags, bras, and draftcards, as well as works of art and architecture—often serve as potent "ammunition on the cultural battlefield."[79] Tangentially related to the propitiation priority, particularly since devotional and socioeconomic motivations ought not be conceived as mutually exclusive, such strategic exercises in "antibuilding" are, nonetheless, usually linked foremost to variations on the politics priority (II-C).[80]

More directly pertinent to the propitiation priority are the sorts of ritualized destruction of architecture that serve as necessary prerequisites to regenerative rebuilding, as in, to cite two earlier examples, the Tongo's dismantlement of their village after a headman dies or the ceremonious unbuilding of shrines at Ise.[81] The most piquantly relevant exemplars are, however, those ceremonial ruinations of art and architecture that seem to be motivated less by sociopolitical interests than by a desire to give, as it were, human creations over to the superhuman.

Ancient Mesoamerica again is notable but hardly unique in instantiating this sort of devotion via destruction at all scales. Fine pre-Columbian ceramics and metal objects were frequently broken or "killed," first by deliberate ritual mutilation and then again by being cached in offerings or burials; the vast majority of precious goods dredged from Chichén Itzá's Sacred Cenote, for instance, had endured this fate, as had much of the pottery retrieved from Maya lake sacrifices.[82] Architectural elements and sculptures, such as Maya stelae and huge Olmec stone carvings, were in many cases similarly ritually defaced and then buried.[83] Whole buildings, too, whether for military or offertory motives, were in many cases subjected to what Tozzer termed, "a pre-Columbian desire to mutilate."[84] And, even at the scale of entire pre-Columbian cities, it is plausible (if unlikely) that the enigmatic destructions and abandonments of Teotihuacan and the Classic Petén Maya centers did not eventuate from military or economic crises but, instead, from giant-scale exercises in propitiatory ritual-architectural self-destruction wherein whole settlements were, in some sense, donated or sacrificed to the gods.[85]

Though suspicions of manipulative, heavily politicized motivations are not unwarranted in any of these cases, often the stylized ritualization of defacement, together with the seeming counterproductivity of such spoilage, militates against that as a full explanation. Consequently, the plausibility of truly voluntaristic, largely apolitical incentives deserves our continued hermeneutical attention.

Building as Investment or Petition: Divine Favor, Cosmic Compensation, Karmic Merit

It is important, then, on the one hand, to entertain seriously the eventuality of substantial building projects (and ritualized destructions of artistic productions) that are undertaken without expectation of either sociopolitical or divine recompense—a heuristic possibility epitomized, for instance, by Ruskin's uncompromising Calvinist insistence that Christians are obliged to deliver to God their finest efforts in architecture, as in other of life's challenges, as "an offering of gratitude which is neither to be exhibited nor rewarded, which is neither to win praise nor purchase salvation. . . ."[86] Again though, this may be another of those morphological sets that is, empirically speaking, empty. Ideals of "pure adoration" and selflessness notwithstanding, in practice, virtually never are the rigors and expenses of religious construction shouldered with complete indifference as to some sort of consequent remuneration, either of a cosmological or a temporal sort. Building is, by and large, an investment for which its creators expect some significant return.

It is, therefore, on the other hand, important—to broach a third and last, still closely related, subset of variations on the theme of propitiatory construction—that interpreters also adopt a complementary, somewhat more skeptical hermeneutical approach to religious building practices. In this last group of examples, in which the metaphors of negotiation and reciprocal exchange are more appropriate, I direct attention to building projects that are explicitly pursuant of some sort of personal interest or ritual-architectural petition—construction that is initiated with deliberative expectations of currying divine favor, accumulating merit, or somehow improving one's situation in this life or the next one.

In Hinduism, for example, while temple building is ostensibly undertaken as demonstration of selflessness and devotion, there is nonetheless a very straightforward acknowledgment of the rewards—especially the cosmic rewards—that one can expect as a consequence of well-executed construction. In fact, in India, construction of temples in particular has traditionally been among the premier forums for the accumulation of karmic merit. Stella Kramrisch, for instance, repeatedly stresses both the careful ritual prescriptions that inform each stage of the temple-building process and the salvific rewards that Hindus anticipate upon careful compliance:

> The Hindu temple is built with a fervor of devotion (*bhakti*) as a work of offering and pious liberality, in order to secure for the builder, a place in heaven, which means a higher level of realization. . . .[87]

Similarly, George Michell comments on the numerous references in Hindu literature that describe the merit due the patron of a temple: an early astronomical text, the *Brihat Samhita,* says, "Let him who wishes to enter the worlds that are reached by meritorious deeds of piety and charity build a temple to the gods."[88] The *Agni Purana,* one of the eighteen major collections of classical mythology, similarly describes temple building as the paradigmatic strategy for the expiation of sins:

> He who attempts to erect temples for gods is freed from the sins of a thousand births. . . . The construction of a temple for a deity dissipates even the sin of Brahamancide. By building a temple one reaps the fruit which he does not even by celebrating a sacrifice. By building a temple one acquires the fruits of bathing at all the sacred shrines. . . .[89]

And, one of the *Shilpa Shastra* texts, the *Shilpa Prakasha,* a medieval Orissan Sanskrit work on temple architecture, goes so far as to explain that correctly constructing a *shikharamalini* (*vimanamalini*), "the best and greatest of temples," virtually guarantees escape from the pain of transmigration:

> By erecting such a piece of architecture (Viśvakarmāṅga) he will definitely attain liberation (mokṣa). In this world he will always have peace, wealth, grain and sons.
>
> By the attainment of mastery in art (śilpa siddhi) he has not to undergo another birth. The knowledge of art (śilpa-vidyā) is always best and gives all bliss.
>
> By proficiency in the art of building (gaṭhana-karma) inexhaustible merit is acquired. . . .[90]

Moreover, in addition to providing individuals an avenue to cosmic liberation, Hindu temple building similarly conduces to more worldly and more communal sorts of rewards (thus merging the propitiation priority

[III-C] with that of politics [II-C]).[91] Though imposing the burdens of large-scaled building projects can certainly be a means of repression and exploitation,[92] in principle at least, by orchestrating the erection of a temple, an Indian ruler not only enhanced his own (temporal and) other-worldly status, he likewise served the entire community by providing his subjects the facilities wherein they might pursue their own spiritual rewards. Furthermore, the construction of a temple rewarded the king with enduring fame, perhaps even an oddly paradoxical immortality insofar as, according to the *Shilpa Prakasha*, "everything vanishes with time, only a monument lasts forever."[93] In other words, then, though ostensibly built as an expression of devotion and piety, the construction of a Hindu temple could, in a somewhat ironic manifestation of the superabundance of architecture, serve at once to provide self-aggrandizement for a king and to demonstrate the sort of selflessness that would enhance his status after death. The *Shilpa Prakasha*, for instance, explains:

> That King, who for his fame (kīrti rūpeṇa) erects a monument, a Śākti temple with a pure mind, in an auspicious moment,
>
> And who completes the work according to rules without obstructions, will go to the abode of Śiva.[94]

Similarly evincing this notion of architectural construction in the interest of cosmic compensation, inaccessibly sited Jain temples in South India were built, in some cases, less for congregational use than as exercises in social virtue and meritorious action.[95] Also, in the case of Buddhism, Edward Conze (actually discussing images rather than buildings, though the principle would seem to apply to architecture as well) first acknowledges the karmic merit that one enjoys as a consequence of devotion to the finished product: "it is believed that the prosperity of a nation depends on honouring those images."[96] But then Conze stresses even more strongly the cosmic rewards that are the consequence of actually creating those religio-artistic objects: "To produce and to multiply sacred images was held to be highly meritorious, and in periods of exalted faith, the manufacture of images almost assumed the profusion of a natural force."[97]

The wide currency of this confidence that one is certain to accumulate great merit as a consequence of temple building, in fact, lends a measure of credence to the suspiciously roseate impressions of travelers in contemporary Tibet that the laborious construction of Buddhist monasteries not only pleases the patron deity but thrills the workers as well. According to one such happy account:

> Tibetan labor gangs working on communal projects are habitually cheerful; but where we find them labouring to rebuild monasteries, men and women, old and young, working voluntarily together, there is a veritable carnival in progress . . . one of the pilgrim's strongest impressions may be the songs and radiant faces of a gang of girls stomping the new floors of the temples.[98]

And, even in Islam, despite its profoundly different epistemology, the large expenditure of funds on public mosques is usually explained as a religious obligation, and the consequent mosque itself as an offering to Allah. There is, after all, as Nader Ardalan reminds us, a saying of the Prophet that "he who builds a mosque for God, God will build for him a similar one in Paradise."[99]

Building and Healing: Contexts and Constructions for Health and Prosperity

One last subset of variations on this notion of purposeful, strategically prehensive building deserves special, if brief, comment: namely, the sometimes very tight connection between ritual-architectral connstruction and healing. Occasionally, buildings or monuments are, in fact, constructed expressly in order to dramatize a one-time petition for a very specific divine remedy. In seventh-century Nara, Japan, for instance, as supplication for a cure to the eye disease of his consort, Emperor Temme ordered the erection of the Yakushi-ji, a temple enshrining an image of Yakushi, the Buddha of Healing.[100]

More often, however, architecture facilitates healing in a rather more generalized and less direct fashion by providing a special context in which the efficacy of curative rituals is significantly enhanced. Reflecting one sort of a merger of the homology priority (I-A) with that of propitiatory healing (III-C), Evenk shamans of Siberia, not unlike healers in innumerable tribal contexts, erect a special tent as a microcosmic replica of the universe, complete with a center post that represents the cosmic tree and presumably channels potent energies from the upper world down to the earth, in order to provide a favorable context for their curing rituals.[101] Or, merging the homology priority with that of propitiation in a somewhat different way, often the ritual-architectural facilitation of healing is grounded in an analogy between religious structures and the human body. Noting, for example, the homologized correspondences between Hindu temples and both the human body and the structure of the universe (as discussed in chapter 14 with respect to homologized building), Burckhardt goes a step further to postulate an identity between the building and its builders so that, in some sense, to raise or refurbish a Hindu temple constitutes a kind of salubrious therapy. As he explains it:

> the architect of the temple identifies himself with the building and with that which it represents; thus each phase of the architectural task is equally a phase of spiritual realization. The artist confers upon his work something of his own vital force; in exchange he participates in the transformation which that force undergoes by virtue of the sacramental and implicitly universal nature of the work.[102]

Demonstrating yet another sort of link between the homology priority and propitiation, Keith Critchlow discusses the location, orientation, and construction of houses in rural Japan as a kind of "protective medicine."[103] Emphasizing the parallels between Japanese design and building processes and the practices of both Chinese acupuncture and *feng shui,* Critchlow explains that the appropriate siting and arrangement of architectural constructions is crucial, not only because it fosters the bodily and mental health of the human builders (while inauspicious siting could eventuate in illness or even death), but also because correct building facilitates the proper working of the world and even the cosmos. As he explains it, "the dwelling position is considered beneficial to the health of the environment if it is placed well and enables the inhabitants to perform their role of nourishing, tending and harmonising the vicinity."[104]

Finally, Navajo sand painting, another of these religioartistic circumstances in which the end product is (in principle) wholly valueless outside of the ritual processes of its construction, and thus unlamentably destroyed at the ceremony's completion, demonstrates a merger of curative propitiation (priority III-C) with concerns for the commemoration of divinity (II-A) and sacred history (II-B). According to Gary Witherspoon's account, the sand paintings depict the Diyin Dine'e and other deities in the context of significant mythical episodes, thereby, in a sense, inviting them to return to the earthly realm and attend to ailing human beings: "the symbolic representation of various sacred beings and things is considered to be effective in attracting them to the ceremonial hogan and thus enabling the patient to absorb their curative power."[105] The "building" of a sand painting, then, allows the patient to identify with a mythological culture hero who has suffered a similar malady—as Witherspoon explains, "in the curing ritual the patient follows in the footsteps of the hero in the myth . . ."[106]—and, therefore, one hopes anyway, to participate in the mythological resolution of the disease.

The Fiction of Finished Architecture: Building as Ritual and Ritual as Building

In sum, several quite specific observations could be adduced from this inventory of propitiative ritual-architectural phenomena, another of those categories that seems to scream for more extensive treatment. We might, for instance, enhance our appreciation of the paired use and "uselessness" of sacred architecture by observing the wide currency of a seemingly compulsive need to build even where there is no apparent need of buildings, an urge to repair that which is not damaged, or to squander scarce resources on overbuilt monuments with little apparent practical or socially redeeming value. Propitiatory building should remind us, then, of the claims, which were made in volume 1, concerning the singular adeptness of buildings, and even more of building processes, as vehicles both for the expression of human creativity and for the expression of awarenesses of and obligations to the transhuman.[107]

In a more strictly methodological vein, we might observe and then work to avoid the undue extrapolation of Abrahamic metaphors of covenant and of dickering with divine negotiation partners into cultural contexts where that sort of bargaining with God does not apply. We might put in doubt the implicit assumption that a work of art or architecture's greatest (or "real") significance, either for indigenous users or academic interpreters, begins when they are completed, by noticing that very often constructional processes are of considerably greater consequence than the eventual products. And we could note also, for instance, the necessity of balancing a generous-minded hermeneutic of retrieval, which enables us to take seriously the indigenous logic that issues in seemingly profligate and counterproductive building practices, and the more skeptical hermeneutic of suspicion that can ascertain the unspoken but still tangible and maybe insidious interests that are served by art and architecture ostensibly dedicated to the Other.

Perhaps the largest and most salient observation in the context of this hermeneutics of sacred architecture, however, has to do with intensified appreciations of the profoundly kindred, more-than-analogous relationship between *building* buildings and *experiencing* buildings. That is to say, these queries into the propitiation priority ought to help us appreciate, on the one hand, that, for the purposes of academic interpretation, processes of construction themselves are advantageously conceived (or problematized) as "ritual-architectural events"—and thus as occasions of (indigenous) hermeneutical reflection and apprehension.[108] Building and making, as should be fairly obvious by now, are often (though not always) highly stylized, "ritualized" practices, amenable to all of the heuristic interrogations scholars apply to other ceremonialized activities.

But, on the other hand, we need to appreciate the less obvious, equally important converse—that ritual-architectural events, including those ritual performances that in no way alter the physicality of the built works, are also occasions of "building." This hermeneutics of sacred architecture is, in other words, based upon an insistence that neither buildings nor beholders be imagined as fixed and solid entities; the experience of architecture is *not,* I (and others) have argued, an occasion of a knowing human subject recovering and deciphering the meanings hidden in an increasingly well-known architectural object.[109] Alternatively, as outlined in my reflections on the eventfulness of religious architecture, both buildings and beholders are transformed in each (successfully productive) occasion of their dynamic interaction.

In actual construction processes, then, where bricks and beams are being laid in place, and the physical shapes as well as the meanings are very clearly being transfigured and rearranged, we find the quintessential instantiation of that which we already knew about human apprehensions of architecture —that they are fluid, multivalent, interactive, and productive, and thus transformative of both the human actors and the built forms. Viewed in this light, all ritual-architectural events are, in principle, occasions of creative construction; all seriously committed ritual participants, even those who never lift a trowel or hammer, are, in an important sense, builders. Moreover, all buildings are, to an important degree, perpetually under construction; never are they "done" in the sense of fixing and fully stabilizing their meanings. From considerations of the propitiatory priority (III-C), we learn again that all religious buildings are, for all time—that is, for the entire duration of their ritual-architectural reception careers—being continuously re-created, rebuilt, and remodeled. The idea of the fully finished building is a fiction that cannot be sustained.

Twenty-four | Sanctuary: Refuges of Sacrality (Priority III-D)

> The door is the boundary between the foreign and the domestic worlds in the case of the ordinary dwelling, between the profane and the sacred worlds in the case of the temple. Therefore to cross the threshold is to unite oneself with a new world.
>
> Arnold van Gennep, 1909[1]

> When the gazelle fled from the san ctuary of Mecca,
> It became the prey of the hunter.
>
> Muhammad Iqbal, 1915[2]

> How is this possible [for humans to make the transition from nature to the "city"]? How can man withdraw himself from the fields? Where will he go, since the earth is one huge, unbounded field? Quite simple; he will mark off a portion of this field by means of walls, which set up an enclosed, finite space over against amorphous, unlimited space. Here you have the public square.
>
> José Ortega y Gasset, 1932[3]

THE EMERGENCE AND MAINTENANCE of urban life constitute perhaps the most momentous turn in both the histories of religion and architecture.[4] According to the traditional foundation legend of Rome, Romulus established the city by plowing a ditch around the Palatine hill, a circular line that designated the eventual perimeter of the town's walls. When his twin, Remus, thoughtlessly jumped over the furrow, Romulus immediately slew him and premonished, "thus perish any who leaps over my walls."[5] The *sulcus primigenius,* or initial furrow, was deserving of reverence because it marked an inviolate boundary that circumscribed a sacred precinct, termed in this case the *mundus,* or world, a downsized universe of perfection and order within the wider, wilder landscape.

Likewise, the hero of the *Epic of Gilgamesh,* if a failure in other ways, nonetheless, according to Jonathan Smith's analysis, won a measure of security for his people by maintaining the walls of the city of Uruk as a defense—both symbolic and military—against the threat of the desert. Smith explains that:

> The walled city is a symbolic universe which serves . . . as an "enclave," "a strategic hamlet" against the boundless, the chaotic desert. The desert, which is a place of utter desolation, of cosmic and human emptiness—the place called "the howling waste of the desert" (Dt. 32: 10), the "land not sown" (Jer. 2:2), the land of "no-kingdon-there" (Is. 34: 12), the place "in which there is no man" (Jb. 38; 26)—is an active threat, constantly seeking to breach the walls.[6]

Or, to return to José Ortega y Gasset's reflections on the difficult and profound transformation from life in the "unbounded field" of nature to that of an urban existence, he maintains that the walled confines of the city define a "lesser, rebellious field, which secedes from the limitless one, and keeps to itself." In his view, walled urban space is

> a space *sui generis,* of the most novel kind, in which man frees himself from the community of the plant and the animal, leaves them outside, and creates an enclosure apart that is purely human, a civil space.[7]

Analogously, though marked somewhat more subtly and less permanently, the traditional *hocoka,* or camp circle, of the Oglalas defined a space inside which everything was irrefutably Oglala, safe, knowable, and auspicious; outside the *hocoka* were the enemies and inconsistencies of everyday life, evil spirits, or, in some contexts, the threatening encroachments of European-Americans.[8] The stone circles of the British Isles have been interpreted similarly, not only as delimitations of sacred from profane space, but also as spiritual barriers that prevent the ghosts of those buried within the circle from leaving their graves.[9] And, worlds away, even the arrangements of oversized portals and passageways on many American university campuses were designed explicitly to formalize and enforce the boundaries between "town and gown" by creating "a symbolic barrier between the college and the world outside."[10] The many-gated campus of Princeton, for instance, was projected in Ralph Adams Cram's 1906 plan as "a citadel of learning and culture . . . a walled city against materialism"; and the elaborate gateway entrances to Bowdoin College have been lauded by some (and dispraised by others) for serving "visibly to exclude the *profanum vulgus.*"[11]

Though radically mismatched in other respects, the motif of walled cities, the Oglala *hocoka,* Stonehenge, and the gated entryways to American colleges each epitomize the final entry to this morphological framework: sanctuary (priority III-D) is a mode of ritual-architectural presentation and apprehension that is dedicated to enclosing space, to carving from the generalized pedestrian environment a hermetic refuge of sacrality or a retreat from the mundane, to cordoning off a zone of purity and perfect order, in short, to distinguishing an inside from the outside.

Outside and Inside, Ordinary and Exceptional: Thresholds, Boundaries, and Limits

In the words of Mircea Eliade, for whom this dimension of the symbolics of sacred space, like that of homology (priority I-A), is an especially prominent theme, what I am calling the sanctuary mode involves the acknowledgment (or perhaps the construction) of a "threshold"[12]—that is, a boundary, a limit, or a frontier between two modes of being, between the profane and the sacred.[13] Outside, in Eliade's view, the *homo religiosus* has a not-altogether rewarding experience of the ordinary and mundane, of chaos, confusion, and danger; inside, however, one presumably experiences the security and the "Reality" and the sense of "Being" that comes only via accessibility to "the Sacred."[14]

Moreover, we learn from plenteous cross-cultural examples of Eliade and countless others—again, this is a heuristic possibility that, in its broad strokes, almost no scholars fail to recognize—that this urgency for clearly picketing, barricading, or otherwise partitioning the exceptional from the prosaic manifests itself in every architectural medium and scale. There are very modest examples like that of four Maya priests (not unlike their Japanese counterparts) holding a rope to tether off a temporary sacred context for the performance of the *emku,* or Yucatecan coming-of-age ceremony.[15] The same logic would seem to be operating in all sorts of more permanent constructions—from simple railings around altars, to elaborate inner sanctums and courtyard precincts, to the walling of whole metropolises, as in the case of the Parisian revetments that Kenneth Frampton unsubtly describes as the protection of "the 'civilization' of the city from the 'idiocy' of the countryside."[16]

Besides these horizontal expressions of the sanctuary mode (III-D), differentiations in height and verticality—from squat podiums and daises, to stairways and house heights, to inaccessible mountain-sited retreats—can serve not only to designate ascending ranks of sociopolitical privilege (as noted in chapter 19), but also increments or gradations of relative sacrality.[17] Or, to cite an even more ingenious ritual-architectural means of differentiating that which is normal from that which is special, the pre-Hispanic designers at work in the lush tropical forests of southern Mesoamerica, for instance, relied on blocky monumental forms accentuated by rigid straight lines and bright colors, which, as Broda explains, "created an artificial order in contraposition to nature; [such design tactics] imposed a new structure, a 'human order' upon the 'natural order.'"[18]

Implemented by whatever means, the sanctuary mode has as its priority the segregation of exceptional places from the randomness and arbitrariness of the world at large. In Edward Tenner's phrase, the abuttals and gates that enclose cities, ceremonial precincts, and campuses, which are now (and probably always) more often metaphorical barriers than enforceable deterrents to entry and exit, "provide a brave front to the terrors of the times."[19] Sanctuary shelters and enclosures enable the appearance, however illusory, of perfection, if only within tightly circumscribed boundaries. Jonathan Smith, whose emphasis on the social construction of "sacred spaces" via the sanctification of apparently ordinary places and buildings makes his work also especially relevant here,[20] well captures the matter when he explains how the careful grooming of a temple space adduces to a kind of hermetic isolation within which every detail can be arranged with such deliberation and meticulous order that nothing random or insignificant is allowed to remain. Thus, as he explains:

> When one enters a temple, one enters marked-off space (the usual example, the Greek *temenos,* derived from *temno,* "to cut") in which, at least in principle, nothing is accidental; everything, at least potentially, demands attention. The temple serves as a focusing lens, establishing the possibility of significance by directing attention, by requiring the perception of difference. Within the temple, the ordinary (which to any outside eye or ear remains wholly ordinary) becomes significant, becomes "sacred," simply by being there.[21]

Indirect and Exclusive: More Imperfect Generalizations

Defined in this broad fashion, one is hard pressed to find any ceremonial situation in which the sanctuary priority does not assert itself in one way or another. This option may seem, at first, to be essentially synonymous with many generic conceptions of "sacred space." The requisite circumscription of some kind of bounded enclosure obtains not only in relation to all of the orientational and commemorative priorities, but also in relation to each of the other presentational modes; theatrically arranged ritual contexts (III-A), for instance, are "sanctuaries" of sorts, and nearly all contemplative (III-B) and propitiatory (III-C) ritual-architectural initiatives require cordoning off some sort of privileged precinct. Nonetheless, in order to isolate this as a distinct morphological option, I can offer a couple of provisional, again strictly heuristic, distinctions.

Where contemplation modes (III-B)—epitomized by the pilgrim's experience of the mandala architecture of Borobudur or by the anagogical agenda of Gothic cathedrals—are characterized by direct and purposeful apprehensions of the actual architectural forms, which thus serve in those cases as the foci of sustained devotional attentions, sanctuary modes (III-D) are characterized by more *in*direct relationships between worshipers and built features. The sanctuary mode, like that of theater (III-A) in this respect, is usually concerned, *not* with the presentation and apprehension of actual objects of devotion, but with the construction of a ritual ambience, a background, or stage setting, which can then serve to facilitate any number of very different sorts of subsequent ceremonial proceedings. Even immediately after the event, however, again not unlike many theatric arrangements, ritual participants may have considerable difficulty in describing in any detail the physical aspects of the ceremonial environment. Sanctuary spaces often succeed by their inconspicuousness.

Yet, unlike the embracing, inclusive pageant spaces and public spectacles typically associated with the theatric mode (III-A), the deployment of the sanctuary mode (as I define it) is invariably characterized by a measure of exclusion and restricted access. Instead of persuading even reticent onlookers into involvement, often by appeals to emotion, sanctuary configurations more often guard the integrity of the occasion by limiting involvement to some select socioreligious contingency. Sanctuary spaces fence in and fence out, thus blocking access, insulating and protecting the sanctity, or maybe insidious secrecy, of the ceremonial (or not so ceremonious) proceedings.

Again, however, specific historical examples provide better and more provocative heuristic leads than do these sorts of very imperfect generalizations. Three instances—concerning the respective emergences of Jewish synagogues, Roman architecture, and Cistercian monasteries—each of which demonstrates clearly the deliberate rejection of other ritual-architectural priorities in favor of the sanctuary mode, may suffice to introduce the theme.

Jewish Synagogues and Roman Temples: The Play of Priorities

Jews, consonant with their celebrated iconoclasm, are, however (in)appropriately, sometimes awarded credit as "the first to voluntarily assemble to erect a structure for prayer and study, and *not to house a visible God.*"[22]

Though claims both to chronologic priority and drastic discontinuity to past practice are overstated, according to this argument, the architecture and institution of the synagogue (from the Greek word meaning "assembly" or "assembling together"), which arose largely in response to the destruction of the Jerusalem Temple, was, in spirit and use, the very opposite of the ancient Near Eastern temple or, for that matter, of the tabernacle and the Jewish temple of earlier times.[23] Instead of monuments to the glory of God, "symbolic houses of God," or cultic centers for offering sacrifices (all of which foreground variations on the commemoration of divinity [priority II-A]), synagogues were originally conceived simply as meetinghouses for prayer—that is, sanctuary spaces—the efficacy of which depended neither on any specific physical form nor on location.

The early synagogue constituted, therefore, ironically, a special place in which Jews experimented with the possibility that one's devotional obligations to God could be fulfilled in any place, not only in the now-desecrated Temple. Since these structures had more the character of schools than shrines, the architecture was called upon to do somewhat less; the design agenda was more modest. Instead of marking the site of some hierophanic manifestation of God (as in cases of the homology priority, I-A) or even the site of some fateful event in Jewish sacred history (as in the case of priority II-B), synagogues were located wherever there was a community of Jews, providing, in a sense, a kind of "portable fatherland."[24] Moreover, unlike most exhortative, inclusivistic, theatrically arranged ritual contexts (mode III-A), there was little attempt to beckon to or even allow the involvement of outsiders. Likewise, the notion that worshipers would meditate directly upon the actual architectural features (as in the contemplative mode, III-B) was repugnant to iconoclastic Jews. And, unlike most propitiatory exercises in building (III-C), including the erection of the Jerusalem Temple, both the synagogue's visual appearance and mode of construction (or expropriation of previous structures) were largely inconsequential so long as the congregation was, in the end, afforded a safe interior space in which to study the Torah, pray, and foster a sense of community in diaspora.

A second, similarly strong demonstration of the historical ascendancy of the sanctuary priority and of a building agenda of containment, control, and exclusion, though stimulated by quite different sociocultural forces, comes in Vincent Scully's account of the transition from Hellenistic to a radically divergent tradition of Roman building.[25] Recall that in Scully's view, the classic Greek temple was outstanding both for its reciprocal relationship with nature, its "outward-looking design," as he terms it, and for its sculptural representation of the abstract attributes of specific deities, such as Hera, Demeter, Artemis, or Aphrodite (which made those temples suitable as a featured example of one sort of the divinity priority [II-A]).[26] While wide open in a certain respect, classic Greek temples provided virtually no sheltering space, and thus served less as "ritual contexts" per se, into which officiants and worshipers entered, than as sculpture-like objects of meditation and reflection, in Scully's phrase "articulated sculptural bodies," which were viewed and appreciated from outside (thus instantiating the contemplative mode of presentation and apprehension [priority III-B]).

The incentives and uses of Roman building were, however, Scully argues, profoundly different in virtually all important respects. Instead of an intimate integration of architecture and nature wherein apprehensions of the built forms were inseparable from those of the features of the landscape, Roman builders aimed for complete disconnectedness from the landscape—that is, for the creation of highly restrictive sanctuary spaces (a clear expression of priority III-D). "Roman theatres, like those at Orange in southern France and Aspendos in Asia Minor," Scully explains, "were intended, like most Roman buildings, to provide an enclosed experience totally shut away from the outside world."[27]

In a military empire like that of Rome, then, the objectives of security and dominion ascended to priority even in the realm of explicitly religious architecture so that, unlike the classic Greek temple's sculptural analogy to the attributes of a deity, the Roman temple was rigidly symmetrical, logical, self-sufficient, and bastioned.[28] Again venturing to accomplish somewhat less (religiously speaking) with the actual built forms, the fabric of the Roman structure was no longer itself holy; it, like the Jewish synagogue, simply enclosed space. The temple at Lykosoura, for instance, "is in no way intended to be a solemn physical embodiment of its god but is purely a shell enclosing space"; alternatively, Scully concludes, "the volume of space to be created . . . is the determinant of the design."[29]

Bernard of Clairvaux and Cistercian Monasteries: Quintessential Exemplars

The third, perhaps the most obvious and fully elaborated, historical illustration of the ascendency of the sanctuary mode are monasteries, and the building agenda of Saint Bernard of Clairvaux and his Cistercians, to which I have already alluded at several points, provides a consummate monastic example. Bernard is especially instructive for our purposes, first, because of his explicit, fully informed, and vehement rejection of the similarly Catholic logic that had eventuated in the opulent decoration, sculpture, stained glass, and towers of Cluny; he rejected, in other words, the appropriateness of decidedly theatric modes of ritual-architectural presentation (III-A).[30] Even more famously well documented and equally adamant (though somewhat qualified) is Bernard's patent dismissal of the anagogical Gothic machinations of his contemporary, Abbot Suger (and thus of contemplation modes, III-B).[31] Not only did Bernard reject the proposition that Christian ritual-architectural agenda should work to further the socioeconomic interests of the state; he also dismissed the notion, which Suger promulgated, that a Christian church building could serve in some tangible sense as "the house of God."[32]

Alternatively, Bernard, in formulating the design of Cistercian communities, imagined that the church ought to be first and foremost an oratorium, the place of the soul's communion with God, a kind of sanctuary within a sanctuary, insofar as he believed also that the entire monastery complex ought to be a pristine, autonomous refuge wherein all energies were enlisted in perfect conformity to the Rule of Saint Benedict.[33] Life in the Cistercian cloister was to be an image and foretaste of paradise, an ideal that Bernard termed *paradisus claustralis*.[34] The monastic ideal espoused then and now required a lifestyle of compromiseless devotion to God:

> Everything in our life tends to protect us from the turmoil of the world and of our passions, to guarantee us solitude of the spirit, the heart and the will, in order that our monasteries may be sanctuaries of silence filled with the fragrance of prayer. . . .[35]

To achieve that ideal, then, unlike the overtly politicized ritual-architectural agenda of Abbot Suger, Bernard (who was hardly oblivious to the wider, more worldly ramifications of his plan of action) opted for a monochromatic architecture of simplicity and geometric clarity.[36] Instead of stimulating the senses, he aspired to austere architectural configurations that would quiet them; instead of winning converts, he aimed to facilitate the ideals of poverty, retreat from the world, and a renewed spirit of Benedictine regulation. It is ironic, then, but perhaps not too surprising, that Bernard's economical plan for Clairvaux won sufficient acclaim that it was repeated in some 742 Cistercian monasteries, virtually all of which were located at similarly remote rural sites—and each of which provides, among other things, quintessential instantiation of the sanctuary mode of ritual-architectural presentation and apprehension (priority III-D).[37]

The singularity and singular success of Bernard's program notwithstanding, Cistercian communities, morphologically akin in this respect to Jewish synagogues and Roman temples, constitute only the most unequivocal of countless historical circumstances in which the construction of some sort of ritual-architectural receptacle or wrapper—a sanctuary space—provides the decisive means for realization of a specific religiosocial aspiration. The exceptionally wide—and widely omnifarious—deployment of sanctuary modes requires, however, that we settle again for a sampling of particularly prominent heuristic possibilities rather than a comprehensive arrangement of available alternatives. As one last exercise in hermeneutical calisthenics, consider, therefore, permutations on three broad themes that raise particularly evocative interpretive questions: 1) the preparatory sanctification of ritual contexts; 2) sanctuary spaces that facilitate an engagement between worshipers and the divine; and 3) sanctuary spaces that express and enforce a set of sociopolitical concerns.

Preparatory Sanctifications of Ritual Context: Allurement via Sanctuary

This first theme bears most directly on matters of allurement and instigation—the front half of the ritual-architectural situation—insofar as it deals with the preparation of the sorts of pure and sanctified contexts that will ensure the appeal, integrity, and efficacy of the subsequent rites and ceremonies. This is the precautionary groundwork of ritualization; the limbering, grooming, and requisite foreshadowing that enables the ceremonial climax; the "pre-ritual," as it were. Three not mutually exclusive variations on the leitmotif deserve special note: a) the appropriation of natural sanctuaries, which are considered already inherently sanctified; b) the sanctification (or purification) of apparently prosaic places or human constructions; and c) the sanctification (or purification) of persons, that is, the ritual participants and officiants themselves.

Appropriations of Natural Sanctuaries: Claiming, Enhancing, and Building Caves

Perhaps the most elemental strategy for the sanctification of place—and one that links the sanctuary priority especially with the symbolism of the center and the notion of charged hierophanic places (that is, with homology, priority I-A)—is the expropriation of some sort of natural sanctuary, most obviously a cave, or "a womb of the earth" as they are so often conceived, which is alluring already by virtue of some seemingly inherent cosmological or mythological significance. In innumerable situations—the spectacular system of underground passageways at Balankanche near Chichén Itzá is but one of literally hundreds of Native American examples[38]—traditional peoples have adopted or confiscated natural caves as ritual-architectural sanctuaries with the confidence that such caverns are intrinsically potent places, in Eliade's terms, hierophanies, centers, or *axis mundis*, where the efficacy of their ritual propitiations will be greatly intensified.[39]

Even these "discovered" ritual contexts, however, require major and periodic cleansings and (re)sanctifications. In most cases, such natural sanctuaries are significantly enhanced, as with the famed prehistoric paintings that embellish the caves of Lascaux in southwestern France. Often, caves are so vastly enlarged and refined that any natural enclosure is entirely subsumed (but not forgotten), as in the case of the spectacular Buddhist rock-cut cave temples at Ajanta in a remote portion of the Deccan, in India, where the mountainside was sculpted into an incredible complex of cells, assembly halls, and chapels, which apparently supported a large and enduring monastic population.[40]

Perhaps more common, though, are those circumstances in which the sanctity and potent rebirth symbolism of caves and grottos is architecturally (re)created quite apart from any natural cavern (demonstrating, among other things, a more heavily conventionalized mode of allurement [priority I-B]). Burial chambers, for instance at Hagar Qim in Malta, are very often designed to resemble caves, presumably in the interest of facilitating the deceased's return to the earth.[41] In India, among similarly prevalent non-funerary exemplars, Michael Meister explains not only how sacred images have for centuries typically been housed in small cavities referred to as "womb-houses," or "germ-houses," but also how textual allusions to the Hindu temple as a cave-like opening into the earth were eventually translated into whole constructions with unmistakably cave-like appearances: in the early fifth century at Udaigiri, in Central India, for example, "the cave was made an actuality, not a metaphor, carved out by architects from the living rock as a means to make manifest the form of divinity present within."[42]

Of the many relevant pre-Columbian Mesoamerican exemplars—notably the cave-like "earth monster" temples of the Río Bec–Chenes area—Richard Townsend comments on the sense in which the Mt. Tlaloc temple enclosure in the mountains outside the Aztec capital was "a diagrammatic womb of the earth, containing the source of water and regenerative forces."[43] And even in Christian architecture, the symbolism of caves and wombs, whether deliberate or unconscious, has been and remains tremendously important. Responding to the notion that the Holy Spirit has feminine qualities, such as the hovering "always with you" quality of a mother, Stephen DeStaebler, for instance, considers:

> The church has become the mother faith and its architecture reflects that symbolism. I am fascinated how certain churches have become thinly veiled female vessels. The European church plan of a long nave, transept, apse, narthex and domes, like Saint Mark's in Venice, are so obviously the splayed female form. The space is the female space, and I think this womb-imaging is crucial.[44]

Sanctifications of Places and Structures: The Impermanence of Purification

Besides coopting and (re)creating the intrinsic allure of caves, either of which nonetheless requires extensive ritual maintenance, the preparatory sanctification of a ritual context even more often involves the ritual transformation of some seemingly ordinary space or architectural configuration into an ambience of extraordinary purity (a means of preparatory allurement that links the sanctuary mode [III-D] even more closely with that of conventionality [I-B]). India again provides an array of instructive examples. Stella Kramrisch notes that the prospective site of a Hindu temple must meet numerous special requirements even to be considered; there needs to be (as Eliade would emphasize) something inherently powerful about that spot in the wider landscape. But then, once selected—or discovered—an intensely elaborate set of conventionalized rites also must be observed in order to "officially" sanctify the site (that is, "artificial" and socially strategic procedures of the sort that J. Z. Smith is inclined to emphasize). Kramrisch explains, for instance, that, among other sorts of ritual primping, the ground should be "rendered as level as the surface of water or of a mirror" and then "mandalized" or made "a perfect square."[45]

Also observing this Indian practice of preparatory sanctification via the mandalization of space, Andreas Volwahsen notes that "even though this was not necessary for practical reasons," the Aryans were fond of fencing in sacred trees, sacrificial places, and even whole towns, thereby transforming prosaic elements of the landscape into perfectly ordered "little cosmoses."[46] In the same vein, Paul Oliver explains how, prior to the construction of a house in rural India, a *pundit,* or Hindu priest, will embark on a complex regime of ritual procedures in order to ready the site:

> the *pundit* . . . marks the positions of the corner poles and coconuts are broken in a ritual intended to ensure the safety of the building. The householder digs the hole for the centre post and the coconut milk is poured into it. Nine coloured bean seeds, signifying the planets, are buried in the hole, invoking the protection of Vishnu, Lord of the Universe. Evil spirits are warded off with bunches of sacred mango leaves tied to the top of the house post, so that they protect the dwelling and ensure the prosperity of its occupants.[47]

Only following the ritual grooming of the site, Oliver says, can actual construction of the house proceed according to similarly detailed (and conventionalized) ceremonious prescriptions, the rules of the *shastras*.

It is crucial to note, however—elaborate ritual-architectural strategies for circumscribing some sort of requisite ambience of purity and efficacy notwithstanding—that the sanctification of space is only rarely conceived as a permanent, once-and-for-always process.[48] Informed again by Smith's insight that "there is nothing that is inherently sacred or profane" and that "these are not substantive categories, but rather situational or relational categories, mobile boundaries that shift according to the map being employed,"[49] we should not be surprised that, in many cases, the purity and sanctity of a place (or a structure) is perceived as fleeting in the extreme so that, almost immediately following the ritual event, that privileged context may revert to its thoroughly undistinguished status—a phenomenon that is often more disturbing to outsiders than to the actual ritual participants themselves.

Western observers in China, for instance, have been puzzled, and sometimes offended, by an apparent lack of boundaries between the sacred and worldly in Chinese culture. Even so sensitive a scholar as J. J. M. DeGroot was irked that cardplayers, coolies, hawkers, and "vagabonds" all make themselves at home in the temples of Amoy, thus giving these places the air of "cabarets" rather than sites to consecrated worship. DeGroot consequently complained that

> Chinese have so little respect for their temples that it happens that at the end of a day's journey, one finds the building where one might spend the night already occupied, not by men, but by animals; the villagers have put their animals there lacking a better stable.[50]

Jean DeBernardi, however, more attuned to the transient sanctity of these buildings, contends that

> Clearly, [DeGroot] only observes these temples at moments when they are not being put to ritual use: presumably during temple fairs when the gods are invited and considered to be immanent in their images, or during spirit medium performances when the gods possess humans, behavior is rather different.[51]

Noting this dynamically fluctuating cycle of sanctification and desanctification in Japan, Fred Thompson and D'Arcy Fenton emphasize that instead of hosting public festivals in a fixed and permanent social-ceremonial space, such as the central square of traditional Western cities, the principal religiosocial space of the Japanese town is a fluid, linear space—namely, the street—which is, in other words, an ordinary public space that is periodically, but only temporarily, transformed into a sacred ceremonial context. And then, once the *matsuri,* or festival, is completed, the street reverts to its prosaic and utilitarian status. As Thompson and Fenton conclude, the Japanese "know that with every tide there is an ebb and flow: [thus, in the context of the festival] space is flooded with the *kami* spirit, only to be replaced by everyday life after *matsuri.*"[52]

In a similarly urban though otherwise very different context, Father Cobo ridiculed the Incas' complex regimen of purificatory preparation that required, among other ritual preliminaries to important festivals and sacrifices, that the city of Cuzco be purged of "undesirables." In preparation for the festivities, Cobo explains:

> First, all the people from the provinces and all the people with their ears torn or any other lesion or physical defect, such as the hunchbacked, crippled, and deformed, were made to leave the city. . . . They were unfortunate men, and their misfortune might very well dampen the good fortune of everyone else. Dogs were also made to leave town so that they would not howl. . . .[53]

Following each Inca ceremony, however, all of these "unfortunates" were allowed to return. The city was, in a sense, desanctified and routine affairs resumed.

Finally, William Powers, if more even-handed in his assessment, provides parallel evidence of the transient nature of the sanctification of place when he observes that contemporary Oglalas are not concerned in the least that the sweat lodges in which they carry out their most sacred purificatory rituals, at other times—which means most of the time—become playgrounds for children, "meeting places for ants, spiders, grasshoppers and flies," and even regular stopping places for urinating dogs:[54]

> when not in use the [sweat lodge] structures look rather pitiful: a dome made of willow saplings stuck in the ground, bent over, and tied in place with cloth strips or rope. There is something exceedingly profane about them when not in use. . . .[55]

Yet, with the advent of some ceremonial occasion, the "potential sacrality" of the Oglala sweat lodge is, in a sense, activated. A host of ritual prohibitions are put into effect, whereupon entry and exit to that place is, at least for the duration of the ritual, subject to very strict regulation.[56]

Sanctifications of Persons: Transitional Spaces of Cleansing and Purification

Once sanctified, the sweat lodge provides a ritual-architectural context of purification through which all Oglala ritual participants pass prior to their involvement in vision quests, Yuwipi (healing) ceremonies, or sun dances. Thus, besides exemplifying this notion of the preparatory and periodic sanctification of places or buildings, the Oglala sweat lodge also provides an instructive example of another important permutation on allurement via the sanctuary mode: the preparatory sanctification of persons.[57] Very often, in other words, the sanctuary priority (III-D) finds expression in the construction of temporary, preparatory refuges to which ritual celebrants retreat for a matter of hours, days, or even months, either to cultivate a sense of renewal or to purify themselves in advance of their participation in the main ritual event.

In the Maya world, for instance, remote, usually austere, though carefully maintained, constructions are often enlisted to facilitate preliminary, transitional ritual-architectural events that refresh and cleanse the main ritual actors, both religiously and psychologically, prior to their participation in more public ceremonial celebrations. Bishop Las Casas reported that the Maya in Guatemala were "accustomed to separate from their wives and take up residence in special men's houses near the temples for 60, 80, or even 100 days before some great festival"; and Bishop Diego de Landa wrote that before major ceremonies in Yucatan, "all had to sleep, not in their homes, but in houses which for the time of the penance were near the temples."[58]

In a morphologically resemblant vein, Nancy Shatzman Steinhardt explains that in traditional China the emperor would retreat temporarily to the Hall of Abstinence (*Tsai-kung*), a moat-encircled enclosure, where he would fast in preparation for the annual sacrificial rites at the Altar of Heaven (*T'ien-t'an*).[59] Japan likewise provides innumerable apposite examples. Robert Ellwood describes how the Shinto priests retire for several days to the Purification House (*Saikan*) of the Ise shrine prior to officiating at the *Kanname-sai,* or Harvest Festival (discussed in chapter 23, on propitiation, priority III-C):

> During this preliminary period [the priests] wear only pure white clothes, eat only food prepared in the Purification House over a "pure fire" (made by wood friction with an archaic string-and-axle device) and are allowed no outside communication except with the Shrine Office and the Imperial Messengers. Nothing impure—that is, primarily, nothing pertaining to blood, sickness, decay, or death—is to reach their five senses.[60]

Arata Isozaki's description of the cave-like *muro,* structures where Japanese initiates retreated in order to fast prior to their ceremonial passage into adulthood, demonstrates even more piquantly the sort of transformative and regenerative experiences that are facilitated by isolated sanctuary places. According to Isozaki,

> these *muro* were plastered over to shut off all contact with the outside air. Entering them, abiding there awhile, and then emerging was a kind of death and resurrection. . . . There was no need of a door to provide free entrance and exit since sudden transformation and emergence were expected. For the same reason, the egg shape was ideal.[61]

And even the Zen rock garden and monastery (or *zendo*), albeit on a larger, longer, and more elaborate scale, are designed—not unlike many Christian monasteries and hermitages—to be experienced only temporarily, as a kind of preparatory sanctification. As D. T. Suzuki explains, although the garden and *zendo* are privileged sanctuaries for developing insight, they are not meant to substitute for the outside world. A Zen garden, he says, is a "passing shelter," a picture of the universe that provides permanent sanctuary only in the enlightenment that it catalyzes, a way-station of sorts:

> When something of this ideal is firmly grasped, the monk takes leave of the Zendo and begins his real life among his fellow-beings, as a member of the great community known as the world.[62]

In sum, sanctuary modes of presentation and apprehension very often serve most prominently in wider ritual processes (or styles of life) as strategies of allurement, insofar as they expedite the preparatory sanctification or purification of places, buildings, and/or the ritual actors themselves. In preliminary sanctifications of this sort, which demonstrate especially well the transformative experience of ritual-architectural contexts, whole built ambiences serve as metaphorical thresholds, gateways, or liminal spaces through which one must pass—but not stay—enroute to participation either in some alternative mode of living or in some more substantial ritual proceeding.

The utility of sanctuary modes is not, however, confined to these sorts of purificatory preludes, which are, we should note, strikingly similar across cultural contexts. Even the subsequent ritual events for which these preliminary practices pave the way—more public events that are both more substantively complex and far more diversified—invariably require the clear demarcation of some sort of restrictive, manicured performative ambience. Turning attention now toward the content, or back half, of these architectural events, though settling again for a sampling rather than a full survey, the alliances between this presentational mode and the respective commemoration of divinity (II-A) and of politics (II-C) present particularly intriguing possibilities.[63]

Sanctuary Modes and Commemorations of Divinity: Appealing to Humans and Gods

Looking at ways in which sanctuary spaces might facilitate some sort of direct interaction between human ritual participants and the divine—though again comparison is complicated greatly by culturally specific conceptions of the supernatural—we can distinguish two large, again not mutually exclusive, sets of options by considering the problem from both directions. That is to say, there are, on the one hand, innumerable sanctuary-like configurations that are designed primarily to enhance human mental concentration, to ready the ritual participants, as it were. And, on the other hand, there are those configurations that are intended primarily to enhance or entice the presence of the sacred, to draw some sort of divine presence into the ritual-architectural context.

Architectural Enhancements of Mental Concentration: Monasteries and Gardens

The former option is more obvious: namely, the construction of a realm of distractionless quiet where devotees are allowed, or sometimes forced, to focus their intellectual energies solely on worship and meditation. Again, monastic examples—one being the Cistercian endeavor to create the perfect environment for contemplation, penance, and liturgical service—provide abundant and consummate illustrations of this initiative to relieve one's mind of the turmoils and passions of the world in order that all mental effort might be concentrated on divine introspection. Likewise insulating itself from transitory culture fashion, the Zen monastery's creation of an "unchanged and unchanging" locus of stillness, purity, and silence in the midst of ephemerality and sensation, a refuge that intentionally avoids (in the short run) any reference to the outside world, is intended to capacitate the acquisition of Zen discipline—that is, of a focused human mindset.[64]

Or, expressing the sanctuary priority in a rather more lush fashion, the courtyard gardens of Islamic Iran provide refuges of calm serenity via the cultivation of verdant oases with plants and pools, which contrast radically with both their urban surroundings and with the wider environ's hot, arid plateau.[65] Ardalan and Bakhtiar, for instance, call the walled courtyard gardens of Iran "recapitulations of paradise" and describe them as providing a special kind of quiet that evokes a special level of spiritual concentration, and thus access to divinity, with a "foretaste of heaven" (a claim that is often, not inconsequentially, invoked also in relation to Cistercian monasteries). These Muslim gardens, the experience of which is intended to be simultaneously soothing and intense, define and isolate a "sacred place within which the soul can be sensed and the spiritual quest fulfilled."[66]

Architectural Enticements of the Divine: Attracting Gods and Redirecting Energy

Besides the fairly straightforward provision of ambiences of repose and meditation that quiet the minds and focus the mental energies of worshipers, a somewhat more subtle, though still very common, sort of collusion between sanctuary modes (III-D) and divinity commemoration (II-A) involves the arrangement of built forms in such a way that deities and sacred forces are directed into the ritual-architectural ambience—and, thus, made accessible to human devotees. As noted earlier, myriad Hindu sanctuaries—for instance, the rock-cut temple at Ellora, which was designed as a replica of Shiva's mythological mountain home of Kailasa, a kind of home away from home for the god—are built with the explicit hope of summoning a divinity to reside there and to dispense his or her favors on the builders and patrons.[67] Maya and Aztec temples, Babylonian ziggurats, Greek oracle temples, Tibetan Buddhist monasteries, and even Gothic cathedrals, all of which were conceived, according to some interpretations, as "deity domiciles," may have been constructed in a fashion that was intended to please specific divinities, and thus to entice those entities to come inhabit those structures, if not permanently, at least on special occasions.[68]

Demonstrating even more clearly the deployment of sanctuary modes in the interest of the commemoration of divinity (broadly defined) is the Oglala holy man's assiduous preparation of the context for a Yuwipi healing ceremony or "sing."[69] In anticipation of those events, an otherwise ordinary house or garage is cleared out and purged of all furniture and "white man's things," which are replaced by a specially constructed altar and a cosmologically homologized *hocoka* (or "camp circle"), demarcated by stringing a cord with offerings of tobacco between willow cane staffs that are either driven into the ground or perhaps supported by coffee cans half-filled with dirt. Then the room is sealed up tight, even to the point of nailing shut doors and windows so as to allow neither (living) people nor light to pass in or out of the room. Only when prepared in that fastidious fashion can the temperamental, mischievously unpredictable spirits be expected to visit the Yuwipi meeting and assist in the healing. Closing up the space thus opens up possibilities.

Even more fascinating exemplification of this variation on the sanctuary theme comes in the architecturization of the Japanese concept of *ma* and in the concerted effort to lure *kami* energy into the ritual-architectural context. *Ma* refers to the "interval" between two (or more) spatial or temporal things or events, and thus carries meanings such as gap, opening, space between, or, like the related term *kekkai,* areas of "pregnant nothing."[70] According to Richard Pilgrim, Japanese designers prize the intervals and gaps between buildings because, by their openness and purity, these are the spaces most receptive to *ki,* or the spiritual power of *kami:*

> Although these spaces may be located within shrine buildings or, for example, caves, their paradigmatic model is the cleared out, white rock-covered spaces surrounding shrines or even predating shrines—spaces variously referred to as *shiki, yuniwa, iwakura, kekkai, and tamajari.*[71]

Especially in ancient Shinto, these open spaces often framed a single tree, rock, or pillar (*himorogi, yashiro, yorishiro, iwasaka*), which acts as a kind of magnet or target for the sacred power of *kami.* In the words of Matsuoka Seigow:

> rather than not know at all where *kami* might make its temporary appearance, our ancestors took to demarcating an "area of *kami*" by enclosing a

particular space with twisted rope thus sanctifying it in preparation for the visit of *kami*. This area was called *kekkai*.[72]

Thus, in *ma*-inspired architecture, all obstacles are cleared away, all distractions silenced. Space is opened up, cleared out, and purified in anticipation of the coming and going of *kami;* a gap or crevice is created in the mundane, a "negative space," a sacred *ma,* a vacuum into which rushes the formless energy (*ki*) of *kami*. Pilgrim says, "such experimental 'places' evoke, by their very nature, a sense of reality characterized by a dynamic, active, changing, poetic immediacy."[73]

In short, then, whether designed to cultivate human sensibilities or, as in the case of the architecture of *ma,* actually to draw divine presences or energy into the ritual-architectural context, the sanctuary mode (III-D) and the commemoration of divinity (II-A) provide an especially congenial pairing.

Sanctuary Modes and Commemorations of Politics: Avoiding and/or Engaging Society

An equally evocative, if quite different, set of hermeneutical questions arises from observations of the interactivity between sanctuary modes and the ritual-architectural expression of socioeconomic structures and hierarchies (the politics priority, II-C). Tenner notes, for instance, that in Western Europe and America, in the era after gunpowder, "Most of all, the gate became, and remains, *the* architectural symbol of power"; after that, he says, "gatecraft ornamented statecraft."[74] Yet, as Tenner knows, in all eras and contexts, not only the ramparts and battlements that held attackers at bay, but also flimsy gauze curtains, subtle differentiations in height, and small deviations in the texture of a floor have served to announce and enforce (or, occasionally, to contest) claims to sociopolitical power and privilege. Among innumerable relevant permutations, three alternatives stand out: sanctuary spaces that facilitate, respectively, a) a complete rejection of society, b) an exemplary model for society, or c) a mechanism of exclusion, which reinforces prevailing patterns of privilege and hierarchy.

Complete Rejections of Society: Architectures of Total and Permanent Withdrawal

By contrast to the earlier examples of sanctuary places that facilitate transitional, preparatory sorts of purification, the first, and perhaps most radical, of these more overtly politicized alternatives involves ritual-architectural sanctuaries that are constructed in the interest of a permanent and total isolation from mainstream society. The stuff of hermits and monks, solitary troglodytes and cenobitic sisterhoods, here we are concerned with the fabrication of entirely self-sufficient, alternative worlds, which are detached as thoroughly as possible from "the evils" and tedium of ordinary consociation. Examples of this sort of world-renouncing, self-imposed ritual-architectural quarantine, whether by individuals or alternative communities, are abundant and, at least as a morphological option, (seemingly) straightforward enough to require only small comment.[75]

Retreating from society rather than aspiring to transform it, German pietist Conrad Beissel, for instance, opted first for a completely eremitical life-style before eventually (in 1732) being persuaded to found the community of Ephrata, Pennsylvania, an Anabaptist settlement, which was nonetheless, as Sibyl Moholy-Nagy notes, "all withdrawal—withdrawal from hostile co-settlers, withdrawal from the Indians, and withdrawal from the temptations of the material world."[76] Proximate Shaker communities, too, were apparently less interested in fomenting social change than in concretizing, building on earth, their idea of the world as it should be in the days of the second coming of Christ. Shakers believed that by creating a community in the way that they envisioned God would have designed it, a kind of built foretaste of heaven (again echoing one element of Bernard's aspiration), they were carrying out the grandest of tributes to their creator.[77]

The nearly inaccessible cave complexes or "rock monasteries" that are scattered throughout the Bulgarian region, apparently founded in relation to the Byzantine teaching of Hesychasm in the thirteenth or fourteenth centuries, though again completely different in outward appearance, seem to derive from the similar initiative of a community to disconnect itself completely and forever from mainstream society. As Antoniy Handjiyski explains, adherents to Hesychasm believed that the sole possibility for achieving union with God depended upon a complete rejection of the world and everything carnal, concentrating instead within themselves on repentance and prayer: "That is why they withdrew to live in distant inaccessible niches and caves which they turned into churches and monks' cells by additional labours."[78]

Participants in these communities, and countless others like them, have, it might appear, abandoned entirely any expectations of changing public values or opinions or of bringing society at large more into synch with their alternative ideals. Instead, these reclusive communities carved out a special place, closeted and disassociated from the wider world where they could, without compromise, pursue their (ostensibly) entirely otherworldly priorities—an initiative that invariably poses very special ritual-architectural requirements.

Exemplary Models for Society: Prototypes of Religiopolitical Perfection

While examples of radical ritual-architectural seclusion and complete disconnectedness from sociality may seem, at first glance, to be very common, in actual practice the detachment is seldom so complete as it might initially appear. In fact, if we exercise a more suspicious hermeneutic, we are faced with the prospect of another morphological option that is nearly empty of historical exemplars. Even Hesychastic troglodytes, for instance, although presumably aspiring for complete uninvolvement in society, eventually—if perhaps unwittingly—functioned as a tool for sociopolitical oppression. Handjiyski explains:

> The ascetic and mystical character of Hesychasm coincided with the interests of the ruling class. The feudal aristocracy and the church saw in the Hesychastic ideology a convenient means of diverting the people's attention from the acute social problems of the day and turning it to passive acceptance of the existing order and system. That is why in 1360 Tsar Ivan Alexander officially recognized Hesychasm.[79]

Given the apparently inevitable politicization of even the most dissocial (or antisocial) religious movement, there are, empirically speaking, far fewer (if any) built environments that effect a complete detachment from society than there are of this second option: namely, sanctuary configurations that serve (or are intended to serve) as paradigms or prototypes of socioreligious perfection. These are built enclosures that will have, to the extent adherents' hopes are realized, very significant ramifications in the wider body politic, albeit in a somewhat indirect fashion.

Cistercian monasteries, again instructive examplars, appear at first to be the perfect demonstration of bastioned, architecturally abetted seclusion and disinterest in wider society. In these largely self-contained rural compounds, the routine of an ostensibly nonproselytizing order, deliberately cut off from the world, is arranged so as to enable monks to devote their entire lives to the pursuit of mystical union with God. Cistercian contemplatives (seem to) embrace a kind of elective obliviousness to the desires and ambitions that complicate the religious lives of even the most duteous laity.

Closer scrutiny of this tradition of Catholic isolationism—and particularly of its modern inheritors, like the Trappist Gethesemani in Kentucky—suggests, however, a more complex and interactive relationship between the world inside and the world outside the monastery. Although not so closed to the wider world as traditional Cistercian monasteries, Gethsemani—which has, for instance, a guesthouse and an early morning mass that is open to the public—an oddly famous monachal settlement, nevertheless participates in the remoteness, quiet, and separation from the world of its European predecessors. Architecturally, this isolation is reinforced, not only by the secluded location, but also by the sheer massiveness of the Enclosure wall, which serves a mostly symbolic function; by the absence of clocks, radios, and telephones; and by the presence within the enclosure of all facilities necessary for self-sufficiency. Once a monk has taken his vows of stability, he never again leaves the Enclosure. Only lay brothers, novices, and the occasional necessary exceptions—most notably, Thomas Merton—ever see the outside world again.

And yet, as Merton's writings, which are largely responsible for the ironic celebrity of this cenobitic community, repeatedly emphasize, Gethsemani, while of course fostering a sense of disconnectedness from society and maybe even a preview of paradise for the cloistered residents, does, in some important sense, reach out to the public sphere. Alluding often to his own personal struggles in appreciating fully the social responsibility of the contemplative life, Merton maintains that the ultimate purpose of Gethsemani-as-sanctuary is not mere removal from the world in order to advance the very private spirituality of the monks (though it does achieve that); nor is it simply a (re)creation of heaven on earth (though it is conceived as that as well). The monks are there foremost, Merton says, to pray for the world. Consequently, they do see themselves as performing an important public service; and, even more relevant to the present morphological option, they understand themselves as constituting an example of perfect devotion and full commitment to God, an ideal that everyone in the world might, to some extent, emulate.[80]

In other words, while "sanctuary" most often connotes withdrawal from society, other, probably more common utilizations of sanctuary modes of ritual-architectural presentation and apprehension work almost oppositely: in the interest of testing and showcasing some sort of exemplary socioreligious model. Cloistered communities may serve, then, not only as laboratory spaces, sites of religious research and development, as it were—that is, as highly controlled environments in which, on some small scale, alternative models of living and worshiping are conceived and tried out—but also as museum-like sites, or perhaps exhibit halls, where the results of those experiments are put on display and wider audiences are invited to participate in the alternative ideas and practices. Thus, instead of isolated and secret hideaways, in many cases, at least according to the internal logic of the participants, sanctuary ambiences ought to be positioned under the spotlight, or the microscope, in order to articulate and display the virtues of an idealized pattern, a microcosmic model not only of religious devotion but of sociopolitical order as well.[81]

Muslim mosques, for instance, especially the original mosques of Medina, served not only as places of prayer, but also as the principal civic centers and thus as focusing lenses for the political, economic, and social as well as spiritual lives of Muhammad's followers; as Ziyaud-Din Desai explains, "all the important activities affecting their daily life, unless they were contrary to the basic tenants of Islam, took place in one or the other part of the mosque."[82] Instead of a disconnectedness from the world, the earliest mosques provided the most public forums for displaying and disseminating the (as yet unrealized) ideals of perfect Muslim worldliness. Even later, after these sanctuary structures began to assume a somewhat more limited role as places specifically for the worship of God, Desai explains that, nonetheless, "It is in the mosque in which the Islamic concepts of equality and brotherhood have found true and complete demonstration."[83] Though the pertinent socioreligious ideals are perhaps expressed more with dogmatic certainty than experimental tentativeness, the mosque space (and the same could be said for the sanctuary spaces of Sikh shrines, Baha'i temples, and even Puritan meetinghouses)[84] provides both a kind of social critique and a prototypical model for that which believers feel should—but does not—obtain in the wider world.

Where sanctuary modes are very often utilized in the service of counter-hegemonic commentaries on, or iconoclastic challenges to, the prevailing social order (note that Bernard's initiative would also fall into that category), such modes of presentation can, however, in other cases, be employed in order to bolster the maintenance of the status quo. Clifford Geertz, for example, provides very strong evidence of that sort of largely conservative alliance between this mode of presentation and the commemoration of temporal authority (priority II-C) when he discusses the workings of what he terms the "Doctrine of the Exemplary Center" in the religiopolity of Indic Java. He notes first that the arrangement of the king's court and capital conforms, albeit imperfectly, to the world of the gods and is thus (after the fashion of the homology priority, I-A) "a visible likeness of an invisible realm." But then Geertz also emphasizes an ulterior, more worldly motive:

> The court, its activities, its style, its organization, its whole form of life . . . also provides an ideal toward which life outside the court, in the kingdom as a whole, ought properly to aspire, upon which it should seek to model itself, as a child models upon a father, a peasant upon a lord, a lord upon a king, and a king upon a god.[85]

The religiopolitical court space of the Javanese king constitutes, in other words, a ritual-architectural sanctuary distinct from the wider kingdom, not by its transcendence or immunity from the prevailing religious and sociopolitical standards, but by its paradigmatic demonstration—its focused intensification—of those standards:

> Indeed, from a religious point of view, that is the court's basic function and justification—to disseminate civilization by displaying it, to shape society by presenting it with a microcosmic expression of macrocosmic form which it can attempt, as well as it is able, to imitate.[86]

Reinforcements of Sociopolitical Hierarchy: Architectures of Exclusion

A third, closely related, and equally politicized variation on the sanctuary mode involves the ritual-architectural articulation and enforcement of hierarchies of sociological exclusion, in other words, the correlation of exclusivistic access to sanctuary spaces with sociopolitical empowerment and privilege (or, conversely, the correlation of *in*accessibility to sanctuary spaces with sociopolitical *dis*empowerment). Historical exemplars of this notion of architecture as a mechanism for the maintenance of socio-religious privilege—or, more affirmatively stated, as a guardian of proper socioreligious order—are legion.

The simple two-room plan of the pre-Hispanic Zapotec *yohepèe* in the Oaxacan region of Mexico, literally the "house of *pè*" (that is, of wind, breath, or spirit), provides a very basic and lucid expression of this heuristic possibility. The outer room of the *yohepèe,* which one encounters first at the top of the stairway entrance, was open to anyone who wished to make an offering. The actual sacrifices, however, were performed on an altar called the *pecogo,* or *pe-quie* (the stone of *pè*), in a second, "more sacred" room to which no layperson was ever admitted; this inner space was the exclusive preserve of the native ritual specialists.[87]

Epitomizing the same theme rather more elaborately, the layout of Hindu temples very often defines a kind of concentric sociosacred hierarchy, so that moving from the periphery of the temple toward the inner sanctum involves an experience both of increasing spiritual potency and of increasingly restrictive access. Accordingly, as Michell explains, the most sacred chamber of the Hindu temple is accessible only to the most privileged elite:

> The interior spaces of temples are arranged to promote the movement of the devotee from the outside towards the sanctuary through a series of enclosures which become increasingly sacred as the sanctuary is approached. At the final stage in the penetration towards the centre, when the doorway of the sanctuary is reached, the priests take over from the worshipper and conduct offerings to the image of the deity inside the sanctuary. This is undertaken on behalf of the worshipper who must wait outside but who follows the movements of the priests, accompanying their actions symbolically.[88]

Albeit in less explicitly religious contexts, several circumstances addressed earlier—the concentric layout of Maya villages, wherein the proximity of one's house to the center of the settlement was directly correlated with wealth and prestige, or the carefully enforced sociospatial patterns in the dwellings of the Navajo, Amazonian Tukanoans, or Indonesian Sa'dan Toraja[89]—likewise evince this juxtaposition of priorities. The processionary experience of mandala architectures like that of Angkor Wat, which features passage through microcosm within microcosm within microcosm, also demonstrates very well this sociosanctuary notion of ascending levels of exclusion. At that famed Cambodian monument, the access of visitors is increasingly restricted through a complex series of gateways, terraces, and galleries until eventually some—but not all—are allowed to reach the main sanctuary and central tower, a pivotal space that is not only the most religiously powerful but the most sociologically exclusive.[90]

Likewise, if somewhat less symmetrical than the cosmogrammatic layout of Angkor Wat, the Second Temple at Jerusalem displays an even more intense correlation of graduated sacrality and segregation according to social status. Not only was the Inner Court of Herod's Temple, which was reserved exclusively for Jews, cordoned off from the Court of the Gentiles, the interior temple space was additionally partitioned by a series of walls, balconies, and levels into the Court of the Women, the Court of Israelites, and the Court of the Priests, which was closed to all but the clergy and their assistants.[91] And the core of the sanctuary was furthermore subdivided into the *hekal,* or holy place, the entrance to which was framed by inscriptions that threatened death to any non-Jew who might dare to enter (see Acts 21:28ff.), and, most exclusive of all, the *debir,* or Holy of Holies, an empty space screened by a double curtain that even the high priests were allowed to penetrate only annually, on the Day of Atonement.[92]

More elaborate still, yet equally demonstrative of this notion of hierarchical sociospatial sanctuaries, is Nelson Wu's explication of what he terms "graduated privacy" in the layout of Beijing and its houses, a context in which "the passing of each gateway is a penetration into the depths of someone's privacy."[93] At the hugest scale, the Great Wall of China defines a collective sense of privacy that excludes "barbarians" and "outsiders." Next, Beijing's civic privacy is guarded both militarily and symbolically by the high walls of the city proper; and then, ensuring the privacy of the emperor, the Forbidden City is encircled by yet another elegant and imposing wall.[94] In more plainly residential contexts, the notions of "graduated privacy" and meticulously restricted access similarly inform the layout of the individual domestic compounds within the city: First, the yard is separated from the street by walls that, as Wu notes, provide only a partial privacy by screening the view but not the many sounds and smells of the street;[95] next, the protruding eaves of the house provide another layer of partial privacy, "privacy from heaven or from the 'Heavenly See'" (which is a fascinating notion in itself); and then, inside the house, there is a succession of intermediate courtyard spaces before reaching the "total privacy" of the *an,* the inner or "dark" rooms of the residence, which only family members and the most intimate guests are ever allowed to enter.[96]

This complexly tiered architectural arrangement, for which we can find innumerable cross-cultural if less elaborate morphological parallels, works, therefore, to facilitate a fastidious protocol regarding how various visitors are ushered into the house, a complex system of Chinese etiquette that amounts to a kind of hierarchy of access based on social status.[97] Outside the front gate is, in Wu's terms, "the world of strangers." At the next levels, merchants or peddlers might be invited through the first doorway to show their wares; and friends and honored guests, "or a messenger from the emperor for that matter," are allowed to penetrate somewhat deeper into the porch and intermediate courtyard, the *ming* (or "bright") room. The core of the house, however, is reserved exclusively for family members and relatives.[98]

Morphology, Sacrality, Superabundance: The Relativity of Inside and Outside

In closing, though presenting some new problems, this consideration of the so-termed sanctuary mode of ritual-architectural presentation and apprehension (priority III-D), the eleventh of eleven categorical options in the heuristic framework, serves also to epitomize and reinforce numerous concerns that are at issue in the entire prolegomenon to the hermeneutics of sacred architecture. Specifically, this last chapter refocuses attention on broad insights, caveats, and cautionings with respect to three very large, constantly relevant matters: morphological comparison, "sacred space," and the "occasionality" and superabundance of religious architecture.

First, regarding what I have termed "the specific and modest ambitions of morphology,"[99] this chapter's provisional tri-partitioning of pertinent possibilities into preparatory sanctifications of ritual contexts and actors versus more content-specific deployments of sanctuary modes in the respective service of commemorations of divinity (priority II-A) and of sociopolitical authority (priority II-C)—three very large sets of possibilities that were then sliced and resliced—ought to remind us of the always heavily overlapping and never fully systematic categorizations that morphology provides. The version of "significant organization" that operates in these exploratory discurses remains insinuative, I hope evocative, but nonetheless, for author and probably readers, frustratingly noncomprehensive. Here the differences between heuristic morphology and those versions of typology and classification that endeavor to provide more definitive conclusions should be especially apparent.

Moreover, the staccato presentation of illustrative historical (and nonhistorical) "cases," which in this chapter and others requires sometimes jarring leaps from one cultural context to another, ought to remind us both of the stimulative potential of unlikely (usually synchronic) comparative juxtapositions and of the dire difficulties of respecting the idiosyncrasies not only of specific cultures but also of subcultural communities and individuals. Trafficking to the end in snapshots and vignettes, this sort of sweeping morphological reconnaissance may demonstrate—if by omission—the rich interpretive rewards that only more sustained, particularistic empirical inquiry can provide. This work carries interpreters to—but not across—a threshold of a different sort, a point of departure from which they are invited to reenter their own more specialized, more rigorously contextualized researches with a widened catalog of leading questions and suggestive cross-cultural analogues. Morphology making, itself a kind of building process, is only, as I have claimed from the outset, an interim phase in the wider hermeneutics of sacred architecture. It is, at its best, only a catalyst or spur to deeper and more tightly focused inquiries.

Second, in relation to the infamous category of "sacred space," consideration of the sanctuary priority (III-D) brings the discussion full circle to the initial treatment of the homology priority (I A). As with that opening morphological option, we face here a set of concerns that enjoys a very high profile in Mircea Eliade's omnipresent work and, thus, in countless academic treatments of religious architectures in myriad cultural contexts. Virtually no student of religious architecture fails to acknowledge, in part anyway, the sense in which built configurations work to enclose perimeters within which some special rules and possibilities obtain. Here again, then, I rechart and nuance the old maps of well-walked territories rather than cutting fully fresh new trails.

Moreover, the discussion of the sanctuary priority brings back to center-stage the competing claims and presumptions concerning what makes a space or building "sacred." Here, especially, we feel the tension, which is present throughout this entire field of inquiry, between indigenous and academic claims about the "discovery" of inherently powerful places and commentators who are bent on exposing the sociohistorical processes whereby ontologically unremarkable places and buildings are somehow invested with a status of exceptionality.[100] In either case, however, we ought to learn from this section that the (apparently) inherent sacrality of place, a cave or a temple location, does not lessen the requirements for ritual sanctification and, perhaps, as in the cases of Hindu temple sites mentioned earlier, does precisely the opposite. The innate sacrality of a space never, I would wager, translates into an exemption from ritual precautions and recognition.

Furthermore, this incomplete inventory of variations on the sanctuary theme ought to persuade us that a space's or building's "sacredness" is, with rare exception, neither a permanent nor an absolute black-or-white condition. The sacrality of even the most revered natural or "found" sanctuary is vulnerable to defilement, and thus desacralization; and nearly all built contexts, to some degree participating in the obviously transient sacrality of multi-use Oglala sweat lodges and Yuwipi rooms, require periodic ritual cleansing or "recharging." Additionally, as Nelson Wu's discussion of "graduated privacy" so well demonstrates, the sacrality of a specific architectural context, built or even found, is seldom if ever a flatly definite, yes-or-no matter. Whether the increments of privilege are expressed horizontally, in the concentric layouts of towns and buildings, or vertically, in ascending platforms or terraces, we should appreciate by now that the sacredness of space is not an objective condition but a situational, relative, and relational one that arises from the dynamically interactive (eventful) engagements between people and architectural configurations.

Third and finally, reflections on sanctuary modes of presentation and apprehension again bring to the foreground the "occasionality" and superabundance of sacred architecture, which constitute the very foundation of this hermeneutics of sacred architecture. To reiterate that central theme one last time, built configurations that cordon off and enclose reveal with the most unmistakable clarity the inadequacy of imagining that religious buildings have unified and stable meanings; and therefore, such configurations demonstrate the equally unmistakable advantages of constituting (or problematizing) studies of sacred architecture in terms of situational events rather than in terms of what are presumed to be the "real," once-and-for-all meanings of buildings.

That is to say, because enactments of the sanctuary priority (III-D) invariably eventuate in explicit differentiations between an outside and an inside (or a series of insides), interpreters need to appreciate that every ritual-architectural enclosure engenders, at the very least, two profoundly different sorts (or sets) of human experiences: those of the insiders and those of persons who are not allowed inside. The built accoutrements of sanctuary—particularly the gates, passages, and doorways that constitute the actual thresholds and zones of transition—are quintessentially ambiguous (and thus particularly multivalent) architectural features insofar as they both keep in and keep out.[101] Palisades and portals present not just one but a wide range of experiential possibilities insofar as they repel and restrict access, but also invite entry and exit; depending on one's view, they either welcome or rebuff.

Here especially, then, the estimable advantages—the necessity, in fact—of holding the interpretive focus on the experiential apprehensions and "receptions" of architecture rather than on built forms per se should be beyond refute. Sanctuary configurations provide the most conspicuous demonstration that what is experienced, say, from the inside, by those who are allowed privileged access, as safe and reliable, in Eliade's terms "sacred" and "real," may, from the outside, be apprehended as nearly the opposite—as forbidding, remote, inaccessible, dangerous, perhaps as "sacred" in the wrong way, that is, as impenetrable and repellant rather than alluring. In the design and apprehension of religious sanctuaries, even more obviously than in other spheres, *including* is, necessarily, *excluding*. Providing a sense of belonging to an elect few is, necessarily, to cultivate a sense of alienation in others.[102]

To end, then, characteristically, with a case in point: critical, empirically minded hermeneuts need to recognize the serious limitations of plausible, but not very comprehensive, assessments like that of Thomas Merton, which suggests that the so-termed Enclosure at Our Lady of Gethesemani in Kentucky engenders an experience of calm, security, belonging, and contemplative proximity to God. The walled Enclosure may be, as Merton maintains, the frame in which to display an exemplary model of prayerful existence—but it is also much more. Appreciating the always-diversified, rebellious, and revalorative apprehensions of such substantial forms, we have to suspect that those idealized sensations of calm and worshipful repose are not apposite even for all the resident monks on all occasions. And, we can be quite certain that, from the perspective of visitors, the very same feature evokes not only reverent respect but, variously, terror, intimidation, guilt, longing, confusion, or, perhaps, relief that one has *not* been compelled to enter into the sterility of this closed world. A reflective and candid entry from the journal of a young visitor to the Kentucky monastery provides, in fact, eloquent testimony to several of those possibilities and, therefore, a fitting, final reminder of the irrepressible superabundance of sacred architecture, the acknowledgment of which furnishes hermeneutical interpreters both their most daunting challenges and their most intriguing prospects:

> [Behind the] Abbey is the Enclosure. This is a big, walled-in area that is open only to monks. It covers a few hundred acres. . . . The wall of the Enclosure is one of the most *real* walls I have ever seen . . . real in the fact that it definitely separates something from Something. One world from another. . . . I cannot imagine setting foot inside the Enclosure. It would be a travesty, a violation. Maybe the air is different, containing some element of X. Maybe the trees, the figures are all insubstantial. . . . Who knows? It is not a place I can go.[103]

Appendix | An Expanded Morphology of Ritual-Architectural Priorities

IN THE SPIRIT OF SUMMATION AND EXPEDIENCE, this appendix provides what amounts to a set of worksheets, which might be utilized in the operationalization of the methodological reflections expounded in the two volumes of *The Hermeneutics of Sacred Architecture*. Relying throughout on the metaphor of a hermeneutical dialogue between scholars and specific ritual-architectural situations, I provide here a series of leading questions and statements in relation to each of the eleven ritual-architectural priorities—questions and statements that, I hope, might serve to initiate and sustain those sorts of interrogational, interpretative conversations.

Conceived firstly as a catalog of possibilities that can aid in the composition of ritual-architectural reception histories, this morphologic framework may prove serviceable in several respects. In its preliminary, least imaginative utilization, the appendix could serve as a kind of checklist, which enumerates an extended pattern of hermeneutical questioning, that students of sacred architecture can bring to bear on whatever specific ritual-architectural circumstance has captured their interest. Interpreters are, in other words, encouraged to ask over and over again: How and to what extent are various permutations of each of the ritual-architectural priorities relevant to that specific circumstance? And how do those configurations of priorities, sub-priorities, and sub-sub-priorities change or stay the same over time? In more ingenious utilizations, the wide array of morphological possibilities could stimulate researchers (or perhaps designers) to give serious consideration to versions of the interrelations between built forms, ritual processes, and human experiences that might otherwise have escaped their attentions, thus providing points of departure for endlessly diversified avenues of interpreting (and making) architecture.

The outline, which follows in most cases the order of the discussions in each individual chapter of volume 2, is, therefore, like the entire project, suggestive rather than exhaustive, heuristic rather than conclusionary. Nearly all the selected examples are also drawn directly from those chapters and thus cited here only in a highly elliptical fashion.

I. Architecture as Orientation: The Instigation of Ritual-Architectural Events

Homology (priority I-A): Sacred architecture that presents a miniaturized replica of the universe and/or conforms to a celestial archetype.

Recall that the notion of ritual-architectural homology refers to several themes that are very prominent in the work of Mircea Eliade. This set of possibilities should not, though, be considered as coextensive with Eliade's work, nor as a blanket endorsement of his redoubted theory of sacred space.

Consider, for example, the non–mutually exclusive applicability of the following four variations on (or dimensions of) the homology theme:

1. Architectural expressions of hierophany or an earthly manifestation of "the sacred":

   This involves the acknowledgment of (apparently) intrinsically powerful places and natural features (e.g., rocks, caves, mountains, springs, or other geographical anomalies), where it is believed that a numinous or "sacred" power has made its presence felt.

   Note that such sites are, from the perspective of the faithful, considered to have been designated by "sacred" or extranatural agencies and thus "discovered" rather than created by any sort of human activity, including ritual.

   Note, moreover, that, for the sort of hermeneutical analysis advocated here, it is important for scholars to take seriously indigenous claims that "the sacred" has manifested itself in some particular place without, however, passing judgment on the ontological viability of those indigenous claims.

2. Architectural imitations of celestial precedents or "archetypes":

   This involves constructions or construction processes conceived as earthly replications (or reiterations) of mythical, "primordial," or heavenly buildings or building processes (e.g., the Temple of Solomon, which is described in the *Letter to the Hebrews* as "a copy and a shadow of the heavenly sanctuary").

Note that architectural configurations conceived as modeled after (or reiterative of) mythical precedents are especially relevant also to the commemoration of sacred history (priority II-B), particularly the subcategory of ritual-architectural commemorations of cosmogony.

3. Architectural expressions of *imago mundi*, or cosmogrammatic ordering:

   This possibility, which constitutes the quintessence of the homology theme, involves constructions that are conceived as downsized replicas of the universe, or "images of the world" (e.g., the house plan of the Sa'Dan Toraja of Indonesia, a domicile that is explicitly conceived and constructed as a reduced version of the entire Toraja cosmological system). Builders and users imagine in these cases that there is a direct parallelism between the macrocosm (i.e., the universe at large) and the architectural microcosm (i.e., the earthly built form).

   Note that this version of homologized building may entail a replication of the structure of the universe at any architectural scale (e.g., at the scale of altars, rooms, buildings, cities, or whole territories, as in the Inca *ceque* system). Such homologizing architectural practices serve often to reflect (or effect) the unification of space, time, colors, biological species, body parts, social structure, political affiliations, etc.

4. Architectural expressions of *axis mundi*, or the symbolism of the center:

   This exceptionally prevalent possibility (which Eliade and others have instantiated in countless cultural contexts) involves architectural configurations that are located at, or oriented with respect to, a cosmic center, or "world axis." Orientation with respect to a cosmic center invariably entails as well a preoccupation with the cardinal directions.

   Note again the possibility that a construction that is conceived as located at the "center of the world," thus enabling special access to other cosmic realms, finds expression at all scales (e.g., rooms, habitations, temples, villages, or, as in the case of ancient Chinese capital cities, whole empires).

More generally, note that, the deployment of such homologizing building practices is, in most cases, preparatory rather than summational: homologized building is most often a means of ritual-architectural allurement, which serves to capture the interest of onlookers and to invite their participation—but almost never constitutes the total, or even primary, significance of an architectural event.

Finally, note also that, irrespective of Eliadean claims to universality, in the sacred architectures of numerous historical contexts (e.g., classical Greece), the infamous categories of hierophany, *imago mundi, axis mundi,* and symbolism of the center are largely or wholly irrelevant.

Convention (priority I-B): Sacred architecture that conforms to standardized rules and/or prestigious mythicohistoric precedents.

Recall that the convention priority refers to architectural constructions and building processes that explicitly conform to standardized (or conventionalized) stipulations and rules. The authority of such architectural conventions and prescriptions may, however, derive from innumerable and very different sorts of sources.

Consider, for example, the non–mutually exclusive applicability of the following three broad sets of variations on the convention theme:

1. Architectures that conform to universalistic principles and proportions that are (considered to have been) derived from largely empirical observations of the natural world:

   This widespread possibility may include, for instance, the replication in architecture of abstract laws of measure and proportion (e.g., sacred ratios, magic numbers, or secret rhythms) that have been variously adduced from any—or usually all—of the following:

   a. Observations of natural phenomena (e.g., Renaissance adducements of the "first principles of Nature" from observations of plants, animals, weather, and the movements of stars and planets);
   b. Measurements of human anatomy (e.g., Alberti's meticulous studies of bodily proportions);
   c. Analyses of sound and music (e.g., Augustine's reliance on studies of music in the formulations of his aesthetics of number and proportion); and/or

d. Mathematical and geometrical calculations (e.g., Chinese *feng shui* geomantic schemes or the rich Sufi tradition of "symbolic and qualitative mathematics").

Note that architectural conventions of this sort may be variously recorded in building manuals (e.g., the abundance of ancient Egyptian manuals of "correct" construction and Renaissance rulebooks of architectural proportion, spacing, and style); narrative canonical codes (e.g., the vast Hindu *Shilpa Shastra* literature); and/or schematic diagrams (e.g., Chinese "magic squares" or Hindu mandala diagrams).

Note also that in some instances (e.g., in the Italian Renaissance context) the guiding priority for architectural design is exact (or ostensibly objective) conformity to universal rhythms and proportions; but in other instances (e.g., in the layout of ancient Greek city states), the first priority seems to be the appearance of perfect order and regularity, which may actually require compromising objective architectural proportions.

2. Architectures that conform to axiomatic stipulations that are (considered to have been) delivered by divine revelation or decree:

   Architectural prescriptions that are mandated by a god may be variously recorded in personal testimony, in oral tradition, and/or in sacred scripture (e.g., Qur'anic design standards that are understood to have been decreed directly by Allah or the divinely given design directives that appear in the Torah and Jewish halakic literature).

3. Architectures that conform to precedents that are (considered to have been) established by prestigious historical and/or mythical predecessors:

   This exceptionally widespread possibility depends less on conformity to abstract cosmic principles than on the faithful imitation of revered mythicohistorical precedents (e.g., "the Ancients"). Often, this involves deliberate "archaisms," that is, the copying of architectural elements (e.g., building forms and styles, iconographic and pictorial elements, or orientations and alignments) that were established in some earlier, or even contemporaneous, context (e.g., the widespread Mesoamerican practice of reproducing artistic and architectural patterns believed to have been "invented" by the highly esteemed mythicohistorical Toltecs).

> Note that, because such deliberately archaic building practices are often in the service of establishing (an appearance of) continuity with prestigious mythicohistorical forebears, these imitative practices are often directly relevant also to the commemoration of sacred history (priority II-B) and the commemoration of politics (priority II-C).

More generally, note that, the convention priority (unlike the homology priority, I-A) is to some considerable extent relevant to virtually all ritual-architectural circumstances. Conformity to ritual-architectural conventions is similar to homologized building, however, insofar as it serves most often as a means of establishing an aura of order and legitimacy, and thus making buildings and occasions alluring—but adherence to convention (again like homology) almost never constitutes the total, or even primary, significance of a ritual-architectural event.

Finally, note also that, in many cases, deliberate deviation from well-established ritual-architectural conventions is at least as provocative and powerful as faithful conformity to those conventions.

Astronomy (priority I-C): Sacred architecture that is aligned or referenced with respect to celestial bodies or phenomena.

Recall that the astronomy priority has an ambiguous status in the morphology insofar as orientations and referencings with respect to celestial features, sometimes neglected in the past, are of central importance in a few ritual-architectural contexts but are largely irrelevant in many, if not most, other contexts.

Recall also that, despite the cross-cultural abundance of elaborate ancient monuments that were clearly designed to observe the movements of celestial bodies, very seldom (particularly in "traditional" contexts) is the significance of astronomically oriented, ostensibly religious architecture exhausted in the acquisition of "empirical data." The incentives for ancient astronomers were, it seems, very different from those of their contemporary counterparts.

Nonetheless, consider how the astronomy theme may be applicable to each of the respective components of the twofold ritual-architectural situation:

1. With respect to astronomy and allurement (the front half of the ritual-architectural situation):

   Astroarchitectural references, when coordinated with other orientational strategies, can substantially enhance the appearance of harmony and conformity to a generalized world order, and thus enhance the legitimacy—and the allure—associated with a specific ritual-architectural circumstance. Two, often complementary, possibilities deserve consideration:

   a. In conjunction with homologized orientation (priority I-A), astronomical features and alignments often serve as one more element that is integrated into some larger cosmogrammatic scheme (e.g., as in the Inca *ceque* system, wherein observational sky phenomena were integrated into a complex system of homological correlations involving not only spaces and times but also occupations, tribute responsibilities, and kinship and marriage groups); and
   b. In conjunction with conventionalized orientation (priority I-B), observable sky phenomena are sometimes integrated into the ritual-architectural context as a means of strengthening the appearance of conformity to (ostensibly) universal rhythms and principles. This may require the deliberate "distortion" (or enhancement) of empirically derived astronomical information (as in the Classic Maya's frequent and willful manipulation of astronomical "data" in order to synchronize sky phenomena both with the conventionalized recording of past events and the scheduling of future ones).

2. Also with respect to strategies of allurement, though somewhat more aggressively and more distinctively connected to astronomy:

   Ritual-architectural choreographers may, on occasion, find ways to capitalize on some predictable sky phenomenon (an eclipse, a solar equinox, or the reappearance of Venus or a comet) as the means for strategic scheduling of a ceremony (e.g., Maya coronations or reaffirmations of kingship that were scheduled in conjunction with the arcane but regular movements of Venus and the sun).

   Note that invitations of this sort, which can be both highly dramatic and often coercive, usually depend on the "ritual-architectural enhancement of nature" (e.g., the "serpent of light" phenomenon at Chichén Itzá).

That is to say, the dramatically alluring astroarchitectural effect is visible only as a consequence of the strategic integration of natural sky phenomena and humanly constructed elements. Without the carefully designed built forms, there is no "celestial" effect.

Note also that, because such ritual-architectural events require and demonstrate special predictive knowledge, they may sometimes engender orientational sensations that are better characterized as "active control" of the future than as "passive harmony" with past (conventionalized) practices or with present (homologized) cosmic realities. That, however, is very difficult to assess.

3. With respect to astronomy and the presentation of substantive meanings and messages (the back half of the ritual-architectural situation):

   Though the most salient uses of celestially aligned features probably come in relation to strategies of allurement, astroarchitectural orientations—which work, in a sense, to incorporate sky phenomena into the ritual context—can likewise substantially enhance the presentation and apprehension of meanings that bear on each of the four commemorative priorities. Consider, for instance:

   a. Astronomical orientations in conjunction with commemorations of divinity (e.g., alignments that enhance the worship of celestial bodies that are variously conceived as sun, sky, and "storm" gods, such as Zeus, Indra, Rudra, Baal, Jupiter, and Thor);
   b. Astronomical orientations in conjunction with commemorations of sacred history (e.g., enhancements of storytelling via alignments to constellations that are conceived as mythological sites or actors, as in the cases of Native Americans, Africans, Polynesians, and Australian aborigines);
   c. Astronomical orientations in conjunction with commemorations of sociopolitical concerns (e.g., alignments that work to enhance the astrocosmologically sanctioned authority of a ruler, such as the frequently close associations between kingship and the sun); and
   d. Astronomical orientations in conjunction with commemorations of the dead (e.g., alignments that enhance devotion to esteemed ancestors, as was apparently the case with numerous British megaliths, most notably, Stonehenge).

II. Architecture as Commemoration: The Content of Ritual-Architectural Events

Divinity (priority II-A): Sacred architecture that commemorates, houses, and/or represents a deity, divine presence, or conception of ultimate reality.

Recall that analyses and cross-cultural comparisons of ritual-architectural commemorations of divinity are especially complicated—and enlivened—by the enormous diversity of culturally specific conceptions of gods and other supernatural entities and presences.

Nonetheless, consider the applicability of the following four sets of non–mutually exclusive variations on the divinity theme:

1. The personification or divination of natural "architectural" features of the landscape:

   This possibility, which integrates naturally occurring architectonic elements into the ritual context, may entail either:

   a. Conceiving of geological or biological features, the "architecture of nature" as it were (e.g., mountains, stones, trees, and lakes), as divinities, culture heroes, and/or ancestors (e.g., as among Australian aborigines); or
   b. Orienting built forms and ritual activities toward natural features that are somehow mythologized and/or divinized (e.g., as in the reciprocal relations between classical Greek temples and the landscape, wherein the experience of the buildings entails and requires also the experience of the broader natural surroundings).

2. Architecture that is conceived as the actual body of a deity:

   In these cases, built forms are equated, or "literally" identified, with (the body of) a divinity, most prominently, a goddess of the earth (e.g., Cretan palaces, which are conceived as the body of the Minoan earth goddess, and thus as "living organisms").

   Note that often the ritualized entry into such god-like (or earth-like) architectural features is conceived as a kind of symbolic death, whereupon exit from the structure enables a cathartic sensation of rebirth (as in the supposed ritual use of Maya zoomorphic, "earth-monster" temples).

3. Architecture that is conceived as an abode, residence, or house of a deity or divine presence:

   Such "deity domiciles," which are designed with the hope of luring a divinity to take up permanent or periodic residence in that sheltering space, are often conceived as earthly replicas of the god's mythological or heavenly home (e.g., Hindu temples built as replicas of Shiva's mythological mountain home of Kailasa).

   Note also that, where deities are regarded as residing in the architectural space (either permanently or periodically), the ritualized interactions between human devotees and divinities (who may be more specifically present in anthropomorphic images, icons, or statues) can variously take the form of:

   a. Honoring, entertaining, or pampering a god (e.g., the feeding and washing of gods at many Hindu temples);
   b. Petitioning or propitiating a god (e.g., fertility rites in innumerable contexts);
   c. Consulting or soliciting advice from a god (e.g., oracle temples in ancient Greece or China); and/or
   d. Holding a god captive (e.g., Aztec cases in which the gods of conquered peoples were confined to a special temple, or those Greek cases in which deity statues were literally restrained with chains).

4. Architecture that is conceived as a built expression of the attributes of a divinity:

   Built forms of this sort, which often have more the character of sculptures than shelters, express or invoke in some abstract fashion the qualities or the "notion" of a deity, a divine presence, or a conception of ultimate reality.

   Though the most obvious exemplars are constructions built to commemorate a specific, largely anthropomorphic deity (e.g., classical Greek temples dedicated, respectively, to Hera, Demeter, Artemis, and

Aphrodite), consider also the following, less straightforward, overlapping variations on this theme:

a. Architectural expressions of a nonanthropomorphic conception of ultimate reality (e.g., architectural expressions of the Buddhist Dharma);
b. Architectural expressions of specific conceptions of existential dilemma and possible solutions (e.g., Hindu architecturizations of the notions of karma-regulated rebirth and *moksha*, or liberation from rebirth);
c. Architectural expressions of subtle and specific theologies (e.g., triangular or three-tiered architectural allusions to the three elements of the Christian Trinity);
d. Architectural configurations designed to avoid depicting (an Abrahamic) God, but disclosing an intuition of the nature and transcendence of God (e.g., in the evocative geometrical designs of Muslim mosques); and
e. Architecture that simply provides a context to meet in order to think, study, and talk about a diety that cannot be confined to any particular earthly place (e.g., those Jewish synagogues or Protestant church contexts in which the absolute transcendence of God is accentuated).

More generally, note also that there is a strong possibility that the commemoration of divinity (priority II-A) is most notable by its omission or highly restricted relevance. With respect, for instance, to the complex matters of idolatry, iconoclasm, and aniconism, both indigenous (especially Abrahamic) and academic claims concerning a deliberate and complete avoidance of any version of the artistic commemoration of divinity are quite common. Actual historical practice, however, nearly always belies those ostensible claims to the total evasion of any representation of God.

Sacred History (priority II-B): Sacred architecture that commemorates an important mythical, mythicohistorical, or miraculous episode or circumstance.

Recall that "sacred history" is employed here as a broad designation that encompasses foundational and authoritative stories concerning variously mythical, miraculous, and historical circumstances, groups, and individuals. Accordingly, narratives belonging to either of the oft-contested categories of "myth" and "history" (as well as legend, fable, folktale, etc.) are directly pertinent.

Consider, for example, the applicability of the following five sets of non–mutually exclusive variations on the sacred history theme:

1. Architectural configurations that serve simply as the stage-setting or backdrop for the reenactment of notable mythic, historic, and/or miraculous episodes:

   Note that such very common configurations (e.g., countless stages, amphitheaters, daises, or dance platforms) are nearly always connected to theatric modes of presentation and apprehension (priority III-A).

2. Ritual-architectural commemorations of cosmogony:

   With respect to architectural embodiments of creation stories, consider, for instance:

   a. Construction (or remodeling) processes that are patterned after a cosmogony, which may entail either:

      i. Building practices that are explicitly conceived by the builders as reiterative of the creation of the world (e.g., the erection of Hindu temples); and/or
      ii. Building practices that, in the view of academic interpreters, are reiterative of a cosmogonic pattern and logic (e.g., interpretations of the sensations of renewal and exhilaration that accompany the construction of some Christian churches).

      Note that instances of these sorts of ritualized, cosmogonically reiterative, building processes are directly related both to the homology priority (I-A) and to one sort of permutation of the propitiation priority (III-C).

   b. Completed architectural configurations that express, and thus facilitate reenactments of, cosmogonic themes (e.g., the moat-encircled Angkor Wat, which is a direct expression of a Southeast Asian creation story).

3. Ritual-architectural commemorations of mythicohistorical episodes or occurrences:

In these cases, the episodes, or "happenings," being commemorated may be conceived as either:

a. Strictly "mythical" insofar as they are understood to have occurred in some primordial, timeless era or dimension (e.g., the Aztec story of the birth of the war god Huitzilopochtli, which is reenacted at the Templo Mayor); or
b. One-time "historical" episodes insofar as the events are understood to have occurred in ordinary human time, perhaps on some specifically dated occasion. Where such unique occurrences are commemorated, consider whether they are conceived as either:

    i. "Miraculous" insofar as they entailed some extrahuman agency (e.g., the apparition of a god, angel, or virgin); or
    ii. Exceptional but strictly human accomplishments (e.g., the discovery of new lands, victory in battle, or insight in law-making).

4. Ritual-architectural commemorations of mythicohistorical individuals or personages:

    In these cases, which often entail the consolidation of various attributes of excellence and good character (or maliciousness and bad character) in a single individual, consider, for instance, whether the figure being commemorated is conceived as:

    a. Wholly nonhuman, such as a mythical beast, animal, trickster, or culture hero (in which case, there is a merger with the commemoration of divinity [priority II-A]);
    b. Human but in some sense divine or transhuman (e.g., Egyptian pharaohs or Jesus Christ); or
    c. Strictly human (e.g., a military leader, such as Napoleon, or a religio-political leader, such as Martin Luther King, Jr.).

5. Ritual-architectural commemorations of mythical places, sites, or locations:

    In these cases, in which the "power of place" or geography of sacred history becomes as important as, or even more important than, the specific events or individuals, consider, for instance:

a. Circumstances in which direct physical contact with the place is required (e.g., journeys to the pilgrimage sites of Mecca, Lourdes, or Banaras); and
b. Circumstances in which efforts are made to, in some sense, "transfer the sanctity" or "bring home" the place, either by carrying away ampullae, water, or dirt (as in St. Helen's transfer of dirt from Mount Calvary to Rome), or perhaps by building a replica of the place in some other location (as in Friar Caimi's replication of the Holy Land in Italy).

More generally with respect to sacred history (priority II-B), consider also the possibilities either of relative indifference toward or ineffectiveness in the expression of narrative themes via art and architecture. In those cases, this priority could be most notable by its limited applicability (e.g., in assessments of the nonnarrative quality of Olmec art as opposed to the decidedly storiological art of Izapa).

Additionally, recall that it will be important to discern, to the extent possible, whether, in the context of the specific ritual-architectural commemorations of sacred history, human participants' apprehensions of the respective mythicohistorical episodes and individuals are conceived more as:

- Pedagogical: that is, simply as occasions of intellectualized learning, remembering, or paying homage (e.g., as in most museums or celebrations of national holidays where people imagine themselves as simply "recalling" significant events and people); or
- Experiential and participatory: that is, as occasions of somehow reliving or reactualizing those exceptional events, and perhaps even, in some sense, "becoming" those mythicohistorical individuals (e.g., as in claims that participants in the Eucharist are actually made present to the Passion of Jesus).

Politics (priority II-C): Sacred architecture that commemorates, legitimates, or challenges socioeconomic hierarchy and/or temporal authority.

Recall that "politics" is a shorthand designation that directs attention to the roles of architecture and ritual not only in relation to the exercise of explicitly governmental force and authority but also in relation to the perpetuation (or subversion) of any sort of social or economic hierarchy. The sweep of relevant issues is, in other words, wide in the extreme.

Nonetheless, consider the applicability of the following three sets of non–mutually exclusive variations on the politics theme:

1. Ritual-architectural configurations that reflect and perpetuate the prevailing social hierarchy:

   Such status quo–reinforcing configurations may occur at all scales—from room furnishings, to individual buildings, to village layouts, to the spatial arrangement of whole regions or empires. Moreover, architectural strategies for reinforcing socioeconomic hierarchies may entail:

   a. Horizontal arrangements (e.g., in the concentric layouts of Maya villages or Chinese cities in which proximity to the town center is correlated with social status); and/or
   b. Vertical arrangements (e.g., in the relative heights of the houses of various Hindu castes or in the design of multilevel Japanese houses).

2. Ritual-architectural configurations that challenge, undermine, and (maybe) change the prevailing social hierarchy:

   Consider the following variations on the theme of social critique via architecture:

   a. Configurations that (temporarily) suspend or ignore wider social differentiation (e.g., Muslim mosques, inside which the social distinctions that obtain in the outside world are erased or suspended).

      Though (ostensibly) designed to criticize and challenge social conventions, note that ritual-architectural designs that enable periodic suspension or avoidance of the wider socioeconomic hierarchy may actually serve in the long run to reinforce rather than undermine the status quo.

   b. Configurations that protest, subvert, and (are intended to) change the status quo (e.g., the doorways and shapes of Sikh or Baha'i temples, which are intended to express classless unity and openness to all).

These are, generally speaking, "bottom-up" configurations, as it were, insofar as they are initiated by "the disenfranchised" (e.g., revolutionaries or social critics with limited economic and political resources who initiate "counter-designs" or "guerilla buildings"). In these cases, the long-term socioeconomic effects are often negligible.

c. Configurations that (are intended to) override the prevailing social order and/or to authorize a transition of authority.

   These are, generally speaking, "top-down" configurations, insofar as they are initiated by "the enfranchised" (e.g., rulers and leaders with substantial economic and political resources). With respect to these better-financed ritual-architectural initiatives, which are more likely to succeed in effecting long-term social change, consider especially two possibilities:

   i. Ritual-architectural projects undertaken in relation to peaceful transitions of authority (e.g., coronations, ascensions, and inaugurations); and
   ii. Ritual-architectural projects undertaken in relation to forcible takeovers of authority (e.g., invasions, military victories, conquests, and colonization).

3. Ritual-architectural configurations that serve more explicitly governmental functions:

   Consider, for instance, the following variations on the theme of ritual-architectural strategies employed in governance and statecraft:

   a. Configurations that glorify a particular ruler:

      Such projects—which may commemorate either divine or human and either living or deceased rulers—may be initiated either by the ruler himself or herself (e.g., as in the Great Pyramid at Giza, which was built by and for the pharaoh Cheops) or by someone else (e.g., posthumous memorials like the Washington Monument, which nonetheless also serve strategic governmental functions).

   b. Configurations that facilitate day-to-day governmental operations:

This often entails the construction of a (ritual) context for stylized debate and decision making (e.g., parliamentary chambers, congressional headquarters, or courtrooms).

c. Configurations that provide (symbolic) expression of the strength and stability of the state and/or other religiocivic institutions:

With respect to these sorts of strategies, which are generally pursued with the greatest urgency when centralized states are expanding or imperiled, consider especially three possibilities:

i. Religiocivic integration via ritual-architectural means:

This often entails persuading reticent people in peripheral territories of their necessary respect for, and allegiance to, a hegemonic center. This may include either the replication in the periphery of architectural elements from the center (e.g., the Quiché Mayas' construction in the outlying reaches of their empire of garrisons that were scaled-down copies of the civic buildings of their capital) or other means of architectural standardization imposed by a centralized authority.

ii. Constructions of religiocivic identity via ritual-architectural means:

This often entails the construction and public showcasing of a distinguished pedigree (e.g., the Aztecs' reliance on architecture and ritual in the perpetration of a legitimating but largely fictive Toltec pedigree; or the strategic imitation of Greco-Roman, European, and Egyptian architectural motifs on the Washington Mall).

iii. Blunt intimidation via ritual-architectural means:

This often entails vivid displays of past military victories (e.g., monuments in several contexts that depict conquerors standing on the necks or heads of the vanquished); or the presentation of "aggressively foreign" styles (e.g., the colonial royal palace of the British in India, which stood in deliberately stark contrast to indigenous architectural styles).

More generally, recall that, with all of these strategic, manipulative expressions of the politics priority (II-C), it is especially important to investigate whether the ritual-architectural ploys "worked" in the sense of successfully solidifying or changing social circumstances and sentiments. In this realm especially—where the ritual-architectural failure rate, as it were, is especially high—watch for disparities between design intentions and subsequent apprehensions.

The Dead (priority II-D): Sacred architecture that commemorates revered ancestors and/or other deceased individuals or groups.

As with the divinity priority (II-A), specific analyses and cross-cultural comparisons of the ritual-architectural commemoration of the dead are especially complicated—and enlivened—by the enormous diversity of culturally specific conceptions not only of death and the "afterlife" but also of human bodies and lived existence.

Nonetheless, consider the applicability of the following three sets of non–mutually exclusive variations on the theme of the commemoration of the dead:

1. Architectural configurations that facilitate "bodiless memorializing":

   Two very different sorts of strategies for architecturally commemorating the dead (variously conceived) that are undertaken largely irrespective of actual bodily remains deserve special consideration:

   a. Architectural configurations that commemorate strictly mythical ancestors, "the dead that never lived," so to speak, who thus have no bodily remains (e.g., Dogon houses and sanctuaries designed to honor esteemed "ancestors" who have, at no point in their existences, lived as ordinary humans); and
   b. Architectural configurations that commemorate "the fully dead," that is, (mythico)historical individuals who, after death, are not expected to exercise any direct influence on earthly affairs, and whose personhood is not directly connected to their bodily remains (e.g., modern Western, "secularized" monuments to the dead, which include no bodily remains and have a primarily pedagogical or museum-like character). Two prominent, overlapping possibilities include:

i. Group or collective bodiless memorials (e.g., the Holocaust Memorial Museum or the Vietnam Veterans Memorial in Washington, D.C., neither of which depends on actual bodily remains for its efficacy); and
ii. Individual-specific bodiless memorials: This may entail statues, monuments, or buildings that were constructed expressly to commemorate deceased individuals, but that include no bodily remains (e.g., public monuments like the Lincoln and Jefferson Memorials). Or this may entail more obviously utilitarian architectural constructions that are dedicated to, and often named after, specific deceased individuals (e.g., stadiums, hospitals, bridges, parks, streets, school or church additions, or smaller architectural elements like balconies, bells, or windows).

2. Architectural configurations that serve as the actual embodiment, re-actualization, or transmutation of the dead:

   This includes variations on the less obvious notion of architecture (broadly speaking) that, in some direct and important sense, *is* the dead. Though, again, usually undertaken largely irrespective of actual bodily remains, these artistic and architectural configurations are conceived as facilitating a kind of "conquest of death" in that they keep the deceased present and "alive." Consider the following possibilities:

   a. Configurations in which ancestors are embodied in natural stone features or stone constructions (e.g., British megaliths or Hindu rock-cut shrines, both of which seem to rely on an equation between the timeless permanence of stone and the ongoing existence of dead ancestors); and
   b. Configurations in which ancestors are embodied in media other than stone (e.g., those practices in which famous or obscure people are "kept alive" in wood or wax carvings, paintings, photographs, or computer imaging).

3. Architectural configurations designed for the assiduous treatment and accommodation of the physical, bodily remains of the (un)dead:

   This includes the more obvious possibility of actual tombs and burials of dead bodies. Consider, among prominent possibilities, the following, non–mutually exclusive variations on more explicitly mortuary architecture:

a. Mortuary domiciles: architectural configurations designed to house and pamper the (un)dead, enabling them to continue ostensibly routine domestic lives (e.g., Etruscan tombs that were conceived as "veritable underground houses");
b. Mortuary refuges: architectural configurations designed either as:

   i. Permanent resting places (e.g., the cave-like burial chambers at Hagar Qim, Malta, which, like countless "tomb wombs," provided places where the [un]dead were returned to their ostensible places of origin); or
   ii. Temporary places of waiting: tomb spaces from which the (un)-dead are expected to move on to some more permanent posthumous destination (e.g., Jewish, Christian, or Muslim burials where the body "sleeps" until eventual resurrection [or condemnation]).

c. Funerary vehicles of transport (e.g., Polynesian, ancient Egyptian, or Viking tombs, which were variously designed as chariots, boats, or other conveyances that could facilitate the [un]dead's perilous passage to some more permanent posthumous destination);
d. Mortuary gates, "crossing places," or points of ontological transition: that is, *axis mundi*–like burial sites where the (un)dead—and often the living—might "cross over" into other worlds or dimensions (e.g., according to some interpretations, Egyptian graves, Buddhist stupas, or Hindu *tirtha*s, which are explicitly conceived as "sacred fords");
e. Mortuary prisons or places of confinement: burial configurations designed to police or incarcerate the (un)dead so that they do not "come back" and cause harm (e.g., massive Haitian tombs, which block dangerous interactions between the dead and the living);
f. Mortuary palaces: burial configurations (e.g., Egyptian pyramids and some Inca and Maya funerary monuments) that are designed so as to enable (un)dead rulers to continue, even posthumously, their exercises of authority; and
g. Mortuary memorials and museums: burial configurations, which are usually associated with heavily rationalized conceptions of death (e.g., in the context of the French Revolution), that are designed primarily for the living either to learn about and imitate the dead or to use and exploit the dead in their constructions of identity.

More generally, note as well that, very often, instances of the commemoration of the dead (priority II-D) also serve as strategies of allurement, that is, in the front half of the architectural situation rather than the back half. Particularly notable are those exceedingly common situations in which the presence of bodily remains provides ritual-architectural contexts with a heightened aura of auspiciousness and sanctity (e.g., as in innumerable cases of the burial of martyrs or esteemed church leaders in the floors or patios of Christian churches). The mere presence of the remains of the (un)dead, even if the deceased are never explicitly mentioned, can substantially enhance the allure of a ritual-architectural context.

III. Architecture as Ritual Context: The Presentation of Ritual-Architectural Events

Theater (priority III-A): Sacred architecture that provides a stage setting or backdrop for ritual performance.

Recall that "theatric" modes of ritual-architectural presentation and apprehension are distinguished from other modes by the following criteria:

- Inclusive strategies of allurement insofar as the designer's incentive usually is to invite, cajole, or sometimes force even reticent onlookers, or "spoilsports," into involvement. (This is contrasted to sanctuary modes [III-D], in which the characteristic incentive is to exclude and restrict participation.)
- Indirect apprehensions of architecture insofar as the built forms contribute to the creation of an ambience or backdrop for ritual performance. (This is contrasted to contemplation modes [III-B], in which architectural elements serve as direct, purposeful objects of attention and meditation.)

Recall also that theatric modes, particularly in relation to allurement, often depend heavily on "affective" appeals to emotion and stimulation of the senses. Show, spectacle, ostentation, pomp and panache, shock, seduction, and amazement—these are the watchwords of theatric presentation.

Consider, for example, how theatric modes of presentation and apprehension may be applicable to each of the respective components of the twofold ritual-architectural situation:

1. With respect to theatric modes of allurement (i.e., the front half of the ritual-architectural situation):

Theatric allurement—which, by definition, involves the aggressive solicitation of involvement—may entail the presentation of dramatic architectural spaces that seduce, affect, or amaze a solitary individual (e.g., when an individual wanders into a spectacularly elaborate Baroque cathedral at a time when no formal proceedings are underway). The more prominent instances of theatric allurement, however, involve carefully scheduled interactions between ritual performers and an audience of onlookers (who constitute ritual actors of a different sort). Characteristically theatrical choreographic arrangements include the following options:

a. Stationary stages, stationary audiences:

   Ritual-architectural configurations of this familiar sort facilitate the presentation of ceremonial performances on a fixed podium or stage for a similarly stationary assembly of onlookers (e.g., the spectacular "pageant spaces" of pre-Columbian Mesoamerica, as well as countless more modest church, classroom, and cinema layouts where a seated audience faces a speaker, screen, or ensemble of singers, dancers, or actors).

b. Ambulatory actors, stationary audiences:

   This very common alternative entails ritual-architectural configurations that facilitate ceremonial movement along processional ways or parade routes past a largely fixed audience or reviewing stand (e.g., longitudinal Christian basilicas like that which hosted the sumptuous liturgical processions at Cluny or, more prosaically, ordinary streets that provide the context for occasional civic or religious parades).

c. Ambulatory actors, ambulatory audiences:

   In these configurations, onlookers are transformed into ritual actors in the most literal sense since they are compelled not simply to watch, but to join in and move in fully physical ways (e.g., by making the choreographed passage through a Minoan labyrinth, a Chinese garden, or perhaps along the route defined by the Stations of the Cross). In this particularly aggressive mode of theatric allurement, the option of passivity is largely removed (e.g., at a very large scale, the

Hajj requires Muslims to undertake the actual journey to Mecca; or, at a more modest scale, many Christian liturgies require worshipers to undertake the actual journey to the altar space to receive the Host).

2. With respect to theatric presentations and apprehensions of meanings and messages (i.e., the back half of the ritual-architectural situation):

   Dramatic presentational means are perhaps most important for the substantive content of ritual-architectural events insofar as they serve to intensify the effect and/or affect—that is, to enhance the "quality of knowledge"—of the information that is presented in those contexts. Consider ways in which theatric modes may work in conjunction with each of the four commemorative priorities:

   a. Theatric modes in conjunction with commemorations of divinity (priority II-A):

      This common combination may entail either ambulatory ritual-architectural arrangements (e.g., the very widespread practice of elaborately choreographed processions in which deity images are carried through temples or streets) or more stationary arrangements (e.g., in Greek oracle temples, Hindu temples, or Tibetan Buddhist monasteries—all of which are, though, contexts in which theatrical elaborations are ostensibly undertaken more in the interest of attracting and impressing gods than human devotees).

   b. Theatric modes in conjunction with commemorations of sacred history (priority II-B):

      This is a particularly salient combination of priorities, ranging from rudimentary architectural configurations (e.g., simple crèche constructions where the birth of Jesus is reenacted for Christmas audiences) to the supra-elaborate (e.g., Bernini's creation of whole baroque environments in which worshipers could relive the mysteries of various episodes in Catholic sacred history).

   c. Theatric modes in conjunction with commemorations of sociopolitical concerns (priority II-C):

This is an exceedingly prevalent and, quite often, highly effective combination of priorities. The most prominent exemplars, which often have an air of intimidation and manipulation, are elaborately, dramatically staged religiocivic ceremonials (e.g., the pomp of Balinese theater states, Japanese royal funerals, or Aztec human sacrifices—all of which are designed to consolidate or redirect public opinion).

d. Theatric modes in conjunction with commemorations of the dead (priority II-D):

Among numerous permutations of this combination, the most obvious are elaborate public funerals (e.g., the Japanese royal funerals just mentioned, or the similarly dramatic West African Tamberma funeral performances, which are staged in domicile-theater structures, elaborately designed to facilitate just such occasions).

Note, more generally, that in virtually all exercises of theatric presentational modes it is important to examine not only the composition of the actors, but also the usually careful constitution and choreography of the audience. The strategic recruitment of beholders (e.g., for Aztec sacrifices or Japanese royal funerals) will determine in large part the impact such occasions have.

Note also that no other priority in the morphology draws nearly so many negative and dismissive assessments as theatric modes of presentation. The disapprobation occurs at two levels. "Indigenous" religious practitioners (e.g., Bernard of Clairvaux) very often deliberately reject the sensory stimulation of theatric modes in favor of what they regard as more suitably cerebral or exclusive alternatives (which are usually achieved via contemplative [III-B] or sanctuary [III-D] modes). Academic students of architecture and religion also very often (and not always with sufficient warrant) dismiss characteristically theatrical configurations as garishly "ritualistic," and thus meretricious and superficial and/or unsubtly propagandistic.

Contemplation (priority III-B): Sacred architecture that serves as a prop or focus for meditation or devotion.

Recall that the distinguishing criterion for, what I term, contemplation modes of ritual-architectural presentation and apprehension is the direct and purposeful reliance on architectural features as foci of meditation or concentration. (This is contrasted to theatric [III-A] and sanctuary [III-D] modes, in which architectural elements contribute to an ambience or backdrop for ritual performance and are thus experienced only indirectly.)

By that definition, then, it is important to remember that not every occasion of meditation qualifies as an occasion of architecture-assisted contemplation per se. Many "contemplative" experiences of architecture are quiet, cerebral, elitist, and apparently mystical; but others are loud, unsophisticated, and more bluntly didactic than abstract.

Recall also, "architectural" foci of contemplation are broadly enough conceived to include not only buildings but also doorways, ceilings, facade decorations, windows, sculpture, paintings, altar ornaments, even light—any of which may serve as an aid to spiritual exercise, education, and/or ascent.

Nonetheless, consider how contemplative modes of presentation and apprehension may be applicable to each of the respective components of the twofold ritual-architectural situation:

1. With respect to contemplative modes of allurement (i.e., the front half of the ritual-architectural situation):

   Ritual-architectural instigation via contemplative modes involves the presentation of architectural configurations and elements that can serve as supports, guides, or, perhaps, "maps" to some sort of devotional experience. Two sorts of tensions are particularly important with respect to these modes of engendering involvement in ritual-architectural events:

   a. The motivations and incentives for participation in architecture-assisted contemplation, which tend to divide between two contrastive possibilities:

      i. Optional and voluntary participation:

         In many cases, people elect to participate in contemplative apprehensions of architecture because they perceive the occasion as an opportunity for spiritual growth (e.g., as in the case of most pilgrims' decisions to journey to and ascend the architectonic mandala of Borobudur). Such participants thus enter the occasion with hopeful enthusiasm, often animated by individualistic and idiosyncratic motivations.

ii. Compulsory and coerced participation:

In other cases, participation in contemplative apprehensions of architectural elements is either obligatory (e.g., in the mandatory viewing of religious or political propaganda films) or at least unavoidable (e.g., in the case of inadvertent exposure to large public murals depicting historical, religious, or political themes). Participants in these cases may, then, be either indifferent or even resistant to serious consideration of the ideas being presented.

b. The socioreligious constitution of the participants in architecture-assisted contemplation, which also divides between two contrastive possibilities:

i. Exclusive and esoteric participation:

In many cases, the invitations to devotion that such contemplative occasions extend appeal only to an educated or trained elite (e.g., the spiritually expert as it were, monks or mystics). Thus, contemplative modes can work like sanctuary modes of allurement (III-D) to restrict access and guard the integrity of the occasion.

ii. Inclusive and popular participation:

In other cases, the foci of devotion that are presented (e.g., stained-glass windows or narrative murals) are directed especially at an unschooled or unlettered audience. In these cases, contemplative modes work more like exhortative theatric modes of allurement (III-A) to beckon and coax reticent onlookers into involvement.

2. With respect to contemplative modes for the presentation and apprehension of meanings and messages (i.e., the back half of the ritual-architectural situation):

Contemplative modes may serve to express messages with respect to each of the four commemorative priorities; but note that in each case the pertinent messages may be either: highly rarified, cerebral, and abstract (e.g., the metaphysical insights engendered by the upper galleries of Borobudur); or more plainly educative and even didactic (e.g., the storiological reliefs in the lower galleries of Borobudur, which depict the punishments and rewards that are the consequences of improper and proper behavior).

Recall also that the vehicles of presentation—that is, the "architectural" foci of worshipers' concentration—may be, variously: elaborate, complex, and abstract (e.g., the intricate floral and geometric designs that adorn Persian mosques); elaborate, complex, and explicitly representational (e.g., the veristic depiction of people and events in paintings, statuary, or stained glass); very plain (e.g., the roughhewn forms in Zen rock gardens); totally natural (e.g., rocks, waterfalls, or canyons); or even inadvertent or accidental (e.g., scratches on the floor or water stains on the walls of a church, which may also become important foci for contemplation).

Consider some of the most prominent ways in which contemplation modes may work in conjunction with each of the four commemorative priorities:

a. Contemplative modes in conjunction with commemorations of divinity (priority II-A):

   This is a particularly prevalent pairing, though here again comparative matters are complicated by specific and highly diversified conceptions of divinity that range from the personalistic to the highly rarified. Nonetheless, consider the following particularly salient possibilities, which, in a sense, range from the literal to the abstract:

   i. Worship of, concentration on, and direct interaction with anthropomorphic idols, sculptures, or images of divinity, during which devotees may imagine themselves in intimate "conversation" with their gods (e.g., the washing or pampering of Hindu deity images or the "face-to-face" consultation of anthropomorphic gods in Greek oracle temples);
   ii. Concentration or reflection on "god-like" architectural features, including whole buildings, that are conceived either as the "body" of a divinity (e.g., Maya "earth monster" temples) or as an abstract

representation of the attributes of a divinity (e.g., sculpture-like classic Greek temples); and

iii. Realizations of divinity via meditation or concentration on more fully abstract, nonanthropomorphic architecture features, (e.g., the Sufi reliance on abstract floral or geometrical designs as a means of ascending from the manifest to the hidden; the Gothic reliance on patterns of light and shadow as a means of "anagogical illumination"; or the Buddhist practice of focused meditation on mandalas as a means of "psychic integration" or "waking up").

b. Contemplative modes in conjunction with commemorations of sacred history (priority II-B):

The esoteric meditations of spiritual experts may sometimes rely on narrative or personalistic images (e.g., pictures of esteemed founders or gurus). But even more prominent instances of this common pairing of priorities involve more popular (nonelite), educative circumstances in which lay worshipers reflect upon artistic depictions of exemplary behavior (e.g., paintings, stained-glass windows, and relief carvings that depict the life histories of Catholic saints, the Buddha, or other mythicohistorical figures).

c. Contemplative modes in conjunction with commemorations of sociopolitical concerns (priority II-C):

Though contemplative modes are perhaps most famously prominent in (ostensibly) apolitical circumstances (e.g., as means of transcending the illusions of this world), such modes of art-assisted devotion may also be used to engender loyalty, respect, and/or fear of the state or other socioeconomic institutions (e.g., Abbot Suger's pragmatic reliance on Gothic architectural elements as a means of communicating a quite specific religiopolitical agenda to a largely illiterate audience).

d. Contemplative modes in connection with commemorations of the dead (priority II-D):

Another very common pairing of priorities, this may entail either personalistic reflection on some sort of funerary monument (e.g., privately contemplating a grave marker as a means of maintaining contact with a dead relative) or more collective reflections (e.g., public celebrations that focus on a crypt or other architectural memorial to a revered ancestor).

More generally, recall also the quite common possibility of deliberate and (ostensibly) complete rejections of any form of art-assisted devotion, in which case contemplation modes of presentation and apprehension are most notable by avoidance. Such explicit rejections of the contemplation mode, which are often more a matter of rhetoric than actual practice, are usually (e.g., in the Abrahamic traditions) connected to unease over idolatry or attachment to worldly things.

Note, then, that a certain ambivalence or condescending attitude toward art-assisted spirituality is evident in the writings not only of many historical religious figures (e.g., Eusebius, Augustine, and Bernard of Clairvaux), but also of many contemporary academics (e.g., those whose work reflects, either explicitly or inadvertently, Protestant suspicions concerning the value of art as an aid to worship).

Propitiation (priority III-C): Sacred architecture and processes of construction designed to please, appease, and/or manipulate "the sacred" (however variously conceived).

Recall that the so-termed propitiation priority constitutes a special case. Somewhat differently than with the other three modes of presentation and apprehension, hermeneutical inquiries in this area will require working to understand the motivations, incentives, and "logic" that animate ritual activities—particularly ritualized building activities—that are "propitiatory" in the very broadest sense.

Note also that, as in the closely related area of divinity commemoration (priority II-A), empirical analyses and cross-cultural comparisons of propitiatory practices are complicated—and enlivened—by the extreme diversity of culturally specific conceptions of the supernatural.

Nonetheless, consider the applicability of the following non–mutually exclusive variations on the theme of propitiation, which can be arranged in two distinct, though very broad, sets:

1. Propitiatory ritual uses of standing (already-built) architecture:

   With respect to architectural arrangements that facilitate and enhance propitiatory activities, two quite different sorts of ritual logic (which presuppose two quite different sorts of cosmological orientations) are particularly prominent:

   a. Architectural configurations that facilitate ritual interactions—particularly reciprocal negotiations—with a personalized deity or other sort of supernatural being (e.g., bargaining with a god, requesting the assistance of an [un]dead ancestor, or placating a troublesome demon or ghost).

      Note that such negotiative ritual logic is very widespread (e.g., especially in relation to Abrahamic conceptions of a covenant or contractual, give-and-take relationship between human communities and an anthropomorphic god). But, beware also that the notions of buying, bartering, and/or begging for divine dispensation are too often invoked as the default explanation for all sorts of cross-cultural propitiatory practices (e.g., in glib explanations of the logic of sacrifice as a bartering between naïve natives and supposedly temperamental gods of rain, hunting, or war).

      Note, moreover, that, while most deity-directed propitiatory practices are designed to win the favor of those transhuman entities, it is also important to give serious consideration to the viability of ritualized expressions of adoration, humility, and respect for divine beings that are undertaken irrespective of expectations of any direct recompense.

   b. Architectural configurations that facilitate propitiatory activities that are not directed at any personalized deity or spirit (and thus do not really qualify as "ritual negotiations"). The logic of this quite different set of options, in which gods play little or no role (and which thus strains the label "propitiation"), has often escaped the attention of scholars. Two closely related possibilities are especially prominent:

      i. Rituals designed to maintain and/or manipulate a cosmic equilibrium (e.g., Melanesian cargo cults or Kwakiutl potlatch, both of which, according to some interpretations, depend upon a logic of cosmic redistribution and exchange); and

ii. Rituals designed to stimulate and/or channel the flow of some sort of impersonal, fluid-like spiritual energy or force (e.g., those interpretations of Aztec human sacrifice that feature the cosmic circulation of *tonalli* and other vital energies).

2. Architectural construction (or destruction) processes that are themselves conceived as propitiatory ritual:

Though expediting construction processes and cutting costs may be taken-for-granted goals in most contemporary Western contexts, not infrequently, building processes have been (and are) deliberately complicated, or "ritualized," in response to incentives that are regarded as more important than efficiency and cost-effectiveness. Consider the following variations on the exceptionally diversified and widespread theme of building (and "unbuilding") as propitiatory ritual:

a. (Re)building for periodic renewal:

Among innumerable versions of renewal, or "starting fresh," via construction—many of which require as well preparatory ritual destructions of architecture—three possibilities are especially prominent:

i. Constructional reiterations of cosmogony (e.g., the building of Hindu temples, which is often explicitly conceived as the founding and building of a new world). This (and the next option) are, then, directly relevant also to versions of homologizing building (priority I-A);
ii. (Re)building or remodeling according to a regularized schedule (e.g., ancient Mesoamerican practices of embellishing pyramid temples at the end or beginning of various calendrical cycles). This may actually entail perpetual, nonstop rebuilding (e.g., at the Ise shrine of Japan where, in order to have a new shrine ready every twenty years, reconstruction is essentially continuous); and
iii. (Re)building according to a strategic though irregular schedule, which may entail:

(1) (Re)building in order to formalize a transition of authority or the onset of a new political era (e.g., the relocation and construction of a new South African Tongo village each time that a headman dies and another is appointed);

(2) (Re)building scheduled according to the availability of scarce resources (e.g., the embellishment of Indonesian Toraja origin-houses "whenever the descendants of the house feel they can afford it"); and

(3) (Re)building in relation to personal life crises (e.g., as a means of marking one's new status after a rite of passage or marriage; or, perhaps, as in the case of the Torajas, to reaffirm one's cultural identity).

b. Building as a demonstration of devotion, sacrifice, or offering:

Construction (or other artistic production) is sometimes undertaken with particularly "pure" motives insofar as (ostensibly) no immediate reward is anticipated. Consider, for instance, the following heavily overlapping possibilities on the theme of "building for the Wholly Other":

i. Building as an expression of gratitude or thanksgiving for some good fortune (e.g., Babylonian kings' construction of temples expressly "in recognition of the services rendered them by the divine powers");

ii. Building as fulfillment of a sacred vow (e.g., construction in fulfillment of a promise made to a god or saint who helped one through a crisis); and

iii. Building as a freely given "gift to God" or as a display of "pure adoration," humility, or commitment to supernatural authority (e.g., the erection of Shaker meetinghouses, which is explicitly conceived as a collective expression of devotion to God).

Note that architectural elements and works of art that are wholly inaccessible to human view (e.g., paintings hidden away deep in caves, carvings on the downsides of sculptures, or decoration in passageways too narrow to pass) may also be conceived as "gifts to God."

Note, moreover, that seemingly excessively large or elaborate construction projects (e.g., lavish Gothic cathedrals, Barcelona's phantasmagoric Sagrada Familia, or the mammoth temple of Karnak) could conceivably (and ironically) be interpreted as huge-scaled offerings, and thus expressions of a willingness to put divine interests before human ones.

c. Building as investment or petition:

Distinct from the previous set of options, this entails construction undertaken as a deliberate and self-conscious strategy for currying divine favor and/or cosmic advantage. Consider several possibilities, which are again based on distinct sorts of propitiatory logic:

i. Building in the interest of the accumulation of (say, covenental or karmic) merit and/or as a means of enhancing one's prospects after death (e.g., numerous Buddhist, Jain, and especially Hindu texts explicitly describe temple construction as among the surest means of enhancing one's rebirth status);
ii. Building as redress for wrongdoing or expiation of sin (e.g., the Jain temple of Mount Abu in western India, supposedly built as an act of penance by a leader who had caused considerable bloodshed in pacifying a rebellion);
iii. Building as means of ensuring one's immortality through enduring fame and, to that extent, "conquering death" (which may have been one incentive for Egyptian pharaohs' erection of their massive pyramid tombs); and
iv. Building in the interest of healing, which may entail either the creation of an efficacious context in which to do healing (e.g., Siberian Evenk shamans' erection of a special cosmogrammatic tent in which to practice their curing rituals), or a more direct analogy between healing and building (e.g., in the "building" of a Navajo sand painting).

d. Ritualized destruction and defacement—or the "unbuilding"—of architecture:

Several variations on the common practice of deliberate defacing and/or dismantling of art and architecture, based on several different sorts of incentives, deserve consideration:

i. Destruction of architecture as requisite preparation for rebuilding (e.g., at the Ise shrine in Japan, where the dismantlement of structures, apparently a symbol of the impermanence of all things, proceeds with nearly the same ceremoniousness as the rebuilding);

ii. Destruction as a means of delivering one's artistic productions to the "Wholly Other" (e.g., the very common practice in Middle and South America of ritual "killing" of vessels or figurines before depositing them in offertory caches); and

iii. Destruction of architecture as a political statement of force and/or intimidation (e.g., Spanish colonial destructions of indigenous temples and shrines, which were often replaced by Catholic churches). Such practices, though clearly expedient, nonetheless served to announce, via ritual-architectural means, the beginning of a "new era."

Sanctuary (priority III-D): Sacred architecture that provides a refuge of purity, sacrality, or perfection.

Recall that so-termed sanctuary modes of presentation and apprehension, which are, to some important extent, relevant to virtually every ritual-architectural situation, are distinguished from other modes by the following criteria:

- "Exclusive" strategies of allurement insofar as the designer's incentive usually is to restrict access and thus guard the integrity of the architectural space and/or ritual proceedings. (This is contrasted to theatric modes [III-A] in which the characteristic incentive is to coax reticent onlookers into involvement.)
- "Indirect" apprehensions of architecture insofar as the built forms contribute to the creation of an ambience or backdrop for ritual performance. (This is similar to the stage-setting of theatric modes [III-A] but unlike contemplation modes [III-B], in which architectural elements serve as direct objects of attention and meditation.)

Consider some of the countless ways in which sanctuary modes of presentation and apprehension may be applicable to each of the respective components of the twofold ritual-architectural situation:

1. With respect to sanctuary modes of allurement (i.e., the front half of the ritual-architectural situation):

By far the most prominent uses of sanctuary modes of allurement and instigation involve the requisite preparation of various elements of the ritual-architectural situation. Three variations on (or dimensions of) preparatory sanctification deserve special consideration:

a. Appropriation of natural "sanctuaries," particularly caves:

   Though generally imagined as inherently sacred places (e.g., hierophanies or *axis mundis*, which already afford special access to gods and other cosmic realities), natural cave-sanctuaries (e.g., the underground passageways at Balankanche, near Chichén Itzá, which hosted Maya rituals, probably for centuries) are, nonetheless, nearly always ritually embellished and enhanced (e.g., the famous prehistoric paintings in the caves of Lascaux, France). Hierophanies, too, require ritual sanctification.

   Note also that, very often, architectural elements (e.g., niches or burial chambers) or whole buildings are designed to resemble caves, thus participating in the "womb-house" symbolism of caves (e.g., many Hindu and Maya temples that have unmistakably cave-like visages).

b. Preparatory sanctification of apparently ordinary places or human constructions:

   This possibility, which is perhaps the most signal dimension of the sanctuary priority, involves the performance of ritual procedures whereby a previously ordinary place or building is cleansed, purified, sanctified, and thus made ready for ritual use (e.g., the cleansing and sanctification of a Japanese street prior to a *matsuri,* or ritual procession, or the resanctification of an Oglala sweat lodge prior to a ceremony).

   Note that such ritual procedures usually provide only situational and temporary sanctification and thus must be repeated periodically (e.g., both Japanese streets and Oglala sweat lodges revert to prosaic status immediately following their ritual usages).

c. Preparatory sanctification of human ritual actors:

Very often this will entail the construction of a building or special context to which either ritual specialists or lay participants repair (for hours, days, or perhaps weeks) to be cleansed and purified prior to their involvement in the main ritual event (e.g., the Chinese *Tsai-kung,* or Hall of Abstinence, to which the emperor would retreat before important ceremonies, or the Japanese cave-like *muro* to which initiates retreat for fasting prior to their ceremonial passage to adulthood).

2. With respect to the presentation and apprehension of messages and meanings (i.e., the back half of the ritual-architectural situation), consider ways in which sanctuary modes may work in conjunction with each of the four commemorative priorities:

a. Sanctuary modes in conjunction with commemorations of divinity (priority II-A):

This is a particularly common and salient pairing of priorities. Sanctuary spaces may facilitate felicitous and productive interactions between humans and the divine (however conceived) via either of the following means:

i. Enhancement of mental concentration (e.g., in a Cistercian or Zen monastery where all attentions are focused on meditation and prayer; or in an Iranian or Chinese classical garden where all worldly distractions are removed); and
ii. Enticement or luring of sacred entities or forces into the ritual context (e.g., Hindu temples designed to lure a specific god to reside there, Japanese *ma*-inspired architecture designed to lure *kami* energy into the ritual context, or Oglala Yuwipi rooms designed to lure spirits in the healing ceremony).

b. Sanctuary modes in conjunction with commemorations of sacred history (priority II-B):

This common possibility—in which sanctuary modes often work in close connection with theatric ones (III-A)—may entail the provision of an exceptional place (and time) in which to reenact, and thus re-experience, important mythical or miraculous circumstances.

c. Sanctuary modes in conjunction with commemorations of socio-political concerns (priority II-C):

This particularly salient and diversified pairing of priorities, which usually capitalizes on the symbolism attendant with privileged access to some highly restricted ritual-architectural context, may take any of the following forms:

i. Sanctuaries that effect a complete rejection of wider society:

This possibility, which involves retreat from mainstream society rather than attempts to change it, requires architectural configurations that facilitate long-term seclusion, isolation, and self-sufficiency (e.g., Anabaptist and Shaker communities or Hesychast and Cistercian monasteries—any of which may be conceived as fabricated "foretastes of heaven," that is, refuges designed to attain a measure of perfection that cannot be realized in society at large).

ii. Sanctuaries that display an exemplary model or idealized prototype for wider society:

This possibility, which reflects greater aspirations to social change, often entails the architectural provision of both laboratory-like spaces for research and development, as it were, of religiosocial alternatives (e.g., in experimental communities or long-established monastic orders), and museum-like spaces in which to showcase the viability and efficacy of those alternatives.

Note that many secluded communities (e.g., the Trappist monks at Gethesemani), which appear at first to have effected a complete rejection of society, are actually (and sometimes explicitly) providing exemplary models for society, and thus for social change. Seclusion from society ought not be equated too quickly with either indifference to or disdain for society.

iii. Sanctuaries that provide a mechanism for hierarchical exclusion:

This possibility, which contributes to the reinforcement rather than the realignment of extant socioeconomic boundaries, often involves architectural configurations that segregate "insiders" from "outsiders" or higher social groups from lower ones (e.g., the Jerusalem Temple's rigorously enforced separation of Jews from gentiles, clergy from laity, men from women).

Particularly notable in this respect are ritual-architectural expressions (and reinforcements) of hierarchies of relative sacrality and socioeconomic privilege (e.g., the complex expression of "graduated privacy" in the layout of traditional Chinese cities and homes, wherein tiered social differences translate into different levels of access to built spaces).

d. Sanctuary modes in conjunction with commemorations of the dead (priority II-D):

This may entail the provision of specially restricted spaces for, variously, the preparation of dead bodies, the posthumous placement of the dead, and the visitation of the dead (e.g., morgues, funeral homes, and cemeteries). Virtually all mortuary architectural configurations, which serve to separate the living from the dead, rely to a significant degree on sanctuary modes of presentation and apprehension.

Notes

Preface to Volume Two

1. I borrow the notion of "open site" from Michel Foucault, *The Order of Things: An Archaeology of the Human Sciences* (London and New York: Tavistock/Routledge, 1974), xii. Foucault explains: "I should like this work to read as an open site. Many questions are laid out on it that have not yet found answers; and many of the gaps refer to earlier works or to others that have not yet been completed, or even begun."

Introduction | A Pedagogical Intent

1. Amos Ih Tiao Chang, *The Tao of Architecture* (Princeton: Princeton University Press, 1956), 42.

2. Bruno Zevi, *Architecture as Space: How to Look at Architecture*, trans. Milton Gendel, ed. Joseph A. Barry, rev. ed. (New York: Horizon Press, 1974), 21.

3. Italo Calvino, *If On a Winter's Night a Traveler*, trans. William Weaver (San Diego: Harcourt Brace and Co., 1981), 145.

4. Stella Kramrisch, "Indian Varieties of Art Ritual," in *Myths and Symbols: Studies in Honor of Mircea Eliade*, ed. Joseph M. Kitagawa et al. (Chicago: University of Chicago Press, 1969), 115.

5. Jonathan Z. Smith, *Drudgery Divine: On the Comparison of Early Christianities and the Religions of Late Antiquity* (Chicago: University of Chicago Press, 1990), 36. Smith writes: "The 'unique' is an attribute that must be disposed of, especially when linked to some notion of incomparable value, if progress in thinking through the enterprise of comparison is to be made." I still, however, regard it is as useful (as Smith's own work aptly demonstrates) to image specific historical phenomena, say specific apprehensions of religious architecture, as, in an important respect, "unique." Regarding the productive tension between sensations of "the unique" and "the analogous," see the quotation from Jonathan Z. Smith, "Adde Parvum Parvo Magnus Acervus Erit," in his *Map Is Not Territory: Studies in the History of Religions* (Leiden: E. J. Brill, 1978), 243, cited below at the onset of chapter 13.

6. Lawrence E. Sullivan, *Icanchu's Drum: An Orientation to Meaning in South American Religions* (New York: Macmillan, 1988), 19. Regarding the inevitability of comparison in both the experience and interpretation of architecture, see volume 1, chapter 11, "Significant Alternatives: Modes, Contexts, and Sequences of Architectural

Comparison," where I previously invoked this quotation from Sullivan. It is noteworthy, for example, that the strategic claim to the singularity or incomparability of the Second Temple of Jerusalem—"He who has not set eyes upon the structure of Herod has not yet seen a structure of beauty in all his life" (cited by Meir Ben-Dov, *Jerusalem, Man and Stone: An Archaeologist's Personal View of the City* [Tel-Aviv: Modan, 1990], 54)—is, in fact, a comparative statement.

7. I should note, as I did in volume 1, that a much attenuated exposition of this framework of ritual-architectural priorities and a parallel set of essays that focus primarily on Mesoamerican architecture appear in chapter 3 of my *Twin City Tales: A Hermeneutical Reassessment of Tula and Chichén Itzá* (Niwot: University Press of Colorado, 1995). That earlier work was written "inside" this one insofar as early drafts of this project preceded that book but later drafts came well after that work was finished.

8. Regarding this important point on the superiority of observation over imagination (as I noted in chapter 11), I am indebted to the anecdotes of art instructors about how students called upon to draw faces, trees, and houses from memory invariably produced bland, stereotypical images; when they were allowed to work from actual models, however, their drawings took on a completely different level of detail, idiosyncrasy, and nuance. Likewise, hermeneutical reflection that is nourished only by prevailing disciplinary paradigms and personal recollections is certain to be impoverished.

9. Juan Eduardo Campo, *The Other Sides of Paradise: Explorations into the Religious Meanings of Domestic Space in Islam* (Columbia: University of South Carolina Press, 1991), 1.

10. I should note that in the ten years since the original conception of most elements of these essays the study of sacred space and architecture has definitely advanced in prolific and, I think, fortuitous ways. Many of my complaints concerning essentialized and reified meanings of religious architectures and places have already been answered, though—and this is an important qualification—I have *not* undertaken to integrate that newer literature into the present work. For particularly instructive comments on and demonstrations of that progress—specifically explorations of the extent to which sacred spaces (and buildings) are invariably "contested spaces"—see the editors' introduction together with the seven essays in *American Sacred Space,* ed. David Chidester and Edward T. Linenthal (Bloomington: Indiana University Press, 1995).

Thirteen | A Morphological Agendum

1. Joachim Wach, *The Comparative Study of Religions,* ed. with an intro. by Joseph M. Kitagawa (New York: Columbia University Press, 1958), 25–26.

2. Smith, "Adde Parvum Parvo Magnus Acervus Erit," in his *Map Is Not Territory,* 243.

3. Staale Sinding-Larsen, *Iconography and Ritual: A Study of Analytical Perspectives* (Oslo: Universitetsforlaget AS, 1984), 129.

4. See volume 1, chapter 10, "Insignificant Organization: Comparative Orderings of Architecture."

5. See volume 1, chapter 11, "Significant Alternatives: Modes, Contexts, and Sequences of Architectural Comparison."

6. Swedish botanist Carolus Linnaeus devised classifications not only of plants and animals, but also of minerals and even diseases. On the classificatory enterprises of George Cuvier, one of the great French naturalists of the early nineteenth century, see his *Animal Kingdom, Arranged according to Its Organization; Forming the Basis for a Natural History of Animals, and an Introduction to Comparative Anatomy* (London: Wm. S. Orr and Co., 1840).

7. See volume 1, chapter 11, "Significant Alternatives: Modes, Contexts, and Sequences of Architectural Comparison."

8. With respect to the insidiousness of classification, see, most prominently, Michel Foucault, *The Order of Things*. Also see Bruce Lincoln, "The Tyranny of Taxonomy," chapter 8 in his *Discourse and the Construction of Society: Comparative Studies of Myth, Ritual, and Classification* (New York: Oxford University Press, 1989).

9. Sullivan, *Icanchu's Drum*, 20.

10. In volume 1, see especially chapter 3, "Conversation and Play: The Eventfulness of Architecture."

11. It is exceedingly difficult (and beyond the scope of this project) to make clear distinctions between morphology and, for example, typology, structuralism, phenomenology, and hermeneutics, particularly because each of these describes such a heterogeneous set of methodological practices. Nonetheless, note that Sullivan, *Icanchu's Drum*, 20–21, contends that morphology, unlike Lévi-Straussian structuralism, "does not draw connections at the level of structures abstracted from what lies beyond (or below) the semantic level, but it makes connections precisely at the level of meaning recognized by the cultures studied." Thus, Sullivan (701, n. 79) agrees with Adrian Marino that comparative morphology is more correctly located, not with structuralism, but with contemporary philosophical, aesthetic, semiological, semiotic, literary-critical, and cultural-linguistic schools of interpretation. Sullivan also notes Julien Riès's use of the terms "comparative phenomenology" and "comparative hermeneutics" to describe the way the morphological method juxtaposes various cultural interpretations of reality; but Sullivan himself contends that (his) morphology is not phenomenology, "to which it could, however, lead in the construction of an anthropology" (21). Regarding distinctions between morphological, typological, and phenomenological comparison, also see Jonathan Z. Smith, "Adde Parvum Parvo Magnus Acervus Erit," in his *Map Is Not Territory*, 240–64; and idem, "In Comparison a Magic Dwells," in his *Imagining Religion: From Babylon to Jonestown* (Chicago: University of Chicago Press, 1982), 22–26.

12. Joachim Wach, in *The Sociology of Religion* (Chicago: University of Chicago Press, 1944), chapter 1, among other places, endorses "types" and "typology" as the most dexterous mediators between particular cases and universal themes. Also see Joachim Wach, *Types of Religious Experience, Christian and Non-Christian* (Chicago: University of Chicago Press, 1951). Regarding Wach's enthusiasm for typological approaches, Joseph Kitagawa ("Verstehen and Erlosung: Some Remarks on Joachim Wach's Work," *History of Religions* 13 [February 1974]: 40) explains that: "To be sure, Wach is not advocating the sheer amassing of historical data; what is important to him is discovering the principle that structures historical facts and events without which it would be impossible to find meaning in the configurations of the vast amount of data that are available to us."

13. Eliade often invoked Goethe's morphology of plants as his preeminent model for a morphology of religions; see, for instance, Mircea Eliade, *Ordeal by Labyrinth: Conversations with Claude-Henri Rocquet,* trans. Derek Coltman (Chicago: University of Chicago Press, 1982), 142. On Eliade's Goethe-informed notion of morphology, see also Norman J. Girardot's introduction to *Imagination and Meaning: The Scholarly and Literary Worlds of Mircea Eliade,* ed. Norman J. Girardot and Mac Linscott Ricketts (New York: Seabury Press, 1982), 3–4. It should become clear, I hope, both that my project owes an enormous debt to Eliade's seminal work on sacred space and that I am determined to find fresher, more critical alternatives. Regarding the morphology of plants devised by Goethe (who first coined the word morphology), Smith describes it as "fundamentally ahistorical while employing the most complex dialectic between the universal and the particular, between ideal and [real] experience, between idea and appearance, between Being and history"; Smith, "Adde Parvum Parvo Magnus Acervus Erit," in his *Map Is Not Territory,* 256.

14. Smith, "Adde Parvum Parvo Magnus Acervus Erit," in his *Map Is Not Territory,* 243. Smith is not at this point speaking specifically about morphology.

15. This quote comes from Sullivan, *Icanchu's Drum,* 18, where Sullivan is actually addressing the status of myth. After citing Eliade's *Patterns in Comparative Religion* as "the most pathbreaking and widely known application of morphology to the study of religion" (701, n. 78), Sullivan writes that his own work "reevaluates morphology in light of a generation of significant advances in hermeneutics." Regarding the relationship between a morphology of symbolic forms and the recounting of their history, also see Lawrence Sullivan, "A History of Religious Ideas," *Religious Studies Review* 9 (January 1983): 13–22. Sullivan is not, of course, accountable for my invocation of his morphological project in relation to mine. For earlier but still relevant remarks on morphological methods applied to religious studies, see Charles H. Long, "From History to Phenomenology," *The History of Religions: Essays in Methodology,* ed. Mircea Eliade and Joseph M. Kitagawa (Chicago: University of Chicago Press, 1959).

16. See especially volume 1, chapter 4, "Order and Variation: The Twofold Pattern of Ritual-Architectural Events."

17. Sullivan, *Icanchu's Drum,* 20.

18. Regarding "typological series" and the "fundamentally ahistorical" organizational criteria of morphology, which is relevant to my framework (though I'd prefer the term "nonhistorical"), see Smith, "Adde Parvum Parvo Magnus Acervus Erit," in his *Map Is Not Territory,* 256–59; and idem, "In Comparison a Magic Dwells," in his *Imagining Religion,* 23. Smith's observation, that "Fundamentally, morphology allows the arrangement of individual items in a hierarchical series of increased organization and complexity" (*Imagining Religion,* 23), is less relevant to my enterprise, which, though not value-free, is not (deliberately) a hierarchical arrangement.

19. Smith ("Adde Parvum Parvo Magnus Acervus Erit," in his *Map Is Not Territory,* 256) explains that "Linnaeus had proposed that his taxonomy represented a closed immutable system which reflected the world of nature conceived as a fixed order of permanent structures."

20. Regarding Max Weber's notion of "ideal-types," which (though often erroneously reified by subsequent scholars) are empirically informed abstractions that are nowhere historically manifest in their purest forms, but that provide commodious points of reference for the subsequent interpretation of all sorts of specific historical circumstances, see his "'Objectivity' in Social Science and Social Policy," in his *Methodology in the Social Sciences* (Glencoe, Ill.: Free Press, 1949), 90–100. Also see Ben Nefger, "The Ideal-Type: Some Conceptions and Misconceptions," *The Sociological Quarterly* 6 (spring 1965): 166–74.

21. Alternatively to Weber (and less applicably to my project), for Joachim Wach's notion of "types," see his *Types of Religious Experience, Christian and Non-Christian,* where he makes, for example, typological distinctions between church, denomination, and sect; and Joachim Wach, *Sociology of Religion,* where he constructs typologies of religious expression, experience, cult-group, religious organization, religious society, and religious leadership. I should note, however, that the differentiation between Weber's "ideal-types" and Wach's "types," particularly in the ways subsequent scholars have (mis)used them, is hardly absolute.

22. Regarding this colloquial expression, I am indebted to old Wyoming logger Charles E. Sayer, for whom seemingly every bend in the road and every patch of timber worked as a stimulus (or a segue) to a story or, as he would say, "puts me in the mind of" an insight or an episode from his youth; only after he began the narration did the less than obvious (though nearly always important) association between that feature in the landscape and subsequent reflection become apparent.

23. T. Burns, "The Comparative Study of Organisations," in *Methods of Organizational Research,* ed. Victor Harold Vroom (Pittsburgh: University of Pittsburgh Press, 1967), 127, includes an apt description of the heuristic status of the categories

in this framework; Burns writes: "The objects of classification are not organisations or parts or attributes of organisations but analytical concepts and frames of reference within which methodological procedures can be designed and comparative studies usefully made."

24. Sullivan, *Icanchu's Drum,* 9.

25. Ibid., 10.

26. My contention is, in other words, that the construction of a framework of possibilities ought not, and does not necessarily, constitute a limitation of possibilities. Alternatively, it can and should be a strategy for expanding the range of possibilities, that is, for bringing to light possibilities not yet imagined.

27. Sullivan, *Icanchu's Drum,* 21. It is largely as a consequence of this matter of "mutually exclusive features," which he finds ill-advised in this case, that Sullivan avoids, with a few exceptions, taking a typological approach toward the religious symbols of South America; see p. 701, n. 80.

28. For helpful remarks and bibliography with respect to Egyptian pyramids, see J. D. Ray, "Egyptian Pyramids," *Encyclopedia of Religion,* ed. Mircea Eliade (New York: Macmillan, 1987), 12:111–13.

29. See Alastair Laing, "Central and Eastern Europe," in *Baroque and Rococo: Architecture and Decoration,* ed. Anthony Blunt (New York: Harper and Row, 1978), 172.

30. On Cluny, to which I will return later, see Wolfgang Braunfels, *Monasteries of Western Europe: The Architecture of the Orders* (Princeton: Princeton University Press, 1972), chapter 4.

31. See ibid., chapters 4 and 5.

32. The contrasting ritual-architectural priorities that inform, respectively, Cluny, Gothic cathedrals, and Cistercian monasteries are discussed more fully below in part 3, "Architecture as Ritual Context: The Presentation of Architectural Events," where I will also provide more technically specific explications of the ways that I am using terms like "theatrical presentation" and "contemplation."

33. See volume 1, chapter 5, "Allurement and Coercion: The Front Half of the Ritual-Architectural Situation."

34. See volume 1, chapter 6, "Transformation and Productivity: The Back Half of the Ritual-Architectural Situation."

35. Not unlike my notion of heterogeneous ritual-architectural priorities, Zevi (*Architecture as Space,* 73ff.) discusses the "variety of needs" and "multiplicity of factors . . . with the predominance of one, now of another, [which] have acted to give rise to various conceptions of space." Zevi mentions specifically the complex interplay between what he terms social premises, intellectual premises, technical premises, and formal and aesthetic premises.

36. Nelson I. Wu, *Chinese and Indian Architecture: The City of Man, the Mountain of God, and the Realm of Immortals* (New York: George Braziller, 1963), 14. Wu aptly notes in his discussion of Indian ceremonial architecture that "a small

mound of sand made between the two hands of a brahmin on the holy shore of the Dhanushkodi" (see his plate 4) provides as "valid" an example as any elaborate, large-scale structure.

37. I am informed at this point by Wendy Doniger's plea, in the context of a very critical review of Joseph Campbell, that, "Out of respect for them [i.e., Hindus and Navajos, and, by extension, all peoples that we might be studying], we must take the trouble to get the stories right." Wendy Doniger, "A Fire in the Mind," review of *The Life of Joseph Campbell*, by Stephen Larsen and Robin Larsen, *New York Times Book Review*, 2 February 1992, 7–8.

38. Also, recalling the layering of indigenous and academic hermeneutical (and comparative) situations—see the section in chapter 3, "The Layering of Hermeneutical Situations: Architectural Experience and Interpretation"—we ought to keep in mind that this is, at many points, a morphological organization of (academic) interpretations of (academic) interpretations of (indigenous) interpretations of architecture, that is, a book about books about apprehensions of architecture.

39. One is reminded at this point of Edmund Leach's stinging criticism of Eliade; in "Sermons by a Man on a Ladder," *New York Review of Books*, 20 October 1966, Leach writes that, among other academic atrocities, "Eliade is a literary scholar. What matters to him is that everything he says should be based on what someone else has put in a book. The printed word is authority enough. . . ." While I certainly concur with Leach's anthropological call for historical (and ethnographic) rigor, I am, at the same time, arguing that we should be forthright in admitting that research in our areas of historical specialization can very often be enriched by interpretive possibilities that come to our attention via all sorts of works—even works that might not meet the most rigorous historical standards. In short, mistakes, hoaxes, and half-truths can be useful in expanding the range of interesting (if only provisional) hermeneutical questions, which we might eventually bring to our more rigorously contextualized studies of specific sacred architectures.

40. On the marvelous, mythical city of Tollan, see Davíd Carrasco, *Quetzalcoatl and the Irony of Empire: Myths and Prophecies in the Aztec Tradition* (Chicago: University of Chicago Press, 1982), chapter 2.

41. On the "visionary world of the Jewish geographical imagination," see Martha Himmelfarb, "The Temple and the Garden of Eden in Ezekiel, the Book of Watchers, and the Wisdom of ben Sira," in *Sacred Places and Profane Spaces: Essays in the Geographics of Judaism, Christianity, and Islam*, ed. Jamie Scott and Paul Simpson-Housley (New York: Greenwood Press, 1991), 63–78; the entire article is relevant in this regard. Jonathan Z. Smith, in *To Take Place: Toward Theory in Ritual* (Chicago: University of Chicago Press, 1987), chapter 3, develops a whole series of important general insights into sacred space on the basis of his interpretation of the temple visions of Ezekiel 40–48.

42. On the idealized plan of the Chinese city laid out in the *Code Book of Works* (*K'ao-kung chi*), see Wu, *Chinese and Indian Architecture,* 37. On other ideal city plans, including images of the "Heavenly Jerusalem," see Helen Rosenau, *The Ideal City: Its Architectural Evolution in Europe,* 3d ed. (London: Methuen, 1983), 10–11, 24, 27.

43. See ibid., 11.

44. See Edward Snow, "The Language of Contradiction in Bruegel's *Tower of Babel,*" *Res: Anthropology and Aesthetics* 5 (spring 1983): 40–48.

45. See ibid., 24; and Braunfels, *Monasteries of Western Europe,* chapter 3, "The St. Gall Utopia."

46. On the "geographic imagination" of Sufi poetry, see Annemarie Schimmel, "Sacred Geography of Islam," in *Sacred Places and Profane Spaces,* ed. Scott and Simpson-Housley, 163–75.

47. Regarding Jataka tales of the Bodhisattva's mythical efforts as a master architect, see Ananda Coomaraswamy, *The Transformation of Nature in Art* (New York: Dover Publications, 1956), 205–6, n. 74.

48. Regarding the notion of virtual, unbuilt architecture, see Robert Harbison, *The Built, the Unbuilt, and the Unbuildable: In Pursuit of Architectural Meaning* (Cambridge, Mass.: MIT Press, 1992), especially chapter 6.

49. See Lincoln, "The Tyranny of Taxonomy," chapter 8 in his *Discourse and the Construction of Society.*

50. Sullivan (*Icanchu's Drum,* 6) notes, with respect to obstructions to a clear view of South American religions and values, that "our own interpretive constructs stand in the way of understanding."

51. Sinding-Larsen, *Iconography and Ritual,* 179, where he expresses his lack of confidence in "the 'anthology' method, that of basing theory and analysis on scattered pickings from heterogeneous materials."

52. Ibid.

53. See Lincoln, "The Tyranny of Taxonomy," chapter 8 in his *Discourse and the Construction of Society,* 137ff., where he cites Durkheim, Mauss, and the more recent work of Pierre Bourdieu as notable precedents in his insistence on the social functions of classificatory logic.

54. Ibid., 137.

55. Regarding the insidiousness and distortions of architectural classifications, see chapter 10, "Insignificant Organization: Comparative Orderings of Architecture."

56. I alluded at several points in volume 1 to the notion of a "hermeneutical wager" in the sense that Paul Ricoeur uses that term in his *Symbolism of Evil,* trans. Emerson Buchanan (Boston: Beacon Press, 1967), 355–57.

57. Though I will not address it in this work, a fifth possible use and reward of this morphological framework involves its heuristic utility in evoking new possibilities for practicing architects. My optimism that historians of religions' morphological interpretations can serve, among other purposes, as provocative reservoirs

for contemporary design work is informed by Eliade's comment that he was spurred on to finish another book about the structure of sacred spaces and the symbolism of dwellings, towns, temples, and palaces by the fact that he had received letters from architects saying that his earlier books "have given them valuable insight into the meaning of their profession." See Mircea Eliade, *Ordeal by Labyrinth,* 29–30.

58. Of the immense literature on Maya stelae and interminable controversy over their possible significances, Michael D. Coe, *Breaking the Maya Code* (New York: Thames and Hudson, 1992), provides among the most thorough accounts of the history of the debate.

59. See Tatiana Proskouriakoff, "The Lords of the Maya Realm," *Expedition* 4 (autumn 1961): 14–21; reprinted in Leo Deuel, *Conquistadors without Swords: Archaeologists in the Americas* (New York: Schocken Books, 1967), 384–90.

60. Regarding debate over the pre-Columbian significance of Maya stele, see also Jones, *Twin City Tales,* 277, n. 140.

61. In volume 1, see especially chapter 10, "Insignificant Organization: Comparative Orderings of Architecture."

62. Regarding the imperfect, though not altogether wrong, generalization that Egyptian pyramids were first and foremost tombs while Mesoamerican pyramids were only sometimes, and even then in just an ancillary fashion, burial monuments, see Jones, *Twin City Tales,* 245–48.

63. See Abbot Suger, *On the Abbey Church of St.-Denis and Its Art Treasures,* ed. and trans. Erwin Panofsky, 2d ed. (Princeton: Princeton University Press, 1979), which will be discussed at some length below in chapter 22, "Contemplation: Props for Devotion."

64. While Renaissance architecture is obviously much closer to the Gothic than either the Tibetan or Algonquin examples with respect to time, geography, stylistic appearance, and religiocultural orientation, morphological analysis reveals that Renaissance builders largely eschewed the notion of architecture as a support for meditative contemplation (that is, they devalued priority III-B) in favor of an architecture that conforms perfectly to a set of abstract principles of proportion, which is, as we'll see in chapter 15, a hallmark of the convention priority (I-B).

65. All of these Mesoamerican possibilities are treated with much greater detail in Jones, *Twin City Tales.* Note also, as another example of the way in which geographic differences might be reassessed in terms of differences in ritual-architectural priorities, the observation in George Michell, *The Hindu Temple: An Introduction to Its Meaning and Forms* (Chicago: University of Chicago Press, 1988), 159, that Hindu temples outside of India, particularly in Southeast Asia (and especially the great temple complexes at Ankor in Cambodia), are distinctive by "their ability to create an architectural layout that embodies elements of myth." This might be articulated and explored with reference to the relative applicability of the priority for commemorating sacred history (II-B) in each of those two geographic regions.

66. See Robert Adams Ivy, *Fay Jones: The Architecture of E. Fay Jones, FAIA* (Washington, D.C.: American Institute of Architects Press, 1992), especially the section on sacred spaces (pp. 30–95) and specifically on Thorncrown Chapel (pp. 32–45). The prize for the best work in American architecture in the 1980s was awarded by the American Institute of Architects, who also designated Jones one of the country's "ten most influential living architects" (13).

67. E. Fay Jones, quoted in ibid., 35.

68. Regarding Fay Jones's adherence to "organic principles," see ibid., 22–25.

69. E. Fay Jones, quoted in ibid., 32 and 36.

70. That is, these eleven ritual-architectural priorities are relevant to all of the various (types of) protocols of architectural apprehension—including, for instance, architects' intentions, indigenous apprehensions, and academic interpretations—which I discussed in the final subsections of chapter 12.

71. Regarding the framework's diachronic comparative utility in projects other than—or in addition to—the composition of architectural reception histories, morphological analyses of ritual-architectural priorities can, on occasion, expose the dubiousness of diffusionist claims based simply on such formal parallels as, for instance, the extravagant theories of transoceanic migrations derived almost exclusively from specious resemblances in the architectural decorations of China, Africa, and the Americas, which are described in Robert Wauchope, *Lost Tribes and Sunken Continents: Myth and Method in the Study of American Indians* (Chicago: University of Chicago Press, 1962). For a demonstration of how this sort of morphological analysis can contribute significantly to the evaluation of specific historical problems, such as migratory patterns and intrasite relations, see Jones, *Twin City Tales,* chapter 4.

72. See in volume 1, chapter 12, the section "Revalorization and Empirical Veracity: Respecting the Particular, Irregular, and Unforeseen."

73. Victor Wolfgang Von Hagen, *Frederick Catherwood, Archt.* (New York: Oxford University Press, 1950), 32–33, among innumerable relevant sources, describes the complex career of the Temple of Jupiter-Baal and Catherwood's visit there in the 1830s.

74. See James S. Duncan, "The Power of Place in Kandy, Sri Lanka: 1780–1980," in *The Power of Place: Bringing Together Geographical and Sociological Imagination,* ed. John A. Agnew and James S. Duncan (Boston: Unwin Hyman, 1989), 185–200.

75. Ibid., 186.

76. Ibid., 192.

77. While this British architectural program did quite thoroughly jettison the sorts of strategies of architectural allurement implied by the homology priority (I-A), it would be viable to suggest that, by contrast, instead of jettisoning the concern for expressing mythological themes in public architecture (sacred history, priority II-B), the British basically substituted a Eurocentric mythology for a Buddhist one.

78. Duncan, "The Power of Place in Kandy, Sri Lanka," 198.

79. For a synoptic enumeration of the hermeneutical questions suggested by this volume, see the appendix, "An Expanded Morphology of Ritual-Architectural Priorities."

80. See Jones, *Twin City Tales,* particularly chapter 4, where I have applied this sort of morphologic procedure to a specific historical problem, namely, the uncanny formal similarity between the architectural remains of Tula and Chichén Itzá.

Part One | Architecture as Orientation

1. Ermilo Abreu Gomez, *Canek: History and Legend of a Maya Hero,* trans. Mario L. Davila and Carter Wilson (Berkeley and Los Angeles: University of California Press, 1979), 37.

2. These lines are attributed to Thomas Jefferson (1801) in John Bach McMaster, *History of the People of the United States, from the Revolution to the Civil War,* 6 vols. (New York: D. Appleton and Company, 1895), 2:586.

3. Kevin Lynch, *The Image of the City* (Cambridge, Mass.: MIT Press, 1960), 4.

4. Mircea Eliade and Lawrence E. Sullivan, "Orientation," in *Encyclopedia of Religion,* ed. Eliade, 11:105.

5. See Mircea Eliade, *A History of Religious Ideas,* trans. Willard R. Trask, vol. 1 (Chicago: University of Chicago Press, 1978), 3–5. In the same vein, Gottfried Richter considers that the sensation of walking down the sphinx-lined avenue toward the tall pointed obelisk at the entrance to an Egyptian temple marks a crucial turning point wherein humans experience the "power of uprightness" in an unprecedented way: "Man is beginning to stand erect. . . . As he stands up he wakes up. . . ." Gottfried Richter, *Art and Human Consciousness,* trans. Burley Channer and Margaret Frohlich (Spring Valley, N.Y.: Anthroposophic Press, 1982), 18.

6. Mircea Eliade, *The Sacred and the Profane: The Nature of Religion,* trans. Willard R. Trask (New York: Harcourt, Brace Jovanovich, 1959), 23.

7. Charles H. Long, *Significations: Signs, Symbols, and Images in the Interpretation of Religion* (Philadelphia: Fortress Press, 1986), 7. On religion as "cosmic orientation," also see Charles H. Long, *Alpha: The Myths of Creation* (Chico, Calif.: Scholars Press, 1963), 18–19.

8. Jonathan Z. Smith, "The Influence of Symbols upon Social Change: A Place on Which to Stand," *Worship* 44 (October 1970): 472; reprinted as chapter 6 of Smith's *Map Is Not Territory.* Davíd Carrasco has repeatedly quoted and embellished this line, for instance, in his *Quetzalcoatl and the Irony of Empire,* 104.

9. James W. Fernandez, "Location and Direction in African Religious Movements: Some Deictic Contours of Religious Conversion," *History of Religions* 25 (May 1986): 352–67.

10. Ibid., 361–67. Fernandez's remarks on African colonization as "reorientation" resonate with Octavio Paz's creative interpretation of the Spanish

Conquest of Mexico as an occasion of catastrophic "disorientation," and, thus, the post-Conquest embrace of Catholicism by Mesoamerican Indians as a desperate attempt to retrieve "a sense of their place on earth"; see Octavio Paz, *The Labyrinth of Solitude: Life and Thought in Mexico* (New York: Grove Press, 1961), 89–90.

11. I lift this characterization of the archaic context from Lawrence E. Sullivan, "Astral Myths Rise Again: Interpreting Religious Astronomy," *Criterion* 22 (winter 1983): 17.

12. Paul Kirchhoff's unpublished notebooks; quoted in Johanna Broda, "Astronomy, *Cosmovision* and Ideology in Pre-Hispanic Mexico," in *Ethnoastronomy and Archaeoastronomy in the American Tropics,* ed. Anthony F. Aveni and Gary Urton (New York: New York Academy of Sciences, 1982), 103.

13. George Kubler, "The Design of Space in Maya Architecture," in *Miscellanea Paul Rivet, octogenario dicata* (Mexico: Universidad Nacional Autonoma de Mexico, 1958), 516.

14. Carrasco, *Quetzalcoatl and the Irony of Empire,* 1.

15. Regarding an "orientation motive" at Teotihuacan, see Anthony F. Aveni, *Skywatchers of Ancient Mexico* (Austin: University of Texas Press, 1980), 218–21. Several of Aveni's works will provide featured examples in chapter 16, "Astronomy: Predictions and Enhancements of Nature."

16. See Johanna Broda, "Astronomy, *Cosmovision,* and Ideology in Pre-Hispanic Mesoamerica"; and idem, "Templo Mayor as Ritual Space," in Johanna Broda, Davíd Carrasco, and Eduardo Matos Moctezuma, *The Great Temple of Tenochtitlan: Center and Periphery in the Aztec World* (Berkeley and Los Angeles: University of California Press, 1987).

17. Annemarie Schimmel, "Sacred Geography in Islam," in *Sacred Places and Profane Spaces: Essays in the Geographics of Judaism, Christianity, and Islam,* ed. Jamie Scott and Paul Simpson-Housley (New York: Greenwood Press, 1991), 164. Schimmel quotes and comments on this line from a Persian poem by the Indo-Muslim philosopher-poet Muhammad Iqbal (1877–1938).

18. See Elisabeth Stroker, *Investigations in Philosophy of Space,* trans. Algis Mickunas (Athens: Ohio University Press, 1987), chapter 1, "The Attuned Space." In Stroker's formulation, "Attuned space is encountered in a pre-reflective orientation toward the world. Such orientation to space is an immediate affinity with the world. For an attuned being to be in another 'space' and to live in another 'world' are expressions identical in meaning." Ibid., 20.

19. Yi-Fu Tuan, *Space and Place: The Perspective of Experience* (Minneapolis: University of Minnesota Press, 1977).

20. Susanne Langer, *Philosophy in a New Key: A Study in the Symbolism of Reason, Rite, and Art,* 4th ed. (Cambridge, Mass.: Harvard University Press, 1960), 289; quoted, for instance, by Smith, *Map Is Not Territory,* 146.

21. Likewise speaking to the important connection between architecture and orientation, the preamble of the [United States] National Historical Preservation

Act of 1966 promotes legislation protecting existing buildings "as a living part of our community life and development in order to give a sense of orientation to the American people"; quoted unapprovingly by Anthony Jackson, *Reconstructing Architecture for the Twenty-First Century: An Inquiry into the Architect's World* (Toronto: University of Toronto Press, 1995), 14.

22. Titus Burckhardt, *Sacred Art in East and West: Its Principles and Methods,* trans. Lord Northbourne (London: Perennial Books, 1967), 24.

23. Christian Norberg-Schulz, "Meaning in Architecture," in *Meaning in Architecture,* ed. Charles Jencks and George Baird (New York: George Braziller, 1969), 225–26.

24. See Christian Norberg-Schulz, *The Concept of Dwelling: On the Way to Figurative Architecture* (New York: Rizzoli, 1985).

25. Sibyl Moholy-Nagy, *Native Genius in Anonymous Architecture in North America* (New York: Schocken Books, 1976), 21. With respect to the reliance on architecture as a guarantor against chaos, the rhetoric of Modernist architecture, for instance, and the International Style was fueled, in large part, by a confidence that the social chaos and physical rubble left by World War I—a circumstance of collective disorientation—could be rectified and repaired, and a new, more healthy orientation could be effected, by an architecture of crisp regularity, rigorous order, and clean white or glass facades.

26. Christian Norberg-Schulz, for instance, emphasizes the atypicality of Michelangelo and the Mannerists' rejection of harmony in his *Meaning in Western Architecture* (New York: Praeger, 1975), 130. There are, of course, any number of other cases in which conflict, doubt, and incongruity supersede harmony and all-encompassing order as design parameters for sacred architecture. Consider a smattering of cross-cultural examples: 1) Whitney S. Stoddard (*Art and Architecture in Medieval France* [New York: Harper and Row, 1966], 279–326) describes French flamboyant and rayonnant architecture that, while looking like baroque, does not stem from confidence (as did the baroque) but rather from disillusionment, nominalism, and skepticism; 2) Alfonso Ortiz (*The Tewa World* [Chicago: University of Chicago Press, 1969], 134–37) demonstrates that there are intentional asymmetries in Tewa Indian ritual and architecture, but that those asymmetries are resolved over longer spans of time; and 3) Irving Goldman (*Mouth of Heaven: An Introduction to Kwakiutl Religious Thought* [Huntington, N.Y.: Robert E. Krieger Publishing Company, 1975], chapter 9) shows that in Kwakiutl cosmology, and thus architecture, interdependence between realms is more important than perfect parallelism between those realms.

27. See particularly Smith's criticism of Eliade's emphasis on a "locative world view" to the neglect of a "utopian world view" in Smith, "The Wobbling Pivot," in his *Map Is Not Territory,* 88–103. Long, with respect to creation myths, has also recognized the limitations of thinking in terms of perfect harmony: "While . . . the cosmogonic myth orients, synthesizes and integrates the world, a complete

harmony is seldom achieved . . . threats and antagonisms are usually identifiable in the myth. As a matter of fact, they are made clearer in light of the definitive structure of the cosmogonic myth"; Long, *Alpha: The Myths of Creation,* 30–31.

28. Recall Robert Venturi's *Complexity and Contradiction in Architecture* (New York: Museum of Modern Art, 1966), discussed in volume 1, chapter 6.

29. Virtually equating "religion" and "orientation," as several historians of religions are wont to do (not unlike equating religion with cosmology or worldview), may have the disadvantage of privileging the cognitive realm of thought or belief over that of action or practice (thus perpetuating certain post-Reformation biases): conceiving of religion primarily as "orientation to sacred reality" has, however, the advantage of holding a focus on human experience (which is consistent with the hermeneutical perspective of this work), while holding open the matter of the ontological status of that so-termed "sacred reality."

30. In volume 1, see especially chapter 4, "Order and Variation: The Twofold Pattern of Ritual-Architectural Events."

Fourteen | Homology

1. *The Mahabharata, Anusasan Parvan,* chapter 108, verses 16–18, as translated in J. H. Dave, *Immortal India,* vol. 1 (Bombay: Bharatiya Viyda Bhavan, 1959), xiv; quoted in Surinder Mohan Bhardwaj, *Hindu Places of Pilgrimage in India: A Study in Cultural Geography* (Berkeley and Los Angeles: University of California Press, 1973), 84.

2. Mircea Eliade, *Patterns in Comparative Religion,* trans. Rosemary Sheed (New York: Sheed and Ward, 1958), 379; originally published as *Traite d'histoire des religions* (Paris: Payot, 1949). Burckhardt, *Sacred Art in East and West,* 39, n. 1, provides a perspective very similar to that of Eliade when he contends that "In primitive civilizations every dwelling is regarded as an image of the cosmos, the house or the tent 'contains' and 'envelopes' man on the model of the great world."

3. Bernard Tschumi, *Architecture and Disjunction* (Cambridge, Mass.: MIT Press, 1996), 90.

4. See, for instance, W. Brede Kristensen, *The Meaning of Religion: Lectures in the Phenomenology of Religion,* trans. John B. Carman (The Hague: M. Nijhoff, 1960); G. van der Leeuw, *Religion in Essence and Manifestation,* trans. J. E. Turner (New York: Harper and Row, 1963); and idem, *Sacred and Profane Beauty: The Holy in Art,* trans. David E. Green (New York: Holt, Rinehart and Winston, 1963). Among many relevant works by Mircea Eliade, see his *Cosmos and History: The Myth of the Eternal Return,* trans. Willard R. Trask (Princeton: Princeton University Press, 1954); and idem, *The Sacred and The Profane,* especially chapter 1, "Sacred Space and Making the World Sacred." Shigeru Matsumoto, in "The Meaning of Sacred Places As Phenomenologists of Religion Understand It," *Tenri Journal of Religion* 10 (October 1969): 46–56, discusses how this phenomenological approach

to sacred space arises in response to earlier evolutionary approaches to religion.

5. On the differences, but general compatibility, between Kristensen's notion of "Ancient" versus "Classical" orientations to the world, Eliade's notion of "archaic" versus "modern" consciousness, and van der Leeuw's use of the terms "primitive" and "modern," see Matsumoto, "The Meaning of Sacred Places," 46–49.

6. Kristensen, *The Meaning of Religion,* 359–60.

7. Ibid.

8. Ibid., 358.

9. Ibid., 360. Note also that, with Kristensen's emphasis on the connection between the "holiness of a place" and the "holiness of a god," we see immediately the interpenetration of ritual-architectural priorities—in this case, homology (I-A) and the commemoration of divinity (II-A).

10. On hierophanies, or the "irruption" of the sacred into the profane, see, among countless relevant possibilities, Eliade, *The Sacred and the Profane,* 21; or idem, *Myth and Reality,* trans. Willard R. Trask (New York: Harper Colophon Books, 1963), 6. For criticism of that notion, see Smith, "The Wobbling Pivot," in his *Map Is Not Territory,* 92ff.

11. See, for instance, Eliade, *Cosmos and History,* 3.

12. Eliade, *Patterns in Comparative Religion,* 368.

13. See Smith, *To Take Place: Toward Theory in Ritual,* chapter 1, "In Search of Place." By now, numerous scholars have commented on the contrast between these two fundamentally different approaches to the status of "sacred space," usually by reference to Jonathan Smith's explicit critique of Eliade's work. Among the clearest of those discussions comes in the editors' introduction to *American Sacred Space,* ed. David Chidester and Edward Linenthal, 5–9, in which they differentiate between "substantial" or phenomenological approaches (linked particularly to Rudolf Otto, van der Leeuw, and Eliade) and the "situational" or sociological approaches (most prominently linked to Emile Durkheim, Arnold van Gennep, Claude Lévi-Strauss, and Jonathan Smith), which those editors regard as considerably more fruitful. Unlike most summary discussions of the problem, however, Chidester and Linenthal additionally point to important contrasts between Eliade's largely apolitical theory of sacred space and that of van der Leeuw, who, in their view, by his heavy reliance on the category of "power," made an advance insofar as, "even if unintended, Van der Leeuw laced his analysis with hints of a politics of sacred space." Ibid., 7.

14. Eliade, *Patterns in Comparative Religion,* 369. Note that I will return in chapter 24 to the matter of what makes a place or building sacred, the sanctuary priority (III-D).

15. See, for instance, Eliade, *The Sacred and the Profane,* chapter 1.

16. While van der Leeuw (*Religion in Essence and Manifestation,* 393) says that a place becomes sacred when it is "selected" by human beings, he is actually quite close to Eliade in emphasizing the "mystery" and "awe-inspiring character" that

causes that place to be selected; he emphasizes, for instance, that "Man adds not at all to Nature" (394). Therefore, both Eliade and van der Leeuw (as would Kristensen) stand in radical contrast to Jonathan Smith's (Durkheim-informed) position about the sanctification of arbitrary places, discussed below in chapter 24, on sanctuary architecture (priority III-D).

17. See Eliade, *Patterns in Comparative Religion,* 369.

18. Ibid.

19. Ibid.

20. It is worth emphasizing that van der Leeuw's and Eliade's claims about the intrinsic potency of certain places, if suspect as a totally comprehensive explanation of sacred space (a universalistic status that many scholars have been willing to afford it), do, nonetheless, provide an intriguing language for addressing what I'd term the "alluring" quality of hierophanic and homologized architectures. Van der Leeuw (*Religion in Essence and Manifestation,* 401), for instance, contends that sacred places "attract the faithful to them in a literal sense," and then cites as an example the sanctuary of Minahassa in the Dutch West Indies, which is named "the callers" because "the stones forming it call back the villagers from the foreign regions, or in other words arouse home-sickness in their breasts." As I noted in chapter 5 of volume 1, "Allurement and Coercion: The Front Half of the Ritual-Architectural Situation," this alluring quality is particularly apparent at pilgrimage sites, which, according to van der Leeuw, constitute "a sort of home" so that "whole peoples and religious communities can have their home: the Jews, Jerusalem, Mohammedans, Mecca, and Christians, Rome" (401). Van der Leeuw's notion of "home-sickness" finds a parallel in Eliade's famous conception of "nostalgia for paradise," which he describes (in *Patterns of Comparative Religion,* 383–84) as the *homo religiosus*'s desire to participate in the sacred, "to transcend the human condition and regain a divine state of affairs like the state of man before the Fall." And because that transcendence can be effected, not everywhere, but only at those houses, temples, palaces, and cities that are conceived as being situated at the "Center of the World," *homo religiosus* are consequently drawn—or "allured"—to those special places. For a Jew to travel to Jerusalem, for instance, is, in Eliade's terms, to journey to a place that is preeminently "real," a place that exhibits a "superabundance of reality."

21. Regarding *axis mundi* and the "symbolism of the center," see Eliade, *Myth of the Eternal Return,* chapter 1; idem, *Patterns in Comparative Religion;* and idem, *The Sacred and the Profane,* chapter 1. There seems little need to review again the plethora of instances of sacred architecture that have been interpreted in terms of these concepts. Alternatively, and more trenchant in this regard, see the startlingly iconoclastic critique of Eliade by Smith, *To Take Place,* chapter 1, wherein Smith claims that "the 'Center' is not a secure pattern to which data may be brought as illustrative; it is a dubious notion . . ." (17).

22. Eliade, *The Sacred and the Profane,* 22; emphasis his.

23. Ibid.

24. See ibid., 50–65.

25. See, for instance, Thomas Barrie, *Spiritual Path, Sacred Place: Myth, Ritual, and Meaning in Architecture* (Boston and London: Shambhala, 1996), 3–4, 164; or Tschumi, *Architecture and Disjunction,* 76.

26. The list of detractors who condemn Eliade's theory of sacred space *indirectly,* often by focusing on his political affiliations and thus putting in doubt his entire interpretive program, continues to grow. Among those focusing more specifically (and thus, for us, much more interestingly) on problems related directly to sacred space, Jonathan Z. Smith is the most prominent: see especially "The Wobbling Pivot," in his *Map Is Not Territory,* 92ff.; and "In Search of Place," chapter 1 of his *To Take Place: Toward Theory in Ritual.* For a concise summary of shifting approaches to sacred space (away from Eliade), see Roger Friedland and Richard D. Hecht, "The Politics of Sacred Place: Jersualem's Temple Mount/*al-haram a-sharif,*" in *Sacred Places and Profane Spaces,* ed. Scott and Simpson-Housley, especially a subsection entitled "Aesthetics or Politics of Sacred Space," 24–28. In a similar vein, also see the editors' introduction to *American Sacred Space,* ed. Chidester and Linenthal, 1–20. Gregory D. Alles, "Surface, Space, and Intention: The Parthenon and the Kandariya Mahadeva," *History of Religions* 28 (August 1988): 1–36, also provides among the most nuanced and critically constructive assessments of Eliade's model of sacred space. In Alles's view, this model is deficient, because "orientation" (in the sense in which Eliade describes it), is *not* important in all religious architectures; moreover, imposing "symbolic" interpretations on historical sacred architectures (which is a procedure deriving from the hermeneutical analysis of texts) obfuscates and reduces perhaps more than it explains (35). Thus, Alles writes: "It has been clear for years that Eliade's peculiar categories—the center, *axis mundi, imago mundi*—are helpful in some contexts (e.g., India) but totally inadequate in others (e.g., Greece)" (36). Also, by the way, it is noteworthy methodologically that Alles's extended (and very illuminating) comparison of two historically unrelated architectures—the Parthenon and the Kandariya Mahadeva —constitutes an excellent example of another sort of morphological (other than appearance-based) comparison. Were his conclusion (re)organized with respect to my heuristic framework, we could note, for instance, profound morphological differences between the two cases in relation to the priorities of homology (I-A) and divinity (II-A), but surprising morphological parallels in relation to the ritual-architectural commemoration of politics (priority II-C), that is, the way in which the respective architectural features of each structure are designed to express a very specific notion of "religiopolitical power" (see especially 32–34).

27. For example, Mary Lee Nolan describes medieval European cult-formation legends that explain how a relic or a miraculous image "chose" a particular locale as the most appropriate place for its veneration; Mary Lee Nolan, "The European Roots of Latin American Pilgrimage," in *Pilgrimage in Latin America,* ed. N. Ross

Crumrine and Alan Morinis (New York: Greenwood Press, 1991), 32–36. Rosenau (*The Ideal City*, 23) discusses similarly miraculous medieval accounts, such as that in the "Fundatio Ecclesiae Hildensemensis," which describes how a spectacularly selective snowfall or frost provided the outline of a ground plan for a new basilica. Yet, quite obviously, in many other situations—most Protestant churches or Jewish synagogues, for instance—more prosaic siting parameters take precedence, and, in fact, worshipers vehemently deny that the sacred has manifested itself more fully in that one place than in any other.

28. This very fundamental issue about the *discovery* of sacred places versus the *creation* or *sanctification* of sacred places might likewise be articulated in terms of a tension between respective concerns for homology (priority I-A) and sanctuary (priority III-D) and will be discussed again more fully in chapter 24, which addresses that latter option.

29. See Alles, "Surface, Space, and Intention: The Parthenon and the Kandariya Mahadeva," where he discusses the irrelevance of Eliade's categories to classical Greek architecture.

30. It should be clear, I hope, that while I am relying most heavily on Eliade for my exposition of this first morphological priority (homology, I-A)—a notion that I regard as central to his work—I do not intend this category as coterminous with his full theory of sacred space. Ideas from Eliade will be featured again, for instance, in relation to my expositions of priorities for the commemoration of sacred history (II-B) and the dead (II-D) as well as in relation to the sanctuary priority (III-D).

31. Smith (*Map Is Not Territory*, 151–53) concisely summarizes Cornelius Loew's term "cosmological conviction" and then deploys it in his own exposition of "locative world views" (on which nearly all of Eliade's work concentrates) as opposed to "utopian world views" (which, Smith shows, Eliade largely neglects). It is noteworthy also that, in my morphological terms, those locative world views invariably entail strong exercises of the homology priority while their utopian counterparts largely eschew that priority.

32. See Roxana Waterson, "The House and the World: The Symbolism of the Sa'Dan Toraja House Carvings," *Res: Anthropology and Aesthetics* 15 (spring 1988): 35–60.

33. See Mircea Eliade, *Shamanism: Archaic Techniques of Ecstasy*, trans. Willard R. Trask (Princeton: Princeton University Press, 1972), 262–63.

34. I. W. Mabbett discusses architectural homologization with respect to Mount Meru and summarizes the landmark work of Paul Mus on Borobudur as a cosmogram in "The Symbolism of Mount Meru," *History of Religions* 23 (August 1983): 76. Hiram W. Woodward provides a concise, though provocative, interpretation of Borobudur (to which I will return in chapter 22, on the contemplation priority, III-B) in "Borobudur and the Mirrorlike Mind," *Archaeology* 34 (November-December 1981): 40–47. And Paul Wheatley discusses Angkor Thom and the traditional Chinese city with direct reference to Eliade's model of sacred

space in *The Pivot of the Four Quarters: A Preliminary Enquiry into the Origins and Character of the Ancient Chinese City* (Chicago: Aldine, 1971), 437–38.

35. Diana Eck discusses the city of Banaras as a mandala and representation of the universe in *Banaras: City of Light* (Princeton: Princeton University Press, 1982), 146, 256, 283–84, 322. On the principle of homology in the Hindu temples, besides Mabbett, "The Symbolism of Mount Meru," see Michell, *The Hindu Temple,* part 1; and Burckhardt, *Sacred Art in East and West,* chapter 1.

36. See Romi Khosla, "Architecture and Symbolism in Tibetan Monasteries," in *Shelter, Sign, and Symbol: An Exploratory Work on Vernacular Architecture,* ed. Paul Oliver (Woodstock, N.Y.: Overlook Press, 1977), 71–83.

37. Fred W. Clothey (*Rhythm and Intent: Ritual Studies from South India* [Madras: Blackie and Son, 1983], 149–51) discusses the tantric principle known as the *Vastupurusha Mandala,* which underwrites a homology between the portions of a ritual room, the limbs of a human body, and the regions of the cosmos. Clothey also explains how the *yaka calai* is constructed as a literal image of Vedic and Puranic cosmologies and, moreover, provides a splendid example in which the dedication of the Hindu temple is explicitly homologized to the founding of a cosmos.

38. See Clark E. Cunningham, "Order in the Atoni House," in *Right and Left: Essays on Dual Symbolic Classification,* ed. Rodney Needham (Chicago: University of Chicago Press, 1973), 204–38.

39. Alexander-Phaedow Lagopoulos, in "Semiological Urbanism: An Analysis of the Traditional Western Sudanese Settlement," in *Shelter, Sign, and Symbol,* ed. Oliver, 206–18, stresses particularly the Dogon conception of the longhouse as a "cosmic egg" in which the "plan of the house is converted into a sort of summary of its three-dimensional spatial reality" (210). With respect to West African vernacular architecture, David Dalby explains that in Hausa, the principal language in the eastern half of the West African Savannah, *garii,* the basic term for individual settlement, i.e., a village or town, can be used on a flexible scale to refer to any category of human settlement or territorial unit up to the whole world itself. See David Dalby, "The Concert of Settlement in the West African Savannah," in *Shelter, Sign, and Symbol,* ed. Oliver, 197–205, especially p. 203.

40. On Salteaux village arrangement, see A. Irving Hallowell, *Culture and Experience* (Philadelphia: University of Pennsylvania Press, 1955), 187–201; discussed by Tuan, *Space and Place,* 87, 92. Joseph G. Jorgensen, *The Sun Dance Religion: Power for the Powerless* (Chicago: University of Chicago Press,1972), 177–205, discusses the cosmic design of Ute and Shoshone sun-dance lodges.

41. On Shaker meetinghouses, see Belden C. Lane, *Landscapes of the Sacred: Geography and Narrative in American Spirituality* (New York: Paulist Press, 1988), 132–51.

42. Keith Critchlow explores the intriguing possibility of an architecture that not only homologizes time and space, but also acupuncture and the health of an

individual at various times of the day; "*Niike*: The Siting of a Japanese Rural House," in *Shelter, Sign, and Symbol,* ed. Oliver, 219–26. On homologization in Japanese temples, see Bruno Taut and Shiro Hiral, trans., *Fundamentals of Japanese Architecture* (Tokyo: Kokusai Bunka Shinkokai, 1936); cited in *Shelter, Sign, and Symbol,* ed. Oliver, 37 n. 71. Richard B. Pilgrim, "Intervals (*Ma*) in Space and Time: Foundations for a Religio-Aesthetic Paradigm in Japan," *History of Religions* 25 (February 1986): 255–77, also adeptly explores the homologization of space and time in Japanese architecture. Allan G. Grapard discusses the progressive expansion of the concept of mandala until the entire country of Japan came to be viewed as sacred space, or *shinkoku,* that is, a "divine nation" in "Flying Mountains and Walkers of Emptiness: Toward a Definition of Sacred Space in Japanese Religion," *History of Religions* 20 (February 1982): 214–18.

43. Broda ("Astronomy, *Cosmovision,* and Ideology in Pre-Hispanic Mexico," 81–85) strikes very close to the issue of homology when she describes "cosmovision" as "the structured view in which the ancient Mesoamericans combined their notions of cosmology into a systematic whole." All of the Mesoamerican examples addressed in this paragraph are discussed, some at greater length, in Jones, *Twin City Tales;* see especially pp. 216–19. For numerous additional, excellent examples of homologized Maya architecture not discussed here, see Karen Bassie-Sweet, *At the Edge of the World: Caves and Late Classic Maya World View* (Norman: University of Oklahoma Press, 1996), chapter 3, "Cosmograms."

44. Joyce Marcus, "Territorial Organization of the Lowland Classic Maya," *Science* 180 (1973): 911–16. Linda Schele extends Marcus's hypothesis about a pan-regional cosmological orientation in Maya site planning, emphasizing particularly Palenque's role in that scheme as "the western portal to the Underworld . . . the place where the sun and the moon died," and Copán's conception as "the eastern portal out of the Underworld, or into it, whichever way you want it"; Linda Schele, "Sacred Sites and World-Views at Palenque," in *Mesoamerican Sites and World-Views: A Conference at Dumbarton Oaks, October 16–17, 1976,* ed. Elizabeth P. Benson (Washington, D.C.: Dumbarton Oaks, 1981), 108, 110 and 115.

45. See Wheatley, *Pivot of the Four Quarters,* which provides extensive documentation of the homologized layouts of cities in seven zones of "primary urban generation," including Mesoamerica.

46. J. Eric S. Thompson, *Maya History and Religion* (Norman: University of Oklahoma Press, 1970), 215, 291; and Robert Redfield and Alfonso Villa Rojas, *Chan Kom: A Maya Village* (Chicago: University of Chicago Press, 1934), 114, among many works, address quadripartite Maya village organizations.

47. Regarding the interpretation of buildings at the Maya sites of Cerros, Uaxactún, and Tikal as "miniature models of the world," see Elizabeth P. Benson, "Architecture as Metaphor," in *Fifth Palenque Round Table, 1983,* vol. 7, ed. Merle Green Robertson (San Francisco: Pre-Columbian Art Research Institute, 1985); and David A. Freidel, "Cultural Areas and Interaction Spheres: Contrasting

Approaches to the Emergence of Civilization in the Maya Lowlands," *American Antiquity* 44 (1979): 36–54.

48. Rudolph van Zantwijk discusses the cosmogrammatic quality of the Templo Mayor in "The Great Temple of Tenochtitlan: Model of Aztec Cosmovision," in *Mesoamerican Sites and World-Views,* ed. Benson, 71–86.

49. Alfred M. Tozzer interprets various tripartite columns at Chichén Itzá in this way in *Chichén Itzá and Its Cenote of Sacrifice: A Comparative Study of Contemporaneous Maya and Toltec,* Memoirs of the Peabody Museum, 11–12 (Cambridge, Mass.: Harvard University, 1957), 119.

50. See, for instance, Benson, "Architecture as Metaphor," 188; and Janet Catherine Berlo, "Artistic Specialization at Teotihuacan: The Ceramic Incense Burner," in *Pre-Columbian Art History: Selected Readings,* ed. Alana Cordy-Collins (Palo Alto, Calif.: Peek Publications, 1982), 90–99.

51. I am following primarily the excellent account of the Barasana provided by Stephen Hugh-Jones, *The Palm and the Pleiades: Initiation and Cosmology in Northwest Amazonia* (Cambridge: Cambridge University Press, 1979). See also Christine Hugh-Jones, *From the Milk River: Spatial and Temporal Processes in Northwest Amazonia* (Cambridge: Cambridge University Press, 1979).

52. Thompson (*Maya History and Religion,* 195–96, 214–19) discusses the Maya conceptions of the universe as an iguana and of the world as set within a house; this interpretation of Maya cosmology, now hotly contested, is strikingly similar to the Barasana cosmology.

53. Hugh-Jones, *The Palm and the Pleiades,* 150.

54. Ibid., 108–9.

55. Ibid., 219.

56. Burr Cartwright Brundage makes passing remarks on the *ceque* system, explaining how Cuzco "mirrored the cosmos" in *Two Earths, Two Heavens: An Essay Contrasting the Aztecs and the Incas* (Albuquerque: University of New Mexico Press, 1975), 27. He also notes (38) how the entire system expressed the vision of one individual, Pachacuti. Victor Von Hagen gives a less rigorous discussion of the *ceque* system that is nonetheless useful in pointing out the social microcosmic character of Cuzco in *The Realm of the Incas* (New York: New American Library, 1961), 126–31. He cites sixteenth-century chronicler Cieza de León to document a political strategy of "enforced ethnicity" whereby representatives of tribes conquered by the Incas were forced to live in Cuzco but maintain their distinctive dress and customs; in this way the city became a microcosm of the social ideal of unity in diversity (and thus demonstrates a merger of homology [priority I-A] and commemoration of politics [priority II-C]). For another sixteenth-century account of the *ceque* system, see Father Bernabé Cobo, *Inca Religion and Customs,* trans. and ed. Roland Hamilton (Austin: University of Texas Press, 1990), chapter 13.

57. R. T. Zuidema, *The Ceque System of Cuzco: The Social Organization of the Capital of the Inca* (Leiden: Brill, 1964), concentrates on the social dimensions of

the *ceque* system. Idem, "The Inca Calendar," in *Native American Astronomy,* ed. Anthony F. Aveni (Austin: University of Texas Press, 1977), 219–59, concentrates on archeoastronomical dimensions.

58. I have benefitted also from the summary of Zuidema's work in Aveni, *Skywatchers of Ancient Mexico,* 302–5.

59. See Zuidema, *The Ceque System of Cuzco,* 210–12.

60. The "space-time concept" articulated by Seigfried Giedion in *Space, Time, and Architecture* (Cambridge, Mass.: Harvard University Press, 1967), as well as the Bauhaus's preoccupations with the architectural unification of space and time, for instance, both belie that the agendum of homologizing unification via architecture is solely the preserve of traditional or "archaic" settings. For astute comments on Giedion's "space-time concept," see also Charles Jencks, "History as Myth," in *Meaning in Architecture,* ed. Charles Jencks and George Baird (New York: George Braziller, 1969), 252–55. By contrast, however, presenting an intriguing sort of example of the abdication of the homology priority, other contemporary architectural theorists—Françoise Choay, for one, exploring in this case the semiology of the Parisian built environment—applaud the modern demise of rigorous systems of homology and strict rules of correspondence in city planning because, as Choay explains, "in freeing ourselves from the former spatial framework, we gain mobility, subtlety and richness for our symbolic devices—that is, we have increased our mobility and possibility of choices"; Choay, "Urbanism and Semiology," in *Meaning in Architecture,* ed. Jencks and Baird, 34.

61. Matsumoto, "The Meaning of Sacred Places," 56.

62. Tschumi, *Architecture and Disjunction,* 90.

63. John B. Carlson provides one of the more thorough (among countless) discussions of the calendrical symbolism of the Castillo in "A Geomantic Model for the Interpretation of Mesoamerican Sites: An Essay in Cross-Cultural Comparison," in *Mesoamerican Sites and World-Views,* ed. Benson, 179–87. Regarding the Pyramid of the Niches, see George Kubler, *The Art and Architecture of Ancient America: The Mexican, Maya, and Andean Peoples,* 3d ed. (New York: Penguin Books, 1984) 137–41. Jones, *Twin City Tales,* provides an extended discussion of strategies of allurement at Chichén Itzá (377–89); and a much briefer account of those at El Tajin (217–19).

Fifteen | Convention

1. Vitruvius, *The Ten Books on Architecture,* trans. Morris Hicky Morgan (New York: Dover Publications, 1960), 117. Vitruvius's manuscript is variously dated from the time of the reign of Augustus to the early centuries of the common era. I have, of course, reproduced only a tiny portion of Vitruvius's intensely detailed prescriptions for proper proportioning in the Doric order.

2. Coomaraswamy, *The Transformation of Nature in Art,* 24–25.

3. Tschumi, *Architecture and Disjunction,* 88. A version of the article in which this quotation appears, "The Pleasure of Architecture," originally appeared in *Architectural Design,* March 1977.

4. Andrea O. Dean discusses the controversy of Barragan's selection for the Pritzker prize, largely because he "has worked virtually in isolation, avoiding all controversy, following no mentor nor prevailing school and attracting few followers," in "Luis Barragan, Austere Architect of Silent Spaces," *Smithsonian* 10, no. 8 (November 1980): 153.

5. See volume 1, chapter 4, "Order and Variation: The Twofold Pattern of Ritual-Architectural Events." It is noteworthy also, though I cannot develop this theme in this short chapter, that both the design and experience of conventionalized architecture are, in an important sense, occasions of comparison; most obviously, continuity with convention cultivates a sensation of similarity, while departures from conventionality engender a (productive) sensation of difference. See volume 1, chapter 11, "Significant Alternatives: Modes, Contexts, and Sequences of Architectural Comparison."

6. In this short treatment of conventionality and sacred architecture I am compelled to jettison almost entirely remarks about two particularly relevant, controversial issues. First is the debate regarding how designers, not to mention lay users, acquire a specific set (or maybe *sense*) of ritual-architectural conventions—whether through education, literary erudition, professional experience, or perhaps simply via life in a particular built environment. See Pascal Boyer, *The Naturalness of Religious Ideas: A Cognitive Theory of Religion* (Berkeley and Los Angeles: University of California Press, 1994) on the analogous problem, which also remains very poorly understood, of the acquisition of "world views" or "religious ideas"; or see Catherine Bell, *Ritual Theory, Ritual Practice* (New York: Oxford University Press, 1992), 69ff., with respect to the similarly elusive process by which one acquires a culturally specific "sense of ritual." The second debate concerns the social, even moral, consequences of conventionalization in architecture. Bernard Tschumi (*Architecture and Disjunction,* 10), for instance, uses the term architectural "paradigm-taboos" with direct reference to Thomas Kuhn's *The Structure of Scientific Revolutions* and then comments on what he regards as the untoward consequences of such "hidden" architectural conventions. By contrast, Titus Burckhardt (*Sacred Art in East and West,* 8) expresses the less critical, still widespread view that the "force of tradition [which] is perpetuated without difficulty, in a quasi-organic manner," adduces to architectures that are, in the end, actually liberating and enlivening. Both issues, of course, deserve much greater discussion.

7. Otto von Simson's iconoclastic, widely renowned *The Gothic Cathedral: Origins of Gothic Architecture and the Medieval Concept of Order* (Princeton: Princeton University Press, 1956), though provocative in the extreme and considerably more "eventful" than most art historical works, raises several basic problems. Among the most pressing for me in the context of this morphology are: 1) how, in the case of

the Gothic, to reconcile the concern for abstract, rarified Augustinian aesthetics of proportion with popular pilgrimage fervor for miracles and relics; 2) how to reconcile the conception of space as heterogeneous and hierophanic, which he claims is characteristic of the Gothic ambience, with the proportional subdivision of homogeneous space, which is also apparently a Gothic preoccupation; and 3) how, if von Simpson is correct, to distinguish the ritual-architectural priorities of the Gothic from those of the Renaissance.

8. The distinction between the homology priority (I-A) and the convention priority (I-B) may actually be clearer in the realm of time than of space. Here, Eliade's distinction between adherence to the "myth of the eternal return" (which implies a temporalized sort of homology) and the endorsement of linear history (which connotes a more conventionalized view of time) is relevant. However, working out that analogy and the possibility of an evolutionary relationship between the two types of priorities raises too many problems to pursue here.

9. Von Simson, *The Gothic Cathedral,* 35–37.

10. Ibid., xvii–xviii.

11. If one operates with a radical constructivist view, then a compelling case could be made that *all* historical apprehensions of architecture, including those that I addressed with respect to the homology priority (I-A), are conventionalized, that is, no apprehensions are really objective or "natural" per se insofar as they all reflect cultural and historical contingencies. Still, I will be arguing that the morphological distinction between homology and convention is heuristically useful.

12. It is very plausible that these three sorts of related options—homologized architecture based on heavily empirical observations, rationalized compliance with abstract principles, and rote conformity to codified prescriptions—constitute a general pattern of historical development, but thus far I am not comfortable positing it as such. Morphological comparison suffices for now.

13. Vincent Scully has connected the advent of architectural adherence to universalistic principles to the growth of philosophical speculation in postclassic Greece; see *The Earth, the Temple, and the Gods: Greek Sacred Architecture,* rev. ed. (New Haven: Yale University Press, 1979), 198–201, 210. In his view, where the classic temple is "a particularly active embodiment of a specific kind of power" (thus participating particularly in the commemoration of the divinity priority [II-A]), the postclassic Greek temple is conceived as "a correct, generalized abstraction" (thus instantiating primarily the convention priority [I-B]). Scully's discussion of the "purely geometrical control of space developed by Hippodamian city planning" (187ff.) is also directly relevant to this sort of rationalized (or conventionalized) architecture. Regarding the important role of formulas and rules of proportion in the layout of Roman cities, see Joseph Rykwert, *The Idea of a Town: The Anthropology of Urban Form in Rome, Italy, and the Ancient World* (Princeton: Princeton University Press, 1976), chapter 3, "Square and Cross."

14. Whitney S. Stoddard (*Art and Architecture in Medieval France* [New York:

Harper and Row, 1972], 58) connects the architectural adherence to universalistic principles to medieval European magic numbers and finds many examples in the Romanesque.

15. Rudolf Wittkower, *Architectural Principles in the Age of Humanism* (New York: W. W. Norton, 1971), part 4, is tremendously useful in distinguishing between Gothic and Renaissance architectures but decidedly "uneventful" insofar as in that work Wittkower has very little to say about the use of buildings or the spectator's point of view. Instead, he is concerned primarily with understanding the intentions of the architect (which, in my view, constitutes only one among several specific sorts of protocols of ritual-architectural apprehension), but that he does very effectively.

16. My discussion of Alberti owes particularly to Joan Gadol, *Leon Battista Alberti: Universal Man of the Early Renaissance* (Chicago: University of Chicago Press, 1969).

17. For Alberti's *De re aedificatoria*, see Leon Battista Alberti, *The Ten Books of Architecture* (New York: Dover Publications, 1986), which is a reprint of James Leoni's 1755 translation. Alberti's treatise (not unlike Vitruvius's treatise) is filled with detailed recommendations, such as the following: "In making of Stair-ca*f*es with Steps, [the Ancients] recommend the making of the Steps in odd Numbers, and e*f*pecially in their Temples: Becau*f*e they *f*aid that by this Means we always *f*et our right Foot into the Temple fir*f*t, which was accounted a Point of Religion" [sic]; book 1, chapter 13.

18. Regarding Sebastiano Serlio's *Tutte l'opere d'architettura* (1531–51), see Sebastiano Serlio, *The Five Books of Architecture* (New York: Dover Publications, 1982), which is an unabridged reprint of the 1611 English edition of this work. Wittkower (*Architectural Principles in the Age of Humanism,* 18) characterizes Serlio's treatise as "pedestrian and pragmatic, consisting of a collection of models rather than expressions of principle. . . . we can not expect to find here any of Alberti's philosophical concepts." On Serlio's treatise, also see Peter Murray, *The Architecture of the Italian Renaissance* (New York: Schocken Books, 1963), 196–200.

19. Regarding Giacomo Barozzi da Vignola's rulebook, *Regola delli cinque ordini d'architettura* (1562), see William R. Ware, *The American Vignola,* 5th ed. (Scranton, N.J.: International Textbook Company, 1923). For a concise discussion of Vignola and his treatise, see Murray, *The Architecture of the Italian Renaissance,* 200–208.

20. Andrea Palladio's treatise, *Quattre libri dell'architettura* (1570), is available in English as Palladio, *The Four Books of Architecture*(New York: Dover Publications, 1965). This treatise is concerned almost entirely with practical issues, though arranged very rationally and precisely. Wittkower (*Architectural Principles in the Age of Humanism,* 21ff.) stresses Palladio's continuity with Alberti; by contrast, James Ackerman (*Palladio* [New York: Penguin Books, 1966], 25–29) claims that Serlio was Palladio's most influential model.

21. Here again I am indebted to Gadol, *Leon Battista Alberti.*

22. The analogy between the human body and architecture appears in many cultural contexts and participates in several categories of the present framework of architectural priorities. The Renaissance correlation of bodily proportions and architecture, such as that by Alberti, is patentedly oriented with respect to universalistic principles (that is, convention, priority I-B); but the Hindu-Tantric mandalization of both human bodies and architectonic spaces (see Giuseppe Tucci, *The Theory and Practice of the Mandala,* trans. Alan Houghton Brodrick [London: Rider and Co., 1961], iii; and Clothey, *Rhythm and Intent,* 149) is much more directly relevant to the homology priority (I-A). To take another example, the Maori's triple analogy of house rafters, human ribs, and reproductive organs—the rafters of the house are decorated with representations of male and female genitalia because reproductive organs are considered to be the ribs of the "Human House"—is an even stronger demonstration of the homology of human body and architecture (priority I-A); see Oliver, *Shelter, Sign, and Symbol,* 17. And, the Aztec homologization of time, space, and body parts, as in the case of the strange figure of Camaxtli, the Mexican god of fate, in the Codex Borgia, likewise participates primarily in the homology priority. For a reproduction of this illustration, see Peter Tompkins, *Mysteries of the Mexican Pyramids* (New York: Harper and Row, 1976), 120.

23. Alberti's careful studies of anatomy, biology, music, and so forth notwithstanding, a case could be made that his preeminent resource is Vitruvius's text and, in his own oft-repeated term, "the Ancients," in which case these "universal principles" really derive less from empirical observations of nature (the first of three broad subvariations on the convention priority) than from prestigious historical antecedents (the third of my three subvariations on the convention priority).

24. While Vitruvius's *Ten Books of Architecture* contains no real theory of proportion, it is a crucial concern for him; see 109 and 130.

25. Wittkower, *Architectural Principles in the Age of Humanism,* part 4.

26. Le Corbusier, *The Modulor—A Harmonious Measure to the Human Scale Universally Applicable to Architecture and Mechanics* (Cambridge, Mass.: Harvard University Press, 1954).

27. Le Corbusier contends that his scheme is valid largely because, "More than these thirty years past, the sap of mathematics has flown through the veins of my work, both as an architect and a painter; for music is always present within me" (ibid., 129). On the continuity and discontinuity between Alberti and Le Corbusier (to which I will return toward the end of this chapter), see Rudolph Arnheim, "A Review of Proportion," in Rudolph Arnheim, *Toward a Psychology of Art* (Berkeley and Los Angeles: University of California Press, 1966), 102–11.

28. On the Babylonian Code of Hammurabi, see Hans G. Kippenberg, "Codes and Codification," in *Encyclopedia of Religion,* ed. Eliade, 3:554–55.

29. On ancient Egyptian artistic conventions, see Erik Iversen, *Canon and*

Proportions in Egyptian Art, 2d ed. (Warminster, England: Aris and Phillips Ltd., 1975). See Kurt Lange and Max Hirmer, *Egypt: Architecture, Sculpture, Painting in Three Thousand Years* (London and New York: Phaidon, 1968), on Imhotep as an architect (pp. 380–401) and as a god (pp. 445, 530–31).

30. See J. G. Davies, *Temples, Churches, and Mosques: A Guide to the Appreciation of Religious Architecture* (Oxford: Basil Blackwell, 1982), 6–11.

31. See Richter, *Art and Human Consciousness,* 53. Richter's interpretation of Egyptian pyramids follows that of Ernst Bindel, *Die agyptischen Pyramiden: Als Zeugen vergangener Mysterienweisheit,* 4th ed. (Stuttgart: Verlag Freies Geistesleben, 1975).

32. See C. A. Doxiadis, *Architectural Space in Ancient Greece* (Cambridge, Mass.: MIT Press, 1972), 3–5, 16–23.

33. Ibid., 16–23. As noted below in chapter 16, this Greek orientational strategy finds a morphological parallel in the hypothesis of Horst Hartung, "Alignments in Architecture and Sculpture of Maya Centers: Notes on Piedras Negras, Copán, and Chichén Itzá," in *Ibero-Amerikanische Archiv* (Berlin), n.s., 10 (1984): 237, wherein the orientation of the Maya site of Copán appears to have a "starting point" on the stairway of Temple 11, from which spreads a system of cardinal lines, right angles, and isosceles triangles.

34. Nader Ardalan and Laleh Bakhtiar, *The Sense of Unity: The Sufi Tradition in Persian Architecture,* Publications of the Center for Middle Eastern Studies, no. 9 (Chicago: University of Chicago Press, 1973), 96. Ardalan and Bakhtiar provide extensive remarks on and examples of architectural (especially Persian) manifestations of Sufi conceptions of "the mathematics of proportion." See especially 21–31, where they accentuate the difference between a traditional Muslim "symbolic and qualitative mathematics" and Renaissance mathematics; and p. 96, where they address the specific cases of the dome of Shaykh Lutfullāh Mosque and the colonnade of Maydān-i-Shāh.

35. Regarding the very heavy reliance on geometrical schemes in Islamic architecture, specifically at the Dome of the Rock, see Titus Burckhardt, *Art of Islam: Language and Meaning* ([London]: World of Islam Festival Publishing Company, 1976), 9–14; and for a whole series of relevant remarks and examples of geometry and proportionality in Islamic architecture, see his chapter 4, "The Sphere and the Cube."

36. See Burckhardt, *Art of Islam,* 70.

37. See Yossi Katz, "The Jewish Religion and Spatial and Communal Organization: The Implementation of Jewish Religious Law in the Building of Urban Neighborhoods and Jewish Agricultural Settlements at the Close of the Nineteenth Century," in *Sacred Places and Profane Spaces,* ed. Scott and Simpson-Housley, 3–7.

38. See ibid., 6–16.

39. Regarding the continuity of traditional Jewish spatial and architectural conventions in American Christianity, Belden Lane (*Landscapes of the Sacred,* 110)

notes that the preferred layout of New England Puritan towns was explicitly "[p]atterned after instructions in the Pentateuch for the placement of the tabernacle and its adjacent tents of the tribes of Israel, . . . [a] centripetal focus of space [that] gave expression to the close bonds of covenent."

40. See Margaret E. Kenna, "Icons in Theory and Practice: An Orthodox Christian Example," *History of Religions* 24 (May 1985): 345–68.

41. For a recent translation, see Paul Hetherington, *The "Painter's Manual" of Dionysius of Fourna* (London: Sagittarius Press, 1974). Regarding contemporary manifestations, "The Icon Maker," an article by Kathleen Vyn in the *Chicago Tribune*, 25 December 1985, sec. 5, pp. 1–2, describes the ongoing construction of Saint Joseph's Ukrainian Catholic Church on the northwest side of Chicago proceeding with meticulous conformity to the prescriptions in the "Painter's Manual."

42. Concerning Asian (as well as African and Native American) parallels to Western systems of architectural proportioning, see Rykwert, *The Idea of a Town,* chapter 5, "The Parallels."

43. *Jataka*, 6:332; cited by Coomaraswamy, *The Transformation of Nature in Art,* 205–6, n. 74.

44. One place to enter the vast literature on Chinese *feng shui* and building manuals is Evelyn Lip, *Feng-Shui: Environments of Power: A Study of Chinese Architecture* (London: Academic Editions, 1995).

45. Regarding the similarly extensive literature on "magic squares," see Charles D. Orzech, "Seeing Chen-Yen Buddhism: Traditional Scholarship and the Vajrayana in China," *History of Religions* 29 (November 1989), especially 111–12, n. 69, where he provides several pertinent sources on such "astrological" texts and practices in Hindu and Islamic as well as Chinese traditions.

46. See Jeffery Meyer, "*Feng-shui* of the Chinese City," *History of Religions* 18 (November 1978): 139–50, which emphasizes especially the *Lo-ching chieh* in the discussion of *feng shui* handbooks. Also see Else Glahn, "Unfolding the Chinese Building Standards: Research on the *Yingzao fashi*," in Nancy Shatzman Steinhardt et al., *Chinese Traditional Architecture* (New York: China Institute in America, Chinese House Gallery, 1984), 47–58; and Wu, *Chinese and Indian Architecture,* 36–44.

47. At that point, then, the convention priority (I-B) is especially closely aligned to what I will describe as the propitiation priority (III-C).

48. The merger of these two traditions is noted in Marwyn S. Samuels and Carmencita Samuels, "Beijing and the Power of Place in Modern China," in *The Power of Place,* ed. John A. Agnew and James S. Duncan (Boston: Unwin Hyman, 1989), 204.

49. See ibid. and Wheatley, *Pivot of the Four Quarters.* Meyer ("*Feng-shui* of the Chinese City," 150) argues that, while the prescriptions in *feng shui* texts operate at the scales of graves, houses, and small structures, at the scale of whole cities the complexity escalates wildly, so that "the scope for personal eccentricities and varia-

tion is vast, [thus, in the end] the *feng-shui* of the city is unpredictable."

50. Wu, *Chinese and Indian Architecture,* 114, n. 2.

51. Paul Oliver describes the reliance on rules of the *shastras*, or Hindu manuals, in the preparation of the site of a contemporary Indian house, and then notes the seemingly obvious parallels in Chinese *feng shui* and Japanese *hogaku* in *Dwellings: The House across the World* (Austin: University of Texas Press, 1987), 167–69. Oliver's introduction in *Shelter, Sign, and Symbol,* ed. Oliver, 15, includes a brief discussion of Chinese planning and the *K'ao-kung chi* (Code book of works) in the *Li chi* (Book of rites), which expounds design canons that apply to both town and temple organization. Andreas Volwahsen discusses the application of traditional building principles at the levels of house, village, and city in *Living Architecture: Indian,* trans. Ann E. Keep (New York: Grosset and Dunlop, 1969), chapter 2.

52. Ramacandra Kaulacara, *Śilpa Prakāśa: Medieval Orissan Sanskrit Text on Temple Architecture,* trans. and annotated Alice Boner and Sadasiva Rath Sarma (Leiden: E. J. Brill, 1966), 83. In her introduction to this manual, Boner contends that it was apparently transcribed some time in the eighteenth century. (An *angula* is a unit of measure equal to one finger's breadth or eight barley corns.) K. V. Soundara Rajan (*An Invitation to Indian Architecture* [New Delhi: Arnold-Heinemann, 1984], 19–20, 32) cites and comments on the intense detail of similar *Shilpa Shastra* passages; and Clothey, *Rhythm and Intent,* 183–84, likewise discusses the *Shilpa Shastra* in helpful ways.

53. See Burckhardt, *Sacred Art in East and West,* 17–43. The logic of mandalas, particularly as applied to the architecture of Borobudur in Java, will be discussed more fully in chapter 22, on the contemplation priority (III-B).

54. See Michael W. Meister, "Measurement and Proportion in Hindu Temple Architecture," *Interdisciplinary Science Reviews* 10 (September 1985): 248–58.

55. Stella Kramrisch, *The Hindu Temple,* 2 vols. (1946; reprint, Delhi: Motilal Banarsidass, 1976), 1:6.

56. Ibid., preface; quoted by Sankar Prosad, *Hindu Religious Art and Architecture* (Delhi: D. K. Publications, 1982), 95.

57. Mathuram Bhoothalingam, *Movement in Stone: A Study of Some Chola Temples* (New Delhi: Soumani Publications, 1969), 14.

58. Coomaraswamy, *The Transformation of Nature in Art,* 114.

59. Michell, *The Hindu Temple,* 78.

60. Ibid.

61. Kramrisch, *The Hindu Temple,* 1:37, nn. 58, 228; quoted by Meister, "Measurement and Proportion in Hindu Temple Architecture," 249.

62. Kramrisch, *The Hindu Temple,* 1:37.

63. Meister, "Measurement and Proportion in Hindu Temple Architecture," 249–51.

64. This is a particularly clear instance in which to note that both the design and experience of conventionalized architecture are, in an important sense, occa-

sions of comparison insofar as faithful adherence to the mandala patterns would engender a sensation of *similarity,* while departure would enable a productive sensation of *difference.*

65. Regarding abstract proportionality in Mesoamerican architecture, after searching the pre-Columbian data explicitly in search of "sacred ratios" and measuring schemes that parallel those of the Chinese geomantic tradition of *feng shui,* Carlson ("A Geomantic Model for the Interpretation of Mesoamerican Sites," 202) is forced to conclude that "the presence of these factors in Mesoamerica is, at best, speculative." He does nevertheless anticipate, not inappropriately, that, "since the Classic Maya had a penchant for numerical complexity coupled with arithmetic exactitude, we may yet discover complex geometrical and mathematical relationships in their site plans and architecture" (202). Promising progress along those lines comes in Anthony F. Aveni and Horst Hartung, "Precision in the Layout of Maya Architecture" in *Ethnoastronomy and Archaeoastronomy in the American Tropics,* ed. Anthony F. Aveni and Gary Urton (New York: New York Academy of Sciences, 1982), 71–77, where they discuss a number of arcane and precise pre-Columbian systems of "radians," "multiple orthogonal axes," and "conceptual lines" that intersect in right angles, form isosceles triangles, and converge on noteworthy points. It is somewhat ironic, morphologically speaking, that Aveni and Hartung, pathfinders in the discernment of astronomical orientations in Mesoamerican buildings (that is, astronomy, priority I-C), have, in the case of the Nunnery Complex at Uxmal, provided a stellar example that, while not entirely without celestial references, is preeminently an inward-looking exercise in orientation with respect to abstract principles of geometry (that is, an exercise of the convention priority, I-B). For similar sorts of conclusions at other sites, see Hartung, "Alignments in Architecture and Sculpture of Maya Centers, 223–40.

66. This version of the convention priority, then, again broaches on the matter of ritual-architectural commemoration of sacred history (priority II-B).

67. Pardeep Singh Arshi, *Sikh Architecture in Punjab* (New Delhi: Intellectual Publishing House, 1986), 142.

68. Alberti, *The Ten Books of Architecture,* is filled with explicit appeals to Vitruvius and "the Ancients." Regarding more current instances of architectural imitation, Tom Wolfe, for instance, comments on Yale University's deliberate reiteration of the prestigious architectures of Oxford and Cambridge in *From Bauhaus to Our House* (New York: Pocket Books, 1981), 56.

69. Pre-Columbian art historians, most notably George Kubler, have been tireless in documenting and debating who copied whom, though much less assiduous in discerning the indigenous logic of such imitation (a matter to which I will return momentarily). Regarding the heuristic merits and limitations of such efforts, see the section "Organization by Tradition: Reuniting Architectural Parents and Offspring," in chapter 10 of volume 1. Also see Herbert J. Spinden, *A Study of Maya Art: Its Subject Matter and Historical Development* (1913; reprint, New York: Dover

Publications, 1975), 175, for an intriguing distinction between "the archaistic" and "the truly archaic" in Maya art.

70. See Aveni, *Skywatchers of Ancient Mexico,* 240–41.

71. E. Wyllys Andrews, "Dzibilchaltún," in *Supplement to Handbook of Middle American Indians,* vol. 1 (Austin: University of Texas Press, 1981), 330–31, discusses the imitation of the Teotihuacan alignment at Dzibilchaltún in northern Yucatan.

72. Moreover, it is noteworthy that sometimes old Mesoamerican architectural elements were retrieved and borrowed with little or no understanding of their original usages; for example, J. Eric S. Thompson (*Maya Archaeologist* [Norman: University of Oklahoma Press, 1963], 260) describes how, in the Río Bec area, the reverence for antique hieroglyphic stelae was so uninformed that most of the old blocks of inscriptions were re-erected upside down and in ridiculous combinations.

73. On the Aztecs' astute expropriation of Toltec artistic and religious traditions, see Carrasco, *Quetzalcoatl and the Irony of Empire,* especially chapter 3.

74. Regarding the ritual-architectural fabrication of a "continuity of tradition," see volume 1, chapter 5, "Allurement and Coercion: The Front Half of the Ritual-Architectural Situation."

75. I explore at some length the prospect of a similar, though more widely eclectic, program of ritual-architectural allurement at the pre-Hispanic capital of Chichén Itzá, in Jones, *Twin City Tales;* see especially pp. 377–89.

76. Meister ("Measurement and Proportion in Hindu Temple Architecture") particularly emphasizes the increasing secrecy over time associated with the knowledge of ritual grids and the extreme care with which a Hindu architect would select only a few disciples who would be taught the principles behind the architecture they had created.

77. In regard to Alberti's ideas about the transformative potential of art and architecture, see David Freedberg, *The Power of Images: Studies in the History and Theory of Response* (Chicago: University of Chicago Press, 1989), 44–47.

78. Umberto Eco, *The Aesthetics of Thomas Aquinas,* trans. Hugh Bredin (Cambridge, Mass.: Harvard University Press, 1988), 85.

79. As noted earlier, on the continuity and discontinuity between Alberti and Le Corbusier, see Arnheim, "A Review of Proportion," in his *Toward a Psychology of Art,* 102–11.

80. See, respectively, Richter, *Art and Human Consciousness,* 53; and Davies, *Temples, Churches, and Mosques,* 10.

81. Ikhwān al-Ṣafā'; quoted in Seyyed Hossein Nasr, *Science and Civilization in Islam* (Cambridge, Mass.: Harvard University Press, 1968), 157, and in Ardalan and Bakhtiar, *The Sense of Unity,* 27.

82. See Ardalan and Bakhtiar, *The Sense of Unity,* 5, 21.

83. See Michell, *The Hindu Temple,* 73.

84. Ibid.

85. Meister ("Measurement and Proportion in Hindu Temple Architecture," 249, 256) also twice makes the intriguing though somewhat puzzling claim that the use of grids helped to "guard" the Hindu temple.

86. See Kenna, "Icons in Theory and Practice."

87. Regarding explicit calls for, and demonstrations of, greater attentiveness to "the politics of sacred space," see, for example, both the editors' introductions and numerous of the subsequent essays in *Sacred Places and Profane Spaces,* ed. Scott and Simpson-Housley, and *American Sacred Space,* ed. Chidester and Linenthal.

88. In volume 1, see chapter 12, "Multifarious Revalorization: The Composition of Ritual-Architectural Reception Histories."

89. In chapter 12, see especially the section "The Selectivity of Reception Histories: Protocols of Architectural Apprehension."

90. See ibid. for elaboration on that line of argumentation.

Sixteen | Astronomy

1. Stanley Looking Horse; quoted by Ronald Goodman, *Lakota Star Knowledge: Studies in Lakota Stellar Theology* (Rosebud, S.D.: Sinte Gleska College, 1990), 17. Goodman cites Stanley Looking Horse as one of the elders he had interviewed in the eight years previous to the publication of *Lakota Star Knowledge.*

2. Peter C. Chemery, "Sky: Myths and Symbolism," *Encyclopedia of Religion,* ed. Eliade, 13:346.

3. Anthony F. Aveni, "Introduction: Whither Archaeoastronomy?" in *World Archaeoastronomy,* ed. Anthony F. Aveni (Cambridge: Cambridge University Press, 1989), 10.

4. Lawrence E. Sullivan, in "Astral Myths Rise Again: Interpreting Religious Astronomy," *Criterion* 22 (winter 1983): 12–13, addresses the significance of Charles François Dupuis, *Origine de tous les cultes* (originally 1798), and the Panbabylonianists in the history of the study of the relationship between astronomy and religion. F. Max Müller, foremost spokesman for the school of "nature mythology," connected the origin of religion with the human experience of the sun (particularly sunrises) and the sky, because those phenomena seemed to best express the infinite; see F. Max Müller, *Nature Religion* (London: Longmans, Green, 1889). Raffaele Pettazzoni, *The All-Knowing God: Researches into Early Religion and Culture,* trans. H. J. Rose (London: Methuen and Co., 1956); and idem, "The Supreme Being: Phenomenological Structure and Historical Development," in *The History of Religions: Essays in Methodology,* ed. Mircea Eliade and Joseph M. Kitagawa (Chicago: University of Chicago Press, 1959), 59–66. Pettazzoni emphasizes the essentially ambivalent structure of all-seeing, celestial supreme beings of the sky. Similarly foundational studies include E. O. James, *The Worship of the Sky-God: A Comparative Study in Semitic and Indo-European Religion* (London: University of London, Athlone Press, 1963); W. Brede Kristensen, "The Worship of Sky and Celestial

Gods," chapter 3 in his *The Meaning of Religion;* and Mircea Eliade, "The Sky and Sky Gods," chapter 2 in his *Patterns in Comparative Religion.* In regard to these (and other) seminal theories of celestial and supreme beings, also see Lawrence E. Sullivan, "Supreme Beings," *Encyclopedia of Religion,* ed. Eliade, 14:166–81.

5. Sullivan, "Astral Myths Rise Again," 13. The archaeoastronomical literature is vast and very rapidly growing. Among particularly important works, see *Archaeoastronomy in the New World,* ed. Anthony F. Aveni (Cambridge: Cambridge University Press, 1982); *Archaeoastronomy in the Old World,* ed. D. C. Heggie (Cambridge: Cambridge University Press, 1982); and *World Archaeoastronomy,* ed. Aveni. For background, also see John F. Michell, *A Little History of Astro-Archaeology: Stages in the Transformation of a Heresy* (London: Thames and Hudson, 1977, 1989). C. L. N. Ruggles (*Megalithic Astronomy: A New Archaeological and Statistical Study of 300 Western Scottish Sites,* B.A.R. British Series, 123 [Oxford: British Archaeological Reports, 1984], 13) is another (like Sullivan) to use the term "explosion" to describe the increase in ethnoastronomical interest and knowledge in the 1970s and early 1980s.

6. Archaeoastronomy, now the most vogue and encompassing of the terms, is the interdisciplinary study of ancient peoples' view of the cosmos as gleaned from both the written and unwritten record; ethnoastronomy studies the astronomic understandings of contemporary peoples; and astroarchaeology, a less current term (though one that may actually be more directly relevant to the present discussion) is defined by Aveni (*Skywatchers of Ancient Mexico,* 4) as "the study of the astronomical principles employed in ancient works of architecture and the elaboration of a methodology for the retrieval and quantitative analysis of astronomical alignment data."

7. I borrow this subtitle from Aubrey Burl, "Science or Symbolism: Problems of Archaeo-astronomy," *Antiquity* 54 (November 1980): 191–200.

8. Ruggles (*Megalithic Astronomy,* 14) notes: "Indeed, albeit perhaps for wrong motives, it was upon the design of British megalithic monuments that archaeoastronomical investigations concentrated during the early emergence of the subject."

9. I borrow the term the "numerate disciplines" from Ruggles (ibid., 14–15), who also comments on the "continuing lack of communication (and at times much contention)" between these two sets of researchers.

10. Peter Lancaster Brown devotes seven chapters of *Megaliths, Myths, and Men: An Introduction to Astro-Archaeology* (New York: Taplinger Publishing Company, 1976) to reconstructing the Stonehenge debate in great detail. Benjamin C. Ray provides the pertinent older bibliographic information on Stonehenge before presenting his own "new theory" in "Stonehenge: A New Theory," *History of Religions* 26 (February 1987): 225–7.

11. Though this is not the place to inventory the vast literature on Stonehenge, see Norman Lockyer, *Stonehenge and Other British Stone Monuments Astronomically Considered,* 2d ed. (London: Macmillan, 1909); A. Thom and A. S. Thom, "The

Astronomical Foresights Used by Megalithic Man," *Archaeoastronomy* 2 (1980): 90–94; A. Thom, A. S. Thom, and H. A. W. Burl, *Megalithic Rings: Plans and Data for 229 Monuments in Britain,* B.A.R. British Series, 81 (Oxford: British Archaeological Reports, 1980); and Gerald S. Hawkins and John B. White, *Stonehenge Decoded* (Garden City, N.Y.: Doubleday, 1965).

12. See R. J. C. Atkinson, *Stonehenge,* rev. ed. (Harmondsworth: Penguin Books, 1979); Glyn E. Daniel, *The Megalithic Builders of Western Europe* (New York: Praeger, 1958); Jacquetta Hopkins Hawkes, *History in Earth and Stone: Prehistoric and Roman Monuments in England and Wales* (Cambridge, Mass.: Harvard University Press, 1952).

13. Commenting on the then-new interpretations of the monument as an observatory, Jacquetta Hawkes ("God in the Machine," Antiquity 16 [September 1967]: 174) observes that "Every age has the Stonehenge it deserves—or desires." Also see Aveni, "Introduction: Whither Archaeoastronomy?" and C. L. N. Ruggles, "Recent Developments in Megalithic Astronomy," both in *World Archaeoastronomy,* ed. Aveni. Note additionally in this respect, though I will not pursue it here, that the many interpretive positions in the long Stonehenge debate could be organized, to considerable advantage I think, according to the respective categories in this morphology.

14. In volume 1, see chapter 12, especially the section "The Selectivity of Reception Histories: Protocols of Architectural Apprehension."

15. Sullivan ("Astral Myths Rise Again," 14–15) discusses the inappropriateness of the typical dichotomy between megaliths as either "astronomical observatories" (i.e., "scientific") or "ceremonial centers" (i.e., "religious").

16. Regarding the "layering" of hermeneutical situations in indigenous and academic apprehensions of architecture, see the final section of chapter 3 in volume 1.

17. Anthony F. Aveni, *Conversing with the Planets: How Science and Myth Invented the Cosmos* (New York: Times Books, 1992).

18. The general issue of correction, adjustment, and manipulation of the Maya calendar has been discussed at great length. See, for instance, Spinden, *A Study of Maya Art,* 111, 140, and 143; J. Eric S. Thompson, *The Rise and Fall of Maya Civilization* (Norman: University of Oklahoma Press), 177–78; and Michael D. Coe, *The Maya,* 3d ed. (London: Thames and Hudson, 1984), 158–59. More recently (and more interestingly) Aveni, in *Skywatchers of Ancient Mexico,* 187, 190, among other places, has discussed the willful distortion of empirical astronomical data by the ancient Mesoamericans.

19. See Tozzer, *Chichén Itzá and Its Cenote of Sacrifice,* 36, 256, where he recounts Morley's explanation of the "curious coincidence" by which the katun date of 8 Ahau in the Maya calendar is repeatedly the recorded date for important events in Yucatan history; Tozzer himself contributes several more examples of Toltecs, Itzás, and Aztecs engaging in similar sorts of willful distortion.

20. Linda Schele, "Sacred Site and World-View at Palenque," in *Mesoamerican*

Sites and World-Views, ed. Elizabeth P. Benson (Washington, D.C.: Dumbarton Oaks, 1981), 104.

21. Broda, "Astronomy, *Cosmovision,* and Ideology in Pre-Hispanic Mesoamerica," 100.

22. Ruggles (*Megalithic Astronomy,* 13) also warns of the specially daunting pitfalls of ethnocentrism with respect to ethno- and archaeoastronomy (particularly in archaeological contexts) and, consequently, the necessity of studying astronomical practices, to the extent possible, in their respective social contexts. Aveni's remarks in his introduction to *World Archaeoastronomy,* ed. Aveni, 10 (quoted at the onset to this chapter), about the possibility that "ancient" and "scientific" perspectives on astronomy are "absolutely different" are likewise relevant in this regard. While I applaud this attentiveness to the particularity of social context, I must nonetheless (as consistent with the position outlined in volume 1, especially chapter 1, "Lineages and Legacies: The Universality of Hermeneutical Reflection") offer the following caveat: I would continue to maintain that an even more serious problem than that of Western scholars overriding their ethnocentrism to appreciate how different ancients' interpretive understandings of the sky may be from their own (which is the problem accentuated, for instance, by Schele, Broda, Ruggles, and Aveni) is the more explicitly hermeneutical problem of overriding lingering positivistic tendencies in order to appreciate how different Western interpretive understandings are from the way that Western scholars continue to imagine that they are. As I've maintained, appreciating the universal aspect of hermeneutics in that sense will also lead us to an appreciation of the particularity of sociohistorical contexts.

23. There are, for example, innumerable individual pre-Columbian Mesoamerican structures that served, at least in part, as observatories for collecting predictive astronomical data, the most renowned being the Caracol at Chichén Itzá; see Anthony F. Aveni, Horst Hartung, and Sharon L. Gibbs, "The Caracol Tower at Chichén Itzá: An Ancient Astronomical Observatory?" *Science* 188 (June 1975): 977–85. Aveni (*Skywatchers of Ancient Mexico,* 165) has shown how, at Copán and Palenque, whole cities acted as superlunary registers of celestial data. For an interesting (and eventful) discussion of an ancient Chinese observatory, see Nancy Shatzman Steinhardt, "The Han Ritual Hall," in *Chinese Traditional Architecture,* ed. Steinhardt et al., 73–76.

24. Clemency C. Coggins, for instance, considers that the famous Structure E-VII sub at Uaxactún, the earliest known Maya pyramid, which is routinely designated as an "observatory," was not only constructed to observe celestial cycles; it also "symbolized the completion" of those cycles and, moreover, was designed as the backdrop for a specific predictive ritual "associated with the casting of seed in divination and with auguries of the named Katun"; Clemency C. Coggins, "The Shape of Time: Some Political Implications of a Four-Part Figure," *American Antiquity* 45 (October 1980): 731–32. Coggins's discussion of this structure is parti-

cularly apt because she makes her case by contrasting the primary usage of E-VII sub as a "calendrical ritual" (i.e., homology, priority I-A) and E-VII sub as a "locus of ancestor veneration ritual" (i.e., commemoration of the dead, priority II-D) with what she considers to be its primary significance as astroarchitecture with a divinatory intention (i.e., astronomy, priority I-C).

25. Recall that the *ceque* system was a featured example of the homology priority (I-A) in chapter 14; and see R. T. Zuidema, "Inca Observations of the Solar and Lunar Passages through Zenith and Anti-Zenith at Cuzco," in *Archaeoastronomy in the Americas,* ed. Ray A. Williamson (Los Altos, Calif.: Ballena Press; College Park, Md.: Center for Archaeoastronomy, 1981), 319–42. Also demonstrating astronomy's role in a more widely homologized conception both of architecture and ritual, Herman W. Conrad ("Pilgrimage as Cyclical Process," in *Pilgrimage in Latin America,* ed. Crumrine and Morinis, 123–38) provides compelling evidence that the movements of the sun, moon, and stars were the inspiration for Maya pilgrimage so that, instead of journeying along direct routes, pilgrims travel "cyclically," thus replicating "the heavenly pilgrimage of astral bodies."

26. Wu (*Chinese and Indian Architecture,* 37), however, expresses doubt that such ideas were ever in the minds of the designers. Among other astro-homology examples, E. O. James (*From Cave to Cathedral: Temples and Shrines of Prehistoric, Classical, and Early Christian Times* [New York: Frederick A. Praeger, 1965], 138) explains that the seven stages of the tower of the temple of Marduk at Babylon, called *Etemenanki,* or "the house of the foundation of heaven and earth," apparently corresponded to the seven principal celestial bodies (the sun, the moon, and five planets known to the Babylonians), thus giving the ziggurat "a cosmic connotation" insofar as it was an earthly reproduction of the celestial abode of the gods. Ernest H. Short (*A History of Religious Architecture,* 3d rev. ed. [London: Eyre and Spottiswoode, 1951], 24) makes the similar suggestion that in the case of the Assyrian palace at Khorsabad, built by King Sargon (722–705 B.C.E.), "there seem to have been seven stages, dedicated respectively to the sun, the moon, and the five planets known to the Babylonians."

27. See Bassie-Sweet, *At the Edge of the World: Caves and Late Classic Maya World View,* 46.

28. It is notable that Herbert Spinden (*Ancient Civilizations of Mexico and Central America* [New York: American Museum of Natural History, 1917], 144) already implied a distinction in ancient Mesoamerican astronomy between the personification of celestial bodies and the consideration of abstract celestial rhythms and cycles.

29. See Kenneth Frampton, "Labor, Work and Architecture," in *Meaning in Architecture,* ed. Jencks and Baird, 156. Note also that this Roman design solution actually relies on astronomy to exercise what I will describe in chapter 24 as the sanctuary priority (III-D).

30. On the orientation of Christian churches, particularly in England, see Peter

Hammond, *Liturgy and Architecture* (London: Barrie and Rockliff, 1960), 3–4. Note also the morphological parallel between this Christian astro-conventional practice and the ancient Mesoamerican practice of imitating prestigious, though nonfunctional astronomical alignments (discussed in chapter 15).

31. Note also that perhaps an even more elemental type of astro-architecture comes in those structures that house meteorites, or "stones from heaven," such as the modest constructions in which the Buriats of Siberia place the "rain stones" to which they offer propitiatory sacrifices in times of drought or, much more famously, the Ka'bah at Mecca. On the Ka'bah's possible involvement in more subtle astronomical associations, see David A. King, "Astronomical Alignments in Medieval Islamic Religious Architecture," in *Ethnoastronomy and Archaeoastronomy in the American Tropics,* ed. Aveni and Urton, 303–12.

32. Regarding the Incas' "idolatrous" worship of the statue of the sun, see the sixteenth-century account of Father Bernabé Cobo, *Inca Religion and Customs,* chapter 5. Also see Zuidema, "Inca Observations of the Solar and Lunar Passages," 319–42.

33. Jean Rhys Bram, "Sun," *Encyclopedia of Religion,* ed. Eliade, 14:138, suggests that, despite this spectacular monument at Rhodes, there was apparently little direct worship of the sun in ancient Greece.

34. Though improbable, the suggestion has been made that the Nazca lines, large abstract shapes and animal figures carved into the surface of the desert in Peru, depict earthly representations of celestial gods. For a very wide spectrum of views on the indigenous intentions behind the Nazca lines, begin with *The Lines of Nazca,* ed. Anthony F. Aveni (Philadelphia: American Philosophical Society, 1990).

35. The supposed astronomical significance of the Serpent Mound is controversial. See Robert Fletcher and Terry Cameron, "Serpent Mound: A New Look at an Old Snake in the Grass," *Ohio Archaeologist* 38, no. 1 (winter 1988); and William F. Romain, "Symbolic Associations at the Serpent Mound," *Ohio Archaeologist* 41, no. 3 (summer 1991).

36. Gary Urton, in "Ethnoastronomy," *Encyclopedia of Religion,* ed. Eliade, 5:177–82, provides a number of examples of personified and mythologized celestial features among South American tribes.

37. See Aubrey Burl, *Prehistoric Astronomy and Ritual* (Aylesbury: Shire Publications, 1983), chapters 4–5.

38. Ray ("Stonehenge: A New Theory," 277) notes that as early as the twelfth century Geoffrey of Monmouth had interpreted Stonehenge as a memorial to the dead.

39. The interpretation of Stonehenge offered by Aubrey Burl, *Rites of the Gods* (London: J. M. Dent and Sons, 1981), which accentuates the veneration of revered ancestors, will be addressed again more thoroughly in chapter 20, where I concentrate on the commemoration of the dead (priority II-D).

40. See Bram, "Sun," 134–43.

41. See Steinhardt, "The Han Ritual Hall," in *Chinese Traditional Architecture,* ed. Steinhardt, 73–76.

42. To give an example of the sometimes extreme selectivity of astroarchitectural concerns: the Japanese, despite their proximity to the rich astrological traditions of China and Korea (and despite Shinto's preoccupations with the sun), somewhat surprisingly—at least in the assessment found in Arata Isozaki, "Floors and Internal Spaces in Japanese Vernacular Architecture," *Res: Anthropology and Aesthetics* 11 (spring 1986): 55—"had little interest in the stars; instead they developed a strong awareness of the east-west axis based on the movement of the sun that largely determined the rhythm of their lives." Isozaki connects the Japanese disinterest in the stars with an ancient tendency to close themselves up in dwellings when night came.

43. See John A. Eddy, "Medicine Wheels and Plains Indian Astronomy," in *Native American Astronomy,* ed. Aveni, 147–70.

44. See Brown, *Megaliths, Myths, and Men,* 11.

45. Eliade, *A History of Religious Ideas,* 1:37.

46. Ruggles, *Megalithic Astronomy,* 13. I do not mean to imply that Ruggles adheres to any simple hypothesis concerning the historical connections between parallel developments in agriculture and astronomy. He is, in fact, cautious to avoid such generalizations.

47. I borrow the phrase "conceptualization of duration" from ibid.

48. The divinatory presage of an eclipse or the helical rising of Venus, for example, implies a kind of mental mastery over the forces of nature, a higher order of orientation, and even a previously unacknowledged confidence (or perhaps arrogance) in one's autonomy and security as a human being. With respect to Greek sacred architecture, Scully (*The Earth, the Temple, and the Gods,* 198–210) alludes to something like this distinction between harmony with nature and control over nature when he contends that, where the classical Greek temple incorporated and merged with the landscape, the relationship of the postclassical temple to the landscape was one of dominance and control.

49. Though his remarks have no explicit connection either with architecture or astronomy, I am informed here by Charles Long's contention in *Alpha: The Myths of Creation,* 17, that "human life represents a particular mode of being—a mode of being which is continuous with nature on one level and discontinuous on another level."

50. Van der Leeuw (*Sacred and Profane Beauty,* 24–25) develops the distinction between "passive harmony" and "active control" in connection with two types of sacred dance and makes no direct reference to its applicability with respect to architecture.

51. *Li chi,* quoted by Nancy Shatzman Steinhardt, "Altar to Heaven Complex," in *Chinese Traditional Architecture,* ed. Steinhardt, 140.

52. Ruggles (*Megalithic Astronomy,* 14) comments on the fortuitous ethno-

historical and ethnographic evidences that are available for Mesoamerican archaeoastronomical research but absent in British work. Aveni, in his introduction to *World Archaeoastronomy,* ed. Aveni, 3–12, likewise comments on the basic differences between the studies of Old and New World archaeoastronomy.

53. On the exceedingly long, rich, and continuing tradition of astro-archaeological study in Mesoamerica, see Jones, *Twin City Tales,* 226–28.

54. Regarding ancient Mesoamericans' supposed fatalistic and predictive obsessions, see the representative assessment of Muriel Porter Weaver, *The Aztecs, Maya, and Their Predecessors: Archaeology of Mesoamerica* (New York: Seminar Press, 1972), 93.

55. Schele, "Sacred Site and World-View at Palenque," 105.

56. See Marion Hatch, "An Hypothesis on Olmec Astronomy with Special Reference to the La Venta Site," in *Papers on Olmec and Maya Archaeology,* Contributions of the University of California Archaeological Research Facility, 13 (Berkeley: University of California, Department of Anthropology, 1971).

57. Coggins ("Shape of Time," 735) reflects on the ritual integration of rainy skies, Tlaloc, and the solar year at Teotihuacan.

58. Regarding two circumstances in which "coincidences" of multiple sky phenomena may have been exploited, see, first, remarks on the biannual occurrence of the helical rising of the Pleiades and the zenith passage of the sun at Teotihuacan, discussed by Anthony Aveni, "Concepts of Positional Astronomy Employed in Ancient Mesoamerican Architecture," in*Native American Astronomy,* ed. Aveni, 3–19; and by John B. Carlson, "The Case for Geomagnetic Alignments of Precolumbian Mesoamerican Sites—The Maya," *Katunob: A Newsletter-Bulletin on Mesoamerican Anthropology* 10 (June 1977): 78–79. And second, for remarks on a scenario in which the classic Maya seized upon the simultaneous inferior conjunction of Venus and a solar zenith passage as the day for an extravagant heir designation ceremony that involved a ritual battle and the final celebration of the victors, see Carlson, "Ancient Skies," 27–28.

59. It is important to note that the apprehension of some celestial phenomena, such as comets and eclipses, requires less ritual-architectural "enhancement" than others. I am specially concerned, however, with those phenomena—helical risings and solstice and equinox passages—that would go entirely unnoticed without the choreography of a special view.

60. For fuller interpretation and bibliography relative to the "serpent of light" phenomenon at Chichén Itzá, see Jones, *Twin City Tales,* 381–83. Jean-Jacques Rivard provides an interesting Eliadean interpretation of the Castillo equinox phenomenon in "A Hierophany at Chichén Itzá," in *Miscellaneous Series,* no. 26 (Greeley: University of Northern Colorado, 1971). And Clemency C. Coggins ("A New Sun at Chichén Itzá," in *World Archaeoastronomy,* ed. Aveni, 260–75) provides a fresh interpretation of the "serpent of light" phenomenon as an element in a New Fire ceremony celebrated at Chichén Itzá.

61. The "Copán Temple 22-Sun-Venus-maize-kingship event," as I've chosen to call it, is a particularly fortuitous example because the same circumstance has been subject to sophisticated archaeoastronomical scrutiny by Anthony Aveni, "The Real Venus-Kukulcan in the Maya. Inscriptions and Alignments" (revised version of paper presented at the Sixth Mesa Redonda de Palenque, Mexico, June 1986); and to ethnohistorical, ritual interpretation by Mary Ellen Miller, "The Meaning and Function of the Main Acropolis, Copán," in *The Southeast Classic Maya Zone: A Symposium at Dumbarton Oaks, 6–7 October 1984,* ed. Elizabeth Hill Boone and Gordon R. Willey (Washington, D.C.: Dumbarton Oaks Research Library and Collection, 1988). Also see Michael P. Closs, Anthony F. Aveni, and Bruce Crowley, "The Planet Venus and Temple 22 at Copán," *Indiana* 9 (1984): 221–47.

62. Hartung ("Alignments in Architecture and Sculpture of Maya Centers," 237) interprets the orientation of Copán in terms of a "starting point" on the stairway of Temple 11, from which spreads a system of cardinal lines, right angles, and isosceles triangles. (In that case, Copán's orientational strategy is [as noted above in chapter 15] morphologically similar to the one that Doxiadis, in *Architectural Space in Ancient Greece,* 16–23, attributes to ancient Greek cities.) Alternatively, Anthony F. Aveni and Horst Hartung, in *Maya City Planning and the Calendar* (Philadelphia: American Philosophical Society, 1986), 15, offer a different explanation of Copán's orientation based on three general zones, each with its own alignment.

63. Aveni ("The Real Venus-Kukulcán," 28) compares the "outliers" located around the periphery of Copán to the *huacas* of Cuzco's *ceque* system and conjectures that those "outliers" could have functioned as "spatial/territorial boundary markers" or "calendrical markers."

64. Ibid., 21–28. My brief summary does not do justice to Aveni's explanation of the relation between the window in Temple 22 and Venus; his argument is bolstered by the abundant Venus iconography on Temple 22.

65. I am following the summary of Mary Miller's work on Copán presented by Aveni in ibid., 29–30.

66. Ruggles, *Megalithic Astronomy,* 13.

Part Two | Architecture as Commemoration

1. J. B. Jackson, *The Necessity for Ruins, and Other Topics* (Amherst: University of Massachusetts Press, 1980), 91. J. G. Davies ("Architecture," *Encyclopedia of Religion,* ed. Eliade, 1:383) notes that "the two terms [monument and memorial] are synonymous—the one from *moneo,* 'to remind,' and the other from *memor,* 'to remember.'"

2. Moholy-Nagy, *Native Genius in Anonymous Architecture in North America,* 11.

3. Henri Lefebvre, *The Production of Space,* trans. Donald Nicholson-Smith (Oxford and Cambridge, Mass.: Basil Blackwell, 1991), 143.

4. Where chapter 5 (volume 1), "Allurement and Coercion: The Front Half of the Ritual-Architectural Situation," provided the basis for this volume's three chapters on architecture as orientation, it is chapter 6, "Transformation and Productivity: The Back Half of the Ritual-Architectural Situation," that provides the basis for these four chapters on architecture as commemoration.

5. See Hans-Georg Gadamer, *Truth and Method* (New York: Crossroad, 1984), 138.

6. Marilyn R. Waldman's astute observations regarding "comparison as a social act" were discussed in chapter 11 of volume 1, particularly in the section entitled "The Indigenous Experience of Architecture as a Comparative Act."

7. See Gadamer, *Truth and Method,* 139–40.

8. Jackson, *The Necessity for Ruins,* 91. Jackson, a student of "the history of American monumental art," contrasts "traditional monuments," which remind us of our obligations, and "modern or vernacular monuments," which simply try "to explain" (91–93).

9. Ibid., 91.

10. Ibid., 91–92.

11. In volume 1, see chapter 8, "Architecture as 'Mute Text'? Literary and Alternative Vehicles of Intelligibility."

12. For a discussion of the architecture of Santini Aichel, see Alastair Laing, "Bohemia and Franconia," in *Baroque and Rococo,* ed. Blunt, 265–67.

13. Ibid.

14. Soundara Rajan (*Invitation to Indian Architecture,* 41) describes several instances, beginning in the twelfth century, of chariot-type *mandapa*s in India.

15. See Wu, *Chinese and Indian Architecture,* 22.

16. See *Memorial Stones: A Study of Their Origin, Significance, and Variety,* ed. S. Settar and Gunther D. Sontheimer (Dharwad: Institute of Indian Art History, Karnatak University, 1982).

17. See Edward T. Linenthal, *Sacred Ground: Americans and Their Battlefields,* 2d ed. (Urbana: University of Illinois Press. 1993).

18. Donald Robertson (*Pre-Columbian Architecture* [New York: George Braziller, 1963], 11) says of Maya stelae: "so directly do they adhere to their architectural role that they were, in the strict sense of the phrase, sculptural architecture rather than mere sculptural monuments."

19. Wolfe (*From Bauhaus to Our House,* 18) discusses the pedagogic design of the House of Successions. Other good examples of the contemporary architectural commemoration of ideology in the same book are Geritt Rietveld's Schroder House, which commemorates the principle of "expressed structure"; the campus of the Illinois Institute of Technology, which commemorates the philosophy of Mies van der Rohe; and the Yale box and Barcelona chair, which were the icons of design for "the common man." Ibid., 25–27, 42, 53–55.

20. Regarding the "simulated [Maya] temples" of the Río Bec and Chenes areas

of Yucatan, see H. E. D. Pollock, "Architecture of the Maya Lowlands," in *Archaeology of Southern Mesoamerica*, ed. Gordon R. Willey, vols. 2–3, *Handbook of Middle American Indians* (Austin: University of Texas Press, 1965), 2:427–28; or Kubler, "The Design of Space in Maya Architecture," 515. Kubler stresses particularly the priority of exterior volumes over interior spaces that is characteristic of much of Mesoamerican architecture; it is, in his phrasing, not "elaborate shelter" but "monumental form . . . [that] commemorates a valuable experience by distinguishing one space from others in an ample and durable edifice."

21. Stanley Abercrombie, *Architecture as Art: An Aesthetic Analysis* (New York: Van Nostrand Reinhold, 1984), 125–29, includes this and a number of other instances of blatantly informational architecture. Harbison, *The Built, the Unbuilt, and the Unbuildable,* 172–73, includes comments on similar sorts of examples, like Jean-Jacques Lequeu's stable that has the form of a giant cow.

22. See John W. Dixon, Jr., "The Christology of Michelangelo: The Sistine Chapel," *Journal of the American Academy of Religion* 55 (fall 1987): 503–33. For other ways in which architecture can reflect and explore exceedingly subtle Christian theological messages, see Peter Hammond, *Liturgy and Architecture* (London: Barrie and Rockliff, 1960), 30; and Edward Snow, "The Language of Contradiction in Bruegel's *Tower of Babel,*" *Res: Anthropology and Aesthetics* 5 (spring 1983), particularly 41, 43, 44, 46.

23. See Michael W. Meister and Joseph Rykwert, "Afterword: Adam's House and Hermits' Huts: A Conversation," *Res: Anthropology and Aesthetics* 15 (spring 1988): 29.

24. Davies, *Temples, Churches, and Mosques,* 37.

25. Von Hagen, *Realm of the Incas,* 129–31, quotes Cieza de León's account. The murals of Tlaloc's paradise at Tepantitla, near Teotihuacan, are a possible parallel to this architectural commemoration of the pristine, pre-urban lifestyle; see Kubler, *Art and Architecture of Ancient America,* 54, 66–67.

26. Among discussions of this phenomenon is Pál Kelemen, *Medieval American Art,* 2 vols. (New York: Macmillan, 1943), 1:75–76.

27. In chapter 15, on conventionalized allurement, see especially the section "Deliberate Archaisms and Mythicohistoric Precedents: Mesoamerican Examples."

28. Regarding the complexity and diversity of motives for architectural imitation, recall the "principle of disjunction" explained in Erwin Panofsky, *Renaissance and Renascences in Western Art,* 2d ed. (New York: Harper and Row, 1969). For a concise summary of Panofsky's "principle of disjunction" as it applies to Mesoamerica and admonishments against facile presumptions of continuity in meaning just because forms are replicated, see George Kubler, "Period, Style, and Meaning in Ancient American Art," in *Ancient Mesoamerica: Selected Readings,* ed. John A. Graham (Palo Alto, Calif.: Peek Publications, 1981), 22.

29. See Robert E. Fry, "Revitalization Movements among the Postclassic Maya," in *The Lowland Maya Postclassic,* ed. Arlen F. Chase and Prudence M. Rice (Austin: University of Texas Press, 1985), 129.

30. An extended exposition of this interpretation of the motivations and means by which architectural elements from Tula and other sites were reproduced at Chichén Itzá appears in chapter 4 of Jones, *Twin City Tales.*

31. In volume 1, see chapter 12, "Multifarious Revalorization: The Composition of Ritual-Architectural Reception Histories."

32. Moholy-Nagy, *Native Genius in Anonymous Architecture in North America,* 11.

Seventeen | Divinity

1. Wu, *Chinese and Indian Architecture,* 21.

2. Wim Swaan, *The Gothic Cathedral* (New York: Park Lane, 1984), 51.

3. I am using the Revised Standard Version. Burckhardt (*Sacred Art in East and West,* 48) quotes a slightly different version of this New Testament passage with the gloss that it is in accordance with these lines that "the symbolism of the Christian temple rests on the analogy between the temple and the body of Christ."

4. See, for instance, the works of the sixteenth-century Dominican missionary to the Indians of Central Mexico, Fray Diego Durán, *Book of the Ancient Gods and Rites and the Ancient Calendar,* trans. and ed. Fernando Horcasitas and Doris Heyden (Norman: University of Oklahoma Press, 1971); and idem, *The History of the Indians of New Spain,* trans. Doris Heyden (Norman: University of Oklahoma Press, 1995).

5. Joyce Marcus ("Archaeology and Religion: A Comparison of the Zapotec and the Maya," in *Ancient Mesoamerica,* ed. John A. Graham [Palo Alto, Calif.: Peek Publications, 1981], 299–305), in the context of an incisive challenge to the stock notion that the Classic Maya and other indigenous Americans had a vast "pantheon" of "gods," attributes the origin of this misconception to the classical educations of the early Spanish chroniclers, "including knowledge of the ancient Greco-Roman pantheon which served as their model for an 'idolatrous' religion." Regarding attempts to be more sensitive to the cultural specificity of indigenous conceptions of the supernatural, see also Nancy Troike, "Fundamental Changes in the Interpretation of the Mixtec Codices," in *Ancient Mesoamerica,* ed. Graham, 282–83.

6. Note, among many many exemplars, Jeanette Mirsky, *Houses of God* (Chicago: University of Chicago Press, 1965).

7. Scully, *The Earth, the Temple, and the Gods,* 1.

8. In volume 1, see especially chapter 3, "Conversation and Play: The Eventfulness of Architecture."

9. Scully, *The Earth, the Temple, and the Gods,* 56. In addition to this laudable sensitivity to religious dispositions, ceremonial usages, and thus the eventful character of architecture, Scully makes the appealing suggestion that sacred architecture (like myth and ritual) is involved in a "double reconciliation," reconciling the human with his physical environment, and also reconciling the earthly realm with the realm of the gods (47, 55).

10. Ibid., chapter 2.

11. Nikos Kazantzakis (*Report to Greco,* trans. P. A. Bien [New York: Simon and Schuster, 1965], 149) contrasts Cretan architecture with that of mainland Greece. Also see Morton P. Levitt, *The Cretan Glance: The World and Art of Nikos Kazantzakis* (Columbus: Ohio State University Press, 1980), 7–8.

12. Scully, *The Earth, the Temple, and the Gods,* 35.

13. Ibid., 42–43.

14. Ibid., 46.

15. Ibid.

16. Kubler ("The Design of Space in Maya Architecture," 515) argues that Maya architecture is not "elaborated shelter." Scully (*The Earth, the Temple and the Gods,* 62) states explicitly that the classic Greek temple is totally unique, *not* a "solid mass like an Egyptian or Maya pyramid"; but, it seems to me that, as sculptural commemorative architectures, the Mesoamerican and classic Greek cases actually have much in common.

17. With respect to classic Greek temples' role as "ritual contexts," they are probably best conceived as foci for devotion and reflection, and thus instantiations of what I will discuss in chapter 22 as the contemplation mode of ritual-architectural presentation and apprehension (priority III-B).

18. Scully, *The Earth, the Temple, and the Gods,* 55.

19. Michell, *The Hindu Temple,* 60.

20. Michael W. Meister ("On the Development of a Morphology for a Symbolic Architecture: India," *Res: Anthropology and Aesthetics* 12 [autumn 1986]: 33) contends that "Temples to house images of divinity developed relatively late in India. . . ." He then traces that development with special concern for the differences between North and South India.

21. See David Miller, "Religious Institutions and Political Ethics in Bhubaneswar," in *Transformation of a Sacred Town: Bhubaneswar, India,* ed. Susan Seymour (Boulder: Westview Press, 1980), 83.

22. See Volwahsen, *Living Architecture: India,* 140–41. The temple at Nachna was likewise patterned after Shiva's Mount Kailasa; see Meister, "On the Development of a Morphology for a Symbolic Architecture," 35. And Michell (*The Hindu Temple,* 69) explains how a temple patterned after a celebrated mythological mountain like Kailasa or Meru "becomes an architectural facsimile of the sacred places of the gods, providing for the worshipper the merit that would be his through an actual visit to the mountains."

23. Soundara Rajan (*An Invitation to Indian Architecture,* 22–23) gives examples of several *unda-deul,* sunken shrine-type temples. A morphological parallel comes in those ancient Egyptian "toilet ceremonies" in which "Each morning the cult image was asperged, censed, anointed, vested, and crowned." See J. G. Davies, "Architecture," *Encyclopedia of Religion,* ed. Eliade, 1:387.

24. Michell, *The Hindu Temple,* 62; emphasis added.

25. Soundara Rajan, *An Invitation to Indian Architecture,* 15. S. G. F. Brandon (*Man and God in Architecture and Ritual: A Study of Iconography, Architecture, and Ritual Action as Primary Evidence of Religious Belief and Practice* [New York: Charles Scribner's Sons, 1975], 96) is another of many to comment on the sense in which the "fabric [of the Hindu temple] is thought of as constituting a form of body in which the deity manifests itself."

26. Kramrisch, *The Hindu Temple,* 2:360. Also see Stella Kramrisch, "The Temple as Puruṣa," in *Studies in Indian Temple Architecture,* ed. Pramod Chandra (New Delhi: American Institute of Indian Studies, 1975). To cite another example from India (though in the Buddhist tradition), Mabbett ("The Symbolism of Mount Meru," 75) explains the sense in which the stupa, "the shrine or cult object at which the otherwise inaccessible divinity was worshipped turned into the divinity in person"; consider, for instance, the personified stupa of Swayambunath, Nepal, where the eyes painted on all sides of the tower keep an imperious watch over the Kathmandu Valley. Interestingly, Mabbett seems to be describing an evolution in the architectural commemoration of divinity from abstract to more literal, the opposite of that which Scully sees in the history of Greek sacred architecture.

27. Michael W. Meister, "Hindu Temples," *Encyclopedia of Religion,* ed. Eliade, 14:370.

28. Wu, *Chinese and Indian Architecture,* 21.

29. Kramrisch, *The Hindu Temple,* 2:360.

30. See Meister, "On the Development of a Morphology for a Symbolic Architecture," 40.

31. Though pursuing this is beyond the scope of the current project, it should not go unnoticed that nearly all of the examples marshaled to illustrate the supposedly "literal equation" of architectural forms and divinity are drawn from cultures that have been stigmatized as "primitive" or "archaic," while the more "abstract" variations on the commemoration of divinity theme lead me to discussions of the Abrahamic traditions. That disparity is, almost certainly, more a reflection of the dynamic of Western intellectual history than of empirical understandings and apprehensions of architecture. In fact, in candor, the notion of organization on a spectrum from "literal to abstract" (which connotes too easily "blunt to sharp" or "crude to sophisticated") is discomforting but perhaps serviceable until a better organizing principle emerges.

32. It is particularly difficult in these cases to maintain a differentiation between the commemoration of divinity (priority II-A) and the commemoration of sacred history (priority II-B); both clearly apply.

33. Ronald M. Berndt, "Identification of Deity through Land: An Australian Aboriginal View," in *Approaches to Iconology,* ed. Hans G. Kippenberg et al. (Leiden: E. J. Brill, 1985–86), 267. Also with respect to the Australian divinization (and mythologization) of features of the landscape, see Amos Rapoport, "Australian Aborigines and the Definition of Place," in *Shelter, Sign, and Symbol,* ed. Oliver, 38–51.

34. Cobo, *Inca Religion and Customs,* 10. Father Cobo, not surprisingly, has a very difficult time understanding indigenous conceptions of divinity. Regarding extreme Inca veneration for a "crag" beside which was constructed the great sanctuary of Titicaca, see ibid., 96–97.

35. Kenzo Tange and Noboru Kawazoe, *Ise: Prototype of Japanese Architecture* (Cambridge, Mass.: MIT Press, 1965), 39.

36. A very different sort of Japanese example of architecture as the body of a god is the Daibutsu of Kamakura, the colossal bronze image of Amida, which was cast by Ino Goroemon in the thirteenth century and then hollowed out to form a chapel literally inside the body of the divinity; see Short, *A History of Religious Architecture,* 106–7.

37. Paul Gendrop ("Dragon-Mouth Entrances: Zoomorphic Portals in the Architecture of Central Yucatan," in *Third Palenque Round Table, 1978, Part 2,* ed. Merle Greene Robertson, Palenque Round Table Series, vol. 5 [Austin: University of Texas Press, 1980], 138–50) describes the stylistic variation and geographic distribution of dragon-mouth entrances. He is in general accord with Eric Thompson that the facades of Central Yucatan temples represent Itzam Na, "the multifaceted creator god"; Gendrop likewise accepts the traditional assessment that the long-nosed masks that are typically associated with these facades are representations of Chaac, the Maya god of rain.

38. Thompson, *Maya History and Religion,* chapter 7, includes a famous discussion of "the major gods of the Maya pantheon," with special attention to Itzam Na. The phrase "triple identification" is my term for Thompson's suggestion that there was a (homologizing) equation of Itzam Na, the Maya universe, and the serpent-mouth temples.

39. Marcus ("Archaeology and Religion," 299–305), who comments on the untoward and still-lingering imposition of Greco-Roman conceptions of divinity onto the Maya, issues a strong challenge to Eric Thompson's widely circulated view that the Classic Maya worshiped a vast "pantheon" of "gods." Daniel Schávelzon also addresses the controversial status of Maya "deities" and specifically Thompson's assessments of the supereminence of Itzam Na in "Temples, Caves, or Monsters? Notes on Zoomorphic Facades in Pre-Hispanic Architecture," in *Third Palenque Round Table, 1978, Part 2,* ed. Robertson.

40. Benson, "Architecture as Metaphor," 185. Benson apparently sees her interpretation as complementary rather than antithetical to Eric Thompson's earlier interpretation. Note also that Benson's intimations of the ritual use of serpent-mouth temples as reiterating "the ancient emergence from the primordial cave" also bears directly on the commemoration of sacred history (priority II-B).

41. Karl A. Taube ("The Teotihuacan Cave of Origin: The Iconography and Architecture of Emergence Mythology in Mesoamerica and the American Southwest," *Res: Anthropology and Aesthetics* 12 [autumn 1986]: 51–82) suggests parallels between the symbolism and usages of Southwest kivas and Mesoamerican con-

structions. Of innumerable sources on kivas, also notable in the context of the present discussion is Vincent Scully, *Pueblo: Mountain, Village, Dance,* 2d ed. (Chicago: University of Chicago Press, 1989).

42. See Lloyd St. Alcorn, *The Serpent Mound* (New York: New York American Library, 1989); Fletcher and Cameron, "Serpent Mound: A New Look at an Old Snake in the Grass"; or Romain, "Symbolic Associations at the Serpent Mound." The controversial Nazca lines are also viably interpreted as enormous commemorations of divinity; see *The Lines of Nazca,* ed. Aveni.

43. See Spinden, *A Study of Maya Art,* 15–16.

44. Coe, *Maya,* 90.

45. Broda ("Templo Mayor as Ritual Space," 64) bases her assessment of the Templo Mayor as a voracious earth monster particularly on the iconography of Cihuacoatl-Coatlique-Coyoxauhqui and on the Tlaltecuhtli representations on relief stones.

46. See Kelemen, *Medieval American Art,* 1:61.

47. See Weaver, *The Aztecs, Maya, and Their Predecessors,* 54.

48. See, among many possibilities, Brundage, *Two Earths, Two Heavens,* 80.

49. Bassie-Sweet, *At the Edge of the World,* 117.

50. Davies, "Architecture," 382.

51. See also Baruch A. Levine, "Biblical Temple," *Encyclopedia of Religion,* ed. Eliade, 2:202–17.

52. Swaan, *The Gothic Cathedral,* 51.

53. Short, *A History of Religious Architecture,* 19–20.

54. Fred Thompson and D'Arcy Fenton ("*Matsuri:* The Binding of Secular and Ceremonial Space in Kakunodate, Japan," *Res: Anthropology and Aesthetics* 13 [spring 1987]: 140) describe two sorts of *yama*: *okiyama*, the big mountain, which is a stationary construction, and *hiki-yama,* the pulling mountain, which is a mobile wagon that is pulled around the town.

55. Kenzo Tange, "Religion and the Treatment of Space in Japanese Architecture," in Tange and Kawazoe, *Ise: Prototype of Japanese Architecture,* 33. With respect to Japanese spaces that are designed to attract or entice the sacred, consider also the architecturalization of the concept of "*ma,*" and the concerted effort to lure or direct *kami* energy into the ritual-architectural context, which I discuss in chapter 24 relative to the sanctuary priority; see especially the subsection in that chapter entitled "Architectural Enticements of the Divine: Attracting Gods and Redirecting Energy."

56. See L. Austine Waddell, *Tibetan Buddhism* (New York: Dover Publications, 1972), 287.

57. Romi Khosla, "Architecture and Symbolism in Tibetan Monasteries," in *Shelter, Sign, and Symbol,* ed. Oliver, 81.

58. Freedberg, *The Power of Images,* 82–85. Actually, all of Freedberg's fifth chapter, "Consecration: Making Images Work," is very relevant to the present discussion.

59. Coomaraswamy, *The Transformation of Nature in Art,* 156.

60. Clothey, *Rhythm and Intent,* 186–200.

61. Coomaraswamy (*The Transformation of Nature in Art,* 157) works to counter stereotypes that Hindus are either a great deal more (or less) superstitious than Westerners by noting that, even in India, "the image *per se* is neither [typically regarded as the] God nor any angel, but merely an aspect or hypostasis (*avasthā*) of God, who is in the last analysis without likeness (*amūrta*), not determined by form (*arūpa*), trans-form (*para-rūpa*)."

62. E. O. James, *From Cave to Cathedral: Temples and Shrines of Prehistoric, Classical, and Early Christian Times* (New York: Frederick A. Praeger, 1965), 99.

63. As a place to begin with respect to the oracle at Delphi, see Jan Bremmer, "Delphi," *Encyclopedia of Religion,* ed. Eliade, 4:277–78.

64. On the history of chaining images and statues, see Freedberg, *The Power of Images,* 74–77.

65. I will address in a somewhat fuller fashion the ambivalence in the Abrahamic traditions concerning the mixed utility and dangers of art and architecture in chapter 22, "Contemplation: Props for Devotion."

66. See Davies, *Temples, Churches, and Mosques,* 91.

67. Hammond, *Liturgy and Architecture,* 154.

68. Burckhardt, *Sacred Art in East and West,* 101. The Qur'anic doctrine of *tawhid* regards Allah as utterly transcendent and totally distinct from the natural world he has created and, consequently, no facet of human existence or of nature—least of all a painting or statue—can be identified with him. Useful bibliography on the issue of Islamic strictures against images is found in Freedberg, *The Power of Images,* 451, n. 4.

69. See Freedberg, *The Power of Images,* 56.

70. Regarding the (re)statement of that familiar view, see Minoru Ooka, *Temples of Nara and Their Art,* trans. Dennis Lishka (New York: Weatherhill, 1973), 40. More interestingly, Susan L. Huntington, in "Early Buddhist Art and the Theory of Aniconism," *Art Journal* 49 (winter 1990): 401–8, argues that there was in fact no "aniconic period" in Buddhist art.

71. Freedberg, *The Power of Images,* 55.

72. Ibid., 54. In the same vein, Coomaraswamy (*The Transformation of Nature in Art,* 162) stresses that "iconolatry" is not "an ignorant or useless practice fit only for spiritual children"; instead, it is the expression of "a human necessity."

73. Freedberg, *The Power of Images,* 55.

74. Ibid., chapter 4, also presents evidence that controverts the claim of pure aniconism in each of these contexts. Also, note that Marilyn Waldman, personal communication, observes that, among the Abrahamic traditions, claims to aniconism are nearly always self-descriptions, (though she, like Freedberg here, also regards those claims as nearly always empirically fallacious); with that in mind, she makes the suggestion that such claims may actually be strategically comparative statements, which serve to announce the superiority of one's god over others—

bluntly put, "your god(s) can be confined in an image or building, but our God cannot."

75. In my rubric, idealized injunctions of orthodoxy, such as prohibitions against image-making, constitute "one sort of protocol of architectural apprehension"; on-the-ground interactions with buildings that variously conform to, ignore, or subvert those injunctions constitute other protocols of apprehension; and academic interpretations constitute still another sort of protocol. See chapter 12, "Multifarious Revalorization: The Composition of Ritual-Architectural Reception Histories."

76. See Huntington, "Early Buddhist Art and the Theory of Aniconism."

77. Ibid., 406. Huntington traces the history of "the traditional aniconic theory" to its first explicit articulation by twentieth-century scholar Alfred Foucher.

78. Lois Ibsen al-Fārūqī, "An Islamic Perspective on Symbolism in the Arts: New Thoughts on Figural Representation," in *Art, Creativity, and the Sacred: An Anthology in Religion and Art,* ed. Diane Apostolos-Cappadona (New York: Crossroad, 1984), 164–78. This notion that art and architecture can "disclose an intuition" raises questions that will be addressed below in chapter 22 with respect to the contemplation priority (III-B).

79. Ibid., 170–71.

80. On the ambivalence of Jewish attitudes toward art, see David Altshuler and Linda Altshuler, "Judaism and Art" in *Art, Creativity, and the Sacred,* ed. Apostolos-Cappadona, 155–63.

81. See Burckhardt, *Sacred Art in East and West,* 48–49.

82. Ibid., 49.

83. Regarding explicit and profound differences between the Eastern church's receptivity to the Neoplatonic notion that spiritual power can actually be present in material objects such as icons or even buildings and, by contrast, the official Roman view, which held that the images were not in themselves holy, so that any veneration before an image of Christ is in reality a veneration of Christ and not of the image, see Sinding-Larsen, *Iconography and Ritual,* 103.

84. The experience of Gothic cathedrals will be explored more fully in chapter 22 with respect to the contemplation priority (III-B).

85. Davies, "Architecture," 390. Demonstrating the creative commemoration of Christian divinity at a somewhat larger scale, Belden Lane (*Landscapes of the Sacred,* 110–14) discusses how the preferred town layout of the similarly iconoclastic New England Puritans, a configuration that radiated out concentrically from a central meetinghouse, gave geographic and architectural expression to Puritan covenant theology and their sense of a special relationship to God.

86. Burckhardt (*Sacred Art in East and West,* 49–50) attributes this interpretation to medieval Christian liturgists, Durant de Mende and Honorius d'Autun, and likewise suggests the parallel to the Hindu symbolism of Purusha.

87. See Laing, "Central and Eastern Europe," in *Baroque and Rococo,* ed. Blunt, 217. Irving Lavin (*Bernini and the Crossing of Saint Peter's* [New York: New York University Press, 1968], 17) likewise discusses the representation of the Trinity at

Saint Peter's, the Latern, and the church of Santa Maria dei Monti in Rome. And Sinding-Larsen (*Iconography and Ritual,* 92) explains how in the medieval mosaic program at San Marco in Venice the three main cupolas "are probably meant as an allusion to the three persons in the Trinity and illustrate the Concept of the Church in a universal sense as being 'full of the Trinity.'" Also, Harbison (*The Built, the Unbuilt, and the Unbuildable,* 70–71) has remarks on English Mannerist Thomas Tresham's "Triangular Lodge," which provides a somewhat more eccentric expression of the Trinity.

88. Consider, for instance, the subtle theological conceptions of Christology expressed in the plan of the cathedral of Chartres where: "the left-hand bay, situated to the North of the central bay is dedicated to the Christ ascending Heaven; the right-hand bay, situated to the South of the central bay, is dedicated to the Virgin and to the nativity of the Christ; [and] the central bay, the real 'Royal gate,' presents Christ in Glory, according to the apocalyptic vision of St. John." Burckhardt, *Sacred Art in East and West,* 92–93.

89. See Hammond, *Liturgy and Architecture,* 11. Hammond considers that "The task of the contemporary architect . . . is to create architectural forms that embody the theological vision of the twentieth century as the characteristic forms of Gothic expressed that of the twelfth."

90. Sinding-Larsen (*Iconography and Ritual,* 104) discusses the chronic disparity between "official" and "ordinary" attitudes toward Christian iconography.

91. Ibid., 34.

92. Ibid.

Eighteen | Sacred History

1. Ernst Cassirer, *The Philosophy of Symbolic Forms,* vol. 2, *Mythical Thought,* trans. Ralph Manheim (New Haven: Yale University Press, 1955), 92; quoted by Hans-Joachim Klimkeit, "Spatial Orientation in Mythical Thinking as Exemplified in Ancient Egypt: Considerations toward a Geography of Religions," *History of Religions* 14 (May 1975): 277.

2. Amos Rapoport, "Australian Aborigines and the Definition of Place," in *Shelter, Sign, and Symbol,* ed. Oliver, 42.

3. Lane, *Landscapes of the Sacred,* 11.

4. Mircea Eliade (*The Quest: History and Meaning in Religion* [Chicago: University of Chicago Press, 1969], 85) defines "sacred history" as "the fabulous epoch [between the creation of the world and historical time] when the ancestors were roaming about the land." I have expanded the term in both directions to include the cosmogony proper and the mythicohistorical events of the postprimordial era.

5. John Ruskin, *The Seven Lamps of Architecture* (1849; New York: Noonday Press, 1971), 69–70. It is interesting to contrast Ruskin's attitude about the commemorative potential of architecture with the almost antithetical position of

Russell Sturgis's "Address" in *American Architect and Building News,* 1890: "Architecture as a fine art has nothing to do with the arts of expression . . . the business of buildings is not to tell tales about the world . . . or of humanity, or of theology"; quoted by Abercrombie, *Architecture as Art,* 125.

6. Ruskin, *The Seven Lamps of Architecture,* 69–70.

7. The term "undoubtedly mythologic" is found in William Henry Holmes, *Archaeological Studies among the Ancient Cities of Mexico* (Chicago: Field Columbian Museum, 1895–97), 196, where it describes the architectural decoration at the Maya site of Palenque; and I borrow the term "mytho-esthetic motifs" from Victor Wolfgang von Hagen, *Frederick Catherwood, Archt.* (New York: Oxford University Press, 1950), caption to plate XV.

8. John Lloyd Stephens, *Incidents of Travel in Yucatan* (1843; New York: Dover Publications, 1963), 1:96.

9. Diego de Landa, *Relación de las cosas de Yucatán,* trans. and ed. Alfred M. Tozzer, Peabody Museum of American Archaeology and Ethnology, Papers, 18 (Cambridge, Mass.: Peabody Museum, 1941), 179. Robert M. Carmack (*The Quiché Mayas of Utatlán: The Evolution of a Highland Guatemala Kingdom* [Norman: Oklahoma University Press, 1981], 208–9, 284ff.) discusses how the mythological dramas performed on such "plaza platforms" served political as well as entertainment functions.

10. The stage-setting function of architecture will be explored more fully below in chapter 21, on the theater priority (III-A).

11. Eliade, *The Sacred and the Profane,* 45; emphasis his.

12. See, among many relevant sources, Meister, "On the Development of a Morphology for a Symbolic Architecture: India," 37.

13. Burckhardt, *Sacred Art in East and West,* 52. Mieke Bal (*Lethal Love: Feminist Literary Readings of Biblical Love Stories* [Bloomington: Indiana University Press, 1987], 115) notes that the verb that describes the creation of gender in Genesis is the verb for construction that refers specifically to architecture and the construction of buildings, which suggests (to me) that every Judeo-Christian act of construction could, in some vague sense, be conceived as a reiteration of cosmogony. This notion of building as ritual raises questions that will be addressed more fully in chapter 23 in relation to propitiation (priority III-C).

14. Jackson (*The Necessity for Ruins,* 19–35, 89–102) entertains this possibility.

15. Robert Heine-Geldern, *Conceptions of State and Kingship in Southeast Asia,* Data Paper no. 18 (Ithaca, N.Y.: Southeast Asia Program, Cornell University, 1956), 19. Mabbett ("The Symbolism of Mount Meru," 71, 82) and Michell (*The Hindu Temple,* 23) also comment on the cosmogonic significance of the Angkor Wat balustrade. Also see Donatella Mazzeo and Chiara Silva Antonini, *Monuments of Civilization: Ancient Cambodia* (New York: Grosset and Dunlap, 1978); and Joan Lebold Cohen, *Angkor: Monuments of the God-Kings* (New York: Harry N. Abrams, 1975).

16. Brandon, *Man and God in Architecture and Ritual,* 92. Brandon also addresses the Egyptian case.

17. Gary Urton provides a book-length exploration of the significance and history of the Incas' Pacaritombo origin myth in *The History of a Myth: Pacariqtambo and the Origin of the Inkas* (Austin: University of Texas Press, 1990). On Pacaritombo, also see Brundage, *Two Earths, Two Heavens,* 3–4, 38; and Cobo, *Inca Religion and Customs,* 12–17.

18. Michael Coe, "Religion and the Rise of Mesoamerican States," in *The Transition to Statehood in the New World,* ed. Grant D. Jones and Robert R. Kautz (Cambridge: Cambridge University Press), 168.

19. See Taube, "The Teotihuacan Cave of Origin."

20. Weaver, *The Aztecs, Maya, and Their Predecessors,* 63.

21. Spinden, *Ancient Civilizations of Mexico and Central America* (originally 1917), 217.

22. Richard Townsend, "The Mt. Tlaloc Project," in *To Change Place: Aztec Ceremonial Landscapes,* ed. Davíd Carrasco (Niwot: University Press of Colorado, 1991), 30.

23. Waterson, "The House and the World: The Symbolism of Sa'Dan Toraja House Carvings," 37.

24. Gary Witherspoon, "Beautifying the World through Art (Navajo)," in *Native North American Art History: Selected Readings,* comp. Zena Pearlstone Mathews and Aldona Jonaitis (Palo Alto, Calif.: Peek Publications, 1982), 219; or Gary Witherspoon, *Language and Art in the Navajo Universe* (Ann Arbor: University of Michigan Press, 1977), 167ff.

25. Davíd Carrasco ("Templo Mayor: The Aztec Vision of Place," *Religion* 2 [1981]: 284–85) and Broda ("Templo Mayor as Ritual Space," 45), among others, interpret Aztec human sacrifice in terms of Huitzilopochtli's birth.

26. See Laing, "Central and Eastern Europe," in *Baroque and Rococo,* ed., Blunt, 165–296. Another strong example of this sort comes in Laing's discussion (p. 269) of the pilgrimage church of the Wies (1746–54), the final masterpiece of Dominikus Zimmermann and the seat of one of the most enduring pilgrimages in Bavaria, which was built specifically to commemorate and perpetuate the miraculous event wherein a crude image of the Scourged Christ at the Column was seen to have shed tears.

27. See Friedland and Hecht, "The Politics of Sacred Place: Jersualem's Temple Mount/*al-haram a-sharif,*" 22ff.

28. See Burckhardt, *Sacred Art in East and West,* 112; or Clinton Bennet, "Islam," in *Sacred Place,* ed. Jean Holm with John Bowker (London and New York: Pinter Publishers, 1994), 103–7.

29. Clothey, *Rhythm and Intent,* 78.

30. See Surinder Mohan Bhardwaj, *Hindu Places of Pilgrimage in India* (Berkeley and Los Angeles: University of California Press, 1973), 98. These are

actually two options in a four-part scheme that Bhardwaj outlines; he does not explicitly correlate these two options with "mythical" versus "miraculous" episodes.

31. For some alternative interpretations of the relief at Mamallapuram, see Michael Edwardes, *Indian Temples and Palaces* (London: Paul Hamlyn, 1969), 61–64. Also see Mirsky, *Houses of God,* 52–54; and Michell, *The Hindu Temple,* 46–48.

32. See Short, *A History of Religious Architecture,* 89–90, 95; Edwardes, *Indian Temples and Palaces,* 37–51; or Volwahsen, *Living Architecture: Indian,* 89–134.

33. Richter (*Art and Human Consciousness,* 111–13) discusses the triumphal arch as Rome's major form of "self-expression" (and provides a picture of the Arch of Titus).

34. Kenna, "Icons in Theory and Practice," 360.

35. Howard Hibbard, *Bernini* (Baltimore: Penguin Books, 1965). Bernini's work is discussed more fully in chapter 21 in relation to the theater priority (III-A).

36. Dixon, "The Christology of Michelangelo," 524.

37. Arshi, *Sikh Architecture in Punjab,* 19–20.

38. Sardar Surinder Singh Johar, *The Sikh Gurus and Their Shrines* (Delhi: Vivek Publishing, 1976). Pardeed Singh Arshi says that because of this principle of organization Johar's work "acquired the character only of a mere inventory of Sikh shrines, and could not serve the need of an architectural study"; Arshi, *Sikh Architecture in Punjab,* 15.

39. Regarding the detailed reliefs of the life of Gautama see Woodward, "Borobudur and the Mirrorlike Mind," 40–47.

40. Edward Conze, *Buddhism: Its Essence and Development* (New York: Harper and Row, 1951), 79. Caityas are similar to stupas, though originally stupas contained relics of the Buddha while caityas did not; over time, as the Buddha's relics became increasingly difficult to obtain, the distinction gradually vanished. See Hirakawa Akira, "Stupa Worship," *Encyclopedia of Religion,* ed. Eliade, 14:92–96.

41. Short, *A History of Religious Architecture,* 98.

42. Ibid.

43. Anthony Blunt, in his introduction to *Baroque and Rococo,* ed. Blunt, 10, and Laing, in "Central and Eastern Europe," in the same volume, 221, discuss the strong affirmation of saints and relics in the Council of Trent, and the consequent developments in architecture.

44. Blunt, introduction to *Baroque and Rococo,* ed. Blunt, 10.

45. See Rapoport, "Australian Aborigines and the Definition of Place," in *Shelter, Sign, and Symbol,* ed. Oliver, 42ff.

46. The priority of *place* over that of sacred historical *episode* or *personage* is evident, for instance, 1) at those pilgrimage sites that multiple traditions esteem for quite different reasons, as in the Jewish, Christian, and Muslim enthusiasm for Jerusalem; and 2) at those pilgrimage sites, like Chalma in Mexico, that are usurped by conquering peoples (in this case, first by the Aztecs, then by the Spaniards), who explain the significance of the place in terms of quite different sacred stories but to

which pilgrims continue to flock, largely irrespective of the new explanations.

47. Eck, *Banaras: City of Light,* 256.

48. It is noteworthy that the sort of commemorations of the places of sacred history being described here are also very relevant to Eliade's notion of "hierophanies" or "hierophanic places" addressed in chapter 14 in relation to the homology priority (I-A).

49. Pilgrimage is an exceedingly complex phenomenon that participates in virtually all the categories in this framework of ritual-architectural priorities.

50. On a more modest scale, Tepoztlán, the Central Mexican pueblo renowned across indigenous Mesoamerica as the site of the legendary discovery of the intoxicating drink *pulque* and, thus, invariably linked to debauchery and orgy, was the goal of a more rambunctious style of commemorative pilgrimage, but one that, nonetheless, preserved a mythological event by connecting it inextricably to a particular parcel of sacred geography. See Oscar Lewis, *Tepoztlán: Village in Mexico* (New York: Holt Rinehart and Winston, 1960); and, on Tepoztlán's relationship to the origins of the *pulque* cult, also see Henry B. Nicholson, "The Octli Cult in Late Pre-Hispanic Central Mexico," in *To Change Place,* ed. Carrasco, 181.

51. Richard C. Martin, "Muslim Pilgrimage," *Encyclopedia of Religion,* ed. Eliade, 11:341, cites a version of the *talbiyah,* the prayer of *ihrām* (consecration) uttered as pilgrims pass the markers of the sacred territory upon entry to Mecca, which reads: "Here I am, O Lord! What is Thy command?"

52. Richard Krautheimer, *Rome: Profile of a City, 312–1308* (Princeton: Princeton University Press, 1980), 85–86.

53. Ibid.

54. Ibid., 82–87. Similarly, on the sociopolitical import of pilgrimage, Victor Turner and Edith Turner (*Image and Pilgrimage in Christian Culture: Anthropological Perspectives* [New York: Columbia University Press, 1978], 51ff.) discuss how the Spaniards successfully exploited pilgrimage fervor in their missionary agenda in Mexico. They also discuss how the "pilgrimage ethic" in Europe, with its emphasis on "holy travel" and the benefits flowing from such travel, may well have helped to create the communications networks that later made mercantile and industrial capitalism a viable national and international system (234). Furthermore, von Simson (*The Gothic Cathedral,* 6–7) has argued the important role of pilgrimage in the growth of cities, marketing systems, and roads in Europe. Likewise, pilgrimage plays an absolutely crucial role in Paul Wheatley's theory of urban genesis in *Pivot of the Four Quarters,* chapter 3. And, for comments regarding the very important sociocultural implications of pilgrimage in India, see Bhardwaj, *Hindu Places of Pilgrimage in India,* 7; and David G. Mandelbaum, *Society in India* (Berkeley and Los Angeles: University of California Press, 1970), 2:402.

55. See William H. McNeill, *Mythistory and Other Essays* (Chicago: University of Chicago Press, 1986), especially chapter 1, "Mythistory, or Truth, Myth, History, and Historians."

56. See, for instance, Freedberg, *The Power of Images,* 128.

57. Ronald Grimes, *Symbol and Conquest: Public Ritual and Drama in Sante Fe, New Mexico* (Ithaca, N.Y.: Cornell University Press, 1976), 71.

58. Lavin, *Bernini and the Crossing of Saint Peter's,* 34–35.

59. Ibid., 25. Lavin, moreover, contends that Bernini's design for the Crossing of Saint Peter's is a continuation of that "topographical transfusion," so that Saint Peter's likewise becomes Jerusalem, the place where salvation was achieved and is continually renewed (35).

60. See Edward T. Linenthal, "Locating Holocaust Memory: The United States Holocaust Memorial Museum," in *American Sacred Space,* ed. Chidester and Linenthal, 241–53. Linenthal (244) credits the quotation concerning the significance of the soil from American military cemeteries to architect James Ingo Freed. It is plausible to argue that the principal initiative in this case, by contrast to other examples in this section, is to "transport" visitors to the "sacred sites" of the Holocaust rather than to "transfer the sanctity" of those sites to Washington, D.C.; but, noting particularly that the design and siting of this memorial museum was also explicitly intended to integrate the Holocaust into "the American story" (see 222–24), I would venture that both sorts of movement are at issue in virtually all these cases.

61. Bhardwaj, *Hindu Places of Pilgrimage in India,* 86.

62. Ibid.

63. Freedberg, *The Power of Images,* 192.

64. See ibid., 196–200.

65. On Puritan, Shaker, and Mormon attempts to create "New Jerusalems" in America, see Lane, *Landscapes of the Sacred,* 114–18, 132–40.

66. See Candace Slater, "The Literature of Pilgrimage: Present-day Miracle Stories from Northeast Brazil," in *Pilgrimage in Latin American,* ed. Crumrine and Morinis, 181–83.

67. Michell, *The Hindu Temple,* 159.

68. See Lindsay Jones, "Conquests of the Imagination: Maya-Mexican Polarity and the Story of Chichén Itzá," *American Anthropologist* 99 (June 1997): 275–90.

69. For a typical bipartioning of Chichén Itzá art into Maya versus Mexican (or Toltec), see George Brainerd, *The Maya Civilization* (Los Angeles: Southwest Museum, 1954), 82–83, 93. Also see Jones, *Twin City Tales,* chapter 1.

70. John Graham, "Antecedents of Olmec Sculpture at Abaj Takalik," in *Pre-Columbian Art History,* ed. Cordy-Collins and Stern, 9–10.

71. Ibid.

72. Tatiana Proskouriakoff, *A Study of Classic Maya Sculpture,* Publication 593 (Washington, D.C.: Carnegie Institution of Washington, 1950), 4–5.

73. Elizabeth P. Benson (*Maya World* [New York: Thomas G. Crowell, 1967], 83) makes the same argument that, "whereas Maya sculpture had a narrow range of subject matter, mural painting was apparently much freer and more telling."

74. Schele, "Sacred Site and World-View at Palenque," 96.

75. Ibid., 99.

76. Ibid., 104.

77. See chapter 16, on astronomy and allurement, particularly the section entitled "Allurement via the Ritual-Architectural Enhancement of Nature: Mesoamerican Examples."

78. Bhardwaj (*Hindu Places of Pilgrimage in India,* 203–6) describes the process of writing a *sthala purana,* that is, a local "ancient account" that establishes a link between a given local place and some part of the wider Sanskritic tradition; if the efforts of the enterprising priest succeed, "the grafted aura of antiquity grows [and] the place may assume a higher stature and enter the 'great tradition' of Hinduism." He provides two very intriguing examples.

79. It is worth noting that, were we to slice the phenomenon of ritual-architectural commemorations of sacred history another way, we could demonstrate three importantly different possibilities: Sometimes what is being represented in the works of art and architecture are whole stories, full narrative sequences, as, for example, in the elaborate arrangement at Angkor Wat where "the whole city became a representation of the churning of the primeval milk ocean by gods and demons . . ." (Heine-Geldern, *Conceptions of State and Kingship in Southeast Asia,* 19). Narrative mural depictions of battles, treaty signings, or "discoveries" or divine apparitions may provide the most obvious instantiation of that storiological possibility. More often, however, what is represented in the works of art and architecture are "mythologems" (or "historio-gems"), that is, particularly significant themes and motifs that are largely extracted from their respective narrative contexts, as in the case of the pictographic iconography on the walls and friezes at the Toltec capital of Tula, which depict over and over again the image of a serpent eating (or maybe vomiting) a skeletal human figure (see Jones, *Twin City Tales,* 328–32). In those cases we can imagine that it is the rituals and, even more, the cultivated imaginations of the visitors and ritual participants that fill out the relevant narrative plots. Or, in many cases, what is represented seems to be an even more abstracted idea or insight—for example, in the case of ancient Mexican art, the reiterative images of a serpent eating its own tail or the paradoxically juxtaposed images of fire and water, both of which are discussed in Laurette Séjourné, *Burning Water: Thought and Religion in Ancient Mexico,* trans. Irene Nicholson (Berkeley: Shambhala, 1976), 99–126. These cases, which may qualify more as a kind of ritual-architectural exegesis on sacred history than as plainer reiteration of stories, depend even more heavily on a foreknowledge of the wider mythicohistorical background.

Nineteen | Politics

1. John Maass, "Where Architectural Historians Fear to Tread," *Journal of the Society of Architectural Historians* 28 (March 1969): 7.

2. Gary Ebersole, *Ritual Poetry and the Politics of Death in Early Japan* (Princeton: Princeton University Press, 1989), 266. Ebersole acknowledges a debt to David I. Kertzer, *Ritual, Politics, and Power* (New Haven: Yale University Press, 1988).

3. Tschumi, *Architecture and Disjunction,* 22.

4. On architecture (particularly in contrast to literature) as a distinctive sort of "vehicle of intelligibility," a term borrowed from Lawrence Sullivan, see volume 1, chapter 8, especially the section entitled "Textual Tyranny and Alternative Vehicles of Intelligibility."

5. Thucydides *History of the Peloponnesian War* 1.10.1 (Loeb Classical Library); quoted by Alles, "Surface, Space, and Intention: The Parthenon and the Kandariya Mahadeva," 27.

6. Short (*A History of Religious Architecture,* 23–24) suggests this connection between Sargon's palace at Khorsabab, which was built in the eighth century B.C.E., and that of Louis XIV. Anthony Blunt ("Baroque and Rococo," in *Baroque and Rococo,* ed. Blunt, 130, 133) discusses the Place Vendôme and the earlier Place des Victoires, which were royal squares "designed first and foremost to glorify the king [Louis XIV] whose statues they framed" and, moreover, Louis XIV's conception of monarchy as reflected in explicitly ecclesiastical buildings. Kent C. Bloomer and Charles W. Moore (*Body, Memory, and Architecture* [New Haven: Yale University Press, 1977], 12) comment on the placement of Louis XIV's bed at Versailles and likewise allude to a sense in which the gardens there symbolize an integration of nature and imperial authority.

7. See Christopher Tadgell, "France," in *Baroque and Rococo,* ed. Blunt, 123–24.

8. Harbison, *The Built, the Unbuilt, and the Unbuildable,* 42–43.

9. For an indictment of the project, see Samir al-Khalil, *The Monument: Art, Vulgarity, and Responsibility in Iraq* (Berkeley and Los Angeles: University of California Press, 1991); and Peter Partner, "In Saddam's Arms," *New York Review,* 25 April 1991, 8–11.

10. Abbot Suger believed that the king of France was a "vicar of God" and that the authority and unity of France were symbolized and vested in the Abbey of Saint-Denis. See Abbot Suger, *On the Abbey Church of St.-Denis,* 2. Von Simson (*The Gothic Cathedral,* 89) argues that Suger's two principal strategies for implementing his master plan in the sphere of politics were the manipulation of the Carolingian histories and the prodigious rebuilding of Saint-Denis.

11. Kerry Downes, "England," in *Baroque and Rococo,* ed. Blunt, 159.

12. Soundara Rajan, *Invitation to Indian Architecture,* 51.

13. Sankar Prosad Ghosh (*Hindu Religious Art and Architecture* [Delhi: D. K. Publications, 1982], 120) notes that the Hindu temple is, among other things, "a symbol of the prestige and wealth of the founder."

14. The *ceque* system of Peru was a featured example in chapter 14, on homologized architecture (priority I-A).

15. Stanley Tambiah, *World Conqueror and World Renouncer: A Study of*

Buddhism and Polity in Thailand against a Historical Background (Cambridge: Cambridge University Press, 1976), chapter 7.

16. Heine-Geldern, *Conceptions of State and Kingship in Southeast Asia,* 24. Mabbett ("The Symbolism of Mount Meru," 79–81) explains that "in much of Southeast Asia, royal legitimacy was sanctified in great measure by the construction of an impressive shrine rather than a secular palace, as a symbolic Mt. Meru and ritual center of the kingdom."

17. Lefebvre, *The Production of Space,* 221.

18. Friedland and Hecht, "The Politics of Sacred Place: Jerusalem's Temple Mount/*al-haram a-sharif,*" 25. Writing in 1991, they could introduce this study with the not unreasonable claim that they were addressing "an almost entirely overlooked element in the study of sacred places—their intimate connection with politics" (23).

19. In addition to my discussion of Eliade's model of sacred space in chapter 14, see Mircea Eliade, "Sacred Architecture and Symbolism," in *Symbolism, the Sacred, and the Arts,* ed. Apostolos-Cappadona, 105–29.

20. Friedland and Hecht ("The Politics of Sacred Place: Jerusalem's Temple Mount/*al-haram a-sharif,*" 24–28, in a section entitled "Aesthetics or Politics of Sacred Space") provide a concise and critical summary of the shift away from Eliade's model of sacred space toward approaches that better attend to the matters of politics. The shift in emphasis from the "poetics of sacred space" to the "politics of sacred space" is also succintly reviewed and affirmed in the editors' introduction to *American Sacred Space,* ed. Chidester and Linenthal, 5–16; those authors then propose "contested space" as the most salient category for attending to apparently inevitable struggles over the legitimate ownership, use, and (re)interpretation of sacred sites (16–20), a methodological prospect that is well demonstrated by the seven subsequent American case studies in that volume. Also see above, in chapter 14, the section entitled "Recovering Eliade: Heuristic Options and (Would-be) Interpretive Panaceas."

21. Friedland and Hecht, "The Politics of Sacred Place: Jerusalem's Temple Mount/*al-haram a-sharif,*" 55.

22. Maass ("Where Architectural Historians Fear to Tread," 3–8), some thirty years ago, complained that modern architectural historians exhibited, among other faults, a "Bourgeois Standard" and a "Racial Bias" that privileged the study of Western or European pedigreed monuments to the near exclusion of all other contexts and genres of building; he concluded that the architectural historian should be trained additionally in the social sciences, economics, political history, literature, and psychology.

23. David Watkin, *The Rise of Architectural History* (London: Architectural Press, 1980), 183. Watkin, who is especially concerned with architectural history in England, attributes this growing concern for the social context of architecture primarily to the influence of Marxist theories from the 1950s through the 1970s; he

associates this approach in art history especially with the work of Arnold Hauser and of Dvorak's pupil, Frederick Antal.

24. Ibid.

25. Isozaki, "Floors and Internal Spaces in Japanese Vernacular Architecture," 66.

26. Oliver, introduction to *Shelter, Sign, and Symbol,* ed. Oliver, 17; Oliver quotes from Father M. C. Nieubarn, *Church Symbolism,* trans. Rev. John Waterreus (London: Sands and Co., 1910), 45.

27. Edmund W. Sinnott, *Meetinghouse and Church in Early New England* (New York: McGraw-Hill, 1963), 7.

28. On Navajo hogans, see Oliver, *Dwellings,* 155. On Amazonian Tukanoan community houses, see ibid., 165. With respect to the architectural accoutrements of gender and sexuality in a very different context, note that Michel Foucault (*The History of Sexuality,* vol. 1, *An Introduction,* trans. Robert Hurley [New York: Vintage Books, 1988], 27–28) discusses how the architectural layout of secondary schools in eighteenth-century Western Europe, both in classrooms and dormitories, was among the principal mechanisms for monitoring and controlling the precocious sexuality of children, which was regarded at that point as a "public problem."

29. Waterson, "The House and the World: The Symbolism of Sa'Dan Toraja House Carvings," 35.

30. Waterson (ibid.) explains that while only a select minority of nobles are allowed to live in these *tongkonan,* or family origin-houses, every Toraja person traces his or her descent through one of these houses.

31. Oliver, *Dwellings,* 24.

32. Landa, *Relación de las cosas de Yucatán,* 62; quoted and discussed by Tozzer, *Chichén Itzá and Its Cenote of Sacrifice,* 73, 83. Subsequent settlement pattern studies have challenged the archaeological viability of Landa's ideas of Mayapán planning and particularly their over-generalization to other Maya sites; see Diane Z. Chase, "Ganned But Not Forgotten: Late Postclassic Archaeology and Ritual at Santa Rita Corozal, Belize," in *The Lowland Maya Postclassic,* ed. Arlen F. Chase and Prudence M. Rice (Austin: University of Texas Press, 1985), 104–25.

33. Carmack, *The Quiché Mayas of Utatlán,* 159–64.

34. Marwyn S. Samuels and Carmencita Samuels ("Beijing and the Power of Place in Modern China," 206) describe separate gates to Beijing and explain that, so rigorously enforced were the cosmological and social conventions, "one approached [traditional Beijing] in awe, not to mention fear, careful to observe every nuance of the ritual aimed to affirm and proclaim one's fealty and reverence for the Harmony and Virtue of the Imperial and Confucian Order." Note also the fascinating discussion of "graduated privacy" in the layout of Beijing and its houses provided by Nelson Wu, *Chinese and Indian Architecture,* 32–34, which I discuss in chapter 24 relative to the sanctuary priority (III-D).

35. Volwahsen, *Living Architecture: Indian,* 57.

36. For a "walk through" of the various ascending levels at Xochicalco, see Carrasco, *Quetzalcoatl and the Irony of Empire,* 126–33. More generally, Kubler ("The Design of Space in Maya Architecture," 528–29) notes "differentiation by height" as "a cardinal objective of the American Indian architect in all periods and all regions," and then cites several pre-Columbian sites (not including Xochicalco) to illustrate the concept of "the ascending ranks of courts rising in hierarchic order."

37. Ardalan and Bakhtiar, *The Sense of Unity: The Sufi Tradition in Persian Architecture,* 70.

38. Ibid.

39. Jean DeBernardi, "Space and Time in Chinese Religious Culture," *History of Religions* 31 (February 1992): 258.

40. Isozaki, "Floors and internal Spaces in Japanese Vernacular Architecture," 59.

41. Ibid.

42. Regarding architecture as social critique, Watkin (*The Rise of Architectural History,* 184) says: "It ought to be pointed out that there is no reason why an architect, artist or patron should not escape from rather than 'express' what the ruling orthodoxy of the day regards as 'reality.'"

43. Edwardes, *Indian Temples and Palaces,* 137.

44. Arshi, *Sikh Architecture in Punjab,* 94. Arshi repeats: "It has been claimed that the four gateways symbolize the spirit of casteless society that the [Sikh] religion stands for" (106).

45. See Anthony A. Lee, ed. *Circle of Unity: Baha'i Approaches to Current Social Issues* (Los Angeles: Kalimat Press, 1984).

46. Madeline C. Zilfi, *The Politics of Piety: The Ottoman Ulema in the Postclassical Age, 1600–1800,* Studies in Middle Eastern History, no. 8 (Minneapolis: Bibliotheca Islamica, 1988), 129–30. On the exemplary demonstration of the ideals of brotherhood and equality in Muslim mosques, also see Ziyaud-Din Desai, *Mosques of India,* 3d ed. (New Delhi: Ministry of Information and Broadcasting, Government of India, 1979), 6–7. Also note that this and parallel cases are discussed in a subsection of chapter 24, on the sanctuary priority (III-D), entitled "Exemplary Models for Society: Prototypes of Religiopolitical Perfection."

47. Robertson, *Pre-Columbian Architecture,* 20–21.

48. Tange and Kawazoe (*Ise: Prototype of Japanese Architecture,* 191) summarize this story from the *Kojiki,* the mythicohistorical "Chronicle of Ancient Events" (completed in 712 C.E.).

49. Tschumi, *Architecture and Disjunction,* 8.

50. Ibid., 8–9, 44.

51. Ibid., 10–11.

52. Ibid., 45.

53. The limitations (and virtues) of architecture as an instrument of socio-

political change are closely aligned with the limitations (and virtues) of architecture as a specific sort of resource for the academic study of religion, which I inventoried in volume 1, chapter 9, "Studying Buildings by Decision or Default: Architecture's Evidential Promise."

54. As Tschumi (*Architecture and Disjunction,* 10–11) notes, the greatest transformative rewards of that sort of subversive architectural activity, either personally or sociologically speaking, will usually lie not in the finished object, but in the collective constructional activity, which, to borrow from Frantz Fanon, constitutes an "action in order to become conscious of one's existence," or, in Tschumi's phrase, "the revelation through building of realities and contradictions of society." Note also that this sort of transformative constructional activity will be addressed again in chapter 23 with respect to the propitiation priority (III-C), under the rubric "building as ritual."

55. Raymond Sidrys, "Megalithic Architecture and Sculpture of the Ancient Maya," in *Papers on the Economy and Architecture of the Ancient Maya,* ed. Raymond Sidrys (Los Angeles: Institute of Archaeology, University of California, 1978), 155–57.

56. See Hilary Sumner-Boyd and John Freely, *Strolling through Istanbul: A Guide to the City,* 4th ed. (Istanbul: Redhouse Press, 1989), 11ff.

57. Short (*A History of Religious Architecture,* 52) describes Augustus's building campaign by saying, "the Greek statues in the streets and temples of Rome were so numerous that it was said that the city had two populations, one of flesh and blood, the other of marble and bronze." Short also cites the profusion of explicitly commemorative religiocivic monuments that filled Rome: especially prominent on a seemingly endless list of exemplars are the Temple of Concord, built by Camillus to commemorate the reconciliation of the Patricians and the Plebians in 367 B.C.E.; the Arch of Severus, dedicated in 203 B.C.E. in memory of the Parthian victories; and the Arch of Titus, which commemorates the conquest of Jerusalem in70 C.E. (56–58).

58. H. P. L'Orange, *Art Forms and Civic Life in the Late Roman Empire* (Princeton: Princeton University Press, 1965), 75.

59. G. H. S. Bushnell (Bushnell, *Ancient Arts of the Americas* [New York: Frederick A. Praeger, 1965], 215) writes of Inca conquest architecture: "the same standardized type of building is found wherever the Inca conquests reached, from Ecuador, to Chile and northwest Argentina. . . . Many of the coastal buildings were put up to dominate older sites like the sanctuary of Pachacamac, where a great terraced platform towers above the remains of the older shrines." Von Hagen (*Realm of the Incas,* 51, 133, 145, 200, and 202) makes similar points.

60. Krautheimer, *Rome: Profile of a City,* 31–34.

61. Ibid., 177–79.

62. It is particularly ironic, given the ambiguous historical reality of Constantine's building program, that, in the twelfth-century rebirth of Rome, the Benedictines

(among others) would invoke Constantine and Saint Peter's as the paradigm for an architecture that can underwrite a union of church and state. Wittkower (*Architectural Principles in the Age of Humanism,* 5), for instance, shows that even in the fifteenth century Alberti was still enamored of the "Constantinian paradigm."

63. George Cowgill, "Rulership and the Ciudadela: Political Inferences from Teotihuacan Architecture," in *Civilization in the Ancient Americas: Essays in Honor of Gordon R. Willey,* ed. Richard M. Leventhal and Alan L. Kolata (Albuquerque: University of New Mexico Press; Cambridge, Mass.: Peabody Museum of Archaeology and Ethnology, Harvard University, 1983), 329–32.

64. Ibid., 330. It is interesting, morphologically speaking, that, while the Inca is alive in his palace, it is an operative bureaucratic center (primarily an instance of the commemoration of politics, priority II-C), but once he dies, the same building is, by prearrangement, transformed into a tomb-shrine, or *huaca* (commemoration of the dead, priority II-D).

65. Cowgill (ibid., 331) acknowledges that his interpretation of the Ciudadela as one of the central symbols of the state, apart from any specific ruler and apart from the day-to-day operation of government, directly follows from the interpretation of René Millon. Cowgill considers that the royal palaces of Montezuma and his predecessors to the Aztec throne are somewhat more like the Chimu temples in their correlation with specific individuals.

66. With respect to the artistic commemoration of specific individuals at Teotihuacan, Weaver (*The Aztecs, Maya, and Their Predecessors,* 136), basing her opinion on work by Kubler, Millon, and Sanders, suggests that after 500 C.E. there is "a trend away from purely religious symbolism toward individual glorification and warfare."

67. Sir Banister Fletcher, in the 1946 preface to his *A History of Architecture on the Comparative Method for Students, Craftsmen, and Amateurs,* 13th ed. (New York: Charles Scribner's Sons, 1946), ix, continues that observation with the less certain claim that "To-day it is the turn of the people as a whole to become the patron of this the oldest of the arts" (ix).

68. See James, *From Cave to Cathedral,* 102, 113.

69. The interpretation of J. D. Ray, in "Egyptian Pyramids," *Encyclopedia of Religion,* ed. Eliade, 12:111–13, suggests this shift in emphasis.

70. Michell, *The Hindu Temple,* 53.

71. Ibid., 54.

72. See, for instance, Heine-Geldern, *Conceptions of State and Kingship in Southeast Asia,* 24; and Mabbett, "The Symbolism of Mount Meru," 79–81.

73. Michell, *The Hindu Temple,* 53. These posthumous commemorations, of course, likewise demonstrate the ritual-architectural commemoration of sacred history (priority II-B) and of the dead (priority II-D). Demonstrating a regional disparity of enthusiasm for the ritual-architectural glorification of specific individuals, Michell notes that, "Portraits of the royal patrons of temples in the

buildings themselves are rare in India. Temple architecture in Nepal [however] sometimes incorporates commemorative stone columns, upon which an image of the ruler is placed facing the principal entrance to the temple" (53).

74. James (*From Cave to Cathedral,* 61) credits this interpretation to Martin P. Nilsson, *The Minoan-Mycenaen Religion and Its Survival in Greek Religion,* 2d rev. ed. (Lund: C. W. K. Gleerup, 1950), 438ff.

75. Early-twentieth-century Mayanist Sylvanus Morley, quoted by Deuel, *Conquistadors without Swords,* 383. Deuel provides a brief historiographical account of the controversy (383–87). Thomas A. Joyce (*Maya and Mexican Art* [London: "The Studio," Ltd., 1927], 41) argues that Maya human representation was conventionalized and impersonal: "portraiture, as we understood it, did not exist." And Spinden (*A Study of Maya Art,* 23) says, "it is exceedingly doubtful whether any [Maya] sculptures were seriously intended as portraits of individual chiefs or priests."

76. Ignacio Bernal (*Mexican Wall Paintings of the Maya and Aztec Period* [New York: New American Library of World Literature, 1963], 16) cites Miguel Covarrubias as his authority for concluding that the regalia, ornaments, and accessories of office are far more important than human figures in Maya murals. Similarly, with respect to Maya sculpture, Bushnell (*Ancient Arts of the Americas,* 106) concludes that "most examples give the impression that the office mattered more than the man."

77. See, for instance, Linda Schele and Mary Ellen Miller, *The Blood of Kings: Dynasty and Ritual in Maya Art* (New York: Braziller; Fort Worth, Texas: Kimball Art Museum, 1986). John Lloyd Stephens (*Incidents of Travel in Central America, Chiapas, and Yucatán* [1841; New York: Dover Publications, 1969], 1:139, 153–58) deserves credit for anticipating this position in the mid-nineteenth century.

78. See especially volume 1, chapter 7, "Use and Uselessness: The Special Case of Architecture."

79. Among the particular problems with the present tripartite division of religiocivic ritual-architectural subpriorities is the somewhat distorting intimation that the first and especially the third options are "symbolic," while the second is not; but, as the forthcoming example of Winston Churchill and the House of Commons ought to demonstrate, even architectural facilitations of routine governmental affairs depend upon the strategic deployment of symbols.

80. Sir Winston Churchill, 28 October 1943, in a speech to the House of Commons; quoted in Anita Abramovitz, *People and Spaces: A View of History through Architecture* (New York: Viking Press, 1979), 10–11.

81. Ooka, *Temples of Nara and Their Art,* 18.

82. Tamaru Noriyoshi, "Buddhism in Japan," *Encyclopedia of Religion,* ed. Eliade, 2:428.

83. Nancy Shatzman Steinhardt, "The Han Ritual Hall," in Steinhardt et al., *Chinese Traditional Architecture,* 74.

84. Friedrich Katz, *The Ancient American Civilizations,* trans. K. M. Lois Simpson (New York: Praeger, 1972), chapter 13, describes how much more thoroughly integrated the Inca empire was than either the Maya or especially the Aztec empire.

85. See John S. Henderson, *The World of the Ancient Maya* (Ithaca, N.Y.: Cornell University Press, 1981), 232. The strength of the materialist position in Mesoamerican studies has insured that this political character of architecture and ritual has been very well documented; Kubler (*Art and Architecture in Ancient America,* 41) cites Cecelia Klein and Johanna Broda (somewhat unfairly I think) as exemplars of the "hard materialist" approach that has class struggle as a dominant theme and in which "the place of art is reduced . . . to propaganda for the state."

86. See E. Wyllys Andrews, V, "Dzibilchaltún," in *Supplement to the Handbook of Middle America Indians,* vol. 1 (Austin: University of Texas Press, 1981), 329, 332.

87. Kelemen (*Medieval American Art,* 1:38, 48) contrasts the Aztec remodeling of Malinalco with their more typically disinterested occupation of Mitla, where "they seem to have left little impression on the place."

88. Carrasco (*Quetzalcoatl and the Irony of Empire,* chapter 3) discusses at length ways in which the Aztecs and numerous other groups legitimated their claims to authority with reference to the mythicohistorical Toltecs. I describe this and parallel examples above, in chapter 15, particularly in the section entitled "Deliberate Archaisms and Mythicohistorical Precedents: Mesoamerican Examples."

89. Michael L. Blakey, "Man and Nature, White and Other," in *Decolonizing Anthropology: Moving Further toward an Anthropology of Liberation,* ed. Faye V. Harrison (Washington, D.C.: American Anthropological Association, 1991), 18.

90. Another very different instantiation of the ritual-architectural quest after pedigree comes in the eighth-century Hindu temple at Kanchipuram dedicated to Vaikunthaperumal, an aspect of Vishnu; Michell (*The Hindu Temple,* 54) explains that the interior walls of the colonnade around the courtyard are covered with carved panels that recount "the whole history of the Pallava kings from which scholars have been able to reconstruct the dynastic chronology." In another very different historical circumstance, the lengths to which one might go to connect oneself to a prestigious architectural tradition is caricatured by Joao V (1707–1750), the Portuguese king who, frustrated in his attempt to attract a major Italian architect to Portugal, had a chapel constructed entirely in Rome, blessed by Pope Benedict XVI, then dismantled and shipped to Lisbon where it was re-erected in the church of Sao Roco. See Blunt, "Baroque and Rococo," in *Baroque and Rococo,* ed. Blunt, 323.

91. Spinden (*A Study of Maya Art,* 21–22, 178), for instance, compares the bound human figures in Maya bas reliefs at Tikal and Naranjo, among other places, to ancient Far Eastern conquest monuments that picture the foot of the king on the neck of a captive.

92. Similar to Montejo's palace in Merida, but more drastic still, is that archi-

tectural event in which the Incas led captives in triumph through Cuzco, forced them to lie prone in front of the Sun Temple, and then trod on their necks to symbolize victory. See von Hagen, *Realm of the Incas,* 200.

93. See Spinden, *A Study of Maya Art,* 221.

94. John Pohl, "The Significance of Human Sacrifice in the Codex Zouche-Nuttal" (paper presented at the annual meeting of the Society for American Archaeology, New Orleans, 1977). Broda ("Templo Mayor as Ritual Space," 41) similarly discusses how, at the main temple of the Aztecs, "it was political power transformed into supernatural power by means of sacrifice."

95. Edwardes, *Indian Temples and Palaces,* 178.

96. Ibid.

97. Ibid., 186.

98. Ibid.

99. See volume 1, chapter 7, "Use and Uselessness: The Special Case of Architecture"; or Gadamer, *Truth and Method,* 138–39.

100. Richard Townsend, "Coronation at Tenochtitlan," in *The Imagination of Matter: Religion and Ecology in Mesoamerican Traditions,* ed. Davíd Carrasco, B.A.R. International Series, 515 (Oxford, England: B.A.R., 1989), 155–88.

101. Ibid., 406. Regarding the ingenious instigation of highly political ritual-architectural events, Clemency C. Coggins ("The Zenith, the Mountain, the Center, and the Sea," in *Ethnoastronomy and Archaeoastronomy in the American Tropics,* ed. Aveni and Urton, 115) reviews the correlation of the revered imagery of zenith and center, the movement of the sun, and the experience of the volcano of Tacana (that is, cosmology, astronomy, and geography) with the specific privileges and demands of rulership in the kingship rituals of Izapa, Chiapas. The Izapa kingship ritual that she describes seems to follow much the same pattern as the so-called Copán Temple 22-Sun-Venus-Maize-Kingship event discussed in chapter 16 relative to the astronomy priority (I-C), insofar as astronomical and homologized orientations are used to instigate an architectural event that communicates the specifics of Izapa rulership. And, similarly, Carolyn Tate describes how a jaguarian-anthropomorphic motif known as the Cauac Monster, originally an apolitical and universalistic depiction of the devouring and regenerative earth (and, as such, perfectly suited to initiating a ritual-architectural event), was later enlisted as a stylized pedestal by specific Maya leaders, and thus became an emblem of the legitimacy of their rulership; see Carolyn Tate, "The Maya Cauac Monster's Formal Development and Dynastic Contexts," in *Pre-Columbian Art History,* ed. Cordy-Collins and Stern, especially 33 and 52.

102. Tschumi (*Architecture and Disjunction,* 44–45), for instance, comments critically on the oversimple presuppositions of behaviorism, "according to which individual behavior could be influenced by the organization of space."

103. See especially volume 1, chapter 12, "Multifarious Revalorization: The Composition of Ritual-Architectural Reception Histories."

104. Jacques Maquet, *The Aesthetic Experience: An Anthropologist Looks at the Visual Arts* (New Haven: Yale University Press, 1986), 221. Maquet contends that, in response to fear about the polysemic character of visual symbols, totalitarian regimes will "try to dry up the two sources of those symbols—aesthetic excellence and conceptualism." Then, he notes, "This is, in fact, what happened in Stalin's Russia and Hitler's Germany."

105. Ronald L. Grimes, in his *Ritual Criticism: Case Studies in Its Practice, Essays on Its Theory* (Columbia: University of South Carolina Press, 1990), chapter 9, "Infelicitous Performances and Ritual Criticism," comments on the prevailing hesitancy of scholars to entertain the possibility that most rituals, in some sense, fail, and then presents a "typology of infelicitous ritual."

Twenty | The Dead

1. Father Bernabé Cobo, in chapter 18, "Of the Different Types of Tombs They Had," of his *Inca Religion and Customs,* 246.

2. Arthur Mercier, *Le Sépulture chrétienne en France d'après, les monuments du XIe au XVIe siècle* (Paris, 1855); quoted by Michel Ragon, *The Space of Death: A Study of Funerary Architecture, Decoration, and Urbanism,* trans. Alan Sheridan (Charlottesville: University Press of Virginia, 1983), 147.

3. Tschumi, *Architecture and Disjunction,* 74. The essay containing this quotation, "Architecture and Transgression," originally appeared in *Oppositions* 7 (winter 1976).

4. Robert Auzelle, *Dernières demeures* (Paris, 1965); quoted by Ragon, *The Space of Death,* 119.

5. Cobo, *Inca Religion and Customs,* 39–43.

6. Pedro de Cieza de León, *The Travels of Pedro de Cieza de León, A.D. 1532–50,* trans. and ed. Clements R. Markham (London, 1864); quoted by von Hagen, *Realm of the Incas,* 110.

7. Moholy-Nagy, *Native Genius in Anonymous Architecture,* 144.

8. Raymond Decary, *La mort et les coutumes funéraires à Madagascar* (Paris: Maisonneuve et Larose, 1962); quoted by Ragon, *The Space of Death,* 35–36.

9. See Suzanne Preston Blier, "The Dance of Death: Notes on the Architecture and Staging of Tamberma Funeral Performance," *Res: Anthropology and Aesthetics* 2 (autumn 1981): 107–43. More will be said on the Tamberma in chapter 21, on the theater priority, III-A.

10. Joseph M. Kitagawa, personal communication.

11. I would note in candor that, of the treatments of the eleven ritual-architectural priorities in this morphology, I am least satisfied with this chapter on commemorations of the dead. I have failed to convince myself, for instance, that the presence or absence of bodily remains (which I foreground in this essay) is actually a particularly (relatively) significant organizational criterion for historians

of religions. Substantially different and stronger efforts are, I hope, forthcoming. Such work could capitalize more fully on, among many possibilities, Howard Colvin, *Architecture and the After-Life* (New Haven: Yale University Press, 1991); James Steven Curl, *A Celebration of Death: An Introduction to Some of the Buildings, Monuments, and Settings of Funerary Architecture in the Western European Tradition* (London: Batsford, 1993); Edward T. Linenthal, *Sacred Ground: Americans and Their Battlefields;* idem, *Preserving Memory: The Struggle to Create America's Holocaust Museum* (New York: Viking Press, 1995); and Peter Metcalf and Richard Huntington, *Celebrations of Death: The Anthropology of Mortuary Ritual,* 2d ed., rev. (Cambridge: Cambridge University Press, 1991).

12. In chapter 18, on sacred history (priority II-B), see the section entitled "Mythicohistorical Personages: Ritual-Architectural Expressions of Excellence," nearly all of which is directly relevant to commemorations of the dead (priority II-D).

13. Marcel Griaule, *Conversations with Ogotemmêli: An Introduction to Dogon Religious Ideas* (London: Oxford University Press for the International African Institute, 1965).

14. Ibid., 93.

15. Ibid., 99.

16. Ibid.

17. In that sense, then, the design of Dogon houses and sanctuaries participates equally in the commemoration of the dead (II-D) and of sacred history (II-B).

18. It is important to keep stressing that what I am presenting here is a morphological possibility, not an empirical observation; empirically speaking, it is rare even in highly rationalized contexts for people to be fully indifferent about the status and whereabouts of physical remains. Moreover, we could note the seeming inconsistency of maintaining, on the one hand, that the deceased are "fully dead," yet, on the other hand, feeling compelled to "honor" the dead or "the memory of the dead," which raises even more questions.

19. Again, see, in chapter 18, the section entitled "Mythicohistorical Personages: Ritual-Architectural Expressions of Excellence."

20. Burl, *Rites of the Gods.* Burl's consideration of megalith ritual constitutes a pleasant contrast to Glyn Daniel's important, more strictly archaeological work, *The Megalith Builders of Western Europe* (London: Hutchinson, 1958), which, besides tending to objectify these monuments, is problematic because it antedates both the carbon-14 dating revolution and most of the serious work on the archaeoastronomical significance of megaliths. Among other important and relevant works by Aubrey Burl, see his *Stone Circles of the British Isles* (New Haven: Yale University Press, 1976) and *Prehistoric Avebury* (New Haven: Yale University Press, 1979).

21. Burl's (and others') analyses of these infamous megaliths—paragons of architectural superabundance—are useful in reminding us again of the interpenetrability and artificiality of morphological categories. Where virtually all interpreters

now acknowledge, with still varying enthusiasm, significant astronomical alignments (exercises of the astronomy priority [I-C]), additional interpretive opinions range over nearly the entire heuristic framework. Many note, for instance, that stone circles of the British Isles encapsulated a sacred space within the prosaic landscape (thus instantiating the sanctuary priority [III-D]). Others (for instance, Burl, *Rites of the Gods,* 71) stress that the chambered tombs in the same area served as stage-like backdrops for cult practice in their forecourts (thus evincing the relevance of the theater priority [III-A]), or that the megalithic temple-tombs were the loci of prayerful petitions of news and favors (propitiation [priority III-C]). It has even been claimed, albeit unconvincingly, that some megaliths were intended as gigantic symbolic representations of mythological animals (thus exemplifying a variation of the sacred history priority [II-B]) or perhaps even as formalized representations of deities (thus instantiating the divinity priority [II-A]); for example, James (*From Cave to Cathedral,* 88) notes that the attempt of William Stukeley, in *Abury: A Temple of the British Druids, and Some Others Described* (London, 1743), pp. 32 et seq., "to interpret the lay of the entire monument [of Avebury] as a symbolic representation of a serpent, with the Overton Sanctuary as its head and the Beckhampton Avenue as its tail, cannot be taken seriously." It is also noteworthy that English architect Inigo Jones, after careful measurements, mistook Stonehenge for the ruins of a proportional Roman temple, in which case that version of the convention priority (II-B) that accentuates adherence to universal principles would have been especially important; see Wittkower, *Architectural Principles in the Age of Humanism,* 143.

22. Burl, *Rites of the Gods,* 47–50. Burl himself does not differentiate quite so systematically between these five stages as I do.

23. Ibid., 61.

24. Ibid., 143.

25. Ibid., 197–99.

26. Ibid., 201.

27. Ruggles (*Megalithic Astronomy,* 305) considers that his more thorough statistical analysis supports Burl's general conclusions about lunar orientations at megalithic burial and ceremonial sites. Be that as it may, in my view, with respect to the twofold pattern of ritual-architectural events, it is probably more useful to imagine the astronomical alignments of megaliths in terms of strategies of instigation and mechanisms for the "right timing" (that is, as exercises of the astronomy priority [I-C]), which initiate architectural events wherein people can commemorate and communicate with their (un)dead ancestors (thus instantiating priority II-D).

28. V. Gordon Childe, *The Dawn of European Civilization* (London: Kegan Paul, Trench, Trubner and Co.; New York: Alfred A. Knopf,1925), 284–85; here he addresses specifically French megalithic culture.

29. Ray, "Stonehenge: A New Theory," 269. Though I appreciate Ray's assess-

ment, I would not emphasize so strongly the connections with the physical remains of the dead.

30. For a concise summary and bibliography of Robert Heine-Geldern's extensive work on megaliths, see Eliade, *A History of Religious Ideas,* 1:123–24, 411.

31. Ibid., 115.

32. Ibid., 124.

33. Sullivan ("Astral Myths Rise Again," 15) is in perfect accord with Eliade on this point.

34. There is, in other words, a parallel between the direct identification of megaliths and the dead and the direct identification of, say, the Cretan palace and the body of the Minoan goddess, as discussed in chapter 17 with respect to the divinity priority (II-A). In that chapter, see especially the section "Architecture as the Body of God: Personified Landscapes and Earth Monsters."

35. Lefebvre, *The Production of Space,* 221.

36. I borrow the phrase "intense aversion to littleness" from Bernard Rudofsky, *The Prodigious Builders: Notes toward a Natural History of Architecture* (New York: Harcourt Brace Jovanovich, 1977), 95. Also with respect to the important religious significance of sheer size, specifically in relation to Egyptian pyramids, see G. van der Leeuw, *Sacred and Profane Beauty,* 206–8, where van der Leeuw considers that building at a massive, monumental scale is the most obviously effective strategy for expressing the power of "the Holy" in architecture. And John Ruskin, in *The Seven Lamps of Architecture,* with respect to "the lamp of power" (chapter 3), notes that the relative majesty of architecture depends more on the impression of sheer size than on any other attribute of the design. We ought also to remember, however, that many scholars, for a variety of reasons, share the assessment of Gottfried Richter (*Art and Human Consciousness,* 11) that "massiveness has nothing to do with monumentality." For a range of relevant opinions, see, in volume 1, chapter 7, the section entitled "Architecture as Utilitarian and Transutilitarian."

37. Adrian Stokes considers that "the love of stone" (or the art of "stone blossom") is the premier characteristic of one mode of Renaissance art. Though Stokes is not particularly concerned with stone in relation to the commemoration of the dead, his remarks are apt. See *The Image in Form: Selected Writings of Adrian Stokes,* ed. Richard Wollheim (New York: Harper and Row, 1972), 14.

38. Regarding cross-cultural instantiation of the symbolism of rocks and stones, see Eliade, *Patterns in Comparative Religion,* chapter 6.

39. Doris Heyden, "Caves, Gods, and Myths: World-Views and Planning in Teotihuacán," in *Mesoamerican Sites and World-Views,* ed. Benson, 10. Heyden is directly influenced by Eliade.

40. Adrián Recinos, trans., *Popol Vuh: The Sacred Book of the Quiché Maya,* trans. Delia Goetz and Sylvanus G. Morley (Norman: University of Oklahoma Press, 1950), 190, 205–6, 225, reconstructs this account of Nacxit's (that is, Quetzalcoatl's) gift of stone to the Quiché from references in both the *Popol Vuh*

and the *Título de los señores de Totonicapán,* the two principal Quiché literary sources. Regarding the wider significance of stones for Mesoamericans, Recinos (190, n. 13; 209, n. 3; and 225, n. 2) notes that the Yucatecan cosmogonic account in *The Chilam Balam of Chumayel* says that "God" was hidden in a stone when there was neither earth nor day, and that later he left that stone, fell into a second stone, and there declared his divinity (*Kuil*). Recinos considers the crucial theme here to be "the constant association of the divinity with stone" (190), but more recent research suggests that, in Mesoamerica, the commemoration of ancestors was actually more relevant than the commemoration of deities—thus, morphologically speaking, the leading priority is "the dead" (priority II-D) rather than "divinity" (priority II-A).

41. Soundara Rajan, *Invitation to Indian Architecture,* 26–27.

42. Mabbett, "The Symbolism of Mount Meru," 74.

43. See, for instance, Tange and Kawazoe, *Ise: Prototype of Japanese Architecture,* 166–67. In the same vein, Mirsky (*Houses of God,* 6) suggests that there was often an identity between stone pillars and gods as, for instance, at the Canaanite stone at Hazor in northern Israel, with carved hands raised to the sun, at the Temple of Solomon, in the Indus Valley, at Ur, and in Egypt where the stone obelisk "stood for the sun god Amon-Re."

44. See Braunfels, *Monasteries of Western Europe,* 74; or Thomas Merton, *The Waters of Siloe* (New York: Harcourt, Brace, 1949), 14. Merton affirms that, from a Trappist or Cistercian view, stone speaks directly of poverty and contemplation.

45. Ragon, *The Space of Death,* 77. Ragon says: "This sacred stool is kept in the house of the ancestors. Each New Year the stools are taken out and whisky or gin is offered to them."

46. Freedberg, *The Power of Images,* 231. He continues by arguing that "We fear the lifelike because the dead substance of which the object is made may yet come alive."

47. Ibid., 440.

48. Ibid., 439–40; see also 315.

49. Where my allusions to *feng shui* in chapter 15 with respect to the convention priority (I-B) accentuated the important role of the codified design prescriptions contained in ritual and divination texts such as the *Chou li* (The rites of the Chou dynasty) and the *I ching* (Book of changes), my emphasis here is on the crucial ritual-architectural role of bodily remains in *feng shui* planning.

50. See Joseph Needham, *Science and Civilization in China,* vol. 4, *Physics and Physical Technology,* pt. 1, *Physics* (Cambridge: Cambridge University Press, 1962); cited by Carlson, "A Geomantic Model for the Interpretation of Mesoamerican Sites," 164.

51. The *Tsang-shu* of Kuo P'u; quoted both by Hong-Key Yoon, "Geomantic Relationships between Culture and Nature in Korea, *Asian Folklore and Social Life Monographs,* vol. 88 (Taipei, Formosa: Orient Cultural Service, 1976), 26, and by

Carlson, "A Geomantic Model for the Interpretation of Mesoamerican Sites," 170.

52. See Meyer, "*Feng-shui* of the Chinese City," 139–50; Else Glahn, "Unfolding the Chinese Building Standards: Research on the *Yingzao fashi,*" in *Chinese Traditional Architecture,* Steinhardt et al.; and Wu, *Chinese and Indian Architecture,* 36–44.

53. At this point, the convention priority (I-B) is especially closely aligned to what I will describe in chapter 23 as the propitiation priority (III-C).

54. Usually (though not always), the bones of the dead, rather than the flesh, are most highly esteemed. Notably, Native Americans, Oceanians, and the early peoples of northern Europe, among others, exposed deceased bodies to the air and to birds of prey before the skulls and bare bones, as it were, were more carefully preserved. On the typical priority of bones over flesh, see Ragon, *The Space of Death,* 10–11, 76. Regarding the prestige of bones in Mesoamerica, Landa (*Relación de las cosas de Yucatán,* 18–19, 120, 123, 131) describes the Yucatec practice of cremating the bodies, but preserving the skulls, of important people—a practice that Eric Thompson confirmed archaeologically and interpreted as evidence of an ancestor cult among the aristocracy of Yucatan and, possibly, Guatemala. Carlson, "A Geomantic Model for the Interpretation of Mesoamerican Sites," 193; Tozzer, *Chichén Itzá and Its Cenote of Sacrifice,* 218–19; and Coe, *The Maya,* 131, all make use of these references. And Bartolomé de Las Casas says that the cadavers of famous Quiché lords were burned and their bodies joined together with gold thread and precious stones to form "mummies" that were entombed and held in great veneration by people who burned incense and made sacrifices to them during important temple ceremonies; Bartolomé de Las Casas, *Apologética historia de las Indias,* vol. 1 of *Historiadores de las Indias,* Nueva biblioteca de autores espanoles, 13, 15 (Madrid: Bailly, Bailliere e hijos, 1909), 630; quoted by Carmack, *The Quiché Mayas of Utatlán,* 194.

55. Carlson ("A Geomantic Model for the Interpretation of Mesoamerican Sites," 190–93), who is specifically concerned to locate Mesoamerican parallels to *feng shui,* notes several myths and practices in which pre-Columbian Americans in that region connect their prosperity and, in fact, their very existence to a rebirth from ancestral bones. Or, in a quite different, rather more grisly testament to the prestige of bones and body parts (and a vivid demonstration of the linked priorities of homology [I-A], politics [II-C], and the dead [II-D]), Ragon (*The Space of Death,* 10) explains how, in late-eighteenth-century France, the Convention heard (and rejected) a proposal that "the body of Louis XIV be cut up into eighty-three pieces, one piece being sent to each of the eighty-three French departments to fumigate the eighty-three trees of liberty."

56. Oliver (*Dwellings,* 38) explains that, in the case of the Fulani compounds of Bé, "When a member of the family died the body would be interred near the guest hut but the deceased's own hut would be abandoned. Soon the puddled earth would be used for the building of another hut nearby."

57. Ibid., 156. Among the Maya, similar practices of abandoning a house upon the death of a family member seem to have obtained; see, for instance, J. Eric S. Thompson, *Maya Archaeologist,* 90.

58. Ragon, *The Space of Death,* 36.

59. Ibid., 26.

60. Ibid., 34.

61. Kelemen, *Medieval American Art,* 1:47.

62. Ragon, *The Space of Death,* 27.

63. Ibid.

64. Ibid., 34.

65. Ibid., 45.

66. Claude Lévi-Strauss, *Tristes Tropiques,* trans. John and Doreen Weightman (New York: Atheneum, 1974), 232.

67. Mirsky, *Houses of God,* 5.

68. Ragon, *The Space of Death,* 58.

69. Ibid., chapter 8, explores the history of this notion of "the vegetal setting of death."

70. Ibid., 208.

71. Ibid., 66.

72. Decary, *La mort et les coutumes funéraires à Madagascar;* cited by Ragon, *The Space of Death,* 68. Ragon also notes that the image of the boatman for the final crossing likewise appears in Greece, Rome, China, and Brittany.

73. Ragon, *The Space of Death,* 68 n. 5.

74. Ibid., 19.

75. See Eliade, *The Sacred and the Profane,* chapter 1.

76. Leonardo López Luján, *The Offerings of the Templo Mayor of Tenochtitlan,* trans. Bernard R. Ortiz de Montellano and Thelma Ortiz de Montellano (Niwot: University Press of Colorado, 1994).

77. See, for instance, Coe, *The Maya,* 103.

78. I will return to this notion of offerings of the dead as "gifts to the gods" in chapter 23, on the propitiation priority (III-C).

79. Ragon, *The Space of Death,* 7.

80. Ibid., 13.

81. See, for instance, Hirakawa Akira, "Stupa Worship," *Encyclopedia of Religion,* ed. Eliade, 14:92–96.

82. Bhardwaj, *Hindu Places of Pilgrimage in India,* 71.

83. Ragon, *The Space of Death,* 16.

84. Ibid.

85. Ibid., 26.

86. Moholy-Nagy, *Native Genius in Anonymous Architecture,* 88.

87. Mirsky, *Houses of God,* 20.

88. See, for instance, Leonard H. Lesko, "Egyptian Religion," *Encyclopedia of Religion,* ed. Eliade, 5:48.

89. Ragon, *The Space of Death*, 27.
90. Cobo, *Inca Religion and Customs*, 39.
91. Ibid., 37.
92. In the same vein, Brundage (*Two Earths, Two Heavens*, 48) explains how the Inca emperor Pachacuti directed that eight previous rulers be "remade" as mummies and then had each carried in a litter to public events, visitations, and meals, treated in every way as if each were alive and still carrying on his rule. Apparently, these rulers could have been remade as stone effigies rather than mummified bodies (in which case, it is actually a better instance of the transmutation of the dead into stone than of the assiduous treatment of physical remains).
93. Coe (*The Maya*, 103) describes the Temple of the Inscriptions and considers that the most appropriate term is "funerary temple" because it captures the dual sense in which the Maya used their pyramid structures as "burial grounds," often intruding innumerable graves into an older substructure, but continuing to carry on ceremonies in the superstructure; also see Carlson, "A Geomantic Model for the Interpretation of Mesoamerican Sites," 196.
94. The most obviously relevant morphological possibilities are the ritual-architectural commemoration of a mythicohistoric individual (one variation on the sacred history priority [II-B]) and the glorification of an individual ruler and strategic construction of prestigious pedigrees (a couple of variations on the politics priority [II-C]). Recall that the Temple of the Inscriptions figured large in my summary discussion of what Linda Schele termed Palenque's "mythology of kingship" in the section in chapter 18 entitled "Mythistory Commemoration as the Back Half of the Architectural Situation: A Maya Example"; also see, in chapter 16 on the astronomy priority (I-C), the section entitled "Allurement via the Ritual-Architectural Enhancement of Nature: Mesoamerican Examples."
95. Benson, "Architecture as Metaphor," 185.
96. Carlson, "A Geomantic Model for the Interpretation of Mesoamerican Sites," 195–99.
97. Kelemen, *Medieval American Art*, 1:47.
98. Marcus ("Archaeology and Religion," 298–301) argues that the Spaniards never understood Zapotec royal ancestor worship and that their distortions have persisted until today. Specifically, she makes a compelling cases that, despite the fact that these stone images found in the Oaxaca temples have usually been considered "idols" representing "gods," those images actually represent ancestors, particularly deceased rulers, whose actual physical remains were housed in elaborately decorated masonry vaults that formed the foundations for the same temples.
99. Fabrizio Mancinelli, *Catacombs and Basilicas: The Early Christians in Rome* (Florence: Scala Books, 1981), 7.
100. Merton, *The Waters of Siloe*, 26–27.
101. Compte de Volney, *Voyage en Syrie et en Egypte* (Paris, 1787); quoted by Ragon, *The Space of Death*, 220.
102. Colvin, *Architecture and the After-Life*, 374.

103. Ragon, *The Space of Death,* 221. All of Ragon's chapter 16, "The Revolution in Funerary Practice from 1789 to the Restoration," is exceedingly relevant here.

104. Baron Haussmann apparently made these remarks in a proposal to the Senate, 5 April 1867; quoted in ibid., 267.

105. Ibid., 264, 269. Also relevant to the notion of the tomb as museum, Ragon argues that, "Certain churches, too, which are, or have never been anything other than, storehouses of illustrious corpses have also become cemetery-museums: Westminster Abbey in London, the Panthéon and Invalides in Paris, the chapel of the abbey church of Saint-Denis, the memorial of Louis XVI, the chapel of Notre-Dame-de-Consolation" (90).

106. See the discussion of Tamberma funeral performances in chapter 21, on the theater priority (III-A).

107. Lefebvre, *The Production of Space,* 221.

108. Ibid.

109. Ibid.

110. Maquet, *The Aesthetic Experience,* 104.

Part Three | Architecture as Ritual Context

1. Lao Tzu, *Tao-te-ching* (Shanghai: Commercial Press, 1929), vol. 307, chapter 11; translated and quoted by Chang, *The Tao of Architecture,* 7.

2. Sinding-Larsen, *Iconography and Ritual,* 9. His work deals specifically (and almost exclusively) with Christianity.

3. Mark Wigley, *The Architecture of Deconstruction: Derrida's Haunt* (Cambridge, Mass.: MIT Press, 1993), 62.

4. Braunfels, *Monasteries of Western Europe,* 132.

5. Franciscans and Dominicans are, of course, not wholly ambivalent about their religious structures. Nowhere is this more clear than in colonial New Spain where church building was a very high priority and a major pillar of the spiritual conquest of Mexico. For example, Tozzer's footnotes to Diego Landa's *Relación de las cosas de Yucatán* (e.g., 74–75, n. 335; and 177, n. 925) include several telling references to Franciscan friars making the Indians work on "the very sumptuous monasteries which they have built without ceasing to build"; and Lesley Byrd Simpson (*Many Mexicos,* 4th rev. ed. [Berkeley and Los Angeles: University of California Press, 1966], 75, 86–87) has some astute remarks on "the architectural conquest" of Mexico by the Mendicant orders and on the transplantation of "the Renaissance tradition of magnificence; the more beautiful the church the greater the glory to God, and the greater credit to themselves."

6. Bruno Zevi (*Architecture as Space,* 295) considers that Lao-tzu is one of far too few who has "affirmed that the reality of a building does not consist in the four walls and the roof, but in the space enclosed—the living space."

7. While the unevenness of this quadripartite morphological arrangement of

modes of ritual-architectural presentation requires particularly heavy qualification, I hope to demonstrate how considerations of the relevance, play, and contestation of these presentational priorities might prove particularly rewarding in at least four quite different respects. First, in the realm of synchronic comparison, appeal to these four modes of ritual-architectural presentation can assist both in the critical (re)evaluation of other scholars' largely non-historical (often non-eventful) cross-cultural architectural comparisons and in the formulation of new cross-cultural comparisons and orderings that are more satisfactorily attentive to the "occasionality" of architecture. Gottfried Richter (*Art and Human Consciousness,* 38), for example, ventures the following oft-repeated (objectifying) contrast between the presumed design tactics of Egyptian pyramids and Babylonian ziggurats: where the former "closes itself off entirely from the outside world. . . [concealing] its mysterious life in deeply hidden, inaccessible corridors and chambers," with the ziggurat "all this is exactly reversed" insofar as "the ziggurat was built for what would take place on its outer surface." Instead of automatically dismissing such formalistic comparisons as irretrievably decontextualized (but without simply accepting them at face value), we can reevaluate and recast those interpretive observations with respect to the four presentational morphological options by noting that the design of Egyptian pyramids seems to reflect the predominance of the sort of exclusivity and limited access that is characteristic of sanctuary presentational modes (priority III-D), while the ziggurat configuration reflects the predominance of the sort of inclusiveness and spectatorial appeal that is characteristic of theatric presentational modes (priority III-A). Translating such standard, formalist architectural assessments into these morphological categories, though not the most daring of interpretive procedures, is a kind of hermeneutic of retrieval that should serve both to raise the comparative inquiry to a more eventful level and, eventually, if one performs enough of these translations, to formulate more nuanced, more "religiously significant" cross-cultural orderings of architecture.

Second, in the realm of diachronic comparison, reflecting on the relevance of these four morphological options also provides a means of (re)assessing the shifts in presentational strategies that are at issue in the transitions between historically related building agendas. For instance, in chapter 24, I will show how Vincent Scully's description of the historical transition from the "outward-looking design" of the classic Greek temple to that of Roman sacred architecture, which facilitated "an enclosed experience totally shut away from the outside world" (Scully, *Greek Sacred Architecture,* 194), could be usefully reassessed as a transition from largely theatrical presentational modes (III-A), and perhaps contemplative modes (III-B) inasmuch as ritual participants' attentions were focused directly on the sculptural aspects of the Hellenistic temple (and the landscape), to sanctuary modes (III-D) in which the prevailing building agenda in Roman temples was one of containment, control, and exclusion. Charting the play and contest of presentational modes that are evident in the direct historical interactions between the extravagant agenda of Cluny, Abbot Suger's different but similarly elaborate design for Saint-Denis, and Saint Bernard's contrastively reclusive plan for Cistercian monasteries (all contiguous cases that will be featured in subsequent chapters) provide even stronger examples of the ways in which translating and problematizing even very heavily studied circumstances into the less familiar rubric of these presentational priorities can work both to clarify the relevant historical dynamics and to locate instructive cross-cultural parallels.

Third, in the realm of intellectual history and the hermeneutics of suspicion, the four presentational priorities also provide a means for (re)assessing various academic debates and hypotheses and, thus, often, for challenging stereotypes and timeworn interpretive prejudices. For example, early Mesoamericanist scholars and antiquarians, focusing particularly on the ostentatious, arguably garish and gaudy appearance of pre-Columbian buildings such as the Puuc facades of central Yucatan, structures that are totally coated with face-like masks and stylized geometric designs, routinely imagined indigenous ritual-architectural events as spectacles of glitz and gore—that is, as though the overwhelmingly dominant presentational priority was that of the theater mode (III-A), an assessment that served to reconfirm the condescending, Eurocentric view that indigenous art and religion were largely without substance or sophistication. "Highly theatrical," "dramatic," and "showy," are, in other words (in this case and most others), pejorative, dismissive terms, which are often applied to the architectures and rituals of "others" but seldom to one's own. Widening the range of interpretive options, however, raises at least two seriously neglected but equally viable sets of possibilities, both of which would show indigenous ritual-architectural programs in much more favorable light. Specifically, this portion of the morphological framework entreats scholars to entertain the prospects, first, that the elaborate convolutes of Mesoamerican architectural ornamentation might have been conceived as built expressions of respect or obedience to some Mesoamerican deity (thus suggesting the preponderance of one version of the propitiatory mode [III-C]) or, second, that such ornamental elaborations served primarily as props for meditative devotion (thus suggesting the preeminence of the contemplation mode [III-B]), a highly plausible alternative that has very seldom been seriously considered in indigenous contexts.

And fourth, most intriguingly I think, with respect to the composition of ritual-architectural reception histories, these four presentational categories also provide a means for exploring and charting the diverse, fluctuating apprehensions of a single ritual context over either long or very short spans of time. One could chronicle, for instance, fluctuations in modes of architectural presentation and apprehension that are deliberately cultivated by opening and closing the light moveable side-walls of Japanese Buddhist pavilions (see Burckhardt, *Sacred Art in East and West,* 140). Or, one could organize and analyze the rapid succession of very different kinds of relations between worshipers and architectural forms that are at issue in a situation like that in Ardalan and Bakhtiar's detailed (and highly eventful) rendition of the choreographed experience of moving through the intensely complex, "vein-like" system of urban portals and pedestrian pathways in the bazaar of Isfahan, Iran, and, specifically, through the walled quarter of the Masjid-i-Jāmiʿ mosque (*The Sense of Unity,* 96–127). In their rich description, the route to the Masjid-i-Jāmiʿ, the "symbolic heart" of the bazaar, commences at the periphery of the city with a sumptuous ceremonial way, a "super pathway" lined with trees and punctuated with an elaborate system of water channels and fountains, which instantiates perfectly one sort of manifestation of the theatric mode of presentation (III-A); upon entering a gateway into the actual Masjid-i-Jāmiʿ quarter, the bazaar route guides visitors through a sequence of dark and narrow covered passageways, before eventually opening back outside into the light of a serene courtyard grove with lush greenery and pools, a space they describe as a kind of "recapitulation of paradise," which thus presumably engenders a particularly tranquil "sanctuary-like" apprehension (III-D) (pp. 105–6); and then, providing the final transition and climax to this ambulatory route, the path leads inside again, through a great portal into the magnificent domed sanctuary of the Masjid-i-Jāmiʿ mosque proper where one is confronted with a stunning array of geometrical and calligraphic brickwork designs. Thus, in the end, according to Ardalan and Bakhtiar, it is the meditative apprehension of these decorative brick surfaces inside the dome—that is, the direct and sustained engagement of architectural forms and ornaments characteristic of the contemplation mode (III-B)—that completes the transformative experience of the Masjid-i-Jāmiʿ and provides a cathartic sensation of "ultimate reintegration" (p. 108).

Twenty-one | Theater

1. Diego López de Cogolludo, *Historia de Yucatán,* 1688, regarding human sacrifice at the Adivivo Pyramid in Uxmal, Yucatan; quoted by John L. Stephens, *Incidents of Travel in Yucatan* (1846; New York: Dover Publications, 1963), 1:192–93.

2. Ali Shariati, *Hajj* (Bedford, Ohio: Free Islamic Literatures Incorporated, 1977), ix–x.

3. Richard Buchanan, "Declaration by Design: Rhetoric, Argument, and Demonstration in Design Practice," in *Design Discourse: History, Theory, Criticism,* ed. Victor Margolin (Chicago: University of Chicago Press, 1989), 103.

4. I borrow the apt term "pageant-spaces" from Kubler, "The Design of Space in Maya Architecture," 528.

5. López de Cogolludo, *Historia de Yucatán;* quoted by Stephens, *Incidents of Travel in Yucatan,* 1:192.

6. Inga Clendinnen, *Ambivalent Conquests: Maya and Spaniard in Yucatan, 1517–1570* (Cambridge: Cambridge University Press, 1987), 114–17. Clendinnen comments on Bishop Landa's "superb theatrical sense" in orchestrating both building and ritual productions, specifically elaborately staged Inquisitional autos de fé,

which served at once to intimidate the Indians and to allow his friars "to become habituated to the exercise of violent physical domination while distancing their actions from the zone of the personal and the personally culpable" (115).

7. Landa, *Relación de las cosas de Yucatán,* 119.

8. Frederick Catherwood, *Views of Ancient Monuments in Central America, Chiapas, and Yucatan* (London: Owen Jones, 1844); reprinted in von Hagen, *Frederick Catherwood, Archt.,* 126–29. Catherwood seems to have simply extrapolated William Prescott's notion of Aztec ritual (which I will address later this chapter) into the Maya context. Stephens seems to have used López de Cogolludo as his main inspiration for Maya ritual; Stephens,*Incidents of Travel in Central America, Chiapas, and Yucatan,*1:143. Also see idem, *Incidents of Travel in Yucatan,* 1:192–93.

9. Francisco de Fuentes, writing of Guatemala in about 1700; cited by Stephens, *Incidents of Travel in Central America, Chiapas, and Yucatan,* 1:131.

10. Spinden, *A Study of Maya Art,* 96. Similarly, Kubler (*Art and Architecture of Ancient America,* 217) agrees that "a primary platform [of Copán], rightly called the acropolis . . . provides a theatrical setting for the ball court."

11. Kelemen, *Medieval American Art,* 1:57–61. William Henry Holmes's and George Kubler's comments on the apparently highly theatrical character of pre-Columbian ritual at Monte Albán in Oaxaca could be added to the present list of examples. Also relevant are the remarks of William Prescott, Johanna Broda, and Davíd Carrasco concerning the theatrics of Aztec human sacrifice, which are quoted toward the end of this chapter.

12. If, as Freedberg (*The Power of Images,* 432) emphasizes, a thorough consideration of the *response* to art and architecture must acknowledge, "the relations between sentiment and sensation on the one hand and knowledge on the other," the theatric priority (III-A) is concerned primarily with the former—that is, with the sensations of pleasure, awe, fascination, terror, disgust, and surprise that religious buildings are wont to evoke.

13. Regarding his notion of "structures of feeling," Raymond Williams (*Marxism and Literature* [Oxford: Oxford University Press, 1977], 132) says: "The term is difficult, but 'feeling' is chosen to emphasize a distinction from more formal concepts of 'world-view' or 'ideology'. . . . We are talking about characteristic elements of impulse, restraint, and tone; specifically affective elements of consciousness and relationships: not feeling against thought, but thought as felt and feeling as thought: practical consciousness of a present kind, in a living and interrelating continuity."

14. James W. Fernandez, "Persuasions and Performances: Of the Beast in Every Body . . . And the Metaphors of Every Man," in *Myth, Symbol, and Culture,* ed. Clifford Geertz (New York: W. W. Norton, 1971), 39–60.

15. Debate as to the relationship between ritual and emotion has been a prominent theme in the work of such seminal scholars as Durkheim, Freud, Radcliffe-Brown, and Victor Turner as well as a host of contemporary anthropologists. Catherine Lutz and Geoffrey M. White, in their article "The Anthropology of

Emotion," *Annual Review of Anthropology* 15 (1986): 405–36, provide an exceedingly useful review of anthropological research on emotion in the decade between 1975 and 1985. On theories of the relationship between ritual and emotion, see especially p. 413. Their article ends with "a comparative framework for the study of emotions" and a statement of optimism about the possibility of cross-cultural comparison (427–31).

16. See Paul Ekman, *The Face of Man: Expressions of Universal Emotions in a New Guinea Village* (New York: Garland STPM Press, 1980); and idem, "Expression and the Nature of Emotion," in *Approaches to Emotion,* ed. Klaus R. Scherer and Paul Ekman (Hillsdale, N.J.: Erlbaum, 1984), 319–43. For concise remarks on Ekman's work, also see Lutz and White, "The Anthropology of Emotions," 410–11.

17. Lutz and White ("The Anthropology of Emotions," 417–27) discuss, on the one hand, the increasing appreciation that emotions are invariably embedded in socially constructed categories, and, on the flip side, a growing tendency to grant emotions an a priori pan-cultural status as opposed to being seen as culturally created.

18. Wittkower, *Architectural Principles in the Age of Humanism,* 20–30. Note that the correspondence between the respective medieval and Renaissance conceptions of the godhead and respective rectangular and round church shapes also provides an excellent exemplification of alternative ritual-architectural commemorations of divinity (priority II-A).

19. Murray (*The Architecture of the Italian Renaissance,* 118, 125) discusses circular Christian martyria and argues that this was Bramante's intention for Saint Peter's.

20. In contrast to Murray, Wittkower (*Architectural Principles in the Age of Humanism,* 24–26) argues that Bramante intended Saint Peter's to be a symbol of God's perfection.

21. A number of authors discuss the history and controversy of the sixteenth-century rebuilding of Saint Peter's. Besides Wittkower, *Architectural Principles in the Age of Humanism,* pt. 1; and Murray, *The Architecture of the Italian Renaissance,* 124–25; see Blunt, introduction to *Baroque and Rococo,* ed. Blunt, 25–26.

22. Zevi (*Architecture as Space,* 78–85), for instance, explains that the most significant Christian modification of the Roman basilica involved shifting the principal entrance of the basilica from the long side of the building to the short (or front) side, accentuating the longitudinal axis of the church, and thus forcing one's attention along a processionary path that culminates at the altar. Davies (*Temples, Churches, and Mosques,* 95–96), among many, also comments on the dramatic effect of the "basilica as path." Also see Stoddard, *Art and Architecture in Medieval France,* 53.

23. Braunfels, *Monasteries of Western Europe,* 51.

24. Jean Leclercq ("Prayer at Cluny," *Journal of the American Academy of Religion* 51 [December 1983]: 651–65) argues that the Cluny monks were afforded at least as much time for private, nonritualized prayer, for reading, meditation, and

other cultural activities as their counterparts in other monasteries. In the context of this article, Leclercq cites several of his own earlier works in which he discusses the wide margin for personal freedom and room for private prayer that Cluniac monks enjoyed.

25. Bates Lowry, *Renaissance Architecture* (New York: George Braziller, 1971), 13. He speaks particularly of the intended visual effect of Brunelleschi's Foundling Hospital.

26. This very typical praise of the Parthenon's visual adjustments is found in H. Arthur Klein and Mina Klein, *Great Structures of the World* (Cleveland: World Publishing, 1968), 86–87.

27. While not a "religiously significant" principle of organization, J. G. Davies's efforts in working with "a dual typology that divides [all] structures into the categories of path and place" is somewhat useful in surveying the range of modes of theatrical ritual-architectural presentation. See Davies, *Temples, Churches, and Mosques,* 15ff.; and idem, "Architecture," 391–92.

28. Jorge E. Hardoy, *Pre-Columbian Cities,* trans. Judith Thorne (New York: Walker and Company, 1973), 106–13. As an enclosure that shuns exterior views, Monte Albán's Great Plaza demonstrates a strong exercise of the sanctuary priority (III-D).

29. Holmes, *Archaeological Studies among the Ancient Cities of Mexico,* 221. Holmes's uncharacteristic reflections on Monte Albán, which actually constitute one of the rarely eventful commentaries in his important work, was cited and discussed in volume 1, in the introduction to part 1, "The Experience of Architecture."

30. Kubler, *Art and Architecture of Ancient America,* 163.

31. A 1934 lecture in Rome by Walter Gropius; quoted in Siegfried Giedion, *Walter Gropius* (London: Architectural Press, 1954), 154; cited by Hammond, *Liturgy and Architecture,* 42.

32. Hammond, *Liturgy and Architecture,* 42.

33. Ibid., 42–43.

34. Ibid.

35. Buchanan, "Declaration by Design: Rhetoric, Argument, and Demonstration in Design Practice," 103.

36. Regarding ambulatory ritual performances, Grimes (*Symbol and Conquest,* chapter 2) makes a number of heuristically useful observations about the differences and similarities between pilgrimages, processions, and parades.

37. Ebersole, *Ritual Poetry and the Politics of Death in Early Japan,* 40.

38. There is an enormous fund of literature on Mesoamerica processional ways. In the Maya area, Thomas Gann, *Mystery Cities* (London: Gerald Duckworth and Co., 1925), 103–27, is among the earliest to explore the network of causeways, or *sacbe* ("white roads"), that crosshatches Yucatan. Gann concludes, "It was completely useless . . . the only explanation was a purely ceremonial road or *via sacre.*"

And, for Central Mexico, George Kubler, *The Iconography of the Art of Teotihuacan,* Studies in Pre-Columbian Art and Archaeology, no. 4 (Washington, D.C.: Dumbarton Oaks, 1967), 12, discusses the famous Miccaotli (or "Street of the Dead") at Teotihuacan and the "strongly marked liturgical character" of the site in general. Also see Antonio Bustillos Carrillo, *El Sacbe de los Mayas,* 2d ed. (Mexico, D.F.: B. Costa-Amic Editor, 1974); and regarding processional roads among the Inca, see Victor Wolfgang von Hagen, *The Highway of the Sun* (London: Victor Gollancz, 1955).

39. William Bullock, *Six Months' Residence and Travels in Mexico* (London: John Murray, 1824), 146, 152–53. Stephens (*Incidents of Travel in Central America, Chiapas, and Yucatan,* 1:210–20, 215–17, 153–54) likewise comments on the prevalence and elaboration of processions in nineteenth-century Mexico.

40. See, for instance, Michell, *The Hindu Temple,* 65.

41. Hammond, *Liturgy and Architecture,* 47. In the same vein, Norberg-Schulz (*Meaning in Western Architecture,* 75–91) discusses the procession through the longitudinal Romanesque form as a metaphor for the teleological salvation route of Christianity.

42. Shariati, *Hajj,* ix–x.

43. Davies, *Temples, Churches, and Mosques,* 36.

44. Ibid.

45. Kiyohiko Munakata ("Mysterious Heavens and Chinese Classical Gardens," *Res: Anthropology and Aesthetics* 15 [spring 1988]: 75) discusses the different sorts of "dynamic sequences of passages" that one would experience in open corridors, covered corridors, and half-walled corridors of Chinese classical gardens.

46. Borobudur is discussed more fully in chapter 22, in relation to the contemplation priority (III-C).

47. For relevant remarks on Le Corbusier, see Geoffrey Broadbent, "Meaning in Architecture," in *Meaning in Architecture,* ed. Jencks and Baird, 58.

48. Here again I am informed (albeit indirectly) by Buchanan, who contends that: "This is what makes the emotive argument of a design so powerful and persuasive: it collapses the distance between the object and the minds of the users, leading them to identity with the expressive movement and allows it to carry them where it will. . . ." Buchanan, "Declaration by Design: Rhetoric, Argument, and Demonstration in Design Practice," 103.

49. Lawrence E. Sullivan ("Sound and Senses: Toward a Hermeneutics of Performance," *History of Religions* 26 [August 1986]: 5) borrows from Hannah Arendt and takes the term "quality of knowledge" from Dell Hymes, *"In Vain I Tried to Tell You": Essay in Native American Ethnopoetics* (Philadelphia: University of Pennsylvania Press, 1981), 81, in order to make this distinction between performance and "brute behavior."

50. Another particularly strong example of funerary histrionics (and thus of a blending of commemorations of the dead [priority II-D] with theatric modes of

presentation [priority III-A]) comes in chapter 1 of Gary Ebersole's *Ritual Poetry and the Politics of Death in Early Japan,* where he discusses the elaborate Japanese staging of public recitations of a whole series of different forms of imperial funeral laments and poems designed to pacify ancestral spirits. A small portion of Ebersole's work is discussed below in relation to blendings of politics (priority II-C) and theatrical presentation (III-A).

51. Blier, "The Dance of Death: Notes on the Architecture and Staging of Tamberma Funeral Performances," 107–43.

52. Blier explains that as Tamberma men approach old age, often they will commission grander and more spacious homes; she says, "such men are, in essence, designing theatres that will be used for their own funerals"; ibid., 126.

53. Ibid.

54. Ibid., 122. At points during the funeral performance, the house itself is identified with its deceased owner; Blier quotes one Tamberma elder who explains that, at the funeral, "we [speak of the house and] say that it is a man and it is dead. . . . We call the house *takoukyeta* (the dead house)" (114).

55. Ibid., 124.

56. Ibid., 123. Blier's remarks on the native Tamberma audience's critical reaction to the funeral performance are tantalizingly brief.

57. Davies (*Temples, Churches, and Mosques,* 15–17), for instance, considers that the configuration of ancient Egyptian temples, ramps, and hypostyle halls constituted "monumental processional sequences."

58. Recall that in chapter 17, on the commemoration of divinity (priority II-A), Vincent Scully's interpretation of the Cretan palaces was a featured example with respect to the morphological possibility of architecture conceived as the body of a god or goddess, and his interpretation of the sculptural attributes of classical Greek temples was deployed to exemplify the possibility of architecture conceived as an abstract expression of the attributes of a deity.

59. In chapter 17, on the commemoration of divinity (priority II-A), see especially the section entitled "Architecture as the House of God: Deity Domiciles and Sacred Shelters."

60. With respect to the last of those instances, Davies (*Temples, Churches, and Mosques,* 63) reminds us that the classical Greek theaters of Athens, Delos, Delphi, and Sparta were all designed originally for performative rituals in honor of Dionysius, "with the spectators as so many members of a religious congregation."

61. Another exceptionally vivid, large-scale exemplification of the theatrical presentation of sacred history comes in the massive assemblage of sanctuaries constructed above the town of Vallaro, Italy (discussed in chapter 18 in relation to sacred history [priority II-B]), a project that originated in the late fifteenth century with Friar Minor Bernardino Caimi's ambitious plan to replicate in the mountains of Italy, and thus make available to participation, the most famous sites of the Holy Land, which he himself had visited. See Freedberg, *The Power of Images,* 192–201.

Owing to the efforts of subsequent builders on through the nineteenth century, pilgrims and visitors to Varallo can now tour a whole cluster of chapels depicting a succession of biblical scenes beginning in the first little sanctuary with Adam and Eve standing amid an architecturally contrived Edenic paradise, and then culminating some forty-five chapels later with an elaborate version of Christ's passion. Freedberg explains that the architectural spaces, paintings and sculptures deploy "every conceivable device to particularize, familiarize, and make vivid" the images and events of this Christian sacred history (196). Of the affective power of these chapels, Freedberg writes: "The journey to the last of the chapels and the sanctuary in the little town at the summit of the mountain becomes increasingly compelling, the views ever more ravishing; and by the end every possible emotion has been engaged in the course of our participation in what, on the face of it, may seem mere representation. . . . Only the most intellectual of people will have attempted to resist the automatic transition from seeing to empathy and involvement. . . " (196). Thus, in these ritual-architectural events, while the religiomythical events and protagonists are made present to pilgrims in stunningly veristic panoramas and statuary rather than in live performances—via painted, stone, and ceramic actors, if you will—the mode of presentation is, nevertheless, highly theatrical and powerfully emotive.

62. Rudolf Wittkower, *Art and Architecture in Italy, 1600 to 1750* (Harmondsworth, Middlesex: Penguin Books, 1958), 199; quoted by Hibbard, *Bernini*, 151.

63. Richter, *Art and Human Consciousness,* 213.

64. Lavin, *Bernini and the Crossing of Saint Peter's,* 18ff.

65. Here I should note again the nonmutual exclusivity (or slippage) of morphological categories, insofar as all of Bernini's work—sculpture and architecture —evokes emotion of the sort associated with the theater priority; but where the architectural spaces may (or may not) be apprehended *indirectly* (as one expects in the case of the theater mode), his sculpture is generally apprehended more *directly,* as befits the contemplation mode (III-B). The remarks found in Hibbard, *Bernini,* 138, for instance, remind us that Bernini's *Ecstasy of St. Teresa* works as a prop for contemplation.

66. See Hibbard, *Bernini,* 144–48.

67. Ibid., 155.

68. Clifford Geertz, *Negara: The Theatre State in Nineteenth-Century Bali* (Princeton: Princeton University Press, 1980), 13, 120 and 123.

69. Ibid., 13.

70. Clifford Geertz, "Centers, Kings, and Charisma: Some Reflections on the Symbolics of Power," in his *Local Knowledge: Further Essays in Interpretive Anthropology* (New York: Basic Books, 1983), 125. Ebersole (*Ritual Poetry and the Politics of Death in Early Japan,* 40) uses the same quotation from Geertz as a point of departure to talk about the religiopolitical dynamics of imperial excursions in early Japan.

71. Ebersole, *Ritual Poetry and the Politics of Death in Early Japan,* 1–5. The Japanese royal family's principal strategy involved the creation and dissemination of a "mythistory," or religiopolitical ideology, that announced family members' direct descent from Amaterasu, the Sun Goddess and, consequently, their temporal preeminence. Obviously then, while Ebersole concentrates especially on the religiopolitical dimensions of this circumstance, his rich analysis likewise vividly demonstrates the effectiveness of theatrical ritual-architectural presentation in the commemoration of the dead (priority II-D), of sacred history (priority II-B), and, to an extent, of divinity (priority II-A).

72. Along with the dead body, all of the women who had been sexually intimate with the deceased, together with their servants and handmaidens, were likewise secluded within the *mogari no miya,* often for several months. Ibid., 125–27.

73. Ibid., 169–70. Ebersole takes issue with the stock assessments of most scholars that these early Japanese rituals simply served the essentially conservative function of maintaining the existing power structure and order or preserving a timeless Japanese religiosity; instead, he emphasizes the sense in which these funerary rituals served as "political tools" and "the ways in which these early rituals were used to challenge and offer alternatives to the status quo" (266).

74. Ibid., 265.

75. Ibid., 137. Emphasizing that these poems were publicly recited and not privately written pieces, Ebersole argues that, "public expressions of pure personal emotion were largely curtailed and all expressions were highly stylized . . ." (270).

76. See ibid., 169.

77. William H. Prescott, *The Conquest of Mexico* (1843), 45; quoted in Catherwood, *Views of Ancient Monuments in Central America, Chiapas, and Yucatan* (1844); reprinted in von Hagen, *Frederick Catherwood, Archt.,* 126.

78. Broda, "Templo Mayor as Ritual Space," 40–41.

79. Ibid.

80. Davíd Carrasco, "Templo Mayor: The Aztec Vision of Place," *Religion* 2 (1981): 292; or idem, *Quetzalcoatl and the Irony of Empire,* 186.

81. In volume 1, chapter 3, see especially the subsection "The (Inter)Activity and Performance of Architecture."

82. Gadamer, *Truth and Method,* 118. Also see Hans-Georg Gadamer, "The Festival Character of Theatre," in *The Relevance of the Beautiful and Other Essays,* trans. Nicholas Walker, ed. Robert Bernasconi (Cambridge: Cambridge University Press, 1986), 58–59; or the section of chapter 3 of volume 1 cited in the previous note.

83. On the "double mediation" of architecture, which is related to Gadamer's "concept of decoration," see Gadamer, *Truth and Method,* 139–40; or in volume 1, chapter 4, see the section entitled "The Concept of Decoration: Architecture's 'Double Mediation.'"

84. That formulation of the relation between the pilgrim and the pyramid

appeared in the section of volume 1, chapter 4, cited in the previous note.

85. In volume 1, see chapter 3, "Conversation and Play: The Eventfulness of Architecture."

86. See Gadamer, *Truth and Method,* 139–40.

87. Saint Bernard, quoted in Louis J. Lekai, *The Cistercians: Ideals and Reality* (Kent, Ohio: Kent State University Press, 1977), 263.

88. See Catherine Bell, *Ritual Theory, Ritual Practice* (New York and Oxford: Oxford University Press, 1992), part 1; and Talal Asad, *Genealogies of Religion: Discipline and Reasons of Power in Christianity and Islam* (Baltimore: Johns Hopkins University Press, 1993), chapter 2. Both comment at length on the post-Enlightenment, post-Reformation construction of the category of "ritual."

89. For a much fuller exposition of the ideas in this paragraph, see Lindsay Jones, "Conquests of the Imagination: Maya-Mexican Polarity and the Story of Chichén Itzá," *American Anthropologist* 99, no. 2 (1997): 275–90; and idem, *Twin City Tales,* chapter 1.

90. Miguel Covarrubias, *Indian Art of Mexico and Central America* (New York: Knopf, 1957), 273.

91. See H. E. D. Pollock, "Architecture of the Maya Lowlands," in *Handbook of Middle American Indians: Archaeology of Southern Mesoamerica,* vol. 2 (Austin: University of Texas Press, 1965), 434–35, for remarks on the unprecedented "spaciousness of planning" in "Toltec Maya" architecture; Weaver, *The Aztecs, Maya, and Their Predecessors,* 225–27, for comments on the commitment to "maximum spectator participation, pomp and ceremony" in the "Toltec Maya" style at Chichén Itzá; and Sylvanus G. Morley, "Chichén Itzá: An American Mecca," *National Geographic Magazine* 47 (January 1925): 82, on the "gloriously robed" Toltec priests at Chichén Itzá.

92. Bernal, *Mexican Wall Paintings of the Maya and Aztec Period,* 21.

93. See Jones, "Conquests of the Imagination: Maya-Mexican Polarity and the Story of Chichén Itzá."

94. See Lutz and White, "The Anthropology of Emotion," 409ff., for very helpful remarks on the implications of romantic versus rationalist views for the cross-cultural study of emotion.

Twenty-two | Contemplation

1. From Abū Ḥāmid al-Ghazālī, *Iḥyā 'ulūm al-dīn* (The Revival of the religious sciences), in Margaret Smith, *Al-Ghazālī, the Mystic* (London: Luzac and Co., 1944), 111; quoted by Ardalan and Bakhtiar, *The Sense of Unity,* 3.

2. Maquet, *The Aesthetic Experience: An Anthropologist Looks at the Visual Arts,* 166. Maquet discusses the differences between "contemplation" and cognition in chapter 13; in chapter 14, he discusses the differences between "contemplation" and affectivity.

3. Freedberg, *The Power of Images,* 161.

4. See, for instance, James Early, *The Colonial Architecture of Mexico* (Albuquerque: University of New Mexico Press, 1994), 122–24.

5. In the same vein, even more often sequential morphological shifts in a single individual's apprehension of a building or context reflect a kind of two-stage succession wherein, first, as a prerequisite to meditation, the individual enters some sort of delimited sacred space or precinct, thus instantiating the sanctuary mode of apprehension (III-D). Then, possibly within just a few minutes, the beholder encounters a statue, an icon, a pool, a fountain, or some architectural form on which she fixes her attention as a focus for meditative reflection, thus shifting at that point into a more contemplative mode (III-B). Among countless examples of that pattern, Ardalan and Bakhtiar (*The Sense of Unity,* 68) imply this sort of two-stage process when they describe how in Islamic Iran, particularly in urban areas, it was necessary first to wall off gardens and courtyards in order to create a paradisiacal isolation "within which the soul can be sensed and its spiritual quest fulfilled" (thus instantiating the sanctuary mode, III-D), and then, "within this tranquil space, the placement of the traditional pool provides a center as a positive direction for the creative imagination" (thus instantiating the contemplative mode, III-B). Or, similarly, the same authors (ibid., 124) describe innumerable situations like the small, roofless side courts in the Masjid-i-Shāh, which the visitor first experiences as "harbors of solitude and shade" (or a sanctuary space, III-D), but which, subsequently, provide judiciously placed objects—in this case, a simple stone slab sundial—that serve as foci of devotion that "stimulate the imagination" (or props for contemplation, III-B).

6. It is perhaps also worth noting at the outset that there is in this entire chapter a special challenge, and a special awkwardness in the required grammar, insofar as I am working to address architectural "objects (or foci or props) of contemplation," but, consistent with the methodological directives outlined in volume 1, in nonobjectifying (eventful and situational) ways.

7. Maquet, *The Aesthetic Experience: An Anthropologist Looks at the Visual Arts,* 165–66.

8. Ibid., 166. The phrase "insight-oriented processes" is also borrowed from Maquet. On the self-abandonment, risks, and rewards implicit in participation in ritual-architectural events, see especially chapters 5 and 6 in volume 1.

9. On the viability and problems of imagining the experience of architecture as an occasion of reading a text-like built form, see especially chapter 8, "Architecture as 'Mute Text'? Literary and Nonliterary Vehicles of Intelligibility."

10. Freedberg, *The Power of Images,* 161–62. Chapter 8 in Freedberg's book is exceptionally relevant and helpful for this discussion of the contemplation priority.

11. Mabbett ("The Symbolism of Mount Meru," 77–78), for instance, notes the sense in which both Mount Meru and Borobudur have been interpreted as mandalas.

12. Tucci, *The Theory and Practice of the Mandala,* vii. Even the two-dimensional mandala paintings that Tucci describes are replete with explicitly architectural imagery: the Tantric Mandala of rDorjeac'an, the Holder of the Diamond, is, for instance, described as a "palace" (*vimana*; in Tibetan, *zal yas k'ang*) and a "walled city" (39–43).

13. Khosla, "Architecture and Symbolism in Tibetan Monasteries," 76.

14. Ibid. Romi Khosla also explains, in *Buddhist Monasteries in the Western Himalaya* (Kathmandu, Nepal: Ratna Pustak Bhander, 1979), that in the early period in Tibet, whole monastery complexes were laid out according to mandala plans, and even where the layout of the monastery was forced to conform to the lay of the land—as at Hemis, for instance—the mandala model was preserved in the individual temple rooms. Also see Jack Finegan, *Tibet: A Dreamt of Image* (New Delhi: Tibet House, 1986).

15. Mabbett ("The Symbolism of Mount Meru," 76) discusses architectural homologization with respect to Mount Meru and summarizes the landmark work of Paul Mus on Borobudur as a cosmogram. Regarding the cosmogrammatic quality of these monuments, see also Mircea Eliade, "Barabudur, the Symbolic Temple," in *Symbolism, the Sacred, and the Arts,* ed. Apostolos-Cappadona, 130–42, for remarks that are also very indebted to Mus's work. Also see Wheatley, *The Pivot of the Four Quarters,* 437–38, for a discussion of Angkor Thom with direct reference to Eliade's model of sacred space.

16. See, for instance, Bernard Groslier and Jacques Arthaud, *The Arts and Civilization of Angkor,* trans. Eric Ernshaw Smith (New York: Frederick A. Praeger, 1957), 99.

17. See Woodward, "Borobudur and the Mirrorlike Mind," 43. My whole discussion of Borobudur is indebted to this article.

18. Brandon, *Man and God in Art and Ritual,* 57.

19. Khosla, "Architecture and Symbolism in Tibetan Monasteries," 78.

20. In chapter 21, on the theater priority (III-A), see especially the subsection on "Ambulatory Actors and Audiences: Participatory Processions and the Experience of Movement."

21. Woodward, "Borobudur and the Mirrorlike Mind," 45.

22. Ibid.

23. Woodward (ibid., 43–46) argues that Borobudur needs to be interpreted in an international Buddhist context, and that there is actually a historical connection between Borobudur and Kukai, the founder of Japanese Shingon Buddhism.

24. Ibid., 45.

25. Allan Grapard's description ("Flying Mountains and Walkers of Emptiness: Toward a Definition of Sacred Space in Japanese Religion," 209) of the liberating transformation facilitated by concentration on Japanese mandalas is likewise relevant to the pilgrim's experience of ascending Borobudur (though he does not make that connection explicit). He explains: "A practitioner of Esoteric Buddhism

'enters' a mandala through its gate, invokes the divinities which are represented, and identifies with them one after the other until reaching the center, in which there is a representation of the cosmic Buddha from which all other Buddhas and their lands emanate. The practitioner goes from the manifestation to the source, from the form to the essence, and finally reaches the realization that form and essence are two-but-not-two."

26. Ardalan and Bakhtiar (*The Sense of Unity*, 31) write: "As the Manifest is a spatial externalization, so man begins his intellectual search by relating to space. This relation must of necessity be structured so that the intellect may function and not dissipate. The mandala as a symbol of emanation and reabsorption provides this structure." The most specific example of Islamic "mandala-aided" contemplation that Ardalan and Bakhtiar provide comes from Edward Granville Browne, *A Year amongst the Persians* (London: Adam and Charles Black, 1950), 161, wherein Brown recounts a conversation with a "philosopher" who explains his regime of forty days of solitary meditation: "[This philosopher] spends the greater part of this time in incantation in the Arabic language, which he recites within the area of the mandal[a] or geometric figure, which he must describe in a certain way upon the ground . . . the operator must not . . . above all, quit the mandal[a] else he will lose the result of his pain." See Ardalan and Bakhtiar, *The Sense of Unity*, 133–34, n. 13.

27. See Séjourné, *Burning Water: Thought and Religion in Ancient Mexico*, 89–96; Irene Nicholson, *Mexican and Central American Mythology* (London: Paul Hamyln, 1967); and Frank Waters, *Mexico Mystique: The Coming Sixth World of Consciousness* (Chicago: Swallow Press, 1975), 141–42, 180–81. Waters speaks about pre-Columbian "mandala symbols" that "evoke a psychic effect from all [their] imparted meanings."

28. Waters (*Mexico Mystique*, 140–42) discusses Seler's allusions to mandala-like symbolism in his commentary on the Codex Borgia, which was first published in German, 1904–9.

29. Thompson, *The Rise and Fall of Maya Civilization*, 74–75.

30. I will return in the conclusion to this chapter to the problem of Western scholars' neglect of the relevance of the contemplation mode (III-B) in indigenous contexts.

31. Richter, *Art and Human Consciousness*, 15; emphasis his. Richter makes no explicit mention of Tucci.

32. Ibid., 17.

33. Ibid., 15. This is, of course, exemplary, to a lesser extent I think, of the sort of participatory processional ritual-architectural event that was discussed in the last chapter in relation to theatric presentation (priority III-A). Moreover, Richter's references to the Egyptian temple as "the house of one's body" (see, for example, 20) speak of a kind of homologized architecture (priority I-A); and his notion of penetrating deeper and deeper into a "holy of holies" will become relevant in chapter 24 with respect to the sanctuary priority (III-D).

34. Mirsky, *Houses of God,* 40. She argues that, "the sculpture [and architecture of Hinduism] was intended to awaken, inspire, inform, and fortify the worshipper for contemplation—not as has been thought, for idolatry."

35. Michell (*The Hindu Temple,* 61) insists: "Paramount is the identification of the divinity with the fabric of the temple or, from another point of view, the identification of the form of the universe with that of the temple."

36. Stella Kramrisch, "Wall and Image in Indian Art," in *Exploring India's Sacred Art: Selected Writings of Stella Kramrisch,* ed. Barbara Stoler Miller (Philadelphia: University of Pennsylvania Press, 1983), 254. Kramrisch cites the *Shilparatna* (16.II4), a text on architecture compiled in the sixteenth century, as her authority for this direct worship of the Hindu temple itself.

37. Michell, *The Hindu Temple,* 61.

38. Ibid., 62; emphasis added.

39. In other words, where I noted in the last chapter that the most likely pairings of the theater mode (III-A) and commemorations of divinity (priority II-A) occur in relation to "houses of god" (which qualify as *places* of worship), the other two, more sculptural variations on the divinity priority, that is, where architecture is conceived either as the body of god or as an abstract representation of a deity's attributes (which qualify more as *objects* of worship), are both commonly paired with the contemplation mode (III-B).

40. Relying on Harold Osborne, Maquet (*The Aesthetic Experience: An Anthropologist Looks at the Visual Arts,* 166) writes: "In the Western philosophical tradition of aesthetics, as well as in the Buddhist tradition of meditation, ego is considered an obstacle to contemplation. The beholder should be disinterested, that is, not self-interested, and the mediator should be non-attached, that is, not self-attached. In the dialectic of contemplation, selflessness is a condition of the contemplative mode of consciousness and at the same time a consequence of it. Selflessness makes contemplation possible and thus is reinforced by contemplation."

41. Thus, in regard to ritual-architectural instigation, generally speaking, the contemplation mode (III-B) is more like the sanctuary mode (III-D) and the propitiation mode (III-C) than it is like the theatrical mode (III-A). Toward the end of this chapter I will note important exceptions to that general rule.

42. On the tension in Abrahamic (and other) traditions between enthusiasm and disdain for the reliance on artistic images in relation to commemorations of divinity (priority II-A), see especially the section in chapter 17 entitled "Architecture and the Attributes of God: Iconoclasm and Aniconism."

43. Altshuler and Altshuler, "Judaism and Art," in *Art, Creativity, and the Sacred,* ed. Apostolos-Cappadona, 159.

44. Ibid.

45. Ibid.

46. Lois Ibsen al-Fārūqī, "An Islamic Perspective on Symbolism in the Arts," in *Art, Creativity, and the Sacred,* ed. Apostolos-Cappadona, 170–71.

47. Ibid.

48. See Burckhardt, *Sacred Art in East and West,* chapter 9. Also see Burckhardt, *Art of Islam,* 12ff., where he elaborates on his statement that "At the same time, this application to architecture of a qualitative—and not a purely quantitative—geometry, has a speculative, contemplative aspect. . . ."

49. Al-Fārūqī, "An Islamic Perspective on Symbolism in the Arts," 174.

50. Burckhardt, *Sacred Art in East and West,* 111. Ardalan and Bakhtiar (*The Sense of Unity,* 45) likewise discuss how "the experience of these repeated [arabesque] patterns establishes the ideal of infinity."

51. Ardalan and Bakhtiar (*The Sense of Unity,* 21) explain that because, from the Sufi perspective, "all of creation is an emanation from the One . . . It follows that all shapes, surfaces, and lines are arranged in conformity with the proportions inherent in nature and reflect ideal systems of beauty. Resting on an objective foundation, independent of man and his subjective tastes, a beauty is attained that is general, universal, and eternal."

52. See, for instance, ibid., 2–3, for brief excerpts from Afḍal al-Dīn al-Kashani (fourteenth century) and Abū Ḥāmid al-Ghazālī (eleventh century) to the effect that the visible world is but a symbol of the invisible.

53. Abū Bakr Siraj ul-Din, *The Book of Certainty* (London: Rider and Co., 1952), 50; quoted in Ardalan and Bakhtiar, *The Sense of Unity,* 132.

54. On the way in which the divinely inspired works of Sufi artists are especially "able to lead man to higher states of being and ultimately to Unity," see Ardalan and Bakhtiar, *The Sense of Unity,* 7, 10.

55. For an extended discussion of the crucial role of geometry and mathematics in Sufi architecture, see, ibid., 21–30.

56. On the decisive role of calligraphy in Sufi architecture, see ibid., 45.

57. Regarding Sufi contemplation on the painting in Persian miniatures, Seyyed Hossein Nasr, in an address to the Iranologist Congress, Tehran, May 1968 (quoted by Ardalan and Bakhtiar, *The Sense of Unity,* 33), explains: "By conforming strictly to the heterogeneous and qualitative conception of space, the Persian miniature succeeded in transforming the plane surface of the miniature to a canvas depicting grades of reality, and was able to guide man from the horizon of material existence and also profane and mundane consciousness, an intermediate world with its own space, time, movement, colors and forms where events occur in a real but not necessarily physical manner, the world which the Muslim philosophers of Persia have called the 'imaginal world' (*mundus imaginalis*) or the *alam-i-khayal.*"

58. Abū Ḥāmid al-Ghazālī, *Iḥyā 'ulūm al-dīn,* 1:242; quoted in Smith, *Al-Ghazālī, the Mystic,* 111–12; cited by Ardalan and Bakhtiar, *The Sense of Unity,* 29.

59. Ardalan and Bakhtiar, *The Sense of Unity,* 79.

60. Ibid.

61. Freedberg, *The Power of Images,* 164. Also see p. 87, where Freedberg explains that: "Since the Neo-Platonists believed that one ascended by stages to the realm of pure intellect and spirit, they self-evidently had to make place for material

symbols of the divine; and because the intermediate role of images between man and god was most crucially and dramatically seen in theurgical practices, a confusion swiftly arose between Neo-Platonism and theurgy." Again, Freedberg's chapter 8, "*Invisibilia per visibilia:* Meditation and the Uses of Theory," has been exceedingly useful in formulating this section on Christianity in relation to the contemplation priority (though Freedberg does not discuss Abbot Suger or Gothic architecture).

62. See ibid., 161.

63. Ibid., 164–65, discusses the vast influence of Dionysius the Areopagite (or Pseudo-Dionysius). For a sensitive reading of Pseudo-Dionysius's theory of anagogical illumination and its legacy, Freedberg appeals to Ernst Kitzinger, "The Cult of Images in the Age before Iconoclasm," *Dumbarton Oaks Papers* 8 (1954): 83–150.

64. See Freedberg, *The Power of Images,* 162.

65. Gregory the Great, *Lib. IX, Epistola LII Ad Secundinum* (Migne *PL* 77.990–91); quoted by Freedberg, *The Power of Images,* 164. Gregory was apparently only indirectly indebted to Pseudo-Dionysius.

66. Suger, *On the Abbey Church of St.-Denis and Its Art Treasures,* ed. Panofsky. On the uniqueness of Abbot Suger's treatise, in addition to Panofsky's thorough introduction to Suger's treatise, see von Simson, *The Gothic Cathedral,* 102.

67. Suger, *On the Abbey Church of St.-Denis and Its Art Treasures,* ed. Panofsky; quoted by Erwin Panofsky on page 21 of his introduction to that treatise. Also, it is interesting here, with respect to alternative "protocols of architectural apprehension" (see chapter 12 in volume 1), to note that Suger is adopting a kind of dual role: as the designer of the architectural work, and thus perpetuator of idealized (probably not very empirical) apprehensions; and as an "indigenous" user and beholder of the space, who might then be expected to deliver more reliably empirical accounts of how the work is actually apprehended by at least some of its patrons.

68. Note that Woodward ("Borobudur and the Mirrorlike Mind," 47) hypothesizes that Borobudur may have had more gilded, "mirrorlike" surfaces than is typically acknowledged, and that these surfaces symbolized elements of existence that were "reflected" and without "real" existence.

69. Though I am focusing on Gothic cathedrals' exemplification of the contemplation priority (III-B), there are certainly important ways in which those constructions also participate, albeit in somewhat less remarkable ways, in those other priorities as well. Wim Swaan (*The Gothic Cathedral,* 31), for instance, reminds us of the nonmutual exclusivity of these presentation modes with his engaging description of the Gothic cathedral's consecration, which begins, in his view, with "pure 'theatre'" (III-A). Particularly notable in Swaan's account of that occasion is how, while the bishop leads a splendid procession toward the new cathedral, one of his clergy plays the role of an evil spirit who lurks inside the church in ambush (*quasi latens*); but, as the procession makes its approach, according to Swaan, "the vanquished 'evil spirit' slipped out into the crowds and the bishop and procession entered the cathedral for the consecration ceremony."

That symbolic cleansing of the cathedral, then, also instantiates the relevance of the sanctuary priority (III-D).

70. Claude Lévi-Strauss, "The Effectiveness of Symbols," in his *Structural Anthropology,* trans. Claire Jacobson and Brooke Grundfest Schoepf (New York: Basic Books, 1963), 186–205.

71. Panofsky's introduction to Suger, *On The Abbey Church of St.-Denis and Its Art Treasures,* ed. Panofsky, 21.

72. Gadol, *Leon Battista Alberti,* 101.

73. Von Simson, *The Gothic Cathedral,* 38–39, 109.

74. Abbot Suger, quoted in Panofsky's commentary on Suger, *On the Abbey Church of St.-Denis and Its Art Treasures,* ed. Panofsky, 203.

75. Gregory the Great, *Lib. IX, Epistola IX Ad Serenum Episcopum Massiliensem* (Migne *PL* 77.1128–29); quoted by Freedberg, *The Power of Images,* 163.

76. On Suger's fidelity to the "'national' state" of France, see Lefebvre, *The Production of Space,* 257.

77. Panofsky, introduction to Suger, *On the Abbey Church of St.-Denis and Its Art Treasures,* ed. Panofsky, 13.

78. For a very helpful summary of Aquinas's view that the institution of images in the Church was indispensable for the instruction of the unlettered, see Freedberg, *The Power of Images,* 162, where he explains how Aquinas's enthusiasm for the use of images in Christian devotion shifted the emphasis somewhat away from that of rarefied mystical insights (the commemoration of divinity, priority II-A) and toward more popular issues like the exemplary behavior of saints (the commemoration of sacred history, priority II-B). Freedberg (163–66) also explains how Aquinas's contemporary, Bonaventure, in his famed *Journey of the Mind towards God,* widened the anagogical view even further to argue that, in fact, *all* created things in the sensible world—including pictures of created things—might lead the mind of the contemplator to eternal God. In so doing, Bonaventure, like Aquinas and Suger, directs our attention to a set of ritual-architectural events that depend upon the direct and purposive engagement of art and architectural forms (i.e., on contemplative modes of ritual-architectural presentation, III-B), but that are, both in the sociology of their participants and in terms of their content, anything but elitist and esoteric. On Aquinas's contention that "men apprehend intelligibles through sensibles," see Turner and Turner, *Image and Pilgrimage in Christian Culture,* 234–35, where they invoke this dictum to explain what is happening in Marian pilgrimage, and, in so doing, articulate the sense in which Catholic pilgrimage churches participate in the contemplation priority.

79. See Maquet, *The Aesthetic Experience: An Anthropologist Looks at the Visual Arts,* 165–66; discussed earlier in the chapter.

80. All of volume 1 is concerned with the cultivation of nonobjectifying interpretive approaches to sacred architecture, but see especially chapter 3, "Conversation and Play: The Eventfulness of Architecture."

81. Sinding-Larsen (*Iconography and Ritual,* 30) notes this relief of boredom as one of the "auxiliary" or nonliturgical functions that Christian images might serve in addition to what he terms their "formal function," that is, their officially prescribed role in the liturgy (29).

82. Dorinne Kondo, "The Way of Tea: A Symbolic Analysis," *Man* 20 (June 1985): 293. See also Sen'ō Tanaka and Sendō Tanaka, *The Tea Ceremony* (Tokyo, New York, London: Kodansha International, 1973), chapter 2.

83. While the "self-annihilating" experience of such Zen rock gardens involves a very direct and sustained concentration on architectural forms (or on rocks and sand anyway), the verb "contemplate" may be particularly misleading here insofar as to contemplate something typically connotes staying, at some level, distant from the object under consideration; it suggests a subject-object relation. In Zen, however, according to Toshihiko Izutsu, *The Interior and Exterior in Zen Buddhism,* Eranos Lectures, 1 (Dallas: Spring Publication, 1975), 27, the goal of meditation is a "complete self-identification" with the stones and sand: "something which is absolutely undifferentiated and undivided; it is Awareness pure and simple with neither subject or object." For another helpful description of the way in which the inscrutable arrangement of elements in the Zen garden is designed to pull one into an abstract meditation, see Mark Holborn, *The Ocean in the Sand: Japan, from Landscape to Garden* (Boulder, Colo.: Shambhala Press, 1978), 64–65.

84. Panofsky, in his introduction to Suger, *On the Abbey Church of St.-Denis and Its Art Treasures,* ed. Panofsky, provides a very useful account of the tenuous relationship between Suger and Bernard.

85. See Lekai, *The Cistercians,* 263.

86. Lekai provides these useful quotations from Saint Bernard (ibid.). Note also that the same ambivalence toward art persists among twentieth-century Cistercians, particularly Trappists. Thomas Merton (*Seeds of Contemplation* [Norfolk, Conn.: New Directions, 1949], 163), for instance, explains that the elaborate iconography in the basilica of the Trappist monastery of Gethesemani in Kentucky and the Stations of the Cross and other statuary on the grounds are all designed as aids to contemplation—and are very useful in that respect. But, contrary to Suger's reliance of such artistic devices, Merton is emphatic that these works of art, under no circumstances, should be confused with "the sanctity or with the pure love which is the substance of true contemplation." For Merton, while art may assist in contemplative meditation, it is certainly not indispensable.

87. Regarding the colonialist biases of the modern academic study of religion, see Charles H. Long, "A Post-Colonial Approach to the Study of Religion," *Religious Studies News* 3 (May 1995): 4–5.

88. The Classic Maya, for instance (among other indigenous peoples whose character has been imagined along the lines of "noble savages"), would constitute such an exception insofar as they have been routinely (mis)represented as contemplatives and mystics. In fact, to reflect on the intellectual history of Mesoamerican

studies, it would be possible (as I have argued in "Conquests of the Imagination: Maya-Mexican Polarity and the Story of Chichén Itzá") to see the romanticizing distortions of contemplative modes (point one in this conclusion) as operating in Western representations of the Maya, while the pejorative, condescending distortions of such practices (point two in this conclusion) operate most strongly in the representation of pre-Columbian Central Mexicans.

89. Regarding both the general tendency to neglect the possibility of contemplative modes of ritual-architectural presentation and apprehension in pre-Columbian contexts and the specific likelihood of reliance on such modes in the Zapotec-Mixtec region of Oaxaca and the Puuc, Río Bec–Chenes region of central Yucatan, see Jones, *Twin City Tales,* 254–58, 352–56.

Twenty-three | Propitiation

1. Bartolomé de las Casas, *Apologética historia de las Indias,* paraphrasing a prayer the Indians of Guatemala recited during human sacrifices; quoted by Recinos, *Popol Vuh: The Sacred Book of the Quiché Maya,* 226–27; and by Thompson, *Maya History and Religion,* 192.

2. Ruskin, *The Seven Lamps of Architecture,* 25. Ruskin makes this remark in reference to architecture and "the lamp of sacrifice."

3. Chang, *The Tao of Architecture,* 44. Recall that a more extended version of this quotation was cited and discussed in volume 1, chapter 7, "Use and Uselessness: The Special Case of Architecture."

4. Robert Redfield, *Folk Culture of Yucatan* (Chicago: University of Chicago Press, 1941), 230.

5. Recall the more politicized contestation over this place described by Friedland and Hecht, "The Politics of Sacred Place: Jerusalem's Temple Mount/*al-haram al-sharif,*" which I discussed in chapter 19 relative to the politics priority (II-C).

6. Mordechai Ha'cohen, "Sanctity, Law, and Customs," chapter 4 in Meir Ben-Dov, Mordechai Naor, and Zeev Aner, *The Western Wall,* trans. Raphael Posner (New York: Adama Books, 1983), 89.

7. See Meir Ben-Dov, *Jerusalem Man and Stone: An Archaeologist's Personal View of His City,* trans. Yael Guiladi (Tel-Aviv: Modan Publishing House, 1990), 57.

8. Ha'cohen, "Sanctity, Law, and Customs," 96.

9. Recall the discussion of the limitedness of the heuristic inquiry—to which god is this temple dedicated?—in chapter 17, on the ritual-architectural commemoration of divinity (priority II-A).

10. Stephens (*Incidents of Travel in Yucatan,* 1:52) notes that the name given by the Spaniards to the large structures of America was "adoratorio," implying that they were essentially places for petitioning favor from the deities.

11. See the sixteenth-century quotation from Bishop Bartolomé de las Casas cited at the beginning of this chapter.

12. Thompson, *Maya History and Religion,* 170.

13. Redfield, *Folk Culture of Yucatan,* 115, 128.

14. Thomas A. Lee, *Jmetic Lubton: Some Modern and Pre-Hispanic Maya Ceremonial Customs in the Highlands of Chiapas, Mexico,* Papers of the New World Archaeological Foundation, 29 (Provo, Utah: New World Archaeological Foundation, Brigham Young University, 1972); Evon Z. Vogt, *The Zinacantecos of Mexico: A Modern Maya Way of Life* (New York: Holt, Rinehart and Winston, 1970); and George Foster, *Tzintzuntzan: Mexican Peasants in a Changing World* (Boston: Little, Brown, 1967). Although the third of these is a study of a village in Michoacán rather than the Maya area, Kenneth Pearce (*The View from the Top of the Temple: Ancient Maya Civilization and Modern Maya Culture* [Albuquerque: University of New Mexico Press, 1984), 155, 174, 247) uses all three sources as support for a "logic of bargain or contract" among the Maya.

15. Marcus, "Archaeology and Religion," 299.

16. Johanna Broda, "The Sacred Landscape of Aztec Calendar Festivals: Myth, Nature, and Society," in *To Change Place,* ed. Carrasco, 84.

17. Ibid.

18. Ibid., 101.

19. For example, as some but not all of these Mesoamericanist interpreters acknowledge, even where a generally arbitrational logic does obtain, often—as in Chinese ancestral rites wherein descendants honor and placate their (un)dead relatives with offerings of food, drink, and money—the supernatural partners in propitiatory ritual mediation might be revered ancestors or spirits of the dead rather than deities per se (thus, the practice coincides more tightly with the commemoration of the dead [priority II-D] than with that of divinity [priority II-A]). Evon Vogt, for instance, in his "Some Aspects of the Sacred Geography of Highland Chiapas," in *Mesoamerican Sites and World-Views,* ed. Benson, 120–25, provides strong evidence that in most cases, the highland Maya, at least, are propitiating ancestors rather than deities.

20. Spanish distortions of indigenous Mesoamerican conceptions of divinity were also discussed in chapter 17.

21. Alfredo López Austin's *The Human Body and Ideology: Concepts of the Ancient Nahaus,* trans. Thelma Ortiz de Montellano and Bernard Ortiz de Montellano, 2 vols. (Salt Lake City: University of Utah Press, 1988), brings to the attention of scholars a remarkably different picture of Aztec conceptions not only of the human body but also of divinity, the cosmos, and ritual than those which had prevailed since the sixteenth century. For summary remarks on some of the most salient revisions, see Davíd Carrasco, *Religions of Mesoamerica: Cosmovision and Ceremonial Centers* (San Francisco: Harper and Row, 1990), 65–70.

22. Regarding "sympathetic causation," see James, *From Cave to Cathedral,* 17, 36–37.

23. Regarding the logic of Melanesian cargo cults, see Smith, *Map Is Not Territory,*

304–8. For a fresh interpretation of Kwakiutl potlatch redistribution, see Irving Goldman, *The Mouth of Heaven: An Introduction to Kwakiutl Religious Thought* (Huntington, N.Y.: Robert E. Krieger Publishing Company, 1981), 122–43.

24. See Goldman, *The Mouth of Heaven,* 85, 123–24.

25. On the endless reinterpretation of the concept of covenant among Jews, Christians, and Muslims, see Delbert R. Hillers, "Covenant," *Encyclopedia of Religion,* ed. Eliade, 4:133–37.

26. Walter Gropius, *The New Architecture and the Bauhaus,* trans. P. Morton Shand (Cambridge, Mass.: MIT Press, 1965), 43.

27. See volume 1, chapter 7, "Use and Uselessness: The Special Case of Architecture."

28. Ruskin, *The Seven Lamps of Architecture,* 17.

29. Ibid., 27.

30. For example, Heyden ("Caves, Gods, and Myths: World-Views and Planning in Teotihuacan," 12) makes explicit use of Eliade to explain how, in Mesoamerica, building and the settling of new territories "reiterated the cosmogony."

31. Clothey (*Rhythm and Intent,* 183), for instance, describes building the Hindu temple as "founding a world." Soundara Rajan (*An Invitation to Indian Architecture,* 25) recounts the celebrated and ancient practice of renewing the building materials of Hindu temples; his specific example is the Jagannath temple in Puri (Orissa), where rites of renewal coincide with the twelve-year sidereal period of Jupiter.

32. On Barasana longhouse construction as reiterative of cosmogony, see Hugh-Jones, *The Palm and the Pleiades: Initiation and Cosmology in Northwest Amazonia,* 28.

33. On the construction of Oglala sun dance lodges, see the famous account in *The Sacred Pipe: Black Elk's Account of the Seven Rites of the Oglala Sioux,* ed. Joseph Epes Brown (Middlesex, England: Penguin Books, 1971), chapter 5. On the Oglala *hocoka,* see William K. Powers, *Oglala Religion* (Lincoln: University of Nebraska Press, 1977), 41–42.

34. Mieke Bal, *Lethal Love: Feminist Literary Readings of Biblical Love Stories* (Bloomington: Indiana University Press, 1987), 115.

35. Burckhardt, *Sacred Art in East and West,* 52.

36. See Landa, *Relación de las cosas de Yucatán,* 18, for mention of the many changes of residence; and p.206, for the oft-cited account of the ritual destruction and replacement of household utensils.

37. Tozzer, *Chichén Itzá and Its Cenote of Sacrifice,* 35.

38. George C. Vaillant, in *Aztecs of Mexico: Origin, Rise, and Fall of the Aztec Nation* (Garden City, N.Y.: Doubleday, 1944), 92, contended that the pyramid at Tenayuca was rebuilt according to fifty-two-year cycles, but that notion has since been challenged. Kubler (*Art and Architecture of Ancient America,* 89), for example, holds tentatively to Vaillant's position.

39. For helpful background on Ise, see Robert S. Ellwood, "Harvest and Renewal at the Grand Shrine of Ise," *Numen* 15 (November 1968): 165–90; and Tange and Kawazoe, *Ise: Prototype of Japanese Architecture.*

40. John Burchard, introduction to Tange and Kawazoe, *Ise: Prototype of Japanese Architecture,* 9. Burchard attributes this assessment of Ise's appearance to Fosco Maraini.

41. Ellwood, "Harvest and Renewal at the Grand Shrine of Ise," 167.

42. This is Kenzo Tange's assessment; see Tange and Kawazoe, *Ise: Prototype of Japanese Architecture,* 14.

43. Ellwood ("Harvest and Renewal at the Grand Shrine of Ise," 181) explains that in the context of the Kanname-sai, the culminating event of Ise's annual liturgical cycle, "the presentation of offerings and its corollary, petition in the form of prayer or norito, is in fact accomplished three times at each of the main shrines."

44. See Kenzo Tange's portion of Tange and Kawazoe, *Ise: Prototype of Japanese Architecture,* 14ff.

45. Burchard, introduction to Tange and Kawazoe, *Ise: Prototype of Japanese Architecture,* 9.

46. Ellwood ("Harvest and Renewal at the Grand Shrine of Ise," 187–90) provides a concise summary of this set of ceremonies that he refers to as the *Shikinen Sengu,* or Ritual Year of Rebuilding of the Grand Shrine, the "consummate rite" of Ise.

47. For a helpful chronology of the Ise Shrine, see Tange and Kawazoe, *Ise: Prototype of Japanese Architecture,* 169–200. Also see Noboru Kawazoe, "The Ise Shrine," *Japanese Quarterly* 9 (July-September, 1962): 285–92.

48. Ellwood, "Harvest and Renewal at the Grand Shrine of Ise," 189.

49. Noboru Kawazoe, in Tange and Kawazoe, *Ise: Prototype of Japanese Architecture,* 202. Similarly, alluding specifically to Ise, Yi-Fu Tuan (*Space and Place,* 190) notes that, in "Oriental" buildings, "the form is more important than the particular substance, which is corruptible. Form can be resurrected whereas the matter of which it consists inevitably decays." Tuan, moreover, contrasts this characteristically Eastern acknowledgment of impermanence with a Western aspiration to, in a sense, defeat (or transcend) transience by constructing buildings that are intended to last forever. Tuan's interpretation of Ise is, in other words, more like that of Kawazoe than Ellwood.

50. Broda, "Templo Mayor as Ritual Space," 42.

51. Martín Alfonso Tovilla, *Relaciones histórico-descriptivas de la Verapaz el Manché y Lacandón en Guatemala* (1635); quoted by Carmack, *The Quiché Mayas of Utatlán,* 194–95. Carmack considers the archaeological evidence for this "rewhitening" agenda (295).

52. Oliver, introduction to *Shelter, Sign and Symbol,* ed. Oliver, 7–8; his principal source is Henri A. Junod, *The Life of a South African Tribe* (London: Macmillan, 1927).

53. Jacques Soustelle, *The Four Suns: Recollections and Reflections of an Ethnologist in Mexico,* trans. E. Ross (New York: Grossman Publishers, 1971), 115–19.

54. Waterson, "The House and the World: The Symbolism of Sa'Dan Toraja House Carvings," 36.

55. Ibid., 58.

56. See Oliver, *Dwellings,* 70.

57. On the other hand, Oliver notes that "As the ability to build a house, or at least to contribute to the process, is required of every man in some societies, or of every woman and child in others, the builder's craft often carries little status" (ibid.).

58. Regarding Evelyn Underhill's notion of "pure adoration," see her *Worship* (New York: Harper, 1937).

59. James, *From Cave to Cathedral,* 137. James explains that this kingly building initiative had a mythical precedent in the *Enuma elish* account of an episode in which, after Marduk had defeated and destroyed Tiamat and the forces of chaos, the gods showed their gratitude to him by building a shrine.

60. See Volwahsen, *Living Architecture: Indian,* 150.

61. See Kenneth Banta, "In Poland: A Monument to Catholicism's Power," *Time,* 28 December 1987, 56.

62. See Short, *A History of Religious Architecture,* 47. Burckhardt (*Sacred Art in East and West,* 40, n. 10) says that Solomon abstained from using any iron tools in the original construction of the Temple in Jerusalem, in memory of the manner in which the primitive altar of the Israelites had been built.

63. The Shaker meetinghouse, though perhaps the plainest of all their large buildings, was nonetheless revered as the most important; it was the one building in the community painted entirely white, the color that represented purity and that was also the most expensive paint to produce at the time. See Paul Rocheleau, *Shaker Built: The Form and Function of Shaker Architecture* (New York: Monacelli Press, 1994); and Julie Nicoletta, *The Architecture of the Shakers* (Woodstock, Vt.: Countryman Press, 1995).

64. Gaudi's perhaps apocryphal response is cited by Margot Hornblower, "Heresy or Homage in Barcelona," *Time,* 28 January 1991, 92. Also see James Johnson Sweeney and Josep Lluis Sert, *Antoni Gaudi,* rev. ed. (New York: Praeger, 1970).

65. Here, again, the relative order of ritual-architectural priorities—such as whether propitiatory (III-C) or political (II-C) incentives are most strongly operative in relation to some architectural construction project—would have to be assessed, to the extent possible, on an eventful, case-by-specific-case basis. That is to say, where designers and sponsors of a large project like the Sagrada Familia may (or may not) be concerned most about their political and economic interests, others laboring on the project may (or may not) be exercising more specifically propitiatory motives.

66. Henry Wadsworth Longfellow's poem "The Builders" would seem to par-

ticipate in this attitude of art for the Wholly Other insofar as he writes, in part:

In the elder days of Art,
Builders wrought with greatest care
Each minute and unseen part;
For the Gods see everywhere.

67. The notion of "art for the Wholly Other" raises some intriguing questions concerning who and what constitute the (intended) audiences or beholders in these sorts of propitiatory ritual-architectural events. Again, in the context of this subsection of the discussion of the propitiation priority (III-C), I would urge interpreters to give serious consideration to the plausibility of transhuman "beholders."

68. Brandon, *Man and God in Architecture and Ritual,* 6.

69. Ibid.

70. Brandon makes the less than compelling contention that "It is generally agreed by prehistorians that the purposes of these [Palaeolithic cave] paintings was [religio-]magical." Ibid.; also see 25ff.

71. Though largely concentrated on the main temple of the Aztecs, López Luján's *The Offerings of the Templo Mayor of Tenochtitlan* nonetheless provides the most thorough and nuanced available interpretive study of the logic (or, in his view, "language") of pre-Columbian offertory caches. Regarding the ubiquity of such caches, Thompson (*Maya Archaeologist*, 163), for instance, generalizes that "an offering was placed in every Maya structure when it was dedicated or enlarged"; Benson, *Maya World,* 91, includes a generalized discussion of typical locations and contents of Maya caches.

72. Pre-Columbian Mesoamerica provided several of the featured examples on theatric modes of ritual-architectural presentation and apprehension (priority III-A), covered in chapter 21.

73. Bushnell, *Ancient Arts of the Americas,* 135. The ancient Egyptian practice of sealing up the sumptuous pyramids once the king who had built it had been buried, so that no one ever again set foot inside them, provides another relevant parallel here.

74. Ian Graham, in conversation with David Adamson; quoted in David Grant Adamson, *The Ruins of Time: Four and a Half Centuries of Conquest and Discovery among the Maya* (New York: Praeger, 1975), 258; Ghirlandajo (1449–1494) was one of the finest Florentine painters of frescoes and a master of Michelangelo.

75. Ruskin (*The Seven Lamps of Architecture,* 27) contributes the very relevant general rule that "we should consider an increase of apparent labor as an increase of beauty in the building." Raymond Sidrys ("Megalithic Architecture and the Sculpture of the Ancient Maya"), among others, attempts to calculate the prodigious labor to build the Mesoamerican, particularly Maya, buildings.

76. Holmes, *Archaeological Studies among the Ancient Cities of Mexico,* 250–52.

77. See Ruskin, *The Seven Lamps of Architecture*, 29–30.

78. Harbison, *The Built, the Unbuilt, and the Unbuildable,* 37. He also comments on the irony that, where monuments and architecture are concerned, "Strength can be an incentive to wreck. Castles and fortifications have probably been the most often deliberately disabled ('slighted' is the funny expression for this) than other kinds of constructions."

79. Sabra J. Webber, *Romancing the Real: Folklore and Ethnographic Representation in North Africa* (Philadelphia: University of Pennsylvania Press, 1991), 212. I have added works of art and architecture to the list of possibilities Webber notes.

80. Regarding the desecration and resacralization of architecture as a political statement, consider the Golden Temple, or Harimandir (discussed in chapter 19 in relation to the politics priority [II-C] and specifically in relation to the ritual-architectural protests against the caste system). Edwardes (*Indian Temples and Palaces,* 137–41) recounts how three different times during the mid-eighteenth century, as reprisals for Sikh attacks on the Afghans, parts of the Harimandir were destroyed and the sacred pool was ritually polluted by being filled with the entrails of cows; in each case, the temple was repaired and the pool ritually cleansed so that religious services could be resumed.

81. Note also that Robert E. Fry ("Revitalization Movements among the Post-classic Lowland Maya," in *The Lowland Maya Postclassic,* ed. Chase and Rice, 129–35) discusses the pervasiveness of the Maya tradition of ritual destruction of art and architecture, and especially its possible relationship to "revitalization movements."

82. Tozzer, *Chichén Itzá and Its Cenote of Sacrifice,* 197, recounts the "killing" of offerings at Chichén Itzá and elsewhere; Deuel (*Conquistadors without Swords,* 378–80) discusses the phenomenon of "ceremonially smashed" pottery and underwater archaeology; Thompson (*Maya History and Religion,* 180) comments on the pervasiveness and resilience of Maya offerings to lakes; and Bushnell (*Ancient Arts of the Americas,* 135) laments the fact that most of the bowls retrieved from New Mexican burials had been ritually "killed."

83. Muriel Weaver, in her *The Aztecs, Maya, and Their Predecessors,* discusses the deliberate destruction and burial of Maya stelae at Tikal (p. 160) and at Kaminaljuyú (83); and of Olmec stone carvings in the Gulf Coast area (51–45).

84. Tozzer, *Chichén Itzá and Its Cenote of Sacrifice,* 259, n. 16.

85. Weaver (*The Aztecs, Maya, and Their Predecessors,* 139), following René Millon, discusses the sudden, catastrophic, and total destruction of Teotihuacan, seemingly from within; and Munro Edmonson ("Some Post-Classic Questions about the Classic Maya," in *Ancient Mesoamerica: Selected Readings,* ed. Graham, 225) suggests that the "destruction" of Classic Maya cities may have been largely ritual and symbolic, and that the "abandonment" was probably an evacuation by the ruling dynasty rather than the total population.

86. Ruskin, *The Seven Lamps of Architecture,* 26.

87. Kramrisch, *The Hindu Temple,* 2:142.

88. See Michell, *The Hindu Temple,* 50.

89. The *Agni Purana;* quoted in *Sacred Texts of the World: A Universal Anthology,* ed. Ninian Smart and Richard D. Hecht (New York: Crossroad Publishing, 1982), 226.

90. Ramacandra Kaulacara, *Śilpa Prakāśa: Medieval Orissan Sanskrit Text on Temple Architecture,* 122.

91. Evoking a happy image not unlike that of a convivial, community-spirited barn-raising, Sankar Prosad Ghosh (*Hindu Religious Art and Architecture,* 120), for instance, emphasizes the very positive socioeconomic ramifications of the collective initiative required to erect a Hindu temple: "An aggregation of the goodwill, genius and economic resources of the community were made to further [the] joint undertaking—that of establishing a temple. . . . Lucrative livelihood for hundreds of artisans, specialist and non-specialist workers were provided by the building of a temple." Recall also that in the section of chapter 19 entitled "Suspending, Undermining, or Overriding the Status Quo: Subversives and Conquerors," I discussed Bernard Tschumi's contention that the greatest transformative rewards of subversive "guerilla architecture," either personally or sociologically speaking, will usually lie not in the finished object, but in the collective constructional activity—as Tschumi (*Architecture and Disjunction,* 10–11) phrases it, "the revelation through building of realities and contradictions of society."

92. Some less convivial, more exploitative exercises of construction with respect to the politics priority (II-C) were noted in chapter 19. Consider, for instance, remarks on the exploitation of native labor to construct the great churches of New Spain in Tzvetan Todorov, *The Conquest of America: The Question of the Other,* trans. Richard Howard (New York: Harper and Row, 1983), 137.

93. *Shilpa Prakasha*; cited by Michell, *The Hindu Temple,* 50.

94. Ramacandra Kaulacara, *Śilpa Prakāśa: Medieval Orissan Sanskrit Text on Temple Architecture,* 123.

95. Ibid., 91.

96. Conze, *Buddhism: Its Essence and Development,* 80.

97. Ibid.

98. Keith Dowman, *The Power-Places of Central Tibet: The Pilgrim's Guide* (New York: Routledge and Kegan Paul, 1988), 10–11. Andrew Powell (*Living Buddhism* [New York: Harmony Books, 1989], 172), while providing a somewhat more moderate description, is, nonetheless, similarly impressed by the enthusiasm that contemporary Tibetans bring to the building task; regarding the "modest amount of reconstruction" going on at Sera, one of the great Gelug-pa monasteries, he says: "On most days two or three dozen local people can be seen struggling with baskets of earth and stones, and gradually new buildings in the traditional style rise from among the ruins of the old. Certainly one could wish for no clearer demonstration of the continuing vitality of Buddhism in Tibet today."

99. Nader Ardalan cites this saying of the Prophet in *The Aga Khan Award for Architecture,* Booklet Describing Program, 3d ed. (Philadelphia: Aga Khan Awards, 1980), 18.

100. See Ooka, *Temples of Nara and Their Art*, 12–13.

101. See Esther Pasztory, "Shamanism and North American Indian Art," in *Native North American Art History*, comp. Mathews and Jonaitis, 16. Pasztory bases her remarks on the Evenk primarily on A. I. Anisimov, "The Shaman's Tent of the Evenks and the Origin of the Shamanistic Rite," in *Studies in Siberian Shamanism*, ed. Henry N. Michael (Toronto: University of Toronto Press for the Arctic Institute of North America, 1963), 84–123.

102. Burckhardt, *Sacred Art in East and West*, 33.

103. Critchlow, "Niike: The Siting of a Japanese Rural House," in *Shelter, Sign and Symbol*, ed. Oliver, 219–26.

104. Ibid., 226.

105. Witherspoon, "Beautifying the World through Art (Navajo)," in *Native North American Art History*, comp. Mathews and Jonaitis, 220.

106. Ibid., 219. On sand painting, also see Witherspoon, *Language and Art in the Navajo Universe*, 167ff.

107. See especially chapter 7, "Use and Uselessness: The Special Case of Architecture."

108. I should note also, though without a chance to elaborate here, that, to the extent that construction processes are conceived as exercises in hermeneutical reflection, those processes are also exercises in comparison. See especially volume 1, chapter 11, "Significant Alternatives: Modes, Contexts, and Sequences of Comparison."

109. See especially part 1, "The Experience of Architecture," in volume 1.

Twenty-four | Sanctuary

1. Arnold van Gennep, *Rites of Passage*, trans. Monika B. Vizedom and Gabrielle L. Caffee (Chicago: University of Chicago Press, 1960), 20; originally published as *Les rites de passage* (Paris: E. Nourry, 1909).

2. Muhammad Iqbal, *Asrar-i khvudi* (The secrets of the self) (Lahore: n.p., 1915); quoted by Annemarie Schimmel, "Sacred Geography in Islam," in *Sacred Places and Profane Spaces*, ed. Scott and Simpson-Housley, 166. Schimmel explains, "As hunting and killing is forbidden in the sacred precincts, the Muslims can live safely as long as they cling to the *haram* [the sacred space around the Ka'bah], undisturbed like the gazelles and the pigeons, but as soon as they leave the *haram* they are vulnerable and can easily fall prey to fatal foreign influences."

3. José Ortega y Gasset, *The Revolt of the Masses* (New York: W. W. Norton and Company, 1932), 152; quoted by George F. Andrews, *Maya Cities: Placemaking and Urbanization* (Norman: University of Oklahoma Press, 1975), 7.

4. On the profound transition from rural to city life in seven different zones of "primary urban generation," see the seminal work of Paul Wheatley, *The Pivot of the Four Quarters*, especially chapter 3.

5. *Encyclopaedia Britannica,* 1965 ed., 19:151–52. Eliade emphasizes that the foundation of Rome and Romulus's plowing of the circular ditch is tantamount to a cosmogony; Mircea Eliade, *Occultism, Witchcraft and Cultural Fashions: Essays in Comparative Religions* (Chicago: University of Chicago Press, 1976), 22–23. The example is invoked to similar ends in Eliade and Sullivan, "Orientation," *Encyclopedia of Religion,* ed. Eliade, 11:105–6, where they stress also, after the fashion of the homology priority (I-A), that Rome was conceived as a detailed, microscopic image of the cosmos, built around a life-giving center. On the importance of this foundation legend, see also Rykwert, *The Idea of a Town,* chapter 1, "Town and Rite: Rome and Romulus."

6. Jonathan Z. Smith, "The Influence of Symbols on Social Change: A Place on Which to Stand," in Smith, *Map Is Not Territory,* 136. With respect to the deliberate and complete segregation of the sacred and profane, Smith appeals especially to Mary Douglas, *Purity and Danger: An Analysis of Concepts of Pollution and Taboo* (London: Routledge and Kegan Paul, 1978).

7. Ortega y Gasset, *The Revolt of the Masses,* 152.

8. See Powers, *Oglala Religion,* 41.

9. See Burl, *Rites of the Gods,* 164.

10. Edward Tenner, "Gate Fever," *Harvard Magazine* (September-October 1988), 31. Tenner credits this assessment of the gate towers (specifically at Princeton University) to Paul Venable Turner, *Campus: An American Planning Tradition* (New York: Architectural History Foundation; Cambridge, Mass.: MIT Press, 1984).

11. Tenner ("Gate Fever," 31) provides this quoted line from Ralph Adams Cram's plan for Princeton and credits the quotation concerning Bowdoin College to "the critic" Montgomery Schuyler.

12. Though Eliade (among others) very often writes of "thresholds" in this respect (for instance, *The Sacred and the Profane,* chapter 1), the wide currency of that term, as exemplified in the opening quote to this chapter, is more appropriately traced to Arnold van Gennep's *Rites of Passage.* Note, though, that van Gennep adheres to an explicitly Durkheimian notion of "sacred" and "profane," which thus aligns his perspective of "sacred space" more closely with that of Jonathan Smith than of Eliade.

13. See Eliade, *The Sacred and the Profane,* 25–26, 49.

14. Davies ("Architecture," 385) formulates the problem in a fashion very similar to that of Eliade: "The sacred place, defined by the religious building or precinct, is first of all a means of ensuring the isolation and so the preservation of both the sacred and the profane. The wall that keeps the one out also serves to keep the other in; it is the demarcation line (*demeans, tempus, templum*) between the two worlds. But within the sacred enclosure, the profane world is transcended and hence the existence of the holy place makes it possible for humans to pass from one world to another. . . ."

15. See Landa, *Relación de las cosas de Yucatán,* 103–4, 153. Karen Bassie-Sweet

(*At the Edge of the World: Caves and Late Classic Maya World View,* 26) notes this example from Landa and then contributes a parallel Maya case of a "tying dance" at Copan in which a cord was apparently stretched around four inner columns, presumably in order to form "a quadrilateral space just as the deities tied off the quadrilateral world." Pilgrim ("Intervals [*Ma*] in Space and Time: Foundations for a Religio-Aesthetic Paradigm in Japan," 265–67) provides a Japanese parallel to this idea of a temporarily roped off sacred precinct, which I discuss later in this chapter.

16. Kenneth Frampton ("Labour, Work and Architecture," in *Meaning in Architecture,* ed. Jencks and Baird, 155) suggests that inside the walls of the city (Paris, in this case) is "culture" and outside is "nature."

17. In chapter 19, on the politics priority (II-C), recall especially the section entitled "Reflecting, Reinforcing, and Perpetuating the Status Quo: Scales and Heights," which addressed the relative heights of Hindu houses, pre-Columbian ceremonial plazas, Muslim palaces, Chinese shrines and altars, and Japanese (Shinto) floors and stairways—all examples that could be invoked in this permutation on the sanctuary mode of presentation (III-D).

18. Broda, "Astronomy, *Cosmovision,* and Ideology in Pre-Hispanic Mesoamerica," 101. Broda argues that Mesoamerican architecture has within it two opposing tendencies: first, the tendency to achieve harmony with nature by creating an architectural replica (which recalls Scully's discussion of Greek architecture that integrates and dialogues with nature, but is actually most relevant to the homology priority [I-A]); and, second, the tendency to differentiate architecture from the natural surroundings (which is more like Roman architecture and especially relevant to the sanctuary priority [III-D]).

19. Tenner, "Gate Fever," 32.

20. It is worth noting here (and I will address this again in the closing reflections to this chapter) that throughout this discussion of the sanctuary priority, there is a strong tension between the conception of "sacred space" as "discovered" (as Eliade implies) and that of sacred space as "socially constructed" (as Jonathan Smith insists).

21. Smith, *To Take Place: Toward Theory in Ritual,* 104.

22. Abramovitz (*People and Spaces,* 76) borrows this line from Paul Thiry, Richard M. Bennett, and Henry L. Kamphoefner, *Churches and Temples* (New York: Reinhold Publishing Co., 1953), 3J; Abramovitz's emphasis.

23. Abramovitz, *People and Spaces,* 76. Mirsky (*Houses of God,* 105) repeats a very similar argument about the origins of the Jewish synagogue.

24. See Mirsky, *Houses of God,* 105.

25. See Scully, *The Earth, the Temple, and the Gods,* chapter 10.

26. In chapter 17, on the divinity priority (II-A), see the section entitled "Greek Gods and Temples: Three Variations on a Theme."

27. Scully, *The Earth, the Temple, and the Gods,* 194.

28. Ibid., 211–12. Note also that Richter (*Art and Human Consciousness,* 75–77)

contrasts the "outward orientation" of the Greek temple, not with its Roman counterpart, but with the "strong inward orientation" of the Egyptian temple, which instantiates, among other things, an exercise of the sanctuary mode.

29. Scully, *The Earth, the Temple, and the Gods,* 202–3. L'Orange (*Art Forms and Civic Life in the Late Roman Empire,* 70–85) discusses how the Romanesque Christian basilica, which is directly indebted to this Roman tradition, perpetuates the stratagem of designing space-enclosing volumes from the inside out.

30. Regarding Cluny, see the section entitled "Architecture, Emotion, and Liturgy: Ritual-Architectural Cultivations of Affect" in chapter 21.

31. The distinction between the respective building agendas of Saint Bernard and Abbot Suger is a central issue in Panofsky's introduction to Abbot Suger's treatise, *On the Abbey Church of St.-Denis and Its Art Treasures.* That interesting contrast could be further illumined, I think, by the use of Victor Turner's categories "iconophilia" (or image lovers) versus "iconoclast" (or image breakers); see, particularly, Turner and Turner, *Image and Pilgrimage in Christian Culture,* 234–36, 253. Also relevant is the discussion of two alternative types of Christian theological aesthetics —namely, naturalism, or "abundant means," and asceticism, or "scanty means"—found in van der Leeuw, *Sacred and Profane Beauty,* 177–89, 303–27.

32. Bernard and the Cistercians were not, however, totally unsympathetic to art (as they are often portrayed); on the aesthetic sensibilities of Cistercians, see Freedberg, *The Power of Images,* 301–3. I hope that it is clear at this point in my discussion why a contemplative like Bernard actually rejects what I term the contemplation mode (priority III-B) in favor of the sanctuary mode (priority III-D).

33. See, for instance, Braunfels, *Monasteries of Western Europe,* chapter 5.

34. Von Simson, *The Gothic Cathedral,* 44. Note also that Braunfels (*Monasteries of Western Europe,* 37–46) discusses the astonishing plan for "an ideal Carolingian monastery," which was found in the library of Saint Gall; this is perhaps an even stronger example of an attempt (never realized) at constructing a place that would provide a foretaste of paradise.

35. *Le Directoire Spirituel des Cisterciens Reformes* (Bricquebec, 1910), chapter 6, pp. 34–37; Cf. the English translation by a monk of New Melleray (Gethsemani, 1946); quoted in Merton, *The Waters of Siloe,* xxvii.

36. Modern proponents of "functionalism" and "nonbourgeois architecture" (for example, the Bauhaus architects) adopt white, beige, gray, and black as their colors and champion a stark simplicity of form, all choices that resemble those of the Cistercians. The formal coincidence is particularly intriguing and ironic, given the radically different intentions of the two groups; see Wolfe, *From Bauhaus to Our House,* 24–27, for a satirical discussion of the so-termed functionalist ideal. Also, it is noteworthy that the Cistercian priorities of detachment and isolation are manifest even more radically in the medieval French charterhouses, where Carthusian hermits literally pass their entire existences in an architectural envelope; see, for instance, Braunfels, *Monasteries of Western Europe,* chapter 6.

37. Note, however, that this imitation and standardization among Cistercian monasteries represent not only the replication of sanctuary modes of presentation and apprehension (III-D) but also that of highly conventionalized architecture (priority I-B).

38. On this cave near Chichén Itzá, see E. Wyllys Andrews, IV, *Balankanche: Throne of the Tiger Priest,* Publication 32 (New Orleans: Middle American Research Institute, 1970). For a more general and more extensive treatment of caves in Mesoamerica, see Doris Heyden, "An Interpretation of the Cave underneath the Pyramid of the Sun in Teotihuacan, Mexico," *American Antiquity* 40 (April 1975): 131–47; idem, "Caves, Gods, and Myths: World-View and Planning in Teotihuacan," in *Mesoamerican Sites and World-Views,* ed. Benson, 1–35; and Bassie-Sweet, *At the Edge of the World: Caves and Late Classic Maya World View.*

39. Besides caves, another particularly intriguing sort of natural "sanctuary" comes in Johanna Broda's description of Pantitlán (which means "amid the flags"), the famous whirlpool (or drain) within the Lake of Tezcoco around which the Aztecs built a kind of enclosure inside the water that was marked by flag-like banners, the *cuenmantli,* which were characteristic of the cult of the rain gods. A site for pre-Columbian child sacrifice and always a dangerous place for shipwrecks, according to Fray Diego Durán, *Historia de las Indias de Nueva Espana,* ed. Angel María Garibay (Mexico City: Porrua, 1967), 1:88–91; during the rainy season water gushed forth at this place, while during the dry season it was thick, salty, and smelled bad. See Broda, "The Sacred Landscape of the Aztec Calendar: Myth, Nature, and Society," in *To Change Place,* ed. Carrasco, 87, 95.

40. On the Buddhist cave temples at Ajanta, see Edwardes, *Indian Temples and Palaces,* 37–52. For more general remarks on the widespread appropriation of caves as sanctuaries, see Brandon, *Man and God in Architecture and Ritual,* 89.

41. Hagar Qim was cited with other relevant examples of cave-burials in chapter 20, on the commemoration of the dead (priority II-D).

42. Meister, "On the Development of a Morphology for a Symbolic Architecture: India," 35. Meister contends that "The major metaphors in the minds of Hindu temple architects—as expressed both in texts and in foundation inscriptions—were those of the body of the temple as mountain and the sanctum as cave or womb (garbha) opening the earth to the approach of the worshiper. . . ." On the Hindu homologization of cave, womb, and temple, also see Kramrisch, *The Hindu Temple,* 1:162–63. For an interesting (and highly eventful) discussion of the architectural (re)creation of caves in Chinese gardens, and particularly the intriguing notion of *tung-t'ien* (or "cave-heavens"), that is, caves that are conceived somehow as entryways into heaven, see Munakata, "Mysterious Heavens and Chinese Classical Gardens," 64–88.

43. Richard F. Townsend, "The Mt. Tlaloc Project," in *To Change Place,* ed. Carrasco, 29. In a similar vein, the so-termed Earth Monster temples of the Río Bec and Chenes areas in the Maya zone (discussed in chapter 17, on the divinity priority

[II-A], as architectural "bodies" of god) also seem to have afforded a regenerative ritual-architectural experience of (re)entering the womb of the earth and then being (re)born upon exiting.

44. Stephen DeStaebler, in Stephen DeStaebler and Diane Apostolos-Cappadona, "Reflections on Art and the Spirit: A Conversation," in *Art, Creativity, and the Sacred,* ed. Apostolos-Cappadona, 27. Apostolos-Cappadona echoes his sentiments concerning the womb-like experience of many Christian churches when she writes: "Galla Placidia is like entering (or reentering) the womb; you feel the protective warmth all around you even in the darkness. When you are in the Rothko Chapel, it is dark and cool: characteristics of Jung's anima. This is an incredible experience. Then you walk outside into the blazing Houston sun as Barnett Newman's *Broken Obelisk* emerges from the reflecting pool. This male-female dichotomy was unconscious and not the architect's intention" (27). Additionally, recall (as mentioned in chapter 20) that, like the crypts in the Christian churches of Europe, Ragon (*The Space of Death,* 58) interprets the cave-burials of the Greeks and the famous catacombs in Rome as (maybe latent) reflections of an abiding fascination with the earth as "universal uterus" from which people are born and then ultimately return.

45. See Kramrisch, *The Hindu Temple,* 1:15–17.

46. Volwahsen, *Living Architecture: Indian,* 92.

47. Oliver, *Dwellings,* 167.

48. Jonathan Z. Smith, in "The Temple and the Magician," in Smith, *Map Is Not Territory,* 182, correlates his broad distinction between "locative" and "utopian world views" with, respectively, a very useful distinction between permanent sacred centers, specifically temples, and places of temporary sacrality that are sanctified by the magician's power.

49. Smith, "The Bare Facts of Ritual," in Smith, *Imagining Religion,* 55.

50. J. J. M. DeGroot; quoted by DeBernardi, "Space and Time in Chinese Religious Culture," 254.

51. DeBernardi, "Space and Time in Chinese Religious Culture," 254.

52. Thompson and Fenton, "*Matsuri:* The Binding of Secular and Ceremonial Space in Kakunodate, Japan," 151.

53. Cobo, *Inca Religion and Customs,* 145. At this point Cobo is speaking specifically about the Coya Paymi, an annual festival just prior to the rainy season in which the ancient Peruvians asked Viracocha if he would see fit to prevent sickness that year in Cuzco and throughout the Inca empire. Regarding similar preparation for the Itu festival, see p. 151.

54. William K. Powers, *Yuwipi: Vision and Experience in Oglala Ritual* (Lincoln: University of Nebraska Press, 1982), 25.

55. Ibid., 24. Powers notes, for instance, that, "It is partly this tolerance that makes the sweat lodge potentially sacred; like humans it is subject to the whims of nature and must abide by its relentless impositions" (25).

56. The famous accounts of Oglala medicine man Black Elk also emphasize repeatedly the preparatory—but not permanent—(re)sanctifications whereby virtually any ordinary place can be transformed into a sacred center; he explains, for instance, "By constructing the altar in this manner, we see that everything leads into, or returns to, the center; and this center which is here, but which we know is really everywhere, is *Wakan-Tanka*." *The Sacred Pipe: Black Elk's Account of the Seven Rites of the Oglala Sioux,* ed. Brown, 89–90. By contrast, Nelson Reed describes a circumstance in the village of Chan Santa Cruz (today, Felipe Carrillo Puerto) in which the natives' holy sanctuary was so thoroughly defiled by whites that, even once it was reclaimed, all their efforts at resanctifying the place were unsuccessful; Nelson Reed, *The Caste War of Yucatan* (Stanford: Stanford University Press, 1964), 250–51.

57. Note that the sweat lodge also provides the Oglalas a ritual-architectural context for closure and reflective interpretation, as participants in vision quests and Yuwipi ceremonies also routinely pass through a sweat ceremony at the end as well as the beginning of the larger ritual process. See, for instance, Powers, *Yuwipi: Vision and Experience in Oglala Ritual,* 80–83.

58. Thompson (*Maya History and Religion,* 172–75) describes preparation for Maya ceremonies, citing not only Las Casas and Landa but a number of strong ethnographic references; and Tozzer (*Chichén Itzá and Its Cenote of Sacrifice,* 76) gives more sources on the same issue. Also relevant here is the remote Guatemalan *raxaja,* or "green house" (so named because this temporary hut was kept ever new and pure with fresh leaves that were continually replaced as they dried out), where a Quiché Maya priest would do penance for up to a year, bleeding himself and offering gifts to the deities; Las Casas's description of this Guatemalan refuge is summarized in Carmack, *The Quiché Mayas of Utatlán,* 198. This same example is cited in Alfredo López Austin, *Hombre-dios: Religión y política en el mundo náhuatl* (México: Universidad Nacional Autónoma de México, 1973), 106; and Nigel Davies, *The Toltecs until the Fall of Tula* (Norman: University of Oklahoma Press, 1977), 292–93.

59. Steinhardt, "Altar to Heaven Complex," in Steinhardt et al., *Chinese Traditional Architecture,* 142–44.

60. Ellwood, "Harvest and Renewal at the Grand Shrine of Ise," 172–73; also see 181.

61. Isozaki, "Floors and Internal Spaces in Japanese Vernacular Architecture," 58.

62. Daisetz Teitaro Suzuki, *The Training of the Zen Monk* (1934; New York: Globe Publishing, 1991), 115.

63. This is not, of course, to say that there are not important interactions between the sanctuary mode (III-D) and the respective commemoration of sacred history (priority II-B) and of the dead (priority II-D).

64. On the "unchanged and unchanging" character of the Zen garden and

monastery as sanctuary, see, for example, Loraine E. Kuck, *The World of the Japanese Garden: From Chinese Origins to Modern Landscape Art* (New York: Weatherhill, 1968), 163–71. Also, in the context of an exceedingly useful (and eventful) treatment of different ways in which Chinese gardens constitute "separate worlds," Munakata ("Mysterious Heavens and Chinese Classical Gardens," 67–69) provides some general contrasts between Japanese and Chinese gardens.

65. On such expressions of the sanctuary priority that eventuate in the ritual-architectural recapitulation of paradise or heaven in other contexts, see Davies, "Architecture," 385, where he notes that the name Babylon itself literally means "gate of the gods," and Jacob at Bethel declared: "This is the gate of Heaven." Davies also notes: "In the same realm of ideas is to be found the royal doors that provide access through the iconostasis to the altar of the Eastern Orthodox church and the 'Gates of Paradise,' which is the name given by Michelangelo to Lorenzo Ghiberti's sculpted doors at the Florence Baptistery."

66. According to Ardalan and Bakhtiar (*The Sense of Unity,* 68) the Safavid Hasht Bihisht, or "Garden of the Eight Paradises," for instance, "quite literally recreates a dynamic paradise not only in its overall plan but in the very concept of its central pavilion." Ardalan and Bakhtiar also explain that the layout of the courtyard of Masjid-i-Jāmiʿ in Isfahan (which I discussed in chapter 21 in relation to the theatrical mode [III-A]) "conforms to the ancient iconography of the recapitulation of paradise" (106).

67. See (as noted in chapter 17) Volwahsen, *Living Architecture: India,* 140–41.

68. These (and other) examples of "deity domiciles" were discussed in chapter 17 with respect to divinity commemoration (priority II-A); see especially the section in that chapter entitled "Architecture as the House of God: Deity Domiciles and Sacred Shelters."

69. On the careful preparation of the context for a Yuwipi ceremony, see Powers, *Yuwipi: Vision and Experience in Oglala Ritual,* chapter 4, "Preparing for the Singing," 38–44.

70. Pilgrim, "Intervals (*Ma*) in Space and Time," 255–77, is my main source for the discussion of *ma*. By collapsing the distinction between time and space, *ma*-inspired architecture also participates in the homology priority (I-A); see particularly ibid., 255–56. Gunter Nitschke connects *ma* explicitly with architecture, in "'Ma': The Japanese Sense of 'Place' in Old and New Architecture and Planning," *Architectural Design* 36 (March 1966), which Pilgrim uses. Also see Richard B. Pilgrim, "Foundations for a Religio-Aesthetic Tradition in Japan," in *Art, Creativity, and the Sacred,* ed. Apostolos-Cappadona, 138–54.

71. Pilgrim, "Intervals (*Ma*) in Space and Time," 263.

72. Matsuoka Seigow, "Aspects of *Kami,*" in *Ma: Space-Time in Japan* (New York: Cooper-Hewitt Museum, n.d.); quoted by Pilgrim, "Intervals (*Ma*) in Space and Time," 262. Pilgrim (p. 263) explains that the term *kekkai* persists in Buddhism to describe the special room in a temple set aside for a priest's spiritual renewal, a

ritual event reminiscent of the Shinto practice of regenerative seclusion, especially in caves, tombs, and *tama-bako* ("soul-boxes"), which—though containing nothing—are filled with sacred power to be imparted to those who have entered them. The strategy of demarcating a sacred space with ropes finds direct parallels in Maya, as noted earlier in this chapter.

73. Pilgrim, "Intervals (*Ma*) in Space and Time," 266. Regarding parallels to the evocative, instigatory power of architecturally engendered voids in other historical contexts, consider Wach, *The Sociology of Religion,* 40, 381, on the Quaker reliance on silence to initiate worship; or, more directly, van der Leeuw, *Sacred and Profane Beauty,* 207–8, on the architectural fabrication of "emptiness" in the Islamic mosque wherein the denial of all content is advanced as the catalyst to spiritual receptivity. On the significance (and I'd say superabundance) of "the free space" around built forms, Amos Ih Tiao Chang (*The Tao of Architecture,* 67) offers the following reflections: "The conscious spacing between individual forms can achieve more than visual unity and clarity. As we have mentioned, a free space seen from many viewpoints in time would have a multiplicative value much beyond its mere physical quality and appearance. In a visual sense, proper allowance for space between and around buildings would inherently allow for man's experience of a richer variety from changing points of view and fuller understanding of an architectural composition."

74. Tenner, "Gate Fever," 30–31.

75. Regarding the variety of ways in which architectural sanctuaries can facilitate a complete detachment from the mainstream social world, prisons, of course, by forcibly segregating that portion of society that refuses to obey its laws, constitute an extreme (if desanctified) expression of the sanctuary mode (III-D). Prisons are intriguing in this context because, somewhat ironically, prestige and empowerment come with being outside rather than inside. Conversely, however, explicitly religious structures, in many cases, operate as sanctuaries in the sense that they provide refuges that are exempted from the ordinary strictures of the law. Taking a famous example from the Greek classical world, for instance, Davies ("Architecture," 388) recounts how Demosthenes sought sanctuary in the Temple of Poseidon on the island of Calauria in 322 B.C.E. Davies also explains that, in the post-Constantinian era, Christian church buildings were included in the same class as pagan temples—that is, as specially holy places—so that the right of fugitives to remain under the protection of their god became legally recognized and, in Western Europe, continued to be so for centuries; in England it was not until 1723 that all rights of sanctuary were finally declared null. For an especially intriguing case of a fugitive seeking refuge in a colonial Mexican Catholic church, which spawned fascinating debates between the civil and ecclesiastical notions of sanctuary, see Simpson, *Many Mexicos,* 147. The case of Panama president Manuel Noriega successfully eluding the American military by seeking refuge in a Catholic church in 1990 provides a more contemporary, yet equally intriguing, example.

76. Moholy-Nagy, *Native Genius in Anonymous Architecture in North America,* 60.

77. See, for instance, Rocheleau, *Shaker Built: The Form and Function of Shaker Architecture;* and Nicoletta, *The Architecture of the Shakers.*

78. Antoniy Handjiyski, *Rock Monasteries,* trans. Marguerite Alexieva (Sofia: Septemvri State Publishing House, 1985), 5. Handjiyski (p. 6) considers that, while there is no doubt that some of the Bulgarian rock monasteries did come into existence as refuges for Hesychast anchorites, others originated as early as the tenth century and many continued to be used well after Bulgaria fell under Ottoman domination.

79. Handjiyski, *Rock Monasteries,* 5–6.

80. Thomas Merton (*The Waters of Siloe,* xix) writes: "No monastery can accomplish much in the material order. Its greatest work is spiritual. In a world in which men have forgotten the value of prayer, it is the monks who pray for the world and for all those in the world who have forgotten how to pray."

81. Note that in this more obviously politicized permutation, sanctuary modes of presentation (III-D) are operating quite similarly to theatric modes (III-A), which are, as noted in chapter 21, especially often paired with commemorations of politics (priority II-C).

82. Desai, *Mosques of India,* 5.

83. Ibid., 6–7.

84. On morphological, sociopolitical parallels between Muslim mosques, Sikh shrines, Baha'i temples, and Puritan meetinghouses, in chapter 19, on the politics priority (II-C), see specifically the sections entitled "Reflecting, Reinforcing, and Perpetuating the Status Quo: Scales and Heights" and "Suspending, Undermining, or Overriding the Status Quo: Subversives and Conquerors." Both of those sections treat numerous examples that are pointedly relevant to this permutation of the sanctuary priority.

85. Clifford Geertz, *Islam Observed: Religious Development in Morocco and Indonesia* (Chicago: University of Chicago Press, 168), 36.

86. Ibid. Note that in Geertz's example the sanctuary mode (III-D) merges especially closely with that of the theater priority (III-A).

87. Marcus ("Archaeology and Religion," 299, 311) explains that this arrangement of a "highly sacred inner room" and a "less sacred outer room" is characteristic of the Maya as well as the Zapotecs. Similar floor plans abound throughout Mesoamerica.

88. Michell, *The Hindu Temple,* 67.

89. All of these examples and the Maya case were cited in the section of chapter 19 entitled "Reflecting, Reinforcing, and Perpetuating the Status Quo: Scales and Heights." Oliver (*Dwellings,* 156) explains that the Navajo hogan demarcates an inviolate boundary inside which behavior is marked by such strict prohibitions that one may not even look into the structure without permission.

90. See Groslier and Arthaud, *The Arts and Civilization of Angkor,* 97ff.

91. There is some controversy regarding the precise arrangement of Herod's Temple, but see, for instance, Short, *A History of Religious Architecture,* 48; or James, *From Cave to Cathedral,* 188–89, 370, n. 110.

92. James, *From Cave to Cathedral,* 188–89.

93. Wu, *Chinese and Indian Architecture,* 33.

94. Ibid., 43.

95. Ibid., 32.

96. Wu (ibid., 34) explains: "Theoretically, the number of courtyards one could have, and the accompanying sense of depth in privacy, was determined by one's status."

97. Ibid. Quoting the *Li chi* (Book of rites; a Han dynasty compilation from accumulated source materials of much earlier periods), Wu explains the meticulous procedure for greeting guests: "The host enters the doorway and turns to the right, and the guest enters and turns to the left. The host proceeds to the eastern stairway, while the guest proceeds to the west. . . . If the guest, for some special reason, such as his inferior social rank, insists upon climbing the eastern stairway, the host must refuse in a most persistent manner; and then the guest may go back to his side and be ready to ascend. In ascending the stairway the guest follows the host's moves; as the host lifts his right foot to ascend the eastern stairs, the guest lifts his left foot to ascend the western stairs" (33).

98. Ibid., 33–34. There are some minor contradictions in Wu's description of who is allowed where in the house, but the general notion of a hierarchy of access is nevertheless unmistakable.

99. See the introduction to this volume.

100. In chapter 14, on the homology priority (I-A), see especially the section entitled "Phenomenology and Hierophany: The Discovery, Not Creation, of Sacred Places."

101. Tenner ("Gate Fever," 27), for instance, comments on the ambiguity of gates, on college campuses and elsewhere, which both repel and invite.

102. In a blunter example of the way in which a single architectural "sanctuary" can engender profoundly different human experiences, a prisoner's experience of confinement, powerlessness, and, no doubt, antipathy in a jail is obviously the opposite of the sensation of security and power that the jailers enjoy.

103. Excerpt from the unpublished journal of Michael Link, (formerly) a graduate student in English at the Ohio State University, dated 30 August 1988.

Select Bibliography

Abercrombie, Stanley. *Architecture as Art: An Esthetic Analysis*. New York: Van Nostrand Reinhold, 1984.

Ackerman, James. *Palladio*. New York: Penguin Books, 1966.

Agnew, John A., and James S. Duncan, eds. *The Power of Place: Bringing Together Geographical and Sociological Imagination*. Boston: Unwin Hyman, 1989.

Alles, Gregory D. "Wach, Eliade, and the Critique from Totality." *Numen* 35 (July 1988): 108–38.

———. "Surface, Space, and Intention: The Parthenon and the Kandariya Mahadeva." *History of Religions* 28 (August 1988): 1–36.

Andrews, George F. *Maya Cities: Placemaking and Urbanization*. Norman: University of Oklahoma Press, 1975.

Apostolos-Cappadona, Diane, ed. *Art, Creativity, and the Sacred: An Anthology in Religion and Art*. New York: Crossroad, 1984.

Arata, Isozaki. "Floors and Internal Spaces in Japanese Vernacular Architecture: Phenomenology of Floors." *Res: Anthropology and Aesthetics* 11 (spring 1986): 54–77.

———. "Of City, Nation, and Style." In *Postmodernism and Japan*, ed. Masao Miyoshi and H. D. Harootunian. Durham, N.C.: Duke University Press, 1989.

Ardalan, Nader, and Laleh Bakhtiar. *The Sense of Unity: The Sufi Tradition in Persian Architecture*. Publications of the Center for Middle Eastern Studies, no. 9. Chicago: University of Chicago Press, 1973.

Arnheim, Rudolf. *The Power of the Center: A Study of Composition in the Visual Arts*. Berkeley and Los Angeles: University of California Press, 1982.

Arshi, Pardeep Singh. *Sikh Architecture in Punjab*. New Delhi: Intellectual Publishing House, 1986.

Atmadi, Parmono. *Some Architectural Design Principles of Temples in Java: A Study through the Buildings Projection on the Reliefs of Borobudur Temple*. Bulaksumur, Yogyakarta: Gadjah Mada University Press, 1988.

Aveni, Anthony F., ed. *Native American Astronomy*. Austin: University of Texas Press, 1977.

———. *Skywatchers of Ancient Mexico*. Austin: University of Texas Press, 1980.

———, ed. *Archaeoastronomy in the New World*. Cambridge: Cambridge University Press, 1982.

———, ed. *World Archaeoastronomy: Selected Papers from the Second Oxford International Conference on Archaeoastronomy, Held at Merida, Yucatan, Mexico, 13–17 January 1986*. Cambridge: Cambridge University Press, 1989.

Aveni, Anthony F., and Sharon L. Gibbs. "On the Orientation of Pre-Columbian Buildings in Central Mexico." *American Antiquity* 42 (October 1976): 509–17.

Aveni, Anthony F., and Horst Hartung. "Precision in the Layout of Maya Architecture." In *Ethnoastronomy and Archaeoastronomy in the American Tropics,* ed. Anthony F. Aveni and Gary Urton. New York: New York Academy of the Sciences, 1982.

———. *Maya City Planning and the Calendar.* Philadelphia: American Philosophical Society, 1986.

Aveni, Anthony F., and Gary Urton, eds. *Ethnoastronomy and Archaeoastronomy in the American Tropics.* New York: New York Academy of Sciences, 1982.

Bachelard, Gaston. *The Poetics of Space.* Boston: Beacon Press, 1964.

Barthes, Roland. *Image, Music, Text.* Ed. and trans. Stephen Heath. New York: Hill and Wang, 1977.

Baxandall, Michael. *Patterns of Intention: On the Historical Explanation of Pictures.* New Haven: Yale University Press, 1985.

Bell, Catherine. *Ritual Theory, Ritual Practice.* New York and Oxford: Oxford University Press, 1992.

Benson, Elizabeth P., ed. *Mesoamerican Sites and World-Views: A Conference at Dumbarton Oaks, October 16–17, 1976.* Washington, D.C.: Dumbarton Oaks, 1981.

———. "Architecture as Metaphor." In *Fifth Palenque Round Table, 1983,* ed. Merle Green Robertson. Palenque Round Table Series, vol. 7. San Francisco: Pre-Columbian Art Research Institute, 1985.

Bernal, Ignacio. *Three Thousand Years of Art and Life in Mexico.* Trans. Carolyn B. Czitron. New York: H. N. Abrams, 1968.

Bhardwaj, Surinder Mohan. *Hindu Places of Pilgrimage in India: A Study in Cultural Geography.* Berkeley and Los Angeles: University of California Press, 1973.

Bhoothalingam, Mathuram. *Movement in Stone: A Study of Some Chola Temples.* New Delhi: Soumani Publications, 1969.

Bleich, David. "Epistemological Assumptions in the Study of Response." In *Reader-Response Criticism: From Formalism to Post-Structuralism,* ed. Jane P. Tompkins. Baltimore: Johns Hopkins University Press, 1980.

Blier, Suzanne Preston. "The Dance of Death: Notes on the Architecture and Staging of Tamberma Funeral Performance." *Res: Anthropology and Aesthetics* 2 (autumn 1981): 107–43.

Bloomer, Kent C., and Charles W. Moore. *Body, Memory, and Architecture.* New Haven: Yale University Press, 1977.

Blunt, Anthony, ed. *Baroque and Rococo: Architecture and Decoration.* New York: Harper and Row, 1978.

Borgeaud, Phillippe. "The Open Entrance to the Closed Palace of the King: The Greek Labyrinth in Context." *History of Religions* 14 (August 1974): 1–27.

Brandon, S. F. G. *Man and God in Art and Ritual: A Study of Iconography, Architecture, and Ritual Action as Primary Evidence of Religious Belief and Practice.* New York: Charles Scribner's Sons, 1975.

Braunfels, Wolfgang. *Monasteries of Western Europe: The Architecture of the Orders.* Princeton: Princeton University Press, 1972.

Broda, Johanna. "Astronomy, *Cosmovision*, and Ideology in Pre-Hispanic Mesoamerica." In *Ethnoastronomy and Archaeoastronomy in the American Tropics,* ed. Anthony F. Aveni and Gary Urton. New York: New York Academy of Sciences, 1982.

———. "Templo Mayor as Ritual Space." In Johanna Broda, Davíd Carrasco, and Eduardo Matos Moctezuma, *The Great Temple of Tenochtitlan: Center and Periphery in the Aztec World.* Berkeley and Los Angeles: University of California Press, 1987.

Brown, Peter Lancaster. *Megaliths, Myths, and Men: An Introduction to Astro-Archaeology.* New York: Taplinger Publishing Company, 1976.

Buchanan, Richard. "Declaration by Design: Rhetoric, Argument, and Demonstration in Design Practice." In *Design Discourse: History, Theory, Criticism,* ed. Victor Margolin. Chicago: University of Chicago Press, 1989.

Burckhardt, Titus. *Sacred Art in East and West: Its Principles and Methods.* Trans. Lord Northbourne. London: Perennial Books, 1967.

———. *Art of Islam: Language and Meaning.* [London]: World of Islam Festival Publishing Company, 1976.

Burl, Aubrey. *Rites of the Gods.* London: J. M. Dent and Sons, 1981.

Bushnell, G. H. S. *Ancient Arts of the Americas.* New York: Frederick A. Praeger, 1965.

Buttimer, Anne, and David Seamon, eds. *The Human Experience of Space and Place.* London: Croom Helm, 1980.

Campo, Juan Edwardo. *The Other Sides of Paradise: Explorations into the Religious Meanings of Domestic Space in Islam.* Columbia: University of South Carolina Press, 1991.

Carlson, John B. "A Geomantic Model for the Interpretation of Mesoamerican Sites: An Essay in Cross-Cultural Comparison." In *Mesoamerican Sites and World-Views: A Conference at Dumbarton Oaks, October 16–17, 1976,* ed. Elizabeth Benson. Washington, D.C.: Dumbarton Oaks, 1976.

———. "The Case for Geomantic Alignments of Pre-Columbian Mesoamerican Sites—The Maya." *Katunob: A Newsletter-Bulletin on Mesoamerican Anthropology* 10 (June 1977): 67–88.

Carmichael, David L., et al., eds. *Sacred Sites, Sacred Places.* London and New York: Routledge, 1994.

Carrasco, Davíd. "City as Symbol in Aztec Thought: The Clue from the Codex Mendoza." *History of Religions* 20 (February 1981): 199–220.

———. "Templo Mayor: The Aztec Vision of Place." *Religion* 2 (1981): 275–97.

———. *Quetzalcoatl and the Irony of Empire: Myths and Prophesies in the Aztec Tradition.* Chicago: University of Chicago Press, 1982.

———. "Star Gatherers and Wobbling Suns: Astral Symbolism in the Aztec Tradition. *History of Religions* 26 (February 1987): 279–94.

———, ed. *To Change Place: Aztec Ceremonial Landscapes.* Niwot: University Press of Colorado, 1991.

Chandra, Pramod. *On the Study of Indian Art.* Cambridge, Mass.: Harvard University Press, 1983.

Chang, Amos Ih Tiao. *The Tao of Architecture.* Princeton: Princeton University Press, 1956.

Chiat, Marilyn Joyce Segal. *Handbook of Synagogue Architecture.* Chico, Calif.: Scholars Press, 1982.

Chidester, David, and Edward T. Linenthal, eds. *American Sacred Space.* Bloomington: Indiana University Press, 1995.

Clifford, James, and George E. Marcus, eds. *Writing Culture: The Poetics and Politics of Ethnography.* Berkeley and Los Angeles: University of California Press, 1986.

Clothey, Fred W. *Rhythm and Intent: Ritual Studies from South India.* Madras: Blackie and Son, 1983.

Cobo, Father Bernabé. *Inca Religion and Customs.* Trans. and ed. Rowland Hamilton. Austin: University of Texas Press, 1990.

Coggins, Clemency C. "The Shape of Time: Some Political Implications of a Four-Part Figure." *American Antiquity* 45 (October 1980): 727–39.

———. "The Zenith, the Mountain, the Center, and the Sea." In *Ethnoastronomy and Archaeoastronomy in the American Tropics,* ed. Anthony F. Aveni and Gary Urton. New York: New York Academy of Sciences, 1982.

Coomaraswamy, Ananda K. *The Transformation of Nature in Art.* New York: Dover Publications, 1956.

Cowgill, George L. "Rulership and the Ciudadela: Political Inferences from Teotihuacan Architecture." In *Civilization in the Ancient Americas: Essays in Honor of Gordon R. Willey,* ed. Richard M. Leventhal and Alan L. Kolata. Albuquerque: University of New Mexico Press; Cambridge, Mass.: Peabody Museum of Archaeology and Ethnology, Harvard University, 1983.

Csikszentmihalyi, Mihaly, and Eugene Rochberg-Halton. *The Meaning of Things: Domestic Symbols and the Self.* Cambridge: Cambridge University Press, 1981.

Davies, J. G. *Temples, Churches, and Mosques: A Guide to the Appreciation of Religious Architecture.* Oxford: Basil Blackwell, 1982.

———. "Architecture." *Encyclopedia of Religion,* ed. Mircea Eliade, vol. 1, 382–92. New York: Macmillan, 1987.

DeBernardi, Jean. "Space and Time in Chinese Religious Culture." *History of Religions* 31 (February 1992): 247–68.

Desai, Ziyaud-Din A. *Mosques of India*. 3d ed. New Delhi: Ministry of Information and Broadcasting, Government of India, 1979.

Dillenberger, Jane. *Image and Spirit in Sacred and Secular Art*. Ed. Diane Apostolos-Cappadona. New York: Crossroad, 1990.

Dixon, John W., Jr. "The Christology of Michelangelo: The Sistine Chapel." *Journal of the American Academy of Religion* 55 (fall 1987): 503–33.

Ebersole, Gary L. *Ritual Poetry and the Politics of Death in Early Japan*. Princeton: Princeton University Press, 1989.

Eck, Diana L. "India's *Tirthas*: 'Crossings' in Sacred Geography." *History of Religions* 20 (May 1981): 323–44.

———. *Banaras: City of Light*. Princeton: Princeton University Press, 1982.

Edwardes, Michael. *Indian Temples and Palaces*. London: Paul Hamlyn, 1969.

Eilberg-Schwartz, Howard. *The Savage in Judaism: An Anthropology of Israelite Religion and Ancient Judaism*. Bloomington: Indiana University Press, 1990.

Eliade, Mircea. *The Myth of the Eternal Return*. Trans. Willard R. Trask. Princeton: Princeton University Press, 1954.

———. *Patterns in Comparative Religion*. Trans. Rosemary Sheed. New York: Sheed and Ward, 1958.

———. *The Sacred and the Profane: The Nature of Religion*. Trans. Willard R. Trask. New York: Harcourt Brace Jovanovich, 1959.

———. *A History of Religious Ideas*. Trans. Willard R. Trask. 3 vols. Chicago: University of Chicago Press, 1978–1988.

Ellwood, Robert S. "Harvest and Renewal at the Grand Shrine of Ise." *Numen* 15 (November 1968): 165–90.

al-Fārūqī, Lois Ibsen. "An Islamic Perspective on Symbolism in the Arts: New Thoughts of Figural Representation." In *Art, Creativity, and the Sacred: An Anthology in Religion and Art*, ed. Diane Apostolos-Cappadona. New York: Crossroad, 1984.

Faure, Bernard. "Space and Place in Chinese Religious Tradition." *History of Religions* 26 (May 1987): 337–56.

Fernandez, James W. "Location and Direction in African Religious Movements: Some Deictic Contours of Religious Conversion." *History of Religions* 25 (May 1986): 352–67.

Fletcher, Banister. *A History of Architecture on the Comparative Method for Students, Craftsmen, and Amateurs*. 13th ed. New York: Charles Scribner's Sons, 1946.

Folch-Serra, Mireya. "A Postmodern Conversation." *Queen's Quarterly* 95 (autumn 1988): 618–40.

Foucault, Michel. *The Order of Things: An Archaeology of the Human Sciences*. London and New York: Tavistock/Routledge, 1974.

Freedberg, David. *The Power of Images: Studies in the History and Theory of Response*. Chicago: University of Chicago Press, 1989.

Friedland, Roger, and Richard D. Hecht. "The Politics of Sacred Place: Jersualem's Temple Mount/*al-haram a-sharif.*" In *Sacred Places and Profane Spaces: Essays in the Geographics of Judaism, Christianity, and Islam,* ed. Jamie Scott and Paul Simpson-Housley. New York: Greenwood Press, 1991.

Fuson, Robert H. "The Orientation of Maya Ceremonial Centers." *Annals of the Association of American Geographers* 3 (1969): 494–511.

Gadamer, Hans-Georg. *Truth and Method.* New York: Crossroad, 1975.

———. *Philosophical Hermeneutics.* Trans. and ed. David E. Linge. Berkeley and Los Angeles: University of California Press, 1976.

———. *The Relevance of the Beautiful and Other Essays.* Trans. Nicholas Walker. Ed. Robert Bernasconi. Cambridge: Cambridge University Press, 1986.

Gadol, Joan. *Leon Battista Alberti: Universal Man of the Early Renaissance.* Chicago: University of Chicago Press, 1969.

Geertz, Clifford. *The Interpretation of Cultures: Selected Essays.* New York: Basic Books, 1973.

———. *Local Knowledge: Further Essays in Interpretive Anthropology.* New York: Basic Books, 1983.

Gendrop, Paul. "Dragon-Mouth Entrances: Zoomorphic Portals in the Architecture of Central Yucatan." In *Third Palenque Round Table, 1978, Part 2,* ed. Merle Greene Robertson. Palenque Round Table Series, vol. 5. Austin: University of Texas Press, 1980.

———. *Compendio de arte prehispánico.* México, D.F.: Editorial Trillas, 1987.

Gendrop, Paul, and Doris Heyden. *Mesoamerican Architecture.* New York: Harry Abrams, 1974.

Ghosh, Sankar Prosad. *Hindu Religious Art and Architecture.* Delhi: D. K. Publications, 1982.

Goldman, Irving. *The Mouth of Heaven: An Introduction to Kwakiutl Religious Thought.* Huntington, N.Y.: Robert E. Krieger Publishing Company, 1981.

Gombrich, E. H. *Art and Illusion: A Study in the Psychology of Pictorial Representation.* Princeton: Princeton University Press, 1972.

Gordon, B. L. "Sacred Directions, Orientation, and the Top of the Map." *History of Religions* 10 (February 1971): 211–27.

Gould, Peter, and Rodney White. *Mental Maps.* Harmondsworth: Penguin Books, 1974.

Grapard, Allan G. "Flying Mountains and Walkers of Emptiness: Toward a Definition of Sacred Space in Japanese Religion." *History of Religions* 20 (February 1982): 195–221.

Gray, Stuart A. *Edwardian Architecture: A Biographical Dictionary.* London: Gerald Duckworth and Co., 1985.

Grieder, Terence. *Origins of Pre-Columbian Art.* Austin: University of Texas Press, 1982.

Gunn, Giles. *The Interpretation of Otherness: Literature, Religion, and the American Imagination.* New York: Oxford University Press, 1979.

———. *The Culture of Criticism and the Criticism of Culture.* New York: Oxford University Press, 1987.

Hallowell, A. Irving. "Cultural Factors in Spatial Orientation." In A. Irving Hallowell, *Culture and Experience.* Philadelphia: University of Pennsylvania Press, 1955.

Hammond, Peter. *Liturgy and Architecture.* London: Barrie and Rockliff, 1960.

Handjiyski, Antoniy. *Rock Monasteries.* Trans. Marguerite Alexieva. Sofia: Septemvri State Publishing House, 1985.

Harbison, Robert. *The Built, the Unbuilt, and the Unbuildable: In Pursuit of Architectural Meaning.* Cambridge, Mass.: MIT Press, 1992.

Hardoy, Jorge E. *Pre-Columbian Cities.* Trans. Judith Thorne. New York: Walker and Company, 1973.

Hartung, Horst. "Consideraciones sobre los trazos de centros ceremoniales Mayas," in *Actes du XXXVIIIe congrès international des Americanistes, 1968,* vol. 4, 17–26. Munich: K. Renner, 1969–1972.

———. "Ancient Maya Architecture and Planning: Possibilities and Limitations for Astronomical Studies." In *Native American Astronomy,* ed. Anthony F. Aveni. Austin: University of Texas Press, 1977.

———. "Alignments in Architecture and Sculpture of Maya Centers: Notes on Piedras Negras, Copán, and Chichén Itzá." *Ibero-Amerikanische Archiv,* n.s., 223–40. Berlin: Colloquim Verlag Berlin, 1986.

Heine-Geldern, Robert. *Conceptions of State and Kingship in Southeast Asia.* Data Paper No. 18. Ithaca, N.Y.: Southeast Asia Program, Cornell University, 1956.

Heyden, Doris. "An Interpretation of the Cave underneath the Pyramid of the Sun in Teotihuacan, Mexico." *American Antiquity* 40 (April 1975): 131–47.

———. "Caves, Gods, and Myths: World-Views and Planning in Teotihuacan." In *Mesoamerican Sites and World-Views: A Conference at Dumbarton Oaks, October 16–17, 1976,* ed. Elizabeth P. Benson. Washington, D.C.: Dumbarton Oaks, 1981.

Hibbard, Howard. *Bernini.* Baltimore: Penguin Books, 1965.

Holm, Jean, with John Bowker, eds. *Sacred Place.* London and New York: Pinter Publishers, 1994.

Holmes, William Henry. *Archaeological Studies among the Ancient Cities of Mexico.* Chicago: Field Columbian Museum, 1895–97.

Holub, Robert C. *Reception Theory: A Critical Introduction.* London and New York: Methuen, 1984.

Hugh-Jones, Stephen. *The Palm and the Pleiades: Initiation and Cosmology in Northwest Amazonia.* Cambridge: Cambridge University Press, 1979.

Hung, Wu. "Tiananmen Square: A Political History of Monuments." *Representations* 35 (summer 1991): 84–117.

Huntington, Susan L. *The Art of Ancient India: Buddhist, Hindu, Jain.* New York and Tokyo: Weatherhill, 1985.

———. "Early Buddhist Art and the Theory of Aniconism." *Art Journal* 49 (winter 1990): 401–8.

Ingarden, Roman. *Ontology of the Work of Art: The Musical Work, the Picture, the Architectural Work, the Film*. Trans. Raymond Meyer with John T. Goldthwait. Athens: Ohio University Press, 1989.

Inoue, Mitsuo. *Space in Japanese Architecture*. Trans. Horoshi Watanabe. New York and Tokyo: Weatherhill, 1985.

Iser, Wolfgang. *The Act of Reading: A Theory of Aesthetic Response*. Baltimore: Johns Hopkins University Press, 1978.

———. "The Reading Process: A Phenomenological Approach." In *Reader-Response Criticism: From Formalism to Post-Structuralism*, ed. Jane P. Tompkins. Baltimore: Johns Hopkins University Press, 1980.

Isozaki, Arata. "Floors and Internal Spaces in Japanese Vernacular Architecture: Phenomenology of Floors." *Res: Anthropology and Aesthetics* 11 (spring 1986): 55–77.

Jackson, J. B. *The Necessity for Ruins, and Other Topics* (Amherst: University of Massachusetts Press, 1980).

James, E. O. *From Cave to Cathedral: Temples and Shrines of Prehistoric, Classical, and Early Christian Times*. New York: Frederick A. Praeger, 1965.

Jauss, Hans Robert. "Literary History as a Challenge to Literary Theory." *New Literary History* 2 (autumn 1970): 7–37.

———. *Aesthetic Experience and Literary Hermeneutics*. Trans. Michael Shaw. Minneapolis: University of Minnesota Press, 1982.

———. *Toward an Aesthetic of Reception*. Trans. Timothy Bahti. Minneapolis: University of Minnesota Press, 1982.

Jencks, Charles A. *The Language of Post-Modern Architecture*. 5th rev. enl. ed. London: Academy Editions, 1987.

Jencks, Charles A., and George Baird, eds. *Meaning in Architecture*. New York: George Braziller, 1969.

Johnsen, Harald, and Bjornar Olsen. "Hermeneutics and Archaeology: On the Philosophy of Contextual Archaeology." *American Antiquity* 57 (July 1992): 419–36.

Jones, Lindsay. *Twin City Tales: A Hermeneutical Reassessment of Tula and Chichén Itzá*. Niwot: University Press of Colorado, 1995.

Joyce, Thomas Athol. *Maya and Mexican Art*. London: "The Studio," Ltd., 1927.

Kelemen, Pál. *Medieval American Art*. 2 vols. New York: Macmillan, 1943.

Kenna, Margaret E., "Icons in Theory and Practice: An Orthodox Christian Example." *History of Religions* 24 (May 1985): 345–68.

Kennedy, Roger G. *Architecture, Men, Women, and Money in America, 1600–1860*. New York: Random House, 1985.

Khosla, Romi. "Architecture and Symbolism in Tibetan Monasteries." In *Shelter, Sign, and Symbol: An Exploratory Work on Vernacular Architecture*, ed. Paul Oliver. Woodstock, N.Y.: Overlook Press, 1977.

Klein, Cecelia F. "Woven Heaven, Tangled Earth: A Weaver's Paradigm of the Mesoamerican Cosmos." In *Ethnoastronomy and Archaeoastronomy in the American Tropics,* ed. Anthony F. Aveni and Gary Urton. New York: New York Academy of Sciences, 1982.

Klemm, David E. *Hermeneutical Inquiry.* 2 vols. Atlanta: Scholars Press, 1986.

Klimkeit, Hans-Joachim. "Spatial Orientation in Mythical Thinking as Exemplified in Ancient Egypt: Considerations Toward a Geography of Religions." *History of Religions* 14 (May 1975): 266–81.

Klotz, Heinrich. *The History of Postmodern Architecture.* Trans. Radka Donnell. Cambridge, Mass.: MIT Press, 1988.

Kohl, David G. *Chinese Architecture in the Straits Settlements and Western Malaya: Temples, Kongsis, and Houses.* Kuala Lumpur: Heinemann Asia, 1984.

Kramrisch, Stella. *The Hindu Temple.* 2 vols. 1946. Reprint, Delhi: Motilal Banarsidass, 1976.

———. *Exploring India's Sacred Art: Selected Writings of Stella Kramrisch.* Ed. Barbara Stoler Miller. Philadelphia: University of Pennsylvania Press, 1983.

Krautheimer, Richard. *Rome: Profile of a City, 312–1308.* Princeton: Princeton University Press, 1980.

Kubler, George. "The Design of Space in Maya Architecture." In *Miscellanea Paul Rivet, octogenario dicata.* México, D.F.: Universidad Nacional Autónoma de México, 1958.

———. *The Shape of Time: Remarks on the History of Things.* New Haven: Yale University Press, 1962.

———. *The Iconography of the Art of Teotihuacan.* Studies in Pre-Columbian Art and Archaeology, no. 4. Washington, D.C.: Dumbarton Oaks, 1967.

———. "History—or Anthropology—of Art?" *Critical Inquiry* 1 (June 1975): 757–67.

———. "Period, Style, and Meaning in Ancient American Art." In *Ancient Mesoamerica: Selected Readings.* Ed. John A. Graham. Palo Alto, Calif.: Peek Publications, 1981.

———. *The Art and Architecture of Ancient America: The Mexican, Maya, and Andean Peoples.* 3d ed. New York: Penguin Books, 1984.

Kuck, Loraine E. *The World of the Japanese Garden: From Chinese Origins to Modern Landscape Art.* New York: Weatherhill, 1968.

Lakai, Louis J. *The Cistercians: Ideals and Reality.* Kent, Ohio: Kent State University Press, 1977.

Lane, Belden C. *Landscapes of the Sacred: Geography and Narrative in American Spirituality.* New York: Paulist Press, 1988.

Lavin, Irving. *Bernini and the Crossing of Saint Peter's.* New York: New York University Press, 1968.

Leeuw, Gerardus van der. *Sacred and Profane Beauty: The Holy in Art.* Trans. David E. Green. New York: Holt, Rinehart and Winston, 1963.

Lefebvre, Henri. *The Production of Space*. Trans. Donald Nicholson-Smith. Oxford and Cambridge, Mass.: Basil Blackwell, 1991.

Linge, David E. Introduction to *Philosophical Hermeneutics,* by Hans-Georg Gadamer. Trans. and ed. David E. Linge. Berkeley and Los Angeles: University of California Press, 1976.

Long, Charles H. *Alpha: The Myths of Creation*. Chico, Calif.: Scholars Press, 1963.

———. *Significations: Signs, Symbols, and Images in the Interpretation of Religion*. Philadelphia: Fortress Press, 1986.

L'Orange, H. P. *Art Forms and Civic Life in the Late Roman Empire*. Princeton: Princeton University Press, 1965.

Maass, John. "Where Architectural Historians Fear to Tread." *Journal of the Society of Architectural Historians* 28 (March 1969): 3–8.

Mabbett, I. W. "The Symbolism of Mount Meru." *History of Religions* 23 (August 1983): 64–83.

Macrae-Gibson, Gavin. *The Secret Life of Buildings: An American Mythology for Modern Architecture*. Cambridge, Mass.: MIT Press, 1985.

Maquet, Jacques. *The Aesthetic Experience: An Anthropologist Looks at the Visual Arts*. New Haven: Yale University Press, 1986.

Marcus, George E., and Michael M. J. Fischer. *Anthropology as Cultural Critique: An Experimental Moment in the Human Sciences*. Chicago: University of Chicago Press, 1986.

Marcus, Joyce. "Territorial Organization of the Lowland Classic Maya." *Science* 180 (1973): 911–16.

———. "Archaeology and Religion: A Comparison of the Zapotec and Maya." In *Ancient Mesoamerica: Selected Readings,* ed. John A. Graham. Palo Alto, Calif.: Peek Publications, 1981.

Margain, Carlos R. "Pre-Columbian Architecture of Central Mexico." In *Archaeology of Northern Mesoamerica,* ed. Gordon F. Ekholm and Ignacio Bernal, vol. 10 of *Handbook of Middle American Indians*. Austin: University of Texas Press, 1971.

Margolin, Victor, ed. *Design Discourse: History, Theory, Criticism*. Chicago: University of Chicago Press, 1989.

Marquina, Ignacio. *Arqitectura Prehispánica*. 2d ed. México, D.F.: Instituto Nacional de Antropología e Historia, 1964.

Martin, James Alfred, Jr. *Beauty and Holiness: The Dialogue between Aesthetics and Religion*. Princeton: Princeton University Press, 1990.

Matsumoto, Shigeru. "The Meaning of Sacred Places as Phenomenologists of Religion Understand It." *Tenri Journal of Religion* 10 (October 1969): 46–56.

Meister, Michael W. "Mandala and Practice in Nagara Architecture in North India." *Journal of the American Oriental Society* 99 (April-June, 1979): 204–19.

———. "Measurement and Proportion in Hindu Temple Architecture." *Interdisciplinary Science Reviews* 10 (September 1985): 248–58.

———. "On the Development of a Morphology for a Symbolic Architecture: India." *Res: Anthropology and Aesthetics* 12 (autumn 1986): 33–50.

Metcalf, Peter, and Richard Huntington. *Celebrations of Death: The Anthropology of Mortuary Ritual.* Cambridge: Cambridge University Press, 1991.

Meyer, Jeffery F. "*Feng-shui* of the Chinese City." *History of Religions* 18 (November 1978): 138–55.

Meyer, Leonard B. *Emotion and Meaning in Music.* Chicago: University of Chicago Press, 1956.

———. "Meaning in Music and Information Theory." *Journal of Aesthetics and Art Criticism* 15 (June 1957): 412–21.

———. "Some Remarks on Value and Greatness in Music." *Journal of Aesthetics and Art Criticism* 17 (June 1959): 486–500.

Michell, George. *The Hindu Temple: An Introduction to Its Meaning and Forms.* Chicago: University of Chicago, 1988.

Miller, Mary Ellen. *The Art of Mesoamerica: From Olmec to Aztec.* London: Thames and Hudson, 1986.

Mirsky, Jeanette. *Houses of God.* Chicago: University of Chicago Press, 1965.

Mitchell, Tom. "The Product as Illusion." In *Design after Modernism,* ed. John Thackera. Gloucester: Thames and Hudson, 1988.

Mitchell, W. J. T. *Iconology: Image, Text, Ideology.* Chicago: University of Chicago Press, 1986.

Moholy-Nagy, Sibyl. *Native Genius in Anonymous Architecture in North America.* New York: Schocken Books, 1976.

Munakata, Kiyohiko. "Mysterious Heavens and Chinese Classical Gardens." *Res: Anthropology and Aesthetics* 15 (spring 1988): 61–88.

Murray, Peter. *The Architecture of the Italian Renaissance.* New York: Schocken Books, 1963.

Nicholson, Henry B. "Preclassic Mesoamerican Iconography from the Perspective of the Postclassic: Problems in Interpretational Analysis." In *Origins of Religious Art and Iconography in Preclassic Mesoamerica,* ed. Henry B. Nicholson. Los Angeles: UCLA Latin American Center Publications, 1976.

Nitschke, Gunter. "'*Ma*': The Japanese Sense of 'Place' in Old and New Architectural Planning." *Architectural Design* 36 (March 1966): 412–21.

Norberg-Schulz, Christian. *Intentions in Architecture.* Cambridge, Mass.: MIT Press, 1965.

———. "Meaning in Architecture." In *Meaning in Architecture,* ed. Charles A. Jencks and George Baird. New York: George Braziller, 1969.

———. *Meaning in Western Architecture.* New York: Praeger, 1975.

———. *Genus Loci: Toward a Phenomenology of Architecture.* New York: Rizzoli, 1980.

Oliver, Paul, ed. *Shelter, Sign, and Symbol: An Exploratory Work on Vernacular Architecture.* Woodstock, N.Y.: Overlook Press, 1977.

———. *Dwellings: The House across the World.* Austin: University of Texas Press, 1987.

Ooka, Minoru. *Temples of Nara and Their Art.* Trans. Dennis Lishka. New York: Weatherhill, 1973.

Ortiz, Alfonso. *The Tewa World: Time, Space, Being, and Becoming in a Pueblo Society.* Chicago: University of Chicago Press, 1969.

Osmen, Sarah Ann. *Sacred Places.* New York: St. Martin's Press, 1990.

Panofsky, Erwin. *Gothic Architecture and Scholasticism.* New York: Meridian Books, 1957.

Pardeep Singh Arshi. *Sikh Architecture in Punjab.* New Delhi: Intellectual Publishing House, 1986.

Parsons, Michael J. *How We Understand Art: A Cognitive Developmental Account of Aesthetic Experience.* Cambridge: Cambridge University Press, 1987.

Pasztory, Esther. "Masterpieces in Pre-Columbian Art." *Actes du XLIIe congrès international des Americanistes, 1976,* vol. 7, 377–90.

Pilgrim, Richard B. "Intervals (*Ma*) in Space and Time: Foundations for a Religio-Aesthetic Paradigm in Japan." *History of Religions* 25 (1986): 255–77.

Pinxton, Rik, Ingrid van Dooren, and Frank Harvey. *The Anthropology of Space: Explorations into the Natural Philosophy and Semantics of the Navajo.* Philadelphia: University of Pennsylvania Press, 1983.

Pollock, H. E. D. "Sources and Methods in the Study of Maya Architecture." In *The Maya and Their Neighbors,* ed. Clarence L. Hay et al. New York: Appleton-Century, 1940.

———. "Architecture of the Maya Lowlands." In *Archaeology of Southern Mesoamerica,* ed. Gordon R. Willey. Vols. 2–3 of *Handbook of Middle American Indians.* Austin: University of Texas Press, 1965.

Poole, Fitz John Porter. "Metaphors and Maps: Toward Comparison in the Anthropology of Religion." *Journal of the American Academy of Religion* 54 (fall 1986): 411–57.

Potter, David F. "Prehispanic Architecture and Sculpture in Central Yucatan." *American Antiquity* 41 (1976): 430–38.

Proskouriakoff, Tatiana. *An Album of Maya Architecture.* Norman: University of Oklahoma Press, 1963.

———. "Studies on Middle American Art." In *Anthropology and Art: Readings in Cross-Cultural Aesthetics,* ed. Charlotte M. Otten. Austin: University of Texas Press, 1971.

Prown, David. "Mind in Matter: An Introduction to Material Culture Theory and Method." Winterthur, Del.: Henry Francis du Pont Winterthur Museum, 1982.

Ragon, Michel. *The Space of Death: A Study of Funerary Architecture, Decoration, and Urbanism.* Trans. Alan Sheridan. Charlottesville: University Press of Virginia, 1983.

Rajchman, John. *Michel Foucault: The Freedom of Philosophy.* New York: Columbia

University Press, 1985.

Rapoport, Amos. *The Meaning of the Built Environment: A Nonverbal Communication Approach.* Tucson: University of Arizona Press, 1982, 1990.

Ray, Benjamin C. "Stonehenge: A New Theory." *History of Religions* 26 (February 1987): 225–78.

Richter, Gottfried. *Art and Human Consciousness.* Trans. Burley Channer and Margaret Frohlich. Spring Valley, N.Y.: Anthroposophic Press, 1985.

Ricoeur, Paul. *The Symbolism of Evil.* Trans. Emerson Buchanan. Boston: Beacon Press, 1967.

———. "The Model of the Text: Meaningful Action Considered as Text." *Social Research* 38 (autumn 1971): 529–62.

———. *The Conflict of Interpretations: Essays in Hermeneutics.* Ed. Don Ihde. Evanston, Ill.: Northwestern University Press, 1974.

———. *Interpretation Theory: Discourse and the Surplus of Meaning.* Fort Worth: Texas Christian University Press, 1976.

Robertson, Donald. *Pre-Columbian Architecture.* New York: George Braziller, 1963.

Rose, Margaret A. *The Post-Modern and the Post-Industrial: A Critical Analysis.* Cambridge: Cambridge University Press, 1991.

Rosenau, Helen. *The Ideal City: Its Architectural Evolution in Europe.* 3d ed. London: Methuen, 1983.

Rudofsky, Bernard. *The Prodigious Builders: Notes toward a Natural History of Architecture with Special Regard to Those Species That Are Traditionally Neglected or Downright Ignored.* New York: Harcourt Brace Jovanovich, 1977.

Ruggles, C. L. N., et al. *Megalithic Astronomy: A New Archaeological and Statistical Study of 300 Western Scottish Sites.* B.A.R. British Series, 123. Oxford: B.A.R., 1984.

Ruskin, John. *The Seven Lamps of Architecture.* 1849. Reprint, New York: Noonday Press, 1971.

Rykwert, Joseph. *The Idea of a Town: The Anthropology of Urban Form in Rome, Italy, and the Ancient World.* Princeton: Princeton University Press, 1976.

———. *On Adam's House in Paradise: The Idea of the Primitive Hut in Architectural History.* 2d ed. Cambridge, Mass.: MIT Press, 1981.

Samuels, Marwyn S., and Carmencita Samuels. "Beijing and the Power of Place in Modern China." In *The Power of Place,* ed. John A. Agnew and James S. Duncan. Boston: Unwin Hyman, 1989.

Schavelzon, Daniel. "Temples, Caves, or Monsters? Notes on Zoomorphic Facades in Pre-Hispanic Architecture." In *Third Palenque Round Table, 1978, Part 2,* ed. Merle Greene Robertson. Palenque Round Table Series, vol. 5. Austin: University of Texas Press, 1980.

Schele, Linda. "Sacred Site and World-View at Palenque." In *Mesoamerican Sites and World-Views: A Conference at Dumbarton Oaks, October 16–17, 1976,* ed. Elizabeth P. Benson. Washington, D.C.: Dumbarton Oaks, 1981.

Scott, Geoffrey. *The Architecture of Humanism*. New York: Charles Scribner's Sons, 1925. Reprint, New York: Doubleday Anchor Books, 1954.

Scott, Jamie, and Paul Simpson-Housley, eds. *Sacred Places and Profane Spaces: Essays in the Geographics of Judaism, Christianity, and Islam*. New York: Greenwood Press, 1991.

Scully, Vincent. *The Earth, the Temple, and the Gods: Greek Sacred Architecture*. Rev. ed. New Haven: Yale University Press, 1979.

Shankman, Paul. "The Thick and the Thin: On the Interpretive Theoretical Program of Clifford Geertz." *Current Anthropology* 25 (June 1984): 261–78.

Sidrys, Raymond. "Megalithic Architecture and Sculpture of the Ancient Maya." In *Papers on the Economy and Architecture of the Ancient Maya,* ed. Raymond Sidrys. Los Angeles: Institute of Archaeology, University of California, 1978.

Simson, Otto von. *The Gothic Cathedral: Origins of Gothic Architecture and the Medieval Concept of Order*. Princeton: Princeton University Press, 1956.

Sinding-Larsen, Staale. *Iconography and Ritual: A Study of Analytical Perspectives*. Oslo: Universitetsforlaget AS, 1984.

Smith, Bardwell, and Holly Baker Reynolds, eds. *The City as a Sacred Center: Essays on Six Asian Contexts*. Leiden: E. J. Brill, 1987.

Smith, Jonathan Z. *Map Is Not Territory: Studies in the History of Religions*. Leiden: E. J. Brill, 1978.

———. *Imagining Religion: From Babylon to Jonestown*. Chicago: University of Chicago Press, 1982.

———. *To Take Place: Toward Theory in Ritual*. Chicago: University of Chicago Press, 1987.

———. *Drudgery Divine: On the Comparison of Early Christianities and the Religions of Late Antiquity*. Chicago: University of Chicago Press, 1990.

Snow, Edward, "The Language of Contradiction in Bruegel's *Tower of Babel*." *Res: Anthropology and Aesthetics* 5 (spring 1983): 40–48.

Soundara Rajan, K. V. *Invitation to Indian Architecture*. New Delhi: Arnold-Heinemann, 1984.

Spinden, Herbert J. *A Study of Maya Art: Its Subject Matter and Historical Development*. 1913. Reprint, New York: Dover Publications, 1975.

Steinhardt, Nancy Shatzman, et al. *Chinese Traditional Architecture*. New York: China Institute in America, China House Gallery, 1984.

Stoddard, Whitney S. *Art and Architecture in Medieval France*. New York: Harper and Row, 1972.

Stokes, Adrian. *Smooth and Rough*. London: Faber and Faber, 1951.

———. *The Invitation in Art*. London: Tavistock Publications, 1965.

Stroker, Elisabeth. *Investigations in Philosophy of Space*. Trans. Algis Mickunas. Athens: Ohio University Press, 1987.

Suger, Abbot. *On the Abbey Church of St.-Denis and Its Art Treasures*. Ed. and trans. Erwin Panofsky, 2d ed. Princeton: Princeton University Press, 1979.

Sullivan, Lawrence E. "Astral Myths Rise Again: Interpreting Religious Astronomy." *Criterion* 22 (winter 1983): 12–17.

———. "Sound and Senses: Toward a Hermeneutics of Performance." *History of Religions* 26 (August 1986): 1–33.

———. *Icanchu's Drum: An Orientation to Meaning in South American Religions.* New York: Macmillan, 1988.

———. "'Seeking an End to the Primary Text' or 'Putting an End to the Text as Primary.'" In *Beyond the Classics? Essays in Religious Studies and Liberal Education,* ed. Frank E. Reynolds and Sheryl L. Burkhalter. Atlanta: Scholars Press, 1990.

Tambiah, Stanley J. *World Conqueror and World Renouncer: A Study of Buddhism and Polity in Thailand against a Historical Background.* Cambridge: Cambridge University Press, 1977.

Tange, Kenzo, and Noboru Kawazoe. *Ise: Prototype of Japanese Architecture.* Cambridge: MIT Press, 1965.

Taube, Karl A. "The Teotihuacan Cave of Origin: The Iconography and Architecture of Emergence Mythology in Mesoamerica and the American Southwest." *Res: Anthropology and Aesthetics* 12 (autumn 1986): 51–82.

Thompson, Fred, and D'Arcy Fenton. "*Matsuri:* The Binding of Secular and Ceremonial Space in Kakunodate, Japan." *Res: Anthropology and Aesthetics* 13 (spring 1987): 135–52.

Tichy, Frank. "Order and Relationship of Space and Time in Mesoamerica: Myth or Reality." In *Mesoamerican Sites and World-Views: A Conference at Dumbarton Oaks, October 16–17, 1976,* ed. Elizabeth P. Benson. Washington, D.C.: Dumbarton Oaks, 1976.

Tompkins, Jane P., ed. *Reader-Response Criticism: From Formalism to Post-Structuralism.* Baltimore: Johns Hopkins University Press, 1980.

Townsend, Richard F. *State and Cosmos in the Art of Tenochtitlan.* Studies in Pre-Columbian Art and Archaeology, no. 20. Washington, D.C.: Dumbarton Oaks, 1979.

———. "Pyramid and Sacred Mountain." In *Ethnoastronomy and Archaeoastronomy in the American Tropics,* ed. Anthony F. Aveni and Gary Urton. New York: New York Academy of Sciences, 1982.

———. "Coronation at Tenochtitlan." In *The Imagination of Matter: Religion and Ecology in Mesoamerican Traditions,* ed. Davíd Carrasco. B.A.R. International Series, 515. Oxford: B.A.R., 1989.

Tracy, David. *The Analogical Imagination: Christian Theology and the Culture of Pluralism.* New York: Crossroad, 1981.

———. *Plurality and Ambiguity: Hermeneutics, Religion, Hope.* Chicago: University of Chicago Press, 1987.

Tschumi, Bernard. *Architecture and Disjunction.* Cambridge, Mass.: MIT Press, 1996.

Tuan, Yi-Fu. *Space and Place: The Perspective of Experience.* Minneapolis: University of Minnesota Press, 1977.

Tucci, Giuseppe. *The Theory and Practice of the Mandala, with Special Reference to the Modern Psychology of the Subconscious.* Trans. Alan Houghton Brodrick. London: Rider, 1961.

Turner, Harold W. *From Temple to Meeting House: The Phenomenology and Theory of Place of Worship.* The Hague: Mouton, 1979.

Turner, Victor. "The Center Out There: Pilgrim's Goal." *History of Religions* 12 (February 1973): 191–215.

Turner, Victor, and Edith Turner. *Image and Pilgrimage in Christian Culture: Anthropological Perspectives.* New York: Columbia University Press, 1978.

Venturi, Robert. *Complexity and Contradiction in Architecture.* New York: The Museum of Modern Art, 1966.

Vitruvius. *The Ten Books of Architecture.* Trans. Morris Hicky Morgan. New York: Dover Publications, 1960.

Volwahsen, Andreas. *Living Architecture: Indian.* Trans. Ann E. Keep. New York: Grosset and Dunlop, 1969.

Wach, Joachim. *The Sociology of Religion.* Chicago: University of Chicago Press, 1944.

———. *The Comparative Study of Religions.* Ed. Joseph M. Kitagawa. New York: Columbia University Press, 1958.

Waldman, Marilyn R. *Inviting Prophets and Entertaining Comparisons* (Cambridge: Cambridge University Press, forthcoming).

Waterson, Roxana, "The House and the World: The Symbolism of Sa' Dan Toraja House Carvings." *Res: Anthropology and Aesthetics* 15 (spring 1988): 35–60.

Watkin, David. *The Rise of Architectural History.* London: Architectural Press, 1980.

Wheatley, Paul. *The Pivot of the Four Quarters: A Preliminary Enquiry into the Origins and Character of the Ancient Chinese City.* Chicago: Aldine, 1971.

Wigley, Mark. *The Architecture of Deconstruction: Derrida's Haunt.* Cambridge, Mass.: MIT Press, 1993.

Willey, Gordon R. "Mesoamerican Art and Iconography and the Integrity of the Mesoamerican Ideological System." In *The Iconography of Middle American Sculpture,* ed. Ignacio Bernal et al. New York: Metropolitan Museum of Art, 1973.

Wittkower, Rudolf. *Architectural Principles in the Age of Humanism.* New York: W. W. Norton, 1971.

Wolfe, Tom. *From Bauhaus to Our House.* New York: Pocket Books, 1981.

Wollheim, Richard, ed. *The Image in Form: Selected Writings of Adrian Stokes.* New York: Harper and Row, 1972.

Woodward, Hiram W. "Borobudur and the Mirrorlike Mind." *Archaeology* 34 (November-December 1981): 40–47.

Wu, Nelson I. *Chinese and Indian Architecture: The City of Man, the Mountain of God, and the Realm of Immortals.* New York: George Braziller, 1963.

Zevi, Bruno. *Architecture as Space: How to Look at Architecture*. Trans. Milton Gendel. Ed. Joseph A. Barry. Rev. ed. New York: Horizon Press, 1974.

Zuidema, R. T. *The Ceque System of Cuzco: The Social Organization of the Capital of the Inca*. Leiden: E. J. Brill, 1964.

———. "The Inca Calendar." In *Native American Astronomy*. Ed. Anthony F. Aveni. Austin: University of Texas Press, 1971.

Index to Volume Two